From Page To Screen

From Page To Screen

Children's and Young Adult Books on Film and Video

Joyce Moss and George Wilson, Editors

Gale Research Inc. • DETROIT • LONDON

Joyce Moss
George Wilson

Gale Research Inc. staff

Coordinating Editors: Linda Metzger
Neil E. Walker

Production Director: Mary Beth Trimper
Production Assistant: Mary Winterhalter

Art Director: Arthur Chartow
Interior Designer: Jeanne Moore
Cover Designer: Kelly J. Schwartz
Keyliner: Yolanda Y. Latham

™ This book is printed on acid-free paper that meets the minimum requirements of American National Standard for Information Sciences—Permanence Paper for Printed Library Materials, ANSI Z39.48-1984.

ISBN: 0-8103-7893-0

Printed in the United States of America
Published in the United States by Gale Research Inc.
Published simultaneously in the United Kingdom
by Gale Research International Limited
(An affiliated company of Gale Research Inc.)

To my partner, George Wilson, whose absolute respect for the value of individual creation is the guiding principle of this book.

Contents

Preface

Novelist William Faulkner had already written for the screen. Now director Howard Hawks appealed to Ernest Hemingway to do the same, later adding that he could make a fine film of what he thought was Hemingway's worst story. The director proved his point in *To Have and Have Not* (1945), adapted not by Hemingway but by Jules Furthman and William Faulkner. The only film story ever to involve two Nobel Prize winners (Hemingway and Faulkner), it retains the main character and theme (no man can stand alone), but otherwise departs radically from the original, including events that "occurred" even before the beginning of the novel. In contrast, the film *Pride and Prejudice* (1940) sticks closely to the original, even using Jane Austen's dialog; yet it too deviates in the setting of a few incidents from the novel.

Certainly there are differences between the literary and motion picture media that prompt such deviations. Print depends on solitary creation, a flexible length, and written language to spur mental images. In contrast, film depends on cooperative creation, a fixed length, and the camera to convey visual images. There is a commonality, however, reflected by a repeatedly documented phenomenon: increased interest in a novel once the film has been released. *To Have and Have Not*, for example, ran through three printings while the film was featured in theaters (Gene D. Phillips, *Hemingway and Film* [New York: Frederick Ungar, 1980], p.59).

Books and films begin with the same raw materials: characters whose actions result in a basic story line. It is a further premise of this resource that the initial creator of a story communicates a vision of characters and events that can be captured in the translation from one medium to another, despite, and sometimes even due to, changes in story details. *From Page to Screen* allows the user to explore the relationship between a printed story and its screen adaptations or between a motion picture and the published story that it inspired. It covers literature and films geared to audiences from preschool through the high school years, including both theatrical and nontheatrical screen adaptations. The theatrical films are those productions designed for release in the public theaters or, in this case, on television. In contrast, the nontheatrical films are intended for institutions such as schools and libraries.

Film literature is a relatively young field of research. Only since the early 1970s has there been an effort to collect evaluative information on nontheatrical as well as theatrical films. The nontheatrical film greatly expands the universe of stories that lend themselves to both print and screen versions. It is not confined to a preset 60, 90, or 120 minute time slot, and so can adapt novellas, picture books, and short stories better suited to briefer time slots.

Whether the concern is theatrical or nontheatrical films, few resources have examined books and their related motion pictures for young audiences; in fact, there appears to be no resource that lists the titles available to the public and includes evaluative information on them. Such a resource addresses the needs of both those who acquire product and those who are the end users. Many films, especially the low-priced screen versions, are often unavailable for preview today, and the costs and time involved in selection, even when movies can be obtained, are high. Yet the process is important. The young stand to benefit most from the relationship between a book and film and the inspiration a story in one medium gives to partake of that story in the other. *From Page to Screen* aims to meet these needs.

Introduction

From Page to Screen allows parents, teachers, librarians, media directors, and students to select films that have been adapted from popular literature for young people. Included are more than 750 literary works and information on more than 1400 16mm films, videos, or laser discs adapted from those works. *From Page to Screen* provides a unique link between the film/video and the work of literature on which it was based and serves as a valuable transition between print and nonprint media. At the same time, available reviews, overall film ratings, and purchasing/rental information are also provided in an easy-to-use format.

Selection Criteria

For guidance in selecting the literature that appears in *From Page to Screen*, the authors turned to state education recommendations as well as to librarians and educators. The resulting collection ranges from classic to contemporary literature. Folklore, short stories, novels, plays, songs, poems, and nonfiction books addressed to preschool through twelfth grade audiences are included. Defining the scope of the publication entailed making decisions about the fluctuating dividing line between young adult and adult literature, and the authors relied on their advisors in the education and library fields in making these decisions.

In selecting the film adaptations of the books, the authors' goal was to provide a comprehensive collection of 16mm, video, and laser disc renditions, but their survey is limited to straight adaptations of the literature. Included are adaptations that employ various cinematic techniques, from iconographic to live action to animation. Excluded are ballets, operas, and instructional films with dramatic excerpts from literature.

Organization

From Page to Screen is organized alphabetically according to the titles of the literary works. The literary title and author appears in boldface print followed by publication information and a synopsis of the work. Following each book description is an evaluative listing of the work's cinematic adaptations.

A sample entry from the book is reprinted below.

Yearling, The
Marjorie Kinnan Rawlings.
Illustrated by N. C. Wyeth. Macmillan. 1985. [1938]. Historical fiction.
A post-Civil War farm family in rural Florida includes a lonely boy who raises a pet fawn. When the much-loved animal destroys crops, the boy must kill it.

Yearling, The.
134 min. Color. Live action. Produced by MGM/Sidney Franklin. 1946. Gregory Peck, Jane Wyman, Claude Jarman, Jr.
This fine adaptation is as dramatically wrenching today as when it was initially released. The story reaches far beyond the level of a boy and his pet to the pain involved in growing up. The mother's reluctance to let herself love her only remaining son plays nicely into the boy's experience of love for his pet and is expertly conveyed. An additional bonus is an honest look at the hardships of frontier life.
Reviews: New York Times, Jan. 24, 1947, 18:2; Variety, Nov. 27, 1946
Awards: Academy Awards, Best Cinematography, Best Set Design, Special Oscar for Outstanding Child Actor to Claude Jarmen, Jr.; Golden Globe Award, Best Actor
Audience: Ages 10-Adult
Distributor: MGM/UA Home Video
Videocassette: $19.98
No public performance rights

As the sample demonstrates, the elements that may appear within an entry are:

Book

1. *Book title*
2. *Author*
3. *Publication information* identifies the publisher and date of the most recent in-print edition. The date of the original edition appears in brackets if the book cited is a reprint. Those stories available in multiple editions are so noted.
4. *Genre designation* appears after each book title, identifying the work as one of the following—Adventure, Biography, Concept books, Drama, Fantasy, Folklore, Historical fiction, Humor, Mystery, Nonfiction, Poetry, Realistic fiction, Science fiction, Short stories, Songs. (For short stores, a subgenre—e.g., science fiction—is also noted.)
5. *Book description* provides a brief plot summary.

Films based on the book—When several adaptations of the same book are covered, the screen versions appear in chronological order form earliest to latest release date.

6. *Film title*
7. *Production information* noting the running time, format, production company, release date, and popularly recognized actors appearing in the film.
8. *Film description* includes a brief evaluative commentary comparing the film to the book and pointing out additional items of interest.
9. *Review citations* are provided when available.
10. *Awards* the film has garnered are noted.
11. *Audience* lists a suggested age range, enabling users to identify appropriate films.
12. *Distributor price, and format data* allows users to contact distributors regarding purchase or rental of the listed films and videos. Entries for videos or films without public performance rights close with "No public performance rights" above the two ratings.

Film ratings: Ratings are based on a combination of published reviews and personal screenings by *From Page to Screen*'s authors and contributors. Because the ratings are by nature subjective, users are encouraged to read the cited reviews for additional insights on a given production.

13. *Adaptation ratings* are denoted by book symbols and indicate how closely the film adaptation reflects its literary source. Each film is rated on a three-point scale with three being the highest rating. In a few instances, the film is a companion piece to the print version—for example, *The Astronomers*; in such cases, only a cinematic rating is provided.
14. *Cinematic ratings* are denoted by film reel symbols and indicate the film's strength independent of the book.

Indexes and Appendixes

The following indexes and appendixes are provided to allow maximum access to information in the text:

Appendix of Films for the Hearing Impaired — Lists captioned and silent films and videos and for stories with multiple adaptations notes the particular adaptation available in captioned format.

Film and Video Distributors Appendix — Provides the name, address, and telephone number of individual distributors.

Awards Index — Groups films and videos by the general award, and specifies the prize won.

Age-Level Index — Organizes films by age set, identifying the youngest age grouping for which a given motion picture is suitable.

Subject Index — Classifies literary works into specific subjects based primarily on *Library of Congress Subject Headings* and *Sears List of Subject Headings*.

Author/Film Title Index — Groups works by a single author and lists the titles of films and videos, including those whose titles differ from that of the printed work.

About the Authors

George Wilson, Ed.D., has taught in California public schools and at the University of Southern California, and has served as director of product development at BFA Educational Media (then a division of CBS Educational Publishing), where he spearheaded the production of 490 films for kindergarten through high school audiences. Joyce Moss graduated Summa Cum Laude in English literature, earned an M.S. in Instructional Technology, and served as senior editor of language arts at BFA Educational Media. For the past ten years, Moss and Wilson have independently authored textbooks and library references and consulted on the development of films for young audiences.

Entries in *From Page to Screen* are a result of personal evaluations from screenings of the motion pictures by Moss and Wilson or by the following contributors: Sue-Ellen Beauregard, assistant editor of audiovisual media for the periodical *Booklist*; Denise Donovan, *Booklist* reviewer; Rene Kirby, former editor of *Cinema Circulus Newsletter*, a USC film school alumni publication; and Margaret Murchie, former elementary school teacher and associate editor of language arts films. Additional evaluations have been drawn from a synthesis of reviews published in nationally syndicated journals.

Acknowledgements

Deep appreciation is extended first and foremost to all the film and video companies who so warmly opened their doors and shared their product with the compilers of this resource. A second "thank you" is extended to the outside contributors for the thorough and thoughtful completion of their entries, and to Rena Kleinfeld for her reliably deft word processing. Children who shared their responses to screenings helped validate evaluations; the authors are particularly grateful to five-year-old Phillip and ten-year-old Kathryn. Gratitude is also extended to Linda Metzger and Neil Walker of Gale Research for valuable organizational and content refinements. Finally, a special "thank you" goes to experts in the field, whose clever research suggestions and guidance made possible a task that required the synthesis of a myriad of facts from a plethora of resources. We are especially grateful to:

Children's librarian Eleanor K. MacDonald of the Beverly Hills Public Library

Supervising children's librarian Chris Garcia of the Beverly Hills Public Library

Supervising librarian Judy Kantor of UCLA's Seeds University Elementary School Library

Young adult librarian Nancy Guidry of the Santa Monica Public Library

Reference librarian Raymond Soto of UCLA's Theater Arts Library

Mentor teacher Carol Jago in secondary English at Santa Monica Public High School

Peggy O'Brien, Director of the High School Shakespeare Project at Washington D.C.'s Folger Library

Further gratitude is extended to the Academy of Motion Pictures and the Academy of Television Arts and Sciences for elusive information acquired from their in-house libraries.

Comments and Suggestions

Your comments on this work, as well as your suggestions for future editions, are welcome. Please write Editors, *From Page to Screen*, Gale Research Inc., 835 Penobscot Bldg., Detroit, Michigan 48225-4094; or call toll-free 1-800-347-4253.

From Page to Screen

adherence to book   film rating

Abe Lincoln in Illinois
Robert Sherwood.
Scribner. 1939. Drama.
The play profiles the pre-Presidential years during which Abraham Lincoln alternated as shopkeeper, postmaster, candidate for state legislature, lawyer, and lover.

Abe Lincoln in Illinois.
110 min. Black and white. Live action. Produced by RKO/Max Gordon. 1939. Raymond Massey, Ruth Gordon, Gene Lockhart.
The film achieves a victory in that it brilliantly humanizes a national hero. Ruth Gordon portrays Mary Todd with depth. Raymond Massey is perfectly convincing as Lincoln.
Reviews: *New York Times*, Feb. 23, 1940, 19:2; *Variety*, Jan. 24, 1940
Audience: Ages 14-Adult
Distributor: RKO/Turner Home Entertainment
Videocassette: $19.98
No public performance rights

★★★★★

Abel's Island
William Steig (illus.).
Farrar, Straus & Giroux. 1976. Fantasy.
An elegant and privileged mouse gets swept away by a storm to an island where he learns to survive using only his wits and his creativity.

Abel's Island.
30 min. Color. Animation. Produced by Michael Sporn Animation/Italtoons. 1987. Voices by Tim Curry and Lionel Jeffries.
This beautifully animated film, with its superb voices and chamber music by Arthur Custer, captures the story of Abel, an enchanting mouse who discovers the deeper meanings of love, friendship and creativity through his adventure on an uninhabited island. Abel concludes that full participation is the only way to live, and he returns home excited by life in a way that he has never known before.
Reviews: *Booklist*, Aug. 1988; *Children's Video Report*, Feb./Mar. 1989
Audience: Ages 4-Adult
Distributor: Random House Home Video
Videocassette: $14.95
No public performance rights

Abel's Island.
29 min. Color. Animation. 1988. Voices by Tim Curry and Lionel Jeffries.
A public performance version of the same title offered by Random House Home Video (see above).
Awards: Red Ribbon, American Film

Festival; CINE Golden Eagle; Best Animated Film, Houston Film Festival
Distributor: Lucerne Media
16mm film: $495 **Videocassette:** $295

★★★★★

Accident, The
Carol Carrick.

Illustrated by Donald Carrick. Houghton Mifflin. 1981. [1976]. Realistic fiction.
Chris and his dog are inseparable until the dog is struck and killed by a truck. Chris blames first the world and then himself for the accident but finally comes to grips with the loss and his own tragedy.

Accident, The.
22 min. Color. Live action. Produced by Mark Chodziko. 1985.
A winner of two first place awards for film quality, this is an excellent telling of Carrick's tale about a boy who struggles to cope with losing his dog to an accident.
Awards: *Booklist* Editors' Choice; First Place, National Educational Film and Video Festival
Audience: Ages 7-12
Distributor: Barr Films
16mm film: $520 **Videocassette:** $365
Rental: $50

★★★★★

Across Five Aprils
Irene Hunt.

Tempo Books. 1964. Historical fiction.
Set in southern Illinois, this story follows the effect of the Civil War on the male and female members of the Creighton family.

Across Five Aprils: A Time to Choose.
34 min. Color. Live action. Produced by LCA. 1990.
The family has sons on both sides of the war and their concerns are revealed in dramatizations of key events, bound by effective narrative bridges. This installment deals with the early war years, climaxing with the father's sudden illness. As stated in *Booklist*, "a gifted cast conveys how one household absorbs the personal anguish of the conflict...."
Reviews: *Booklist*, Oct. 1, 1990; *School Library Journal*, Oct. 1990
Awards: *Booklist* Editors' Choice
Audience: Ages 10-Adult
Distributor: Coronet/MTI Film & Video
16mm film: $595 **Videocassette:** $250
Rental: $75

Across Five Aprils: War and Hope.
30 min. Color. Live action. Produced by LCA. 1990.
This continuation of *A Time to Choose* begins with a narrative synopsis of previous events. It proceeds with the torments and concerns of the Creighton family during the last two years of the war. Major events are dramatized intact, and narrative bridges by the youngest son, Jethro, effectively hold the story together. As in the novel, tending the farm falls on Jethro's shoulders during this period. His cousin, a deserter, indirectly draws Jethro into the conflict. As concluded in *Booklist*, "...this faithful adaptation expands both Jethro's and viewers' understanding of war."
Reviews: *Booklist*, Oct. 1, 1990
Awards: *Booklist* Editors' Choice
Audience: Ages 10-Adult
Distributor: Coronet/MTI Film & Video
16mm film: $595 **Videocassette:** $250
Rental: $75

★★★★★

Adventures of a Two-Minute Werewolf, The
Gene DeWeese.

Illustrated by Ronald Fritz. Berkeley. 1986. [1983]. Humor; mystery.
Turning into a werewolf for two minutes at a time, thirteen-year-old Walt puts his unique ability to good use in upsetting the activities of bully burglars.

Adventures of a Two-Minute Werewolf, The.
26 min. Color. Live action. Produced by Scholastic Productions/ABC Weekend Special. 1990. Special appearances by Lanie Kazan and Melba Moore.
Bullied by an older boy, Walt learns he has a special talent—the ability to turn into a werewolf. He and his friend Cindy visit the library to figure out why. Walt also tries to prove himself innocent of burglaries that he is accused of by the bully Stanley. Walt catches the burglar, Stanley, in the act and changes into a werewolf at just the right time. Ending comically, the film shows that the tendency to turn into a werewolf runs in the family.
Reviews: *Booklist*, July 1990; *School Library Journal*, Dec. 1990
Audience: Ages 10-16
Distributor: Aims Media
16mm film: $495 **Videocassette:** $295
Rental: $50

Adventures of a Two-Minute Werewolf, The.
41 min. Color. Live action. 1990. Special appearances by Lanie Kazan and Melba Moore.
A full-length version of the same, abbreviated title also distributed by Aims Media (see above).
Audience: Ages 10-16
Distributor: Aims Media
Videocassette: $99

★★★★★

Adventures of Br'er Rabbit, The
Joel Chandler Harris.
Multiple editions. Folklore and fairy tales.
In the most famous of the Br'er Rabbit tales, the character's luck seems to have run out when he falls into a trap. The rabbit is hopelessly ensnared in a tar baby created by Br'er Fox until his own quick thinking frees Br'er Rabbit, landing him back in the briar patch, where he was "bred and born."

Br'er Rabbit.
30 min. Color. Limited animation. Produced by Rabbit Ears. 1990. Narrated by Danny Glover.
Narrator Glover captures the mounting frustration of Br'er Rabbit as he woos in vain the young tar baby, who is clad in pink skirt and sun hat. A playfully romantic quality enriches the classic and is keenly relayed by Glover's mischievous voice, Henrik Drescher's apt illustrations, and the music of Taj Mahal.
Audience: Ages 5-10
Distributor: SVS/Triumph
Videocassette: $14.95
No public performance rights

★★★★★

Adventures of Huckleberry Finn, The
Mark Twain.
Multiple editions. Adventure.
Huck Finn, a rebellious nineteenth-century youth, flees his home town with the runaway slave Jim. Riding a raft, they drift down the Mississippi River, meeting up with scoundrels and experiencing a stream of sometimes perilous adventures.

Adventures of Huckleberry Finn, The.
88 min. Black and white. Live action. Produced by Joseph L. Mankiewicz. 1939. Richard Thorpe, Mickey Rooney, Walter Connolly.
Hailed as the finest of the adaptations, this Huckleberry Finn dramatizes the

highlights of the novel with depth and understanding of the humor and prejudices of the time. The production is fast moving, from Huck's running away with Jim to their meeting up with scoundrels to Jim's capture and Huck's rescue. Of course, the movie telescopes the novel, leaving out incidents such as Huck's stay with a friendly family, the Grangefords.

Reviews: *New York Times*, Mar. 3, 1939, 21:2; *Variety*, Feb. 15, 1939
Audience: Ages 14-Adult
Distributor: MGM/UA Home Video
Videocassette: $24.98
No public performance rights

Adventures of Huckleberry Finn, The.
107 min. Color. Live action. Produced by Samuel Goldwyn, Jr. 1960. Eddie Hodges, Archie Moore, Patty McCormick.
While this is an entertaining production of the literary classic, it departs from the original with sequences that are new to the story. Huck and Jim take jobs on a riverboat, for example. The dramatization is notable for its strong performances and for river photography that admirably captures the setting of the tale.

Reviews: *New York Times*, Aug. 4, 1960, 19:1; *Variety*, May 11, 1960
Audience: Ages 14-Adult
Distributor: MGM/UA Home Video
Videocassette: $19.98
No public performance rights

Huckleberry Finn.
77 min. Color. Live action. Produced by Steven North. 1975. Ron Howard, Antonio Fargas.
This is a straightforward rendition of the classic, produced for television. While Howard is a convincing Huck, the adaptation on the whole is less than emotionally involving.

Reviews: *Variety*, Apr. 2, 1975
Audience: Ages 14-Adult
Distributor: Fox Video
Videocassette: $19.98
No public performance rights

Adventures of Huckleberry Finn, The.
121 min. Color. Live action. Produced by PBS American Playhouse. 1985. Lillian Gish, Jim Dale, Frederick Forrest, Richard Kiley, Butterfly McQueen, Geraldine Page.
Edited down from the 240 min. PBS broadcast, this entertaining adaptation focuses mainly on Huck's interaction with the fugitive slave Jim.

Audience: Ages 14-Adult
Distributor: MCA/Universal Home Video
Videocassette available
No public performance rights

★★★★★

Adventures of Sherlock Holmes, The
Arthur Conan Doyle.
Multiple editions. Mystery.
Detective Holmes's foe, Moriarty, intends to steal the crown jewels and to throw Holmes off his track by sidetracking him with two murders.

Adventures of Sherlock Holmes, The.
82 min. Black and white. Live action. Produced by Twentieth Century Fox. 1939. Basil Rathbone, Nigel Bruce, George Zucco, Ida Lupino.
The characters of Holmes and Watson are played to the hilt by Rathbone and Bruce. Meanwhile the script pays such close attention to details of the novel that it manages to include Holmes idiosyncrasies, from his playing of the violin to his conducting science experiments.

Reviews: *New York Times*, Sept. 2, 1939, 20:1; *Variety*, Sept. 6, 1939
Audience: Ages 10-Adult
Distributor: Fox Video

Videocassette: $19.98
No public performance rights

Adventures of Sherlock Holmes, The.
147 min. Black and white. Live action. 1939. Basil Rathbone, Nigel Bruce, George Zucco, Ida Lupino.
A laser disc version of the same title offered by Fox Video (see above). Also includes a second feature that involves Holmes, *Voice of Terror.*
Distributor: Image Entertainment
Laser disc: CLV format $49.98
No public performance rights

★★★★★

Adventures of Tom Sawyer, The
Mark Twain.
Multiple editions. Adventure.
Set in Mississippi during the mid-1800s, this classic follows the adventures of Tom and his friends Huckleberry Finn and Becky Thatcher. Tom witnesses a murder in a dark cemetery. He later clears the man unjustly accused of the crime, then is vengefully chased by the true criminal.

Adventures of Tom Sawyer, The.
91 min. Color. Live action. Produced by David O. Selznick. 1938. Tommy Kelly, Jackie Moran, Ann Gillis.
Scenes of the novel are convincingly dramatized, from Tom's conning his friends into whitewashing his fence to Injun Joe's chasing him in a cave to retaliate for Tom's disclosure at the murder trial. Like the novel, this fine production is full of action that proceeds at a swift pace.
Reviews: *New York Times*, Feb. 18, 1938, 23:1; *Variety*, Feb. 16, 1938
Audience: Ages 10-Adult
Distributor: Fox Video
Videocassette: $14.98
No public performance rights

Adventures of Tom Sawyer, The.
91 min. Color. Live action. 1938. Tommy Kelly, Jackie Moran, Ann Gillis.
A laser disc version of the same title offered by Fox Video (see above).
Distributor: Image Entertainment
Laser disc: CLV format $39.98
No public performance rights

Tom Sawyer.
100 min. Color. Live action. Produced by Reader's Digest/United Artists/Arthur P. Jacobs. 1973. Johnny Whitaker, Jodie Foster, Celeste Holm.
This is a spirited musical adaptation in which the songs help advance the story. Clara Blandick is particularly convincing as tenderhearted Aunt Polly and Jodie Foster is thoroughly believable as Becky Thatcher. Shot in Missouri, the film boasts authentic locations.
Reviews: *New York Times*, Mar. 15, 1973, 28:1; *Variety*, Mar. 14, 1973
Audience: Ages 10-Adult
Distributor: MGM/UA Home Video
Videocassette: $19.98
No public performance rights

Tom Sawyer.
76 min. Color. Live action. Produced by Universal. 1973. Josh Albee, Jeff Tyler, Jane Wyatt, Vic Morrow.
Produced for television, this is an adequate rendition of the classic. Vic Morrow makes a particularly wicked Injun Joe.
Reviews: *Variety*, Apr. 4, 1973
Audience: Ages 10-Adult
Distributor: MCA/Universal Home Video
Videocassette available

No public performance rights

Tom Sawyer.
26 min. Color. Animation. Produced by Rankin-Bass. 1989. An abbreviated version, this cartoon-style production changes the story so that Tom and Becky stumble upon Joe counting his treasure in the cave. There is no mention of the murder Joe committed in the cemetery. The production lacks depth and is uninvolving, though its characters are nicely animated.
Audience: Ages 8-12
Distributor: Lucerne Media
Videocassette: $195

★★★★★

Aesop's Fables
Aesop.
Multiple editions. Folklore and fairy tales.
Aesop's fables include tales about a fox that impart morals. "The Fox and the Crow" concerns flattery, "The Fox and the Grapes" deals with rationalization about what is not achieved (sour grapes), and "The Fox and the Stork" shows that the one who laughs last, laughs best.

Three Fox Fables (2nd edition).
11 min. Color. Animation. Produced by Paul Buchbinder. 1984.
Spirited, fun-loving narration in rhyme is set to country western music in this delightful rendition. The fox first flatters a crow into relinquishing a tasty-looking piece of cheese, next decides a bunch of grapes he can't reach is probably sour, and lastly tricks a stork that repays the fox in kind.
Awards: CINE Golden Eagle; Gold Award, Houston International Film Festival
Audience: Ages 4-10
Distributor: Britannica
16mm film: $305 **Videocassette:** $190

★★★★★

Aladdin and the Wonderful Lamp.
Multiple editions. Folklore and fairy tales.
A young wanderer in China stumbles upon a magic ring and a magic lamp. Both empower him to call up genies. The genie of the lamp provides him with riches enough to marry the sultan's daughter. With his new-found powers, Aladdin has a palace built next to the sultan's. His tranquil state of bliss is short-lived. Aladdin's palace and the lamp are soon confiscated by a magician, whom Aladdin must defeat.

Aladdin and His Wonderful Lamp.
9 min. Color. Animation. Produced by Greatest Tales. 1977.
The plot is well told and the animation sporadically charming in this far too condensed version of the old story.
Audience: Ages 4-8
Distributor: Phoenix/BFA Films & Video
16mm film: $230 **Videocassette:** $135
Rental: $44

Aladdin.
22 min. Color. Puppet animation. Produced by Eddie Van Der Madden. 1980.
This lackluster adaptation features unremarkable puppet characters with faces resembling cartoonlike pigs. Although this Australian production follows the basic storyline of the original version, very little atmospheric flavor is retained.
Audience: Ages 6-10
Distributor: Films Inc.
Videocassette: $49

Aladdin and His Wonderful Lamp (Faerie Tale Theatre).
60 min. Color. Live action. A Platypus Production with Lion's Gate Films. 1985. Valerie Bertinelli, Robert Carradine, James Earl Jones, Leonard Nimoy.
James Earl Jones is a magnificent genie, imposing and somewhat fearsome in his thunderous way yet loyal to his boy-man master. The special effects lend a wondrous air to the tale, perhaps the most enchanting one being a magic carpet. The romance between Aladdin and the princess is stressed in this version, making it most appealing to children beyond their primary years.

Audience: Ages 6-Adult
Distributor: Fox Video
Videocassette: $14.98
No public performance rights

★★★★★

Alexander and the Terrible, Horrible, No Good, Very Bad Day
Judith Viorst.
Illustrated by Raymond Cruz. Atheneum. 1972. Realistic fiction.
Anthony relays all the events that went wrong for him one day, from tripping on his skateboard when he gets out of bed to the elevator door closing on his foot to his night light burning out in the dark. His mom says some days are like that, even in the land to which he dreams of escaping—Australia.

Alexander and the Terrible, Horrible, No Good, Very Bad Day.
14 min. Color. Live action. Produced by Bernard Wilets. 1989.
Fine acting brings this story to life as Alexander, one of three brothers, experiences disaster after disaster in his otherwise ordinary day. Like the book, the film brings a smile and a warm feeling of human kinship to the viewer.

Reviews: *Booklist*, Apr. 15, 1989; *School Library Journal*, July 1989
Awards: *Booklist* Editors' Choice; Bronze Plaque, Columbus International Film Festival; Bronze Medal, Houston International Film & Video Festival
Audience: Ages 4-10
Distributor: Aims Media
16mm film: $350 **Videocassette:** $295
Rental: $50

Alexander and the Terrible, Horrible, No Good, Very Bad Day.
14 min. Color. Live action. 1989.
A laser disc version of the same title also distributed by Aims Media (see above).

Distributor: Aims Media
Laser disc: CAV format $295

★★★★★

Alexander Who Used To Be Rich Last Sunday
Judith Viorst.
Illustrated by Raymond Cruz. Atheneum. 1980. Realistic fiction.
Alexander's grandparents give the boy five dollars, and he discovers he has too many ways to spend the fortune.

Alexander Who Used to Be Rich Last Sunday.
14 min. Color. Live action. Produced by Bernard Wilets. 1990.
A humorously painful lesson in how quickly money goes, this film follows Alexander as he spends his new-found wealth on chewing gum, bets he makes with his family, the rental of a snake, punishment for kicking his brother, and so on. The musical accompaniment is a pleasant addition to this lesson in the value of a dollar.

Audience: Ages 4-10
Distributor: Aims Media
16mm film: $350 **Videocassette:** $295
Rental: $50

Alexander Who Used to Be Rich Last Sunday.
14 min. Color. Live action. 1990.
A laser disc version of the same title also distributed by Aims Media (see above).
Distributor: Aims Media
Laser disc: CAV format $295.

★★★★★

Alice's Adventures in Wonderland
Lewis Carroll.
Multiple editions. Fantasy.
Alice follows a white rabbit down a rabbit-hole into a strange world where she shrinks in size after eating a magic mushroom. She meets some memorable characters, such as an elusive Cheshire Cat. Eventually, Alice decides a topsy-turvy world would not be as much fun as she had imagined, and she longs to return home.

Alice in Wonderland.
75 min. Color. Animation. Produced by Walt Disney. 1951. Features the voices of Ed Wynn and Sterling Holloway.
This animated version of Lewis Carroll's classic is light, episodic and uninvolving. The voices of Ed Wynn and Sterling Holloway bring some life to the film, and songs like "I'm Late" have managed to work themselves into our vocabulary. The animation is excellent but the characters fall flat.
Audience: Ages 3-8
Distributor: Buena Vista Home Video
Videocassette: $24.99
No public performance rights

Alice in Wonderland.
75 min. Color. Animated. Produced by Walt Disney. 1951. A laser disc version of the same title offered by Buena Vista Home Video (see above).
Distributor: Image Entertainment
Laser disc: CLV format $36.99
No public performance rights

Alice's Adventures in Wonderland.
22 min. Color. Animation. Produced by Greatest Tales. 1981.
This is a limited exploration of the Lewis Carroll story that recreates some of the escapades of the White Rabbit, Duchess, Mad Hatter, and Queen of Hearts.
Reviews: *School Library Journal*, Dec. 1981
Audience: Ages 8-12
Distributor: Phoenix/BFA Films & Video
16mm film: $470 **Videocassette:** $275
Rental: $66

Alice in Wonderland.
81 min. Color. Live action. Produced by Children's Theatre Company and School of Minneapolis. 1985.
Not up to the zaniness of the Disney film, this is still an engaging musical production by the award-winning theater group.
Audience: Ages 5-12
Distributor: MCA/Universal Home Video
Videocassette available
No public performance rights

Alice in Wonderland.
26 min. Color. Animation. Produced by Rankin-Bass. 1989.
Only highlights of Alice's adventures can be seen in this short animated sketch.
Audience: Ages 8-12
Distributor: Lucerne Media

Videocassette: $195

★★★★★

All Creatures Great and Small
James Herriot.
Bantam. 1977. Biography.
A straightforward story, this centers on a country veterinarian in Yorkshire, England. It concerns his practice in the treatment of animals, and the affection of the people who care for them.

All Creatures Great and Small.
94 min. Color. Live action. Produced by EMI/Venedon. 1974.
The production portrays a tenderness for animals that captures the spirit of the book, which is actually based on events experienced by its veterinarian author James Herriot.
Audience: Ages 10-14
Distributor: Fox Video
Videocassette: 14.98
No public performance rights

★★★★★

All Quiet on the Western Front
Erich M. Remarque.
Multiple editions. Historical fiction.
World War I is seen through the eyes and emotional reactions of young German soldiers and their older leader. The story follows a group from training through battle to their deaths.

All Quiet on the Western Front.
132 min. Black and white. Live action. Produced by Universal. 1930. Lew Ayres, Louis Wolheim, Slim Summerville.
Restored in the 1980s to nearly its original length and strength, this story of World War I from the viewpoint of German soldiers is one of the finest films of all time. It profiles soldiers advancing to certain death, living with rats, suffering wartime hospitals, and so on. Hailed for its realism, the production was described in *Variety* as "the best war picture ever filmed." Its graphic impact has stood the test of time.
Reviews: *New York Times*, Apr. 30, 1930, 19:1; *Variety*, May 7, 1930
Awards: Academy Awards, Best Picture, Best Director
Audience: Ages 12-18
Distributor: MCA/Universal Home Video
Videocassette available
No public performance rights

All Quiet on the Western Front.
130 min. Black and white. Live action. 1930. Lew Ayres, Louis Wolheim.
A laser disc version of the same title offered by MCA/Universal Home Video (see above).
Distributor: MCA/Universal Home Video
Laser disc: CAV format $39.98
No public performance rights

★★★★★

"All Summer in a Day"
Ray Bradbury.
Anthologized in *Twice Twenty-Two* by Ray Bradbury. Doubleday. 1958. Short stories—science fiction.
Sensing that Margot is different, schoolchildren on the planet Venus play a cruel trick on her. They lock her in a closet for the brief two hours during which the sun shines; thereafter it disappears for the next seven years.

All Summer in a Day.
28 min. Color. Live action. Produced by LCA. 1982.
Although too difficult for very young viewers to follow, this is an excellent adaptation of Ray Bradbury's tale. The film ends differently than the short story yet

achieves the same overall effect. "This gripping, unsettling production softens the original story's abrupt conclusion without diminishing its punch." —*Booklist*.

Reviews: *Booklist*, Apr. 15, 1983; *School Library Journal*, Dec. 1983
Awards: Blue Ribbon, American Film Festival; CINE Golden Eagle; "25 Best Films of the Year," *Instructor* Magazine; *Learning* Magazine AV Award
Audience: Ages 10-14
Distributor: Coronet/MTI Film & Video
16mm film: $550 **Videocassette:** $250
Rental: $75

★★★★★

All the Money in the World
Bill Brittain.

Illustrated by Charles Robinson. Harper & Row. 1979. Fantasy.

A leprechaun grants Quentin his wish for all the money in the world, but the boy can't spend any of it because then he won't have all the money in the world. This comical disaster involves the President and angers the citizenry. Finally, Quentin stumbles on a way out of having all the money in the world, and he gets the bicycle he wants in the bargain.

All the Money in the World.
23 min. Color. Live action. Produced by ABC Weekend Specials. 1990.

As in the novel, Quentin is so focused on money that it upsets his friendships and creates a worldwide monetary crisis. The boy cleverly tricks the leprechaun into granting him a final wish, which he uses to undo his wish for all the money in the world. In the end, Quentin learns to appreciate things money can't buy. Special effects such as the magical appearance of the leprechaun enchance the production. Its story, however, falls short of being convincing; the acting is somewhat stilted.

Reviews: *Booklist*, June 1990; *School Library Journal*, Jan. 1991
Audience: Ages 6-12
Distributor: Aims Media
16mm film: $495 **Videocassette:** $295
Rental: $50

★★★★★

"All the Troubles of the World"
Isaac Asimov.

Creative Education. 1988. Short stories—science fiction.

In a future world, scientists have developed a computer, Multivac, that controls virtually everything on earth. The scientists are shocked to find out about an intended murder that is beyond Multivac's ability or inclination to control.

All the Troubles of the World.
23 min. Color. Live action. Produced by Bernard Wilets. 1978.

The Asimov story serves, with little variation, as the script in this well-done movie tale about a world-weary computer. This is a consciousness-raising film about human dependence on machines, which has an unusual, thought-provoking ending.

Audience: Ages 12-18
Distributor: Britannica
Videocassette: $275

★★★★★

Alligators All Around
Maurice Sendak (illus.).

Harper & Row Junior Books. 1962. Concept books.

Associating the letter *a* with "alligators," this is a colorful alphabet book that relates letters to words for objects, concepts, or actions (*y* stands for "yakety yaking").

Alligators All Around.
2 min. Color. Animated. Produced by Sheldon Riss/Weston Woods. 1978. Directed by Maurice Sendak. Music by Carole King.
Set to music and lyrics sung by Carole King, the motion picture is fast-paced and true to the original story. It, like the book, matches concrete as well as abstract ideas to letters (*u* stands for "upside down"). The lively show serves best as an introduction to, or review of, the alphabet.
Audience: Ages 4-8
Distributor: Weston Woods
16mm film: $100 **Videocassette:** $60
Rental: $10 daily

Maurice Sendak Library.
35 min. Color. Animated. Produced by Weston Woods. 1989.
Included in this tape anthology are adaptations of *Alligators All Around*, *Pierre*, *One Was Johnny*, *Chicken Soup with Rice*, *In the Night Kitchen*, and *Where the Wild Things Are.* See individual titles for full descriptions. An additional segment, *Getting to Know Maurice Sendak*, features the author commenting on his work.
Reviews: *Children's Video Report*, Nov. 1, 1990
Audience: Ages 4-8
Distributor: Children's Circle, Weston Woods
Videocassette: $19.95
No public performance rights

★★★★★

"Almos' a Man"
Richard Wright.
Anthologized in *Look Who's Talking*, edited by Bruce Weber. Washington Square Press. 1986. Short stories—realistic fiction.
A black teenager in a Southern household struggles to prove he is a man, purchasing a gun that misfires.

Almos' a Man.
39 min. Color. Live action. Produced by Perspective Films. 1977. LeVar Burton.
A not-too-believable father is the only weakness in this portrayal. Viewers are spared the short story's agonizing description of the boy's trying in vain to save the mule he has shot. Yet the show is ever mindful of the original story. As stated in *Booklist*, "This production catches each detail of life and emotion superbly...."
Reviews: *Booklist*, Dec. 1, 1977
Audience: Ages 12-Adult
Distributor: Coronet/MTI Film & Video
16mm film: $720 **Videocassette:** $250
Rental: $75

Almos' A Man.
39 min. Color. Live action. 1977. LeVar Burton.
A home video version of the same title distributed by Coronet/MTI Film & Video (see above).
Distributor: Monterey Home Video
Videocassette: $24.95
No public performance rights

★★★★★

Amazing Bone, The
William Steig (illus.).
Farrar, Straus & Giroux. 1976. Fantasy.
Pearl, an innocent female pig, happens upon a talking bone that she takes home. It rescues her from a fox and thieves, earning a place in Pearl's family.

Amazing Bone, The.
11 min. Color. Animated. Produced by Michael Sporn Animation/Weston Woods. 1985.
The film has a casual pace that suits the mood of the original tale. Its animation is at the same time imaginative and faithful

to the spirit of the storybook, while the bone's voice is likeably lively.

Reviews: *Booklist*, Feb. 15, 1986; *School Library Journal*, Feb. 1986

Awards: ALA Notable Film; CINE Golden Eagle; Chris Bronze Plaque, Columbus International Film Festival

Audience: Ages 4-8

Distributor: Weston Woods

16mm film: $245 **Videocassette:** $60

Rental: $25 daily

Amazing Bone, The and Other Stories.

33 min. Color. Iconographic and animated. Produced by Weston Woods. 1989.

Included in this tape anthology are adaptations of *The Amazing Bone* (William Steig), *John Brown, Rose, and the Midnight Cat* (Jenny Wagner), *A Picture for Harold's Room* (Crockett Johnson), and *The Trip* (Ezra Jack Keats). See individual titles for full descriptions.

Reviews: *Children's Video Report*, Apr./May 1989.

Audience: Ages 4-12

Distributor: Children's Circle, Weston Woods

Videocassette: $19.95

No public performance rights

★★★★★

American Ghost, An

Chester Aaron.

Illustrated by David Gwynne Lemon. Harcourt Brace Jovanovich. 1974. Adventure.

A storm sends a boy floating downriver through the wilderness in his family's home. Nearby is a deadly pregnant cougar. The boy, terrified of the cougar at first, befriends the animal, and it, in turn, rescues him from two scoundrels.

Cougar.

28 min. Color. Live action. Produced by ABC Weekend Special. 1986. Angus McGinnis, Caroline Yaeger.

While this adaptation is a first-rate adventure tale, it changes several details of the story. The book places the boy Albie alone in the abandoned house during the flood and alone again when he meets up with the cougar. In the film, his spunky younger sister appears, and they share a warm sibling relationship. This relationship is established in the book as well, but there the sister is absent during the flood. The film shows the cougar ferrying the two young people across river to safety, while in the book Albie steers himself to safety. Yet both versions evoke a thrilling sense of adventure built on the same basic storyline.

Reviews: *Booklist*, June 15, 1990

Audience: Ages 8-Adult

Distributor: Aims Media

16mm film: $395 **Videocassette:** $295

Rental: $50

Cougar.

60 min. Color. Live action. Produced by ABC Weekend Special. 1986. Angus McGinnis, Caroline Yaeger.

A full-length version of the same, abbreviated title also distributed by Aims Media (see above).

Distributor: Aims Media

Videocassette: $99

★★★★★

Anansi Stories.

Multiple editions. Folklore and fairy tales.

Anansi is a wiley spider of West Africa whose adventures impart fable-style morals and explanations for how things came to be. The tale "From Tiger to Anansi" explains how Anansi the Spider acquired possession of all stories. The "Hat-Shaking Dance" explains the origin of this dance.

Anansi.
30 min. Color. Limited animation. Produced by Mike Pogue, Mark Sottnick/Rabbit Ears. 1991. Narrated by Denzel Washington.
The production fades in and out of brightly colored illustrations, simulating motion. Narration in black English, without articles in sentences and with novel grammatical structure, lends an authentic note. However, some viewers may find the language difficult to understand.

Audience: Ages 6-10
Distributor: Uni Distribution Corp.
Videocassette: $9.95

★★★★★

Anansi the Spider: A Tale from the Ashanti
Gerald McDermott (illus.).
Henry Holt & Co. 1972. Folklore and fairy tales.
Based on traditional West African folktale, this Caldecott Medal honor book follows the adventures of mischief maker Anansi who can't decide which one of his six sons should be rewarded for saving him from terrible fates.

Anansi the Spider.
10 min. Color. Animation. Produced by Gerald McDermott. 1969.
Different from most film adaptations, where the book came first, this exquisitely animated version preceded Gerald McDermott's Caldecott Medal honor book. The book and film are nearly identical with vivid colors of orange, blue, pink, and black decorating the film and print formats. Distinctive narration and native African background music wonderfully complement this spirited adaptation of a traditional tale of Ghana.

Reviews: *Booklist*, Oct. 1, 1976
Awards: Blue Ribbon, American Film Festival; CINE Golden Eagle
Audience: Ages 6-Adult
Distributor: Films Inc.
16mm film: $225 **Videocassette:** $79

★★★★★

And This Is Laura
Ellen Conford.
Little, Brown & Co. 1977. Realistic fiction.
A girl in a brilliant family lacks confidence until she discovers that she can foretell future events.

Girl with Extra-Sensory Perception, The.
24 min. Color. Live action. Produced by ABC Video. 1980. A not-too-believable family surrounds the star of this show, a girl who has a terrible self-image until she discovers she has a special talent—ESP.

Audience: Ages 8-12
Distributor: Coronet/MTI Film & Video
16mm film: $455 **Videocassette:** $250
Rental: $75

★★★★★

Androcles and the Lion
George Bernard Shaw.
Multiple editions. Drama.
An ancient Roman slave removes a thorn from a lion's paw. Later, in the arena, the lion refuses to eat the slave.

Androcles and the Lion.
98 min. Black and white. Live action. Produced by RKO/Gabriel Pascal. 1952. Jean Simmons, Maurice Evans, Victor Mature.
This is a rather lackluster adaptation, which manages to sustain interest with lines of Shaw's play that survived the transfer to cinema. The man who removes the thorn from the lion labors in his daily occupation as a tailor.

Reviews: *New York Times*, Jan. 15, 1953, 23:2; *Variety*, Oct. 29, 1952

Audience: Ages 14-Adult
Distributor: Janus Films
Videocassette: $88

★★★★★

Andy and the Lion
James Daugherty (illus.).
Penguin USA. 1938. Adventure.
After learning about lions, Andy meets one with a thorn stuck in its paw. He remedies the ill and is later joyfully remembered by the circus lion in a crowd.

Andy and the Lion.
10 min. Gold, black, and white. Iconographic. Produced by Weston Woods. 1986.
The production faithfully tells the tale of Andy's aid to the circus lion and its joy in later spotting the boy in the crowd. While there are appropriate effects, such as band music, motionless characters on screen and the leisurely pace make the show somewhat slow-moving.
Awards: Award of Merit, Columbus International Film Festival
Audience: Ages 4-8
Distributor: Weston Woods
16mm film: $175 **Videocassette:** $60
Rental: $20 daily

★★★★★

Angus Lost
Marjorie Flack.
Doubleday. 1989. [1932]. Realistic fiction.
Angus wanders away from home and begins an adventure that involves the whole town.

Angus Lost.
11 min. Color. Live action. Produced by Gary Templeton. 1982.
Angus, a Scottish terrier, is the center of attention in this charming story. The fine film is so well constructed that the tale unfolds clearly without narration.
Reviews: *Booklist*, May 15, 1983; *Horn Book*, Apr. 1983; *School Library Journal*, Dec. 1983
Audience: Ages 4-8
Distributor: Phoenix/BFA Films & Video
16mm film: $275 **Videocassette:** $175
Rental: $25

★★★★★

Animal Farm
George Orwell.
Multiple editions. Fantasy.
A pig leads a revolution among barnyard animals, but succumbs to the temptation of power.

Animal Farm.
73 min. Color. Animation. Produced by Halas and Batchelor. 1955. Narrated by Gordon Heath, voice by Maurice Denham.
Halas and Batchelor have done a fine job of animating the Orwell story, but their production makes the ending rosier than in the original tale. It is available in its entirety or in two parts (Part 1—32 min.; Part II—41 min.).
Audience: Ages 14-Adult
Distributor: Phoenix/BFA Films & Video
16mm film: $850 **Videocassette:** $475
Rental: $75
Part I **16mm film:** $425 **Videocassette:** $250 **Rental:** $40
Part II **16mm film:** $475 **Videocassette:** $275 **Rental:** $40

Animal Farm.
73 min. Animation. 1955. Narrated by Gordon Heath; voice by Maurice Denham.
A home video version of the same title distributed by Phoenix/BFA Films & Video (see above).

Distributor: Vestron Video
Videocassette: $29.98
No public performance rights

Animal Farm.
73 min. Animation. 1955. Narrated by Gordon Heath; voice by Maurice Denham.
A laser disc version of the same title distributed by Phoenix/BFA Films & Video (see above).
Distributor: Image Entertainment
Laser disc: CLV format $39.95
No public performance rights

★★★★★

Anna Karenina
Leo Tolstoy.
Multiple editions. Realistic fiction.
Wife to the Russian politician Karenin, Anna falls in love with another man, Count Vronsky, and their affair is her undoing as she loses her son, her social standing, and finally her life.

Anna Karenina.
95 min. Black and white. Live action. Produced by David O. Selznick. 1935. Greta Garbo, Frederic March, Basil Rathbone.
Garbo's captivating performance as Anna dominates in this fine adaptation of a novel with two plots, the second being the story of a socially revolutionary estate owner named Konstantine Levin.
Reviews: *New York Times*, Aug. 31, 1935, 16:2; *Variety*, Sept. 4, 1935
Audience: Ages 16-Adult
Distributor: MGM/UA Home Video
Videocassette: $19.98
No public performance rights

Anna Karenina.
96 min. Color. Live action. Produced by Doreen Bergesen. 1985. Jacqueline Bisset, Paul Scofield.
The production is an adequate dramatization of the classic. Scofield gives a winning performance as Anna's cold, politically minded husband.
Audience: Ages 16-Adult
Distributor: Image Entertainment
Laser disc: CLV format $39.95
No public performance rights

★★★★★

Anne Frank: Diary of a Young Girl
Anne Frank.
Multiple editions. Biography.
A Dutch Jewish family hides from the Nazis by living in an attic with a few other Jews. Discovered just before the war ends, they are carted off to concentration camps.

Diary of Anne Frank, The.
151 min. Black and white. Produced by Twentieth Century Fox. 1959. Millie Perkins, Shelley Winters.
Convincing performances convey the emotions surrounding a girl coming of age in the tormentuous atmosphere of hiding from authorities who at any moment may ship her off to the death camps. Shelley Winters won an Oscar for her portrayal of Mrs. Van Dan. If the focus on the hiding seems overlong, the actual waiting was painfully so. This version is based on the play, which, in turn, was adapted from Anne Frank's diaries.
Reviews: *New York Times*, Mar. 19, 1959, 40:1
Awards: Academy Awards, Best Supporting Actress, Best Cinematography, Best Art Direction-Set Decoration
Audience: Ages 12-Adult
Distributor: Fox Video
Videocassette: $79.98

No public performance rights

Diary of Anne Frank, The.
183 min. Black and white. Live action. 1959. Millie Perkins, Joseph Schildkraut.
A laser disc version of the same title offered by Fox Video (see above).
Distributor: Image Entertainment
Laser disc: Widescreen CLV format $79.98
No public performance rights

★★★★★

Anne of Avonlea
Anne of the Island
Anne of Windy Poplars
Lucy Maud Montgomery.
Multiple editions. Realistic fiction.
The above titles are three sequels to *Anne of Green Gables.* Living at home at Green Gables, Anne of Avonlea teaches at the local school, and her foster parent, Marilla, adopts twins. Anne of the Island follows the main character to Redmond College, where she studies and encounters new romance under the jealous eye of her old friend Gilbert. Anne of Windy Poplars concerns her later adventures as principal of a high school.

Anne of Avonlea.
224 min. Color. Live action. Produced by Kevin Sullivan/Walt Disney. 1987. Megan Follows, Colleen Dewhurst.
While this captures some events that occur in all three novels from which it abstracts incidents, it leaves out key events and relationships. There is no dramatization of Anne's adventurous college days, which predominate in Anne of the Island, for example. A romance between Anne and rich Morgan Harris is added to the events from *Anne of Windy Poplars.* On a general level, the plot remains true to the originals. Anne and her old enemy Gilbert become engaged.
Audience: Ages 10-Adult
Distributor: Buena Vista Home Video
Videocassette: $29.95
No public performance rights

Anne of Avonlea.
231 min. Color. Live action. 1988. Megan Follows, Colleen Dewhurst.
A public performance version of the same title offered by Buena Vista Home Video (see above).
Distributor: Direct Cinema
16mm film: $2,495 **Videocassette:** $100

Anne of Avonlea.
231 min. Color. Live action. 1988. Megan Follows, Colleen Dewhurst.
A laser disc version of the same title offered by Buena Vista Home Video (see above).
Distributor: Image Entertainment
Laser disc: CLV format $39.99
No public performance rights

★★★★★

Anne of Green Gables
Lucy Maud Montgomery.
Multiple editions. Realistic fiction.
Matthew and Marilla Cuthbert of Green Gables on Prince Edward Island, Canada, intend to adopt a boy but get instead a spirited, freckle-faced, red-headed girl, Anne. Bright and lively with a penchant for mischief, Anne proves to be an endearing handful.

Anne of Green Gables.
79 min. Black and white. Live action. Produced by RKO/Kenneth MacGowan.

1934. Anne Shirley, Tom Brow, O. P. Heggie.
This is a faithful adaptation with a convincing performance by the female lead, who identified so closely with the heroine she actually adopted her name.

Reviews: *New York Times*, Dec. 22, 1934, 21:1; *Variety*, Dec. 25, 1934
Audience: Ages 10-Adult
Distributor: RKO/Turner Home Entertainment
Videocassette: $19.98
No public performance rights

Anne of Green Gables.
197 min. Color. Live action. Produced by WonderWorks/Walt Disney. 1987. Megan Follows, Colleen Dewhurst, Richard Farnsworth.
The motion picture for the most part sticks closely to the novel. Anne is the same spirited, imaginative character who makes up romantic names for everyday places. The roles seem perfectly cast as the film focuses on Anne's relationships with Marilla, her new friend Diane, her romantic interest Gilbert, and so on. Action is of course telescoped in the dramatization, and a few of the novel's details are changed. The film ends with Anne's preparing to take her teachers' exam; the book closes on the death of her adopted parent Matthew. Also, Anne acts more conceited about Gilbert's affections for her than in the book, but on the whole this is a superb film both technically and dramatically.

Audience: Ages 10-Adult
Distributor: Buena Vista Home Video
Videocassette: $29.95
No public performance rights

Anne of Green Gables.
197 min. Color. Live action. 1985. Megan Follows, Colleen Dewhurst, Richard Farnsworth.
A public performance version of the same title offered by Buena Vista Home Video (see above).

Distributor: Direct Cinema
16mm film: $2,495 **Videocassette:** $100

Anne of Green Gables.
197 min. Color. Live action. 1985. Megan Follows, Colleen Dewhurst, Richard Farnsworth.
A laser disc version of the same title offered by Buena Vista Home Video (see above).

Distributor: Image Entertainment
Laser disc: CLV format $39.99
No public performance rights

★★★★★

Annie and the Old One
Miska Miles.
Illustrated by Peter Parnall. Little, Brown & Co. 1985. [1971]. Realistic fiction.
A Navajo grandmother tells her granddaughter a legend about death that sets the girl off on a plan to keep her grandmother alive.

Annie and the Old One.
15 min. Color. Live action. Produced by Greenhouse Films. 1976.
The beauty of the Navajo countryside and the sensitive, touching story about death are only slightly marred in this film by the weak acting of the grandmother.

Reviews: *Booklist*, May 1, 1977; *Instructor*, Jan. 1977
Audience: Ages 6-10
Distributor: Phoenix/BFA Films & Video
16mm film: $340 **Videocassette:** $205
Rental: $44

★★★★★

"Any Friend of Nicholas Nickleby Is a Friend of Mine"

Ray Bradbury.

Anthologized in *I Sing the Body Electric!*. Knopf. 1959. Short stories—science fiction.

Set in 1929, this short story features a stranger who comes to live with the Nickleby family and claims to be Charles Dickens.

Any Friend of Nicholas Nickleby Is a Friend of Mine.

54 min. Color. Live action. Produced by Rubicon Productions. 1987. Narrated by Ray Bradbury.

Ralph, the boy character, lacks support from the others in the cast. The role of the grandmother is particularly weak in this rendition.

Audience: Ages 13-17
Distributor: Coronet/MTI Film & Video
Videocassette: $125 **Rental:** $75

★★★★★

Apt. 3

Ezra Jack Keats (illus.).

Macmillan. 1971. Realistic fiction.

Sam and Ben, two young boys, search for the source of beautiful harmonica music in a dingy tenement. They find it in the apartment of a blind man, whom they befriend.

Apt. 3.

8 min. Color. Iconographic. Produced by Weston Woods. 1977. Narrated by Charles Turner in consultation with Ezra Jack Keats.

The music and narration complement the story especially well. Though only the camera moves and the show starts slowly, its pace quickens and interest builds to a fine finish. Realistic sounds of apartment life enrich the adaptation.

Awards: Gold Venus Medallion, Virgin Islands International Film Festival

Audience: Ages 6-10
Distributor: Weston Woods
16mm film: $155 **Videocassette:** $80
Rental: $20 daily

★★★★★

Arabian Nights Entertainments.

Multiple editions. Folklore and fairy tales.

Persia's emperor vows to marry a wife a day and have her executed the next morning. One wife, Scheherazade, tells him stories for 1,001 nights to save herself and others. The stories feature Ali Baba and forty thieves, Prince Ahmed and a magic carpet, Aladdin and a magic lamp, and other wondrous subjects.

Thief of Bagdad, The.

190 min. Black and white. Live action. Produced by Douglas Fairbanks. 1924. Douglas Fairbanks, Snitz Edwards, Julanne Johnston.

Reputed as one of the finest films of the silent era, this is a long yet continually entertaining production that adapts various elements from the different tales. Fairbanks plays a thief in old Bagdad who reforms after falling in love with a princess. Deciding that happiness must be earned, he sets out to bring her the rarest object that exists. The quest brings him into contact with fantastic dangers–a cave on fire, a monstrous lizard, moving trees, and so forth. The hero finally rides a winged horse to the moon, where he acquires the rarest object. After returning home, he whisks the princess away from danger on a flying carpet.

Reviews: *New York Times*, Mar. 19, 1924, 19:1; *Variety*, Mar. 26, 1924
Audience: Ages 14-Adult
Distributor: KVC Entertainment
Videocassette: $19.95
Distributor: Video Yesteryear
Videocassette: $49.95
No public performance rights

Thief of Bagdad, The.
190 min. Black and white. Live action. Produced by Douglas Fairbanks. 1924. Douglas Fairbanks, Snitz Edwards, Julanne Johnston.
A laser disc version of the same title distributed by Video Yesteryear (see above).
Distributor: Image Entertainment
Videocassette: $59.95
No public performance rights

Thief of Bagdad, The.
109 min. Color. Live action. Produced by Alexander Korda. 1940. Conrad Veidt, Sabu, John Justin.
This spectacular production is unparalleled in capturing the magical atmosphere of the Arabian Nights adventures on film. Drawing from different tales, the screenplay combines various elements to create an original work. Sabu, confined in a Baghdad dungeon for stealing, is joined by the ruler, Prince Ahmad, who has been overthrown. The pair escape, meet a princess, and are transformed into a dog and a blind beggar. Later, with the help of a magic carpet and a genie, they rescue the princess from an unsavory fate. A steady pace, marvelous set designs, and a stunning score complement the superb performances. The production is reputed as the most outstanding fantasy ever to appear on screen.
Reviews: *New York Times*, Dec. 6, 1940, 28:2; *Variety*, Oct. 16, 1940
Awards: Academy Awards, Best Cinematography, Best Set Design, Best Special Effects
Audience: Ages 14-Adult
Distributor: Videocassette not currently in distribution

Thief of Baghdad, The.
100 min. Color. Live action. Produced by Joseph E. Levine. 1961. Steve Reeves, Georgia Moll, Arturo Dominici.
Reeves embarks on a quest for a blue rose to win the hand of the fair Sultan's daughter in marriage. This is a somewhat updated version in which the hero faces harrowing dangers. He must cross a stretch of boiling lava, outsmart a temptress, and survive a flood. While the production has strong moments, it is surpassed by the earlier remakes.
Reviews: *New York Times*, Aug. 17, 1961, 18:2; *Variety*, July 5, 1961
Audience: Ages 14-Adult
Distributor: New Line Home Video
Videocassette: $59.95
No public performance rights

Thief of Baghdad, The.
100 min. Color. Live action. 1978. Roddy McDowall, Peter Ustinov, Kabir Bedi.
The adaptation is a pleasing rendition with familiar elements from the source material: a genie, a prince, a carefree thief, and a flying carpet. Although entertaining, this version pales beside the 1940 remake.
Audience: Ages 14-Adult
Distributor: Videocassette not currently in distribution

★★★★★

Are You My Mother?
Go, Dog, Go!
The Best Nest.
P. D. Eastman. (illus.).
Random House. 1960. 1961. 1968. Concept books; fantasy.
In *Are You My Mother?* a baby bird wonders if everything it meets is its mother. *Go, Dog, Go!* builds on the concepts of color and direction. Searching for a new home, Mrs. Bird discovers her old one is *The Best Nest.*

Are You My Mother?
25 min. Color. Iconographic. Produced by

Pravis Media/Random House. 1991.
The sound track in these adaptations enhances the storyline, but the lack of movement limits their impact. In *Go, Dog, Go!* a blue dog appears in a red tree, a green dog is up, and other connections are made between two distinct concepts. *The Best Nest* shows Mr. and Mrs. Bird exploring nest possibilities (the mailbox, a shoe) before reaching a conclusion.
Audience: Ages 4-6
Distributor: Random House Home Video
Videocassette: $9.95
No public performance rights

★★★★★

Around the World in Eighty Days
Jules Verne.
Multiple editions. Adventure.
In the 1870s, an English gentleman and his valet experience one adventure after another while traveling around the world in eighty days to win a bet.

Around the World in Eighty Days.
167 min. Color. Live action. Produced by Michael Todd. 1956. David Niven, Robert Newton, Shirley MacLaine.
In its time, this stellar adaptation swept up kudos for its excellence, and it remains a strong, if episodic, production. For today's audiences the dramatization is somewhat slow moving and the American Indian sequence leaves a stereotyped impression. The performances of the lead characters remain superb.
Reviews: *New York Times*, Oct. 18, 1956, 37:1; *Variety*, Nov. 24, 1956
Awards: Academy Awards, Best Picture, Best Screenplay, Best Cinematography, Best Music Score
Audience: Ages 12-Adult
Distributor: Warner Home Video
Videocassette: $29.98
No public performance rights

Around the World in Eighty Days.
179 min. Color. Live action. 1956. David Niven, Robert Newton, Shirley MacLaine.
A laser disc version of the same title offered by Warner Home Video (see above).
Distributor: Pioneer LDCA, Inc.
Laser disc: CLV format $39.98
No public performance rights

Around the World with Willy Fog.
Eight 27-min. segments. Color. Animation. 1988.
The show stars a British lion named Willy Fog and his two cohorts, a French cat and an Italian mouse. Willy is as cool as Phineas Fog in the original while his two cohorts are comic foils in this well-animated series of interrelated episodes. Produced for young children, the eight-part series is loosely taken from the Jules Verne novel. Segments are "The Wagon," "Bon Voyage," "The Mysterious Mademoiselle," "The Temple of Doom," "The Counterfeit Fog," "Bombey Adventure," "The Deadly Jungle," and "The End of the Line."
Audience: Ages 7-10
Distributor: SVS/Triumph
Videocassette: $14.95
No public performance rights

Around the World in Eighty Days.
52 min. Color. Animation. Produced by Rankin-Bass. 1989.
Very limited animation and a rudimentary attempt at scripting dialogue make this a mediocre adaptation.
Audience: Ages 12-Adult
Distributor: Lucerne Media
Videocassette: $295

★★★★★

Arrow to the Sun

Gerald McDermott (illus.).

Penguin. 1974. Folklore and fairy tales.

The vibrantly illustrated Caldecott Medal winner is an adaptation of a Pueblo Indian myth that explores the journey of a young boy in search of his father. The tale explains the transference of the spirit of the Lord of the Sun to the world of men.

Arrow to the Sun.

12 min. Color. Animation. Produced by Gerald McDermott. 1973.

Because author-illustrator McDermott is the producer of this distinctively animated short, the rich colors of the book and film are strikingly similar. Where the book contains more dialogue, this sparsely narrated program relies on the robustly animated images (based on Acoma Indian art) to reflect the young boy's search for his father. Younger viewers may have some difficulty following the meaning of the images.

Reviews: *Booklist*, Sept. 1, 1974; *English Journal*, Nov. 1974

Awards: First Prize, Birmingham Film Festival; CINE Golden Eagle

Audience: Ages 12-Adult

Distributor: Films Inc.

16mm film: $240 **Videocassette:** $79

★★★★★

Arthur the Kid

Alan Coren.

Illustrated by John Astrop. Little, Brown & Co. 1977. Adventure.

Three bungling bandits need a leader and place an ad in the paper. Answered by Arthur, the gang is led into a situation that makes them local heroes.

Arthur the Kid.

24 min. Color. Live action. Produced by ABC Weekend Specials. 1982.

The story will hold young viewers' interests even though it is a bit uneven, slow in developing and abrupt in the end.

Audience: Ages 8-11

Distributor: Coronet/MTI Film & Video

16mm film: $455 **Videocassette:** $250

Rental: $75

★★★★★

Astronomers, The

Donald Goldsmith.

St. Martin's Press. 1991. Nonfiction.

This book was developed concurrently with the production of the film series, and was planned to supplement the films, delving more deeply into the topics listed.

Astronomers, The.

Six 60-min. programs. Color. Live action. Produced by KCET/Los Angeles. 1991. Narrated by Richard Chamberlain.

This excellent six-part program explores major developments and discoveries of recent astronomical history. Subjects are covered in documentary fashion on separate tapes: 1) Where Is the Rest of the Universe?; 2) Searching for Black Holes; 3) A Window to Creation; 4) Waves of the Future; 5) Stardust; 6) Prospecting for Planets. The shows introduce astronomers and topics explored in greater detail in the companion book.

Audience: Ages 14-Adult

Distributor: PBS Video

Videocassette: $19.95 per tape; $129.95 per set with resource guides; $149.95 with companion book

★★★★★

At the Earth's Core
Edgar Rice Burroughs.
Doubleday. 1914. Fantasy.
Two adventurers traveling to the Earth's core encounter prehistoric animals and subhuman creatures.

At the Earth's Core.
90 min. Color. Live action. Produced by Amicus/John Dark. 1976. Doug McClure, Peter Cushing, Caroline Munro, Cy Grant, Godfrey James.
The production, colorful but unsophisticated and at times confusing, is elevated to average by the special effects.
Reviews: *Variety*, June 23, 1976
Audience: Ages 12-18
Distributor: Warner Home Video
Videocassette: $59.95

★★★★★

Autobiography of Miss Jane Pittman
Ernest J. Gaines.
Bantam. 1982. [1971]. Historical fiction.
Once a slave, a 110-year-old black woman recalls the plight of black Americans in the South from the Civil War to the civil rights movement.

Autobiography of Miss Jane Pittman.
110 min. Color. Live action. Produced by Bob Christianson, Rick Rosenberg. 1974. Cicely Tyson, Barbara Chaney, Richard Dysart, Katherine Helmond, Michael Murphy.
Tyson is tremendous as a 110-year-old slave recalling the Civil War days. Made for television, the drama won high acclaim for its personal insight into black American history.
Reviews: *Variety*, Feb. 6, 1974
Awards: Emmy Awards, Outstanding Drama, Outstanding Costume Design, Outstanding Makeup
Audience: Ages 10-Adult
Distributor: Videocassette not currently in distribution

B

adherence to book   film rating

Back to the Future: The Story
Robert L. Fleming.
Putnam. 1985. Science fiction.
A 1980s teenager travels back in time to the 1950s and encounters his future parents as teenagers.

Back to the Future.
116 min. Color. Live action. Produced by Universal/Steven Spielberg. 1985. Michael J. Fox, Christopher Lloyd.
The movie is pure fun, with elements of science fiction and humor deftly interwoven in the witty plot.
Awards: Academy Award, Best Sound Effects Editing
Audience: Ages 12-18
Distributor: MCA/Universal Home Video
Videocassette available
No public performance rights

★★★★★

Bambi
Felix Salten.
Illustrated by Girard Goodenow. Simon and Schuster. 1929. Fantasy.
Bambi learns about life in the forest from his animal friends and about the danger humans can cause from his parents who tell him, "Man can do anything he wants—he is all-powerful." After a huge forest fire, Bambi loses his mother. His father, who was the Prince of the Forest, leaves, and Bambi takes his place.

Bambi.
72 min. Color. Animation. Produced by Walt Disney. 1942. The brilliantly detailed animated film shows how the phases of life parallel the seasons in the forest. It is regarded as one of Walt Disney's finest achievements, with an amazing climactic forest fire segment. Because of the loss of Bambi's mother, the film is not recommended for viewers under five years.
Reviews: *New York Times*, Aug. 14, 1942
Awards: Academy Award, Best Song
Audience: Ages 5-Adult
Distributor: Buena Vista Home Video (not currently in distribution)

★★★★★

Bang the Drum Slowly
Mark Harris.
Buccaneer Books. 1981. [1956]. Realistic fiction.
Playing on a New York baseball team, a star pitcher finds that he has leukemia and comes to depend on his not-so-bright catcher.

Bang the Drum Slowly.
96 min. Color. Live action. Produced by Paramount. 1973. Michael Moriarty, Robert De Niro, Vincent Gardenia, Phil Foster.
Even though Vincent Gardenia received an Academy Award nomination for his role, this film is only slightly above average and seems a little too long for the story.
Reviews: *New York Times*, Aug. 27, 1973, 35:1; *Variety*, Aug. 15, 1973
Audience: Ages 10-Adult
Distributor: Paramount Home Video
Videocassette available
No public performance rights

Bang the Drum Slowly.
98 min. Color. Live action. 1974. Robert De Niro, Michael Moriarty.
A laser disc version of the same title offered by Paramount Home Video (see above).
Distributor: Pioneer LDCA, Inc.
Laser disc: CLV format $29.95
No public performance rights

★★★★★

Banner in the Sky
James Ramsey Ullman.
Harper & Row. 1988. [1978]. Adventure.
A young man decides to follow a famous mountain climber up a slope on which the young man's father had died.

Banner in the Sky.
36 min. Color. Live action. A Disney Educational Production. 1980.
A teenage boy rescues a famous mountain climber at the start of the show, and the action grows thereafter. Beautiful scenery of the Alps adds interest in this excellent film.
Audience: Ages 8-Adult
Distributor: Coronet/MTI Film & Video
16mm film: $690 **Videocassette:** $250
Rental: $75

★★★★★

"Banshee"
Ray Bradbury.
Anthologized in *The Toynbee Convector* by Ray Bradbury. Knopf. 1988. Short stories—mystery.
After an American writer arrives at the Irish home of a moody film director, the director forces the writer to go into the woods to look for the "Banshee."

Banshee.
26 min. Color. Live action. Produced by Seaton McLean for Atlantis Films. 1989. Peter O'Toole, Charles Martin Smith.
Ray Bradbury's chilling screenplay is identical to the prolific author's original short story in which a taunting movie director coerces a talented writer to step into the dark woods to search for the eerie sounding "Banshee."
Audience: Ages 15-Adult
Distributor: Beacon Films
Videocassette: $149 **Rental:** $35

★★★★★

"Barn Burning"
William Faulkner.
Anthologized in *A Modern Southern Reader*, edited by Ben Forkner and Patrick Samway. Peachtree. 1986. Short stories—realistic fiction.
For the sake of justice, a ten-year-old white boy prevents his father-sharecropper from burning yet another barn. There are dire consequences for both father and son.

Barn Burning.
41 min. Color. Live action. 1980. Tommy Lee Jones, Diane Kagen; introduction by Henry Fonda.
Made as an instructional film, this version begins with an unnecessary introduction by Henry Fonda. The story is simply told and easy to understand in this excellent version, which "captures the feeling of Faulkner's tale...." —*Booklist.*

Reviews: *Booklist*, Dec. 1, 1980
Audience: Ages 12-17
Distributor: Coronet/MTI Film & Video
16mm film: $750 **Videocassette:** $250
Rental: $75

Barn Burning.
41 min. Color. Live action. 1980. Tommy Lee Jones, Diane Kagen; introduction by Henry Fonda.
A home video version of the same title distributed by Coronet/MTI Film & Video (see above).

Distributor: Monterey Home Video
Videocassette: $24.95
No public performance rights

★★★★★

Be a Perfect Person in Just Three Days!
Stephen Manes.
Illustrated by Tom Huffman. Houghton Mifflin. 1982. Humor.
Young Milo Crinkley tries to follow the advice of an eccentric author who promises readers they can become perfect in merely three days.

How to Be a Perfect Person in Just Three Days.
58 min. Color. Live action. Produced by Mark R. Gordon/WonderWorks. 1983.
Many changes have been made in this film adaptation of the hilarious book that centers on young Milo Crinkley's quest for perfection. While in the story young Milo reads the advice of quirky Dr. K. Pinkerton Silverfish, the film version sees a more klutzy Milo actually visiting the eccentric doctor, whose final rule is totally different in the film. This professionally polished drama doesn't always convey the novel's originality, sweetness, and humor but is nevertheless entertaining.

Reviews: *Booklist*, Sept. 1, 1985
Audience: Ages 9-12
Distributor: Public Media Video
Videocassette: $29.95
No public performance rights

How to Be a Perfect Person in Just Three Days.
31 min. Color. Live action. Originally produced by Mark R. Gordon/WonderWorks. Abridged edition by LCA. 1984.
An abbreviated version of the same, full-length title distributed by Public Media Video (see above). This version retains the basic plot but omits selected details.

Awards: ALA Selected Film for Young Adults
Distributor: Coronet/MTI Film & Video
16mm film: $550 **Videocassette:** $250
Rental: $75

How to Be a Perfect Person in Just Three Days.
55 min. Color. Live action. Produced by Mark R. Gordon/WonderWorks. 1984.
A full-length version with public performance rights of the same title distributed by Public Media Video (see above).

Distributor: Coronet/MTI Film & Video
16mm film: $750 **Videocassette:** $250
Rental: $75

★★★★★

"Bear, The"
William Faulkner.
Anthologized in *The Uncollected Stories of William Faulkner* by William Faulkner. Random House. 1979. Short stories—adventure.
Hunters near a Mississippi town have told stories about and hunted for one famous bear for years. A boy on his first hunting trip is caught up with the lore of the giant bear, Ben, and is the one hunter to be confronted by the giant.

Bear, The.
26 min. Color. Live action. Produced by Bernard Wilets. 1980.
Faulkner's story of tension and drama begins a little slowly in this film version but comes to the same dynamic climax as in the original short story.
Audience: Ages 12-18
Distributor: Britannica
Videocassette: $295

★★★★★

Bear and the Fly, The
Paula Winter (illus.).
Crown. 1976. Humor.
Without words, this humorous tale follows the antics of a papa bear bent on swatting a bothersome fly.

Bear and the Fly, The.
5 min. Color. Animated. Produced by DMI Productions/ Weston Woods. 1985.
This is a delightfully funny rendition of the story. Like the book, the motion picture is wordless, but the sound effects and movements are marvelous, and the anticlimactic ending is perfectly executed. "The bears' expressive grunts, ear twitchings, orbiting eyes, and lumbering lurches animatedly humanize the characters." —*Booklist*
Reviews: *Booklist*, Aug. 1985; *School Library Journal*, Aug. 1985

Awards: CINE Golden Eagle; Honorable Mention, Columbus International Film Festival
Audience: Ages 4-8
Distributor: Weston Woods
16mm film: $125 **Videocassette:** $60
Rental: $15 daily

Joey Runs Away and Other Stories.
24 min. Color. Iconographic and animated. Produced by Weston Woods. 1989.
Included in this tape anthology are adaptations of *Joey Runs Away* (Jack Kent), *The Most Wonderful Egg in the World* (Helme Heine), *The Cow Who Fell into the Canal* (Phyllis Krasilovsky), and *The Bear and the Fly* (Paula Winter). See individual titles for full descriptions.
Audience: Ages 4-8
Distributor: Children's Circle, Weston Woods
Videocassette: $19.95
No public performance rights

★★★★★

Bear Called Paddington, A
Michael Bond.
Illustrated by Peggy Fortnum. Houghton Mifflin. 1960. Fantasy.
Paddington is a very messy bear. He wraps himself in wallpaper when he helps the Brown family redecorate, floods the bathroom when he takes a bath, and so forth. Yet the bear is so loveable the Browns make him one of the family. Adaptations have also been made from the sequels *More About Paddington, Paddington Helps Out, Paddington Goes to Town, Paddington Marches On, Paddington on Top, Paddington Abroad, Paddington at Large, Paddington at Work, Paddington Takes the Air, Paddington Takes to TV*, and *Paddington's Garden.*

Bear Called Paddington, A (Film 1).
16.5 min. Color. Puppet animation. Produced by Filmfair, London. 1977.

Adapted from *A Bear Called Paddington*, this film covers chapters 1, 2, and 3: "Please Look After This Bear," "A Bear in Hot Water," and "Paddington Goes Underground." Like the chapters in the book, the episodes in the film feature Paddington's entry into the Brown family, his taking a bath, and a shopping trip during which he gets lost.

Audience: Ages 4-10
Distributor: Filmfair Communications
16mm film: $150 **Rental:** $25

Bear Called Paddington, A (Film 2).
16.5 min. Color. Puppet animation. Produced by Filmfair, London. 1977.
Adapted from *A Bear Called Paddington*, this film covers chapters 4, 5, and 8: "A Shopping Expedition," "Paddington and the Old Master," and "A Disappearing Trick." Episodes in the film, like the chapters in the book, feature Paddington shopping for pajamas and ending up in the store window, becoming a painter, and putting on a magic show that makes someone in the audience furious.

Audience: Ages 4-10
Distributor: Filmfair Communications
16mm film: $150 **Rental:** $25

More About Paddington (Film 1).
16.5 min. Color. Puppet animation. Produced by Filmfair, London. 1977.
Adapted from *More About Paddington*, the film covers chapters 1, 2, and 3: "A Family Group," "A Spot of Decorating," and "Paddington Turns Detective." Like the chapters in the book, the film features Paddington taking a picture, decorating the attic, and using a flashlight to play detective.

Audience: Ages 4-10
Distributor: Filmfair Communications
16mm film: $150 **Rental:** $25

More About Paddington (Film 2).
16.5 min. Color. Puppet animation. Produced by Filmfair, London. 1977.
Adapted from *More About Paddington*, the film covers chapters 5, 6, and 7: "Trouble at Number Thirty-two," "Paddington and the Christmas Shopping," and "Christmas." The film, like the chapters in the book, features Paddington discovering snow, a diamond tie pin, and a wishing coin in his Christmas pudding.

Audience: Ages 4-10
Distributor: Filmfair Communications
16mm film: $150 **Rental:** $25

Paddington at Large.
11 min. Color. Puppet animation. Produced by Filmfair, London. 1977.
Adapted from *Paddington at Large*, this film covers chapters 4 and 5: "Paddington Hits the Jackpot" and "An Unexpected Party." Like the chapters in the book, the film features Paddington appearing on a TV quiz show and Paddington cooking up a batch of butter toffee.

Audience: Ages 4-10
Distributor: Filmfair Communications
16mm film: $105 **Rental:** $20

Paddington at Work.
5.5 min. Color. Puppet animation. Produced by Filmfair, London. 1977.
Adapted from *Paddington at Work*, this film covers chapter 6: "Too Much Off the Top." As in the book, Paddington takes a job in a barber shop to help the antique dealer. Mayhem results but the story concludes happily as the chaos ends with a customer buying antiques.

Audience: Ages 4-10
Distributor: Filmfair Communications
16mm film: $50 **Rental:** $10

Paddington Goes to Town.
11 min. Color. Puppet animation. Produced by Filmfair, London. 1977.
Adapted from *Paddington Goes to Town*, this film covers chapters 2 and 3: "Paddington Hits Out" and "A Visit to the Hospital." The film, like the chapters in the book, features Paddington serving as caddy on a golf course and having his head examined in the hospital.
Audience: Ages 4-10
Distributor: Filmfair Communications
16mm film: $105 **Rental:** $20

Paddington Helps Out.
22 min. Color. Puppet animation. Produced by Filmfair, London. 1977.
Adapted from *Paddington Helps Out*, this film covers chapters 2, 3, 5, and 6: "Paddington Makes a Bid," "Do-It-Yourself," "Something Nasty in the Kitchen," and "Trouble at the Launderette." Like chapters in the book, the film features Paddington attending an auction, constructing a magazine rack, and cooking stew with dumplings.
Audience: Ages 4-10
Distributor: Filmfair Communications
16mm film: $197.50 **Rental:** $35

Paddington Marches On.
22 min. Color. Puppet animation. Produced by Filmfair, London. 1977.
Adapted from *Paddington Marches On*, the film covers chapters 1, 3, 4, and 7: "Paddington and the 'Cold Snap,'" "Paddington Makes a Clean Sweep," "Mr. Gruber's Mystery Tour," and "An Unexpected Party." Like the book's chapters, this film features Paddington acting as plumber, engaging in spring cleaning, and visiting a wax museum.
Audience: Ages 4-10
Distributor: Filmfair Communications
16mm film: $197.50 **Rental:** $35

Paddington on Top (Film 1).
5.5 min. Color. Puppet animation. Produced by Filmfair, London. 1977.
Adapted from *Paddington on Top*, this film covers Chapter 2: "Paddington Cleans Up," in which the bear sells vacuum cleaners. As in the book chapter, the film features Paddington purposely making a mess in Mr. Curry's house so he can demonstrate his vacuum cleaner. The only problem is that Mr. Curry's house operates on gas, not electricity.
Audience: Ages 4-10
Distributor: Filmfair Communications
16mm film: $50 **Rental:** $10

Paddington Takes the Air.
11 min. Color. Puppet animation. Produced by Filmfair, London. 1979.
Adapted from *Paddington Takes the Air*, the film covers chapters 1 and 6: "A Visit to the Dentist" and "Paddington Recommended." The film, like the chapters in the book, features a dentist unsettled by a visit from Paddington and a restaurant that mistakes the bear for a food critic.
Audience: Ages 4-10
Distributor: Filmfair Communications
16mm film: $105 **Rental:** $20

Bear Called Paddington, A (Series II).
16.5 min. Color. Puppet animation. Produced by Filmfair, London. 1980.
Adapted from *A Bear Called Paddington*, this film covers chapters 6 and 7 in which Paddington visits the beach and the theater. As in the book, the film features Paddington having his picture taken at the shore, building a sand castle, and playing a role in the theatre.
Audience: Ages 4-10

Distributor: Filmfair Communications
16mm film: $150 **Rental:** $25

Paddington Abroad (Series II).
22 min. Color. Animation. Produced by Filmfair, London. 1980.
Episodes from several books begin with *Paddington Abroad* and include *Paddington's Garden, Paddington Takes the Test, Paddington at the Tower,* and *Paddington Goes to Town.* In these episodes, the bear withdraws money from the bank, plants a rock garden, lays in a hammock, and visits the Tower of London.
Audience: Ages 4-10
Distributor: Filmfair Communications
16mm film: $197.50 **Rental:** $35

Paddington at Large (Series II).
15 min. Color. Puppet animation. Produced by Filmfair, London. 1980.
Adapted from *Paddington at Large,* the film features chapters 2, 6, and 7: "An Outing in the Park," "Trouble in the Bargain Basement," and "Paddington Takes the Stage." Paddington's antics take him into the park, where he meets up with a musical band, into a bargain basement where he is asked to make pancakes, and to a stage show for which he manages the sound effects.
Audience: Ages 4-10
Distributor: Filmfair Communications
16mm film: $142.50 **Rental:** $30

Paddington at Work (Series II).
11 min. Color. Puppet animation. Produced by Filmfair, London. 1980.
Adapted from *Paddington at Work,* the film features chapters 3 and 5: "Paddington Buys a Share" and "Paddington in a Hole." In the film, as in the book, Paddington buys a share of oil and builds a service opening in the wall for a neighbor.
Audience: Ages 4-10
Distributor: Filmfair Communications
16mm film: $105 **Rental:** $20

Paddington Helps Out (Series II).
10.75 min. Color. Puppet animation. Produced by Filmfair, London. 1980.
Adapted from *Paddington Helps Out,* this film covers chapters 1 and 7: "A Picnic on the River" and "Paddington Dines Out." The film, like the chapters in the book, features Paddington falling out of the boat during a family picnic and celebrating the anniversary of his arrival in England.
Audience: Ages 4-10
Distributor: Filmfair Communications
16mm film: $105 **Rental:** $20

Paddington on Top (Film 2).
21.5 min. Color. Puppet animation. Produced by Filmfair, London. 1980.
Adapted from *Paddington on Top,* the film covers chapters 3, 5, 6, and 7: "Paddington Goes to Court," "Keeping Fit," "Paddington in Touch," and "Comings and Goings at Number Thirty-Two." The film, like the book chapters, features Paddington in a courtroom, with a body-building set, at a rugby match, and during a visit from his Aunt Lucy.
Audience: Ages 4-10
Distributor: Filmfair Communications
16mm film: $197.50 **Rental:** $35

Paddington Takes to TV (Series II).
16 min. Color. Puppet animation. Produced by Filmfair, London. 1980.
Adapted from *Paddington Takes to TV,* the film covers chapters 1, 3, and 6: "Paddington Bakes a Cake," "Paddington Clears the Coach," and "Paddington Weighs In." As in the chapters, Padding-

ton bakes an unusual cake, empties the dining car of a train, and visits a weight control clinic.

Audience: Ages 4-10
Distributor: Filmfair Communications
16mm film: $150 **Rental:** $25

Paddington Bear, Vol. 1.
50 min. Color. Puppet animation. Produced by Filmfair, London. 1983.
Eleven brief episodes are combined on a tape that begins with Paddington's induction into the Brown family and ends with his attending an auction. The episodes are adapted from *A Bear Called Paddington, More About Paddington, Paddington at Work*, and *Paddington Helps Out.*

Audience: Ages 4-10
Distributor: Filmfair Communications
Videocassette: $29.95

Paddington Bear, Vol. 2.
50 min. Color. Puppet animation. Produced by Filmfair, London. 1983.
Eleven episodes, new to this five-volume video series, begin with Paddington's building a do-it-yourself magazine rack and end with his playing rugby. The episodes are adapted from *Paddington Helps Out, Paddington on Top, Paddington Marches On, Paddington Takes the Air*, and *Paddington Goes to Town.*

Audience: Ages 4-10
Distributor: Filmfair Communications
Videocassette: $29.95

Paddington Bear, Vol. 3.
52 min. Color. Puppet animation. Produced by Filmfair, London. 1983.
Eleven episodes, new to this five-volume video series, begin with Paddington's spending his first Christmas with the Brown family and ends with his trips to a garden store to get the finishing touch for Mr. Gruber's new patio. The episodes are adapted from *More About Paddington, Paddington on Top, Paddington Abroad, Paddington Helps Out, A Bear Called Paddington, Paddington at Large, Paddington at Work*, and *Paddington Goes to Town.*

Audience: Ages 4-10
Distributor: Filmfair Communications
Videocassette: $29.95

Paddington Bear, Vol. 4.
52 min. Color. Puppet animation. Produced by Filmfair, London. 1983.
Eleven episodes, new to this five-volume video series, begin with Paddington's planting a rock garden and end with his experience in a courtroom. The episodes are adapted from *Paddington's Garden, Paddington Takes the Test, Paddington at the Tower, Paddington at Large, The Great Big Paddington Book, Paddington Takes to TV*, and *Paddington on Top.*

Audience: Ages 4-10
Distributor: Filmfair Communications
Videocassette: $29.95

Paddington Bear, Vol. 5.
57 min. Color. Puppet animation. Produced by Filmfair, London. 1983.
Eleven episodes, new to this five-volume video series, begin with Paddington's being mistaken for a food critic at a restaurant and end with his visiting the hospital to have his head examined. The episodes on this tape are adapted from *Paddington Takes the Air, Paddington Marches On, Paddington at Work, Paddington on Top, Paddington Takes to TV, More About Paddington, Paddington at Large*, and *Paddington Goes to Town.*

Audience: Ages 4-10
Distributor: Filmfair Communications
Videocassette: $29.95

Paddington Bear: Please Look After This Bear.
25 min. Color. Animation. Produced by Filmfair, London. 1983.
An abbreviated home video version of the *Paddington Bear, Vol. 1* title distributed by Filmfair Communications (see above). This version includes the first six of eleven episodes.
Distributor: Buena Vista Home Video
Videocassette: $9.99
No public performance rights

Paddington Bear: Paddington, P.I.
25 min. Color. Animation. Produced by Filmfair, London. 1983.
An abbreviated home video version of the *Paddington Bear, Vol. 1* and *Vol. 2* titles distributed by Filmfair Communications (see above). This version includes the end of Vol. 1 and beginning of Vol. 2, spanning six episodes.
Distributor: Buena Vista Home Video
Videocassette: $9.99
No public performance rights

Paddington Bear: All Paws.
25 min. Color. Animation. Produced by Filmfair, London. 1983.
An abbreviated home video version of the *Paddington Bear Vol. 2* title distributed by Filmfair Communications (see above). This version includes the middle six episodes from Vol. 2.
Distributor: Buena Vista Home Video
Videocassette: $9.99
No public performance rights

Paddington Bear: A Paddington Christmas.
25 min. Color. Animation. Produced by Filmfair, London. 1983.
An abbreviated home video version of the *Paddington Bear, Vol. 2* and *Vol. 3* titles distributed by Filmfair Communications (see above). This version includes the end of Vol. 2 and the beginning of Vol. 3, spanning six episodes.
Distributor: Buena Vista Home Video
Videocassette: $9.99
No public performance rights

Paddington Bear: Backstage Bear.
25 min. Color. Animation. Produced by Filmfair, London. 1983.
An abbreviated home video version of the *Paddington Bear, Vol. 3* title distributed by Filmfair Communications (see above). This version includes the middle six episodes from Vol. 3.
Distributor: Buena Vista Home Video
Videocassette: $9.99
No public performance rights

Paddington Bear: Bargain Basement Bear.
25 min. Color. Animation. Produced by Filmfair, London. 1983.
An abbreviated home video version of the *Paddington Bear, Vol. 3* and *Vol. 4* titles distributed by Filmfair Communications (see above). This version includes the end of Vol. 3 and beginning of Vol 4, spanning six episodes.
Distributor: Buena Vista Home Video
Videocassette: $9.99
No public performance rights

★★★★★

Bearskin
Jacob Grimm and Wilhelm K. Grimm.
Multiple editions. Folklore and fairy tales.
A soldier makes a bargain with the Devil not to wash or cut his hair for seven years and to perpetually wear a bearskin during this period. His adventures lead him into

marriage as a reward for his kindness, which in the end redeems him.

Bearskin.
20 min. Color. Live action. Produced by Tom and Mimi Davenport. 1983.
This adaptation includes more dialogue than narration, dramatizing the tale vividly and accurately down to the soldier's demand that his opponent clean him up at the end of the seven years. The nonverbal communication in meaningful glances, frowns, and smiles enhances the story. At the end, the Devil, as in the original, gloats over having won two souls in exchange for one. He refers to the selfish sisters of the bride, whose deaths are merely described in the film.
Reviews: *Children's Video Report*, May 1985
Audience: Ages 8-12
Distributor: Davenport Films
16mm film: $350 **Rental:** $35
Videocassette: $60 (with public performance rights)
Videocassette: $29.95 (no public performance rights)

★★★★★

Beast of Monsieur Racine, The
Tomi Ungerer (illus.).
Farrar, Straus & Giroux. 1971. Humor.
A retired tax collector refuses to share his prize pears until a mysterious beast wins his friendship.

Beast of Monsieur Racine, The.
9 min. Color. Animated. Produced by Weston Woods. 1975.
This is an aptly crafted version of the story in which children in a beast costume play a hoax on the old pear grower.
Awards: First prize, Children's Category, International Animation Film Festival; Red Ribbon, American Film Festival
Audience: Ages 4-6
Distributor: Weston Woods
16mm film: $215 **Videocassette:** $60
Rental: $20 daily

Rosie's Walk and Other Stories.
32 min. Color. Iconographic and animated. Produced by Weston Woods. 1985.
Included in this tape anthology are adaptations of *Rosie's Walk* (Pat Hutchins), *"Charlie Needs a Cloak,"* (Tomie de Paola), *The Story about Ping* (Marjorie Flack) and *The Beast of Monsieur Racine*. See individual titles for full descriptions.
Audience: Ages 4-8
Distributor: Children's Circle, Weston Woods
Videocassette: $19.95
No public performance rights

★★★★★

Beauty and the Beast
Madame de Beaumont.
Multiple editions. Folklore and fairy tales.
Father angers a beast by plucking a rose for his daughter Beauty. She agrees to the beast's request to move into its palace so that her father will not die.

Beauty and the Beast.
90 min. Black and white. Live action. Produced by Discina International/Lopert Films. 1946. Jean Marais, Josette Day.
In French with subtitles, this is a classic, innovative version that select audiences find spellbinding. Outstandingly filmed, the picture, directed by Jean Cocteau, includes unique props and camera shots that create a surreal effect. The leisurely pace may lose young viewers. For older audiences "it is a fabric of gorgeous visual metaphors...of hypnotic sounds and music...." —*New York Times*
Reviews: *New York Times*, Dec. 24, 1947, 12:2; *Variety*, Dec. 24, 1947
Audience: Ages 10-Adult
Distributor: Janus Films

Videocassette: $88

Beauty and the Beast.
93 min. Black and white. Live action. 1946. Jean Marais.
A laser disc version of the same title offered by Janus Films (see above).
Distributor: The Voyager Company
Laser disc: CAV format $89.95

Beauty and the Beast.
19 min. Color. Puppet animation. Produced by Gaken Company. 1978.
An almost gruesome beast makes this otherwise entertaining puppet show less than appropriate for very young audiences; the medium itself detracts from its use for older, more sophisticated audiences. While the film changes a few details (the plucked rose is red, not white), it follows the original story line and is paced quickly enough to sustain interest.
Reviews: *Booklist*, June 15, 1979
Audience: Ages 5-7
Distributor: Coronet/MTI Film & Video
16mm film: $455 **Videocassette:** $250
Rental: $75

Beauty and the Beast.
11 min. Color. Animation. Produced by Greatest Tales. 1980.
Limited animation along with dark and shadowy scenes make the film an adequate but less-than-ideal adaptation.
Audience: Ages 6-10
Distributor: Phoenix/BFA Films & Video
16mm film: $250 **Videocassette:** $140
Rental: $34

Beauty and the Beast.
12 min. Color. Animated. Produced by Bosustow Entertainment. 1981. Voices of Claire Bloom, James Earl Jones, Michael York.
Tastefully adapted, this animated version follows the traditional story line in which Beauty makes amends for her father's plucking a rose that belonged to the Beast by living with him. The production is well paced for the audience. Based on the retelling by Marianna Mayer (Macmillan, 1978), it remains true to the theme that happiness comes from seeing beneath the surface.
Reviews: *School Library Journal*, May 1982
Audience: Ages 4-8
Distributor: Churchill Media
16mm film: $260 **Videocassette:** $59
Rental: $50

Beauty and the Beast (Faerie Tale Theatre).
50 min. Color. Live action. Produced by Shelley Duvall. 1983. Klaus Kinski, Susan Sarandon.
Susan Sarandon is a splendid Beauty, and the atmosphere is a convincing result of wonderful scenery and fine effects. There is a nice element of realism. The father is more protective of Beauty than in the short fairy tale. Yet the production as a whole is not emotionally rousing, and there is a minor change in the ending. In the movie, the beast-turned-prince explains that his bestial state was punishment for his parents' not believing in fairy tales. Then he and Beauty fly to his far-off kingdom through the clouds.
Audience: Ages 8-Adult
Distributor: Fox Video
Videocassette: $14.98
No public performance rights

Beauty and the Beast (Faerie Tale Theatre).

50 min. Color. Live action. 1984. Klaus Kinski, Susan Sarandon.
A laser disc version of the same title offered by Fox Video (see above).
Distributor: Image Entertainment
Laser disc: CLV format $29.98
No public performance rights

Beauty and the Beast.
27 min. Color. Animation. Produced by Joshua M. Greene. 1988. Narrated by Mia Farrow.
The traditional story is embellished with a few visually enhancing details. When Beauty appears at the Beast's castle, a book opens and tells her to trust her heart, not her eyes, because appearances are full of lies. Mia Farrow performs all the voices in this award-winning, well-paced adaptation, dropping into a gruff tone for the Beast.
Reviews: *Booklist*, Dec. 1, 1989; *U.S. News & World Report*, Jan. 22, 1990; *Video Librarian*, Nov. 1989
Awards: First Prize, Chicago International Festival of Children's Films; CINE Golden Eagle; Bronze Apple, National Educational Film and Video Festival
Audience: Ages 4-8
Distributor: Lightyear Entertainment
Videocassette: $14.98
No public performance rights

Beauty and the Beast.
93 min. Color. Live action. Produced by Golan Globus Productions. 1988. Rebecca De Mornay, John Savage.
The adaptation is slowly paced and unconvincing. It spends considerable time on Beauty's premonition in dreams of the prince, who appears on screen during the dreaming. The effect is contrary to the element of surprise on which the tale hinges.
Audience: Ages 8-12
Distributor: Cannon Video
Videocassette available
No public performance rights

Beauty and the Beast.
12 min. Color. Animated. Produced by David Alexovich. 1990.
Beginning with a brief summary of the plot, this production moves rapidly into the events of the tale. The action progresses quickly, with little depth to the characters or time for viewers to absorb new developments in the story.
Audience: Ages 4-8
Distributor: Britannica
Videocassette: $79

★★★★★

Becket
Jean Anouilh.
Putnam. 1960. Drama.
An English ruler, Henry II, and the Archbishop of Canterbury, Thomas à Becket, suffer a troubled friendship that ends in Becket's assassination.

Becket.
145 min. Color. Live action. Produced by Paramount/Hal B. Wallis. 1964. Peter O'Toole, Richard Burton, John Gielgud.
Excellent performances coupled with outstanding footage shot on location in England bring the stormy, historical relationship to life. The friends' bitter differences erupt over issues of Church and the authority of the crown.
Reviews: *New York Times*, Mar. 12, 1964, 40:2; *Variety*, Mar. 4, 1964
Awards: Academy Award, Best Screenplay; Golden Globe Awards, Best Dramatic Film, Best Actor
Audience: Ages 16-Adult
Distributor: Janus Films

Videocassette: $130

Becket.
148 min. Color. Live action. 1964. Peter O'Toole, Richard Burton.
A laser disc version of the same title offered by Janus Films (see above).
Distributor: Image Entertainment
Laser disc: Widescreen CLV format $49.95

★★★★★

Bedknob and Broomstick
Mary Norton.
Illustrated by Erik Blegvad. Harcourt Brace Jovanovich. 1975. [1957]. Fantasy.
The book is actually a combination of two earlier novels, *The Magic Bed-knob* and *Bonfires and Broomsticks*. In *The Magic Bed-knob*, the three Wilson children visit the English countryside and discover Miss Price, a spinster, who is studying to be a witch. In exchange for their keeping her secret, Miss Price empowers one of their bedknobs with the power to take them anywhere in the present or the past. *Bonfires and Broomsticks* reunites the children with Miss Price; this time they visit seventeenth-century England.

Bedknobs and Broomsticks.
117 min. Color. Live action. Produced by Bill Walsh/Walt Disney. 1971. Angela Lansbury, Roddy McDowall, David Tomlinson.
The film is only minimally based on the characters in the books. It centers around a spinster studying to be a witch in her spare time, who, during World War II, takes three London children to live in the English countryside. They travel to London on a magic bed and end up helping with the war effort. Sometimes referred to as a "poor-man's Mary Poppins," this production has a charm all its own, due to a fine performance by Angela Lansbury, and a wonderful blend of live-action, animation and special effects.
Awards: Academy Award, Special Effects
Audience: Ages 3-Adult
Distributor: Buena Vista Home Video
Videocassette: $24.99
No public performance rights

Bedknobs and Broomsticks.
117 min. Color. Live action. 1971. Angela Lansbury, Roddy McDowall, David Tomlinson.
A laser disc version of the same title offered by Buena Vista Home Video (see above).
Distributor: Image Entertainment
Laser disc: CLV format $36.99
No public performance rights

★★★★★

Ben and Me
Robert Lawson (illus.).
Little, Brown & Co. 1939. Fantasy.
Amos the mouse, his parents and twenty-five brothers and sisters live in a church, and the family is quite poor. So Amos sets out on his own and makes his home in Benjamin Franklin's hat. From this cozy vantage-point, he discovers electricity and travels to France with Ben, where he rescues a family of mice from the dungeon in the Palace of Versailles.

Ben and Me.
21 min. Color. Animation. A Disney Educational Production. 1953. Narrated by Sterling Holloway.
This is a whimsical tale of the life of Benjamin Franklin as told by his mouse, Amos. With tongue in cheek, the film teaches us that it was really Amos who invented the Franklin Stove and his friend Red (The Radical) Jefferson (the mouse who lived in Thomas Jefferson's hat) who

wrote the Declaration of Independence. *Ben and Me* is great fun for all ages.

Audience: Ages 5-12
Distributor: Coronet/MTI Film & Video
16mm film: $500 **Videocassette:** $250
Rental: $75

Ben and Me.
21 min. Color. Animation. A Disney Educational Production. 1953. Narrated by Sterling Holloway.
A home video version of the same title distributed by Coronet/MTI Film & Video (see above).

Distributor: Buena Vista Home Video
Videocassette: $12.99
No public performance rights

Walt Disney Mini Classics: Ben and Me.
61 min. Color. Animation. A Disney Educational Production. 1989. Narrated by Sterling Holloway.
A laser disc version of the same title distributed by Coronet/MTI Film & Video (see above). Also includes a second feature, *Bongo.*

Distributor: Image Entertainment
Laser disc: CLV format $29.99
No public performance rights

★★★★★

"Bernice Bobs Her Hair"
F. Scott Fitzgerald.

Anthologized in *The Short Stories of F. Scott Fitzgerald*, edited by Matthew J. Bruccoli. Scribner. 1989. Short stories—realistic fiction.
Bernice visits her cousin Marjorie, a popular eighteen year old, who ridicules, then helps, then again ridicules Bernice—this time for stealing Marjorie's boyfriend. Bernice retaliates by commiting a vengeful act.

Bernice Bobs Her Hair.
48 min. Color. Live action. Produced by Perspective Films. 1977. Colleen Dewhurst, Shelley Duvall, Veronica Cartwright, Bud Cort.
The film seems to lose the spirit of the short story. The male characters are only superficially developed, and the last event of the tale—the crowning blow for revenge—is lost. While the film begins a bit slowly, the middle is superb and has moments in which Fitzgerald's dialog is used. The footage at the end is dark. Comparing and contrasting this adaptation to the original is particularly revealing.

Awards: CINE Golden Eagle; Red Ribbon, International Short & Documentary Film Festival
Audience: Ages 14-Adult
Distributor: Coronet/MTI Film & Video
16mm film: $835 **Videocassette:** $250
Rental: $75

Bernice Bobs Her Hair.
48 min. Color Live action. 1977. Colleen Dewhurst, Shelley Duvall, Veronica Cartwright, Bud Cort.
A home video version of the same title distributed by Coronet/MTI Film & Video (see above).

Distributor: Monterey Home Video
Videocassette: $24.95
No public performance rights

★★★★★

Big Red
Jim Kjelgaard.

Holiday. 1956. Realistic fiction.
An orphan boy is hired to care for a dog. The dog becomes the boy's greatest

friend and protector, saving him from attack by a mountain lion.

Big Red.
87 min. Color. Live action. Produced by Walt Disney. 1962. Walter Pidgeon, Gilles Payant, Emile Genest.
Walter Pigeon is excellent as the tough-tender owner of the dog. Otherwise, the film adapts the simple tale in straightforward fashion.
Audience: Ages 5-12
Distributor: Buena Vista Home Video (not currently in distribution)

★★★★★

Billy Budd
Herman Melville.
Multiple editions. Adventure.
Young Billy Budd accidentally kills a cruel leader of a British warship, who terrifies the crew. The young culprit must hang for the murder.

Billy Bud.
123 min. Black and white. Live action. Produced by Anglo-Allied. 1962. Robert Ryan, Terrance Stamp, Peter Ustinov.
As in the novel, Billy Budd impresses the audience as a force of good caught in his opposition to the evil officer he kills. The story is difficult to dramatize, making for a production with weaker impact than the version in print.
Reviews: *New York Times*, Oct. 31, 1962, 32:1
Audience: Ages 16-Adult
Distributor: Fox Video
Videocassette: $59.98
No public performance rights

★★★★★

Birdman of Alcatraz
Thomas E. Gaddis.
Amereon. 1955. Biography.
A prisoner confined to a life sentence in Alcatraz becomes an authority on birds after curing an ailing bird that flew into his cell.

Birdman of Alcatraz.
148 min. Black and white. Live action. Produced by United Artists/Hecht-Lancaster. 1962. Burt Lancaster, Karl Malden, Thelma Ritter.
The Birdman communicates better with the animals than with his human warden in this effective but lengthy adaptation.
Reviews: *New York Times*, July 19, 1962, 19:2; *Variety*, June 20, 1962
Audience: Ages 14-Adult
Distributor: MGM/UA Home Video
Videocassette: $19.98

★★★★★

Black Beauty
Anne Sewell.
Multiple editions. Realistic fiction.
Black Beauty passes from one horse master to another, enduring hardships and kindness along the way. The thoroughbred thinks, talks, and feels in the manner of a person.

Black Beauty.
74 min. Color. Live action. Produced by Edward L. Alperson/Twentieth Century Fox. 1946. Mona Freeman, Richard Denning, Evelyn Ankers.
This adaptation features a girl searching for her missing colt; the show bears little resemblance to the novel.
Reviews: *New York Times*, Aug. 30, 1946, 13:2; *Variety*, July 17, 1946
Audience: Ages 8-12
Distributor: Videocassette not currently in distribution

Black Beauty.
106 min. Color. Live action. Produced by Peter Andrews/Malcolm B. Hayworth/ Paramount. 1971. Mark Lester, Walter Slezak, Peter Lee Lawrence.
This version involves Beauty in new adventures outside the novel, among the Irish gypsies, fighting in India, and so forth.
Reviews: *New York Times*, Nov. 25, 1971, 55:1; *Variety*, Sept. 29, 1971
Audience: Ages 8-12
Distributor: Paramount Home Video
Videocassette available
No public performance rights

Black Beauty.
106 min. Color. Live action. 1971. Mark Lester, Walter Slezak, Peter Lee Lawrence.
A laser disc version of the same title offered by Paramount Home Video (see above).
Distributor: Pioneer LDCA, Inc.
Laser disc: CLV format $34.95
No public performance rights

Black Beauty.
49 min. Color. Animation. Produced by William Hanna/Joseph Barbera. 1978.
Nicely animated, this literal adaptation of the novel exposes cruelty and kindnesses in the life of the horse and ends on a sadly comforting note with his last fourteen-year-old master. However, the saga of the horse's trials grows a bit tedious.
Audience: Ages 8-12
Distributor: Hanna-Barbera Home Video
Videocassette: $19.95
No public performance rights

★★★★★

Black Stallion, The
Walter Farley.
Illustrated by Keith Ward. Random House. 1977. [1941]. Adventure.
A boy and a wild stallion become fast friends when they are shipwrecked and make their way alone to a deserted island. Once they return home, a retired jockey shows the boy how exceptional a horse the stallion is.

Black Stallion, The.
117 min. Color. Live action. Produced by United Artists/Francis Coppola. 1979. Kelly Reno, Mickey Rooney, Teri Garr.
Kelly Reno as Alec registers emotions perfectly in keeping with the story, from his determined independence to his stubborn love for the stallion. The production is breathtaking, both riveting and heart-rending, with a long engrossing sequence on the glorious island during which no words were spoken. The mother and the jockey are exceptionally convincing. Some poetic license is taken with the novel, in which Alec is traveling alone, not with his father, when the ship is destroyed by the disastrous storm. The tenderness between the boy and horse is the same, though.
Reviews: *Children's Video Report*, Feb./Mar. 1989; *New York Times*, Oct. 13, 1979, 12:5; *Variety*, Oct. 17, 1979
Audience: Ages 10-Adult
Distributor: MGM/UA Home Video
Videocassette: $19.98
No public performance rights

Black Stallion, The.
117 min. Color. Live action. 1980. Kelly Reno, Mickey Rooney.
A laser disc version of the same title offered by MCA/UA Home Video (see above).
Distributor: Pioneer LDCA, Inc.
Laser disc: CLV format $34.98
No public performance rights

★★★★★

Black Stallion Returns, The
Walter Farley.
Illustrated by Harold Eldridge. Random House. 1982. [1945]. Adventure.
"The Black" is kidnapped to the Middle East, and Alec, the stallion's young owner, journeys there to rescue him. Tribes of the area compete for the animal. Alec ultimately rides it in a customary race.

Black Stallion Returns, The.
93 min. Color. Live action. Produced by Francis Ford Coppola/United Artists. 1983.
Not quite as topnotch as the earlier *Black Stallion*, this production is nonetheless thrilling in its own right. The story line seems more farfetched than in the novel. Alec hightails his way to the Middle East by stowing away alone on an airplane; in the novel, he more realistically sets out with others to retrieve the Black. Still, the excitement never flags. Alec makes a friend, meets a scoundrel, and adapts to customs of the Berber culture. Audience exposure to these customs is an additional plus.
Reviews: *New York Times*, Mar. 27, 1983, 54:4; *Variety*, Mar. 30, 1983
Audience: Ages 10-Adult
Distributor: MGM/UA Home Video
Videocassette: $19.98
No public performance rights

★★★★★

Blackberries in the Dark
Mavis Jukes.
Illustrated by Thomas B. Allen. Knopf. 1985. Realistic fiction.
A young boy makes his annual visit to his grandparents, but this time finds that his grandfather has died.

Blackberries in the Dark.
27 min. Color. Live action. A Disney Educational Production. 1978.
Like the novel, this dramatization is a touching exploration of a grandmother-grandson relationship in which ties are made stronger by the death of the grandfather. The film is a sensitive rendition that moves a bit slowly at times.
Audience: Ages 8-12
Distributor: Coronet/MTI Film & Video
16mm film: $600 **Videocassette:** $375
Rental: $75

★★★★★

Bleak House
Charles Dickens.
Multiple editions. Realistic fiction.
Heirs to an estate spend their lives waiting for the settlement of a lawsuit.

Charles Dickens: Bleak House.
390 min. Color. Live action. Produced by BBC. 1985. Diana Rigg, Denholm Elliott, Robin Bailey.
One theme of the story well served by the adaptation is the negative impact legalities can have on people. However, much of the difficult-to-dramatize novel falters in this adaptation. "Rapid juxtaposition of short scenes, along with sizeable gaps in the story generate a disjointedness that's at variance with the novel's close-knit slow unrolling." —*Times Literary Supplement*
Reviews: *Times Literary Supplement*, June 7, 1985
Audience: Ages 14-Adult
Distributor: Fox Video
Videocassette: $29.98
No public performance rights

★★★★★

Bless the Beasts and the Children
Glendon Swarthout.
Pocket Books. 1984. [1970]. Realistic fiction.
Six boys attempt to set free a herd of buffalo slated to be slaughtered.

Bless the Beasts and the Children.
110 min. Color. Live action. Produced by Columbia/Stanley Kramer. 1971. Billy Mumy, Barry Robins, Miles Chapin.
The good intentions behind this film are quite evident, and the production inspires excitement at times.
Reviews: *New York Times*, Oct. 29, 1971, 29:1; *Variety*, July 14, 1971
Audience: Ages 14-Adult
Distributor: Columbia TriStar Home Video
Videocassette: $59.95
No public performance rights

★★★★★

Blind Men and the Elephant.
Multiple editions. Folklore and fairy tales.
Some blind men try to figure out what they are touching as they feel an animal. They conclude it is like a rope, log, fan, and something beginning and endless.

Whazzat?
9 min. Color. Puppet animation. Produced by Crocus Entertainment. 1975.
Imaginative but unconventional and difficult for young viewers to interpret, this is a non-narrated adaptation starring six clay shapes in puppet-style animation. Among those unfamiliar with the story, only a select audience will not tire from figuring out the events that occur.
Audience: Ages 4-8
Distributor: Britannica
16mm film: $305 **Videocassette:** $190

★★★★★

Blueberries for Sal
Robert McCloskey (illus.).
Viking. 1948. Realistic fiction.
Little Sal goes blueberry picking with her mother and gets mixed up with a bear cub who was likewise following its mother.

Blueberries for Sal.
9 min. Color. Iconographic. Produced by Weston Woods. 1967.
Set to pleasant music, the show is faithful to the original story but somewhat slow-moving.
Audience: Ages 4-6
Distributor: Weston Woods
16mm film: $155 **Videocassette:** $60
Rental: $20 daily

Robert McCloskey Library, The.
58 min. Color. Iconographic and animated. Produced by Weston Woods. 1991.
Included in this tape anthology are adaptations of *Lentil*, *Make Way for Ducklings*, *Burt Dow: Deep-Water Man*, *Blueberries for Sal*, and *Time of Wonder*. See individual titles for full descriptions. An additional segment, *Getting to Know Robert McCloskey*, features the author commenting on his work.
Audience: Ages 4-8
Distributor: Children's Circle, Weston Woods
Videocassette: $19.95
No public performance rights

Mike Mulligan and His Steam Shovel and Other Stories.
33 min. Color. Iconographic and animated. Produced by Weston Woods. 1986.
Included in this tape anthology are adaptations of *Burt Dow: Deep-Water Man* (Robert McCloskey), *Moon Man* (Tomi Ungerer), and *Mike Mulligan and His Steam Shovel* (Virginia Lee Burton). See individual titles for full descriptions.

Audience: Ages 4-12
Distributor: Children's Circle, Weston Woods
Videocassette: $19.95
No public performance rights

★★★★★

Bollo Caper, The: A Fable for Children of All Ages
Art Buchwald.
Illustrated by Elise Primavera. Putnam. 1983. [1974]. Fantasy.
Brought to the United States, a leopard destined to become a fur coat tries to save itself by convincing the government to put it on the endangered species list.

Bollo Caper, The.
23 min. Color. Animated. Produced by Rick Reinert. 1990.
Both humorous and informational, this adaptation remains true to the spirit of the book. The audience gains a perspective on humane treatment of animals from the viewpoint of an animal in a delightfully comical tale that promotes serious thought.
Audience: Ages 8-Adult
Distributor: Aims Media
16mm film: $495 **Videocassette:** $295
Rental: $75

Bollo Caper, The.
23 min. Color. Animated. 1990.
A home video version of the same title distributed by AIMS Media (see above).
Distributor: Strand VCI
Videocassette: $9.98
No public performance rights

★★★★★

Born Free
Joy Adamson.
Random House. 1974. [1960]. Nonfiction.
Joy Adamson and her husband, a game warden in Kenya, adopt the cubs of a dead lioness. Instead of shipping off the cub Elsa to a zoo after she grows up, they train her to survive in the wild.

Born Free.
95 min. Color. Live action. Produced by Open Road/High Road/Atlas/Columbia. 1965. Virginia McKenna, Bill Travers, Geoffrey Keen.
The live wild-animal footage in a natural setting makes this film version captivating.
Reviews: *New York Times*, June 23, 1966, 19:1
Awards: Academy Awards, Best Song, Best Original Score
Audience: Ages 11-Adult
Distributor: Columbia TriStar Home Video
Videocassette: $14.95
No public performance rights

Born Free.
95 min. Color. Live action. 1965. Virginia McKenna, Bill Travers.
A laser disc version of the same title offered by Columbia TriStar Home Video (see above).
Distributor: Image Entertainment
Laser disc: CLV format $39.95
No public performance rights

★★★★★

Bound for Glory
Woody Guthrie.
NAL. 1983. [1943]. Biography.
Folksinger Woody Guthrie leaves Texas during the Dust Bowl of the 1930s, bound for California.

Bound for Glory.
148 min. Color. Live action. Produced by United Artists. 1976. David Carradine, Ronny Cox, Melinda Dillon.
The motion picture is an emotion-rousing document of the Dust Bowl region during the Depression, as this story of the singer's experience veers off into excerpts about union workers, migrant farmers, and the like.

Reviews: *New York Times*, Dec. 12, 1976; *Variety*, Oct. 27, 1976
Awards: Academy Awards, Best Cinematography, Best Music Score
Audience: Ages 14-Adult
Distributor: MGM/UA Home Video
Videocassette: $59.98
No public performance rights

Bound for Glory.
148 min. Color. Live action. 1976. David Carradine, Ronny Cox.
A laser disc version of the same title offered by MGM/UA Home Video (see above).

Distributor: Image Entertainment
Laser disc: CLV format $49.95
No public performance rights

★★★★★

Boy, a Dog, and a Frog, A
Mercer Mayer (illus.).
Dial. 1967. Humor.
A boy and his dog find a frog near a pond and try to catch it. The frog disappears, then reappears in an unexpected place.

Boy, a Dog, and a Frog, A.
9 min. Color. Live action. Produced by Evergreen. 1981.
Like the book, the film is wordless. The story of a boy and his dog caught in a chase with a frog. It has won many of the major film awards for its excellence. The frog in this warm story ends up following the other characters home.

Reviews: *Booklist*, Jan. 15, 1982; *Horn Book*, Dec. 1981; *School Library Journal*, Mar. 1982
Awards: Blue Ribbon, American Film Festival; Best Children's Film, Athens Film Festival; Best Early Childhood Film, Birmingham Film Festival; Best Short Feature, Netherlands Fishkon Film Festival
Audience: Ages 4-8
Distributor: Phoenix/BFA Films & Video
16mm film: $250 **Videocassette:** $155
Rental: $20

★★★★★

Boy and the Dove, The
James Sage.
Photos by Robert Doisneau. Workman. 1978. Realistic fiction.
A boy wants to work in a circus with his pet white dove, but the dove has decidedly different ideas.

Flyaway Dove.
19 min. Color. Live action. 1982.
Directed by the cameraman of the classic "The Red Balloon," the beauty of this film is worth the viewing. Without narration, the story unfolds in lovely pictures and musical soundtrack. The hero(ine) of the story is a girl in the film, and a boy in the book. Still, as described in *School Library Journal*, the film is "an aesthetic delight, bringing good technical quality and timeless imagery together with heart-warming success."

Reviews: *School Library Journal*, Nov. 1982
Audience: Ages 5-11
Distributor: Coronet/MTI Film & Video
16mm film: $350 **Videocassette:** $250
Rental: $75

★★★★★

Boy Who Cried Wolf, The
Aesop.
Multiple editions. Folklore and fairy tales.
A boy tending sheep plays a prank on the townspeople by crying "wolf." When a wolf really arrives, no one responds to his frantic cry, thinking the boy must be joking.

Boy Who Cried Wolf, The.
11 min. Color. Animation. Produced by Greatest Tales. 1981.
While the original story line is faithfully followed, this adaptation mixes a medieval setting with contemporary speech.
Reviews: *School Library Journal*, Oct. 1981
Audience: Ages 6-10
Distributor: Phoenix/BFA Films & Video
16mm film: $255 **Videocassette:** $140
Rental: $34

Boy Who Cried Wolf, The.
17 min. Color. Animation. Produced by Paul Buchbinder. 1983.
Brightly animated, this is also a non-narrated version of the tale, which appears to be set in a strange land and is at times not easily interpreted by someone unfamiliar with the story.
Awards: CINE Golden Eagle
Audience: Ages 8-12
Distributor: Britannica
16mm film: $490 **Videocassette:** $300

Boy Who Cried Wolf/Nate the Great and the Sticky Case.
36 min. Color. Animation/Live action. Produced by Paul Buchbinder. 1983.
A laser disc version of two separate titles also distributed by Britannica (see above).
Distributor: Britannica
Laser disc: CAV format $99

★★★★★

"Boys and Girls"
Alice Munro.
Anthologized in *Dance of the Happy Shades and Other Stories* by Alice Munro. Penguin. 1985. Short stories—realistic fiction.
Munro's short story subtly probes sexual stereotypes from the perspective of a young girl who lives on a fox farm in Canada.

Boys and Girls.
26 min. Color. Live action. Produced by Janice Platt, Seaton McLean, Michael McMillan/Atlantis Films. 1983. Megan Follows, Ian Heath.
This poignant adaptation alters a few details and sequence of events to stress the sexual stereotypes that young Margaret faces while growing up on a rural fox farm. This focus on Margaret's frustration with "girl's roles" and feelings of self-worth strengthens the finely acted drama's impact.
Reviews: *Booklist*, Jan. 1, 1984
Awards: Academy Award, Best Short Film; ALA Selected Film for Young Adults; Blue Ribbon, American Film Festival; Bronze Hugo, Chicago International Film Festival
Audience: Ages 10-18
Distributor: Beacon Films
16mm film: $575 **Videocassette:** $149
Rental: $35

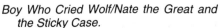

★★★★★

Brave Irene
William Steig (illus.).
Farrar, Straus & Giroux. 1986. Realistic fiction.
A determined daughter weathers a snowstorm to deliver a gown for her ailing seamstress mother.

Brave Irene.
12 min. Color. Limited animation. Produced by DMI Productions/Weston Woods. 1989.
This is a quiet, appealing film that captures the details of the original. The medium heightens the realism of story by bringing alive, for example, the sounds of the whirling snowstorm.
Audience: Ages 6-10
Distributor: Weston Woods
16mm film: $295 **Videocassette:** $150
Rental: $25 daily

Norman the Doorman and Other Stories.
38 min. Color. Iconographic and animated. Produced by Weston Woods. 1989.
Included in this tape anthology are adaptations of *Norman the Doorman* (Don Freeman), *Brave Irene* (William Steig), and *Lentil* (Robert McCloskey). See individual titles for full descriptions.
Audience: Ages 4-8
Distributor: Children's Circle, Weston Woods
Videocassette: $19.95
No public performance rights

★★★★★

Bremen Town Musicians, The
Jacob Grimm and Wilhelm K. Grimm.
Multiple editions. Folklore and fairy tales.
A group of animals who are no longer appreciated by their owners set off for the town of Bremen to join a band. En route the animal friends encounter a group of thieves who have settled into an abandoned house.

Musicians in the Woods.
14 min. Color. Puppet animation. 1962.
The jerky movements of the puppet animation becomes particularly annoying at critical points in the story.
Audience: Ages 5-7
Distributor: Coronet/MTI Film & Video
16mm film: $340 **Videocassette:** $240
Rental: $75

Bremen Town Musicians.
16 min. Color. Puppet animation. Produced by Institut fur Film und Bild. 1972.
Simple puppet animation and lovely background music accents this nicely paced adaptation of the popular Grimm fairy tale. A few minor embellishments to the original story (such as the robbers quibbling over who will go back to the house the animals have inhabited) add rather than detract from the tale.
Audience: Ages 5-10
Distributor: Films Inc.
16mm film: $330 **Videocassette:** $49

Bremen Town Musicians, The.
11 min. Color. Animation. Produced by Greatest Tales. 1981.
Oriental flavor and limited animation notwithstanding, this is one of the finer film adaptations of the popular story.
Reviews: *School Library Journal*, Oct. 1981
Audience: Ages 4-8
Distributor: Phoenix/BFA Films & Video
16mm film: $260 **Videocassette:** $150
Rental: $34

★★★★★

Brian's Song
William Blinn.
Bantam. 1983. [1972]. Drama.
Adapting football player Gale Sayers's true story *I Am Third*, the play concerns football player Brian Piccolo's bout with life-consuming cancer.

Brian's Song.
73 min. Color. Live action. Produced by Screen Gems. 1970. James Caan, Billy Dee Williams, Jack Warden.
The emotionally moving footage details the friendship between the two football stars, Sayers and Piccolo. It reveals the impact Piccolo's cancer has not only on himself but also on his family and the team.
Audience: Ages 14-Adult
Distributor: Columbia TriStar Home Video
Videocassette: $19.95
No public performance rights

Brian's Song.
73 min. Color. Live action. 1970. James Caan, Billy Dee Williams, Jack Warden.
A laser disc version of the same title offered by Columbia TriStar Home Video (see above).
Audience: Ages 14-Adult
Distributor: Image Entertainment
Laser disc: CLV format $39.95
No public performance rights

★★★★★

Bridge Over the River Kwai, The
Pierre Boulle.
Multiple editions. Historical fiction.
British prisoners of war must build for the Japanese a bridge in Southeast Asia, which other British characters plan to destroy.

Bridge on the River Kwai, The.
161 min. Color. Live action. Produced by Horizon. 1957. Alec Guinness, William Holden, Jack Hawkins.
The fine detail in this exceptional production makes it unquestionably convincing. Guinness plays the British prisoner of war, who at first shows hostility to the enemy but ultimately agonizes over the idea of his bridge being shattered.
Reviews: *New York Times*, Dec. 19, 1957, 39:1; *Variety*, Nov. 20, 1957
Awards: Academy Awards, Best Picture, Best Actor, Best Directing, Best Screenplay, Best Cinematography, Best Music Score; Golden Globe Awards, Best Dramatic Film, Best Director, Best Actor
Audience: Ages 14-Adult
Distributor: Columbia TriStar Home Video
Videocassette: $19.95
No public performance rights

Bridge on the River Kwai, The.
161 min. Color. Live action. 1957. William Holden, Alec Guinness.
A laser disc version of the same title offered by Columbia TriStar Home Video (see above).
Distributor: Pioneer LDCA, Inc.
Laser disc: CLV format $39.95
No public performance rights

★★★★★

Bridge to Terabithia
Katherine Paterson.
Illustrated by Donna Diamond. Harper & Row Junior Books. 1977. Realistic fiction.
A story of friendship, tragedy, and deep emotions revolves around two fifth graders who find comfort in a woodland kingdom retreat they call Terabithia.

Bridge to Terabithia.
58 min. Color. Live action. Produced by WonderWorks. 1985. Annette O'Toole, Julian Coutts, Julie Beaulieu.
A superbly acted drama filmed in Canada poignantly dramatizes Katherine Paterson's Newbery-award winning novel. The only variation from the original story finds

Jesse blaming himself for his friend's death, a point not raised in the book.

Reviews: *Booklist*, June 15, 1991
Audience: Ages 9-13
Distributor: Public Media Video
Videocassette: $29.95

★★★★★

Brighton Beach Memoirs
Neil Simon.
Random House. 1984. Drama.
Concerning two Jewish families living in the same building in Brooklyn in the 1930's, *Brighton Beach Memoirs* evokes a way of life in the past.

Brighton Beach Memoirs.
110 min. Color. Live action. Produced by Universal. 1986. Blythe Danner, Bob Dishy, Jonathan Silverman.
Though this adaptation of the Neil Simon play has some sparklingly humorous moments, its richness lies more in its successful recreation of family life in the past. Its central character, the young writer, Eugene, is an adolescent in a small Jewish household to which his aunt and her two daughters have moved. The production captures the ethnic spirit and values of the group.

Reviews: *New York Times*, Dec. 25, 1986, 23:1; *Variety*, Dec. 17, 1986
Audience: Ages 15-Adult
Distributor: MCA/Universal Home Video
Videocassette available
No public performance rights

Brighton Beach Memoirs.
110 min. Color. Live action. 1986. Blythe Danner, Bob Dishy.
A laser disc version of the same title offered by MCA/Universal Home Video (see above).

Distributor: Pioneer LDCA, Inc.
Laser disc: CLV format $34.98
No public performance rights

★★★★★

Broderick
Edward Ormondroyd.
Illustrated by John M. Larrecq. Houghton Mifflin. 1969. Fantasy.
Broderick, a mouse without goals except to get food, learns to read while nibbling books. After reading one book, he decides to become a water surfer.

Broderick.
10 min. Color. Animation. Produced by Art Nelles. 1980.
Art Nelles has created an excellent film version of the popular children's story of a mouse who reads and learns to become a world-famous surfer. The story moves well in spite of limited animation.

Reviews: *School Library Journal*, Feb. 1981
Audience: Ages 5-9
Distributor: Phoenix/BFA Films & Video
16mm film: $235 **Videocassette:** $235
Rental: $31

★★★★★

Brothers Karamazov, The
Fyodor Dostoyevsky.
Multiple editions. Realistic fiction.
A domineering father is murdered in nineteenth-century Russia, and the wrong son among four brothers is convicted for the deed.

Brothers Karamazov, The.
146 min. Color. Live action. Produced by MGM/Avon. 1957. Yul Brynner, Maria Schell, Claire Bloom, Lee J. Cobb, Richard Basehart, William Shatner.
A pleasure-seeking son, a studious son, a religious son, and a fourth who is an

epileptic fill the screen with a complex tale about their experiences with love and tragedy.

Reviews: *New York Times*, Feb. 21, 1958, 18:2; *Variety*, Feb. 19, 1958
Audience: Ages 16-Adult
Distributor: MGM/UA Home Video
Videocassette: $24.98
No public performance rights

★★★★★

"Brown Wolf"
Jack London
Anthologized in *Brown Wolf and Other Jack London Stories.* Macmillan. 1920. Short stories—realistic fiction.
Some people from Boston move to the wilds of northern California and encounter a dog very intent on establishing its own rules for making friends.

Brown Wolf.
26 min. Color. Live action. Produced by LCA. 1972.
An excellent rendition of Jack London's story, the film is a prime vehicle for discussing the human desire to tame or control everything.

Audience: Ages 10-15
Distributor: Coronet/MTI Film & Video
16mm film: $450 **Videocassette:** $250
Rental: $75

★★★★★

Bugs in Your Ears
Betty Bates.
Holiday House. 1977. Realistic fiction.
Carolyn, an eighth grader, has a mother who remarries. Moving into her stepfather's household, the girl has trouble adjusting to her new family.

Family of Strangers, A.
46 min. Color. Live action. Produced by LCA. 1978.
The film is probably of most interest to someone just experiencing the problems of divorce and remarriage as they affect the family. It portrays a warm story of a father struggling to unite a torn family. Captured by both the pacing and the acting, the audience is held strongly until the end.

Awards: Emmy Award, Outstanding Individual Achievement in Children's Programming
Audience: Ages 10-15
Distributor: Coronet/MTI Film & Video
16mm film: $750 **Videocassette:** $250
Rental: $75

Family of Strangers, A.
31 min. Color. Live action. Produced by LCA. 1980.
An abbreviated version of the same title also distributed by Coronet/MTI Film & Video (see above). This version retains the basic plot but omits selected details.

Distributor: Coronet/MTI Film & Video
16mm film: $450 **Videocassette:** $99
Rental: $75

★★★★★

Burt Dow: Deep-Water Man
Robert McCloskey (illus.).
Penguin USA. 1963. Fantasy.
An old, retired fisherman who is swallowed by a whale tries to trick the whale into spitting him out.

Burt Dow: Deep-Water Man.
10 min. Color. Animated. Produced by Weston Woods. 1983.
The details in this production match the original story down to Burt Dow's fishing in a boat named Tidley-Idely. While there is plenty of action, the story line is some-

what simple for the older segment of today's audience.

Reviews: *Booklist*, Oct. 1, 1983; *Horn Book*, Oct. 1983
Audience: Ages 8-12
Distributor: Weston Woods
16mm film: $235 **Videocassette:** $60
Rental: $20 daily

Robert McCloskey Library, The.
58 min. Color. Iconographic and animated. Produced by Weston Woods. 1991.
Included in this tape anthology are adaptations of *Lentil*, *Make Way for Ducklings*, *Burt Dow: Deep-Water Man*, *Blueberries for Sal*, and *Time of Wonder*. See individual titles for full descriptions. An additional segment, *Getting to Know Robert McCloskey*, features the author commenting on his work.

Audience: Ages 4-8
Distributor: Children's Circle, Weston Woods
Videocassette: $19.95
No public performance rights

★★★★★

"Butch Minds the Baby"
Damon Runyon.
Anthologized in *Romance in the Roaring Forties and Other Stories*. William Morrow & Co. 1986. Short stories—adventure.
A one-time gangster turned father, Big Butch agrees to crack a safe if the other thieves will mind his baby at the scene of the crime.

Butch Minds the Baby.
31 min. Color. Live action. Produced by LCA/Park Village. 1982.
Butch, a safecracker attempting to reform, is babysitting when he is tempted to help some of his old friends. The results are comic and sensitive in this well-done version, faithful to the spirit and language of Damon Runyan's short story.

Reviews: *School Library Journal*, Nov. 1983
Audience: Ages 12-Adult
Distributor: Coronet/MTI Film & Video
16mm film: $550 **Videocassette:** $250
Rental: $75

Butch Minds the Baby.
31 min. Color. Live action. Produced by LCA/Park Village. 1982.
A home video version of the same title distributed by Coronet/MTI Film & Video (see above).

Distributor: New World Video
Videocassette: $14.95
No public performance rights

C

adherence to book   film rating

Caddie Woodlawn
Carol Ryie Brink.

Illustrated by Trina S. Hyman. Macmillan. 1973. [1954]. Historical fiction.

The tomboy in a Wisconsin pioneer family of 1864, Caddie Woodlawn has an adventuresome year. The spirited preteen attends school, helps prevent a conflict with the Indians, "entertains" Annabel (her proper cousin from Boston), hunts, and even begins to grow into a lady.

Caddie Woodlawn.

104 min. Color. Live action. Produced by Churchill Entertainment (George McQuilkin, Noel Resnick). 1989. Scanlon Gail, Season Hubley, Emily Schulman.

This version is poignant and faithful to the spirit of the original, although it makes a few telling changes in details. For example, not in the original but in the film, Caddie tries to prevent her uncle from hunting animals instead of helping him in the chase. Her school friend Ella Mae dies in the film, presumably for dramatic effect. Also, her father's hired hand, Robert Ireton, is a rabble rouser instead of the gentle character he is in the novel. The incident of conflict with the Dakota Indians and Caddie's rivalry with her cousin Annabel are magnified in the adaptation. Despite these changes, Caddie's growth and character are aptly and adroitly portrayed.

Reviews: *Booklist*, Dec. 1, 1989; *Detroit Free Press*, May 4, 1990; *Los Angeles Times*, Apr. 21, 1990; *Variety*, Apr. 20, 1990

Awards: Ace Award; Gold Apple, National Educational Film and Video Festival; Parents' Choice Group Award

Audience: Ages 8-Adult

Distributor: Churchill Media

16mm film: $695 **Videocassette:** $375

Rental: $125

★★★★★

Caine Mutiny, The
Herman Wouk.

Doubleday. 1954. Historical fiction.

The captain of a World War II destroyer panics during a typhoon. Naval officers mutiny against the captain, and a court martial follows.

Caine Mutiny, The.

125 min. Color. Live action. Produced by Columbia/Stanley Kramer. 1954. Jose Ferrer, Humphrey Bogart, Van Johnson, Fred MacMurray, E. G. Marshall, Lee Marvin.

There are riveting performances in this topnotch adaptation. Bogart plays the neurotic captain.

Reviews: *New York Times*, June 25, 1954, 17:1; *Variety*, June 9, 1954

Audience: Ages 16-Adult

Distributor: Columbia TriStar Home

Video
Videocassette: $19.95
No public performance rights

Caine Mutiny, The.
125 min. Color. Live action. 1954. Humphrey Bogart, Jose Ferrer.
A laser disc version of the same title offered by Columbia TriStar Home Video (see above).
Distributor: Pioneer LDCA, Inc.
Laser disc: CLV format $39.95
No public performance rights

★★★★★

Call It Courage
Armstrong Sperry (illus.).
Macmillan. 1940. Adventure.
A quiet young man is branded a coward by his peers and sets out on a lonely cruise to prove his courage.

Call It Courage.
24 min. Color. Live action. A Disney Educational Production. 1981.
The story is well told with only mildly emotion-rousing episodes; it is a quiet tale of courage in the South Pacific.
Audience: Ages 8-12
Distributor: Coronet/MTI Film & Video
16mm film: $550 **Videocassette:** $250
Rental: $75

★★★★★

Call of the Wild, The
Jack London.
Multiple editions. Adventure.
Kidnapped from his California home, the dog Buck is sold to mail carriers in the Alaskan gold rush. He proves his mettle, enduring pain, exhaustion, and the rebelliousness of other dogs. Also he befriends a kind human, John Thornton.

Call of the Wild, The.
105 min. Color. Live action. Produced by Harry Alan Towers. 1972. Charlton Heston, Michèle Mercier, Raimund Harmstorf.
This version sticks more closely to the original than the earlier adaptation, but it is flat. Not captured by the film is London's impression of the connection between human and dog in the stark northern wilderness.
Reviews: *Variety*, Mar. 7, 1973
Audience: Ages 12-Adult
Distributor: MPI Home Video
Videocassette: $59.98
No public performance rights

Call of the Wild, The.
100 min. Color. Live action. Produced for television. 1976. John Beck, Bernard Fresson, John McLiam.
This is a good but not spectacular production of the dog's adventures in the Klondike. As in the novel, the dog, Buck, takes center stage in this made-for-television version.
Audience: Ages 12-Adult
Distributor: Videocassette not currently in distribution

Call of the Wild, The.
13 min. Color. Live action. Produced by Asselin for LCA/A CBS Library Special. 1989.
The beauty of the Alaskan setting is alone worth the viewing, and the story of the man who befriends a battered dog is finely told.
Audience: Ages 10-Adult
Distributor: Coronet/MTI Film & Video
16mm film: $320 **Videocassette:** $250
Rental: $75

Call of the Wild.
68 min. Color. Animation. Produced by Vestron. 1989.
A good production for young viewers of the story of a domesticated dog in the wilds of Alaska.
Audience: Ages 10-Adult
Distributor: Vestron Video
Videocassette: $29.98
No public performance rights

★★★★★

Camel Who Took a Walk, The
Jack Tworkov.
Illustrated by Roger Duvoisin. E. P. Dutton. 1974. [1951]. Humor.
In a chain-reaction tale, a tiger spots a camel taking a walk and makes ready to pounce on it. Another animal sets its sights on the tiger and so on, but the camel upsets them all.

Camel Who Took a Walk, The.
6 min. Color. Iconographic. Produced by Weston Woods. 1957.
Despite the limited motion, this short picture aptly brings the story book to life. Its well-narrated text and colorful visuals evoke the humor of the tale and convey the personality of the camel.
Audience: Ages 4-8
Distributor: Weston Woods
16mm film: $140 **Videocassette:** $70
Rental: $20 daily

★★★★★

Cannery Row
Sweet Thursday
John Steinbeck.
Multiple editions. Realistic fiction.
In *Cannery Row*, Steinbeck profiles the endearing but shiftless fringe of seamy characters living on a California waterfront; in *Sweet Thursday* he returns to the scene with the character of a marine biologist.

Cannery Row.
120 min. Color. Live action. Produced by MGM/Michael Philips. 1982. Nick Nolte, Debra Winger, narration by John Huston.
A one-time baseball star, the marine biologist falls in love with a smart-tongued prostitute who lives on the waterfront. John Steinbeck returned to the setting of *Cannery Row* ten years later to write *Sweet Thursday*, which won far less acclaim. The production combines elements from both novels.
Reviews: *New York Times*, Feb. 21, 1982, II, 13:4; *Variety*, Feb. 3, 1982
Audience: Ages 14-Adult
Distributor: MGM/UA Home Video
Videocassette: $19.98
No public performance rights

★★★★★

Canterville Ghost, The
Oscar Wilde.
Multiple editions. Fantasy.
An American family of the late 1800s moves into an English mansion, which upsets the resident ghost. Victoria, the daughter, resolves matters to the ghost's satisfaction.

Canterville Ghost, The.
95 min. Black and white. Live action. Produced by Arthur L. Field/MGM. 1944. Charles Laughton, Robert Young, Margaret O'Brien, Peter Lawford.
Adapted from the original is the premise of a ghost in an English mansion, but other aspects of the story have been changed. In the film, the setting is World War I at a time when some American soldiers sojourn at the castle. The ghost is

reputedly a coward, and one of the soldiers fears he might be, too, so both comically try to prove their bravery.

Reviews: *New York Times*, July 29, 1944, 16:2; *Variety*, May 31, 1944
Audience: Ages 14-Adult
Distributor: MGM/UA Home Video
Videocassette: $19.98
No public performance rights

Canterville Ghost, The.
96 min. Color. Live action. Produced by Columbia Pictures TV/Peter Graham Scott. 1986. John Gielgud, Ted Wass, Andrea Marcovicci.
Gielgud's performance as the spirit brings some humor to this production of the classic tale.

Reviews: *Variety*, Oct. 15, 1986
Audience: Ages 14-Adult
Distributor: Columbia TriStar Home Video
Videocassette: $69.95
No public performance rights

Canterville Ghost, The.
22 min. Color. Animation. Produced by Orkin-Flaum. 1988.
A strong story line and zany animated characters make this a successful adaptation of the story about a would-be-scary ghost who is more comical than frightening. This is an attention-holding film that appeals to a slightly younger audience than the printed tale.

Reviews: *Curriculum Review*, April 1989; *School Library Journal*, Sept. 1989
Audience: Ages 5-10
Distributor: Barr Films
16mm film: $505 **Videocassette:** $355
Rental: $50

Canterville Ghost, The.
57 min. Color. Live action. Produced by Sascha Schneider. 1991. Richard Kiley, Jenny Beck, Shelley Fabares.
Even though numerous details have been changed, the mysterious flavor of Oscar Wilde's short story is retained in this modern video adaptation. The American couple and their children are much younger in this dramatization, which uses an ancient prophecy and curse to explain the presence of the eerie, ultimately friendly specter.

Reviews: *Booklist*, Oct. 15, 1991
Audience: Ages 9-14
Distributor: Public Media Video
Videocassette: $29.95

★★★★★

"Cap for Steve, A"
Morley Callaghan.
Anthologized in *The World of the Short Story*, edited by Clifton Fadiman. Houghton Mifflin. 1986. Short stories—realistic fiction.
The relationship between Steve and his father is further strained when Steve's father accepts money for his son's prized baseball cap.

Cap, The.
26 min. Color. Live action. Produced by Atlantis Films/ the National Film Board of Canada. 1985.
The plot of Callaghan's meaningful short story is retained in this emotionally rending drama involving a young boy, a baseball hero, and a father's weakness for money. Although the filmed version is set in Canada, this has little bearing on the overall effect of the story. Another change of little consequence is the fact that an uncle (not found in the print version) makes an appearance in the drama.

Reviews: *Booklist*, May 1, 1986
Awards: ALA Notable Children's Film; *Booklist* Editors' Choice
Audience: Ages 7-12

Distributor: Beacon Films
16mm film: $575 **Videocassette:** $149
Rental: $35

★★★★★

Caps for Sale
Esphyr Slobodkina (illus.).
William R. Scott. 1947. Humor.
A merchant who sells caps that he wears stacked on his head takes a nap under a tree, during which he mysteriously loses his wares.

Caps for Sale.
5 min. Color. Iconographic. Produced by Weston Woods. 1960.
Though music and a few sound effects are added in this adaptation, its straight retelling and the lack of movement do little to enhance the storybook version.
Audience: Ages 4-8
Distributor: Weston Woods
16mm film: $115 **Videocassette:** $60
Rental: $15 daily

★★★★★

Captains Courageous
Rudyard Kipling.
Multiple editions. Adventure.
A selfish boy falls off an ocean liner into the sea, then is rescued by some Portuguese fishermen who teach him about the realities of life.

Captains Courageous.
115 min. Black and white. Live action. Produced by MGM/Louis D. Lighton. 1937. Freddie Bartholomew, Spencer Tracy, Lionel Barrymore.
Reputed as one of the finest sea stories of all time, the plot is admirably portrayed in this outstanding adaptation. The fishermen insist on completing their three-month voyage before the boy can go home, and in the meanwhile his character changes.
Reviews: *New York Times*, May 12, 1937, 21:1; *Variety*, May 19, 1937
Awards: Academy Award, Best Actor
Audience: Ages 10-Adult
Distributor: MGM/UA Home Video
Videocassette: $19.98
No public performance rights

★★★★★

Case of the Elevator Duck, The
Polly Berrien Berends.
Illustrated by James K. Washburn. Random House. 1973. Mystery.
Gilbert finds a lost duck in the elevator of his apartment house and the two become inseparable, much to Gilbert's dismay. No pets are allowed in the housing project, so searching for the duck's owner calls for some detective work.

Case of the Elevator Duck, The.
17 min. Color. Live action. Produced by LCA. 1974.
Not the usual story about drab tenement life, this is a warm and humorous tale about Gilbert and the bird pet he didn't plan to have. "The film is full of funny, hip lines that will amuse children and adults alike." —*Booklist*
Reviews: *Booklist*, Dec. 15, 1974
Awards: ALA Notable Children's Films; Red Ribbon, American Film Festival
Audience: Ages 5-11
Distributor: Coronet/MTI Film & Video
16mm film: $350 **Videocassette:** $250
Rental: $75

★★★★★

"Casey at the Bat"
William Lawrence Thayer.
Multiple editions. Poetry.

In the top of the ninth inning, the mighty Casey comes to bat with two men out and a chance to win the game.

Casey at the Bat.
9 min. Color. Animation. A Disney Educational Production. 1971.
Zany Disney animation makes this an unforgettable rendition of how Casey let his Mudville team down.

Audience: Ages 5-12
Distributor: Coronet/MTI Film & Video
16mm film: $250 **Videocassette:** $190
Rental: $75

★★★★★

Casey Jones.
Multiple editions. Folklore and fairy tales.
John Luther Jones, the greatest railroad engineer of his time, is represented by Casey Jones as he makes his last train ride.

Casey Jones.
11 min. Color. Limited animation. Produced by Film Associates. 1972.
The words of the original poem are the narrative of this film, which holds an audience well, despite limitations with the animation.

Audience: Ages 7-12
Distributor: Phoenix/BFA Films & Video
16mm film: $265 **Videocassette:** $150
Rental: $35

★★★★★

"Cask of Amontialldo, The"
Edgar Allan Poe.
Anthologized in *The Unabridged Edgar Allan Poe*. Running Press. 1983. Short stories—horror.
A young man is slighted by a nobleman and plans revenge. On the pretense of wine-testing he lures the nobleman into a cellar for his final retribution.

Cask of Amontialldo, The.
18 min. Color. Animation. Produced by Bernard Wilets. 1978.
Produced in iconographic style, using beautifully drawn illustrations of the Poe story and drawing heavily on Poe's words, this is "a stirring dramatization." —*Booklist*

Reviews: *Booklist*, July 15, 1979
Audience: Ages 12-18
Distributor: Britannica
Videocassette: $240

★★★★★

Cat in the Hat
Dr. Seuss (illus.).
Beginner Books. 1966. [1957]. Humor.
Two children left alone on a rainy day are visited by a most unusual cat with magical abilities.

Cat in the Hat.
24 min. Color. Animation. Produced by DePatie-Freling/CBS. 1972.
Originally made for CBS television release, the words and characters of Dr. Seuss's story are enhanced by music and swirling action. This is a delightful experience for young viewers.

Reviews: *Instructor*, Jan. 1973
Audience: Ages 5-10
Distributor: Phoenix/BFA Films & Video
16mm film: $525 **Videocassette:** $315
Rental: $76

Dr. Seuss: The Cat in the Hat.
28 min. Color. Animation. Produced by DePatie-Freleng/CBS, Inc. 1971.
A home video version of the same title distributed by Phoenix/BFA Films & Video (see above).

Reviews: *Variety*, Mar. 17, 1971
Distributor: Fox Video
Videocassette: $9.98
No public performance rights

★★★★★

Cat in the Hat Comes Back, The
Fox in Socks
There's a Wocket in My Pocket!
Theodor S. Geisel and Audrey S. Geisel (illus.).

Beginner Books. 1958. 1965. 1974. Humor.

The Cat in the Hat Comes Back features the return of the Cat in the Hat, who stirs up much mischief and calls for his little "alphabet cats" to save the day. *Fox in Socks* is a clever and complicated set of tongue twisters. In *There's a Wocket in My Pocket*, a word game invents names for imaginary creatures that rhyme with the things they're found in.

Dr. Seuss Beginner Book Videocassette: Cat in the Hat Comes Back; Fox in Socks; There's a Wocket in My Pocket!.

30 min. Color. Iconographic. Produced by Praxis Media, Inc. and Random House Home Video. 1989.

Three excellent adaptations provide amusing lessons in listening and pronouncing. Electronic music mimics a variety of instruments, underscoring the humor. Using both adult's and children's voices to give personality to the characters, the narrator stimulates viewers to "play the story game." *The Cat in the Hat Comes Back* illustrates how solving one problem can create another; *Fox in Socks* plays rhyming games; *There's a Wocket in My Pocket* encourages inventing words.

Reviews: *Children's Video Report*, Oct./Nov. 1989
Awards: Parents' Choice Award
Audience: Ages 3-10
Distributor: Random House Home Video
Videocassette: $9.95
No public performance rights

★★★★★

Catch Twenty-Two
Joseph Heller.

Dell. 1962. Historical fiction.

Set in the Mediterranean on an air-force base during World War II, this story reveals the unfortunate fates of its officers.

Catch Twenty-Two.

122 min. Color. Live action. Produced by John Calley, Martin Ransohoff/Filmways. 1970. Alan Arkin, Bob Newhart, Anthony Perkins, Jon Voight, Martin Sheen, Orson Welles.

The film proceeds at a sluggish pace in this bold attempt to dramatize the insanity of army life captured in the book.

Reviews: *New York Times*, June 25, 1970, 54:1; *Variety*, June 10, 1970
Audience: Ages 15-Adult
Distributor: Paramount Home Video
Videocassette available
No public performance rights

★★★★★

Caterpillar and the Polliwog, The
Jack Kent (illus.).

Prentice-Hall. 1982. Realistic fiction.

A caterpillar excitedly circles a pond, informing the animals she will turn into something else when she grows up. As her friend the polliwog watches, he himself becomes a frog.

Caterpillar and the Polliwog, The.

7 min. Color. Animation. DMI Productions/Weston Woods. 1988.

Brightly animated visuals and realistic sound effects capture the charm of this tale. The polliwog at first thinks he will turn into a butterfly too; the element of surprise adds to the charm of the tale.

Reviews: *School Library Journal*, June 1989

Audience: Ages 4-8

Distributor: Weston Woods

16mm film: $175 **Videocassette:** $110

Rental: $20 daily

Owl Moon and Other Stories.

35 min. Color. Iconographic and animated. Produced by Weston Woods. 1990.

Included in this tape anthology are adaptations of *Owl Moon* (Jane Yolen), *The Caterpillar and the Polliwog* (Jack Kent), *Hot Hippo* (Mwenye Hadithi), and *Time of Wonder* (Robert McCloskey). See individual titles for full descriptions.

Audience: Ages 4-8

Distributor: Children's Circle, Weston Woods

Videocassette: $19.95

No public performance rights

★★★★★

"Celebrated Jumping Frog of Calaveras County, The"

Mark Twain.

Multiple editions. Short stories—humor.

Jim Smiley is willing to bet anything on the jumping ability of his giant frog, Dan'l Webster. When Jim bets against the frog of a stranger, he doesn't realize that Dan'l Webster has been filled with buckshot, making the frog unable to move.

Notorious Jumping Frog of Calaveras County, The.

24.5 min. Color. Animation and live action. Produced by Learning Garden. 1981.

The slow beginning of this film is a distraction before the wild animation cells begin to capture the audience. Although the show has won several awards, one wonders what might have been if the slow start, which introduces Mark Twain, who then tells the frog story, had been eliminated.

Awards: Honorable Mention, Columbus Internaional Film Festival; *Learning* Magazine AV Award

Audience: Ages 8-15

Distributor: Barr Films

16mm film: $550 **Videocassette:** $99

Rental: $50

★★★★★

Changes, Changes

Pat Hutchins (illus.).

Macmillan. 1971. Fantasy.

Using brightly colored blocks, a wooden man and woman embark on a building adventure, creating a house that burns, a fire engine, a barge, a train. They form all the figures from the same set of blocks.

Changes, Changes.

6 min. Color. Animated. Produced by Weston Woods. 1973.

Like the storybook, this film is a wordless celebration of imagination. The animation, in fact, adds to the force of the picture story as the wooden characters visibly change the building blocks from house to fire engine and so on. "This is not a film that will get by with just one showing. Youngsters will be intrigued and motivated by its appeal to their imaginations...." —*Previews*

Reviews: *Horn Book*, Oct. 1973; *Previews* May 1974

Audience: Ages 4-8

Distributor: Weston Woods

16mm film: $175 **Videocassette:** $60

Rental: $20 daily

Five Stories for the Very Young.

30 min. Color. Iconographic and animated. Produced by Weston Woods. 1986.

Included in this tape anthology are adaptations of *Changes, Changes* (Pat

Hutchins), *Harold's Fairy Tale* (Crockett Johnson), *Whistle for Willie* (Ezra Jack Keats), *Drummer Hoff* (Barbara and Ed Emberly) and *Caps for Sale* (Esphyr Slobodkina). See individual titles for full descriptions.

Audience: Ages 4-6
Distributor: Children's Circle, Weston Woods
Videocassette: $19.95
No public performance rights

★★★★★

"Chaparral Prince, A"
O. Henry.

Anthologized in *Collected Stories of O. Henry*, edited by Paul J. Horowitz. Avenel Books. 1979. Short stories—adventure.
A leader of a robbery band becomes a hero when he reads a letter from a young girl to her parents about her plans to escape from the bondage in which she has been placed.

Chaparral Prince, The.
19 min. Color. Live action. Produced by LCA. 1982. John Shea.
A band of robbers who turn out to be heros? A young girl shipped off by her father to work for a tyrant? It's a mix of Robin Hood and Cinderella set in the old west. Everyone in this fantasy performs excellently.

Reviews: *School Library Journal*, Nov. 1983
Audience: Ages 12-Adult
Distributor: Coronet/MTI Film & Video
16mm film: $550 **Videocassette:** $250
Rental: $75

★★★★★

"Charles"
Shirley Jackson

Anthologized in *The Best of Both Worlds*, compiled by Georgess McHargue. Doubleday. 1968. Multiple editions. Short stories—realistic fiction.
A girl goes to kindergarten, where she has difficulty adjusting and concocts a fictitious character to help.

Charles.
12 min. Color. Live action. Produced by Advanced American Communications. 1989.
Not very exciting for young viewers, this is more an adult story about young children than fare for youngsters. Even so it is a story whose conclusion (that her friend is imaginary) is recognizable almost throughout the overly long twelve minutes.

Audience: Ages 4-6
Distributor: Coronet/MTI Film & Video
16mm film: $380 **Videocassette:** $250
Rental: $75

★★★★★

Charlie and the Chocolate Factory
Roald Dahl.

Penguin. 1983. [1972]. Fantasy.
A poor boy wins a visit to a chocolate factory that results in good fortune for his whole family.

Willy Wonka and the Chocolate Factory.
98 min. Color. Live action. Produced by David L. Wolper. 1971. Gene Wilder, Jack Albertson, Peter Ostrum.
Based on an imaginative adventure yarn, the live-action production falls short of the humor and energy that may have been more easily achieved with animation. Despite some appealing performances, the production has little verve.

Reviews: *New York Times*, July 1, 1971, 61:1; *Variety*, May 26, 1971
Audience: Ages 8-10
Distributor: Warner Home Video
Videocassette: $19.98

No public performance rights

Willy Wonka and the Chocolate Factory.
98 min. Color. Live action. 1971. Gene Wilder, Jack Albertson, Peter Ostrum.
A laser disc version of the same title offered by Warner Home Video (see above).
Distributor: Pioneer LDCA, Inc.
Laser disc: CLV format $34.98
No public performance rights

*****

"Charlie Needs a Cloak"
Tomie de Paola (illus.).
Prentice Hall. 1973. Realistic fiction.
This non-fictionlike tale follows Charlie, a shepherd boy, step-by-step as he shears the sheep, washes the wool, and makes a cloak.

"Charlie Needs a Cloak."
8 min. Color. Limited animation. Produced by Weston Woods. 1977.
The slow, matter-of-fact narration corresponds well to the informational content but may lose younger viewers with short attention spans. Showing Charlie cut, pin, and sew promotes concepts of self-sufficiency and male-female equality. "The background music is beautiful." —*Language Arts*
Reviews: *Booklist*, Nov. 15, 1977; *Language Arts*, Oct. 1977
Awards: ALA Notable Film, *Learning* Magazine AV Award; Silver Medal, International Film & TV Festival of New York
Audience: Ages 6-10
Distributor: Weston Woods
16mm film: $195 **Videocassette:** $60
Rental: $20 daily

Rosie's Walk and Other Stories.
32 min. Color. Iconographic and animated. Produced by Weston Woods. 1985.
Included in this tape anthology are adaptations of *Rosie's Walk* (Pat Hutchins), *"Charlie Needs a Cloak,"* (Tomie de Paola), *The Story about Ping* (Marjorie Flack) and *The Beast of Monsieur Racine*. See individual titles for full descriptions.
Audience: Ages 4-8
Distributor: Children's Circle, Weston Woods
Videocassette: $19.95
No public performance rights

*****

Charlotte's Web
E. B. White.
Illustrated by Garth Williams. Harper & Row. 1952. Fantasy.
Charlotte the Spider can write, and her actions save Wilbur the Pig from being butchered.

Charlotte's Web.
85 min. Color. Animation. Produced by Hanna-Barbera. 1973. Voices of Debbie Reynolds, Henry Gibson, Paul Lynde, Charles Nelson Reilly.
Hanna-Barbera outdid itself in an animated film that will hold the attention of young audiences. The script easily matches most Disney productions, but the animation appears a cut below. Besides adding comic sequences and musical numbers, the adaptation takes some liberties with characters that may be objectionable to literary purists. Not in the novel but in the film is the character of a goosling.
Audience: Ages 6-10
Distributor: Paramount Home Video
Videocassette available
No public performance rights

Charlotte's Web.
94 min. Color. Animation. 1973. Voices of

Debbie Reynolds, Henry Gibson, Paul Lynde, Charles Nelson Reilly.
A laser disc version of the same title offered by Paramount Home Video (see above).

Distributor: Pioneer LDCA, Inc.
Laser disc: CLV format $29.95
No public performance rights

★★★★★

Chicken Soup with Rice: A Book of Months

Maurice Sendak (illus.).
Harper & Row Junior Books. 1962. Concept books.
Chicken soup with rice is the theme around which this rhyming, episodic tale of the months of the year unfolds.

Chicken Soup with Rice.
4 min. Color. Animation. Produced by Sheldon Riss/Weston Woods. 1978. Directed by Maurice Sendak. Music by Carole King.
This is a lyrical fast-paced rendition that presents the book of months in song. While the rhyme and animation are appealing, the rapid pace makes the show most suitable for entertainment or review.

Audience: Ages 5-8
Distributor: Weston Woods
16mm film: $125 **Videocassette:** $60
Rental: $15 daily

Maurice Sendak Library.
35 min. Color. Animated. Produced by Weston Woods. 1989.
Included in this tape anthology are adaptations of *Alligators All Around*, *Pierre*, *One Was Johnny*, *Chicken Soup with Rice*, *In the Night Kitchen*, and *Where the Wild Things Are*. See individual titles for full descriptions. An additional segment, *Getting to Know Maurice Sendak*, features the author commenting on his work.

Reviews: *Children's Video Report*, Nov. 1, 1990
Audience: Ages 4-8
Distributor: Children's Circle, Weston Woods
Videocassette: $19.95
No public performance rights

★★★★★

Child's Christmas in Wales, A

Dylan Thomas.
Multiple editions. Nonfiction.
The Welsh poet recalls Christmas in Wales and the joy and magic of that wonderful season.

Child's Christmas in Wales, A.
55 min. Color. Live action. Produced by Atlantis Films/Cypress Films/WTTW. 1987. Mathonwy Reeves, Denholm Elliott.
Except for a few embellishments, this drama (shot in Wales and Canada) faithfully recreates Dylan Thomas' nostalgic reminiscences of delightful Christmas holidays in Wales. In many places, the expressive dialogue follows the book word for word. "This fine dramatization is not to be missed." —*Booklist*

Reviews: *Booklist*, Jan. 1, 1988; *Library Journal*, Nov. 15, 1988; *School Library Journal*, Sept. 1988; *Video Choice*, Dec. 1988; *Video Review*, Dec. 1988
Awards: *Booklist* Editors' Choice; Chris Statuette, Columbus International Film Festival
Audience: Ages 8-Adult
Distributor: Beacon Films
16mm film: $795 **Videocassette:** $149
Rental: $35

★★★★★

Children of a Lesser God
Mark Howard Medoff.
Dramatists Play Service. 1980. Drama.
A new teacher at a school for the deaf is intrigued by the intelligence and beauty of a girl working as a janitor.

Children of a Lesser God.
110 min. Color. Live action. Produced by Paramount. 1986. William Hurt, Marlee Matlin, Piper Laurie.
The success of this film depends largely on the believable performance by Matlin. Her part seems flawless as does the role played by William Hurt. Aside from telling a strong story, the film has the added attraction of broadening understanding of the deaf.
Reviews: *New York Times*, Oct. 3, 1986, C, 5:1; *Variety*, Sept. 24, 1986
Awards: Academy Award, Best Actress; Golden Globe Award, Best Actress
Audience: Ages 12-Adult
Distributor: Paramount Home Video
Videocassette available
No public performance rights

Children of a Lesser God.
110 min. Color. Live action. Produced by Paramount. 1986. William Hurt, Marlee Matlin, Piper Laurie.
A laser disc version of the same title offered by Paramount Home Video (see above).
Distributor: Image Entertainment
Laser disc: CLV format $39.95
No public performance rights

★★★★★

Chocolate War, The
Robert Cormier.
Pantheon. 1974. Realistic fiction.
A student at a Catholic boys school and an acting authority each attempt to cope with a secret student organization that seeks control.

Chocolate War, The.
103 min. Color. Live action. Produced by M.C.E.G. International. 1988. John Glover, Ilan Mitchell-Smith, Wally Ward.
For his own sake, Glover, a teacher, aims to double the amount of chocolates sold for a yearly fund drive. A secret club of bullies forces students to resist Glover in this grim but effective adaptation.
Audience: Ages 13-16
Distributor: Image Entertainment
Laser disc: CLV format $39.95

★★★★★

Chosen, The
Chaim Potok.
Simon and Schuster. 1967. Realistic fiction.
Occurring in New York during the early 1940s, this is the story of a friendship that goes awry due to a family feud between Hassidic and Zionist Jews.

Chosen, The.
108 min. Color. Live action. Produced by Edie and Ely Landau. 1981. Robby Benson, Rod Steiger, Maxmilian Schell.
Emotionally stirring, this adaptation captures the divisiveness that beliefs may cause in human relations. The Hassidic boy's father (Rod Steiger) is a rabbi concerned with preserving his son's lifestyle.
Reviews: *New York Times*, Apr. 30, 1982, C, 5:3
Audience: Ages 16-Adult
Distributor: Fox Video
Videocassette: $59.98

★★★★★

Christmas Carol, A
Charles Dickens.
Multiple editions. Fantasy.
An evil moneylender mistreats his employee's family until he is visited by his ex-partner's ghost and spirits of the past, present, and future. With them come visions of the consequences of greed, which turn him into a different man.

Scrooge.
78 min. Black and white. Live action. Produced by Twickenham. 1935. Sir Seymour Hickes, Donald Calthrop, Athene Seyler.
Sir Seymour Hicks is an impressive Scrooge in this early effort to replay the Dickens story. This is a good production for its time, very faithful to the original story.
Reviews: *New York Times*, Dec. 4, 1935, 11:1; *Variety*, Dec. 11, 1935
Audience: Ages 6-Adult
Distributor: Video Yesteryear
Videocassette: $24.95
No public performance rights

Christmas Carol, A.
69 min. Black and white. Live action. Produced by MGM/Joseph L. Mankiewicz. 1938. Reginald Owen, Terry Kilburn, Gene Lockhart, Kathleen Lockhart.
This is a solid production of the Dickens story, which was released by MGM in black and white, and later colorized. Both the original fine black-and-white production and a colorized version are available, but the colorization does little to enhance the film. "It is good Dickens, good cinema, and good for the soul."—*New York Times*.
Reviews: *New York Times*, Dec. 23, 1938, 16:2
Audience: Ages 8-Adult
Distributor: MGM/UA Home Video
Videocassette: $19.98
No public performance rights

Christmas Carol, A.
70 min. Black and white. Live action. 1938. Reginald Owen, Gene Lockhart.
A laser disc version of the same title offered by MGM/UA Home Video (see above).
Distributor: Pioneer LDCA, Inc.
Laser disc: CLV format $34.98
No public performance rights

Christmas Carol, A.
69 min. Color. Live action. Produced by MGM/Joseph L. Mankiewicz. 1938. Reginald Owen, Gene Lockhart.
A colorized version of the same title also distributed by MGM/UA Home Video (see above).
Distributor: MGM/UA Home Video
Videocassette: $19.98
No public performance rights

Christmas Carol, A.
86 min. Black and white. Live action. Produced by Renown/United Artists. 1951. Alastair Sim, Jack Warner, Kathleen Harrison.
Faithful to the original story, this production gives a classic impression of Scrooge with the help of a fine performance by Alastair Sim. The show moves a bit slowly for today's audiences but remains a perennial favorite. The action that revolves around the ghost is somber, but Kathleen Harrison makes a comic housekeeper.
Reviews: *New York Times*, Nov. 29, 1951, 41:2; *Variety*, Nov. 14, 1951
Audience: Ages 8-Adult
Distributor: Video Communications, Inc.
Videocassette: $19.95
No public performance rights

Christmas Carol, A.
86 min. Black and white. Live action. 1951. Alastair Sim, Jack Warner.
A laser disc version of the 1951 remake of the same title offered by Video Communications, Inc. (see above).
Distributor: Pioneer LDCA
Laser disc price: CLV format $29.95
No public performance rights

Christmas Carol, A.
25 min. Black and white. Live action. Produced by Desmond Davis. 1962. Basil Rathbone.
Basil Rathbone makes an excellent Scrooge in this film that was given authenticity by being shot in Dickensian settings in England.
Audience: Ages 8-Adult
Distributor: Coronet/MTI Film & Video
16mm film: $385 **Videocassette:** $250
Rental: $75

Scrooge.
118 min. Color. Live action. Produced by Cinema Center/Waterbury. 1970. Albert Finney.
A musical version of the story, this features an excellent portrayal of Scrooge by Albert Finney and Guinness's cold and memorable ghost of Christopher Marley. The actors make this a reasonably entertaining film even though there are few memorable songs in the musical production.
Reviews: *New York Times*, Nov. 20, 1970, 29:3; *Variety*, Nov. 4, 1970
Audience: Ages 6-Adult
Distributor: Fox Video
Videocassette: $14.98
No public performance rights

Scrooge.
115 min. Color. Live action. 1970. Albert Finney.
A laser disc version of the same title offered by Fox Video (see above).
Distributor: Image Entertainment
Laser disc: CLV format $34.98
No public performance rights

Christmas Carol, A.
90 min. Color. Live action. Produced by Crocus Entertainment. 1988. Marshall Borden, Stephen D'Ambrose, Jonathan Fuller, Richard Hilger, Gregory Leifeld, J. Patrick Martin, Peter Thoemke.
Far too long and slow, this version is no match for some of the earlier productions, or even the animated release of the same year.
Audience: Ages 8-Adult
Distributor: Videocassette not currently in distribution

Dickens Collection: A Christmas Carol
72 min. Color. Animation. Produced by Children's Video of America. 1988.
For younger audiences this is a colorful and entertaining animated version of the story.
Audience: Ages 5-10
Distributor: Vestron Video
Videocassette: $19.98
No public performance rights

★★★★★

Christmas Every Day
William Dean Howells.
Multiple editions. Fantasy.
Tilly finds that one ornament her father has brought home has wish-granting powers. Her wish, which Tilly comes to regret, is to have Christmas every day. Under that system, the whole town soon finds that Christmas is no longer special.

Christmas Every Day.
20 min. Color. Animation. Produced by Orkin-Falum. 1988.
The film was animated from cells that are not particularly beautifully drawn, making the magic ornament seem less than magical. Otherwise this is a well-developed story animated in cartoon style.

Reviews: *Curriculum Products Review Service*, Apr. 1988
Audience: Ages 5-8
Distributor: Barr Films
16mm film: $485 **Videocassette:** $340
Rental: $50

★★★★★

Chronicles of Narnia
C.S. Lewis

The author has written a series of classic fantasies set in the mythical kingdom of Narnia and based on the overall theme of good conquering evil. Novels in the series are *The Lion, the Witch, and the Wardrobe*; *Prince Caspian*; *The Voyage of the Dawn Treader*; *The Silver Chair*; *The Horse and His Boy*, *The Magician's Nephew*; and *The Last Battle*.

Chronicles of Narnia.
9 hrs. Color. Live action. 1991.
A series of video adaptations of the chronicles of a mythical kingdom, distributed separately or as a set (see *Lion, the Witch, and the Wardrobe, The*; *Prince Caspian*; and *Silver Chair, The*).

Audience: Ages 8-12
Distributor: Publlic Media Video
Videocassette: $79.95 series
No public performance rights

★★★★★

"Chrysanthemums, The." John Steinbeck.

Anthologized in *The Nobel Reader* by J. Eisen and S. Troy.
Potter. 1987. Short stories—realistic fiction.
Set in rural California, this tale focuses on a farm wife's encounter with a traveling salesman who asks her for some potted chrysanthemum seeds. In reality, all he wants is the pots.

Chrysanthemums, The.
23 min. Color. Live action. Produced by Mac and Ava Motion Pictures. 1990. Nina Capriola, Paul Henri.
Well-performed, the story shows how animated and lively Elisa becomes when speaking about chrysanthemums. The man tricks her into planting buds for him and their conversation hints at her aspirations in life extending beyond her role as a farm wife. There is a historical feel to the film. Though a bit slow moving, it is loyal to the original and succeeds well as a period piece.

Reviews: *School Library Journal*, Dec. 1990
Audience: Ages 16-Adult
Distributor: Pyramid Film & Video
16mm film: $495 **Videocassette:** $395
Rental: $75

★★★★★

Cinderella
Charles Perrault.

Multiple editions. Folklore and fairy tales.
A stepdaughter becomes servant to her stepmother and stepsisters, and is forced to sleep among the cinders. When the king of the land sponsors balls to find his son a wife, the steprelatives make Cinderella stay home, but her fairy godmother comes to the girl's rescue. Cinderella attends the balls, with the help of a little magic, then loses a fateful glass slipper that becomes her key to future happiness.

Cinderella.
75 min. Color. Animation. Produced by Walt Disney. 1950. Featuring the voices

of Ilene Woods, Verna Felton, William Phipps.
Walt Disney has adapted the Perrault fairy tale into a more light-hearted story than the original. The movie features animal characters and some comedic elements in the form of two mice named Gus-Gus and Jaq. But the basic rags to riches tales remains, with lot of magic and an enduring musical score.

Reviews: *New York Times*, Feb. 23, 1950
Audience: Ages 4-12
Distributor: Buena Vista Home Video (not currently in distribution)

Rodgers and Hammerstein's Cinderella.
84 min. Color. Live action. Produced by Charles S. Dubin. 1964. Lesley Ann Warren, Ginger Rogers.
A musical production, this adaptation evokes the magic of the classic with special effects and a superb performance by the female lead. Now-classic tunes ("Do I Love You Because You're Beautiful/Or Are You Beautiful Because I Love You") complement the action. Rather than wicked, the stepsisters are silly and ornery but the stepmother is harsh. The show opens with a long overture and includes music that may try the patience of today's youngsters but creates a magic that is worth the wait.

Reviews: *Variety*, Feb. 24, 1965
Audience: Ages 6-10
Distributor: Fox Video
Videocassette: $19.98
No public performance rights

Cinderella.
84 min. Color. Live action. 1964. Leslie Ann Warren, Ginger Rogers. A laser disc version of the same title offered by Fox Video (see above).

Distributor: Image Entertainment
Laser disc: CLV format $34.98
No public performance rights

Cinderella.
26 min. Color. Animation. Produced by Rankin-Bass. 1972.
Cells appear well illustrated but not well animated in a version of Cinderella that leaves a drawn-out impression.

Audience: Ages 4-8
Distributor: Lucerne Media
Videocassette: $195

Cinderella.
11 min. Color. Limited animation. Produced by Ardli Broadcasting Co. 1980.
Unremarkable animation makes this less than the best of the Cinderella adaptations, though it remains true to the classic story.

Audience: Ages 4-8
Distributor: Coronet/MTI Film & Video
16mm film: $280 **Videocassette:** $195
Rental: $75

Cinderella (Faerie Tale Theatre).
60 min. Color. Live action. Produced by Shelley Duvall. 1984. Jennifer Beals, Matthew Broderick, Jean Stapleton.
Several details in this adaptation differ from the classic Perrault tale. The film opens with Cinderella's family learning of her father's death. Later, her stepmother explains that the family mistreats Cinderella because she is graced with beauty and a sweet disposition, qualities absent from herself and her daughters. Otherwise, the adaptation is faithful to the original story line and develops in more depth the relationship between Cinderella and her fairy godmother. They share a warm, joking, tender relationship; at one point the two discuss reality and fantasy. Cinderella questions whether her experience has indeed happened, adding a

dimension not in the original. While the production is also graced with some superb acting, it does not quite evoke the spirit of magic and awe that is inherent in the tale.

Audience: Ages 6-Adult
Distributor: Fox Video
Videocassette: $14.98
No public performance rights

Cinderella.
17.5 min. Color. Animation. Produced by Brian Jackson. 1987.
Brian Jackson has based this film on beautiful, soft drawings, developing it with graceful animation and a gentle narrative. This is among the finest of many Cinderella films.

Reviews: *Curriculum Products News*, Apr. 1988
Audience: Ages 5-10
Distributor: Barr Films
16mm film: $410 **Videocassette:** $290
Rental: $50

Ashpet.
45 min. Color. Live action. Produced by Tom and Mimi Davenport. 1989.
Set in the rural south during World War II, this updated Cinderella retains the basic story line. The fairy godmother is replaced by a benevolent conjure woman, Dark Sally. She tells riddles and tales rapidly in Southern black dialect and transforms Ashpet into a belle for a wartime Victory Dance. Instead of a prince, Ashpet meets a saxophone-playing soldier. As in the original, she loses a slipper that is the key to the soldier's finding her. Their version evokes rich vestiges of American Southern and wartime culture, managing at the same time to remain true to the Cinderella plot.

Reviews: *Video Librarian*, May 1991; *School Library Journal*, July 1990
Awards: CINE Golden Eagle; Chris Award, Columbus International Film Festival; ALA Selected Film for Young Adults
Audience: Ages 12-Adult
Distributor: Davenport Films
16mm film: $550 **Rental:** $55
Videocassette: $60 (with public performance rights)
Videocassette: $29.95 (no public performance rights)

Cinderella.
12 min. Color. Animated. Produced by David Alexovich. 1990.
While the animation in this adaptation is quite lively, an element of humor has been added that detracts from the magical quality of the classic. At film's opening, the stepmother is in the process of teaching her own two daughters how to slurp soup politely. Cinderella is a bit too willing of a workhorse. The prince himself tries to fit the glass slipper on the right maiden, whereas in Perrault's tale one of his attendants is the fitter. Cinderella does not appear exceptionally beautiful in contrast to her wicked stepsisters. Her prince, however, speaks with a French accent in loyalty perhaps to the collector Perrault. As in his version, the stepsisters live happily ever after as Cinderella sees them married to two gentlemen at court.

Audience: Ages 4-8
Distributor: Britannica
Videocassette: $79

★★★★★

Circus Baby, The
Maud and Miska Petersham (illus.).
Macmillan. 1953. Fantasy.
In a story about self-acceptance, a mother and baby elephant try to imitate the habits of circus people.

Circus Baby, The.
6 min. Color. Iconographic. Produced by Weston Woods. 1956.
Though faithful to the storybook, this show is likely to lose all but the youngest of audiences. The fact that the camera, not the characters, moves, in this case appears to reduce their interest value on screen.
Audience: Ages 4-6
Distributor: Weston Woods
16mm film: $115 **Videocassette:** $60
Rental: $15 daily

★★★★★

Civil War: An Illustrated History, The
Geoffrey C. Ward, with film producers Richard and Kenneth Burns.
Illustrated with photographs from multiple sources. Knopf. 1990. Nonfiction.
The story of the Civil War is told through photographs, letters, and live-action re-enactments in this book created from the same sources as were the films.

Civil War, The.
Nine 60-90 min. segments. Color. Live action and still photos. Produced by Florentine Films. 1991.
An outstanding documentary, this series is drawn from old photographs, vintage footage, and letters written during the Civil War. The nine segments follow Confederate and Union soldiers through the war: 1) "The Cause: 1861" (99 min.); 2) "A Very Bloody Affair: 1862" (69 min.); 3) "Forever Free: 1862" (76 min.); 4) "Simply Murder: 1863" (62 min.); 5) "The Universe of Battle: 1863" (95 min.); 6) "The Valley of the Shadow of Death: 1864" (70 min.); 7) "The Most Hallowed Ground: 1864" (72 min.); 8) "War is All Hell: 1865" (69 min.); and 9) "The Better Angel of Our Nature: 1865" (68 min.). The series with public performance rights is purchasable as a package or by single episode.
Awards: Homer Award
Audience: Ages 15-Adult
Distributor: PBS Video
Videocassette: $350 (with public performance rights; $59.95 per episode, except $79.95 for episode 1 or 5)
Videocassette: $179.95 (no public performance rights)

★★★★★

Clan of the Cave Bear
Jean M. Auel.
Crown. 1980. Fantasy.
Some 35,000 years ago, life progressed from the Neanderthal to the Cro-Magnon age. Looking different from the others of her time, a blonde woman is adopted by a swarthy tribe. She wins respect by her skill with weaponry.

Clan of the Cave Bear.
100 min. Color. Produced by Warner/PSO/Guber-Peters/Jozak-Decade/Jones-film. 1986. Daryl Hannah, Pamela Reed.
The beautiful blonde, Ayla, achieves mastery of the tribe's weapons, thereby becoming a medicine woman. Rape and a flash of nudity appear in the production, which is generally quite mindful of the novel on which it is based.
Reviews: *New York Times*, Jan. 17, 1986, C, 32:1
Audience: Ages 16-Adult
Distributor: Fox Video
Videocassette: $14.98
No public performance rights

Clan of the Cave Bear.
100 min. Color. 1986. Daryl Hannah, Pamela Reed.
A laser disc version of the same title offered by Fox Video (see above).
Distributor: Image Entertainment
Laser disc: CLV format $34.98
No public performance rights

★★★★★

Clown of God, The
Tomie de Paola (illus.).
Harcourt Brace Jovanovich. 1978. Folklore and fairy tales.
This heart-rending tale follows a poor boy turned juggler, who experiences success, then grows old and loses it all. He dies performing a final juggling act in a monastery.

Clown of God, The.
10 min. Color. Animated. Produced by Weston Woods. 1982.
A spellbinding show, the motion picture chronicles the legend of the orphan turned juggler. It, like the book, sets the tale in Italy, faithfully animating the characters from juggler to monk to beggar. Strong character voices heighten the realism.
Awards: ALA Notable Film; CINE Golden Eagle; Honorable Mention, National Educational Film and Video Festival
Audience: Ages 5-Adult
Distributor: Weston Woods
16mm film: $235 **Videocassette:** $60
Rental: $20 daily

Christmas Stories.
30 min. Color. Iconographic and animated. Produced by Weston Woods. 1986.
Included in this tape anthology are adaptations of *Morris's Disappearing Bag* (Rosemary Wells), *The Clown of God* (Tomie de Paola), *The Little Drummer Boy* (Katherine Davis, Henry Onrati, and Harry Simeone), and *The Twelve Days of Christmas* (Robert Broomfield).
Audience: Ages 4-Adult
Distributor: Children's Circle, Weston Woods
Videocassette: $19.95
No public performance rights

★★★★★

"Colonel's Lady, The"
W. Somerset Maugham.
Anthologized in *Treasury of English Short Stories*, edited by N. Sullivan. Doubleday. 1985. Short stories—realistic fiction.
A successful gentleman's mistress rises to her own stardom by writing an acclaimed volume of poetry. It prompts her into a revelation about the changing nature of her romantic relationship with the gentleman.

Overnight Sensation.
30 min. Color. Live action. Produced by Jon N. Bloom. 1983. Louise Fletcher, Robert Loggia, Shari Belafonte-Harper.
This riveting adaptation stimulates thoughts not only about marriage but also about the potential and achievements of women. It is an updated version that moves the setting from turn-of-the-century England to present-day America. It also changes the colonel to a successful advertising photographer. Instead of a mistress who writes poetry, he has a wife who writes a novel. The triumph of the show is that, despite these changes, it retains the male-female realizations. The wife's novel is about her affair with a younger man, who is, in fact, her husband in his early years. "A wonderful film to compare with the story...." —*English Journal.*
Reviews: *Booklist*, Apr. 1, 1985; *English Journal*, Nov. 1985; *Library Journal*, May 15, 1985
Awards: Blue Ribbon, American Film Festival; CINE Golden Eagle; Chris Plaque, Columbus International Film Festival
Audience: Ages 16-Adult
Distributor: Pyramid Film & Video
16mm film: $550 **Videocassette:** $225

★★★★★

Come Along with Me
An unfinished novel by Shirley Jackson.

Viking Press. 1968. Humor.
A widow abandons her identity and tries to establish a new life, but she cannot rid herself of her ability to communicate with the spirit world.

Come Along with Me.
60 min. Color. Live action. Produced by Learning in Focus. 1981. Estelle Parsons.
The mix of reality and imagination in this comical tale of a non-conforming widow keeps the audience wondering what will happen next. It is a fine adaptation of the original story.
Reviews: *School Library Journal*, Jan. 1988
Audience: Ages 15-18
Distributor: Monterey Home Video
Videocassette: $24.95
No public performance rights

★★★★★

Connecticut Yankee in King Arthur's Court, A
Mark Twain.
Multiple editions. Fantasy.
A New Englander, hit on the head, awakens in 528 A.D. in England during King Arthur's reign. Using his knowledge of phenomena such as a solar eclipse, he astonishes the inhabitants and saves his own skin.

Connecticut Yankee.
95 min. Black and white. Live action. Produced by Twentieth Century Fox/David Butler. 1931. Will Rogers, Maureen O'Sullivan, Myrna Loy.
Made during the Depression, this film includes some comedy that may be missed by today's viewers. Still amusing are the visual feats, such as the star's lassoing one of King Arthur's knights during a joust. Though the adaptation at times digresses from the literary original, its spirit is successfully conveyed by the production.
Reviews: *New York Times*, June 13, 1963, 29:1; *Variety*, Apr. 15, 1931
Audience: Ages 10-Adult
Distributor: Fox Video
Videocassette: $19.98
No public performance rights

Connecticut Yankee in King Arthur's Court, A.
108 min. Color. Live action. Produced by Robert Fellows/Paramount. 1949. Bing Crosby, Rhonda Fleming, William Bendix, Cedric Hardwicke.
Bing Crosby is his usual easy-going self in a role in which he seems always to be unruffled and in complete control. This is a delightfully light film; its musical numbers capitalize on the stars' talents without disturbing the integrity of the story.
Reviews: *New York Times*, Apr. 8, 1949; *Variety*, Feb. 23, 1949
Audience: Ages 12-Adult
Distributor: MCA/Universal Home Video
Videocassette available
No public performance rights

Connecticut Yankee in King Arthur's Court, A.
108 min. Color. Live action. 1949. Bing Crosby, Rhonda Fleming, William Bendix, Cedric Hardwicke.
A laser disc version of the same title offered by MCA/Universal Home Video (see above).
Distributor: Pioneer LDCA, Inc.
Laser disc: CLV format $34.98
No public performance rights

★★★★★

Contest Kid and the Big Prize, The
Barbara Brooks Wallace.
Illustrated by Gloria Kamen. Abingdon. 1978. Humor.

A boy who is an inveterate enterer of contests wins a month's services of a staid butler, but neither boy nor butler knows how to handle this new situation.

Contest Kid, The.
24 min. Color. Live action. Produced by MTI (An ABC Weekend Special). 1978.
This mildly humorous film adapts a story about youth and age, extroverts and introverts, free and controlled spirits. The adaptation is not as funny as the book suggests it might be.
Audience: Ages 5-12
Distributor: Coronet/MTI Film & Video
16mm film: $450 **Videocassette:** $250
Rental: $75

★★★★★

Contest Kid Strikes Again, The
Barbara Brooks Wallace.
Illustrated by Gloria Kamen. Abingdon. 1980. Humor.
Harvey won Hawkins the butler's services in a contest. When the time for services is ended, Hawkins finds himself unemployed. Harvey decides to help him become an independent chicken rancher.

Contest Kid Strikes Again, The.
24 min. Color. Live action. Produced by ABC Weekend Specials. 1979. Patrick Peterson, Ronnie Scribner.
Pure fun to watch, this is a bright, well-directed motion picture with enough escapade and disaster in it to win audience attention. It begins with Harvey trying to set up his ex-butler in the egg business. Everything that can go wrong does—until the end.
Reviews: *Booklist*, Dec. 15, 1980
Audience: Ages 8-11
Distributor: Coronet/MTI Film & Video
16mm film: $450 **Videocassette:** $240
Rental: $75

★★★★★

"Cop and the Anthem, The"
O. Henry.
Anthologized in *Collected Stories of O. Henry*, edited by Paul J. Horowitz. Avenel Books. 1979. Short stories—humor.
A bum tries in every way to get himself sent to jail for the winter but is successful only after he has changed his mind.

Cop and the Anthem, The.
23 min. Color. Live action. Produced by LCA. 1982.
"Soapy" the bum who wants to go to jail is a lovable character in this story of failed efforts and unexpected success. The film is a delightful dramatization of O. Henry's story "and would be helpful in teaching literature, particularly the use of irony." —*Media and Methods*
Reviews: *Booklist*, Apr. 15, 1983; *Media and Methods*, Jan. 1983; *School Library Journal*, Dec. 1983
Audience: Ages 12-Adult
Distributor: Coronet/MTI Film & Video
16mm film: $550 **Videocassette:** $250
Rental: $75

★★★★★

Corduroy
Don Freeman (illus.).
Penguin USA. 1968. Fantasy.
A toy bear that talks has a department store adventure as he searches for the missing button on his overalls. The next morning the buttonless bear is taken home to the warmth of a friendly black girl.

Corduroy.
16 min. Color. Live action. Produced by Evergreen-Firehouse/Weston Woods. 1984.
This delightful dramatization follows the original story line but adds a few details that are in keeping with it. During his

night of misadventure, Corduroy rides a toy train and falls into a colorful pile of beach balls, but he ends up in little Lisa's arms, as in the original.

Reviews: *Booklist*, May 1985; *School Library Journal*, Aug. 1985

Awards: Blue Ribbon, American Film Festival; ALA Notable Film; Best Early Childhood Film, Birmingham International Film Festival; CINE Golden Eagle

Audience: Ages 4-6

Distributor: Weston Woods

16mm film: $355 **Videocassette:** $60

Rental: $25 daily

★★★★★

Cornelius

Leo Lionni (illus.).

Pantheon. 1983. Fantasy.

Cornelius the crocodile positions himself in a different way. Standing upright, he sees the world as no other crocodile has ever seen it.

Cornelius.

5 min. Color. Animated. Produced by Italtoons. 1986.

This winning adaptation celebrates the powers of imagination, discovery, and being different. The film version remains true to the original manuscript in art and story line, adding appealing music and the magic of movement.

Reviews: *Booklist*, Sept. 1, 1986

Awards: Red Ribbon, American Film and Video Festival

Audience: Ages 3-10

Distributor: Lucerne Media

16mm film: $300 **Videocassette:** $225

Five Lionni Classics—The Animal Fables of Leo Lionni.

30 min. Color. Animation by Giulio Gianini. Produced by Italtoons Corp./Random House Home Video. 1987.

Included in this tape anthology are adaptations of *Frederick*, *Cornelius*, *It's Mine*, *Fish is Fish*, and *Swimmy*. See individual titles for plot summaries. As a package, these animal fables illustrate the power of imagination, the joy of discovery, and the importance of living together in harmony. The screen versions remain true to the original art and manuscripts. Winning animation, along with equally winning music, enhances the charm of the characters and the appeal of the storybooks.

Reviews: *Children's Video Report*, Feb. 1987

Audience: Ages 4-8

Distributor: Random House Home Video

Videocassette: $14.95

No public performance rights

Five Lionni Classics.

30 min. Color. Animation. Produced by Italtoons. 1987.

A public performance package of five separate Lionni titles for libraries, including *Frederick, Swimmy, Cornelius, Fish Is Fish*, and *It's Mine*. See individual titles for plot summaries.

Audience: Ages 4-8

Distributor: Lucerne Media

Videocassette: $325

★★★★★

Count of Monte Cristo, The

Alexandre Dumas.

Multiple editions. Adventure.

Unjustly imprisoned in nineteenth-century France, Edmond Dantes escapes to Monte Cristo Island. There he discovers a treasure with which he plans to take revenge on his imprisoners.

Count of Monte Cristo, The.

119 min. Black and white. Live action. Produced by Edward Small. 1934. Robert Donat, Elissa Landi, Louis Calhern.

Robert Donat is a striking count in this excellent adaptation filmed in the days before color but with big studio casts.

Reviews: *New York Times*, Sept. 27, 1934, 25:2; *Variety*, Oct. 2, 1934
Audience: Ages 12-Adult
Distributor: Videocassette not currently in distribution

Count of Monte Cristo, The.
48 min. Color. Animation. Produced by Hanna-Barbera. 1973.
Directed in its written form to an adolescent or older audience, the story was shortened and edited in this film version to suit a younger audience. It has been described in *Variety* as "an okay adaptation of the Alexandre Dumas classic, scaled down to fit juvenile tastes."

Reviews: *Variety*, Oct. 3, 1973
Audience: Ages 8-12
Distributor: Hanna-Barbera Home Video
Videocassette: $19.95
No public performance rights

Count of Monte Cristo, The.
103 min. Color. Live action. Produced by Norman Rosemont Productions/ITC. 1974. Richard Chamberlain, Tony Curtis.
The production spends considerable time establishing the story, thereby slowing the pace of the whole. It has however, some fine costuming and performances, particularly by Chamberlain as the Count Edmond Dantes.

Reviews: *Variety*, June 2, 1976
Audience: Ages 14-Adult
Distributor: Fox Video
Videocassette: $59.98
No public performance rights

★★★★★

Country Mouse and the City Mouse, The
Aesop.
Multiple editions. Folklore and fairy tales.
A country mouse visits his city cousin but finds life too different and difficult to deal with when he is in the city.

Country Mouse and the City Mouse.
9 min. Color. Limited animation. Produced by Coronet. 1962.
The production qualities of this older version do not reach the level of the later Disney version, but this is still a fine film for young audiences.

Audience: Ages 5-8
Distributor: Coronet/MTI Film & Video
16mm film: $245 **Videocassette:** $170
Rental: $75

Country Cousin, The.
9 min. Color. Animation. A Disney Educational Production. 1986.
Disney gave names to the cousins—Abner and Monty—and made the story so entertaining that the production won an Academy Award in 1936, when it was first released. It is a Disney cartoon at a cartoon's near best.

Awards: Academy Award, Best Cartoon Short Subject
Audience: Ages 5-8
Distributor: Coronet/MTI Film & Video
16mm film: $200 **Videocassette:** $150
Rental: $75

★★★★★

Crack in the Pavement, A
Ruth Howell and Arlene Strong (illus.).
Atheneum. 1970. Realistic fiction.
An inner-city boy sees little excitement around him until he watches a caterpillar follow a crack in the pavement.

Crack in the Pavement, A.
8 min. Color. Animation. Produced by Dan Bessie. 1972.
Without narration and with limited animation this film still manages an adequate telling of this simple story.

Audience: Ages 5-10
Distributor: Filmfair Communications
16mm film: $160 **Videocassette:** $89
Rental: $15

★★★★★

Crow Boy
Taro Yashima (illus.).

Penguin USA. 1955. Realistic fiction.
Set in Japan, this story follows the progress of an unassuming boy named Chibi, who is an outcast until he imitates the voices of crows at a sixth-grade talent show.

Crow Boy.
13 min. Color. Iconographic. Produced by Weston Woods. 1971.
A faithful but static portrayal of the storybook, the film moves slowly.

Audience: Ages 5-9
Distributor: Weston Woods
16mm film: $175 **Videocassette:** $90
Rental: $25 daily

Cry, the Beloved Country
Alan Paton.

Multiple editions. Realistic fiction.
Written when apartheid was official policy in South Africa, the novel follows a black rural preacher to the city, where he learns of the unhappy fates of his prostitute daughter and criminal son.

Cry, the Beloved Country.
96 min. Black and white. Live action. Produced by London Films/Alan Paton. 1951. Sidney Poitier, Canada Lee, Charles Carson.
Adapted to the screen by the novelist himself, this is a powerfully moving yet unsentimental story about a black family under apartheid. It was the first motion picture to deal forcefully with the policy or to expose the appalling living conditions of South African blacks.

Reviews: *Variety*, Jan. 23, 1952
Audience: Ages 15-Adult
Distributor: Monterey Home Video
Videocassette: $69.95
No public performance rights

★★★★★

Curious George
H. A. Rey (illus.).

Houghton Mifflin. 1973. [1941]. Humor.
From Africa, the man with the Big Yellow Hat transports a monkey named George to America. George's curiosity leads him into one scrape after another, taking him to jail, the top of a traffic signal, and the local zoo.

Curious George.
14 min. Color. Animated. Produced by Churchill Media. 1984. Directed by John Matthews.
Using puppet, or three-dimensional animation, this captivating film remains faithful to the original story. It is full of fun and adventure as George the monkey's curiosity leads him from one mishap to the next, beginning with his capture in the jungle and ending in the city zoo. In this well-crafted version, "the female narration balances the dialogue...of the male characters." *—School Library Journal*

Reviews: *School Library Journal*, Nov. 1984
Awards: ALSC Notable Children's Film; Red Ribbon Winner, American Film Festival; CINE Golden Eagle
Audience: Ages 4-8
Distributor: Churchill Media

16mm film: $335 **Videocassette:** $250
Rental: $60

★★★★★

Curious George Goes to the Hospital
H. A. Rey and Margaret Rey.
Illustrated by Margaret Rey. Houghton Mifflin. 1973. [1966]. Humor.
Swallowing a puzzle piece lands George in the hospital, to the delight of the patients in the children's ward. His curiosity causes havoc there, while the story introduces readers to hospital procedures.

Curious George Goes to the Hospital.
15 min. Color. Animated. Produced by Robert Churchill and George McQuilken. 1983.
Using effective dimensional, or puppet, animation, this film faithfully portrays the book of the same title. Moments of pure fun (George rides a go-cart in the children's ward) mix with information about hospital procedures. The story is less a tale of pure entertainment then its predecessor *Curious George*. One of the authors (Margaret Rey) served as an adviser on this film version.
Reviews: *Booklist*, Nov. 1, 1983
Awards: ALSC Notable Children's Film; CINE Golden Eagle; Chris Plaque, Columbus International Film Festival
Audience: Ages 4-8
Distributor: Churchill Media
16mm film: $370 **Videocassette:** $275
Rental: $60

★★★★★

Curious George Rides a Bike
H. A. Rey (illus.).
Houghton Mifflin. 1952. Adventure.
After receiving a bicycle from the man in the yellow hat, George the Monkey starts delivering newspapers. Needless to say his curiosity prevents him from finishing, and he ends up giving quite a performance.

Curious George Rides a Bike.
10 min. Color. Iconographic. Produced by Weston Woods. 1958.
Despite the characters' lack of movement, this is a well-paced visualization of the storybook. The mischief of George the Monkey, from his antics on a wheeled bicycle to his rescue of a baby bear, builds the show into a lively adventure. Fine narration complements the action.
Audience: Ages 4-8
Distributor: Weston Woods
16mm film: $175 **Videocassette:** $60
Rental: $20 daily

Doctor De Soto and Other Stories.
35 min. Color. Iconographic and animated. Produced by Weston Woods. 1985.
Included in this tape anthology are adaptations of *Doctor De Soto* (William Steig), *Patrick* (Quentin Blake), *Curious George Ride a Bike* (H. A. Rey) and *The Hat* (Tomi Ungerer). See individual titles for full descriptions.
Reviews: *Children's Video Report*, Dec. 1985
Audience: Ages 4-8
Distributor: Children's Circle, Weston Woods
Videocassette: $19.95
No public performance rights

★★★★★

Cyrano de Bergerac
Edmond Rostand.
Multiple editions. Drama.
Hampered by an unsightly nose, the gallant soldier Cyrano de Bergerac despairs of winning the love of his cousin Roxanne. He instead acts as the voice for another man she marries, revealing the

truth some fifteen years later, before he dies.

Cyrano de Bergerac.
113 min. Black and white. Live action. Produced by Stanley Kramer. 1950. Jose Ferrer, Mala Powers, William Prince.
Ferrer remains a wholly convincing Cyrano in his Academy-Award winning performance. The ability of the black-and-white footage to evoke a romantic atmosphere, however, has lessened with time.

Awards: Academy Award, Best Actor; Golden Globe Award, Best Cinematography
Audience: Ages 14-Adult
Distributor: Republic Pictures Home Video
Videocassette: $24.98

Cyrano.
46 min. Color. Animation. Produced by William Hanna/Joseph Barbera. 1974.
This is a literal adaptation that faithfully animates the surface of a tale that is actually aimed at an older audience than the production. Those unfamiliar with the plot may experience difficulty keeping track of its thread of events.

Audience: Ages 8-12
Distributor: Hanna-Barbera Home Video
Videocassette: $19.95
No public performance rights

Cyrano de Bergerac.
177 min. Color. Live action. Produced by the Royal Shakespeare Company. 1985. Derek Jacobi.
Theater on film, this performance of the play captures its melodrama and sentimentality with an honesty that makes the production highly appealing. Mr. Jacobi triumphs as Cyrano, filling the role with all the dignity and passion that befits it. The climax of his performance comes during the balcony scene; Jacobi conveys such longing that it is as if Cyrano's soul is rising to the window. Anthony Burgess translated and adapted the play for this three-hour production. As noted in the *New York Times*, he has preserved the rhyme, minimized the heroic couplet, and added some memorable touches. "Anthony Burgess's ingenious translation...serves Rostand's wit while adding a few fillips of its own ('Oh that this too too solid nose would melt,' goes one interpolation.)"

Reviews: *New York Times*, Oct. 17, 1984, III 21:1
Audience: Ages 14-Adult
Distributor: RKO/Turner Home Entertainment
Videocassette available
No public performance rights

D

adherence to book film rating

Danny and the Dinosaur
Syd Hoff (illus.).
Harper & Row Junior Books. 1958. Fantasy.
A playful dinosaur comes to life and wanders out of the museum into town with young Danny and his friends.

Danny and the Dinosaur.
9 min. Color. Animated. Produced by DMI Productions/Weston Woods. 1990.
Like the storybook, the motion picture is a short, imaginative tale about a dinosaur that moves and talks to Danny. It also plays hide and seek with Danny and his friends, giving them an altogether pleasant day.
Audience: Ages 4-8
Distributor: Weston Woods
16mm film: $250 **Videocassette:** $125
Rental: $25 daily

Danny and the Dinosaur and Other Stories.
35 min. Color. Iconographic and animated. Produced by Weston Woods. 1991.
Included in this tape anthology are adaptations of *Danny and the Dinosaur* (Syd Hoff), *The Camel Who Took a Walk* (Roger Duvoisin), *Island of the Skog* (Steven Kellogg), and *The Happy Lion* (Louis Fatio). See individual titles for full descriptions.
Audience: Ages 4-8
Distributor: Children's Circle, Weston Woods
Videocassette: $19.95
No public performance rights

★★★★★

David Copperfield
Charles Dickens.
Multiple editions. Realistic fiction.
Obstacles and personalities (from cruel stepfather to kindly aunt to hypocritical scoundrel Uriah Heep) in David's life are recounted as he grows into young manhood. He ultimately settles down as a novelist with Agnes, who stood staunchly by him, even when he was married to childlike, sickly Dora.

David Copperfield.
130 min. Black and white. Live action. Produced by MGM. 1935. Freddie Bartholomew, Frank Lawton, Lionel Barrymore, W. C. Fields, Maureen O'Sullivan.
This would probably not have been a truer adaptation of the book if Dickens himself had written the screenplay. The cast of superb Hollywood stars portraying memorable characters like the dastardly Uriah Heep (Roland Young), the ne'er-do-well Mr. Micawber (W. C. Fields), and

childish Dora (Maureen O'Sullivan) makes this a film classic.

Reviews: *New York Times*, Jan. 19, 1935, 18:1; *Variety*, Jan. 22, 1935
Audience: Ages 12-Adult
Distributor: MGM/UA Home Video
Videocassette: $19.98
No public performance rights

David Copperfield.
131 min. Black and white. Live action. 1935. Freddie Bartholomew, Frank Lawton, Lionel Barrymore, W. C. Fields, Maureen O'Sullivan.
A laser disc version of the same title offered by MGM/UA Home Video (see above).

Distributor: Pioneer LDSCA, Inc.
Laser disc: CLV format $39.98
No public performance rights

David Copperfield.
72 min. Color. Animation. Produced by Vestron. 1983.
This is an adequate telling of the story for young audiences. The sound and animation are less than inspiring.

Audience: Ages 8-15
Distributor: Vestron Video
Videocassette: $19.98
No public performance rights

★★★★★

Day Boy and the Night Girl, The
George MacDonald.
Illustrated by Nonny Hogrogian. Knopf. 1988. Folklore and fairy tales.
A boy and a girl are kept in separate parts of a house by an evil woman. The boy is never exposed to darkness and the girl never exposed to light until, as teenagers, the two independently become curious about the world around them.

Day Boy and the Night Girl, The.
29.5 min. Color. Live action. Produced by Parasol Group. 1989.
Today's young viewers may find it difficult to imagine two teenagers living in the same house without being aware of each other's presence. However, the beauty of the setting and the handsomeness of the two characters will make believers of most who view this narrated but silently acted story.

Audience: Ages 10-15
Distributor: Barr Films
16mm film: $595 **Videocassette:** $395
Rental: $50

★★★★★

Day of the Jackal, The
Frederick Forsyth.
Bantam. 1982. [1971]. Historical fiction.
British and French secret agents work to uncover and defeat a plan to assassinate Charles De Gaulle.

Day of the Jackal, The.
143 min. Color. Live action. Produced by Universal/Warwick/Universal France. 1974. Michael Lonsdale, Alan Badel, Eric Porter, Cyril Cusack.
The drama of the plot is enough to make this a compelling film. It maintains a clinical, almost detached view in its dramatization of the plot to kill Charles De Gaulle. Yet the motion picture maximizes the tension of the story.

Reviews: *New York Times*, May 17, 1973, 53:1; *Variety*, May 16, 1973
Audience: Ages 15-Adult
Distributor: MCA/Universal Home Video
Videocassette available
No public performance rights

★★★★★

Day They Came to Arrest the Book, The
Nat Hentoff.
Delacorte. 1982. Realistic fiction.
A black student refuses to read Twain's Huckleberry Finn because it uses the word *nigger.* This raises a furor about the issue of censorship in the classroom, which directly involves the viewpoints of the students.

Day They Came to Arrest the Book, The.
47 min. Color. Live action. Produced by Joe Ruby and Ken Spears. 1987. Jonathan Crombie, Real Andrews, Barry Flatman, Ardon Bess.
This stellar adaptation features superb performances. A student journalist single-handedly uncovers de facto censorship of books such as *Catcher in the Rye* and *Grapes of Wrath* from his high school library. A librarian, who was a party to the censorship, breaks her silence and voices her objections in an impassioned plea that seems to sway even the opponents.
Reviews: *Booklist*, Feb. 1, 1989
Awards: ALA Selected Film; Emmy Award, Outstanding Writing of a Children's Special; Bronze Apple, National Educational Film and Video Festival
Audience: Ages 12-Adult
Distributor: Filmfair Communications
Videocassette: $495 **Rental:** $50

★★★★★

"Day's Wait, A"
Ernest Hemingway.
Anthologized in *The Complete Short Stories of Ernest Hemingway.* Scribner. 1987. Short stories—realistic fiction.
John has a fever and thinks he is going to die. Reassured by his father, the boy recovers from influenza.

Day's Wait, A.
14 min. Color. Live action. Produced by Advanced American Communications. 1990.
It's a little difficult to believe that the young, robust looking actor in the story is really ill, or that listening to the prescriptions of the doctor would lead to such a phobia about dying. Otherwise this is a well-produced film.
Audience: Ages 14-Adult
Distributor: Coronet/MTI Film & Video
16mm film: $350 **Videocassette:** $250
Rental: $75

★★★★★

Dear Lovey Hart: I Am Desperate
Ellen Conford.
Little, Brown & Co. 1975. Realistic fiction.
A teenage girl is pressed into writing an advice column for the school newspaper—with disastrous results.

Dear Lovey Hart: I Am Desperate.
32 min. Color. Live action. A Disney Educational Production. 1977.
Teenagers will certainly empathize with Caroline as she tries to make the best of a very difficult situation. The natural acting in this film moves the story along in a brisk fashion.
Audience: Ages 11-17
Distributor: Coronet/MTI Film & Video
16mm film: $665 **Videocassette:** $500
Rental: $75

★★★★★

Death of a Salesman
Arthur Miller.
Penguin. 1976. Drama.
A middle-aged salesman struggles with his family and his work as his life seems to disintegrate.

Death of a Salesman.
115 min. Black and white. Live action. Produced by Columbia/Stanley Kramer. 1951. Frederic March, Kevin McCarthy, Cameron Mitchell, Mildred Dunnock, Howard Smith.
Arthur Miller's play is faithfully reproduced and supplemented by colorful flashbacks. Frederic March is excellent in the character of the salesman.
Reviews: *New York Times*, Dec. 21, 1951, 21:3; *Variety*, Dec. 12, 1951
Audience: Ages 15-Adult
Distributor: Warner Home Video
Videocassette: $19.98
No public performance rights

★★★★★

"Deer in the Works"
Kurt Vonnegut, Jr.
Anthologized in *Welcome to the Monkey House*. Dell. 1974. [1950]. Short stories—realistic fiction.
The publisher of a weekly newspaper applies for a more stable position in publicity with a gigantic manufacturing plant. His first and last assignment is to report on a deer that has strayed into the plant area.

Deer in the Works.
25 min. Color. Live action. Produced by Ron Underwood. 1980.
Only the lighting—or lack of it—detracts from this well-scripted and produced adaptation of the Kurt Vonnegut story about freedom of action.
Awards: Bronze Award, Columbus Film Festival; Silver Award, Houston International Film Festival
Audience: Ages 14-Adult
Distributor: Barr Films
16mm film: $595 **Videocassette:** $99
Rental: $50

★★★★★

Devil and Daniel Webster, The
Stephen Vincent Benét.
Multiple editions. Fantasy.
A New England farmer of the 1800s sells his soul to a Mr. Scratch; a lawyer, Daniel Webster, must rescue the farmer.

Devil and Daniel Webster, The.
89 min. Black and white. Live action. Produced by William Dieterle. 1941. Walter Huston, Edward Arnold, James Craig, Simone Simon, Anne Shirley, Gene Lockhart.
Huston is exceptional as the devil Mr. Scratch. Music, photography, and special effects, along with lively performances, bring the classic to life in style. But the mix of realism and fantasy is not quite believable.
Reviews: *Variety*, July 16, 1941
Awards: Academy Award, Best Music Score
Audience: Ages 12-16
Distributor: Janus Films
Videocassette: $88

Devil and Daniel Webster, The.
104 min. Black and white. Live action. Produced by William Dieterle. 1941. Walter Huston, Edward Arnold, James Craig, Simone Simon, Anne Shirley, Gene Lockhart.
Laser disc versions, with or without public performance rights, of the same title offered by Janus Films (see above).
Distributor: The Voyager Company
Laser disc: CLV format $88 (with public performance rights)
Laser disc: CLV format $49.95 (no public performance rights)

Devil and Daniel Mouse, The.
26 min. Color. Animation. Produced by Patrick Laubert, Michael Hirsch. 1981.
Original music, which was composed and performed by John Sebastian, comple-

ments this animated retelling of the familiar story about an individual who sells his soul to the devil. In this version, after rock performer "Funky Jan" sells her soul, her spunky friend, Daniel Mouse, pleads Jan's case to a jury and judge chosen by the devil himself. Everything except the main theme has been changed in this animated version that seems reminiscent of Saturday morning cartoon fare.

Awards: Chris Statuette, Columbus International Film Festival
Audience: Ages 6-12
Distributor: Beacon Films
16mm film: $550 **Videocassette:** $149
Rental: $35

*****

"Diamond Necklace, The"
Guy de Maupassant.

Anthologized in *The Collected Stories of Guy de Maupassant*. Avenel Books. 1985. Short stories—realistic fiction.

A woman without much money borrows and loses a "diamond" necklace from her wealthy friend. Without telling the friend, the woman and her husband replace the original necklace at their own expense. For the next ten years, they work to pay off the replacement. Then they discover that the original they borrowed was never real but just a cheap imitation.

Necklace, The.
23.25 min. Color. Live action. Produced by Mark Baer and Mark O'Kane. 1979.

Given a decidedly more modern setting than the original story, this is an adequate but not outstandingly faithful telling of the de Maupassant story.

Audience: Ages 14-Adult
Distributor: Filmfair Communications
16mm film: $400 **Videocassette:** $89

Necklace, The.
20 min. Color. Live action. Produced by Bert Van Bork with Clifton Fadiman. 1980.

Beginning with a narrator, this adaptation moves quickly into convincing performances by the necklace borrower, her husband, and her wealthy friend. The setting is updated and might be any large American city as easily as one in France. The film's conclusion, in which the heroine learns the staggering fact that the first necklace was a cheap imitation, is not as much of a surprise ending as in the original tale.

Reviews: *School Library Journal*, Apr. 1981
Awards: CINE Golden Eagle
Audience: Ages 14-Adult
Distributor: Britannica; rental—Penn State University
16mm film: $585 **Videocassette:** $300
Rental: $25

Necklace, The (and Discussion).
34 min. Color. Live action. 1980.

A laser disc version of the same 1980 title also distributed by Britannica (see above). Added to this version is the separate title *What Is a Short Story? A Discussion by Clifton Fadiman.*

Distributor: Britannica
Laser disc: CAV format $129

Necklace, The.
22 min. Color. Live action. Produced by Bernard Wilets. 1981.

There are several film versions of the de Maupassant classic; Britannica distributes two of them. Both are reasonably true to the short story. For adherence to the original and overall quality, this version is one of the finest. Its producer has remained strictly faithful to the author's work.

Reviews: *School Library Journal*, Nov. 1981
Audience: Ages 14-Adult

Distributor: Britannica
Videocassette: $270

★★★★★

Dinky Hocker Shoots Smack!
M. E. Kerr.
Harper & Row Junior Books. 1972. Realistic fiction.
Dinky Hocker's mother is involved in volunteer work. She doesn't pay much attention to Dinky, who is hooked on over-eating.

Dinky Hocker.
30 min. Color. Live action. Produced by Robert Guenette and Paul Asselin for LCA. 1979.
Teenagers are likely to identify with Dinky, the girl left to resolve her own personal conflicts while her mother is too busy to notice. *Booklist* judges the production as one that "extracts the essence of a winning novel."
Reviews: *Booklist*, Jan. 1, 1980; Science Books and Films, Sept./Oct. 1980
Audience: Ages 10-15
Distributor: Coronet/MTI Film & Video
16mm film: $500 **Videocassette:** $250
Rental: $75

★★★★★

"Displaced Person"
Kurt Vonnegut.
Anthologized in *Welcome to the Monkey House*. Dell. 1970. Short stories—realistic fiction.
A black war orphan taunted by his white peers and villagers is led to believe that the first black man he sees is his father.

D. P.
60 min. Color. Live action. Produced by Learning in Focus. 1985. Stan Shaw, Rosemary Leach, Julius Gordon.
Stan Shaw plays the black war orphan and Rosemary Leach is the nun charged with caring for him in a home for boys. Both perform excellently in this highly sensitive film.
Awards: Emmy Award, Outstanding Children's Program
Audience: Ages 10-15
Distributor: Monterey Home Video
Videocassette: $24.95
No public performance rights

★★★★★

Doctor De Soto
William Steig (illus.).
Farrar, Straus & Giroux. 1982. Fantasy.
A mouse dentist refuses to work on harmful animals but then one day is persuaded to treat a sly fox with an ailing tooth. In the end, the mouse outfoxes the fox.

Doctor De Soto.
10 min. Color. Animated. Produced by Michael Sporn Animation Inc./Weston Woods. 1984.
This delightfully funny film captures all the humor of the original. The motion adds comedy as the mouse dentist climbs a ladder to work in his patient's mouth, which waters to chew up the mouse that treats it until the clever dentist paints his "secret formula" on the hungry fox's teeth.
Awards: Ruby Slipper Award, International Children's Film Festival
Audience: Ages 4-8
Distributor: Weston Woods
16mm film: $235 **Videocassette:** $60
Rental: $20 daily

Doctor De Soto and Other Stories.
35 min. Color. Iconographic and animated. Produced by Weston Woods. 1985.
Included in this tape anthology are adaptations of *Doctor De Soto* (William Steig), *Patrick* (Quentin Blake), *Curious George*

Rides a Bike (H. A. Rey), and *The Hat* (Tomi Ungerer). See individual titles for full descriptions.
Reviews: *Children's Video Report*, Dec. 1985
Audience: Ages 4-8
Distributor: Children's Circle, Weston Woods
Videocassette: $19.95
No public performance rights

★★★★★

Dr. Seuss's ABC
I Can Read With My Eyes Shut!
Mr. Brown Can Moo! Can You?
Theodor S. Geisel and Audrey S. Geisel (illus.).
Beginner Books. 1963. 1978. 1970. Concept books.
Dr. Seuss's ABC presents the alphabet, capitals and lower case, while picturing items that begin with each letter. *I Can Read with My Eyes Shut!* shows that nothing much gets read if you keep your eyes shut and a whole lot can be learned when you keep your eyes open. *Mr. Brown Can Moo! Can You?* is a long list of delightful sounds with accompanying pictures—for example, bees "buzz," corks "pop," horses hooves "klop."

Dr. Seuss Beginner Book Videocassette: Dr. Seuss's ABC; I Can Read with My Eyes Shut!; Mr. Brown Can Moo! Can You?.
30 min. Color. Iconographic. Produced by Praxis Media, Inc. and Random House Home Video. 1989.
These are three true-to-the-book films that convey (progressively) how pleasurable reading can be: learning the alphabet, actually reading words, and imitating sounds. A narrator reads the letters and pictures as they appear on screen, inviting viewers to answer questions by sounding out words and by repeating sounds. The lively music and the illustrations keep these basic lessons moving right along, despite the absence of character movement.
Reviews: *Children's Video Report*, Oct./Nov. 1989
Audience: Ages 3-10
Distributor: Random House Home Video
Videocassette: $9.95
No public performance rights

★★★★★

Dog Days of Arthur Cane, The
T. Ernesto Bethancourt.
Holiday House. 1976. Fantasy.
Arthur Cane envies his rich friend Lou and doubts the spiritual heritage of another friend, an African named James. James does a chant over Arthur to make him more understanding and shortly thereafter Arthur changes into a dog. Adventures as a mutt lead him into close quarters with a blind musician-artist, who teaches him about the richest of possessions: friendship, trust, and loyalty.

Dog Days of Arthur Cane, The.
29 min. Color. Live action. Produced by ABC Weekend Special. 1990.
Faithful to the original, this adaptation is both dramatic and comical as Arthur undergoes an experience that jars him into recognition of truly important values. The book presents more detail about his family members and Arthur's alienation from them, while the film moves quickly to his transformation as a dog, his adventures in this role, and his return back to human life. Yet the spirit of the original is aptly conveyed in an entertaining film that promotes moral growth.
Audience: Ages 8-Adult
Distributor: Aims Media
16mm film: $495 **Videocassette:** $295
Rental: $50

Dog Days of Arthur Cane, The.
39 min. Color. Live action. Produced by ABC Weekend Special. 1990.

A full-length version of the same, abbreviated title also distributed by Aims Media (see above).
Audience: Ages 8-Adult
Distributor: Aims Media
Videocassette: $99

★★★★★

Drummer Hoff
Adapted by Barbara Emberley.
Illustrated by Ed Emberley. Prentice-Hall. 1967. Folklore and fairy tales.
Mounting a team effort, soldiers ready a cannon for firing by Drummer Hoff.

Drummer Hoff.
6 min. Color. Animated. Produced by William L. Snyder/Weston Woods. 1969.
Fine, clear narration chants this story in rhyme. The narration quickens as more soldiers and their roles in preparing the cannon unfold. At the end, sound effects enhance the folk rhyme with the delivery of the shot and chirping birds.
Awards: Golden Plaque, Tehran International Film Festival; Honors Award, American Film Festival
Audience: Ages 4-8
Distributor: Weston Woods
16mm film: $175 **Videocassette:** $90
Rental: $20 daily

★★★★★

Drums Along the Mohawk
Walter D. Edmonds.
Multiple editions. Historical fiction.
Young newlyweds settle in pre-Revolutionary War upstate New York, enduring the hardships of pioneer life. Prompted by the British, Iroquois Indians attack.

Drums Along the Mohawk.
103 min. Color. Live action. Produced by Twentieth Century Fox/Raymond Griffith. 1939. Henry Fonda, Claudette Colbert.
A first-rate historical chronicle, the production takes pains to accurately recreate details of the period, down to the flintlock muskets used in combat. The film illustrates the difficulty in adjustment to frontier life, particularly through the character of Lana, the young wife.
Reviews: *New York Times*, Nov. 4, 1939, II:2; *Variety*, Nov. 8, 1939
Audience: Ages 16-Adult
Distributor: Fox Video
Videocassette: $19.98
No public performance rights

Drums Along the Mohawk.
104 min. Color. Live action. 1939. Claudette Colbert, Henry Fonda.
A laser disc version of the same title offered by Fox Video (see above).
Distributor: Fox Video/Image Entertainment
Laser disc: CLV format $39.98
No public performance rights

E

adherence to book   film rating

East of the Sun, West of the Moon.
Multiple editions. Folklore and fairy tales.
A poor family has a chance to become wealthy if the youngest daughter will live for one year with a mysterious white bear, who is really a bewitched prince. When a promise is broken, the castle disappears and the bear's life is threatened, so the girl undertakes a dangerous journey "east of the sun, west of the moon" to rescue him.

East of the Sun, West of the Moon.
30 min. Color. Limited animation. Produced by Rabbit Ears. 1991. Narrated by Max von Sydow.
The music of Lyle Mays combines well with the show's cubist drawings to accentuate the Northern setting of this folk tale. Max von Sydow's deep voice conveys the characters of the hero (the white bear who is a bewitched prince) as well as those of the wind and the trolls. The drawings blend smoothly into one another giving a serene sense of motion, especially during the scenes in which the winds act as couriers of the girl on her mission to save the bear-prince.
Awards: CINE Golden Eagle Award
Audience: Ages 6-10
Distributor: Uni Distribution Corp.
Videocassette: $9.95

★★★★★

18th Emergency, The
Betsy Byars.
Illustrated by Robert Grossman. Penguin. 1973. Realistic fiction.
Mouse writes a derogatory remark about big Marvin, and for a while runs for his life to escape the imagined bully.

Pssst! Hammerman's After You.
28 min. Color. Live action. A Disney Educational Production. 1977.
"Mouse" is not too believable in this story that will comfort big people. Marvin Hammerman's restraint after his very real initial fury at Mouse's prank reveals that big people have feelings, too. In the end everyone turns out to be a hero.
Audience: Ages 8-14
Distributor: Coronet/MTI Film & Video
16mm film: $625 **Videocassette:** $470
Rental: $75

★★★★★

Elephant Man, The
Ashley Montague.
E. P. Dutton. 1971. Biography.
Based on the true story of John Merrick, this tale features a man so deformed that he is a circus freak until he is rescued by a kindly surgeon.

Elephant Man, The.
124 min. Black and white. Live action. Produced by Stuart Cornfield/ EMI/Brooksfilms. 1980. John Hurt, Anthony Hopkins, John Gielgud, Anne Bancroft.
Sensitively dramatized, the story features a human with a head twice the ordinary size, a spine that's twisted, and a right arm that doesn't work. The film covers the Elephant Man's life, from his discovery by the kind doctor to his kidnapping to his return and success in London high society.
Reviews: *New York Times*, Oct. 3, 1980, III, 8:1; *Variety*, Oct. 1, 1980
Awards: British Film Awards, Best Picture, Best Actor, Best Set Design
Audience: Ages 12-Adult
Distributor: Paramount Home Video
Videocassette available
No public performance rights

Elephant Man, The.
124 min. Color. Live action. 1980. John Hurt, Anthony Hopkins.
A laser disc version of the same title offered by Paramount Home Video (see above).
Distributor: Pioneer LDCA, Inc.
Laser disc: CLV format $39.95
No public performance rights

★★★★★

Elephant Who Couldn't Forget, The
Faith McNulty.
Illustrated by Mark Simont. Harper & Row 1987. [1980]. Fantasy.
A young elephant has a memory of his brother's misdeeds that is just too good. It leads this elephant into a great deal of trouble.

Elephant Who Couldn't Forget, The.
10 min. Color. Animated. Produced by LCA. 1981.
This production is a fine portrayal of an animal story with moral lessons for humans.
Reviews: *School Library Journal*, Jan. 1982
Audience: Ages 5-11
Distributor: Coronet/MTI Film & Video
16mm film: $250 **Videocassette:** $200
Rental: $75

★★★★★

Elephant's Child
Rudyard Kipling.
Multiple editions. Fantasy.
This explains how the elephant got its trunk when one little elephant went off to satisfy its insatiable curiosity.

Elephant's Child.
30 min. Color. Iconographic. Produced by Rabbit Ears Productions and Random House Home Video. 1986. Narrated by Jack Nicholson.
Adapted from the edition illustrated by Tim Raglin (Knopf 1985), the show stars an insatiably curious elephant who simply must know what the crocodile eats for dinner. Tim Raglin's charming illustrations and Bobby McFerrin's musical score, with voices singing African rhythms, set the stage perfectly for the Kipling tale. Playing all the many wonderful animal characters, Jack Nicholson draws out Kipling's marvelous touch of humor. The film delights the senses in both watching and listening.
Reviews: *Children's Video Report*, Dec. 1986
Audience: Ages 3-10
Distributor: Random House Home Video
Videocassette: $14.95
No public performance rights

★★★★★

Elmer Gantry
Sinclair Lewis.
Multiple editions. Realistic fiction.
An American salesman turns evangelist in the 1920s and joins a traveling woman preacher, barnstorming through the Midwest.

Elmer Gantry.
146 min. Color. Live action. Produced by United Artists/Bernard Smith. 1960. Richard Brooks, Burt Lancaster, Jean Simmons.
An exposé of commercialized religion in the past, the motion picture advances with gripping performances. It appeals most strongly to select audiences with societal concerns.
Reviews: *New York Times*, July 8, 1960, 16:1; *Variety*, June 19, 1960
Awards: Academy Awards, Best Actor, Best Supporting Actress, Best Screenplay
Audience: Ages 16-Adult
Distributor: MGM/UA Home Video
Videocassette: $19.98
No public performance rights

★★★★★

Elves and the Shoemaker, The
Jacob Grimm and Wilhelm K. Grimm.
Multiple editions. Folklore and fairy tales.
A poor shoemaker is aided by elves who manufacture beautiful shoes each night for him to sell. He repays them with miniature outfits of clothing.

Shoemaker and the Elves, The.
13 min. Color. Puppet animation. Produced by Coronet. 1962.
A slightly enhanced version of the old story unfolds charmingly through the medium of puppets. Featured in this adaptation is a night during which the shoemaker and his wife decide to repay their unknown benefactors not only with new clothes but also with nourishment.
Audience: Ages 5-10
Distributor: Coronet/MTI Film & Video
16mm film: $325 **Videocassette:** $235
Rental: $75

Shoemaker and the Elves, The.
15 min. Color. Puppet animation. Produced by Institut fur Film und Bild. 1971.
Simple puppets set among real objects are used in this recreation, which remains true to the popular tale.
Awards: Chris Plaque, Columbus International Film Festival
Audience: Ages 6-10
Distributor: Films Inc.
16mm film: $320 **Videocassette:** $49

Elves and the Shoemaker, The.
30 min. Color. Animation. Produced by Hanna-Barbera and Hallmark Cards. 1990. Hosted by Olivia Newton-John.
The original is exceedingly short and the adaptation has added to the story with a cat that attacks the clothed elves as they work. The cobbler's dog retaliates and his wife gives the elves new outfits, as in the classic tale. She wants children badly and finds out she is expecting triplets in a slightly trite ending to a generally pleasing show.
Audience: Ages 4-8
Distributor: Hanna-Barbera Home Video
Videocassette: $19.95
No public performance rights

★★★★★

Emil and the Detectives
Erich Kastner.
Scholastic. 1985. [1930]. Mystery.

A schoolboy is robbed on the way to visit his grandmother in 1929 Berlin. Bent on retrieving his money, he captures the thief.

Emil and the Detectives.
99 min. Color. Live action. Produced by Walt Disney. 1964. Walter Slezak, Bryan Russell, Roger Mobley.
Shot in Germany, the production is convincing.
Reviews: *Variety*, Oct. 14, 1964
Audience: Ages 8-12
Distributor: Buena Vista Home Video (not currently in distribution)

★★★★★

Emperor's New Clothes, The
Hans Christian Andersen.
Multiple editions. Folklore and fairy tales.
A scam is pulled over the eyes (so to speak) of a vain emperor by two swindlers posing as tailors who pretend to weave a fine suit of clothing that cannot be seen by the unusually stupid or those unfit for their office. The insecure emperor is so taken in that he parades through town in his birthday suit.

Emperor's New Clothes, The.
28 min. Color. Live action. Produced by Swedish Broadcasting Corp. 1967.
The film begins by explaining how this particular fairy tale relates to Hans Christian Andersen's life, revealing that he was a man ever conscious of his looks. It then launches into a faithful if somewhat lackluster retelling in live action. The costumes and setting suit the tale nicely, but relying only on a narrator to tell the tale has a distancing effect.
Audience: Ages 4-8
Distributor: Britannica
16mm film: $605 **Videocassette:** $300

Emperor's New Clothes, The.
9 min. Color. Animation. Produced by Greatest Tales. 1976.
The emperor doesn't quite get down to the bare facts of his appearance in this film story, which remains clear, amusing, and true to the Andersen tale.
Audience: Ages 4-8
Distributor: Phoenix/BFA Films & Video
16mm film: $230 **Videocassette:** $145
Rental: $30

Emperor's New Clothes, The.
11 min. Color. Live action. Produced by Coronet. 1979. A satisfactory, but not overwhelming, enactment of the old story is played out in pantomime, silhouette, and modern dance. Backgrounds are moved and color-changed to set the mood. Accompanying the visuals are a musical score and straightforward narration.
Audience: Ages 5-8
Distributor: Coronet/MTI Film & Video
16mm film: $280 **Videocassette:** $195
Rental: $75

Emperor's New Clothes, The (Faerie Tale Theatre).
60 min. Color. Live action. Produced by Shelley Duvall. 1986. Alan Arkin, Art Carney, Dick Shawn.
Graced with marvelous performances, this is a truly comical rendition of the classic tale with added dimensions. Art Carney is a swindler, who turns "straight" at the end of the tale, leaving money to the citizens whose fortunes have been robbed through taxation. There is a slapstick element to the comedy and slang phrases abound ("We're dead meat," "let's take the crackpot emperor for everything he's got," and so forth.) The conceit and vanity of the emperor are unmistakable. Though muffled, a profanity is uttered toward the end but it interferes little with the good natured jollity that per-

vades. Even the emperor seems to have fun. He doesn't look too concerned when the tailors present him with the marvelous material and he fails to see it. The ruler simply makes ready to proceed through town dressed only in his royal red shorts. While entertaining, the humor in this version is too sophisticated for the very young.

Audience: Ages 8-Adult
Distributor: Fox Video
Videocassette: $14.98
No public performance rights

Emperor's New Clothes, The.
85 min. Color. Live action. A Golan Globus Production. 1989. Sid Caesar, Robert Morse.
This is a thoroughly comical if somewhat slow-moving adaptation. Complicating the plot is a new thread of romance in that the king has a daughter who falls in love with one of the tailors. The two tailors, in this version, are uncle and nephew, redeemable scoundrels. The nephew puts his love for the princess above his thirst for the king's jewels.

Audience: Ages 8-Adult
Distributor: Cannon Video
Videocassette available
No public performance rights

Emperor's New Clothes, The.
8 min. Color. Animated. Produced by Weston Woods. 1990.
Tied to the retelling of *The Emperor's New Clothes* by Nadine Bernard Westcott (Little, Brown & Co. 1984), this is a wonderfully humorous rendition of the classic tale. The swindlers are delightful rascals. Dressed in his birthday suit, the emperor is visibly embarrassed at the end when he recognizes what a fool his vanity has made of him.

Audience: Ages 4-8
Distributor: Weston Woods
16mm film: $250 **Videocassette:** $125
Rental: $25 daily

Emperor's New Clothes and Other Folktales, The.
30 min. Color. Iconographic and animated. Produced by Weston Woods. 1991.
Included in this tape anthology are adaptations of *The Emperor's New Clothes* (Hans Christian Andersen), *Why Mosquitoes Buzz in People's Ears* (Verna Aardema), and *Suho and the White Horse* (Yuzo Otsuka). See individual titles for full descriptions.

Audience: Ages 4-10
Distributor: Children's Circle, Weston Woods
Videocassette: $19.95
No public performance rights

Emperor's New Clothes, The (Timeless Tales).
30 min. Color. Animation. Produced by Hanna-Barbera and Hallmark Cards. 1990. Hosted by Olivia Newton-John, with Dom De Luise for the emperor's voice.
The charm of the original tale is lost in this animated adaptation that places animals in the roles of people. A lion, of course, is king, and quite a cocky monarch at that. Lines such as "Oh, goody gum drops" issue from his lips. Enemies make ready to attack the kingdom (after the emperor rides a cloud in his birthday suit) but laugh at the ridiculous looking monarch, who inadvertently saves the day.

Audience: Ages 4-8
Distributor: Hanna-Barbera Home Video
Videocassette: $14.95
No public performance rights

Emperor's New Clothes, The.
30 min. Color. Limited animation. Produced by Rabbit Ears. 1990. Narrated by John Gielgud.
Although at times a bit breathless, John Gielgud delivers a spellbinding narration of this story about a vain ruler who is duped by a trio of con men posing as tailors. The dissolve animation techniques and panning from crowd to emperor highlight his final nude parade (viewed from the chest up). Mark Isham's music is perfectly suited to Robert Van Nutt's regal artwork.
Reviews: *Booklist*, Oct. 15, 1990
Audience: Ages 5-10
Distributor: SVS/Triumph
Videocassette: $14.95
No public performance rights

Emperor's New Clothes, The.
25 min. Color. Animation. Produced by Michael Sporn and Italtoons Corps. 1991.
Various inhabitants of a tavern convey the story in this fine adaptation. At times, the production focuses on them and at times it slips into the dramatization of their tale. A journalist visiting the tavern listens closely to the brightly animated characters, who are all delightfully invigorated with distinct personalities of their own. In this version, instead of two scoundrels, one overtaxed citizen, the royal weaver, concocts the invisible-clothes plan.
Audience: Ages 4-8
Distributor: Lucerne Media
16mm film: $495 **Videocassette:** $295

★★★★★

Escape to Witch Mountain
Alexander Key.
Illustrated by Leon B. Wisdom, Jr. Westminister. 1968. Science fiction.
Two young people are endowed with miraculous powers and set out to trace their origins. They are pursued by a villain, and, as it turns out, they come from another planet. The sequel to this novel is *Return from Witch Mountain.*

Escape to Witch Mountain.
97 min. Color. Live action. Produced by Walt Disney. 1974. Ray Milland, Eddie Albert, Kim Richards.
Ray Milland makes an easy-to-take villain in pursuit of two innocent youngsters who possess mystical powers in this children's adventure-mystery. His plan is to have them predict the stock market.
Reviews: *New York Times*, July 3, 1975, 21:1; *Variety*, Mar. 19, 1975
Audience: Ages 8-14
Distributor: Buena Vista Home Video (not currently in distribution)

Escape to Witch Mountain.
26 min. Color. Live action. A Disney Educational Production. 1983. Ray Milland, Eddie Albert, Kim Richards.
This is a lively, emotion-rousing thriller. An abbreviated version of the story, it focuses on the adopted girl with clairvoyance and her brother, trapped by a money-hungry man.
Audience: Ages 10-12
Distributor: Coronet/MTI Film & Video
16mm film: $600 **Videocassette:** $250
Rental: $75

F

adherence to book · film rating

Fall of Freddie the Leaf, The
Leo Buscaglia (illus.).
Charles B. Slack. 1982. Fantasy.
This gentle tale follows the life cycle of a leaf named Freddie, from birth to death. The leaves are personified and Freddie's fear of death is expressed; an older companion leaf reassures Freddie that death is a natural part of life.

Fall of Freddie the Leaf, The.
17 min. Color. Live action. Produced by Bernard Wilets. 1986.
This quiet film centers on a leaf that grows on a tree in a great park and loves its life. The photography remains wondrous throughout, showing the changing colors of seasons, and the production is set to classical music by the composers Mozart and Shubert. While the film is appropriate for younger audiences, the story's lack of vigorous action militates against holding their attention.
Reviews: *Library Journal*, Jan. 1987
Awards: Best of Festival, Birmingham International Educational Film Festival; Bronze Medal, International Film and Television Festival of New York; First Place, National Council on Family Relations
Audience: Ages 4-Adult
Distributor: Aims Media
16mm film: $390 **Videocassette:** $295
Rental: $50

★★★★★

"Fall of the House of Usher, The"
Edgar Allan Poe.
Anthologized in *The Unabridged Edgar Allan Poe*. Illustrated by Suzanne Clee. Running Press. 1983. Short stories—horror.
A boyhood friend, Roderick Usher, sends for the narrator of this story. Beset with a mental ailment, Usher stays confined to his gloomy house in which his sister wastes away. The narrator hastens to the house, where he witnesses a hair-raising scene.

Fall of the House of Usher, The.
30 min. Color. Live action. Produced by Alan P. Sloan. 1976.
As in the short story, Usher is convinced that his sister has been buried alive and her image indeed appears to confirm this. The build up is overlong and, though the acting is convincing, the production as a whole is less so. A viewer watches the production without feeling the terror and suspense the tale intends to engender.
Audience: Ages 14-Adult
Distributor: Britannica
16mm film: $720 **Videocassette:** $300

Fall of the House of Usher, The (and Discussion).
42 min. Color. Live action. 1976.
A laser disc version of the same title also distributed by Britannica (see above). Added in this version is a second title, *A Discussion of Edgar Allan Poe's The Fall of the House of Usher.*
Distributor: Britannica
Laser disc: CAV format $129

House of Usher, The.
16 min. Color. Live action and animation. Produced by Kratky Films. 1985.
The words are those of Edgar Allen Poe. The pictures, actorless, are intended to set the mood of the story rather than to dramatize it. There are angled shots of the haunted house with chairs toppling down, doors opening of their own volition, and so forth. At times, the pictures are effective.
Audience: Ages 14-18
Distributor: Phoenix/BFA Films & Video
16mm film: $300 **Videocassette:** $190
Rental: $30

★★★★★

Fantastic Voyage
Isaac Asimov.
Houghton Mifflin. 1966. Science fiction.
To remove a blood clot from a scientist's brain, a medical team is shrunk and injected into the scientist's bloodstream. One member of the team is a traitor. Asimov's novel is based on the earlier story by Otto Klement and Jay Lewis Bixby, as is the film.

Fantastic Voyage.
101 min. Color. Live action. Produced by Twentieth Century Fox/Saul David. 1966. Stephen Boyd, Raquel Welch.
Creative special effects make this a visually intriguing science fiction film. They combine with the inherently interesting plot line to sustain viewer interest.
Reviews: *New York Times*, Sept. 8, 1966, 43:1; *Variety*, July 27, 1966
Awards: Academy Awards, Best Visual Effects, Best Art Direction—Set Decoration
Audience: Ages 16-Adult
Distributor: Fox Video
Videocassette: $19.98
No public performance rights

Fantastic Voyage.
101 min. Color. Live action. 1966. Stephen Boyd, Raquel Welch.
A laser disc version of the same title offered by Fox Video (see above).
Distributor: Image Entertainment
Laser disc: Widescreen CLV format $49.98

★★★★★

Father Like That, A
Charlotte Zolotow.
Illustrated by Ben Shecter. Harper & Row. 1971. Realistic fiction.
A fatherless boy faced with an assignment decides to write about the father he would like to have.

Father Like That, A.
18 min. Color. Live action. Produced by Philip S. Marshall. 1982.
Though this screen version is somewhat slow-moving, Marshall has produced a soft and tender story of a boy coming to grips with his own feelings.
Audience: Ages 8-12
Distributor: Phoenix/BFA Films & Video
16mm film: $385 **Videocassette:** $250
Rental: $40

★★★★★

Fellowship of the Ring
The Two Towers, The
J. R. R. Tolkien.
Houghton Mifflin. 1965. [1954]. 1967. [1955]. Fantasy.
Different creatures in Middle Earth attempt to gain possession of a potent ring in these two novels.

Lord of the Rings, The.
133 min. Color. Animation and live action. Produced by Fantasy/Saul Zaentz. 1978. Voices of Christopher Guard, John Hurt, William Squire, Michael Sholes.
The production begins well but becomes slow-moving and confusing. Anyone not familiar with the plot may have difficulty figuring out the course of events. Technically, it uses a unique combination of live action and animation. The film ends abruptly without resolving the situation at hand. At the time of production, a sequel was planned.
Reviews: *New York Times*, Nov. 15, 1978, III 21:1; *Variety*, Nov. 8, 1978
Audience: Ages 12-18
Distributor: HBO Video
Videocassette: $29.98
No public performance rights

★★★★★

Fir Tree, The
Hans Christian Andersen.
Multiple editions. Folklore and fairy tales.
Failing to appreciate the natural richness of its life, a young fir tree aspires to become a Christmas tree. It rejoices once it becomes one, little expecting its sorry future in the aftermath.

Fir Tree, The.
32 min. Color. Iconographic. Produced by Institut fur Film und Bild. 1990.
There is an impressive three-dimensional effect to the illustrations, which gives them a lifelike aura. The lack of movement, however, contributes to a slow-paced production.
Audience: Ages 4-8
Distributor: Britannica
Videocassette: $250

Fir Tree, The.
27 min. Color. Live action. Produced by Swedish Broadcasting Co. 1967.
The live action characters look dated, though the production of the fairy tale manages to be convincing in a true life setting. Since the tree, too, is real, it does not, for example, shiver when the narrator says it trembles. He delivers the tale strongly in an authoritative voice, at times slipping into a character. The version is leisurely paced.
Audience: Ages 4-8
Distributor: Britannica
16mm film: $590 **Videocassette:** $300

★★★★★

Fish Is Fish
Leo Lionni.
Pantheon. 1970. Fantasy.
Illustrating how everything has its proper place, this tale features a tadpole that becomes a frog and whets the appetite of a minnow fish for experiences on land.

Fish Is Fish.
5 min. Color. Animated. Produced by Italtoons. 1986.
The near disaster that almost occurs when the minnow tries to join the frog on the bank adds the element of tension in this simple yet profound tale. Fine animation and music enhance the charm of the original.
Reviews: *Booklist*, Sept. 1, 1986
Awards: Special Jury Prize, Chicago International Festival of Children's Films
Audience: Ages 3-10

Distributor: Lucerne Media
16mm film: $300 **Videocassette:** $225

Five Lionni Classics—The Animal Fables of Leo Lionni.
30 min. Color. Animation by Giulio Gianini. Produced by Italtoons Corp./Random House Home Video. 1987.
Included in this tape anthology are adaptations of *Frederick, Cornelius, It's Mine, Fish Is Fish*, and *Swimmy*. See individual titles for plot summaries. As a package, the animal fables illustrate the power of imagination, the joy of discovery and the importance of living together in harmony. The screen versions remain true to the original art and manuscripts. Winning animation, along with equally winning music, enhances the charm of the characters and the appeal of the storybooks.
Reviews: *Children's Video Report*, Feb. 1987
Audience: Ages 4-8
Distributor: Random House Home Video
Videocassette: $14.95
No public performance rights

Five Lionni Classics.
30 min. Color. Animation. Produced by Italtoons. 1987.
A public performance package of five separate Lionni titles for libraries, including *Frederick, Swimmy, Cornelius, Fish Is Fish*, and *It's Mine*. See individual titles for plot summaries.
Audience: Ages 4-8
Distributor: Lucerne Media
Videocassette: $325

★★★★★

Fisherman and His Wife, The
Jacob and Wilhelm Grimm.
Multiple editions. Folklore and fairy tales. An enchanted fish rewards a fisherman for releasing it by granting his wishes. Urged on by his wife, the fisherman makes ever grander requests until the fish punishes the wife for her greed, and the couple ends up with nothing.

Fisherman and His Wife, The: A Tale from the Brothers Grimm.
20 min. Color. Limited animation. Produced by Minimal Produkter, Stockholm/Weston Woods. 1970.
Based on the retelling by Wanda Gag in *Tales from Grimm* (Coward-McCann 1936), this is a reasonably effective version in which the characters have the appearance of moving paper cutouts. The show features only the narrator's voice, no character voices, and is slow-moving.
Audience: Ages 4-8
Distributor: Weston Woods
16mm film: $375 **Videocassette:** $190
Rental: $30 daily

Fisherman and His Wife, The: A Grimm's Fairy Tale.
10 min. Color. Animated. A Bosustow Production. 1977.
This is a richly colored and well-paced rendition of the classic tale, based on the retelling in *Eric Carle's Storybook: Seven Tales by the Brothers Grimm* (Franklin Watts 1976). Loyal to the original in details, this version adds dimension to the character of the fisherman's wife. Yes, she is greedy, but rather than the shrewish woman so often portrayed, there is a softness to her that allows the couple to be happy at the end despite their loss.
Audience: Ages 4-8
Distributor: Churchill Media
16mm film: $225 **Videocassette:** $59
Rental: $50

Folktale from Two Lands.
16.5 min. Color. Limited animation. Produced by Pieter Van Deusen. 1988. Narrated by Walker Edmiston.
Included in this short film anthology are two stories that deal with personal greed, "The Fisherman and His Wife" and "The Stonecutter." The fisherman's wife is more sympathetic here than in other versions. Absent from the show is the element of a storm rising as the wife grows greedier. Like the fisherman's wife, the stonecutter wishes to be more and more powerful until he becomes a mountain. The mountain ironically falls victim to the chisel of a lowly stonecutter. Both adaptations feature very limited animation and story lines that are generally faithful to the originals.
Audience: Ages 5-9
Distributor: Churchill Media
16mm film: $415 **Videocassette:** $310
Rental: $60

Fisherman and His Wife, The.
30 min. Color. Limited animation. Produced by Rabbit Ears (Mark Sottnick). 1989. Narrated by Jodie Foster.
Black silhouettes depict the characters in this tale while color and movement appear in the waves, which turn from blue to gray to black as the wishes of the fisherman's wife become more grandiose and the ire of the magic fish grows. Foster's even reading is subdued and allows the tension to mount steadily, a mood enhanced by the show's music and its striking cutout animation. Backgrounds are in gold and blue.
Audience: Ages 5-10
Distributor: SVS/Triumph
Videocassette: $14.95
No public performance rights

Fisherman and His Wife, The.
30 min. Color. Animation. 1989. Narrated by Jodie Foster.
A laser disc version of the same title offered by SVS/Triumph (see above).
Distributor: Image Entertainment
Laser disc: CLV format $19.95
No public performance rights

★★★★★

Five Chinese Brothers, The
Claire Bishop.
Illustrated by Kurt Wiese. Putnam. 1938. Folklore and fairy tales.
This is the clever folktale of five Chinese brothers, each with a special talent (one has stretchable legs, for example) that helps rescue the brother who is charged with a crime.

Five Chinese Brothers, The.
10 min. Color. Iconographic. Produced by Weston Woods. 1958.
The show gives a complete account of the clever use of their talents by all five brothers—from the one with the iron neck to the one who can hold his breath indefinitely. The brothers, however, remain still while the camera moves due to the filmmaking technique. Though true to the original tale, the film is slow-paced.
Audience: Ages 4-8
Distributor: Weston Woods
16mm film: $175 **Videocassette:** $60
Rental: $20 daily

Mysterious Tadpole and Other Stories, The.
34 min. Color. Animated and Iconographic. Produced by Weston Woods. 1989.
Included in this tape anthology are adaptations of *The Mysterious Tadpole* (Steven Kellogg), *The Five Chinese Brothers* (Claire Bishop), *Jonah and the Great Fish* (Warwick Hutton) and *The*

Wizard (Jack Kent). See individual titles for full descriptions.
Reviews: *Children's Video Report*, Feb./Mar. 1989
Audience: Ages 4-8
Distributor: Children's Circle, Weston Woods
Videocassette: $19.95
No public performance rights

★★★★★

Flight of the Doves
Walter Macken.
Macmillan. 1967. Adventure.
Two orphans escape a mean guardian in England to find their way to their grandmother's farm in Ireland.

Granny Lives in Galway.
26 min. Color. Live action. Produced by Ralph Nelson for LCA. 1973.
With no obligation to sustain an audience for a feature-film time span, this edited version of the 1971 Columbia Pictures release *Flight of the Doves* is actually an improvement over that good feature film. As stated in *Previews*, it is "Exciting and fast paced. Middle-grade children will enjoy the story and the cliffhanger questions raised."
Reviews: *Previews*, Nov. 1974
Audience: Ages 8-14
Distributor: Coronet/MTI Film & Video
16mm film: $395 **Videocassette:** $250
Rental: $75

★★★★★

Flight of the White Wolf
Mel Ellis.
Holt. 1970. Realistic fiction.
A boy's white dog is accused of killing neighboring animals. When the neighbors organize to kill the "white wolf," the boy must take bold steps to save his friend.

Flight of the White Wolf.
11 min. Color. Live action. Produced by Asselin/LCA. 1988.
The film begins and ends with a photo of the book cover. In between is a slow, somewhat stiffly acted film story about a boy's devotion to a white wolf.
Audience: Ages 8-17
Distributor: Coronet/MTI Film & Video
16mm film: $290 **Videocassette:** $220
Rental: $75

★★★★★

"Flying Machine, The"
Ray Bradbury.
Anthologized in *Stories of Ray Bradbury*. Knopf. 1980. Short stories—fantasy.
A young man in fifth-century China invents a flying machine and soars over the emperor's garden. While moved by the flier's account of the beauty of his machine and the world view it provides, the emperor imagines evils the machine might bring. In the end, he has it and the flier destroyed.

Flying Machine, The.
16 min. Color. Live action. Produced by Bernard Selling. 1980.
The emperor in this fifth-century Chinese community portrays just the right uncertainty and agony as he decides what to do with the young man and his flying machine. The setting is beautiful, the dramatization excellent, and the plot faithful to the original. However, the audience level for the film is younger than for the short story.
Audience: Ages 8-12
Distributor: Barr Films
16mm film: $360 **Videocassette:** $250
Rental: $50

★★★★★

Follow My Leader
James B. Garfield.
Illustrated by Robert Greiner. Viking. 1957. Realistic fiction.
A blinded boy, age eleven, adjusts to his situation with the help of a guide dog named Leader and his family and friends.

Follow My Leader.
42 min. Color. Live action. Produced by Bernard Wilets. 1988.
The heart of the story is retained in this film about suddenly becoming blind and adjusting to the situation, but details are changed to improve accuracy. Jimmy, the blinded boy, is eleven years old in the book but in the film is sixteen, the age necessary to receive a guide dog. Spectacular visuals show Jimmy being blinded by a firecracker and the emotion is vividly conveyed as his feelings run the gamut from anger to determination. There is a wealth of information in his learning to find his way by using his fingertips, a braille typewriter, and his guide dog. The pace moves steadily, sustaining audience interest. "*Follow My Leader* is an intense experience, painstakingly produced, that leaves no viewer unaffected."—*School Library Journal*
Reviews: *Booklist*, July 15, 1989; *School Library Journal*, May 1989
Awards: CINE Golden Eagle; Gold Medal, Chicago International Film Festival
Audience: Ages 10-Adult
Distributor: Aims Media
16mm film: $745 **Videocassette:** $495
Rental: $75

Follow My Leader.
29 min. Color. Live action. 1988.
An abbreviated version of the same full-length title also distributed by Aims Media (see above). This version retains the basic plot but omits selected details.
Distributor: Aims Media
16mm film: $545 **Videocassette:** $395
Rental: $75

Follow My Leader.
29 min. Color. Live action. 1988.
A laser disc version of the abbreviated edition of the same title also distributed by Aims Media (see above).
Distributor: Aims Media
Laser disc: CAV format $395

★★★★★

Fool and the Flying Ship, The
Multiple editions. Folklore and fairy tales.
In this Russian folktale, a dimwitted younger brother imitates his older siblings by setting out on a mission to build a flying ship and win the hand of the czar's daughter. The outcome demonstrates, with traditional folk wisdom and humor, that fate smiles on the less-gifted.

Fool and the Flying Ship, The.
30 min. Color. Limited animation. Produced by Rabbit Ears. 1991. Narrated by Robin Williams.
A strong Yiddish influence is apparent in Robin Williams's telling and Henrik Drescher's drawings of the Russian tale. "If you're eaten by wild beasts, don't even think about coming home," the fool's mother shouts at him as he sets off to invent or discover a flying ship and win the daughter of the czar. On his travels, the fool meets a man who can shoot around the world, a more-than-hearty eater, and others who help him ply his suit at court. Music by the Klezmer Conservatory Band heightens the humor of each new challenge faced by the fool and his strangely talented comrades.
Reviews: *Booklist*, June 15, 1991
Audience: Ages 5-10

Distributor: Uni Distribution Corp.
Videocassette: $9.95

★★★★★

Foolish Frog, The
Pete and Charles Seeger.
Illustrated by Miloslav Jagr. Macmillan. 1973. Songs.
A farmer sees a bullfrog that becomes the main character of his folk song at the corner store. The farmer's singing eventually draws everybody (and everything) into the store until it explodes and all is restored to its rightful place.

Foolish Frog, The.
8 min. Color. Animated. Produced by William Bernal of Firebird Films and Loom Productions/Weston Woods. 1973. Music played and lyrics sung by Pete Seeger.
In this case, the film is so delightful that it inspired the book. It is a fun-filled, musical dramatization of the revelry that begins with the farmer's singing of the folk song.
Awards: Red Ribbon, American Film Festival; Chris Certificate, Columbus International Film Festival
Audience: Ages 4-8
Distributor: Weston Woods
16mm film: $195 **Videocassette:** $60
Rental: $20 daily

Strega Nonna and Other Stories.
35 min. Color. Iconographic and animated. Produced by Weston Woods. 1985.
Included in this tape anthology are adaptations of *Strega Nonna* (Tomie de Paola), *Tikki Tikki Tembo* (Arlene Mosel), *The Foolish Frog* (Pete and Charles Seeger) and *A Story—A Story* (Gail E. Haley). See individual titles for full descriptions.
Audience: Ages 4-8
Distributor: Children's Circle, Weston Woods
Videocassette: $19.95
No public performance rights

★★★★★

Forever Free
Joy Adamson.
Harcourt, Brace & World. 1963. Nonfiction.
Elsa and her three cubs are followed and cared for in the Serengeti plains near Lake Victoria, Africa.

Orphan Lions, The.
18 min. Color. Live action. Produced by LCA. 1973.
Edited from *Living Free*, the sequel to the film *Born Free*, this section tells about Elsa's three cubs who are released, recaptured and rereleased in a more favorable environment in the Serengeti. It is an exciting story of harrowing travels in the wilds.
Reviews: *Booklist*, Sept. 1, 1974
Audience: Ages 8-14
Distributor: Coronet/MTI Film & Video
16mm film: $300 **Videocassette:** $250
Rental: $75

★★★★★

Foundling, The
Carol Carrick.
Illustrated by Donald Carrick. Houghton Mifflin. 1987. [1977]. Realistic fiction.
A boy whose dog has died is encouraged to find another one. Seeing a puppy loose in the neighborhood, the boy stops to meet it, but the puppy escapes. There follows a search to locate the abandoned puppy.

Foundling, The.
24 min. Color. Live action. Produced by Mark Chodzka. 1986.

A sequel to *The Accident*, an award winning production, this story of Chris with his new dog is a sensitive tale that is as well done as its predecessor.

Reviews: *Booklist*, Aug. 1986; *Science Books and Films*, Nov./Dec. 1986; *School Library Journal*, Nov. 1986
Audience: Ages 5-10
Distributor: Barr Films
16mm film: $575 **Videocassette:** $400
Rental: $50

★★★★★

Fox Went Out on a Chilly Night, The
Peter Spier (illus.).
Doubleday. 1961. Songs.
A New England folk song, these lyrics are about a father fox who goes after some geese for his family's dinner.

Fox Went Out on a Chilly Night, The.
8 min. Color. Iconographic. Produced by Weston Woods. 1968.
Sung by Molly Scott, the tune covers the fox's capture of a goose and his being chased by the farmer. The melody is resung in the film, its words appearing over the still pictures of characters on screen.

Awards: Honors Award Certificate, American Film Festival
Audience: Ages 6-8
Distributor: Weston Woods
16mm film: $135 **Videocassette:** $70
Rental: $20 daily

Foxfire: A Play Based on Materials from the Foxfire Books.
Susan Cooper, Hume Cronyn, and Jonathan Holtzman.
French. 1983. Drama.
Weaving Appalachian customs from the Foxfire Books into its plot, the play stars Annie Nations. At seventy-nine, she is a widow who lives alone in her Appalachian mountain home. Annie still feels the presence of her departed husband when a land developer urges her to sell her homestead, and her son, a successful singer, urges her to join his family in Florida.

Foxfire.
97 min. Color. Live action. Produced by Marian Rees/Hallmark Hall of Fame. 1987. Hume Cronyn, Jessica Tandy, John Denver.
Adapted by playwright Susan Cooper, this production is the video medium at its finest. The story unfolds through a combination of interaction in the present—largely between Annie and her son Dillard—and flashbacks. The ages of the stars do not change, even in the flashbacks, but their performances are so engrossing that such details are of little consequence. Emotions and customs—love for the homestead, planting by the signs, and so forth—take center stage. Ever present is the conflict between old and new. The land developer has Annie's old land earmarked for new vacation homes. Annie today struggles to let go of her husband's memory and the yesterdays she shared with him. The production, like the literature on which it is rooted, exudes appreciation for times past. As described in *Variety*, "'Foxfire,' based on the play and on the Foxfire books...speaks lots of truth and wisdom; but it also works up good laughs and a sense of what's real and worthwhile in life...."

Reviews: *Variety*, Dec. 16, 1987
Awards: Emmy Awards, Outstanding Lead Actress, Outstanding Art Direction in a Miniseries or Special
Audience: Ages 14-Adult
Distributor: Republic Pictures Home Video
Videocassette: $89.98
No public performance rights

★★★★★

Frankenstein

Mary Wollstonecraft Shelley.

Multiple editions. Science fiction.

A brilliant scientist creates a monster who demands the scientist create a companion monster, a mate. The scientist refuses, precipitating murder.

Frankenstein.

71 min. Black and white. Live action. Produced by Universal. 1931. Boris Karloff, Colin Clive, Mae Clark.

The film is a powerful piece of cinematic horror that set the trend for an entire movie genre. It retains the basic theme of the original novel.

Reviews: *New York Times*, Dec. 5, 1931, 21:2; *Variety*, Dec. 8, 1931

Audience: Ages 12-Adult

Distributor: MCA/Universal Home Video

Videocassette available

No public performance rights

Frankenstein.

71 min. Black and white. Live action. 1931. Boris Karloff, Colin Clive.

A laser disc version of the same title offered by MCA/Universal Home Video (see above).

Distributor: Pioneer LDCA, Inc.

Laser disc: CLV format $34.98

No public performance rights

★★★★★

Freaky Friday

Mary Rodgers.

Harper & Row. 1972. Fantasy.

Thirteen-year-old Annabel Andrews has braces, an unreciprocated crush on a boy, and an irritating little brother. Her mother, Ellen, is tired of taking care of everyone but herself. The two gain a sympathetic understanding for each other after they magically switch personalities for a day.

Freaky Friday.

98 min. Color. Live action. Produced by Ron Miller/Walt Disney. 1976. Jodie Foster, John Astin, Dick Van Patten, Barbara Harris.

The novelist herself adapted the book to the screen. Added to this movie version is a slapstick chase scene at the end. As a consciousness raiser, the film appeals to pre-teen and teenage audiences.

Reviews: *Variety*, Dec. 22, 1976

Audience: Ages 10-Adult

Distributor: Buena Vista Home Video

Videocassette: $19.99

No public performance rights

Freaky Friday.

100 min. Color. Live action. 1976. Jodie Foster, John Astin, Dick Van Patten, Barbara Harris.

A laser disc version of the same title offered by Buena Vista Home Video (see above).

Distributor: Image Entertainment

Laser disc: CLV format $34.99

No public performance rights

Freaky Friday.

24 min. Color. Live action. A Disney Educational Production. 1980.

Young viewers might have difficulty with the transitions in this adaptation of the 1976 feature film; the mother's and daughter's changes in positions do not always seem to be matched by the voices.

Audience: Ages 10-Adult

Distributor: Coronet/MTI Film & Video

16mm film: $550 **Videocassette:** $250

Rental: $75

★★★★★

Freckle Juice
Judy Blume.

Illustrated by Sonia O. Lisker. Four Winds. 1985. [1971]. Realistic fiction.
Andrew Marcus wants freckles so badly that he will do almost anything to get them, including buying a secret formula from Sharon and then getting intensely ill from drinking the concoction. Creating freckles with a blue marking pen proves equally disastrous. Anthony ultimately decides that he likes himself just as he is.

Freckle Juice.
20 min. Color. Animation. Produced by Barrie Nelson. 1987.
The simple storyline is apparently too thin to sustain a film of this length. Its animated characters are ghostlike. The general effect is less than appealing, despite the show's loyalty to the letter and spirit of the picture book.
Reviews: *School Library Journal*, Aug. 1988
Audience: Ages 5-8
Distributor: Barr Films
16mm film: $480 **Videocassette:** $335
Rental: $50

★★★★★

Frederick
Leo Lionni (illus.).

Pantheon. 1987. [1967]. Fantasy.
Frederick the mouse, who muses on the colors of summer and fall while the other mice are busily storing supplies, shows that we all make our own special contributions to life.

Frederick.
6 min. Color. Animation. Produced by Italtoons. 1987.
Set to winning music and art, the animated short captures the spirit of the storybook and enhances it with movement.
Awards: Gold Medal, Atlanta Film Festival
Audience: Ages 3-10
Distributor: Lucerne Media
16mm film: $300 **Videocassette:** $225

Five Lionni Classics—The Animal Fables of Leo Lionni.
30 min. Color. Animation by Giulio Gianini. Produced by Italtoons Corp./Random House Home Video. 1987.
Included in this tape anthology are adaptations of *Frederick*, *Cornelius*, *It's Mine*, *Fish Is Fish*, and *Swimmy*. See individual titles for plot summaries. As a package, the animal fables illustrate the power of imagination, the joy of discovery and the importance of living together in harmony. The screen versions remain true to the original art and manuscripts. Winning animation, along with equally winning music, enhances the charm of the characters and the appeal of the storybooks.
Reviews: *Children's Video Report*, Feb. 1987
Audience: Ages 4-8
Distributor: Random House Home Video
Videocassette: $14.95
No public performance rights

Five Lionni Classics.
30 min. Color. Animation. Produced by Italtoons. 1987.
A public performance package of five separate Lionni titles for libraries, including *Frederick, Swimmy, Cornelius, Fish Is Fish*, and *It's Mine*. See individual titles for plot summaries.
Audience: Ages 4-8
Distributor: Lucerne Media
Videocassette: $325

★★★★★

Free to Be You and Me
Marlo Thomas.
Illustrated under the direction of Samuel N. Antupit.
McGraw Hill. 1987. [1974]. Nonfiction.
Adapted from the film, this collection of song, story, and conversation concerns the importance of children growing into individuals without sexual or racial prejudices.

Free to Be You and Me.
44 min. Color. Puppets, animation, live action. Produced by Marlo Thomas, Carole Hart. 1974. Marlo Thomas, Alan Alda, Harry Belafonte.
This production unfolds like a splendidly entertaining variety show with a host of well-known stars communicating through sequences, song, and conversation. Strong personalities such as Rosey Grier convey convincing messages like "it's okay to cry." Even the puppets in this production are multicultural. A boy wants a doll, a girl wants to race, and so on in a film that fosters acceptance.
Audience: Ages 6-12
Distributor: Vestron Video
Videocassette: $14.98
No public performance rights

★★★★★

Frog and Toad Are Friends
Arnold Lobel (illus.).
Harper & Row Junior Books. 1970. Humor.
The quiet loyalty and companionship of two best friends is exhibited in a string of five ministories: "Spring," "The Story," "A Lost Button," "A Swim," and "The Letter."

Frog and Toad Are Friends.
17.5 min. Color. Animated. Produced by John Matthews for Churchill Media. 1985. Narrated by Arnold Lobel.
Astonishingly realistic three-dimensional animation brings to life the warm friendship of the two characters. Faithful to the book by Arnold Lobel, the film animates its episodes. In "A Swim," for example, Toad is embarrassed about how he looks in a bathing suit. Such easy-to-identify-with situations are enhanced by the film's lifelike, "elaborately contrived sets." —*Booklist*
Reviews: *Booklist*, Nov. 1, 1985; Mar. 15, 1987; *School Library Journal*, Nov. 1985; *Young Viewers*, April 1987
Awards: ALSC Notable Children's Film; CINE Golden Eagle
Audience: Ages 4-8
Distributor: Churchill Media
16mm film: $395 **Videocassette:** $295
Rental: $60

Frog and Toad Are Friends.
27 min. Color. Animation. 1985.
A laser disc version of the same title also distributed by Churchill Media (see above). This version includes a second Churchill title, *Frog and Toad: Behind the Scenes*, in which filmmaker John Matthews explains the dimensional animation technique used in the Frog and Toad films.
Distributor: Churchill Media
Laser disc: CAV format $295

★★★★★

Frog and Toad Together
Arnold Lobel (illus.).
Harper & Row Junior Books. 1972. Humor.
In this sequel to *Frog and Toad Are Friends* (SEE), the pair star in another set of ministories: "The List," "The Garden," "Cookies," "Dragons and Giants," and "The Dream." In this last, Toad dreams he does great deeds, such as walking on a high wire, but he is lonely for Frog, who happens to be by Toad's side when he wakes up.

Frog and Toad Together.
17.5 min. Color. Animated. Produced by Churchill Media/John Matthews. 1987.
There is a wonderfully lifelike quality to this dimensional, or puppet, animation. Of the five vignettes in Lobel's storybook, all but "The List" are vividly and faithfully included in the film. As stated in *Booklist*, "'Dragons and Giants' is a little bit scarier here than in the print version." But overall, the film, like the book, is a warm and gentle celebration of true friendship.
Reviews: *Booklist*, Nov. 15, 1987
Awards: ALSC Notable Children's Film; CINE Golden Eagle.
Audience: Ages 4-8
Distributor: Churchill Media
16mm film: $395 **Videocassette:** $295
Rental: $60

★★★★★

Frog Prince, The
Jacob Grimm and Wilhelm K. Grimm.
Multiple editions. Folklore and fairy tales.
A princess loses her favorite plaything, a golden ball, in the water. Exacting a promise from her to be his companion, a frog rescues and returns the ball. The lovely princess begrudgingly keeps her promise at the insistence of her father, the king, which brings the frog into the palace, where he miraculously turns into a handsome prince.

Frog Prince, The.
7 min. Color. Limited animation. Produced by Halas and Batchelor. 1969.
This is a faithful if somewhat flat retelling, which offers brightly colored illustrations, a brisk pace, and some character dialogue in addition to narration.
Audience: Ages 4-8
Distributor: Britannica
16mm film: $190 **Videocassette:** $190

Frog Prince, The.
86 min. Color. Live action. A Golan Globus Production. 1972. Aileen Quinn, John Paragon, Helen Hunt, Clive Revill.
There are fine elements in this musical adaptation: a lovable king and an enhancement of the friendship between the princess and the frog. Not only is a promise something that must be kept in this rendition but friendship supersedes personal pleasure. The frog winds up in a waterless pit because of a wicked prank and the princess rushes to his rescue in an extension of the traditional plot.
Audience: Ages 6-Adult
Distributor: Cannon Video
Videocassette available
No public performance rights

Tale of the Frog Prince, The.
60 min. Color. Live action. Produced by Shelley Duvall. 1982. Terri Garr, Robin Williams.
Different in several regards from the original story, this adaptation is a sophisticated rendition of the classic. The film, unlike the tale, begins with an incident that shows why a spell was cast on the frog prince. The princess acts like a spoiled child for most of the production. In an incident new to the film, when the frog approaches the royal dining hall, it is sidetracked by a cook intent on preparing frog legs for dinner. In another new incident, the frog fights an insect. The princess finally redeems herself by apologizing for her unappreciative behavior, whereupon the frog changes into an unclothed prince. The outraged king has this strange man in his daughter's bedroom thrown into the dungeon, but a fairy godmother saves the day and explains how the tale ends happily ever after. Viewers may find the humor and some of the dialogue inappropriate for young audiences.
Reviews: *Variety*, Feb. 8, 1984
Audience: Ages 8-Adult

Distributor: Fox Video
Videocassette: $14.98
No public performance rights

Tale of the Frog Prince.
55 min. Color. Live action. 1982. Robin Williams, Terri Garr.
A laser disc version of the same title offered by Fox Video (see above).
Distributor: Image Entertainment
Laser disc: CLV format $29.98
No public performance rights

Frog Prince, The.
51 min. Color. Live action and puppetry. Produced by Jim Henson. 1988.
Young viewers will undoubtedly delight in this rousing version of the fairy tale, which features Kermit the Frog and other Muppet characters. However, with a monster named Sweetums, a princess who cannot speak correctly because of an evil spell (*awful frog* becomes *frawful og*) and a purple-faced witch, there is little in this adaptation that resembles the original Grimm tale.
Audience: Ages 6-10
Distributor: Films Inc.
Videocassette: $49

★★★★★

Froggie Went A-Courtin'
Chris Conover (illus.).
Farrar, Straus & Giroux. 1986. Songs.
A lovable, amorous frog goes courting with typical frog courting antics in this Scottish ballad. The courtship ends happily when the married frog and mouse sail to France, despite the interference of the tomcat at their wedding.

Froggie Went A-Courtin'.
8.5 min. Color. Live action. Produced by Wendy Hershey. 1981.
Not an outstanding production, this is a cute film with young children listening to a storyteller-singer and reenacting the song. The film appears to be more concerned about a proper ethnic mix of actors than about a superior enactment.
Reviews: *School Library Journal*, Sept. 1982; *Booklist*, Oct. 1981; *Early Childhood*, Sept. 1981
Awards: First Place in Language Arts, Chicago Educational Film Festival
Audience: Ages 4-7
Distributor: Barr Films
16mm film: $190 **Videocassette:** $135
Rental: $50

★★★★★

From the Mixed-Up Files of Mrs. Basil E. Frankweiler
Elaine Konigsburg (illus.).
Macmillan. 1967. Adventure.
Feeling unappreciated, a young girl and her even younger brother run away from home and live in the Metropolitan Museum of Art. There they stumble on a mystery about a breathtaking statue that takes them to the mansion of a recluse.

From the Mixed-Up Files of Mrs. Basil E. Frankweiler.
30 min. Color. Live action. Produced by Westfall Productions/BFA. 1978. Features Ingrid Bergman.
Convincing acting combines with the captivating setting of the Metropolitan Museum and excellent pacing to dramatize this story about the determined young girl and her brother. Besides the aristocratic yet tender performance of Mrs. Frankweiler (donator of the statue) by Ingrid Bergman, the film boasts a cameo appearance by Madeleine Kahn as a schoolteacher. The two children are perfectly believable.

Audience: Ages 8-12
Distributor: Phoenix/BFA Films & Video
16mm film: $600 **Videocassette:** $340
Rental: $83

G

adherence to book   film rating

Gabrielle and Selena
Peter Desbarats.
Harcourt Brace Jovanovich. 1968. Realistic fiction.
A black girl and her white friend are bored, so they decide to trade families. One day serves to show the common elements in the lives of the two families.

Gabrielle and Selena.
13 min. Color. Live action. Produced by Bosustow. 1972.
Two charming girls play the lead roles exceptionally well among an otherwise mediocre cast. The production as a whole is nevertheless a highly engaging, gentle story.
Audience: Ages 6-10
Distributor: Phoenix/BFA Films & Video
16mm film: $295 **Videocassette:** $175
Rental: $38

★★★★★

"Game of Catch, A"
Richard Wilbur.
Printed story included with screen version. Short stories—realistic fiction.
A not particularly athletic pre-teenager, who is drawn to baseball, happens upon two more athletic friends playing catch. Left out, he annoys them by insisting he controls all their actions.

Game of Catch, A.
15 min. Color. Live action. Produced by Steven John Ross. 1990.
Strikingly realistic, the film focuses on a twelve-year-old boy whose frustration at being left out results in his professing he has more control in life than he actually does. Soho, the boy, climbs and falls out of a tree while the others play ball. His friends are concerned until they see he is alright. Sadly, his taunts about controlling them continue. The film, like the story, is a thought-provoking work of art.
Audience: Ages 10-Adult
Distributor: Pyramid Film & Video
16mm film: $395 **Videocassette:** $295
Rental: $75

★★★★★

Georgie
Robert Bright (illus.).
Doubleday. 1944. Fantasy.
A likable ghost named Georgie searches for a new house to haunt.

Georgie.
6 min. Color. Iconographic. Produced by Weston Woods. 1956.

This is an adequate screen version that echoes the picture book. As a ghost tale, the film does not create the feeling of suspense that stories in the genre promise to deliver.

Audience: Ages 6-8
Distributor: Weston Woods
16mm film: $140 **Videocassette:** $60
Rental: $20 daily

What's Under My Bed? and Other Creepy Stories.
35 min. Color. Iconographic and animated. Produced by Weston Woods. 1990.
Included in this tape anthology are adaptations of *What's Under My Bed* (James Stevenson), *Georgie* (Robert Bright), *Teeny Tiny and the Witch Woman* (Barbara Walker), and *The Three Robbers* (Tomi Ungerer). See individual titles for full descriptions.

Audience: Ages 4-10
Distributor: Children's Circle, Weston Woods
Videocassette: $19.95
No public performance rights

★★★★★

Ghost Belonged to Me, The
Richard Peck.
Penguin USA. 1975. Fantasy.
A boy is led by the ghost of a young girl to rescue people about to drive over a collapsing bridge.

Ghost Story Classics.
21 min. Color. Animation and live action. Produced by Asselin Productions. 1990. Vincent Price.
Those who enjoy Vincent Price, no matter how exaggerated the dramatics, will enjoy the abbreviated and interrupted accounts of two popular ghost stories that he introduces. *The Ghost Belonged to Me* and *The Legend of Sleepy Hollow* are portrayed in part, but don't expect a conclusion to either story. Vincent Price intervenes to challenge you to create your own story endings.

Audience: Ages 10-14
Distributor: Barr Films
Videocassette: $295 **Rental:** $50

Ghost Belonged to Me, The.
11 min. Color. Live action. A Disney Educational Production. 1981.
This delightful ghost story ends happily as a boy who first doesn't believe in ghosts is joined by a girl ghost in saving the lives of people about to travel over a disintegrating bridge.

Audience: Ages 8-17
Distributor: Coronet/MTI Film & Video
16mm film: $290 **Videocassette:** $220
Rental: $75

★★★★★

"Ghost in the Shed"
Marilyn K. Roach.
Anthologized in *Encounters with the Invisible World.* Thomas Y. Crowell. 1977. Short stories—fantasy.
In this comical ghost story a peddler was killed and buried in a farm shed. Years later, his ghost annoys the new farm tenants by constantly opening the door between the kitchen and the shed, no matter how hard they try to fasten it.

Ghost in the Shed.
8 min. Color. Animated. Produced by Nick Bosustow. 1980. Narrated by George Gobel.
The original ghost story is closely followed in this well-crafted film. More prominent in the film than the print version is the humorous effect of the situation at hand.

Audience: Ages 8-Adult
Distributor: Churchill Media

16mm film: $180 **Videocassette:** $59
Rental: $50

★★★★★

Ghost of Thomas Kempe, The
Penelope Lively.
Illustrated by Antony Jasper Maitland. Dutton. 1978. [1973]. Fantasy.
A boy moves into an old house and accidentally frees an impish ghost intent on tormenting a neighbor lady.

Ghost of Thomas Kempe, The.
48 min. Color. Live action. Produced by ABC Weekend Specials/Teleprograms Inc. 1979.
In this well acted and directed nonsensical story, a boy who moves into a new house accidentally pokes a hole in the wall and unleashes a prank-playing ghost. Only the antagonist, an elderly neighbor woman, is less than believable.
Awards: Honorable Mention, Columbus International Film Festival
Audience: Ages 8-11
Distributor: Coronet/MTI Film & Video
16mm film: $654 **Videocassette:** $250
Rental: $75

★★★★★

"Gift of the Magi"
O. Henry.
Anthologized in *The Gift of the Magi and Other Stories*. Illustrated by Gordon Grant. Reader's Digest. 1987. Short stories—realistic fiction.
A husband and wife each sell their dearest treasures to afford Christmas gifts for one another.

Gift of Love, The.
96 min. Color. Live action. Produced by Osmond Productions. 1978. Marie Osmond, Timothy Bottoms, James Woods.
Greatly adding to the short story, the picture creates a past for its main female character. She is a well-to-do orphan about to enter into an arranged marriage with a socially "acceptable" mate, when she falls in love with a young Swiss immigrant. Afterwards, she struggles with pleasing her relatives or giving herself the Gift of Love. The rather saccharin show features a narrator acting as O. Henry.
Audience: Ages 12-Adult
Distributor: Monterey Home Video
Videocassette: $24.95
No public performance rights

Gift of the Magi, The.
18 min. Color. Live action. Produced by Bert van Bork with Clifton Fadiman. 1980.
A husband sells his watch to buy his wife a comb, but she has sold her hair to buy him a watch chain. So they both receive useless gifts. To viewers unfamiliar with the story, the surprise ending is effectively performed in this faithful adaptation of this touching tale about sacrifice and the spirit of love.
Audience: Ages 12-Adult
Distributor: Britannica; rental—Penn State University
16mm film: $505 **Videocassette:** $295
Rental: $30

Gift of the Magi and *The Magic Shop, The.*
28 min. Color. Live action. 1980.
A laser disc version of the same two titles distributed separately by Britannica (see above).
Distributor: Britannica
Laser disc: CAV format $129

★★★★★

Gingerbread Man, The

Multiple editions. Folklore and fairy tales.
A little old lady bakes a gingerbread cookie in the form of a man who comes to life, runs away, and then is tricked by a fox.

Gingerbread Man, The.
10 min. Color. Limited animation. Produced by Somersaulter and Moats. 1980.
The prizes won by this film are well deserved. It is an accurate retelling of the popular tale, a production that ranks well above average. Distinguished in the United States, it has also achieved recognition in international film festivals.
Awards: CINE Golden Eagle
Audience: Ages 5-8
Distributor: Coronet/MTI Film & Video
16mm film: $265 **Videocassette:** $170
Rental: $75

★★★★★

Girl of the Limberlost, A
Geneva Grace Stratton-Porter.

Dell. 1986. Historical fiction.
This coming-of-age historical novel follows the adventures of a fifteen-year-old girl who finds solace in the Limberlost, a swampy forest near her home that holds the secret to her father's untimely death.

Girl of the Limberlost, A.
105 min. Color. Live action. Produced by Tony Bishop, Ann Eldridge/WonderWorks. 1991.
The video version eliminates many characters and incidents from the book so that it can concentrate on the difficult relationship between the engaging character, fifteen-year-old Elinor, and her stern mother, who at the drama's conclusion reveals the reasons for her rigid, seemingly heartless attitude. While the movie does not strictly adhere to the book's plot, it is an entertaining, involving drama that features authentic costumes and sets.
Reviews: *Booklist*, June 15, 1991
Audience: Ages 10-Adult
Distributor: Public Media Video
Videocassette: $29.95

★★★★★

The Giving Tree
Shel Silverstein (illus.).

Harper & Row Junior Books. 1964. Fantasy.
A tree satisfies a boy's needs, continuing to do so as the boy grows into an adult and then an old man. By this time the tree has been reduced to a mere stump, providing the perfect place for sitting and resting.

The Giving Tree.
10 min. Black and white. Animated. Produced by Nick Bosustow and Shel Silverstein. 1973. Narrated by Shel Silverstein.
This is a quiet film, soothing in its faithful delivery of the storybook. As in the original, the line drawings are limited in color; in the film to blue and black. The style enhances the impact of the theme that giving is joyous.
Reviews: *Your Church*, Mar./Apr. 1984
Awards: Bronze Plaque, Columbus International Film Festival
Audience: Ages 8-Adult
Distributor: Churchill Media
16mm film: $240 **Videocassette:** $180
Rental: $60

★★★★★

Glass Menagerie, The
Tennessee Williams.

NAL. 1987. [1975]. Drama.
In a Southern family, a crippled girl must deal with her mother's fantasies and her brother's idealism.

Glass Menagerie, The.
132 min. Color. Live action. Produced by Universal. 1987. Joanne Woodward, John Malkovich, Karen Allen.
The adaptation "starts out stiffly and gets better as it goes along, with the dinner party sequence its biggest success."—*New York Times*

Reviews: *New York Times*, Oct. 23, 1987, C 14:3; *Variety*, May 13, 1987
Audience: Ages 16-Adult

Distributor: MCA/Universal Home Video
Videocassette available
No public performance rights

Glass Menagerie.
134 min. Color. Live action. 1987. Joanne Woodward, John Malkovich, Karen Allen.
A laser disc version of the same title offered by MCA/Universal Home Video (see above).

Distributor: Pioneer LDCA, Inc.
Laser disc: CLV format $39.98
No public performance rights

★★★★★

Goggles!
Ezra Jack Keats (illus.).
Macmillan. 1987. [1969]. Realistic fiction.
Peter, a young black boy, finds a pair of goggles, and some older boys threaten to take them away. His dog Willie and friend Archie help him outsmart the bullies.

Goggles.
11 min. Color. Live action. Produced by American Communicator/LCA. 1988.
Brandon Adams is the charming finder of the goggles; his bright-eyed portrayal makes this an entertaining live-action adaptation of the story for young viewers.

Reviews: *Booklist*, May 15, 1989
Awards: Silver Award, National Film Festival
Audience: Ages 6-12
Distributor: Coronet/MTI Film & Video
16mm film: $320 **Videocassette:** $250
Rental: $75

Goggles!
6 min. Color. Iconographic. Produced by Weston Woods in consultation with Ezra Jack Keats. 1974. Realistic fiction.
The iconographic production builds with the energy of the chase, effectively creating the impression of movement. Well-narrated, the show conveys the boys' tension and relief. As in the book, the story progresses naturally with only the pictures revealing that the main character is black.

Reviews: *Booklist*, Sept. 15, 1974
Audience: Ages 4-8
Distributor: Weston Woods
16mm film: $140 **Videocassette:** $60
Rental: $20 daily

★★★★★

"Gold Bug, The"
Edgar Allan Poe.
Anthologized in *The Unabridged Edgar Allan Poe.* Running Press. 1983. Short stories—adventure.
A boy visits an island and becomes involved with unsavory characters searching for a lost treasure.

Gold Bug, The.
43 min. Color. Live action. Produced by ABC Children's Weekend Special/LCA. 1980.
As stated in *Media and Methods*, "This film will rivet the attention of its viewers to the screen." The shorter version (see below) of this production, also an excellent adaptation, retains the major elements necessary to the story.

Reviews: *Media and Methods*, Dec. 1980
Awards: ALA Notable Film for Young Adults; Chris Plaque, Columbus International Film Festival; *Learning* Magazine AV Award
Audience: Ages 8-14
Distributor: Coronet/MTI Film & Video
16mm film: $750 **Videocassette:** $250
Rental: $75

Gold Bug, The.
31 min. Color. Live action. Produced by ABC Children's Weekend Special/LCA. 1980.
An abbreviated version of the same, full-length title also distributed by Coronet/MTI Film & Video (see above). This version retains the basic plot but omits selected details.
Distributor: Coronet/MTI Film & Video
16mm film: $500 **Videocassette:** $250
Rental: $75

Edgar Allan Poe's The Gold Bug.
43 min. Color. Live action. Produced by ABC Weekend Special/LCA. 1980.
A full-length, home video version of the same title distributed by Coronet/MTI Film & Video (see above).
Distributor: New World Video
Videocassette: $19.95
No public performance rights

★★★★★

Golden Goose, The
Jacob Grimm and Wilhelm K. Grimm.
Multiple editions. Folklore and fairy tales.
A peasant carries a goose that results in making a solemn princess laugh, so he is entitled to her hand in marriage. Her father attempts to prevent the marriage by devising impossible tasks for the peasant; rewarding him for past generosity, a stranger helps the peasant fulfill them all.

Princess Who Had Never Laughed, The (Faerie Tale Theatre).
60 min. Color. Live action. Produced by Shelley Duvall. 1984. Ellen Barkin, Howie Mandell, Howard Hesseman.
Unlike most Faerie Tale Theatre productions, this one does not begin with a preview of excerpts from the other tales in the series. The production launches into its main story. In this version, the king holds a contest to find the person who can make his daughter laugh. The prize, her hand in marriage, is won by a likable pig farmer, whose tale makes the princess laugh at herself. Some of the other contestants use updated routines, mentioning twentieth-century personalities such as Ed Sullivan and Jack Benny. There is a touching scene between the king and princess, in which he explains how laughter led to the death of her mother, which, in turn, led to his banishing laughter from the kingdom. Some of the dialogue verges on silliness yet elicits smiles. After the princess marries the pig farmer, her father jokes "I never sausage a marriage." In all seriousness, the film, like the tale and variations of it, celebrates laughter.
Audience: Ages 6-Adult
Distributor: Fox Video
Videocassette: $14.98
No public performance rights

★★★★★

Goldilocks and the Three Bears.
Multiple editions. Folklore and fairy tales.
Goldilocks wanders into the home of a mama bear, papa bear, and baby bear. She tries their porridge, their chairs, and their beds before being awakened by the bears' return.

Goldilocks and the Three Bears.
10 min. Color. Animation. Produced by Christianson Productions. 1981.
Though the animation is limited, David Christianson is a master of the style. This rendition of the old story is a lively film that remains faithful to the printed retellings.
Audience: Ages 4-8
Distributor: Phoenix/BFA Films & Video
16mm film: $245 **Videocassette:** $145
Rental: $32

Goldilocks and the Three Bears.
12 min. Color. Animated. Produced by Somersaulter and Moats. 1984.
A weak narrator who seems to be talking down to the audience and mediocre animation slowly reveal the old story.
Reviews: *School Library Journal*, Aug. 1985
Audience: Ages 4-8
Distributor: Coronet/MTI Film & Video
16mm film: $295 **Videocassette:** $210
Rental: $75

Goldilocks and the Three Bears (Faerie Tale Theatre).
60 min. Color. Live action. Produced by Shelley Duvall. 1983. Tatum O'Neal, John Lithgow, Hoyt Axton.
Digressing from the simple, original tale, this dramatization of Goldilocks gives her a host of negative traits, from tampering with other people's things to lying to tricking others into doing her work. The basic plot of the fairy tale in which Goldilocks invades the bears' home and possessions, falling asleep in Little Bear's bed, is retained. Upon being discovered, however, Goldilocks fibs that she is an orphan. She and the bear family become good companions and in the end she sees the error of her ways and learns to tell the truth.
Audience: Ages 6-10
Distributor: Fox Video
Videocassette: $14.98
No public performance rights

Goldilocks and the Three Bears.
47 min. Color. Live action. 1983. Tatum O'Neal, John Lithgow, Hoyt Axton.
A laser disc version of the same title offered by Fox Video (see above).
Distributor: Image Entertainment
Laser disc: CLV format $29.98
No public performance rights

Red Riding Hood/Goldilocks and the Three Bears.
30 min. Color. Limited animation. Produced by Rabbit Ears. 1990. Narrated by Meg Ryan.
In two separate morality tales, young girls run into trouble when they stray from the path or disregard parental advice. Red Riding Hood is swallowed by a wolf; Goldilocks is awakened in the home of three bears by the outraged trio. In the first tale, artist Laszlo Kubinyi introduces the red-topped lass against a soft colored-pencil background. Bolder colors are developed as she dons her red cape and heads into the forest where a silver-coated fox with a walking stick and a French accent lolls-in-wait. The trip to granny's and the outcome follow the conventional story line. The main character in Goldilocks is a spoiled brat with a southern drawl and a "make-me" demeanor. Meg Ryan's accent and grumpy mutterings add freshness to an old favorite.
Reviews: *Booklist*, Nov. 15, 1990
Audience: Ages 4-8
Distributor: SVS/Triumph
Videocassette: $14.95
No public performance rights

★★★★★

Gone with the Wind
Margaret Mitchell.

Macmillan. 1975. [1936]. Historical fiction. Scarlett O'Hara, a self-centered, stubbornly independent Southern belle fails to win the man she loves but survives the Civil War. Meanwhile, a dashing but incorrigible "gentleman," Rhett Butler, falls in love with her.

Gone with the Wind.
220 min. Color. Live action. Produced by MGM/David O. Selznick. 1939. Vivien Leigh, Clark Gable, Olivia de Havilland, Leslie Howard, Hattie McDaniel.
A testimony to motion picture making at its best, this adaptation took great pains to recreate from the novel even the difficult scene about the burning of Atlanta. The characters are full-bodied. As demonstrated by its multiple awards, the motion picture succeeds on a host of levels.
Reviews: *New York Times*, Dec. 20, 1939, 31:2; *Variety*, Dec. 20, 1939
Awards: Academy Awards, Best Picture, Best Actress, Best Supporting Actress, Best Directing, Best Screenplay, Best Cinematography, Best Set Design
Audience: Ages 16-Adult
Distributor: MGM/UA Home Video
Videocassette: $89.98
No public performance rights

Gone With the Wind.
232 min. Color. Live action. 1939. Clark Gable, Vivien Leigh, Olivia de Havilland, Leslie Howard.
A laser disc version of the same title offered by MGM/UA Home Video (see above).
Distributor: Pioneer LDCA, Inc.
Laser disc: CLV format $49.98
No public performance rights

★★★★★

Good Earth, The
Pearl S. Buck.

Multiple editions. Realistic fiction.
A Chinese peasant family endures hardship, then grows wealthy. Over the years, the father loses his precious wife but never relinquishes his ties to the land.

Good Earth, The.
138 min. Black and white. Live action. Produced by MGM/Albert Levin. 1937. Paul Muni, Luise Rainer.
Though the novel is recreated in fine detail, the production has lost some impact over time and is uneven in that the first hour of the film includes most of its drama.
Reviews: *New York Times*, Feb. 3, 1937, 27:1; *Variety*, Feb. 10, 1937
Awards: Academy Awards, Best Actress, Best Cinematography
Audience: Ages 12-Adult
Distributor: MGM/UA Home Video
Videocassette: $19.98
No public performance rights

★★★★★

Goodbye Book, The
Judith Viorst.

Atheneum. 1988. Realistic fiction.
A boy who is about to be left with a babysitter for the first time imagines many unsavory moments with the sitter—all of which turn out not to be the real situation.

Goodbye Book, The.
12 min. Color. Live action. Produced by Bernard Wilets. 1989.
Unimaginative acting and a star who appears to be several years too old to be having the tantrums seen in the film make this otherwise true-to-the-book adaptation a so-so rendition.

Reviews: *School Library Journal*, Feb. 1991
Awards: Bronze Apple, National Educational Film and Video Festival
Audience: Ages 4-8
Distributor: Barr Films
16mm film: $315 **Videocassette:** $195
Rental: $50

★★★★★

Goodbye, Mr. Chips
James Hilton (illus.).
Little, Brown & Co. 1962. [1934]. Realistic fiction.
The English schoolteacher Mr. Chipping, alias Mr. Chips, recounts his life in Brookfield and the scores of boys he tutored.

Goodbye, Mr. Chips.
114 min. Black and white. Live action. Produced by MGM/Victor Saville. 1939. Robert Donat, Greer Garson, Paul Henreid.
Unreservedly sentimental, the film pulls at the heartstrings in detailing the career of Charles Chipping. Viewers follow him from his days as novice teacher to his marriage, which makes him more outgoing, to his elderly years at school. The film tastefully capitalizes on humorous possibilites in the novel.
Reviews: *New York Times*, May 16, 1939, 27:2
Awards: Academy Award, Best Actor
Audience: Ages 12-Adult
Distributor: MGM/UA Home Video
Videocassette: $19.98
No public performance rights

Goodbye, Mr. Chips.
147 min. Color. Live action. Produced by MGM/Arthur P. Jacobs. 1969. Peter O'Toole, Petula Clark, Michael Bryant.
While O'Toole's performance is quite convincing, the production is a musical with songs that contribute little to the action and with an updated conclusion to the story.
Reviews: *Variety*, Oct. 15, 1969
Audience: Ages 12-Adult
Distributor: MGM/UA Home Video
Videocassette: $19.98
No public performance rights

★★★★★

Goose Girl, The
Jacob Grimm and Wilhelm K. Grimm.
Multiple editions. Folklore and fairy tales.
A princess journeys to a distant land to marry a prince. En route, her treacherous chambermaid switches places with her. The princess becomes a lowly goose girl in the distant kingdom until the king himself uncovers the truth.

Goose Girl, The.
18 min. Color. Live action. Produced by Tom and Mimi Davenport. 1984.
This fine live action adaptation moves along swiftly and, as in the printed tale, includes the violent sentence of death for the deceitful serving woman. There is a nice balance of narration and dialogue.
Audience: Ages 5-12
Distributor: Davenport Films
16mm film: $350 **Rental:** $35
Videocassette: $60 (with public performance rights)
Videocassette: $29.95 (no public performance rights)

Goosemaid, The.
10 min. Limited animation. Produced by Institut fur Film und Bild. 1990.
As in the original, the king discovers the true identity of the goosemaid when a fellow worker complains about her strange behavior. The princess-turned-goosemaid does not disclose the truth to the king but to an iron stove within his earshot. After-

wards, the chambermaid is killed for her treachery. The production relies on motionless illustrations and extremely limited animation. Though the colors are vivid and the settings quite convincing, there is a conspicuous lack of movement in this faithfully adapted tale.

Audience: Ages 4-8
Distributor: Britannica
Videocassette: $250

★★★★★

Grapes of Wrath, The
John Steinbeck.

Penguin USA. 1939. Historical fiction.
Forced to migrate from Oklahoma to California because of the 1930s Dust Bowl, farmers experience hardship at a labor camp instead of the better life for which they had hoped.

Grapes of Wrath, The.

129 min. Black and white. Live action. Produced by Twentieth Century Fox/Nunnally Johnson. 1940. Henry Fonda, John Carradine, Jane Darwell.
A film classic, this production continues to receive accolades for riveting performances and its slice-of-past-life realism. The film ends less harshly than the book, without damaging the effect achieved by the novel as a whole.

Reviews: *New York Times*, Jan. 25, 1940, 17:2; *Variety*, Jan. 31, 1940
Awards: Academy Awards, Best Director, Best Supporting Actress
Audience: Ages 16-Adult
Distributor: Fox Video
Videocassette: $19.98
No public performance rights

Grapes of Wrath, The.

128 min. Black and white. Live action. 1940. Henry Fonda, John Carradine, Jane Darwell.
A laser disc version of the same title offered by Fox Video (see above).

Distributor: Image Entertainment
Laser disc: CLV format $49.98
No public performance rights

★★★★★

Grasshopper and the Ants
Aesop.

Multiple editions. Folklore and fairy tales.
In the spring and summer, a grasshopper plays and rests while its ant neighbors work to prepare for winter. When winter arrives, the grasshopper must appeal to the ants for help.

Grasshopper and the Ants, The.

8 min. Color. Animation. A Disney Educational Production. 1979.
Bright and lively, this production with its memorable tunes and usual Disney high-quality animation serves as a fine choice for young viewers who need to be impressed by the value of hard work.

Audience: Ages 5-8
Distributor: Coronet/MTI Film & Video
16mm film: $220 **Videocassette:** $165
Rental: $75

Ant and the Grasshopper, The.

11 min. Color. Limited animation. Produced by Greatest Tales. 1980.
A fun-filled production despite the limited animation, this mostly straightforward adaptation adds some music and dance.

Audience: Ages 4-8
Distributor: Phoenix/BFA Films & Video
16mm film: $255 **Videocassette:** $135
Rental: $33

★★★★★

Great Escape, The
Paul Brickhill.
W. W. Norton. 1950. Nonfiction.
During World War II, allied captives in a German POW camp mount a mass escape through three underground tunnels.

Great Escape, The.
173 min. Color. Live action. Produced by United Artists/John Sturges. 1963. Steve McQueen, James Garner, Richard Attenborough.
Based on a true story, the film quickly achieves and retains a high level of excitement. It concerns a troublesome lot of prisoners, escapees confined in a supposedly escape-proof camp. The story's ending is tragic.
Reviews: *New York Times*, Aug. 8, 1963, 19:1; *Variety*, Apr. 17, 1963
Audience: Ages 14-Adult
Distributor: MGM/UA Home Video
Videocassette: $29.98
No public performance rights

Great Escape, The.
173 min. Color. Live action. 1963. Steve McQueen, James Garner, Richard Attenborough.
A laser disc version of the same title offered by MGM/UA Home Video (see above).
Distributor: Pioneer LDCA, Inc.
Laser disc: CLV format $39.98
No public performance rights

★★★★★

Great Expectations
Charles Dickens.
Multiple editions. Realistic fiction.
The growth of an orphan into a young gentleman unfolds in an adventuresome novel. After he aids a criminal, the orphan is generously but mysteriously repaid for his kindness.

Great Expectations.
100 min. Black and white. Live action. Produced by Universal. 1934. Phillips Holmes, Jane Wyatt, Henry Hull.
This adaptation is much stronger in the first half than the second half. It includes long passages of narrative that show deference to the novel but slow the pace. Considered mediocre when released, the production has paled in contrast to the still outstanding 1946 version.
Reviews: *Variety*, Jan. 29, 1935
Audience: Ages 15-Adult
Distributor: Videocassette not currently in distribution

Great Expectations.
118 min. Black and white. Live action. Produced by Rank/Cineguild. 1946. John Mills, Jean Simmons, Alec Guinness.
With vivid cinematography and directing by David Lean that makes full use of an excellent cast, this production is reputed as one of the finest book adaptations ever.
Reviews: *New York Times*, May 23, 1947, 31:1; *Variety*, Dec. 25, 1946
Awards: Academy Awards, Best Cinematography, Best Art Direction
Audience: Ages 15-Adult
Distributor: Paramount Home Video
Videocassette available
No public performance rights

Dickens: Great Expectations.
118 min. Black and white. Live action. 1946. John Mills, Jean Simmons, Alec Guinness.
A public performance version of the same title offered by Paramount Home Video (see above).
Distributor: Films for the Humanities &

Sciences
Videocassette: $89.95

Charles Dickens: Great Expectations.
299 min. Color. Live action. Produced by BBC. 1981. Gary Sundquist, Graham McGrath, Paul Davies-Prowles, Strafford Johns, Joan Hickson.
Authentic and warmly told, this lengthy adaptation captures the essence of the novel and portrays it with reverence. The performances are superb, from Pip's crotchety older sister to his tenderly affectionate brother-in-law to the haughty Estella whom he grows to love. Pip himself is captivating.
Audience: Ages 14-Adult
Distributor: Fox Video
Videocassette: $29.98
No public performance rights

Great Expectations.
72 min. Color. Animated. 1983.
The cartoon-style production is less than convincing. Though their actions are literally in accord with the novel, the characters are portrayed without depth. The relationship between Pip and his brother-in-law, for example, lacks any special affection. There is no indication of Pip's revulsion when he learns who his true benefactor is, and so forth. The production appeals to a younger audience than the novel.
Audience: Ages 8-12
Distributor: Vestron Video
Videocassette: $19.98
No public performance rights

★★★★★

Great Gatsby, The
F. Scott Fitzgerald.
Scribner. 1961. [1925]. Realistic fiction.
A love story of the Jazz Age, *The Great Gatsby* centers on a bootlegger-dreamer who buys a mansion near the woman of his heart (who is by this time married).

Great Gatsby, The.
146 min. Color. Live action. Produced by David Merrick/Newdon/Paramount. 1974. Robert Redford, Mia Farrow, Bruce Dern, Karen Black.
This well-staged film evokes the period in fine fashion. Yet it conveys only the surface of the novel, without delving into its characters or imparting its themes.
Reviews: *New York Times*, Mar. 28, 1974, 32:1; *Variety*, Mar. 27, 1974
Awards: Academy Awards, Best Costumes, Best Song Score; Golden Globe Award, Best Supporting Actress
Audience: Ages 16-Adult
Distributor: Paramount Home Video
Videocassette available
No public performance rights

Great Gatsby.
146 min. Color. Live action. 1974. Robert Redford, Mia Farrow, Bruce Dern, Karen Black.
A laser disc version of the same title offered by Paramount Home Video (see above).
Distributor: Pioneer LDCA, Inc.
Laser disc: CLV format $39.95
No public performance rights

★★★★★

Great Skinner Strike, The
Stephanie Tolan.
Macmillan. 1983. Realistic fiction.
A mother, who receives many more demands on her time and attention than

offers to help, goes on strike and organizes the neighborhood women.

Mom's on Strike.
46 min. Color. Live action. 1988. Produced by LCA. Mary Kay Place, George Gaynes.
A stimulus to discussion about family roles in the present day, the film is also comic entertainment. The shortened version (see below) is ample to portray a tale that prompts viewers to think about their own family relationships.
Awards: Electra Award, Birmingham International Film & Video Festival
Audience: Ages 12-17
Distributor: Coronet/MTI Film & Video
16mm film: $750 **Videocassette:** $250
Rental: $75

Mom's on Strike.
31 min. Color. Live action. 1988. Produced by LCA. Mary Kay Place, George Gaynes.
An abbreviated version of the same title also distributed by Coronet/MTI Film & Video (see above). This version retains the basic plot but omits selected details.
Audience: Ages 12-17
Distributor: Coronet/MTI Film & Video
16mm film: $595 **Videocassette:** $250
Rental: $75

★★★★★

Great White Hope, The
Howard Sackler.
Dial Press. 1968. Drama.
A black boxer wins the title of world heavyweight champion at the beginning of the twentieth century but experiences difficulties due to his relationship with a white woman.

Great White Hope, The.
103 min. Color. Live action. Produced by Twentieth Century Fox/Lawrence Turman. 1970. James Earl Jones, Jane Alexander.
The film's strengths lie in the vivid recreation of the prejudices of the time and in its Golden Globe-winning central performance by James Earl Jones.
Reviews: *New York Times*, Oct. 12, 1970, 46:1
Awards: Golden Globe Award, Most Promising Newcomer—Male
Audience: Ages 16-Adult
Distributor: Fox Video
Videocassette: $39.98
No public performance rights

★★★★★

Green Eggs and Ham
The Sneetches and Other Stories
Dr. Seuss (illus.).
Random House. 1960. 1961. Humor.
Three stories humorously shed light on a few negative habits—snap judgments, envy, and stubbornness. In *Green Eggs and Ham* (Random House 1960), Sam I Am attempts to share his dish with an unwilling character. *The Sneetches and Other Stories* (Random House 1961) features first a tale that shows Star-Belly Sneetches are no better than Plain-Belly Sneetches. In a second story, "The Zax," a north-bound Zax meets a south-bound Zax, and both of them stubbornly refuse to budge.

Green Eggs and Ham.
9 min. Color. Live action. Produced by DePatie-Freling/CBS. 1974.
Fun for all ages, this produced-for-television adaptation encourages viewers not to make hasty judgments. Few viewers or readers of the book will forget the changing reactions to green eggs with ham. This film is also available in a trilogy of Seuss stories (*Dr. Seuss On the Loose*; below).

Audience: Ages 6-10
Distributor: Phoenix/BFA Films & Video
16mm film: $325 **Videocassette:** $180
Rental: $28

Dr. Seuss: On the Loose.
28 min. Color. Animation. Produced by DePatie-Freleng/CBS, Inc. 1973. Voices of Allan Sherman and Hans Conreid.
The film animates three of the author's tales, concerning The Sneetches, The Zax, and Sam I Am of Green Eggs and Ham. Though the plots remain true to the originals, the production adds songs, so the events proceed at a more leisurely pace.
Reviews: *Variety*, Oct. 31, 1973
Audience: Ages 4-10
Distributor: Fox Video
Videocassette: $9.98
No public performance rights

Dr. Seuss on the Loose.
24 min. Color. Animation. 1974.
A public performance version of the same title distributed by Fox Video (see above).
Distributor: Phoenix/BFA Films & Video
16mm film: $545 **Videocassette:** $315
Rental: $78

★★★★★

Gulliver's Travels
Jonathan Swift.
Multiple editions. Fantasy.
An English physician of the 1600s voyages to other lands. On different occasions, he resides in a realm of miniature people (Lilliput), a country of giants (Brobdingnag), and a land ruled by horses (Houyhnhnm).

Gulliver's Travels.
77 min. Color. Animated. Produced by Paramount/Max Fleischer. 1939.
Gone from this filmed version is the social satire element of the story. The feature has been rendered as a comical, mostly uninvolving fantasy. Episodes from Swift's novel have been discarded, leaving Gulliver on the island of Lilliput and simplifying his experience here. Some of the animation is quite fine, but the whole appears dated and geared toward a younger audience than the novel on which it is based.
Reviews: *New York Times*, Dec. 21, 1939, 29:1; *Variety*, Dec. 20, 1939.
Audience: Ages 6-12
Distributor: Republic Pictures Home Video
Videocassette: $19.98
No public performance rights

Gulliver's Travels.
77 min. Color. Animation. 1939.
A laser disc version of the same title offered by Republic Pictures Home Video (see above).
Distributor: Image Entertainment
Laser disc: CLV format $29.98.
No public performance rights

Three Worlds of Gulliver, The.
100 min. Color. Live action. Produced by Columbia/Charles Schneer. 1960. Kerwin Mathews, Basil Sydney, Mary Ellis.
The film adapts portions of the original, including Gulliver's adventures in Lilliput and Brobdingnag. Geared to young audiences, it dispenses with Swift's integral satire and straightforwardly adapts plot lines. Added to the film version is a new character, Gulliver's fiancée, who accompanies him to the land of the giants.
Reviews: *New York Times*, Dec. 17, 1960, 19:3; *Variety*, Dec. 7, 1960

Audience: Ages 10-14
Distributor: Columbia TriStar Home Video
Videocassette: $69.95
No public performance rights

Gulliver in Lilliput.
108 min. Color. Live action. Produced by BBC with the Sever Network Australia and RCTV. 1986. Andrew Burt, Elizabeth Sladen.
Splendidly realistic, the photography and special effects accomplish the feat of making convincing a live action version of the fantastic satire. The production portrays Gulliver writing of his travels, then launches into a lengthy dramatization of his experience in Lilliput. Gulliver falls in love with a married Lilliputian to the jealous rage of the royal head of state. A fine motivator to further reading, the show closes with the mention of the land of giants.
Audience: Ages 14-Adult
Distributor: Fox Video
Videocassette: $14.98
No public performance rights

H

adherence to book   film rating

Hamlet
William Shakespeare.
Multiple editions. Drama.
The prince of Denmark avenges his father's murder, provoking the death of his sweetheart, mother, stepfather, and himself.

Hamlet.
155 min. Black and white. Live action. Produced by Rank/Two Cities. 1948. Laurence Olivier, Eileen Herlie, Basil Sydney.
While abbreviated by this production, the play is powerfully performed, particularly by Olivier in the role of Hamlet. The four-and-a-half-hour drama is, however, reduced to a two-and-a-half-hour motion picture. In the process, the characters Rosencrantz and Guildenstern have been totally lost.
Reviews: *New York Times*, Sept. 30, 1948, 32:2; *Variety*, May 12, 1948
Awards: Academy Awards, Best Picture, Best Actor, Best Art Direction-Set Decoration, Best Costumes; Golden Globe Awards, Best Foreign Film, Best Actor
Audience: Ages 16-Adult
Distributor: Paramount Home Video
Videocassette available
No public performance rights

Hamlet.
155 min. Black and white. Live action. Produced by Rank/Two Cities. 1948. Laurence Olivier, Eileen Herlie, Basil Sydney.
A public performance version of the same title offered by Paramount Home Video (see above).
Distributor: Films for the Humanities & Sciences
Videocassette: $89.95

Hamlet.
155 min. Black and white. Live action. 1948. Laurence Olivier, Eileen Herlie, Basil Sydney.
A laser disc version of the same title offered by Paramount Home Video (see above).
Distributor: Pioneer LDCA, The
Laser disc: CLV format $39.95
No public performance rights

Hamlet.
114 min. Color. Live action. Produced by Columbia/Leslie Linder/Martin Ransohoff. 1969. Nicol Williamson, Gordon Jackson,

Anthony Hopkins, Judy Parfitt, Marianne Faithfull.
This is a reasonable rendition with some notable moments.

Reviews: *New York Times*, Dec. 22, 1969, 43:1; *Variety*, Dec. 17, 1969
Audience: Ages 14-Adult
Distributor: Columbia TriStar Home Video
Videocassette: $19.95
No public performance rights

Hamlet (The Shakespeare Plays).
222 min. Color. Live action. Produced by BBC. 1980. Derek Jacobi, Patrick Stewart, Claire Bloom.
As described in the *Hartford Courant*, Jacobi portrays Hamlet in unique fashion: "This is a cool, calculating Hamlet, not a man crippled by indecision..." On the whole, the production is finely paced and convincing, with the exception of the settings. The staging of the climactic duel that has Hamlet pitted against Laertes seems contrived, and the locale of the graveyard scene too bare. Still, of all the BBC Shakespeare Plays, *Hamlet* is reputed as one of the finest. This video edition is for institutional use only.

Reviews: *Hartford Courant*, Nov. 10, 1980; *Washington Post*, Nov. 10, 1980; *Los Angeles Times*, Nov. 10, 1980
Audience: Ages 16-Adult
Distributor: Ambrose Video
Videocassette: $249.95

Hamlet.
135 min. Color. Live action. Produced by Warner Bros./Nelson/ICON. 1990. Mel Gibson, Glenn Close, Alan Bates, Paul Scofield.
The production is marked by splendid realism in the setting and a haunting performance by Mel Gibson as Hamlet, which draws viewers into the anguish of the prince. Shakespeare's layering of plot and subplot and their interrelationship comes through. However, the movie has reduced the play by some two hours, in the process reducing its depth. Paul Scofield makes a riveting ghost, and Alan Bates as Claudius imparts an unfounded conviction in his own innocence. The climactic dueling scene is particularly powerful.

Reviews: *Variety*, Dec. 19, 1990
Audience: Ages 16-Adult
Distributor: Warner Home Video
Videocassette: $92.99
No public performance rights

★★★★★

Hand-Me-Down Kid, The
Francine Pascal.
Penguin. 1980. Realistic fiction.
A girl with an older sister has a difficult time with her own identity until friends share their experiences.

Hand-Me-Down Kid, The.
45 min. Color. Live action. Produced by LCA. 1983.
The made-for-television story of sibling rivalry is sometimes humorous, sometimes slow. It appears to have been intended more for guidance than for entertainment.

Audience: Ages 7-12
Distributor: Coronet/MTI Film & Video
16mm film: $750 **Videocassette:** $250
Rental: $75

Hand-Me-Down Kid, The.
31 min. Color. Live action. Produced by LCA. 1983.
An abbreviated version of the same title also distributed by Coronet/MTI Film & Video (see above). This version retains the basic plot but omits selected details.

Audience: Ages 7-12

Distributor: Coronet/MTI Film & Video
16mm film: $500 **Videocassette:** $250
Rental: $75

★★★★★

Hangin' Out with Cici
Francine Pascal.
Penguin. 1977. Realistic fiction.
A fourteen-year-old girl and her mother are at odds until a fantasy takes the girl back in time to witness her mother's fourteenth year.

My Mother Was Never a Kid.
46 min. Color. Live action. Produced by LCA. 1981.
Science Books and Films maintains this adaptation is "entertaining enough to hold even a skeptic's interest," and the American Library Association agrees. This is one of the finest ABC After School Specials. It is distributed also in a short version (see below) that tells the story very well.
Reviews: *Booklist*, May 1, 1982; *School Library Journal*, Mar. 1982; *Science Books and Films*, Jan./Feb. 1982.
Awards: ALA Notable Children's Film; Emmy Award, Outstanding Children's Art Direction/Scenic Design/Set Decoration
Audience: Ages 10-15
Distributor: Coronet/MTI Film & Video
16mm film: $750 **Videocassette:** $250
Rental: $75

My Mother Was Never a Kid.
30 min. Color. Live action. Produced by LCA. 1981.
An abbreviated version of the same title also distributed by Coronet/MTI Film & Video (see above). This version retains the basic plot but omits selected details.
Audience: Ages 10-15
Distributor: Coronet/MTI Film & Video
16mm film: $500 **Videocassette:** $250
Rental: $75

★★★★★

Hansel and Gretel
Jacob Grimm and Wilhelm K. Grimm.
Multiple editions. Folklore and fairy tales.
With little food left for the family, a stepmother prompts her husband to abandon his children in the forest. The sister and brother come upon a house made of bread, cake, and candy. Famished, they bite into it, then discover it belongs to a wicked witch, who eats young children. These two find a way to outwit their captor and return safely home.

Hansel and Gretel.
11 min. Color. Puppet animation. Produced by Ray Harryhausen. 1955.
In a diversion from the line-drawing animation for which he is famous, Ray Harryhausen has created an excellent retelling of the classic story with puppets. The technique, however, suffers in comparison with contemporary animation.
Audience: Ages 6-9
Distributor: Phoenix/BFA Films & Video
16mm film: $230 **Videocassette:** $125
Rental: $28

Hansel and Gretel.
7 min. Color. Animation. Produced by Halas and Batchelor. 1969.
The bright animation and lively narration do not compensate for the limited character dialogue in a tale that lends itself to ample dialogue from the characters. While the retelling is faithful, the pace is so brisk there is little development of suspense.
Audience: Ages 6-9

Distributor: Britannica
16mm film: $190 **Videocassette:** $190

Hansel and Gretel: An Appalachian Version.
16 min. Color. Live action. Produced by Tom and Mimi Davenport. 1975.
Though faithful to the original, this live action adaptation is dominated by the wicked stepmother and the wicked witch. The father and children have nothing to say, so that there is little depth to their characters. The plot unfolds as in the Grimm version, but the effect on the audience is uninvolving.
Audience: Ages 6-12
Distributor: Davenport Films
16mm film: $275 **Rental:** $30
Videocassette: $60 (with public performance rights)
Videocassette: $29.95 (no public performance rights)

Hansel and Gretel.
10 min. Color. Animation. Produced by Greatest Tales. 1981.
Faithfully reenacted, the old story will hold the young audience despite animation that seems slightly stacatto.
Audience: Ages 6-9
Distributor: Phoenix/BFA Films & Video
16mm film: $230 **Videocassette:** $125
Rental: $28

Hansel and Gretel (Faerie Tale Theatre).
51 min. Color. Live action. Produced by Shelley Duvall. 1982. Ricky Schroeder, Joan Collins, Paul Dooley, Bridgette Andersen.
This is a close adaptation of the original tale, in which characters are most convincingly portrayed. There are a few additions to the basic story line. A moral that builds naturally from the story is spelled out: the children learn not to take candy from strangers. A second addition is another boy held captive with Hansel, a companion prisoner who meets his end before the young hero. More than justice is done in this adaptation, though, for the gingerbread children at the witch's house spring back to life at the end, a satisfying touch. Still, the basic plot makes this vivid version too chilling for the very young, and the lengthy dramatization of the short tale is rather slow moving.
Audience: Ages 6-12
Distributor: Fox Video
Videocassette: $14.98
No public performance rights

Hansel and Gretel (Faerie Tale Theatre).
48 min. Color. Live action. 1982. Ricky Schroeder, Joan Collins.
A laser disc version of the same title offered by Fox Video (see above).
Distributor: Image Entertainment
Laser disc: CLV format $29.98
No public performance rights

Hansel and Gretel.
17 min. Color. Limited animation. Produced by Coronet. 1985.
Cell animation that is not the fullest, but is bright and lively, faithfully recreates this well-known fairy tale.
Reviews: *Booklist*, Dec. 1, 1986
Audience: Ages 6-9
Distributor: Coronet/MTI Film & Video
16mm film: $375 **Videocassette:** $250
Rental: $75

Hansel and Gretel.
12 min. Color. Animated. Produced by David Alexovich. 1991.
Well-animated, energetically paced, and brightly colored, this fine rendition changes some minor details of the origi-

nal. The stepmother, without her husband, leaves the children in the forest. When Gretel first attempts to push the witch into the oven she is foiled by the suspecting witch and must outfox her by trying again.

Audience: Ages 6-9
Distributor: Britannica
Videocassette: $79

★★★★★

Happy Birthday, Moon
Frank Asch (illus.).
Prentice-Hall. 1982. Humor.
Bear sets out to get the moon a birthday present. He believes it is answering him when he talks to it and hears the echo of his own voice.

Happy Birthday, Moon.
7 min. Color. Animated. Produced by Weston Woods. 1985.
This is a well-animated, entertaining version of the story. Besides the visibly careful heed paid to the author's art, "...a crisply articulated and roundly expressive narration of the text echoes the bear's...loving wonder." —*Booklist*

Reviews: *Booklist*, Apr. 15, 1986; *School Library Journal*, Mar. 1986
Awards: CINE Golden Eagle; ALA Notable Film
Audience: Ages 4-6
Distributor: Weston Woods
16mm film: $175 **Videocassette:** $60
Rental: $20 daily

Happy Birthday Moon and Other Stories.
30 min. Color. Animated and iconographic. Produced by Weston Woods. 1989.
Included in this tape anthology are adaptations of *Happy Birthday, Moon* (Frank Asch), *Peter's Chair* (Ezra Jack Keats), *The Napping House* (Audrey Wood), *The Three Little Pigs* (Erik Bledgvad), and *The Owl and the Pussy-Cat* (Edward Lear). See individual titles for full descriptions.

Reviews: *Children's Video Report*, Feb./Mar. 1989
Audience: Ages 4-8
Distributor: Children's Circle, Weston Woods
Videocassette: $19.95
No public performance rights

★★★★★

Happy Lion, The
Louise Fatio.
Illustrated by Roger Duvoisin. McGraw-Hill. 1954. Adventure.
Set in France, this is a story about a lion everyone loves until the day he escapes and alarms his one-time friends.

Happy Lion, The.
8 min. Color. Limited animation. Produced by Rembrandt Films/Weston Woods. 1990.
The show faithfully details little François's rescue of the lion in animation that is noticeably limited.

Audience: Ages 4-6
Distributor: Weston Woods
16mm film: $195 **Videocassette:** $100
Rental: $20 daily

Danny and the Dinosaur and Other Stories.
35 min. Color. Iconographic and animated. Produced by Weston Woods. 1991.
Included in this tape anthology are adaptations of *Danny and the Dinosaur* (Syd Hoff), *The Camel Who Took a Walk* (Roger Duvoisin), *Island of the Skog* (Steven Kellogg), and *The Happy Lion* (Louis Fatio). See individual titles for full descriptions.

Audience: Ages 4-8
Distributor: Children's Circle, Weston Woods
Videocassette: $19.95

No public performance rights

★★★★★

Happy Owls, The
Celestino Piatti (illus.).
Atheneum. 1964. [1963]. Fantasy.
In a tale about quarreling, two owls explain to the other barnyard animals how they manage to co-exist peacefully all year.

Happy Owls, The.
7 min. Color. Limited animation. Produced by William L. Snyder/Weston Woods. 1969.
The moral is central to this story, while the action is secondary. This is an instructive but tranquil film with a plot that has selective rather than general appeal.
Audience: Ages 4-6
Distributor: Weston Woods
16mm film: $175 **Videocassette:** $90
Rental: $20 daily

Pigs' Wedding and Other Stories, The.
39 min. Color. Iconographic and animated. Produced by Weston Woods. 1991.
Included in this tape anthology are adaptations of *The Pigs' Wedding* (Helme Heine), *The Happy Owls* (Celestino Piatti), *The Selkie Girl* (Susan Cooper), *A Letter to Amy* (Ezra Jack Keats), and *The Owl and the Pussy-Cat* (Edward Lear). See individual titles for full descriptions.
Audience: Ages 4-8
Distributor: Children's Circle, Weston Woods
Videocassette: $19.95
No public performance rights

★★★★★

Happy Prince, The
Oscar Wilde.
Multiple editions. Fantasy.
Carved into a statue after his death, a prince who was happy in life witnesses the poverty and misery of his city. He beseeches a swallow to pluck the jewels and gold from the statue he now is and distribute them to the needy.

Happy Prince, The.
25 min. Color. Animated. Produced by Reader's Digest with Potterton Productions. 1974. Voices of Christopher Plummer and Cyris Jones.
True to the original, this splendid adaptation shows the statue of the happy prince being dejeweled for the higher purpose of aiding one unfortunate soul and then another. The film is well paced, with a fine balance of dialogue and narration. Like the story, its sadness builds as the prince-statue destroys itself in the process of helping others and the loyal swallow drops to its untimely death. The production gives viewers a revealing look at hardships in the city in stark contrast to the joys of the rich.
Reviews: *Booklist*, Feb. 15, 1975; *English Journal*, Dec. 1975
Awards: CINE Golden Eagle
Audience: Ages 6-10
Distributor: Pyramid Film & Video
16mm film: $495 **Videocassette:** $95
Rental: $75

Happy Prince, The.
8 min. Color. Animation. Produced by Romania Films. 1981.
The limited animation has a watercolor effect. As in the original, there is a curious sadness to the ending of this story about giving to others.
Audience: Ages 6-10
Distributor: Phoenix/BFA Films & Video
16mm film: $175 **Videocassette:** $122.50 **Rental:** $17.50

★★★★★

Hare and the Tortoise, The
Aesop.
Multiple editions. Folklore and fairy tales.
A cockily confident hare races a tortoise and loses.

Tortoise and the Hare, The.
8 min. Color. Animation. A Disney Educational Production. 1954.
In full, Disney-style animation, this version mixes fun and music with a bright, faithful retelling of the old story. The high entertainment value has endured since the production's initial award-winning release in 1934.
Awards: Academy Award, Best Cartoon Production
Audience: Ages 4-10
Distributor: Coronet/MTI Film & Video
16mm film: $225 **Videocassette:** $170
Rental: $75

Hare and the Tortoise, The (2nd edition).
10 min. Color. Animation. Produced by Paul Buchbinder. 1979.
Upbeat music, bright lively animation, and spirited narration make this a winning adaptation of the classic fable. The narrator's delivery and the musical accompaniment add humorous touches that enhance the story.
Reviews: *Booklist*, Apr. 1, 1980
Audience: Ages 4-8
Distributor: Britannica
16mm film: $325 **Videocassette:** $205

Hare and the Tortoise, The (2nd edition)/Whazzat?.
19 min. Color. Animation/Puppet animation. Produced by Paul Buchbinder/Crocus. 1979/1975.
A laser disc version of two separate titles also distributed by Britannica (see above). *Whazzat?* is a non-narrated adaptation of "The Blind Men and the Elephant."
Distributor: Britannica
Laser disc: CAV format $99

★★★★★

Harold and the Purple Crayon
Crockett Johnson (illus.).
Harper & Row Junior Books. 1958. Fantasy.
This imaginative tale has Harold draw his own adventure as he walks. Included in this adventure are the moon, a tree, a path, a hot-air balloon, and Harold's own room.

Harold and the Purple Crayon.
8 min. Color (mainly purple). Animated. Produced by David Piel, Robert Sagalyn, and Stanley Flink/Weston Woods. 1969.
Like the storybook, the motion picture celebrates the imagination. It is quite a simple tale about Harold's fantastic walk; its appeal rests in his clever use of the crayon. Motion enhances the presentation of the plot.
Audience: Ages 4-8
Distributor: Weston Woods
16mm film: $195 **Videocassette:** $60
Rental: $20 daily

★★★★★

Harold's Fairy Tale
Crockett Johnson (illus.).
Harper & Row. 1956. Fantasy.
Using his purple crayon, Harold draws a castle, a king, and an enchanted garden in which nothing grows due to an evil witch.

Harold's Fairy Tale.
8 min. Color (mainly purple and white). Animated. Produced by Weston Woods. 1974.
Complete with king and villain, this fairy tale grows with the movement of Harold's

purple crayon. It is delightfully imaginative and the motion of the medium heightens interest in whatever the crayon may draw next.

Audience: Ages 4-8
Distributor: Weston Woods
16mm film: $195 **Videocassette:** $100
Rental: $20 daily

★★★★★

Harry and the Lady Next Door
Gene Zion.
Illustrated by Margaret Graham. Harper & Row. 1960. Humor.
The dog Harry gets along with everyone except the neighbor next door, who is constantly practicing her singing. Invited to perform at a party, the neighbor overstays her welcome, so Harry decides to do something about the situation.

Harry and the Lady Next Door.
20 min. Color. Live action. Produced by Peter Matulavich. 1989.
Viewers will be disturbed by the neighbor lady's singing long before Harry is driven to action in this sometimes funny film about a dog driven to desperate measures by the constant caterwauling of a nearby neighbor.

Awards: Silver Cindy Award; ALA Notable Children's Film
Audience: Ages 6-12
Distributor: Barr Films
16mm film: $530 **Videocassette:** $370
Rental: $50

★★★★★

Harry the Dirty Dog
Gene Zion.
Illustrated by Margaret Graham. Harper & Row. 1956. Humor.
Harry is a carefree dog with a great dislike for baths. Fleeing a bath, he traverses through the city, growing so grimy that his family almost fails to recognize him.

Harry the Dirty Dog.
18 min. Color. Live action. Produced by Peter Matulavich. 1987.
The dog is outstanding in this story of a pet not inclined to take a bath. Rescued from the pound, the canine star does the finest acting in this gently funny film. Some details of his experience have been changed for a more visual effect, yet the dog emits the same personality in the film and the book. As noted in *School Library Journal*, "Harry loses none of his endearing qualities as he chases cows, jumps fences, and is transformed into a black dog with white spots."

Reviews: *School Library Journal*, Aug. 1988
Awards: Silver Apple, National Educational Film and Video Festival; Ruby Slipper, International Children's Film and Video Festival
Audience: Ages 4-12
Distributor: Barr Films
16mm film: $425 **Videocassette:** $295
Rental: $50

★★★★★

Hat, The
Tomi Ungerer.
Parents Magazine Press/Four Winds. 1970. Fantasy.
The hat in this story travels from one adventure to another, intercepting a falling flower pot, for example, and putting out a fire in a baby's carriage.

Hat, The.
6 min. Color. Iconographic. Produced by Weston Woods. 1982.
This is a well-paced version that sustains interest despite the minimum of movement in film style. The hat itself progresses from one adventure to another, creating the impression of movement.

Reviews: *Booklist*, Oct. 1982; *Horn*

Book, Oct. 1982
Awards: CINE Golden Eagle; Chris Bronze Award, Columbus Film Festival; *Learning* Magazine AV Award
Audience: Ages 4-6
Distributor: Weston Woods
16mm film: $175 **Videocassette:** $90
Rental: $20 daily

Doctor De Soto and Other Stories.
35 min. Color. Iconographic and animated. Produced by Weston Woods. 1985.
Included in this tape anthology are adaptations of *Doctor De Soto* (William Steig), *Patrick* (Quentin Blake), *Curious George Rides a Bike* (H. A. Rey) and *The Hat* (Tomi Ungerer). See individual titles for full descriptions.
Reviews: *Children's Video Report*, Dec. 1985
Audience: Ages 4-8
Distributor: Children's Circle, Weston Woods
Videocassette: $19.95
No public performance rights

★★★★★

Hating Book, The
Charlotte Zolotow (illus.).
Harper & Row. 1969. Realistic fiction.
Two friends have a misunderstanding, which they resolve by confronting one another and discussing the problem.

Hating Movie, The.
15 min. Color. Live action. Produced by Tim Spiedel. 1986.
An accurate adaptation of the book, this impresses the viewer as a too-predictable film. There is little novelty or excitement in this dramatized message on communicating to resolve differences.
Awards: Bronze Award, Houston International Film Festival
Audience: Ages 6-10
Distributor: Phoenix/BFA Films & Video
16mm film: $345 **Videocassette:** $220
Rental: $45

★★★★★

"Haunted Trailer, The"
Robert Arthur.
Anthologized in *Young Witches and Warlocks,* edited by Isaac Asimov, et. al. Harper & Row Junior Books. 1987. Short stories—mystery.
Two girls decide to live in a trailer haunted by four boys. In the end, a compromise sends the ghosts to another home.

Haunted Trailer, The.
24 min. Color. Live action. Produced by ABC Video. 1978.
A trailer salesperson knows his trailer is haunted. Two girls, who are going away to school, decide that a haunted trailer is where they want to live. Four insistent but finally agreeable ghosts inhabit the trailer in what might have been a really comic show—but misses.
Audience: Ages 14-18
Distributor: Coronet/MTI Film & Video
16mm film: $455 **Videocassette:** $250
Rental: $75

★★★★★

Heart Is a Lonely Hunter, The
Carson McCullers.
Bantam. 1970. [1940]. Realistic fiction.
A deaf mute living in a small Southern town helps the people around him.

Heart Is a Lonely Hunter, The.
123 min. Color. Live action. Produced by Warner Seven Arts/Joel Freeman. 1968. Alan Arkin, Sondra Locke, Stacy Keach.

Set in an updated context, the story seems to plod along in spite of fine acting by the leads.

Reviews: *New York Times*, Aug. 1, 1968, 24:1; *Variety*, July 31, 1968
Audience: Ages 15-Adult
Distributor: Warner Home Video
Videocassette: $59.99
No public performance rights

★★★★★

Heidi
Johanna Spyri.
Multiple editions. Realistic fiction.
A young girl goes to live with her embittered grandfather, a recluse in the Swiss Alps. She wins his heart, then brings her invalid cousin, Clara, there. Clara attempts to walk.

Heidi.
88 min. Black and white. Live action. Produced by Twentieth Century Fox/ Raymond Griffith. 1937. Shirley Temple.
As in the original, Heidi longs for the mountain village and Grandfather when she is in the home of the wealthy gentleman, but her stay there positively affects the gentleman's invalid daughter, Clara. Eventually both girls visit Grandfather with dramatic results. The production retains the basic plot of the original but accommodates the talents of the child star, adding a musical number. Tugging on viewers' heartstrings, Temple is well suited to the title role.

Reviews: *New York Times*, Nov. 6, 1937, 14:2; *Variety*, Nov. 10, 1937
Audience: Ages 10-16
Distributor: Fox Video
Videocassette: $19.98
No public performance rights

Heidi.
170 min. Black and white. Live action. 1937. Shirley Temple.
A laser disc version of the same title offered by Fox Video (see above). Also includes a second feature, *Poor Little Rich Girl*, about a child who joins a radio singing act.

Distributor: Image Entertainment
Laser disc: CLV format $49.98
No public performance rights

The Story of Heidi.
93 min. Color. Animated. Produced by Charles Ver Halen, Claudio Guzmán. 1975.
Cartoon-style animation reduces the drama of the novel, though Heidi's lively personality and Grandfather's gruff character are in keeping with the original text. Incidents new to the story have been added in this film version: Heidi brings a wounded bird home and nurses it to health; Heidi gets lost in the fog with Peter; Peter throws a tantrum when Heidi leaves. At Clara's house, Heidi falls victim to dreams of goats and so forth, which the viewer sees on screen. Her emotional changes occur a little too suddenly to be believable. Though there is melodrama in the ending, it has a satisfying effect.

Audience: Ages 6-10
Distributor: Pacific Arts Video
Videocassette available
No public performance rights

Heidi.
105 min. Color. Live action. Produced by Frederick Bragger/James Franciscus. 1979. Jean Simmons, Walter Slezack, Michael Redgrave, Jennifer Edwards.
This is a graceful, heartwarming, engrossing adaptation. Beautifully scripted, it provides character depth, with Clara's fears about walking dovetailing with Grandfather's fears about playing the organ again. The scenery is breathtaking,

the relationship between Clara's governess and father marvelously understated to keep Heidi, Clara, and Grandfather in the foreground. Peter and the goats are there, too.

Reviews: *School Library Journal*, Nov. 1989
Audience: Ages 8-12
Distributor: Vestron Video
Videocassette: $19.98
No public performance rights

★★★★★

Hercules.

Multiple editions. Folklore and fairy tales.
The Greek hero Hercules proves himself worthy of immortality by performing twelve labors. Exceptionally strong, the hero experiences a stream of adventures that also demand courage.

Hercules' Return from Olympus.
13 min. Color. Animation. Produced by Brian Jackson. 1987.
The critical-to-the-story background art of a temple is sometimes not very clear. In this version, a whining Hercules is granted a request to return to earth for a day.

Reviews: *School Library Journal*, Nov. 1988
Audience: Ages 6-12
Distributor: Barr Films
16mm film: $305 **Videocassette:** $215
Rental: $50

★★★★★

Hercules
Hardie Gramatky (illus.).

Putnam. 1960. [1940]. Fantasy.
Unable to compete with motored fire engines, a horse-drawn fire engine called Hercules saves the day when all the "powered" trucks have problems.

Hercules.
11 min. Color. Iconographic. Produced by Weston Woods. 1956.
This rather slow-moving version is nonetheless pointed in its delivery of a tale with a message about changing times and the advantages of old ways.

Audience: Ages 4-8
Distributor: Weston Woods
16mm film: $175 **Videocassette:** $60
Rental: $25 daily

★★★★★

Hero Ain't Nothin' But a Sandwich, A
Alice Childress.

Avon. 1977. [1973]. Realistic fiction.
A thirteen-year-old youth in the black ghetto of Harlem is attracted to drugs while his family fights to guide him on a proper path.

Hero Ain't Nothin' But a Sandwich, A.
107 min. Color. Live action. Produced by Radnitz-Mattel. 1977. Cicely Tyson, Paul Winfield, Larry B. Scott.
Rather than inspiring a natural perception as an outgrowth of a fine story, this adaptation gives the impression of the message being imposed on the audience. The motion picture, though laudable and realistic, has a didactic edge that lessens its effectiveness. Changes from the novel include a shift in setting from Harlem to Los Angeles, in point of view from first person to third person, in number of characters in Benjie's drug world from four to two, and in the sequence of events. Included in the motion picture are some moving scenes and performances. Acting increases the excitement of the novel's rooftop scene in which Benjie's life is at risk.

Reviews: *New York Times*, Feb. 3, 1978, III, 10:1; *Variety*, Dec. 14, 1977

Audience: Ages 12-16
Distributor: Paramount Home Video
Videocassette available

★★★★★

Hi, Cat!
Ezra Jack Keats (illus.).
Macmillan. 1988. Realistic fiction.
A boy finds a stray cat who follows him all day and interferes with his plan for a vaudeville show.

Hi, Cat!.
10 min. Color. Live action. Produced by LCA. 1989.
A very charming Archie helps carry this simple story, which ends with the boy's adopting the cat who followed him all day.
Audience: Ages 5-9
Distributor: Coronet/MTI Film & Video
16mm film: $320 **Videocassette:** $250
Rental: $75

★★★★★

Higglety Pigglety Pop! or, There Must Be More to Life
Maurice Sendak (illus.).
Harper & Row Junior Books. 1967. Fantasy.
Jennie, a pampered though discontented terrier, packs her bag and leaves home to seek independence. She eventually lands the lead role in a production of the World Mother Goose Theatre.

Higglety Pigglety Pop!.
60 min. Color. Live action. Produced by BBC TV. 1985.
An opera version of Sendak's modern fairy tale with music performed by the London Sinfonietta, this rendition follows the book perfectly. The libretti and beautifully intricate set designs, which were created by author Sendak, perfectly complement the characters' gorgeous costumes. The professionally polished, though slow-moving, production contains lyrics that are sometimes difficult to understand.
Audience: Ages 8-Adult
Distributor: Films Inc.
Videocassette: $29.95

★★★★★

Hobbit, The
J. R. R. Tolkien.
Multiple editions. Fantasy.
Bilbo, the hobbit, joins a team of dwarfs on their mission to recover a treasure stolen by a dragon and hidden at a place called Lonely Mountain.

Hobbit, The.
76 min. Color. Animation. Produced by Rankin-Bass. 1977.
This is a fast-paced, literal adaptation that takes no time for character development and never quite draws in viewers.
Reviews: *Variety*, Nov. 30, 1977
Audience: Ages 9-16
Distributor: Warner Home Video
Videocassette: $19.98
No public performance rights

★★★★★

Hoboken Chicken Emergency, The
D. Manus Pinkwater (illus.).
Prentice-Hall. 1977. Humor.
When young Arthur is sent to buy a turkey for Thanksgiving dinner, he returns with a giant 266-pound live chicken named Henrietta who wreaks havoc on the city of Hoboken.

Hoboken Chicken Emergency, The.
58 min. Color. Live action. Produced by Martin Tahse/WonderWorks. 1984. Dick

Van Patten, Peter Billingsley, Gabe Kaplan.
A delightful, finely acted, authentic adaptation of Pinkwater's uproariously humorous story features a perfectly costumed, huge chicken character who will surely entrance viewers.

Reviews: *Booklist*, Nov. 1, 1990
Audience: Ages 6-12
Distributor: Public Media Video
Videocassette: $29.95

★★★★★

Home from Far

Jean Little.

Little, Brown & Co. 1965. Realistic fiction.
After a young girl's twin brother is killed in an automobile accident, the grieving family takes in two foster children to raise.

Home from Far.
26 min. Color. Live action. Produced by Atlantis Films/Seaton McLean, Michael MacMillan, Janice Platt. 1984.
The 1960s setting of the original novel has been updated and many of the subplots have been eliminated in the filmed drama, which concentrates solely on Jenny's adjustment and eventual acceptance of a foster child, Michael, into the family.

Reviews: *Booklist*, Apr. 15, 1985
Audience: Ages 9-12
Distributor: Beacon Films
16mm film: $575 **Videocassette:** $149
Rental: $35

★★★★★

Homer Price

Robert McCloskey.

Penguin USA. 1976. [1943]. Humor.
Homer Price is a youth who stumbles onto one misadventure after another, from catching burglars to handling a nonstop doughnut-making machine. In one instance, Homer and a friend, enthralled with a superhero, witness the actor who plays the superhero experience car trouble. Without superpowers, he relies on the boys to rescue him and they experience a rude awakening about fantasy and reality.

Doughnuts, The.
20 min. Color. Live action. Produced by Weston Woods. 1963.
Homer tries to control a machine that refuses to stop spewing out doughnuts; a customer loses her bracelet in the chaos. The boy solves both problems at once in this faithful, mid-twentieth-century period piece. Unless viewers keep the period in mind, the show seems dated and slow moving.

Audience: Ages 6-10
Distributor: Weston Woods
16mm film: $525 **Videocassette:** $60
Rental: $35 daily

Case of the Cosmic Comic, The.
20 min. Color. Live action. Produced by Weston Woods. 1976.
Set in the 1940s, the visuals in this dramatization appear dated. Lip sync is off, which detracts from the story's believability. The sequence of the film-within-a-film starring the superhero Superduper continues for an extended period, during which audiences are likely to lose interest.

Audience: Ages 6-10
Distributor: Weston Woods
16mm film: $375 **Videocassette:** $60
Rental: $25 daily

Homer Price Stories.
50 min. Color. Live action. Produced by Weston Woods. 1986.
Included in this tape anthology are adaptations of two episodes in the novel

Homer Price: See *The Doughnuts* and *The Case of the Cosmic Comic* for individual film descriptions.

Reviews: *Children's Video Report*, Dec. 1986
Audience: Ages 6-10
Distributor: Children's Circle, Weston Woods
Videocassette: $19.95
No public performance rights

★★★★★

Hop On Pop
Oh Say Can You Say?
Marvin K. Mooney, Will You Please Go Now!
Dr. Seuss (illus.)

Beginner Books. 1963. 1979. 1972. Concept books; humor.
Directed at pre-readers, *Hop On Pop* presents simple rhyming sentences with one-syllable words. *Oh Say Can You Say?* is a set of mini-stories using tongue twisters, alliteration and rhyme. *Marvin K. Mooney, Will You Please Go Now!* deals with how many silly ways you can ask someone to leave.

Dr. Seuss Beginner Book Video: Hop On Pop; Marvin K. Mooney, Will You Please Go Now!; Oh Say Can You Say?.
30 min. Color. Iconographic. Produced by Praxis Media and Random House Home Video. 1989.
Using children's and adult's voices, this delightful video for the ready-to-start-reading set provides practice in listening for sounds, repeating sounds and rhyming sounds. A visual aid has been included in one of the three adaptations. In *Hop On Pop*, simple rhyming sentences with one-syllable words flash on the screen as the narrator reads them.

Reviews: *Children's Video Report*, Oct./Nov. 1989
Audience: Ages 4-8
Distributor: Random House Home Video
Videocassette: $9.95
No public performance rights

★★★★★

Horse That Played Center Field, The
Hal Higdon.

Avon. 1979. [1963]. Fantasy.
A horse is enamored of baseball and gets his opportunity when a local team is losing. Becoming a baseball star brings attention from a group of gamblers.

Horse That Played Centerfield, The.
48 min. Color. Animation. Produced by MTI. 1979.
A clever story unfolds somewhat slowly in this film. Yet the production is generally captivating to young viewers.

Audience: Ages 5-10
Distributor: Coronet/MTI Film & Video
16mm film: $455 **Videocassette:** $250
Rental: $75

★★★★★

Horton Hears a Who
Dr. Seuss (illus.).

Random House. 1962. Humor.
An elephant discovers a dust particle that is home to some creatures called Whos. Horton, the elephant, becomes their protector.

Horton Hears a Who.
24 min. Color. Animation. Produced by Chuck Jones and Theodor Geisel. 1970.
As in the storybook, the other beasts of the jungle suspect that Horton the elephant is out of his mind, which makes protecting the Whos a challenging task.

Reviews: *Variety*, Mar. 25, 1970; *Video Choice*, Nov. 1988
Audience: Ages 4-8
Distributor: MGM/UA Home Video

Videocassette: $12.98
No public performance rights

Dr. Seuss Video Festival, The.
51 min. Color. Animation. 1966.
A laser disc version of *How the Grinch Stole Christmas* and *Horton Hears a Who* offered by MGM/UA Home Video (see above).
Distributor: Pioneer LDCA, Inc.
Laser disc: CLV format $34.98
No public performance rights

★★★★★

Hot Hippo
Mwenye Hadithi.
Illustrated by Adrienne Kennaway. Little, Brown & Co. 1986. Fantasy.
A hippo who wishes the water were his home makes a deal with the all-powerful deity to live there by day.

Hot Hippo.
6 min. Color. Limited animation. Produced by Weston Woods. 1990. Narrated by Terry Alexander.
Not only is the tale faithfully portrayed but it is also enriched with special effects. It is set to the beat of African drums and narrated with an African accent. Like the book, the film features water-color style visuals.
Audience: Ages 4-8
Distributor: Weston Woods
16mm film: $175 **Videocassette:** $90
Rental: $20 daily

Owl Moon and Other Stories.
35 min. Color. Iconographic and animated. Produced by Weston Woods. 1990.
Included in this tape anthology are adaptations of *Owl Moon* (Jane Yolen), *The Caterpillar and the Polliwog* (Jack Kent), *Hot Hippo* (Mwenye Hadithi), and *Time of Wonder* (Robert McCloskey). See individual titles for full descriptions.
Audience: Ages 4-8
Distributor: Children's Circle, Weston Woods
Videocassette: $19.95
No public performance rights

★★★★★

Hound of the Baskervilles, The
Arthur Conan Doyle.
Multiple editions. Mystery.
The detective and his sidekick investigate the murder of a nobleman, whose family has been cursed with haunting by a ghostly hound.

Hound of the Baskervilles, The.
80 min. Black and white. Live action. Produced by Twentieth Century Fox/Gene Markey. 1939. Basil Rathbone, Nigel Bruce.
Recreating the Victorian atmosphere of London in the 1880s, the production captures the setting in the novel. Also present is the suspense created by the original tale. The mystery seems to be solved, but then it continues to unravel. Included in the production is a line at the end that refers to Holmes's drug addiction: "Watson, the needle!"
Reviews: *New York Times*, Mar. 25, 1939, 19:2; *Variety*, Mar. 29, 1939
Audience: Ages 14-Adult
Distributor: Fox Video
Videocassette: $19.98
No public performance rights

Hound of the Baskervilles, The.
148 min. Black and white. Live action. 1939. Basil Rathbone, Nigel Bruce.
A laser disc version of the same title offered by Fox Video (see above). Also includes a second feature, *Holmes Faces Death.*
Distributor: Image Entertainment
Laser disc: CLV format $49.98

No public performance rights

★★★★★

House of Dies Drear, The
Virginia Hamilton.
Macmillan. 1968. Mystery.
A family moves into a spooky, seemingly haunted house that was the former home of a murdered Dutch immigrant who helped slaves escape through Ohio's Underground Railroad.

House of Dies Drear.
107 min. Color. Live action. Produced by Valerie Shepherd and Joseph Dennis. 1991. Howard E. Rollins, Jr., Shavar Ross.
Hamilton's spellbinding mystery is adroitly adapted in this chilling drama that, with its eerie background music and suspenseful scenes, will have youngsters sitting on the edge of their seats until the satisfying climactic conclusion.
Reviews: *Booklist*, Oct. 15, 1991.
Audience: Ages 10-14
Distributor: Public Media Video
Videocassette: $29.95

★★★★★

House on East 88th Street, The
Bernard Waber (illus.).
Houghton Mifflin. 1975. [1962]. Humor.
When they move into their new home, the Primm family finds a crocodile living in the bathtub. Their surprise turns to tender affection when he proves himself useful and endearing.

Lyle, Lyle Crocodile.
24.5 min. Color. Animated. Produced by Michael Sporn Animation and HBO. 1988.
This delightfully comic adaptation has enchanting character voices and animation that retains the spirit of Waber's drawings. "Some additional text and illustrations were necessary for the slim book to become a musical with rhymed lyrics, but the changes do not affect the storyline." —*Booklist*. This edition is for institutional use only.
Reviews: *Booklist*, Feb. 1, 1989; *School Library Journal*, June 1989; *Video Librarian*, Sept. 1989
Audience: Ages 4-8
Distributor: Ambrose Video
Videocassette: $69.95

Lyle, Lyle Crocodile—The Musical.
25 min. Color. Animation. 1988.
A home video version of the same title distributed by Ambrose Video (see above).
Distributor: Video Treasures
Videocassette: $9.99
No public performance rights

★★★★★

House with a Clock in Its Walls, The
John Bellairs.
Dial. 1973. Mystery.
A man dies after having plotted to destroy the world by rigging bombs and setting a clock to trigger them to explode. A man and boy attempt to find the clock before its trigger time. When they do, they also find the ghost of the bomber.

House with a Clock in Its Walls, The.
23 min. Color. Live action. Produced by Diane Asselin. 1991.
An old man and a boy are caught as they discover a clock that has been wired by its ghostly inventor to destroy the world. The search and discovery are interestingly portrayed, but the ending is rather blandly extended in this film.
Audience: Ages 8-14

Distributor: Barr Films
16mm film: $595 **Videocassette:** $395
Rental: $50

★★★★★

How the Grinch Stole Christmas
Dr. Seuss (illus.).
Random House. 1957. Fantasy.
Alone on his mountain, the Grinch manages to ignore people except during Christmas when they sing. One year it decides to steal all the presents to stop Christmas from occurring.

How the Grinch Stole Christmas.
24 min. Color. Animated. Produced by Chuck Jones and Theodore Geisel. 1966. Narrated by Boris Karloff.
The Grinch discovers presents are unnecessary for the spirit of Christmas to prevail, whereupon it returns the presents and joins the fun. Karloff's narration of this story in rhyme conveys its humor, villainy, sadness, and spirit of rejoicing.
Reviews: *Video Choice*, Nov. 1988
Audience: Ages 4-8
Distributor: MGM/UA Home Video
Videocassette: $12.98
No public performance rights

Dr. Seuss Video Festival, The.
51 min. Color. Animation. 1966.
A laser disc version of *How the Grinch Stole Christmas* and *Horton Hears a Who* offered by MGM/UA Home Video (see above).
Distributor: Pioneer LDCA, Inc.
Laser disc: CLV format $34.98
No public performance rights

★★★★★

How to Dig a Hole to the Other Side of the World
Faith McNulty.
Illustrated by Marc Simont. Harper & Row. 1979. Nonfiction.
Readers are taken on a journey to the center of the world to learn about the earth's form.

How to Dig a Hole to the Other Side of the World.
11 min. Color. Animation. Produced by Don and Irra Duga for LCA. 1981.
In keeping with the book, this production is an amusing and joyously creative introduction to the splendors of earth science. The producers have done an excellent job on the traditionally low budget of animated educational films.
Audience: Ages 8-12
Distributor: Coronet/MTI Film & Video
16mm film: $275 **Videocassette:** $215
Rental: $75

★★★★★

Human Comedy, The
William Saroyan.
Dell. 1966. [1943]. Realistic fiction.
The fatherless Macauley family loses Marcus, the eldest son, in World War II. The boy's friend Tobey, an orphan, insists Marcus can never die as long as he lives in the family's hearts.

Human Comedy, The.
117 min. Black and white. Live action. Produced by MGM/Clarence Brown. 1943. Mickey Rooney, Frank Morgan, James Craig, Marsha Hunt.
The film, like the novel, is a sentimental journey to a small town (Ithaca, California) during World War II. Centering on the second son, Homer, who is a telegraph messenger, the film includes a stream of touching vignettes in the manner of the novel.
Reviews: *New York Times*, Mar. 3, 1943, 19:2; *Variety*, Mar. 3, 1943

Awards: Academy Award, Best Original Story
Audience: Ages 12-16
Distributor: MGM/UA Home Video
Videocassette: $24.98
No public performance rights

★★★★★

Humpty Dumpty.
Multiple editions. Folklore and fairy tales.
Humpty Dumpty had a great fall from a wall and nothing in the kingdom could put the poor egg-shaped creature back together again.

Real Story of Humpty Dumpty, The.
24 min. Color. Animated. Produced by Peter Sandar/CINAR/Ronald A. Weinberg. 1990. Voices of Huey Lewis and Glenda Jackson.
The slight nursery rhyme is built into an amusing tale about a walking, talking egg. Rejected, it runs away and becomes privy to a witch's plot to harm a princess. Humpty saves the royal wench. Proudly, but unfortunately, he sits himself on a high wall for the king's men to honor him. Humpty, of course, has a great fall, and as in the nursery rhyme, all the king's men cannot put him back together again...but others can in this delightful expansion of the original.
Audience: Ages 4-8
Distributor: Golden Book Video
Videocassette available

★★★★★

Hunchback of Notre Dame
Victor Hugo.
Multiple editions. Historical fiction.
The year 1482 in France saw the start of an unswerving loyalty and love from the hunchback bell ringer of Notre Dame Cathedral for the gypsy girl Esmeralda, who was ultimately hung as a sorceress.

Hunchback of Notre Dame, The.
93 min. Black and white. Live action. Produced by Universal. 1923. Lon Chaney, Patsy Ruth Miller.
This silent adaptation convincingly recreates medieval Paris and the misshapen man's dogged dedication to the gypsy woman. It concentrates more on the setting and characters than the novel does, and less on the plot. While the picture has obviously taken pains to accurately portray the cathedral and seaminess in the old city, it includes some unrealistic details, such as clean rather than muddy streets.
Reviews: *New York Times*, Sept. 3, 1923, 9:3; *Variety*, Sept. 6, 1923
Audience: Ages 16-Adult
Distributor: Republic Pictures Home Video
Videocassette: $19.98
No public performance rights

Hunchback of Notre Dame, The.
93 min. Black and white. Live action. 1923. Lon Chaney, Patsy Ruth Miller.
A laser disc version of the same title offered by Republic Pictures Home Video (see above).
Distributor: Pioneer LDCA, Inc.
Videocassette: $29.98
No public performance rights

Hunchback of Notre Dame, The.
117 min. Black and white. Live action. Produced by RKO/Pandro S. Berman. 1939. Charles Laughton, Cedric Hardwicke, Maureen O'Hara.
The sets, the performances, the medieval atmosphere are combined to create an exceptionally superb adaptation.
Reviews: *New York Times*, Jan. 1, 1940,

29:2; *Variety*, Dec. 20, 1939.
Audience: Ages 16-Adult
Distributor: RKO/Turner Home Entertainment
Videocassette: $19.98
No public performance rights

Hunchback of Notre Dame, The.
117 min. Black and white. Live action. 1939.
A laser disc version of the same title offered by RKO/Turner Home Entertainment (see above).
Distributor: Image Entertainment
Laser disc: CLV format $39.95
No public performance rights

★★★★★

Hundred Penny Box, The
Sharon Bell Mathis.
Illustrated by Leo Dillon and Diane Dillon. Penguin USA. 1975. Realistic fiction.
Michael sympathizes with his great-great-aunt Dew's need for her hundred penny box, whose coins represent the memories of her life. But his mother aims to dispose of the box so Aunt Dew will live in the present rather than the past.

Hundred Penny Box, The.
18 min. Color. Live action. Produced by Pieter Van Deysen and Leah Miller. 1974.
As in the storybook, the film centers on hundred-year-old Aunt Dew and the young boy Michael, whose mother threatens to burn the hundred penny box full of memories. It is a moving dramatization, marred only by the slightly muffled voice of Aunt Dew, and even this is in character.
Reviews: *Booklist*, Dec. 1, 1979; *Gerontologist*, Feb. 1982
Audience: Ages 8-Adult
Distributor: Churchill Media
16mm film: $360 **Videocassette:** $89
Rental: $60

I

adherence to book   film rating

I Am Not Going to Get Up Today!
The Shape of Me and Other Stuff
Great Day for Up!
Dr. Seuss.
Random House. 1987. 1973. 1974. Humor; concept books.
Nothing can get the main character out of bed in *I Am Not Going to Get Up Today!* (illustrated by James Stevenson). *The Shape of Me and Other Stuff* (illustrated by Dr. Seuss) and *Great Day for Up!* (illustrated by Quentin Blake) deal with concepts of form and direction.

I Am Not Going to Get Up Today!. The Shape of Me and Other Stuff. Great Day for Up!.
25 min. Color. Limited animation. Produced by Sharon Lerner. 1991.
Movement is very limited in these faithful adaptations of three Seuss picture books. Second in the collection is *The Shape of Me and Other Stuff*, which creates a nice illusion of movement with mostly dark shapes against a light background. Words appear on screen along with objects in *Great Day for Up!* A preview of other Beginner Books concludes the tape.
Audience: Ages 4-8
Distributor: Random House Home Video
Videocassette: $9.95
No public performance rights

★★★★★

I Never Sang for My Father
Robert Anderson.
Dramatists Play Service. 1968. Drama.
Ready to move to California, a middle-aged man faces a dilemma when his mother dies and his quarrelsome father opposes his leaving.

I Never Sang for My Father.
92 min. Color. Live action. Produced by Columbia/Jamel. 1969. Gene Hackman, Melvyn Douglas, Dorothy Stickney, Estelle Parsons.
The father tries to prevent the son from getting married, as in the play on which this motion picture is based. Scripted by the playwright himself, the adaptation includes powerful performances that bring the depressing story line to life.
Reviews: *New York Times*, Oct. 19, 1970, 50:1; *Variety*, Oct. 21, 1970
Audience: Ages 14-Adult
Distributor: Columbia TriStar Home Video
Videocassette: $69.95
No public performance rights

★★★★★

"I Sing the Body Electric"
Ray Bradbury.
Anthologized in *The Stories of Ray Bradbury*. Knopf. 1980. Short stories—science fiction.
A family of three children fall under the care of a machine, an electric grandmother, whom they grow to love.

Electric Grandmother, The.
49 min. Color. Live action. Produced by LCA. 1982. Maureen Stapleton.
The film moves along at a more entertaining pace in the shorter version (see below), but both the long and short versions are captivating. Not the least reason for this is the unusual story line, which is grippingly followed. The film softens the short story's abrupt ending, yet its impact remains intact. As stated in *School Library Journal*, "With but minor changes, this adaptation...retains accurately the characterization, plot, and especially the spirit of the original."
Reviews: *School Library Journal*, Sept. 1982
Awards: Blue Ribbon, American Film Festival; CINE Golden Eagle
Audience: Ages 8-Adult
Distributor: Coronet/MTI Film & Video
16mm film: $750 **Videocassette:** $250
Rental: $75

Electric Grandmother, The.
28 min. Color. Live action. 1982. Maureen Stapleton.
An abbreviated version of the same title also offered of Coronet/MTI Film & Video (see above). This version retains the basic plot but omits selected details.
Distributor: Coronet/MTI Film & Video
16mm film: $500 **Videocassette:** $250
Rental: $75

Ray Bradbury's The Electric Grandmother.
50 min. Color. Live action. 1982. Maureen Stapleton.
A home video version of the same, full-length title distributed by Coronet/MTI Film & Video (see above).
Distributor: New World Video
Videocassette: $19.95
No public performance rights

★★★★★

I'll Fix Anthony
Judith Viorst.
Illustrated by Arnold Lobel. Harper & Row. 1969. Realistic fiction.
Scolded and called names by his sibling Anthony, a younger brother imagines all the ways he will surpass this older brother once the young brother reaches the age of six.

I'll Fix Anthony.
13 min. Color. Live action. Produced by Bernard Wilets. 1991.
In keeping with the first-person narrative in the storybook, this adaptation is told by the young boy. There is a minimum of dialogue with alternate voices that enhance the story. The younger brother fantasizes about learning to tell time before his older brother, Anthony, losing his teeth before Anthony, and so on. While characters in the dramatization appear perfectly suited to the story, the action as in the original is a stream of variations on a simple, single theme. It is most appealing to very young audiences.
Audience: Ages 4-6
Distributor: Aims Media
16mm film: $350 **Videocassette:** $295
Rental: $50

★★★★★

"I'm a Fool"
Sherwood Anderson.
Anthologized in *The Portable Sherwood Anderson.* Penguin. 1977. Short stories—realistic fiction.
A nineteen-year-old racetrack hand is filled with remorse when he misrepresents himself to a young lady he loves.

I'm a Fool.
38 min. Color. Live action. 1977. Produced by Learning in Focus. Introduced by Colleen Dewhurst. Ron Howard, Amy Irving.
Slow-paced but charming, the dramatization, like the short story, shows how building a false image can be disastrous. It is preceded by a stiff-sounding, unnecessary introduction. Ending more abruptly than the story, the film has Ron Howard (Andy) speak the title phrase in a moment of self-perception.
Reviews: *Booklist*, June 1, 1978
Awards: ALA Selected Film for Young Adults
Audience: Ages 12-Adult
Distributor: Coronet/MTI Film & Video
16mm film: $685 **Videocassette:** $250
Rental: $75

I'm a Fool.
38 min. Color. Live action. 1977. Introduced by Colleen Dewhurst. Ron Howard, Amy Irving.
A home video version of the same title distributed by Coronet/MTI Film & Video (see above).
Distributor: Monterey Home Video
Videocassette: $24.95
No public performance rights

★★★★★

Ida Fanfanny and the Four Seasons
Dick Gackenbach.
Harper & Row. 1978. Humor.
Ida Fanfanny buys three paintings from a traveling salesman and gets a free one that seems to be magical. The magic painting allows her to experience each season.

Ida Fanfanny and the Four Seasons.
13 min. Color. Animated. Produced by LCA. 1980.
Animated in the light, watercolor style of the book, the film serves as "a colorful introduction to the four seasons. There is ample humor and sprightly music." —*School Library Journal*
Reviews: *School Library Journal*, Mar. 1981
Audience: Ages 5-8
Distributor: Coronet/MTI Film & Video
16mm film: $250 **Videocassette:** $240
Rental: $75

★★★★★

Ida Makes a Movie
Kay Chorao.
Seabury Press. 1974. Realistic fiction.
Ida and her friend Cookie make a movie about ecology that wins a prize in a filmmaking contest as a war protest film.

Ida Makes a Movie.
22 min. Color. Live action. Produced by Playing With Time for LCA. 1980.
The producers were not "playing with time" when they created this very nicely scripted and acted film about truth and the ability of young viewers to deal with real-world problems.
Audience: Ages 7-12
Distributor: Coronet/MTI Film & Video
16mm film: $375 **Videocassette:** $250
Rental: $75

★★★★★

Illustrated Man, The

Ray Bradbury.

Grafton Books. 1985. [1952]. Science fiction.

A man's body is illustrated with a myriad of pictures, which represent a collection of eighteen tales that come to life in this work.

Illustrated Man, The.

103 min. Color. Live action. Produced by Warner/SKM. 1989. Rod Steiger, Claire Bloom, Robert Drivas.

A young wanderer meets tattooed Steiger and sees three stories in Steiger's illustrations. The stories feature Steiger and Bloom as parents of superchildren, Steiger as astronaut, and Steiger and Bloom during a nuclear conflict. In contrast to the print version, the motion picture is slow moving and lacks poetic impact.

Audience: Ages 12-Adult
Distributor: Warner Home Video
Videocassette: $59.99
No public performance rights

★★★★★

Importance of Being Earnest, The

Oscar Wilde.

Multiple editions. Drama.

In this comedy of nineteenth-century manners, two bachelors encounter trouble with possible marriage partners when each assumes the fictitious name Ernest to win the woman he loves.

Importance of Being Earnest, The.

95 min. Color. Live action. Produced by Rank/Javelin/Two Cities. 1952. Michael Redgrave, Dame Edith Evans, Joan Greenwood, Margaret Rutherford.

The witty play appears to be filmed theater rather than being wholly concentrated in the cinema medium. Yet the roles are skillfully performed. The fine acting brings out the humor in this play about turn-of-the-century manners.

Reviews: *New York Times*, Dec. 23, 1952, 17:2; *Variety*, June 18, 1952
Audience: Ages 16-Adult
Distributor: Janus Films
Videocassette: $88

Importance of Being Earnest, The.

95 min. Color. Live action. 1952. Michael Redgrave, Margaret Rutherford.

A home video version of the same title offered by Janus Films (see above).

Distributor: Paramount Home Video
Videocassette available
No public performance rights

★★★★★

"In a Far Country"

Jack London.

Anthologized in *The Unabridged Jack London*, edited by Lawrence Teacher and Richard E. Nicholls. Running Press. 1981. Short stories—realistic fiction.

Stuck in a cabin in the Far North, two men while away the cold season of seemingly endless days during which it remains dark for twenty-four hours. There is foreshadowing that hints at the tragic conclusion—the men, who do not get along, wind up killing each other at the close of the season.

In a Far Country.

53 min. Color. Live action. Produced by William MacAdam/Norfolk. 1980. Narrated by Orson Welles.

Focusing on how poorly the two men get along, the film like the story, shows them waiting. It is full of inaction, other than their bickering, which grows wearisome. Two grave sites in the front yard, and repeated mention of them in the short time span of the film, make the ending quite predictable.

Audience: Ages 14-Adult
Distributor: Britannica
Videocassette: $99

★★★★★

In the Night Kitchen
Maurice Sendak (illus.).
Harper & Row Junior Books. 1970. Fantasy.
In this dream fantasy, a boy falls through the dark into the night kitchen, where he lands in cake batter and bread dough, then flies up the Milky Way galaxy.

In the Night Kitchen.
6 min. Animated. Produced by Kratky Film/Weston Woods. 1987.
This fully animated motion picture matches the story book, the movement adding touches like the bakers in the night kitchen dancing. The fantasy seems more a stream of loosely connected incidents than a continuous tale. Its quick pacing and fanciful plot appeal to the highly imaginative viewer.

Reviews: *Booklist*, Dec. 15, 1987
Awards: CINE Golden Eagle
Audience: Ages 4-8
Distributor: Weston Woods
16mm film: $195 **Videocassette:** $100
Rental: $20 daily

Maurice Sendak Library.
35 min. Color. Animated. Produced by Weston Woods. 1989.
Included in this tape anthology are adaptations of *Alligators All Around*, *Pierre*, *One Was Johnny*, *Chicken Soup with Rice*, *In the Night Kitchen*, and *Where the Wild Things Are*. See individual titles for full descriptions. An additional segment, *Getting to Know Maurice Sendak*, features the author commenting on his work.

Reviews: *Children's Video Report*, Nov. 1, 1990
Audience: Ages 4-8
Distributor: Children's Circle, Weston Woods
Videocassette: $19.95
No public performance rights

★★★★★

"In the Region of Ice"
Joyce Carol Oates.
Anthologized in *The Treasury of American Short Stories*, compiled by Nancy Sullivan. Doubleday. 1981. Short stories—realistic fiction.
A nun who is a college teacher must deal with a male student who seems obsessed with her.

In the Region of Ice.
38 min. Color. Live action. Produced by Peter Werner and Andre Guttfreund. 1977.
The subject matter might not enthrall everyone, but this sensitive film justly deserves the major prizes it has earned—including its Academy Award.

Awards: Academy Award, Best Short Film; ALA Selected Film for Young Adults; Red Ribbon, American Film Festival; Gold Plaque, Chicago International Film Festival
Audience: Ages 14-Adult
Distributor: Phoenix/BFA Films & Video
16mm film: $525 **Videocassette:** $280
Rental: $40

★★★★★

Incredible Journey, The
Sheila Burnford.
Multiple editions. Adventure.
This is the heart-warming tale of three pets—a Siamese cat, an English bull terrier and a Labrador retriever—who make a 250-mile journey across the wilds of

Canada to be with their human family. On the way, they survive threats posed by other animals and by lack of food.

Incredible Journey, The.
80 min. Color. Animation. Produced by James Algar/Walt Disney. 1963. Featuring the voices of Emile Genest, Tommy Tweed, Sandra Scott.
Based on a true story, the film is a superior adaptation for viewers of all ages. The production, set in the wilderness of northern Canada, is worth the viewing for its beautiful scenery in addition to the pets' heart-rending antics. It holds the audience on the strength of its animal appeal, which is continually high. "As gentle, warm and lovely a movie as any pet owner could wish."—*New York Times*

Reviews: *New York Times*, Nov. 21, 1963
Audience: Ages 3-Adult
Distributor: Buena Vista Home Video (not currently in distribution)

Incredible Journey, The.
28 min. Color. Live action. A Disney Educational Production. 1980.
An abbreviated version of the 1963 feature originally distributed by Buena Vista Home Video (see above).

Audience: Ages 8-14
Distributor: Coronet/MTI Film & Video
16mm film: $600 **Videocassette:** $250
Rental: $75

★★★★★

"Interloper, The"
H. H. Munro.
Anthologized in *The Complete Works of Saki.* Dorset Press. 1989. [1976]. Short stories—adventure.
The leaders of two feuding families are trapped by a falling tree. Lying side by side waiting for help, the men have time to think about their foolish fighting. But just as they have agreed to become friends, an ironic turn upsets their earthly plans.

Interloper, The.
21 min. Color. Live action. Produced by Zack and Karen Taylor. 1979.
The setting for this film about two long-feuding families is beautiful, and the story is finely portrayed. Only spatial relationships (two distant men are suddenly trapped by a tree and lie within reach of each other) detract from the believability. The ironic climax demands viewer attention.

Awards: Bronze Award, Houston International Film Festival
Audience: Ages 14-Adult
Distributor: Barr Films
16mm film: $540 **Videocassette:** $99
Rental: $50

★★★★★

Invisible Man, The
H. G. Wells.
Multiple editions. Science fiction.
A mad scientist discovers how to make himself invisible and uses this skill to torment people in a British village. The scientist, an ill-tempered character, is unable to find an antidote to restore himself to human form.

Invisible Man, The.
71 min. Black and white. Live action. Produced by Universal. 1933. Claude Rains, Gloria Stuart, William Harrigan.
Claude Rains is outstanding in this mad scientist role. He has bulk even though he is invisible, so in clothes he can be seen. He first appears dressed with bandages where his head would be. Suspecting him of wrongdoing, the whole countryside is soon in pursuit of this invisible man.

Reviews: *New York Times*, Nov. 18,

1933, 18:4; *Variety*, Nov. 21, 1933
Audience: Ages 14-Adult
Distributor: MCA/Universal Home Video
Videocassette available
No public performance rights

Invisible Man, The.
71 min. Black and white. Live action. 1933. Claude Rains, Henry Travers.
A laser disc version of the same title offered by MCA/Universal Home Video (see above).
Distributor: Pioneer LDCA, Inc.
Laser disc: CLV format $34.98
No public performance rights

★★★★★

Ira Sleeps Over
Bernard Waber.
Houghton Mifflin. 1975. [1972]. Realistic fiction.
A boy needs his favorite toy to support him on his first night away from home. Fearing shame, he leaves the toy home, then discovers his friend has a similar need.

Ira Sleeps Over.
17 min. Color. Live action. Produced by Andrew Sugerman. 1977.
Young viewers are likely to tire of the troublemaking older sister, who is portrayed less than enthusiastically. Still this is a good film from an excellent book.
Reviews: *Booklist*, Feb. 1, 1978
Audience: Ages 6-10
Distributor: Phoenix/BFA Films & Video
16mm film: $365 **Videocassette:** $250
Rental: $30

★★★★★

Island of the Blue Dolphins
Scott O'Dell.
Houghton Mifflin. 1960. Historical fiction.
Set in 1800, this is a story based on fact that features a Chumash Indian girl who survives alone on an island off the coast of California for eighteen years.

Island of the Blue Dolphins.
99 min. Color. Live action. Produced by Universal/Robert B. Tadnitz. 1964. Celia Kaye, Larry Domasin, Ann Daniel.
The film opens by focusing on the young girl Karana's family life, then moves quickly to her father's murder, her people's departure, her brother's death, and her solitary life on the island. Much of the footage progresses without dialogue or narration as we watch her befriending a wild dog, catching abalone, crafting a flute and so on. She utters thoughts aloud, sometimes melodramatically. The telescoping of time is unconvincing, as her physical appearance displays little signs of aging.
Audience: Ages 10-14
Distributor: MCA/Universal Home Video
Videocassette available
No public performance rights

★★★★★

Island of the Skog
Steven Kellogg (illus.).
Dial Books for Young Readers. 1973. Fantasy.
A story on literal and deeper levels, this features mice who escape the threat of animals at home only to persecute a creature whose island they inhabit.

Island of the Skog.
13 min. Color. Iconographic. Produced by Weston Woods in consultation with Steven Kellogg. 1980.
Though a careful adaptation, this film version has moderate appeal. Only the camera moves, yet the story is full of action.

Character voices enhance the telling of the tale.

Reviews: *Booklist*, Oct. 15, 1980
Audience: Ages 4-8
Distributor: Weston Woods
16mm film: $195 **Videocassette:** $60
Rental: $25 daily

Danny and the Dinosaur and Other Stories.

35 min. Color. Iconographic and animated. Produced by Weston Woods. 1991.

Included in this tape anthology are adaptations of *Danny and the Dinosaur* (Syd Hoff), *The Camel Who Took a Walk* (Roger Duvoisin), *Island of the Skog* (Steven Kellogg), and *The Happy Lion* (Louis Fatio). See individual titles for full descriptions.

Audience: Ages 4-8
Distributor: Children's Circle, Weston Woods
Videocassette: $19.95
No public performance rights

★★★★★

It's Mine
Leo Lionni.

Alfred A. Knopf. 1986. Adventure.

Three argumentative frogs learn to live in harmony when a flood forces them to share the same rock.

It's Mine.

5 min. Color. Animated. Produced by Italtoons. 1986.

This engaging adaptation shows the frogs rising to their better selves under the threat of danger. Remaining true to the original art and story line, the production enhances them with highly appealing movement and music.

Reviews: *Booklist*, Sept. 1, 1986
Audience: Ages 3-10
Distributor: Lucerne Media
16mm film: $300 **Videocassette:** $225

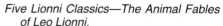

Five Lionni Classics—The Animal Fables of Leo Lionni.

30 min. Color. Animation by Giulio Gianini. Produced by Italtoons Corp./Random House Home Video. 1987.

Included in this tape anthology are adaptations of *Frederick*, *Cornelius*, *It's Mine*, *Fish Is Fish*, and *Swimmy*. See individual titles for plot summaries. Simple yet profound, these animal fables illustrate the power of imagination, the joy of discovery, and the importance of living together in harmony. The film versions remain true to the original art and manuscripts. Winning animation, along with equally winning music by Egisto Macchi, enhances the charm of the characters and the appeal of the storybooks.

Reviews: *Children's Video Report*, Feb. 1987
Audience: Ages 4-8
Distributor: Random House Home Video
Videocassette: $14.95
No public performance rights

Five Lionni Classics.

30 min. Color. Animation. Produced by Italtoons. 1987.

A public performance package of five separate Lionni titles for libraries, including *Frederick, Swimmy, Cornelius, Fish Is Fish*, and *It's Mine*. Each of these titles is also distributed individually by Lucerne Media (see above).

Audience: Ages 4-8
Distributor: Lucerne Media
Videocassette: $325

★★★★★

It's No Crush, I'm in Love
June Foley.
Delacorte. 1982. Realistic fiction.
Amy has a crush on her English teacher until she meets a boy in her class and learns a little about the professor.

It's No Crush, I'm in Love.
31 min. Color. Live action. Produced by LCA/ABC Afterschool Special. 1983.
A lesson in the danger of becoming too enamored with a person's looks, this ABC Special adapts a novel with a telling moral. The production conveys a good lesson and is an adequate film for the low-budget, after-school market.
Reviews: *Booklist*, Feb. 15, 1984; *School Library Journal*, May 1984
Audience: Ages 14-18
Distributor: Coronet
16mm film: $500 **Videocassette:** $250
Rental: $75

★★★★★

It's So Nice to Have a Wolf Around the House
Harry Allard.
Illustrated by James Marshall. Doubleday. 1979. [1977]. Humor.
A wolf tries to repair its bad reputation by helping to bring happiness to an old man who lives alone with his pets. But the wolf is undone by its reputation and roles become reversed between the wolf and the family it aims to help.

It's So Nice to Have a Wolf Around the House.
12 min. Color. Animation. Produced by Paul Fierlinger for LCA. 1979.
The awards won for animation in this film about the wayward wolf attest to its outstanding production qualities. Its producer also demonstrates concern for faithfulness to the book. The combination of writer Harry Allard, artist James Marshall, and animator Paul Fierlinger makes for a superior and involving adaptation, described in *Booklist* as "joyful entertainment." At the same time, it suggests "a wealth of serious discussion possibilities that include responsibility for one's actions and the fate of the elderly."
Reviews: *Booklist*, Mar. 1, 1986
Awards: ALA Notable Children's Film; CINE Golden Eagle
Audience: Ages 5-12
Distributor: Coronet/MTI Film & Video
16mm film: $250 **Videocassette:** $230
Rental: $75

Fables of Harry Allard.
30 min. Color. Animation. 1979.
A home video version of two titles distributed separately by Coronet/MTI Film & Video: *Miss Nelson Is Missing* and *It's So Nice to Have a Wolf Around the House*. See individual titles for full descriptions.
Distributor: New World Video
Videocassette: $14.95
No public performance rights

★★★★★

Ivanhoe
Walter Scott.
Multiple editions. Historical fiction; romance.
In twelfth-century England, a Saxon knight rescues his sweetheart and a traveling Jewess from some Norman evildoers, at the same time upsetting their plot against King Richard the Lion-Hearted.

Ivanhoe.
106 min. Color. Live action. Produced by MGM/Pandro S. Berman. 1952. Robert Taylor, Joan Fontaine, Elizabeth Taylor.
A faithful adaptation, this production lavishly recreates the period. The plot unfolds rather slowly.
Reviews: *New York Times*, Aug. 1, 1952, 8:2; *Variety*, June 11, 1952
Audience: Ages 12-18
Distributor: MGM/UA Home Video

Videocassette: $19.98
No public performance rights

Ivanhoe.
150 min. Color. Live action. Produced by Columbia Pictures TV/Rosemont. 1982. Anthony Andrews, James Mason, Sam Neill, Olivia Hussey.
This is a lively rendition of the classic, with energetic performances and striking photography. At the outset, the adaptation does not focus much on the character Ivanhoe, directing viewers' attention to other elements of the story.
Reviews: *Variety*, Mar. 10, 1982
Audience: Ages 12-18
Distributor: Columbia TriStar Home Video
Videocassette: $19.95
No public performance rights

J

adherence to book   film rating

Jack and the Beanstalk.
Multiple editions. Folklore and fairy tales.
A poor widow sends her son to sell the family's only cow, and to her disappointment he returns with some allegedly magic beans. Tossed outside, the beans grow into a giant stalk. Jack climbs the beanstalk, finding danger and treasures at the castle of a thieving ogre, whom the boy rushes to escape.

Jack and the Beanstalk.
51 min. Color. Animation. Produced by Hanna-Barbera/Gene Kelley. 1961. Gene Kelley.
The show successfully combines animation and live action, but appears slightly dated. Unlike the fairy tale, it has Gene Kelley, the merchant who gave Jack the beans, climb the stalk with the lad, singing and dancing in the process. The acting is splendid, but the whole fails to elicit the tension of the original tale. The pair have adventures in the castle with the ogre, mice, and a cat, then climb down penniless. A fortune rains down on them when they chop off the beanstalk.
Audience: Ages 6-10
Distributor: Hanna-Barbera Home Video
Videocassette: $19.95
No public performance rights

Jack and the Beanstalk.
51 min. Color. Live action. 1966.
A laser disc version of the same title offered by Hanna-Barbera Home Video (see above).
Distributor: Image Entertainment
Laser disc: CLV format $29.95
No public performance rights

Jack and the Beanstalk.
9 min. Color. Animation. Produced by Greatest Tales. 1977.
In this generally accurate adaptation, Jack is depicted as more greedy than foolish in his trading and raiding.
Audience: Ages 4-8
Distributor: Phoenix/BFA Films & Video
16mm film: $230 **Videocassette:** $135
Rental: $30

Jack and the Beanstalk.
11 min. Color. Limited animation. 1980.
The giant is grotesque in this story that ends in the traditional way—happily for the boy and unpleasantly for people who like giants.
Audience: Ages 5-7
Distributor: Coronet/MTI Film & Video

16mm film: $280 **Videocassette:** $195
Rental: $75

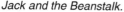

Jack and the Beanstalk (Faerie Tale Theatre).
60 min. Color. Live action. Produced by Shelley Duvall. 1982. Dennis Christopher, Katherine Helmond, Elliott Gould, Jean Stapleton.
This is a delightful *Jack and the Beanstalk*, in which the actors add a touch of humor to the tale. The giant comes across as fearsome yet slow-witted and the added character of his wife enriches rather than detracts from the spirit of the tale. Extending the story line, this adaptation has Jack fulfilling a mission by climbing the beanstalk. He is avenging the death of his father by tackling the mean ogre. As a playful aside, Jack hides from the ogre, and the ogre's wife helps him by stashing him away in her oven. He quips, "You know, this is not Hansel and Gretel," and she replies, "I'm an ogre, not a witch." The basic story line is faithfully followed, despite the additional humor.
Reviews: *Variety*, Feb. 8, 1984
Audience: Ages 4-Adult
Distributor: Fox Video
Videocassette: $14.98
No public performance rights

Jack and the Beanstalk.
Color. Live action. 1982. Dennis Christopher, Katherine Helmond, Elliott Gould, Jean Stapleton.
A laser disc version of the same title offered by Fox Video (see above).
Distributor: Image Entertainment
Laser disc: CLV format $29.98
No public performance rights

Jack and the Beanstalk.
28 min. Color. Limited animation. Produced by Rabbit Ears. 1991. Narrated by Michael Palin.
Very much the English peasants, Jack and his widowed mother are drawn with a nice blend of realism and comic affect. Jack's sale of the family cow and his three journeys up the beanstalk are strictly in keeping with the folktale and result in the transfer of ownership of a bag of gold, a hen that lays golden eggs, and a singing harp from the giant to Jack. Jack's marriage to a princess and Dave Stewart's song at the end are innovations that nevertheless suit the story.
Audience: Ages 4-8
Distributor: Uni Distribution Corp.
Videocassette: $9.95

★★★★★

"Jack of Hearts"
Isabel Huggan.
Anthologized in *The Elizabeth Stories*. Viking. 1987. Short stories—realistic fiction.
Portly Elizabeth, who is tapped to play a male role in a ballet, gains self-confidence after learning how to play poker from her mother's flashy friend.

Jack of Hearts.
26 min. Color. Live action. Produced by Cindy Hamon-Hill, Giles Walder for Atlantis Films & the National Film Board of Canada. 1986. Renee Gersovitz.
In this thoughtful, well-acted drama, preteen Elizabeth learns how to play poker following a humiliating dance recital in which she was forced to play a boy's role. The short story has the poker game taking place on a different night, but the impact of the card game on Elizabeth's self-esteem is the same in both versions.
Reviews: *Booklist*, Nov. 15, 1987
Awards: Second Prize, Chicago International Festival of Children's Films; Honor-

able Mention, National Educational Film & Video Festival
Audience: Ages 9-13
Distributor: Beacon Films
16mm film: $575 **Videocassette:** $149
Rental: $35

★★★★★

"Jack-a-Boy"
Willa Cather.
Anthologized in *Willa Cather's Collected Short Fiction, 1892-1912*, edited by Virginia Faulkner. University of Nebraska Press. 1970. Short stories-realistic fiction.
A family with a young boy moves to an apartment building in New Orleans, where the neighbors are not fond of children. The boy takes this problem into his own hands.

Jack-a-Boy.
28 min. Color. Live action. Produced by Carl Colby. 1980. Fernandez is the charming Jack-a-Boy who beguiles the neighborhood in this New Orleans-set story. As stated in *Horn Book*, "The cinematography is magnificent...the action is carefully paced...and the sound track...is always inviting."
Reviews: *Booklist*, Jun. 15, 1981; *Horn Book*, Apr. 1981
Awards: CINE Golden Eagle
Audience: Ages 10-18
Distributor: Phoenix/BFA Films & Video
16mm film: $525 **Videocassette:** $285
Rental: $45

★★★★★

Jacob Have I Loved
Katherine Paterson.
Harper & Row Junior Books. 1980. Realistic fiction.
Set in the 1940s, this sensitive novel focuses on teenager Louise, who is insanely jealous of her selfish and talented twin sister, Caroline.

Jacob Have I Loved.
57 min. Color. Live action. Produced by Richard Heus/WonderWorks. 1989.
Beautiful Chesapeake Bay settings and excellent performances shine in this outstanding adaptation of Paterson's award-winning novel. The time frame is condensed in the video version, which changes the order of events and does not follow Louise into adulthood. Yet the book's main plot (focusing on a teenager's search for identity) has been faithfully adapted in this entrancing drama.
Reviews: *Booklist*, Oct. 1, 1990
Awards: ALA Notable Film; *Booklist* Editors' Choice 1990; Parents Choice Award
Audience: Ages 12-Adult
Distributor: Public Media Video
Videocassette: $29.95

★★★★★

Jake
Alfred Slote.
Lippincott. 1971. Realistic fiction.
Jake, an eleven-year-old black boy, organizes a baseball team, but he discovers the team is illegal unless he can find it an adult to coach it. The boy, who lives with his musician uncle, also faces the threat of being placed in a foster home.

Rag Tag Champs, The.
48 min. Color. Live action. Produced by ABC Weekend Specials. 1978.
This is a fine production of a story about one boy's efforts to have a home. While it is not immediately clear why Jake is in this personal predicament, viewers are gently drawn to sympathize with him and his bumbling athletes.
Audience: Ages 8-11
Distributor: Coronet/MTI Film & Video

16mm film: $645 **Videocassette:** $250
Rental: $75

Rag Tag Champs, The.
48 min. Color. Live action. 1978.
A home video version of the same title distributed by Coronet/MTI Film & Video (see above).
Distributor: Strand VCI
Videocassette: $12.98
No public performance rights

★★★★★

Jane Eyre
Charlotte Brontë.
Multiple editions. Realistic fiction.
An orphan in Victorian England becomes the governess in a mansion with a melancholy master who grows to love her. Living on the third floor of the mansion is a mysterious woman whose presence clouds Jane's romance.

Jane Eyre.
239 min. Color. Live action. Produced by BBC. 1983. Zelah Clarke, Timothy Dalton.
Hailed as a triumph, this lengthy production excels through the performance of its two main characters as well as the authenticity of its sets.
Reviews: *Times Literary Supplement*, Dec. 30, 1983
Audience: Ages 14-Adult
Distributor: Fox Video
Videocassette: $29.98
No public performance rights

★★★★★

Jason and the Argonauts.
Multiple editions. Folklore and fairy tales.
Jason was the rightful heir to a throne in ancient Greece, which his uncle seized. The uncle promised to forfeit the throne if Jason and his men overcame obstacles and retrieved the golden fleece of a slaughtered ram. They set sail in quest of the Golden Fleece, encountering challenges along the way.

Jason and the Argonauts.
102 min. Color. Live action. Produced by Columbia/Charles H. Schneer. 1963. Todd Armstrong, Nancy Kovack, Gary Raymond.
This is a strong rendition of the legendary tale with exceptional special effects by Ray Harryhausen. The film, like the legend, teems with adventurous action.
Reviews: *New York Times*, Aug. 8, 1963, 19:1; *Variety*, June 5, 1963
Audience: Ages 9-16
Distributor: Columbia TriStar Home Video
Videocassette: $19.95
No public performance rights

Jason and the Argonauts.
104 min. Color. Live action. 1963. Todd Armstrong, Nancy Kovak.
A laser disc version of the same title offered by Columbia TriStar Home Video (see above).
Distributor: Pioneer LDCA, Inc.
Laser disc: CLV format $34.95
No public performance rights

Jason and the Argonauts.
20 min. Color. Animation. Produced by Brian Jackson Films. 1987.
This is probably the best of an interesting mythology series by Brian Jackson distributed by Barr Films; compressing the

major events in the adventures of the Argonauts makes for an action-filled film.

Reviews: *Curriculum Products Review Service*, Apr. 1988
Audience: Ages 8-14
Distributor: Barr Films
16mm film: $470 **Videocassette:** $330
Rental: $50

★★★★★

Jeeter Mason and the Magic Headset
Maggie Twohill.
Bradbury. 1985. Fantasy.
A girl who is not very good at dancing has her life changed by a headset that gives advice.

Jeeter Mason and the Magic Headset.
23 min. Color. Live action. 1987.
The "magic" in this story is not really believable as Jeeter (a girl) drifts through scenes that catapult her from bumbling tap dancer to performing artist, and back again.

Audience: Ages 5-11
Distributor: Coronet/MTI Film & Video
16mm film: $425 **Videocassette:** $250
Rental: $75

★★★★★

"Jilting of Granny Weatherall, The"
Katherine Anne Porter.
Anthologized in *The American Short Story, Vol 2*, edited by C. Skaggs. Harcourt Brace Jovanovich. 1979. Short stories—realistic fiction.
A woman, haunted all her life by the memory of being jilted on her wedding day, holds on to her spiritual strength and her will to live even on her last day.

Jilting of Granny Weatherall, The.
57 min. Color. Live action. Produced by Learning in Focus. 1980. Geraldine Fitzgerald.
Geraldine Fitzgerald is a fine old lady who was once jilted on her wedding day and still is haunted by that event, even though she is surrounded by loving people.

Reviews: *Booklist*, Sept. 15, 1980
Audience: Ages 15-18
Distributor: Coronet/MTI Film & Video
16mm film: $895 **Videocassette:** $250
Rental: $75

Jilting of Granny Weatherall, The.
57 min. Color. Live action. 1980. Geraldine Fitzgerald.
A home video version of the same title distributed by Coronet/MTI Film & Video (see above).

Distributor: Monterey Home Video
Videocassette: $24.95
No public performance rights

★★★★★

Joe Magarac and His U.S.A. Citizen Papers
Irwin Shapiro.
Illustrated by James Daugherty. University of Pittsburgh Press. 1979. [1962]. Folklore and fairy tales.
Joe Magarac is born when he pops out of a furnace. He is a miracle steelworker until he dies in a ladle bucket.

Joe Magarac.
10 min. Color. Limited animation. Produced by Lumin Films. 1971.
Produced with little animation, this adequate production uses art plates as if from a book to tell the story of the steelworker.

Audience: Ages 7-10

Distributor: Phoenix/BFA Films & Video
16mm film: $220 **Videocassette:** $125
Rental: $31

★★★★★

Joey Runs Away
Jack Kent (illus.).
Prentice Hall. 1985. Humor.
Joey, a boy kangaroo, runs away from his crowded home in his mother's pouch.

Joey Runs Away.
8 min. Color. Animated. Produced by Weston Woods. 1988. The animation adds to the humor of the delightful tale as Joey, for example, flies into the sky after moving into a pelican's pouch. The emotions—his fear and his mother's sadness and anger at others who want to move into her pouch—are expressively conveyed through character dialog.
Audience: Ages 4-8
Distributor: Weston Woods
16mm film: $195 **Videocassette:** $110
Rental: $20 daily

Joey Runs Away and Other Stories.
24 min. Color. Iconographic and animated. Produced by Weston Woods. 1989.
Included in this tape anthology are adaptations of *Joey Runs Away* (Jack Kent), *The Most Wonderful Egg in the World* (Helme Heine), *The Cow Who Fell into the Canal* (Phyllis Krasilovsky), and *The Bear and the Fly* (Paula Winter). See individual titles for full descriptions.
Audience: Ages 4-8
Distributor: Children's Circle, Weston Woods
Videocassette: $19.95
No public performance rights

★★★★★

John Brown, Rose and the Midnight Cat
Jenny Wagner.
Illustrated by Ron Brooks. Penguin. 1972. Realistic fiction.
A tender tale, this is about a widow, Rose, and her devoted dog, John Brown, who refuses to share his mistress with the Midnight Cat until Rose grows ill.

John Brown, Rose and the Midnight Cat.
7 min. Color. Iconographic. Produced by Weston Woods. 1982.
This well-paced tale moves right along, revealing not only the actions of the three characters but also their feelings. Superb narration shifts into character voices at appropriate moments.
Reviews: *Booklist*, Oct. 15, 1982
Audience: Ages 8-12
Distributor: Weston Woods
16mm film: $140 **Videocassette:** $60
Rental: $20 daily

★★★★★

John Henry.
Multiple editions. Folklore and fairy tales.
Wielding a hammer, John Henry enters into a steel-driving competition with a machine.

John Henry.
11 min. Color. Animation. Produced by Lumin Films. 1972. Cartoonlike scenes will attract young audiences to the animated picture. In this version of the legend, John Henry, the fastest steel driver, uses two hammers at one time.
Audience: Ages 7-10
Distributor: Phoenix/BFA Films & Video
16mm film: $265 **Videocassette:** $150
Rental: $35

★★★★★

Johnny Appleseed.

Multiple editions. Folklore and fairy tales. A frontiersman who loves nature and peace sets out to beautify the countryside by planting apple seeds.

Johnny Appleseed.
11 min. Color. Animation. Produced by Lumin Films. 1972.
Though the animation is limited, nicely drawn visuals grace this version of Johnny Appleseed's travels and encounters with friends, Indians, and animals.
Audience: Ages 5-11
Distributor: Phoenix/BFA Films & Video
16mm film: $265 **Videocassette:** $150
Rental: $35

Johnny Appleseed.
26 min. Color. Animation. Produced by Rankin-Bass. 1989. In a mix of *Johnny Appleseed* and *Tom Sawyer* (in which Tom connives others into painting his picket fence), this version sees Johnny convincing others to plant apple seeds for him.
Audience: Ages 6-10
Distributor: Lucerne Media
Videocassette: $195

★★★★★

Johnny Tremain
Esther Forbes.

Illustrated by Lynd Ward. Houghton Mifflin. 1943. Historical fiction.
Johnny is a young boy in Boston, a silversmith apprentice, who becomes involved with the Sons of Liberty, the Boston Tea Party, and the Battle of Lexington.

Johnny Tremain and the Sons of Liberty.
80 min. Color. Live action. Produced by Walt Disney. 1957. Hal Stalmaster, Sebastian Cabot, Luana Patten.
The production communicates the excitement of the times, thrusting Johnny simultaneously on the sidelines and into the thick of the action. In contrast to the book, the film version focuses more on the war than on Johnny.
Audience: Ages 10-16
Distributor: Buena Vista Home Video (not currently in distribution)

★★★★★

Jonah and the Great Fish
Warwick Hutton (illus.).

Atheneum. 1984. Bible stories.
A great fish swallows Jonah and he lives in its belly for three days, pleading with the Lord to save him.

Jonah and the Great Fish.
6 min. Color. Iconographic. Produced by Weston Woods. 1984.
This a straightforward adaptation in which the storybook version of this biblical tale unfolds on screen with few embellishments other than music and narration.
Audience: Ages 4-8
Distributor: Weston Woods
16mm film: $140 **Videocassette:** $70
Rental: $20 daily

Mysterious Tadpole and Other Stories, The.
34 min. Color. Animated and Iconographic. Produced by Weston Woods. 1989.
Included in this tape anthology are adaptations of *The Mysterious Tadpole* (Steven Kellogg), *The Five Chinese Brothers* (Claire Bishop), *Jonah and the Great Fish* (Warwick Hutton), and *The Wizard* (Jack Kent). See individual titles for full descriptions.
Reviews: *Children's Video Report*, Feb./Mar. 1989

Audience: Ages 4-8
Distributor: Children's Circle, Weston Woods
Videocassette: $19.95
No public performance rights

★★★★★

Jorinda and Joringel
Jacob Grimm and Wilhelm K. Grimm.
Multiple editions. Folklore and fairy tales.
A witch changes Jorinda into a captive nightingale until her sweetheart, Joringel, finds a means by which to break the spell.

Jorinda and Joringel.
11 min. Color. Limited animation. Produced by Institut fur Film und Bild. 1990.
Nicely animated, the adaptation relies on a straight retelling set to music but without character voices. It is well-paced and moderately involving.
Audience: Ages 4-8
Distributor: Britannica
Videocassette: $250

★★★★★

Journey to the Center of the Earth
Jules Verne.
Multiple editions. Science fiction.
A Scottish professor, accompanied by others, travels down an extinct volcano toward the center of the earth.

Journey to the Center of the Earth.
130 min. Color. Live action. Produced by Twentieth Century Fox/Charles Brackett. 1959. James Mason, Pat Boone.
In this case, the motion picture has enhanced the original writing by including dynamic special effects and the vivid locational footage of the Carlsbad Caverns.
Reviews: *New York Times*, Dec. 17, 1959, 51:1
Audience: Ages 12-Adult
Distributor: Fox Video
Videocassette: $14.98
No public performance rights

Journey to the Center of the Earth.
129 min. Color. Live action. 1959. Pat Boone, James Mason.
A laser disc version of the same title offered by Fox Video (see above).
Distributor: Image Entertainment
Laser disc: CLV format $44.98, Widescreen CLV format $69.98
No public performance rights

★★★★★

Julius Caesar
William Shakespeare.
Multiple editions. Drama.
The tribunes of Rome assassinate the head of state, Julius Caesar, then engage in civil war.

Julius Caesar.
121 min. Black and white. Live action. Produced by MGM/John Houseman. 1953. Marlon Brando, James Mason, John Gielgud, Greer Garson.
This is a fine adaptation of the drama about the plotting, execution, and aftermath of Caesar's assassination. Like the play, the motion picture centers more on Brutus, the well-loved nobleman who joins the assassins, than on Julius Caesar. This production has been celebrated not only for its riveting performances but also for its magnificent setting, which is packed with the statues and icons of ancient Rome.
Reviews: *New York Times*, June 5, 1953, 19:1; *Variety*, June 3, 1953
Audience: Ages 12-Adult
Distributor: MGM/UA Home Video
Videocassette: $19.98

No public performance rights

Julius Caesar.
116 min. Color. Live action. Produced by Commonwealth United. 1969. Richard Johnson, Jason Robards, John Gielgud, Charlton Heston, Robert Vaughn, Richard Chamberlain.
Though not as strong as the 1953 version, this is an adequate remake with a star-studded cast. Caesar's murder and Antony's speech to the Romans come across well. But the crowd scenes seem staged and the performers, with the exception of Heston as Antony, deliver speeches that fall flat. Much of the passion in the play seems forced.
Reviews: *Variety*, June 10, 1970
Audience: Ages 12-Adult
Distributor: Image Entertainment
Laser disc: Widescreen CLV format $39.95
No public performance rights

Julius Caesar (The Shakespeare Plays).
161 min. Color. Live action. Produced by BBC. 1979. Charles Gray, Richard Pasco, Keith Michell.
This is a strong, straightforward rendition of the classic. Charles Gray as Caesar conveys the impression of troubled power demanded by the role. Richard Pasco as Brutus is equally convincing. Made for television, the production uses its sound and picture capabilities to advantage. The actors think (aloud) rather than mouth their soliloquies, and close-up shots make visible the expressions on characters' faces. A few scenes, such as Antony's address at the Forum, call for spectacle, and these are less convincing. Still, the play becomes an intimate experience for the audience. This video edition is for institutional use only.
Reviews: *Los Angeles Times*, Feb. 14, 1979; *Minneapolis Tribune*, Feb. 14, 1979; *New York Times*, Feb. 14, 1979
Audience: Ages 14-Adult
Distributor: Ambrose Video
Videocassette: $249.95

★★★★★

Jungle Book, The
The Second Jungle Book
Rudyard Kipling.
Multiple editions. Adventure. *The Jungle Book* centers on Mowgli, a lone boy, taken in by wolves and raised in the jungle. At one point, he meets a human family, whom he rescues from danger. The last half of the novel features stories of other animals. In the eight tales of *The Second Jungle Book*, the animals share with each other secrets of their East Indian habitat.

Jungle Book, The.
109 min. Color. Live action. Produced by Alexander Korda/W. Howard Greene. 1942. Sabu, Joseph Calleia, John Qualen.
Little related to the original tales, this adaptation features the jungle boy preventing the escape of three robbers. His character is played without depth, though the presence of actual animals commands interest.
Reviews: *New York Times*, Apr. 6, 1942, 19:1; *Variety*, Mar. 25, 1942
Audience: Ages 4-8
Distributor: Republic Pictures Home Video
Videocassette: $19.98
No public performance rights

Jungle Book, The.
78 min. Color. Animation. Produced by Walt Disney. 1967. Featuring the voices of George Sanders, Phil Harris, Louis

Prima, Sebastian Cabot, Sterling Holloway.
This is an animated, musical version of the Rudyard Kipling classic about a boy raised by wolves. Though the film tells a more carefree tale than the book, Mowgli, the "boy-cub," still learns about life from his animal friends and goes through a rite of passage with the king tiger that prepares him for life in the human world. Memorable music and lovable characters give the film widespread appeal. When the animated feature was first released, "kids in the audience stayed raptly glued to the screen." —*New York Times*
Reviews: *New York Times*, Dec. 23, 1967
Audience: Ages 4-10
Distributor: Buena Vista Home Video
Videocassette: $24.99
No public performance rights

Rikki Tikki Tavi.
25 min. Color. Animated. Produced by Chuck Jones. 1975. Narrated by Orson Welles.
Nicely animated, this adaptation from *The Jungle Book* captures the excitement of the story about the mongoose Rikki Tikki. Characters have dimension, and the narration helps establish atmosphere. Orson Welles communicates tension, making an enemy snake sound convincingly frightening.
Audience: Ages 6-10
Distributor: Family Home Entertainment
Videocassette: $14.95
No public performance rights

Jungle Book, The.
Eleven 30 min. episodes. Color. Animation. Produced by Nippon Animation Co. 1990.
Limited animation and squeaky voices tell stories loosely based on the Kipling's *The Jungle Book* and *The Second Jungle Book* in a style seen in Saturday morning cartoons. The half hour segments, sold separately, are 1) *Mowgli Comes to the Jungle*, 2) *Mowgli Comes to the Jungle: The Adventure Continues*, 3) *Alexander's Story*, 4) *The Law of the Jungle*, 5) *A New Friend*, 6) *A Cold Fang*, 7) *Sorry, Baloo!* 8) *More Important than the Law of the Jungle*, 9) *An Old Wolf's Visit*, 10) *A Devil in Mind*, and 11) *A Trip of Adventure.* The cartoon style makes the series most suitable for the very young.
Audience: Ages 4-8
Distributor: Strand/VCI Entertainment
Videocassette: $9.95 each
No public performance rights

★★★★★

Just an Overnight Guest
Eleanor Tate.
Dial. 1980. Realistic fiction.
A black family takes in an abused girl and decides to make her part of their home.

Just an Overnight Guest.
38 min. Color. Live action. Produced by Joanne Mallas. 1983. Richard Roundtree, Rosalind Cash.
The adaptation makes for an inoffensive, if not too exciting, film about abused children. Though the story is set in the context of a black family, the issue is not a racial one.
Audience: Ages 10-18
Distributor: Phoenix/BFA Films & Video
16mm film: $575 **Videocassette:** $315
Rental: $55

★★★★★

Just So Stories
Rudyard Kipling.
Multiple editions. Fantasy.
The collection includes twelve animal fables, accounting for how the elephant got its trunk, how the leopard got its

spots, and so forth. Its stories imagine how animals came to be as they are or why they behave as they do.

How the Elephant Got Its Trunk.
7 min. Color. Limited animation. Produced by LCA. 1970. An inquisitive young elephant angers a crocodile, who pulls the elephant's nose to its present long length. The time span of this film is just right for the story of the "nosey" young elephant.
Reviews: *Booklist*, Jan. 1, 1971
Audience: Ages 5-8
Distributor: Coronet/MTI Film & Video
16mm film: $195 **Videocassette:** $150
Rental: $75

How the First Letter Was Written.
8 min. Color. Limited animation. Produced by LCA. 1970.
When a girl needs to send a message back to her village, the confusion resulting from her poor drawing prompts the villagers to seek a better way to write. This is part of a generally more effective series, though older and shorter than other Just So films from the same distributor.
Audience: Ages 5-8
Distributor: Coronet/MTI Film & Video
16mm film: $195 **Videocassette:** $150
Rental: $75

How the Whale Got His Throat.
8 min. Color. Limited animation. Produced by LCA. 1970.
A whale swallows a sailor and then agrees to free him. Irritated, the sailor takes revenge and changes the whale's eating habits forever. One of the stronger productions based on this Kipling tale, the film is a bright portrayal.
Audience: Ages 5-8
Distributor: Coronet/MTI Film & Video
16mm film: $195 **Videocassette:** $150
Rental: $75

Beginnings of the Armadillos, The (Just So Stories).
11 min. Color. Limited animation. Produced by Coronet. 1984.
Limited in animation, this one in a series of *Just So Stories* films explains how a hedgehog and tortoise escape the painted jaguar by making a transformation that results in the first armadillo. The film is above average entertainment.
Audience: Ages 5-10
Distributor: Coronet/MTI Film & Video
16mm film: $275 **Videocassette:** $170
Rental: $75

Butterfly That Stamped, The (Just So Stories).
11 min. Color. Limited animation. Produced by Coronet. 1984.
Overhearing a butterfly couple's domestic spat, a king with 999 quarreling wives learns a lesson. He takes the same action as the male butterfly and temporarily brings peace to his household.
Audience: Ages 5-10
Distributor: Coronet/MTI Film & Video
16mm film: $275 **Videocassette:** $170
Rental: $75

Cat That Walked by Himself, The (Just So Stories).
16 min. Color. Limited animation. Produced by Coronet. 1984.
When all the animals were wild, including people, the cat was the wildest of them all. It was, in fact, the only "untamable" animal that the clever woman character in the story encountered.
Audience: Ages 5-10

Distributor: Coronet/MTI Film & Video
16mm film: $340 **Videocassette:** $240
Rental: $75

Crab That Played with the Sea, The (Just So Stories).
12 min. Color. Limited animation. Produced by Coronet. 1984.
The king crab was hiding in the deepest ocean when all the other animals were given roles in the world pattern. So the crab played and played until a crafty magician trapped it into a bargain.
Audience: Ages 5-10
Distributor: Coronet/MTI Film & Video
16mm film: $275 **Videocassette:** $170
Rental: $75

Elephant's Child, The (Just So Stories).
12 min. Color. Limited animation. Produced by Coronet. 1984.
One of the most well-known of the Just So Stories, this concerns a curious elephant child and a crocodile that stretches the child's nose to its present length.
Reviews: *School Library Journal*, Dec. 1983
Audience: Ages 5-10
Distributor: Coronet/MTI Film & Video
16mm film: $275 **Videocassette:** $170
Rental: $75

How the Camel Got His Hump.
11 min. Color. Limited animation. Produced by Coronet. 1984.
A reasonably successful adaptation, this production relies on limited animation to tell the story of the camel who refused to work. This camel was given to responding "Humpf" whenever anyone suggested work. The "Humph" was a sufficient answer until he met the Djinn of the desert and felt its magic.
Audience: Ages 5-8
Distributor: Coronet/MTI Film & Video
16mm film: $275 **Videocassette:** $170
Rental: $75

How the Rhinoceros Got His Skin.
11 min. Color. Limited animation. Produced by Coronet. 1984.
A rhinoceros's ill manners and greed turn his smooth skin into ugly folds. This is one of a series of Just So films that is effective and interesting, if limited in movement.
Audience: Ages 5-8
Distributor: Coronet/MTI Film & Video
16mm film: $275 **Videocassette:** $170
Rental: $75

How the Leopard Got His Spots.
11 min. Color. Limited animation. Produced by Coronet. 1984.
The one-color leopard hunts food successfully until his prey learn to hide in the forests. Soon the leopard discovers the value of coloring. A good introduction to protective coloration lies in this story of a leopard who needed to change or starve.
Audience: Ages 5-8
Distributor: Coronet/MTI Film & Video
16mm film: $275 **Videocassette:** $170
Rental: $75

How the Whale Got His Throat.
11 min. Color. Limited animation. Produced by Coronet. 1984.
A whale swallows a man who makes such a commotion that the whale lets him out. On the way, the man changes the whale's eating habits. Adapting one of Kipling's most far-fetched stories, the film is fun because of the unexpected events.
Audience: Ages 5-8

Distributor: Coronet/MTI Film & Video
16mm film: $275 **Videocassette:** $170
Rental: $75

Sing-Song of Old Man Kangaroo, The (Just So Stories).
11 min. Color. Animation. Produced by Coronet. 1984.
A woolly kangaroo wants to change its form and with the help of a dingo (Australian dog) arrives at its present shape within a day.
Audience: Ages 5-10
Distributor: Coronet/MTI Film & Video
16mm film: $275 **Videocassette:** $170
Rental: $75

How the Leopard Got His Spots.
30 min. Color. Limited animation. Produced by Rabbit Ears. 1989. Narrated by Danny Glover.
Early in time the leopard was a champion hunter, a plain gold creature who blended with the high veldt grass and captured unspotted giraffes and greyish, unstriped zebras. With migration to the forest all the animals (except the leopard) developed some sort of camouflage, so it did too. The haunting rhythms of Ladysmith Black Mambazo form an ensnaring backdrop to Danny Glover's droll narration. Faithful to the original, it relates how animals, and people, developed their coloring. The illustrator's (Lori Lohstoeter) rich use of color creates unforgettable jungle scenes.
Audience: Ages 4-10
Distributor: SVS/Triumph
Videocassette: $14.95
No public performance rights

How the Leopard Got His Spots.
27 min. Color. Limited animation. 1989. Narrated by Danny Glover.
A laser disc version of the same title offered by SVS/Triumph (see above).
Distributor: Image Entertainment
Laser disc: CAV format $19.95.
No public performance rights

How the Rhinoceros Got His Skin/How the Camel Got His Hump.
30 min. Color. Limited animation. Produced by Rabbit Ears. 1987. Narrated by Jack Nicholson.
Kipling's classic tales come to life via the enigmatic expressions that illustrator Tim Raglin bestows on all the creatures. Nicholson delivers beautifully restrained narration, disclosing how the two arrogant animals each received their comeuppance. Occasionally, his narrative wanders into sly digressions that enhance the humor in both plot and language.
Reviews: *Booklist*, Feb. 1, 1988
Audience: Ages 4-10
Distributor: SVS/Triumph
Videocassette: $14.95
No public performance rights

How the Rhinoceros Got His Skin/How the Camel Got His Hump.
22 min. Color. Limited animation. 1988. Narrated by Jack Nicholson.
A laser disc version of the same title offered by SVS/Triumph (see above).
Distributor: Image Entertainment
Laser disc: CLV format $19.95
No public performance rights

K

adherence to book   film rating

Kidnapped
Robert Louis Stevenson.
Multiple editions. Adventure.
In eighteenth-century Scotland, David Balfour, upon his father's death, is betrayed by an avaricious uncle who arranges his kidnap. Events lead the boy into the care of Alan Stewart, a soldier-of-fortune who helps David find his way back to the Scottish Highlands and regain his fortune. David becomes involved in the conflict between Scottish highlanders and English rule.

Kidnapped.
95 min. Color. Live action. Produced by Hugh Atwooll/Walt Disney. 1959. Peter Finch, James MacArthur, Peter O'Toole.
The film, though faithful to the book, is long, talky and relatively dull. The inclusion of Highlander and Redcoat politics slows the action.
Reviews: *New York Times*, May 19, 1960
Audience: Ages 8-Adult
Distributor: Buena Vista Home Video
Videocassette: $19.99
No public performance rights

Kidnapped.
97 min. Color. Live action. 1959. Peter Finch, James MacArthur, Peter O'Toole.
A laser disc version of the same title originally offered by Buena Vista Home Video (see above).
Distributor: Image Entertainment
Laser disc: CLV format $34.99
No public performance rights

Kidnapped.
23 min. Color. Live action. A Disney Educational Production. 1979.
An abridged version of the 1959 feature, the film is finely paced; the action moves along quite well in this shortened version. It stands as an exciting adaptation of the Stevenson classic that reflects high Disney quality.
Audience: Ages 12-Adult
Distributor: Coronet/MTI Film & Video
16mm film: $625 **Videocassette:** $250
Rental: $75

★★★★★

Kim
Rudyard Kipling.
Multiple editions. Adventure.
An orphaned boy in India takes to the road, where he meets two characters who change his life: a pious llama and a

horse trader who is actually a British secret agent.

Kim.
113 min. Color. Live action. Produced by MGM/Leon Gordon. 1950. Errol Flynn, Dean Stockwell, Paul Lucas, Robert Douglas, Reginald Owen.
Though much of the atmosphere and historical detail are missing from the motion picture, it succeeds as a rousing adventure tale. Kim is a much deeper character in the novel.
Reviews: *New York Times*, Dec. 8, 1950, 40:4; *Variety*, Dec. 6, 1950
Audience: Ages 12-Adult
Distributor: MGM/UA Home Video
Videocassette: $19.98
No public performance rights

★★★★★

King Kong
Edgar Wallace.
Multiple editions. Science fiction.
A filmmaker and his female star find a legendary ape on an island. The ape falls in love with the female star. Brought to New York, it breaks loose and goes wild in search of its love.

King Kong.
100 min. Black and white. Live action. Produced by Merian C. Cooper. 1933. Robert Armstrong, Fay Wray.
Reputed as the finest monster movie of all time, this rendition boasts outstanding special effects. It launched the monster movie genre. The climax in this film classic occurs in the scene atop the Empire State Building.
Reviews: *New York Times*, Mar. 3, 1933, 12:1; *Variety*, Mar. 7, 1933
Audience: Ages 8-14
Distributor: RKO/Turner Home Entertainment
Videocassette: $19.98
No public performance rights

King Kong.
100 min. Color. Live action. 1933. Robert Armstrong, Fay Wray.
A colorized version of the same title offered in black and white by RKO/Turner Home Entertainment (see above).
Distributor: RKO/Turner Home Entertainment
Videocassette: $19.98
No public performance rights

King Kong.
101 min. Black and white. Live action. 1933. Robert Armstrong, Fay Wray.
A laser disc version of the same title offered by RKO/Turner Home Entertainment (see above).
Distributor: Criterion Collection
Laser disc: CLV format $39.95, CAV format $75.95
No public performance rights

King Kong.
135 min. Color. Live action. Produced by Dino de Laurentiis. 1976. Jessica Lange, Jeff Bridges.
Geared toward a slightly older audience (due to sexual suggestiveness), this one lacks the mythic overtones achieved by the earlier landmark version.
Reviews: *New York Times*, Apr. 4, 1976, II 19:1; *Variety*, Dec. 15, 1976
Audience: Ages 12-16
Distributor: Paramount Home Video
Videocassette available
No public performance rights

King Kong.
135 min. Color. Live action. 1976. Jessica Lange, Jeff Bridges.
A laser disc version of the same title offered by Paramount Home Video (see above).
Distributor: Pioneer LDCA, Inc.
Laser disc: CLV format $35.95
No public performance rights

★★★★★

King Lear
William Shakespeare.
Multiple editions. Drama.
A king divides his royal holdings among his daughters, giving nothing to the one who refuses to flatter him. The king, an addle-brained soul, is later spurned by the daughters he favored and aided by the one he shunned.

King Lear.
137 min. Black and white. Live action. Produced by Filmways-Laterna. 1970. Paul Scofield, Irene Worth, Alan Webb.
Those unfamiliar with the play may experience some difficulty with this stark production filmed in Denmark. There are captivating moments in this grim motion picture, though. It portrays old age in unadorned fashion, refusing to treat sentimentally this individual example of human experience.
Audience: Ages 16-Adult
Distributor: Videocassette not currently in distribution

King Lear (The Shakespeare Plays).
185 min. Color. Live action. Produced by BBC. 1982. Michael Hordern, John Shrapnel, Anton Lesser.
Black-and-white costumes and scant scenery help convey the stark mood of the play. An engrossing performance by Michael Hordern in the title role portrays Lear as a man without power, an individual ill-acquainted with himself even before the division of his kingdom. The show adapts the main plot splendidly, the subplot, less successfully. There are some strong performances and a few unconvincing details, such as characters who speak of crying without shedding tears. This video edition is for institutional use only.
Reviews: *Times Literary Supplement*, Oct 1, 1982, *Los Angeles Times*, Oct. 18, 1982; *Washington Post*, Oct. 18, 1982
Audience: Ages 16-Adult
Distributor: Ambrose Video
Videocassette: $249.95

King Lear.
158 min. Color. Live action. Produced by BBC. 1983. Sir Laurence Olivier, Diana Rigg.
The producers replicated Stonehenge as part of the setting to give it a timeless quality. Their production received high acclaim with minor exceptions—the storm scene whose sound effects muffle Lear's dialog and a few word changes such as "ne'er trust poison" for "ne'er trust medicine." Turning to its strengths, the version focuses more on Lear's suffering and growth than the earlier screen versions did. Sir Laurence Olivier, in his final major screen performance as Lear, earned loud verbal applause. "He may have given a more commanding performance in 1946, but can scarcely have given a more touching one." —*Times Literary Supplement*
Reviews: *Times Literary Supplement*, Apr. 8, 1983; *Wall Street Journal*, Jan. 23, 1984; *Variety*, Apr. 20, 1983
Awards: Emmy Award, Outstanding Lead Actor in a Special
Audience: Ages 16-Adult
Distributor: Films for the Humanities & Sciences
Videocassette: $89.95

King Lear.
158 min. Color. Live action. 1983. Laurence Olivier, Diana Rigg.
A home video version of the same title distributed by Films for the Humanities & Sciences (see above).
Distributor: Kultur Video
Videocassette: $29.95
No public performance rights

★★★★★

King of the Cats
Joseph Jacobs.
Illustrated by Paul Galdone. Houghton Mifflin. 1980. Folklore and fairy tales.
This is a suspenseful tale about a procession of black cats, a gravedigger, and his wife. One of the cats informs the gravedigger he must "tell Tom Tildrum that Tim Toldrum is dead." When the gravedigger repeats this to his wife, his own cat, Old Tom, lets out a shriek and disappears.

King of the Cats.
5 min. Color. Iconographic. Produced by Weston Woods. 1984.
A well-paced version, this show builds suspense and enhances it with sound effects such as the cat's meow. The question "Who's Tom Tilden?" runs ominously through the tale, ending with a harmless answer that alleviates the element of fear yet does not detract from the suspense.
Audience: Ages 4-8
Distributor: Weston Woods
16mm film: $160 **Videocassette:** $50
Rental: $15 daily

★★★★★

King Thrushbeard
Jacob Grimm and Wilhelm K. Grimm.
Multiple editions. Folklore and fairy tales.
A haughty but beautiful princess mocks her suitors. Her father determines to marry her to the first commoner who comes along. After enduring hardship as a poor man's wife, the princess becomes privy to the ruse played on her. Her husband is in fact not a poor man, but one of the suitors she mocked.

Cabbages and Kings.
17.5 min. Color. Animation. Produced by Tim Landry. 1980.
An unusual style features colored backgrounds against which silhouette figures play the roles. The result is a highly entertaining film for young audiences.
Audience: Ages 5-10
Distributor: Barr Films
16mm film: $395 **Videocassette:** $295
Rental: $50

Bristlelip.
20 min. Color. Live action. Produced by Tom and Mimi Davenport. 1982.
This captivating adaptation builds into a humorously rousing tale. On the sober side, the film, like the story, rebukes its main characters for insensitivity and vanity.
Audience: Ages 5-Adult
Distributor: Davenport Films
16mm film: $350 **Rental:** $35
Videocassette: $60 (with public performance rights)
Videocassette: $29.95 (no public performance rights)

★★★★★

Koko's Kitten
Francine Patterson.
Photographs by Ronald H. Cohn. Scholastic. 1985. Nonfiction.
This true account documents a caretaker's efforts with a gorilla and the gorilla's capacity for emotion toward another animal.

Koko's Kitten.
16.5 min. Color. Live action. Produced by The Gorilla Foundation and Churchill Media. 1988. Dr. Francine Patterson.
Most of the footage is so lifelike the viewer feels like an onlooker at the scene. As described in *Booklist*, "Despite the theatrical restaging of the emotion surrounding the kitten's disappearance and demise, the production touchingly documents Koko's honest interactions...."
Reviews: *Booklist*, Aug. 1989
Audience: Ages 4-10
Distributor: Churchill Media
16mm film: $435 **Videocassette:** $325
Rental: $60

★★★★★

Kon-Tiki
Thor Heyerdahl.
Rand McNally. 1960. [1950]. Nonfiction.
Believing that Polynesia was possibly colonized by raft-sailing people from Peru, Thor Heyerdahl attempted the Pacific crossing himself.

Kon-Tiki.
73 min. Black and white. Live action. Produced by RKO Pictures. 1951.
Narrated by the author himself, this film documents his experiences while rafting from Peru to Tahiti.
Reviews: *New York Times*, Apr. 4, 1951, 35:2; *Variety*, Mar. 21, 1951
Awards: Academy Award, Best Documentary
Audience: Ages 12-Adult
Distributor: Janus Films
Videocassette: $88

L

adherence to book film rating

Lady and the Tramp
Walter Elias Disney (illus.).
Crown. 1988. [1980]. Fantasy.
A pedigreed female dog is tormented by two Siamese cats, but then falls in love with a mongrel who is street wise.

Lady and the Tramp.
76 min. Color. Animation. Produced by Walt Disney. 1955.
One of Disney's most charming stories for young viewers features some very humanlike dogs. Disney later produced a book from the movie.
Reviews: *New York Times*, June 24, 1955, 17:1; *Variety*, Apr. 20, 1955
Audience: Ages 5-10
Distributor: Buena Vista Home Video (not currently in distribution)

★★★★★

Lassie Come Home
Eric Knight.
Multiple editions. Adventure.
An English boy must give up his prize collie to a rich man. The collie escapes and, enduring formidable hardships, journeys back from Scotland to his original home in England.

Lassie Come Home.
90 min. Color. Live action. Produced by MGM/Samuel Marx. 1943. Roddy McDowall, Elizabeth Taylor, Donald Crisp.
This is a heartwarming dramatization that captures the spirit of the novel.
Reviews: *New York Times*, Oct. 8, 1943, 15:4; *Variety*, Aug. 18, 1943
Audience: Ages 8-12
Distributor: MGM/UA Home Video
Videocassette: $19.98
No public performance rights

Lassie Come Home.
89 min. Color. Live action. 1943. Roddy McDowall, Elizabeth Taylor, Donald Crisp.
A laser disc version of the same title offered by MGM/UA Home Video (see above).
Distributor: Pioneer LDCA, Inc.
Laser disc: CLV format $34.98
No public performance rights

★★★★★

Last of the Mohicans, The
James Fenimore Cooper.
Multiple editions. Historical fiction.
During the French and Indian War, an English woodsman guides Alice and Cora to a fort with the help of Mohican Indian friends. The girls are captured by an enemy Indian, and one of them dies.

Last of the Mohicans, The.
91 min. Black and white. Live action. Produced by Edward Small. 1936. Randolph Scott, Binnie Barnes, Heather Angel.
This is an action-packed adaptation in the style of Westerns that retains the story line but not the historical emphasis of the novel.
Audience: Ages 14-18
Distributor: International Video Entertainment
Videocassette: $12.95
No public performance rights

Last of the Mohicans, The.
50 min. Color. Animation. Produced by William Hanna/Joseph Barbera. 1976.
For viewers unfamiliar with the story, sorting out the course of events is a challenge in this literal adaptation of a novel directed at an older audience than this animated film.
Audience: Ages 10-14
Distributor: Hanna-Barbera Home Video
Videocassette: $19.95
No public performance rights

★★★★★

"Leader of the People, The"
John Steinbeck.
Anthologized in *The Arbor House Treasury of Nobel Prize Winners*, edited by M. H. Greenberg and C. C. Waugh. Arbor House. 1983. Short stories—historical fiction.
A boy visiting his grandfather is the only family member or friend interested in the grandfather's stories about pioneer days in the Old West.

Leader of the People, The.
24 min. Color. Live action. Produced by Bernard Wilets. 1979.
The lackluster nature of this well-done but unexciting adaptation probably lies in the choice of the original story. Not much happens in this account of an old man's sudden realization that the world has passed him by.
Reviews: *Booklist*, Nov. 1, 1979
Audience: Ages 10-18
Distributor: Britannica
Videocassette: $285

★★★★★

Legend of Bluebonnet, The
De Paola, Tomie (illus.)
Putnam. 1983. Folklore and fairy tales.
To save her people from a terrible drought, a girl sacrifices her most prized possession, a doll made for her by her parents before they died. The gods are pleased and bring rain, then cover the fields with bluebonnet flowers in the girl's honor.

Legend of Bluebonnet, The.
20 min. Color. Live action. Produced by Dimension Films. 1990.
In an inauspicious beginning, a group of children tumble out of a bus to encounter an Indian carver. But the brief beginning soon turns to a finely done dramatization with the story told by the carver turned storyteller. Beautiful scenery and excellent casting make this a superior film.
Audience: Ages 5-10
Distributor: Coronet/MTI Film & Video
16mm film: $475 **Videocassette:** $335
Rental: $50

★★★★★

Legend of Sleepy Hollow, The
Washington Irving.
Multiple editions. Mystery.
Ichabod Crane is an awkward nineteenth-century schoolmaster in love with Katrina van Tassel. His rival, Brom Bones, terrifies Ichabod with a ghost story of the Headless Horseman, who haunts a road Ichabod must travel.

Legend of Sleepy Hollow, The.
33 min. Color. Animation. Produced by Walt Disney. 1949. Narrated and sung by Bing Crosby.
This Disney production, a blend of comedy and the supernatural, features gangly Ichabod Crane and his encounter with the Headless Horseman. Irving's story is a bit more menacing than this video version, but the terror Ichabod feels on a dark lonely night is conveyed intact.
Audience: Ages 8-14
Distributor: Buena Vista Home Video
Videocassette: $12.99
No public performance rights

Legend of Sleepy Hollow, The.
13 min. Color. Limited animation. Produced by Nick Bosustow. 1972. Narrated by John Carradine.
Nicely narrated, this animated tale captures the spirit of Irving's story and augments the humor with its picturesque visualizations. Crane is truly the tall, lanky figure with the enormous appetite that Irving's story describes. Though faithful, there is a tongue-in-cheek quality to this version that makes it more comical than suspenseful.
Awards: Blue Ribbon, American Film and Video Festival; Gold Hugo, Chicago International Film Festival; Jack London Award, National Educational Film and Video Festival
Audience: Ages 10-Adult
Distributor: Pyramid Film & Video
16mm film: $325 **Videocassette:** $195
Rental: $75

Legend of Sleepy Hollow, The.
20 min. Color. Animated. A Disney Educational Production. 1974. Narrated by Bing Crosby.
An abbreviated version of the same full length title offered by Buena Vista Home Video (see above). This version retains the basic plot but omits selected details. It begins with Washington Irving's introductory words and presents a comical Ichabod in his hair-raising experiences, made more dramatic by musical background and interlude. As described in *Landers*, this version is "witty, vigorous, and colorful."
Reviews: *Landers*, June 1975
Audience: Ages 8-Adult
Distributor: Coronet/MTI Film & Video
16mm film: $490 **Videocassette:** $250
Rental: $75

Legend of Sleepy Hollow, The.
30 min. Color. Limited animation. Produced by Rabbit Ears. 1988. Narrated by Glenn Close.
There are plenty of details about the ghost's purported history and the spinning of legends in this adaptation of the classic tale. The horsemanship of Brom Bones and the dancing of the fair Katrina are conveyed in flowing iconography. The final chase uses silhouettes to great advantage; more generally, the fine use of period art serves as an integral part of the video storytelling.
Audience: Ages 5-10
Distributor: SVS/Triumph
Videocassette: $14.95
No public performance rights

Legend of Sleepy Hollow, The.
26 min. Color. Limited animation. 1988.
A laser disc version of the same title offered by SVS/Triumph (see above).
Distributor: Image Entertainment
Laser disc: CLV format $19.95
No public performance rights

Ghost Story Classics.
21 min. Color. Animation and live action. Produced by Asselin Productions. 1990. Vincent Price.
Those who enjoy Vincent Price, no matter how exaggerated the dramatics, will enjoy the abbreviated and interrupted accounts of two popular ghost stories that he introduces. *The Ghost Belonged to Me* and *The Legend of Sleepy Hollow* are portrayed in part, but don't expect a conclusion to either story. Vincent Price intervenes to challenge you to create your own story endings.
Audience: Ages 10-14
Distributor: Barr Films
Videocassette: $295 **Rental:** $50

★★★★★

Lentil
Robert McCloskey (illus.).
Penguin USA. 1940. Realistic fiction.
Lentil saves the day by playing his harmonica when the town band "freezes" just as a visiting dignitary arrives.

Lentil.
9 min. Black and white. Iconographic. Produced by Weston Woods. 1956.
While only the camera moves, this is a well-paced version of the storybook with strong narration and lively harmonica music.
Audience: Ages 4-8
Distributor: Weston Woods
16mm film: $175 **Videocassette:** $90
Rental: $20 daily

Norman the Doorman and Other Stories.
38 min. Color. Iconographic and animated. Produced by Weston Woods. 1989.
Included in this tape anthology are adaptations of *Norman the Doorman* (Don Freeman), *Brave Irene* (William Steig), and *Lentil* (Robert McCloskey). See individual titles for full descriptions.
Audience: Ages 4-8
Distributor: Children's Circle, Weston Woods
Videocassette: $19.95
No public performance rights

Robert McCloskey Library, The.
58 min. Color. Iconographic and animated. Produced by Weston Woods. 1991.
Included in this tape anthology are adaptations of *Lentil*, *Make Way for Ducklings*, *Burt Dow: Deep-Water Man*, *Blueberries for Sal*, and *Time of Wonder*. An additional segment features Robert McCloskey commenting on his work. See individual titles for full descriptions.
Audience: Ages 4-8
Distributor: Children's Circle, Weston Woods
Videocassette: $19.95
No public performance rights

★★★★★

Les Miserables
Victor Hugo.
Multiple editions. Historical fiction.
Unfairly imprisoned for stealing a loaf of bread, Jean Valjean reestablishes himself as a fine citizen after his release but is hounded by an unrelenting inspector.

Les Miserables.
104 min. Black and white. Live action. Produced by Darryl F. Zanuck. 1935. Frederic March, Charles Laughton.

Still regarded as the finest adaptation of the classic, this production succeeds as a faithful and an emotionally rousing adaptation.

Reviews: *New York Times*, Apr. 22, 1935, 14:2; *Variety*, Apr. 24, 1935
Audience: Ages 16-Adult
Distributor: Fox Video
Videocassette: $59.98
No public performance rights

Les Miserables.
104 min. Black and white. Live action. 1935. Frederic March, Charles Laughton.
A laser disc version of the same title offered by Fox Video (see above).

Distributor: Image Entertainment
Laser disc: CLV format $39.98
No public performance rights

Les Miserables.
150 min. Color. Live action. 1978. Produced by ITC. Richard Jordan, Anthony Perkins, Cyril Cusack, John Gielgud.
This convincing made-for-television production serves the classic well. Expressive performances by the cast lend fine interpretations to the characters, with Glenn Jordan in the role of Jean Valjean.

Audience: Ages 16-Adult
Distributor: Fox Video
Videocassette: $59.98
No public performance rights

★★★★★

Letter to Amy, A
Ezra Jack Keats (illus.).

Harper & Row Junior Books. 1968. Realistic fiction.
A quiet story about friendship, this tale concerns Peter's inviting a girl to his party despite what the other boys may think.

Letter to Amy, A.
7 min. Color. Iconographic. Produced by Weston Woods in consultation with Ezra Jack Keats. 1970.
This film version captures all the details of the original, from the blowing away of Peter's letter/invitation to Amy's party gift of a parrot.

Audience: Ages 4-8
Distributor: Weston Woods
16mm film: $140 **Videocassette:** $60
Rental: $20 daily

Pigs' Wedding and Other Stories, The.
39 min. Color. Iconographic and animated. Produced by Weston Woods. 1991.
Included in this tape anthology are adaptations of *The Pigs' Wedding* (Helme Heine), *The Happy Owls* (Celestino Piatti), *The Selkie Girl* (Susan Cooper), *A Letter to Amy* (Ezra Jack Keats), and *The Owl and the Pussy-Cat* (Edward Lear). See individual titles for full descriptions.

Audience: Ages 4-8
Distributor: Children's Circle, Weston Woods
Videocassette: $19.95
No public performance rights

★★★★★

Life on the Mississippi
Mark Twain.

Multiple editions. Nonfiction.
The book is a collection of memories about adventures on the Mississippi River. Once a young man apprenticed to a riverboat pilot, Twain witnesses changes brought by the railroad, Civil War, and mechanization. His recollections of his riverboat piloting days form the basis of this classic account.

Life on the Mississippi.
155 min. Color. Live action. Produced by Nebraska ETV/Peter H. Hunt. 1980. Robert Lansing, David Knell, James Keane.

While the book is a much more detailed recollection of Twain's days on the Mississippi River, this live action adaptation wisely focuses on a shorter time period in the life of the young apprentice riverboat pilot. Twain's mentor, savvy pilot Mr. Bixby, receives prominent attention in this version. At times stirring, the production contains beautiful scenery and aurally pleasing background music performed by the St. Louis Symphony Orchestra.

Audience: Ages 12-Adult
Distributor: MCA/Universal Home Video
Videocassette available
No public performance rights

Life on the Mississippi.
54 min. Color. Live action. 1980. Robert Lansing, David Knell, James Keane.
An abbreviated version of the same title offered by MCA/Universal Home Video (see above). This abridged version is a well-paced, generally stirring production.

Awards: CINE Golden Eagle
Audience: Ages 12-Adult
Distributor: Films Inc.
16mm film: $750 **Videocassette:** $79

★★★★★

Light in the Forest, The
Conrad Richter.
Knopf. 1966. [1953]. Historical fiction.
A child raised from infancy by Indians is returned to his parents as a teenager and finds difficulty adjusting to the white world.

Light in the Forest, The.
93 min. Color. Live action. Produced by Walt Disney. 1958. James MacArthur, Carol Lynley, Fess Parker, Wendell Corey, Jessica Tandy.
An intriguing story for young people is made into a riveting drama in this film adaptation of the Conrad Richter book.

Reviews: *New York Times*, July 11, 1958, 15:2; *Variety*, Apr. 30, 1958
Audience: Ages 8-14
Distributor: Buena Vista Home Video (not currently in distribution)

★★★★★

Like Jake and Me
Mavis Jukes.
Illustrated by Lloyd Bloom. Knopf. 1984. Realistic fiction.
The widowed mother of a young son marries a strong, silent cowboy who has difficulty expressing his feelings toward the son.

Like Jake and Me.
15 min. Color. Live action. A Disney Educational Production. 1989.
The motion picture, like the novel, is an emotion-rousing story to warm the hearts and build hopes in young viewers whose families have been disrupted.

Reviews: *Booklist*, Nov. 15, 1989
Audience: Ages 5-8
Distributor: Coronet/MTI Film & Video
16mm film: $400 **Videocassette:** $280
Rental: $75

★★★★★

Lilies of the Field, The
William E. Barrett.
Drawings by Burt Silverman. Doubleday. 1967. [1962]. Realistic fiction.
A traveling black workman aids some German refugee nuns in building a chapel.

Lilies of the Field.
94 min. Black and white. Live action. Produced by UA/Rainbow/Ralph Nelson. 1963. Sidney Poitier, Lilia Skala.
The performances make this uplifting entertainment in which the characters

come to appreciate one another's point of view.

Reviews: *New York Times*, Oct. 2, 1963, 51:1; *Variety*, July 3, 1963
Awards: Academy Award, Best Actor
Audience: Ages 10-Adult
Distributor: MGM/UA Home Video
Videocassette: $29.98
No public performance rights

★★★★★

Lilith Summer, The
Hadley Irwin.
Feminist Press. 1979. Realistic fiction.
An adolescent girl and an elderly lady are hired to look after each other for the summer. The young girl's resentment changes to care and a new understanding of the elderly in the process.

Lilith Summer, The.
28 min. Color. Live action. Produced by Bernard Wilets. 1985.
Remarkably well performed, this is a touching adaptation of a story that deals realistically with the feelings associated with aging and with relating to the elderly. At first intent only on earning money to buy a bicycle, young Ellen receives companionship and, when she steals a ring, gentle guidance from elderly Lilith. Their brief visit to a nursing home where they see Lilith's friend, who dies in the story, may be difficult for sensitive viewers. The rest of the show focuses on the relationship and growth of understanding between Ellen and Lilith, with a nice balance of action and dialogue.
Awards: ALA Notable Children's Film; CINE Golden Eagle; Gold Apple, National Educational Film and Video Festival
Audience: Ages 8-16
Distributor: Aims Media
16mm film: $545 **Videocassette:** $395
Rental: $50

Lilith Summer, The.
28 min. Color. Live action. 1985.
A laser disc version of the same title also distributed by Aims Media (see above).
Distributor: Aims Media
Laser disc: CAV format $395.

★★★★★

Lion and the Mouse, The
Aesop.
Multiple editions. Folklore and fairy tales.
A mouse convinces a lion not to eat it, promising to return the favor some day. Amused, the lion agrees. Much to its surprise, the lion is subsequently rescued by the mouse from a hunter's trap, learning that no act of kindness is wasted.

Lion and the Mouse, The.
13 min. Color. Live action. Produced by David Alexovich. 1988.
This delightful adaptation boasts energetic pacing and characterization. Vivid, full animation brings the tale to life with an appealing zest that results in pure entertainment and a palatable moral: kindness inspires kindness in return. The production has a humorous tone to it yet an air of authenticity. The lion hunters speak some African words and the lion growls with a vengeance when trapped. The clever mouse is a priceless mix of wit and loyalty.
Audience: Ages 4-8
Distributor: Britannica
16mm film: $330 **Videocassette:** $190

★★★★★

Lion, the Witch, and the Wardrobe, The
C. S. Lewis.
Macmillan. 1988. [1950]. Fantasy.
An evil witch has taken control in the mythical kingdom of Narnia. According to a prophecy, four children and Aslan (the

force of good in the form of a lion) become her undoing.

Lion, the Witch, and the Wardrobe, The.
95 min. Color. Animated. Produced by Children's Television Workshop. 1979.
Less realistic than the 1989 version, this animated adaptation is equally faithful to the original in its dialogue. Characters in this animated version have less personality, though the queen is convincingly evil. The action progresses at a quicker pace.
Reviews: *Variety*, Apr. 4, 1979
Audience: Ages 8-12
Distributor: Vestron Video
Videocassette: $19.95
No public performance rights

Lion, The Witch and the Wardrobe, The.
170 min. Color. Live action. Produced by Paul Stone/BBC/Wonderworks. 1989. Richard Dempsey, Susan Cook, Jonathan R. Scott, Sophie Wilcox, Michael Aldridge.
While vivid costumes and special effects picture the fantastic tale in fine detail, this installment remains distant from its viewers. The progression of events is quite clear, and touches of animation blend tastefully into the live action. Though his role is small, Michael Aldridge makes a splendid professor. The adventures of Narnia continue in *Prince Caspian* and in *The Silver Chair.* See the individual titles for full descriptions.
Audience: Ages 8-12
Distributor: Public Media Video
Videocassette: $29.95
No public performance rights

*****

Lisa and David
Theodore I. Rubin.
Macmillan. 1988. [1961]. Realistic fiction.
Two disturbed teenagers meet and fall in love while attending a special school.

David and Lisa.
94 min. Black and white. Live action. Produced by Continental/Paul M. Heller. 1962. Keir Dullea, Janet Margolin, Howard da Silva.
This is a sensitively handled adaptation of the love story involving a disturbed teenager who begins to flourish because of his relationship with a schizophrenic young woman. The production gives viewers a glimpse into the lives and emotions of the exceptional youth.
Reviews: *New York Times*, Dec. 27, 1962, 5:5; *Variety*, Sept. 5, 1962
Audience: Ages 14-Adult
Distributor: Columbia TriStar Home Video
Videocassette: $69.95
No public performance rights

David and Lisa.
94 min. Black and white. Live action. 1962. Keir Dullea, Janet Margolin.
A laser disc version of the same title offered by Columbia TriStar Home Video (see above).
Distributor: Pioneer LDCA, Inc.
Laser disc: CLV format $34.95

*****

Little Big Man
Thomas Berger.
Dell. 1985. [1964]. Historical fiction.
A white man over a hundred years old looks back on his eventful life in the Old West.

Little Big Man.
149 min. Color. Live action. Produced by Stockbridge/Hiller/Cinema Center. 1970. Dustin Hoffman, Faye Dunaway.
The old-timer's memories are the strand that binds the episodic motion picture. A fictitious character, Little Big Man claims a career that ranges from pioneer to adopted Indian to medicine show veteran to survivor of the massacre at Little Bighorn. The screenplay, though it omits some events in the novel and telescopes others, seems to cover too much ground. While the feature is lengthy, it has some fine moments. It is more flagrantly comic than the original.
Reviews: *New York Times*, Dec. 15, 1970, 53:1; *Variety*, Dec. 16, 1970
Audience: Ages 16-Adult
Distributor: Fox Video
Videocassette: $24.98
No public performance rights

Little Big Man.
149 min. Color. Live action. 1970. Dustin Hoffman, Faye Dunaway.
A laser disc version of the same title offered by Fox Video (see above).
Distributor: Image Entertainment
Laser disc: CLV format $44.98
No public performance rights

★★★★★

Little Drummer Boy, The
Katherine Davis, Henry Onorati, and Harry Simeone.
Illustrated by Ezra Jack Keats. Collier. 1972. [1968]. Songs.
The verses of this Christmas carol follow the familiar plot in nativity tales.

Little Drummer Boy, The.
7 min. Color. Iconographic. Produced by Weston Woods. 1971.
Sung throughout the film, the narrative accompanies visuals in which movement is limited to the camera's traveling over the screen. The singers pronounce most of the lyrics clearly, but a few lines lose clarity in the transmission.
Audience: Ages 4-8
Distributor: Weston Woods
16mm film: $140 **Videocassette:** $60
Rental: $20 daily

Christmas Stories.
30 min. Color. Iconographic and animated. Produced by Weston Woods. 1986.
Included in this tape anthology are adaptations of *Morris's Disappearing Bag* (Rosemary Wells), *The Clown of God* (Tomie de Paola), *The Little Drummer Boy* (Katherine Davis, Henry Onrati, and Harry Simeone), and *The Twelve Days of Christmas* (Robert Broomfield).
Audience: Ages 4-Adult
Distributor: Children's Circle, Weston Woods
Videocassette: $19.95
No public performance rights

★★★★★

Little Engine That Could, The
Olive Beaupre Miller.
Multiple editions. Fantasy.
A little engine that no one thought was very effective proves its value and the importance of determination when it pulls a heavy trainload over the mountain.

Little Engine That Could, The.
10 min. Color. Limited animation. Produced by Coronet. 1963.
Following the original story line, this is a very well-done film with effective, if limited, animation.
Audience: Ages 5-10
Distributor: Coronet/MTI Film & Video

16mm film: $265 **Videocassette:** $185
Rental: $75

★★★★★

Little House, The
Virginia Lee Burton (illus.).
Houghton Mifflin. 1978. [1942]. Fantasy.
A little house in the country is surrounded by noise and lights when the city grows around it.

Little House, The.
8 min. Color. Animation. A Disney Educational Production. 1988. Narrated by Sterling Holloway.
This is a charming story, told from the point of view of a little house overwhelmed by the advances of a nearby city. Sterling Holloway provides just the right narrative voice for the tale.
Audience: Ages 5-10
Distributor: Coronet/MTI Film & Video
16mm film: $225 **Videocassette:** $170
Rental: $75

★★★★★

Little Humpback Horse.
Multiple editions. Folklore and fairy tales.
A silly-looking horse is magical. Its magic helps its young owner win the kingdom from a tyrannical ruler.

Magic Pony, The.
11 min. Color. Animation. A Disney Educational Production. 1971.
An early Disney film, this motion picture displays the full animation and flexibility of characters that have made Disney productions so highly entertaining.
Audience: Ages 4-8
Distributor: Coronet/MTI Film & Video
16mm film: $280 **Videocassette:** $195
Rental: $75

★★★★★

Little Lord Fauntleroy
Francis Hodgson Burnett.
Multiple editions. Realistic fiction.
Cedric Errol, bred in Brooklyn, New York, is heir to a fortune and an English noble title when his father dies. Once in England, he has to win the sympathy of especially his grandfather, who abhors Americans.

Little Lord Fauntleroy.
98 min. Black and white. Live action. Produced by David O. Selznick. 1936. Freddie Bartholomew, C. Aubrey Smith, Dolores Costello, Mickey Rooney.
This adaptation preserves the plot line while heightening the melodrama and sentimentality. The novel, first published in the late 1800s, includes some details that reflect the Victorian attitudes of the time. These have been softened or left out altogether in the film.
Reviews: *New York Times*, Apr. 3, 1936; *Variety*, Apr. 8, 1936
Distributor: Fox Video
Videocassette: $14.98
No public performance rights

★★★★★

Little Match Girl, The
Hans Christian Andersen.
Multiple editions. Folklore and fairy tales.
A penniless young girl is forced to sell matches to passersby during the cold of winter. Caught in a snowstorm, she lights the matches for warmth and has visions, then perishes from the cold.

Little Match Girl, The.
17 min. Color. Puppet animation. Produced by Coronet. 1978.
The limitations of the puppet animation are the only distraction in this otherwise sensitive adaptation of the heart-rending Andersen tale.
Audience: Ages 7-12
Distributor: Coronet/MTI Film & Video
16mm film: $405 **Videocassette:** $250
Rental: $75

Little Match Girl, The.
25 min. Color. Animation. Produced by Michael Sporn and Italtoons Corp. 1990.
Set in present-day New York, the adaptation stars a homeless little girl whose family lives in a subway station. She sells matches in the cold, lights them for warmth, has visions, then collapses, inspiring a city official to pledge more help for the homeless. In this version, but not in the original, the little match girl revives.
Awards: Silver Apple, National Educational Film and Video Festival
Audience: Ages 8-12
Distributor: Lucerne Media
16mm film: $495 **Videocassette:** $295

Little Match Girl, The.
25 min. Color. Animation. Produced by Michael Sporn and Italtoons. 1990.
A home video version of the same title distributed by Lucerne Media (see above).
Distributor: Family Home Entertainment
Videocassette: $14.95
No public performance rights

★★★★★

Little Mermaid, The
Hans Christian Andersen.
Multiple editions. Folklore and fairy tales.
A teenage mermaid saves a young prince from a shipwreck, then beseeches a sorceress to make her human so she can be near the prince. She wants also the chance mortals have to earn an immortal soul. In the transformation, the mermaid forfeits her beautiful voice and gains legs on which walking is cuttingly painful. Ultimately the prince marries another; the mermaid loses her earthly life but gains the opportunity for immortality.

Little Mermaid, The.
25 min. Color. Animated. Produced by Reader's Digest with Potterton Productions. 1974. Narrated by Richard Chamberlain.
Not quite as sad as the original, this version is nevertheless faithful to the basic story line. The little mermaid beseeches the enchantress of the sea to make her human, then loses the prince to the princess he marries. The mermaid's suffering is reflected in the film, though it does not mention the physical pain caused by her human feet.
Audience: Ages 8-Adult
Distributor: Pyramid Film & Video
16mm film: $495 **Videocassette:** $95
Rental: $75

Mermaid Princess, The.
13.5 min. Color. Puppet animation. Produced by Coronet. 1976.
In this version a mermaid princess, freed to travel wherever she will, chances upon a city with a handsome prince with whom she falls in love. When the prince marries another woman, the princess returns to her home in the water. Polished-looking dolls glide through the story with little animation before backdrops that provide little additional information. The film plot is conveyed through the gentle narration.
Audience: Ages 5-8

Distributor: Coronet/MTI Film & Video
16mm film: $340 **Videocassette:** $240
Rental: $75

Little Mermaid, The.
82 min. Color. Animation. Produced by Howard Ashman and John Musker/Walt Disney with Silver Screen Partners IV. 1989. Featuring the voices of Buddy Hackett, Kenneth Mars, Pat Carroll.
In this version Ariel, a teenage mermaid, saves Prince Erik during a shipwreck. Without seeing her, he falls in love with her beautiful voice. She trades her voice for becoming human, then, through the help of her undersea friends, regains her voice and marries Prince Erik. Based very loosely on the much darker Andersen tale, this film radically transforms his melancholy original into happily-ever-after entertainment. The show includes a menacing witch and various ocean villains but nothing too terribly frightening for younger audiences. Apart from its disparity with the original tale, the film is "a happy confluence of lively witty animation and a timeless-sounding Broadwayish score. It's funny, romantic and—OK—scary, just as it should be." —*New York Post*
Reviews: *New York Post*, Nov. 15, 1989; *New York Times*, Apr. 8, 1990
Awards: Academy Awards, Best Music Score, Best Song
Audience: Ages 4-12
Distributor: Buena Vista Home Video (not currently in distribution)
No public performance rights

Little Mermaid, The.
83 min. Color. Animation. Produced by Walt Disney. 1990.
A laser disc version of the same title offered by Buena Vista Home Video (see above).
Distributor: Image Entertainment
Laser disc: CLV format $29.99; CAV format $39.99
No public performance rights

★★★★★

Little Prince, The
Antoine de Saint-Exupery (illus.)
Translated by Katherine Woods. Harcourt Brace Jovanovich. 1943. Fantasy.
A boy from outer space learns about life on the planet Earth from an aviator with misleading advice.

Little Prince, The.
89 min. Color. Live action. Produced by Stanley Donen/Paramount. 1974. Richard Kiley, Bob Fosse, Gene Wilder.
Turned into a musical, the production doesn't have the impact of the classic children's book about a boy counseled on life by a pilot he idolizes.
Reviews: *New York Times*, Nov. 8, 1974, 24:1; *Variety*, Nov. 6, 1974
Audience: Ages 10-12
Distributor: Paramount Home Video
Videocassette available
No public performance rights

Little Prince, The.
88 min. Color. Live action. 1974. Richard Kiley, Bob Fosse.
A laser disc version of the same title offered by Paramount Home Video (see above).
Distributor: Pioneer LDCA, Inc.
Laser disc: CLV format $29.95
No public performance rights

★★★★★

Little Princess, A
Frances Hodgson Burnett.
Multiple editions. Realistic fiction.
The pampered daughter of wealthy Captain Crewe, sent from India to a London boarding school, finds herself penniless when her father seems to die unexpectedly.

Little Princess, The.
93 min. Color. Live action. Produced by Gene Markey/Tox. 1939. Shirley Temple, Richard Greene, Cesar Romero.
Slightly altered to accommodate Shirley Temple's talents, the script nevertheless retains the original story line and mood. A villainous headmistress makes her young border work as a servant when the father is presumed dead. Discovered by the child, he is not dead but an amnesia victim who regains his memory upon seeing his daughter. The charm of the story is reflected in the film and in Temple's winning ways.
Reviews: *New York Times*, Mar. 11, 1939, 21:1; Variety, Feb. 22, 1939
Audience: Ages 8-12
Distributor: Fox Video
Videocassette: $19.98
No public performance rights

Little Princess, A.
165 min. Color. Live action. Produced by Colin Shindler/WonderWorks. 1986.
Containing only a few minor changes from the book version, this charming, lengthy drama that *Booklist* describes as "'Masterpiece Theater' for kids" wonderfully captures the engrossing plot and the flavor of Victorian England.
Reviews: *Booklist*, Oct. 1, 1990
Awards: BAFTA Award, British Emmy; Gold Plaque, Chicago International Film Festival; Parents' Choice Award
Audience: Ages 9-Adult
Distributor: Public Media Video
Videocassette: $79.95
No public performance rights

★★★★★

Little Rabbit's Loose Tooth
Lucy Bate.
Illustrated by Diane De Groat. Crown. 1975. Fantasy.
Little Rabbit's loose tooth finally falls out and Little Rabbit doesn't know what to do with it. She is not sure there is a tooth fairy until she finds a dime under her pillow.

Little Rabbit's Loose Tooth.
12.5 min. Color. Animation. Produced by Advanced American Communications. 1990.
Little Rabbit's tooth wiggles and jiggles and finally falls out into chocolate ice cream in this cleverly animated and beautifully drawn adaptation of a popular children's book.
Reviews: *School Library Journal*, Apr. 1991
Audience: Ages 5-8
Distributor: Coronet/MTI Film & Video
16mm film: $375 **Videocassette:** $250
Rental: $75

★★★★★

Little Red Hen, The.
Multiple editions. Folklore and fairy tales.
The little red hen busily plants, harvests, and grinds wheat into flour without the help of other farm animals, who prove only too willing to partake in the bread she makes.

Little Red Hen, The.
10 min. Color. Live action. Produced by Coronet. 1950.
Drawings are mixed with live action shots of the barnyard animals to make this

early Coronet film a timeless adventure for the viewer.

Audience: Ages 4-8
Distributor: Coronet/MTI Film & Video
16mm film: $255 **Videocassette:** $180
Rental: $75

★★★★★

Little Red Lighthouse and the Great Gray Bridge, The
Hildegard Swift.
Illustrated by Lynd Ward. Harcourt Brace Jovanovich. 1942. Fantasy.
A lighthouse feels unnecessary after the building of a lighted, great gray bridge until one night the lighthouse rushes to a boat's rescue.

Little Red Lighthouse and the Great Gray Bridge, The.
9 min. Color. Iconographic. Produced by Weston Woods. 1955.
Fine narration and music make the story of the Little Red Lighthouse ideal for very young audiences. The wreck of a tugboat turns the show into an adventure. Only the camera moves, yet the film is well-paced.

Audience: Ages 4-6
Distributor: Weston Woods
16mm film: $155 **Videocassette:** $80
Rental: $20 daily

★★★★★

Little Red Riding Hood
Charles Perrault.
Multiple editions. Folklore and fairy tales.
A girl meets a wolf on her way to her grandmother's house. When the wolf threatens the girl and her ailing grandmother, a passing woodsman intervenes.

Little Red Riding Hood.
9 min. Color. Puppet animation. Produced by Ray Harryhausen. 1958.
Faithful to the original story, the film is weakened by puppet characters that are unbelievable.

Audience: Ages 6-9
Distributor: Phoenix/BFA Films & Video
16mm film: $220 **Videocassette:** $140
Rental: $29

Little Red Riding Hood.
13 min. Color. Animation. Produced by DEFA Studios/LCA. 1979.
Colorful backgrounds and animated characters recreate the old folktale very well in this film produced in East Germany.

Audience: Ages 5-8
Distributor: Coronet/MTI Film & Video
16mm film: $255 **Videocassette:** $240
Rental: $75

Brothers Grimm Fairy Tales, The.
35 min. Color. Animated. Produced by DEFA Studios/LCA. 1979.
A home video version of *Little Red Riding Hood* distributed by Coronet/MTI Film & Video. Also included in this tape anthology is a second feature, *The Seven Ravens*. See individual titles for full descriptions.

Distributor: New World Video
Videocassette: $14.95
No public performance rights

Little Red Riding Hood.
17 min. Color. Live action. Produced by Texture Films. 1979.
An imaginative though slow-moving production uses characters wearing Balinese masks to retell the story of Little Red Riding Hood. Set in a lush forest and using a different musical instrument to accompany each character who performs mime,

the tale is creatively acted out in this non-narrated adaptation.

Reviews: *Booklist*, Feb. 15, 1981
Awards: ALA Notable Children's Film, 1982; CINE Golden Eagle Award
Audience: Ages 6-Adult
Distributor: Films Inc.
16mm film: $330 **Videocassette:** $49

Little Red Riding Hood (Faerie Tale Theatre).
60 min. Color. Live action. Produced by Shelley Duvall/a Platypus/Lion's Gate Production. 1983. Malcolm McDowell, Mary Steenburgen, Diane Ladd.
This is a convincingly realistic if slow-moving rendition. Malcolm McDowell, dressed in wolf ears and tail, makes an amusing yet menacing wolf. The movie portrays Little Red Riding Hood as an overprotected child. Grandmother is marvelous. It adds verbal humor (a remark about fang dental floss for the wolf, for example) without detracting from the whole.

Audience: Ages 6-Adult
Distributor: Fox Video
Videocassette: $14.98
No public performance rights

Little Red Riding Hood (Faerie Tale Theatre).
60 min. Color. Live action. 1983. Malcolm McDowell, Mary Steenburgen.
A laser disc version of the same title offered by Fox Video (see above).

Distributor: Image Entertainment
Laser disc: CLV format $29.98
No public performance rights

Red Hiding Hood.
84 min. Color. Live action. Produced by Golan Globus. 1989. Amelia Shankley, Rocco Sisto, Isabella Rosselini.
This is a musical adaptation in which the classic's charm disappears due to plot complications. In a Robin Hood-like vein, the little girl's father has gone to war and her evil uncle becomes the wolf, making life unpleasant for those around him. He itches to marry Red Riding Hood's mother and get the daughter out of the way. Her father returns just in time to cut the wolf open and save his child.

Audience: Ages 6-Adult
Distributor: Cannon Video
Videocassette available
No public performance rights

Red Riding Hood/Goldilocks and the Three Bears.
30 min. Color. Limited animation. Produced by Rabbit Ears. 1990. Narrated by Meg Ryan.
In two separate morality tales, young girls run into trouble when they stray from the path or disregard parental advice. Red Riding Hood is swallowed by a wolf; Goldilocks is awakened in the home of three bears by the outraged trio. In the first tale, artist Laszlo Kubinyi introduces the red-topped lass against a soft, colored-pencil background. Bolder colors are developed as she dons her red cape and heads into the forest where a silver-coated fox with a walking stick and a French accent lolls-in-wait. The trip to granny's and the outcome follow the conventional story line. The main character in Goldilocks is a spoiled brat with a southern drawl and a "make-me" demeanor. Meg Ryan's accent and grumpy mutterings add freshness to an old favorite.

Reviews: *Booklist*, Nov. 15, 1990
Audience: Ages 4-8
Distributor: SVS/Triumph
Videocassette: $14.95
No public performance rights

★★★★★

Little Tim and the Brave Sea Captain
Edward Ardizzone (illus.).
Oxford. 1955. [1936]. Realistic fiction.
Tim, a stowaway on a ship, is left on board during a shipwreck.

Little Tim and the Brave Sea Captain.
11 min. 1976. Iconographic. Produced by Weston Woods. 1976.
The interest builds as Tim stows away, makes himself useful on board, then experiences a shipwreck. Sea shanty music enlivens the show and adds atmosphere. Though the film becomes slow-moving toward the end, "the iconographic simulation of the motion of the sea and the lurching of the steamer add touches that capture the excitement of Tim's experiences." —*Horn Book*
Reviews: *Booklist*, July 1, 1976, *Horn Book*, Aug. 1976
Awards: ALA Notable Film
Audience: Ages 4-8
Distributor: Weston Woods
16mm film: $175 **Videocassette:** $60
Rental: $25 per day

★★★★★

Little Toot
Hardie Gramatky.
Putnam. 1959. [1939]. Fantasy.
An incorrigible little tugboat becomes a hero when it finds a ship threatened by a storm and leads the ship to harbor.

Little Toot.
9 min. Color. Animation. A Disney Educational Production. 1971.
Charming Disney animation and storytelling faithfully replay the book's tale of a small, overzealous tugboat.
Audience: Ages 5-10
Distributor: Coronet/MTI Film & Video
16mm film: $260 **Videocassette:** $195
Rental: $75

★★★★★

Little Women
Louisa May Alcott.
Multiple editions. Realistic fiction.
Little Women follows the March family, including four sisters, through days of growth in a New England town during the 1800s. One sister dies and the others marry; spirited, tomboyish Jo finally settles down with a German professor.

Little Women.
115 min. Black and white. Live action. Produced by RKO/David O. Selznick, Merian C. Cooper, Kenneth MacGowan. 1933. Katherine Hepburn, Paul Lukas, Joan Bennett.
The film successfully details the inner workings and spirit of a family in early America with a sentimentality that echoes the book. Hepburn plays Jo, the aspiring writer, and while all the performances are captivating, hers is particularly exceptional.
Reviews: *New York Times*, Nov. 17, 1933, 22:3; *Variety*, Nov. 21, 1933
Awards: Academy Award, Best Screenplay
Audience: Ages 10-Adult
Distributor: MGM/UA Home Video
Videocassette: $19.98
No public performance rights

Little Women.
122 min. Color. Live action. Produced by MGM/Mervyn Le Roy. 1949. June Allyson, Elizabeth Taylor, Peter Lawford.
Not quite as fine an adaptation as the 1933 motion picture, this production does a reasonable if overly sentimental job of dramatizing the original.
Reviews: *New York Times*, Mar. 11, 1949, 33:2, *Variety*, Feb. 23, 1949
Awards: Academy Award, Best Art Direction-Set Decoration
Audience: Ages 10-Adult
Distributor: MGM/UA Home Video

Videocassette: $19.98
No public performance rights

★★★★★

Long Day's Journey into Night
Eugene O'Neill.
Yale University Press. 1989. [1956]. Drama.
The play profiles the lives in a family: an actor father, a drug-dependent mother, and two sons—an alcoholic and a physically unwell writer.

Long Day's Journey into Night.
178 min. Black and white. Live action. Produced by Ely Landau. 1962. Katherine Hepburn, Ralph Richardson, Jason Robards, Jr.
Exceptionally well performed, the motion picture, like the play, is set in Connecticut in 1912. This screen version captures the physical and emotional agonies experienced by the family members.
Reviews: *New York Times*, Oct. 10, 1962, 57:2; *Variety*, May 30, 1962
Audience: Ages 16-Adult
Distributor: Republic Pictures Home Video
Videocassette: $24.98
No public performance rights

Lorax, The
Dr. Seuss.
Random House. 1971. Fantasy.
The Onceler family lives in a grassy valley with spectacular multicolored trees. Father uses the trees to weave beautiful clothes, which prompts protest from the Lorax, spokesperson for the trees. But the business is successful, so it grows, becomes mechanized, and eventually uses all the trees despite the Lorax's intercessions. Finally, the valley is destroyed and the factory gone; all that is left is a single seed.

Dr. Seuss: The Lorax.
25 min. Color. Animation. Produced by DePatie-Freleng Productions/CBS. 1972.
This is a direct attack on environmental problems generated by industry, and although well animated with the wild characters and habitats characteristic of Dr. Seuss, it is long and the story is a bit overwhelming for young readers. Still, this Seuss production carries the high quality of the others and is one of the most popular environmental films in public and schools libraries.
Reviews: *Children's Video Report*, June/July 1990; *Variety*, Feb. 23, 1972
Audience: Ages 8—12
Distributor: Fox Video
Videocassette: $9.98
No public performance rights

Lorax, The.
25 min. Color. Animation. Produced by DePatie-Freleng Productions/CBS. 1972.
A public performance version of the same title offered by Fox Video (see above).
Distributor: Phoenix/BFA Films & Video
16mm film: $535 **Videocassette:** $300
Rental: $76

★★★★★

Lord Jim
Joseph Conrad.
Multiple editions. Adventure.
A young man becomes chief mate on an unseaworthy craft and, with the rest of the crew, leaves passengers behind and abandons ship during an accident. He then wanders in search of a way to atone for his misdeed.

Lord Jim.
154 min. Color. Live action. Produced by Columbia/Keep. 1965. Peter O'Toole, James Mason, Curt Jurgens.
The film is an uneven adaptation that seems to continue for too long, though the supporting cast is quite strong. Its focus shifts from the introspective character of Jim, which is in keeping with the novel, to the surface level of melodramatic adventures.
Reviews: *New York Times*, Feb. 26, 1965, 18:1; *Variety*, Feb. 24, 1965
Audience: Ages 14-Adult
Distributor: Columbia TriStar Home Video
Videocassette: $19.95
No public performance rights

★★★★★

Lord of the Flies
William Golding.
Multiple editions. Adventure.
A group of English schoolboys are stranded on an island after a plane crash. The boys turn savage.

Lord of the Flies.
91 min. Black and white. Live action. Allen-Hogdon Productions/Two Arts. 1963. James Aubrey, Tom Chapin, Hugh Edwards.
The story of the boys' degeneration is more convincing in print than on film but the adaptation is still engrossing.
Reviews: *New York Times*, Aug. 20, 1963, 37:1; *Variety*, May 22, 1963
Audience: Ages 14-Adult
Distributor: Videocassette not currently in distribution

Lord of the Flies.
90 min. Color. Live action. Produced by Castlerock. 1990. Balthazar Getty, Chris Furrh, Danuel Pipoly.
In this version, the novel's English schoolboys are transformed into an American television-literate crowd. The transformation reduces the story's impact. This is a less effective adaptation than the earlier black-and-white version.
Audience: Ages 14-Adult
Distributor: New Line Home Video
Videocassette available
No public performance rights

Lord of the Flies.
90 min. Color. Live action. 1990. Balthazar Getty, Chris Furrh, Danuel Pipoly.
A laser disc version of the same title offered by New Line Home Video (see above).
Audience: Ages 14-18
Distributor: Pioneer LDCA, Inc.
Laser disc: CLV format $34.98
No public performance rights

★★★★★

Lost Horizon
James Hilton.
Multiple editions. Fantasy.
A consulate member is kidnapped to a Tibetan monastery called Shangri-La. Equipped with Western conveniences, it is a refuge of serenity and long life that will purportedly survive after war destroys the existing world.

Lost Horizon.
118 min. Black and white. Live action. Produced by Columbia/Frank Capra. 1937. Ronald Colman, Jane Wyatt, Edward Everett Horton.
This still-gripping version of the classic leaves out some of the Utopian quality of the novel but nevertheless succeeds as an exceptionally fine and thought-provoking adaptation.
Reviews: *New York Times*, Mar. 4, 1937, 27:1, *Variety*, Mar. 10, 1937

Awards: Academy Awards, Best Film Editing, Best Set Design
Audience: Ages 16-Adult
Distributor: Columbia TriStar Home Video
Videocassette: $19.95
No public performance rights

Lost Horizon.
132 min. Black and white. Live action. 1937. Ronald Coleman, Jane Wyman.
A laser disc version of the same title offered by Columbia TriStar Home Video (see above).
Distributor: Pioneer LDCA, Inc.
Laser disc: CLV format $39.95
No public performance rights

★★★★★

"Lottery, The"
Shirley Jackson.

Anthologized in *The Norton Book of American Short Stories* edited by Peter S. Prescott. Norton. 1988. Short stories—fantasy.
Once a year the townspeople hold a lottery that everyone attends. The "winner," the person who picks the fatal piece of marked paper, gets stoned.

Lottery, The.
18 min. Color. Live action. Produced by Larry Yust with Clifton Fadiman. 1969.
While much of this dramatization focuses on the undramatic action of the townspeople gathering and waiting for the results of the lottery, the suspense nevertheless builds. Small talk by the townspeople about other communities abandoning the lottery raises the issue of change and its consequences. Viewers who have not yet read the story experience shock at its ending.
Audience: Ages 14-Adult
Distributor: Britannica
16mm film: $515 **Videocassette:** $300
Rental: $16 Pennsylvania State University

Lottery, The (and Discussion).
28 min. Color. Live action. 1969.
A laser disc version of the same title also distributed by Britannica (see above). Added to this version is a second Britannica title, *A Discussion of The Lottery.*
Distributor: Britannica
Laser disc: CAV format $129

★★★★★

Louis James Hates School
Bill Morrison (illus.).

Houghton Mifflin. 1978. Realistic fiction.
Louis James decides to quit school and find a job. Some misadventures make him change his mind.

Louis James Hates School.
11 min. Color. Animated. Produced by Paul Fierlinger/LCA. 1980.
The drawings on which the limited animation is based seem almost childlike. Still, this is a reasonably effective film of an interesting story.
Awards: Honorable Mention, Columbus International Film Festival; Reel Winner, *Instructor* Magazine
Audience: Ages 5-11
Distributor: Coronet/MTI Film & Video
16mm film: $225 **Videocassette:** $215
Rental: $75

★★★★★

"Love of Life"
Jack London.

Anthologized in *In a Far Country: Jack London's Tales of the West*, edited by

Dale L. Walker. Jameson Books. 1987. Short stories—realistic fiction.
Harry faces difficult decisions as he struggles through a hostile environment to bring back his load of gold.

Love of Life.
30 min. Color. Live action. Produced by Norfolk Communications. 1981. Narrated by Orson Welles.
Excellent narration carries the viewers through a story set against the stark beauty of Alaska in this upbeat Jack London tale.
Reviews: *Booklist*, May 1, 1982; *Library Journal*, Mar. 1, 1982; *School Library Journal*, Mar. 1982
Awards: ALA Selected Film for Young Adults
Audience: Ages 14-Adult
Distributor: Coronet/MTI Film & Video
16mm film: $450 **Videocassette:** $250
Rental: $75

★★★★★

Luck of Roaring Camp
Bret Harte.
Multiple editions. Realistic fiction.
An orphaned child becomes "The Luck" of Roaring Camp, and especially of the rough miner Kentuck.

Luck of Roaring Camp, The.
28 min. Color. Live action. Produced by LCA. 1982. Randy Quaid.
A gentle comic/tragic story is beautifully portrayed in this award-winning adaptation of Bret Harte's tender tale of mining camp days. Like the original, the excellent retelling concerns emotional and social changes in a tough mining camp. "This tenderly executed production blossoms with warmth, pathos, and humor into a vitalizing adaptation of Bret Harte's touching classic." —*Booklist*
Reviews: *Booklist*, May 1, 1983
Audience: 12-18
Distributor: Coronet/MTI Film & Video
16mm film: $550 **Videocassette:** $250
Rental: $75

★★★★★

"Luke Baldwin's Vow"
Morley Callaghan.
Anthologized in *Saturday Evening Post Stories of 1947*. Random House. 1947. Short stories—realistic fiction.
A boy and his uncle succeed in saving the life of an old blind dog.

Big Henry and the Polka Dot Kid.
51 min. Color. Live action. Produced by LCA. 1977.
This is a tenderly performed tale of a misplaced boy and an aging dog. As described in *Film News*, the film is "a moving story and a rare visual treat...it points out that angry confrontations...are not the only possible responses when children have problems with adults—or with their own peers."
Reviews: *Film News*, Summer 1977
Audience: Ages 8-14
Distributor: Coronet/MTI Film & Video
16mm film: $750 **Videocassette:** $250
Rental: $75

Big Henry and the Polka Dot Kid.
33 min. Color. Live action. 1977.
An abbreviated version of the same full length title also distributed by Coronet/MTI (see above). This version retains the basic plot but omits selected details.
Distributor: Coronet/MTI
16mm film: $550 **Videocassette:** $250
Rental: $75

M

adherence to book film rating

Macbeth
William Shakespeare.
Multiple editions. Drama.
Hearing the prophecy that he will become king, Macbeth takes matters into his own hands by murdering the reigning monarch. Lady Macbeth goes mad and commits suicide. The enemies of Macbeth kill him.

Macbeth.
112 min. Black and white. Live action. Produced by Republic/Orson Welles. 1948. Orson Welles, Jeanette Nolan, Dan O'Herlihy, Roddy McDowall.
This controversial adaptation confines the action to dark, tight settings, its players speaking with sometimes difficult-to-understand Scot accents. The film was rapidly shot in twenty-three days, then rerecorded. Departing from Shakespeare's text, it introduces Christian elements to convey the conflict between good and evil. Strange settings predominate, reducing the importance of the play's dialog. The original tragedy seems to have been lost in the process.
Reviews: *New York Times*, Dec. 28, 1950, 22:6; *Variety*, Nov. 13, 1948
Audience: Ages 14-Adult
Distributor: Republic Pictures Home Video
Videocassette: $19.98
No public performance rights

Macbeth.
112 min. Black and white. Live action. 1948. Orson Welles, Jeanette Nolan, Dan O'Herlihy, Roddy McDowall.
A laser disc version of the same title offered by Republic Pictures Home Video (see above).
Distributor: Image Entertainment
Laser disc: CLV format $39.95
No public performance rights

Macbeth.
140 min. Color. Live action. Produced by Playboy Productions/Caliban. 1971. Jon Finch, Francesca Annis, Martin Shaw.
Directed by Roman Polanski, this is a bloody adaptation that displays bare-bodied flesh in the sleeping walking scene. Shot in Wales, the production has authentic atmosphere. Among its other strengths are a historically realistic social setting that provides a plausible context for Macbeth's mental anguish.
Reviews: *New York Times*, Dec. 21, 1971, 51:1; *Variety*, Dec. 15, 1971
Audience: Ages 14-Adult
Distributor: Columbia TriStar Home Video
Videocassette: $59.95
No public performance rights

Macbeth.
140 min. Color. Live action. 1971. Jon Finch, Francesca Annis, Martin Shaw.
A laser disc version of the same title offered by Columbia TriStar Home Video (see above).
Distributor: Pioneer LDCA, Inc.
Laser disc: CLV format $39.95
No public performance rights

Macbeth.
150 min. Color. Live action. Produced by Trevor Nunn. 1979. Ian McKellen, Judi Dench, John Bowen.
Considered perhaps the finest made-for-television Shakespeare ever, this is an unconventional production. Actors are put in a circle so they themselves are both actors and audience. Costumes range from turtleneck sweaters on the Scottish lords to a black leather-and-boots outfit on Macbeth. The acting is superb, and the close-ups make the screen audience feel the play mirrors themselves. Banquo voices his doubts about Macbeth directly to the audience as if viewers are in the play. Instead of realism, the production stresses ritual—Macbeth's crowning, the organ music, and so forth. Only eight actors appear in a banquet scene that would include many more if realism were the goal, yet the effect is powerful. Ian McKellen, as Macbeth, wears a punk hairstyle and a villanous look, reflecting an inner foulness. Only Macbeth sees the ghost in a scene that has him looking at nothing but a stool, yet the action is convincing. Scene after scene includes captivating minidramas. The lighting helps create a surreal, nightmarish atmosphere without using special effects or tricks. Throughout, the television medium is relegated to a lesser position than the piece of theater.
Audience: Ages 16-Adult
Distributor: Films for the Humanities & Sciences
Videocassette: $149

Macbeth.
148 min. Color. Live action. Produced by Richmond Crinkley, John Goberman. 1982. Maureen Anderman, Phil Anglim, Fritz Sperberg.
Directed by Sarah Caldewell, this television version of a live stage production portrays the tragedy without gimmickry. The early scenes between Macbeth and Lady Macbeth fall flat, but Macbeth's performance grows more convincing as the action progresses. Lady Macbeth's mad scene is riveting, as is the murder scene. In relation to the Macbeth marriage, the adaptation conveys the sense of a relationship gone awry.
Audience: Ages 16-Adult
Distributor: Films for the Humanities & Sciences
Videocassette: $89.95

Macbeth (The Shakespeare Plays).
148 min. Color. Live action. Produced by BBC. 1983. Nicol Williamson, Jane Lapotaire.
Nicol Williamson manages through his performance to convey a complex notion: Macbeth is obsessed not so much with killing off the opposition as with his conscience. His murdering Duncan has offended his own being in the first instance, rendering him vile to himself thereafter. Each new murder he commits is an act of self-punishment. With such a notion underlying his role, the show comes across as a tragedy of the soul. It seems proper that no ghostly apparitions appear in this version. Indicating that the ghosts exist in Macbeth's mind, the camera focuses instead on his reaction to them. Williamson sometimes mumbles, sometimes speaks so rapidly he is hard to understand. His peformance has prompted various reactions, from being overly frenzied to being in keeping with Macbeth's distraught character. This video edition is for institutional use only.
Reviews: *Los Angeles Times*, Oct. 17, 1983; *Times Literary Supplement*, Nov. 18, 1983; *Washington Post*, Oct. 17, 1983

Audience: Ages 16-Adult
Distributor: Ambrose Video
Videocassette: $249.95

★★★★★

Madame Bovary
Gustave Flaubert.
Multiple editions. Realistic fiction.
A French doctor's wife, in search of romance and relief from boredom, deceives her husband with two men, ultimately bringing on her own ruin.

Madame Bovary.
114 min. Black and white. Live action. Produced by MGM/Pandro S. Berman. 1949. Jennifer Jones, James Mason, Van Heflin, Louis Jourdan, Gene Lockhart.
Mason performs as the author Flaubert, defending himself from the censors of his day and disclosing the story in flashback fashion. His tale of the fallen heroine, Madame Bovary, has been toned down in its transference to the screen.
Reviews: *New York Times*, Aug. 26, 1949, 15:2; *Variety*, Aug. 3, 1949
Audience: Ages 16-Adult
Distributor: MGM/UA Home Video
Videocassette: $24.98
No public performance rights

★★★★★

Madeline
Ludwig Bemelmans (illus.).
Penguin USA. 1958. [1939]. Realistic fiction.
Living in a strictly patterned Paris convent school, Madeline is the heroine of a rhymed story about a girl who doesn't always follow the rules. This tale explains, with the help of picturesque Paris scenes, how the young girl turned a case of appendicitis into a major event.

Madeline.
6.5 min. Color. Animated. Produced by Stephen Bosustow. 1952.
Set in Paris, this animated version of the fast-paced tale is told in rhyme to match the storybook. It is a fine and faithful rendition of the original.
Audience: Ages 4-8
Distributor: Churchill Media
16mm film: $165 **Videocassette:** $79
Rental: $60

Madeline: The Musical.
30 min. Color. Animation. Produced by DIC. 1989.
This is a spirited musical adaptation. As described in *Booklist*, the show features "finely detailed animation, lively music, and swift pacing." This edition is for institutional use only.
Reviews: *Booklist*, Feb. 15, 1989; *School Library Journal*, Aug. 1989; *Video Librarian*, May 1989
Audience: Ages 4-8
Distributor: Ambrose Video
Videocassette: $69.95

Madeline.
30 min. Color. Animation. 1989.
A home video version of the same title distributed by Ambrose Video (see above).
Distributor: Video Treasures
Videocassette: $9.99
No public performance rights

★★★★★

Madeline and the Bad Hat
Ludwig Bemelmans (illus.).
Penguin USA. 1957. [1956]. Realistic fiction.

A very bad boy, an ambassador's son, moves next door to Madeline's boarding school in this rhyming tale. He one day gets himself into a jam that changes his subsequent behavior.

Madeline and the Bad Hat.
24 min. Color. Animated. Produced by Ronald A. Weinberg/Christian Davin. 1991. Narrated by Christopher Plummer.
Topnotch animation captures the spirit of the storybook in fine style, with the addition of rhyming songs that meld into the rhyming tale. The production has all the charm of the original, coming to a crowning finish as Pepito, a reformed evildoer, romps with animated animals.
Audience: Ages 4-8
Distributor: Golden Book Video
Videocassette: $14.95
No public performance rights

Madeline and the Bad Hat.
8 min. Color. Animated. A Rembrandt Film. 1990.
Narrated by a woman who might be Madeline's schoolmistress, the show flows nicely and attracts young viewers with its elements of bad and good. The boy thrusts a cat into a pack of dogs but pays for his misdeed. Like the book, the film sets the story in Paris and tells it in rhyme.
Reviews: *School Library Journal*, Apr. 1991
Audience: Ages 4-8
Distributor: Weston Woods
16mm film: $195 **Videocassette:** $100
Rental: $20 daily

Madeline's Rescue and Other Stories about Madeline.
23 min. Color. Animated. Produced by Weston Woods. 1990.
Included in this tape anthology are adaptations of *Madeline's Rescue*, *Madeline and the Bad Hat*, and *Madeline and the Gypsies*. See individual titles for full descriptions.
Audience: Ages 4-8
Distributor: Children's Circle, Weston Woods
Videocassette: $19.95
No public performance rights

★★★★★

Madeline and the Gypsies
Ludwig Bemelmans (illus.).
Penguin USA. 1959. Adventure.
The rhyming tale focuses on Madeline and the ambassador's son, who are left behind on the ferris wheel at a gypsy carnival. The gypsies have the two children perform.

Madeline and the Gypsies.
7 min. Color. Animated. A Rembrandt Film. 1990.
The adventurous tale moves from Madeline and her companion being stuck on top of a ferris wheel to their being sewn inside a lion costume. As in the picture book, the story is told in rhyme.
Reviews: *School Library Journal*, Apr. 1991
Audience: Ages 4-8
Distributor: Weston Woods
16mm film: $195 **Videocassette:** $100
Rental: $20 daily

Madeline's Rescue and Other Stories about Madeline.
23 min. Color. Animated. Produced by Weston Woods. 1990.
Included in this tape anthology are adaptations of *Madeline's Rescue*, *Madeline and the Bad Hat*, and *Madeline and the Gypsies*. See individual titles for full descriptions.
Audience: Ages 4-8
Distributor: Children's Circle, Weston Woods

Videocassette: $19.95
No public performance rights

★★★★★

Madeline's Christmas
Ludwig Bemelmans (illus.).
Penguin USA. 1985. Realistic fiction.
All set to go home for Christmas, Madeline must change her plans, for she is the only healthy one at the sickly boarding school. The story unfolds in rhyme.

Madeline's Christmas.
24 min. Color. Animated. Produced by Ronald A. Weinberg/Christian Davin. 1991. Narrated by Christopher Plummer.
Splendid full animation and complementary songs bring the tale to life with gusto. This is an enchanting adaptation. It adds a few, realistic lines of dialogue and thoughtful visual touches, such as a Santa Claus hat on the house radio. Like the book, the show ends with a brief rhyme about love.
Audience: Ages 4-8
Distributor: Golden Book Video
Videocassette: $14.95
No public performance rights

★★★★★

Madeline's Rescue
Ludwig Bemelmans (illus.).
Penguin USA. 1953. Realistic fiction.
A dog rescues Madeline from the river in this rhyming tale. The girls at Madeline's boarding school adopt the dog as their pet, but the trustees object.

Madeline's Rescue.
7 min. Color. Animated. A Rembrandt Film. 1990.
This story-in-rhyme comes alive in a film with a happy ending. The girls find more than they bargained for when they locate the missing dog.
Audience: Ages 4-8
Distributor: Weston Woods
16mm film: $195 **Videocassette:** $100
Rental: $20 daily

Madeline's Rescue and Other Stories about Madeline.
23 min. Color. Animated. Produced by Weston Woods. 1990.
Included in this tape anthology are adaptations of *Madeline's Rescue*, *Madeline and the Bad Hat*, and *Madeline and the Gypsies*. See individual titles for full descriptions.
Audience: Ages 4-8
Distributor: Children's Circle, Weston Woods
Videocassette: $19.95
No public performance rights

Madeline's Rescue.
24 min. Color. Animated. Produced by Ronald A. Weinberg/Christian Davin. 1991. Narrated by Christopher Plummer.
Splendidly animated, this is a faithful adaptation that is augmented with lyrical song and rhythmic music. There are nice animated touches like Madeline's imagining the dog once its gone, and the screen visualizing it floating by in a cloud.
Audience: Ages 4-8
Distributor: Golden Book Video
Videocassette: $14.95
No public performance rights

★★★★★

Magic Fishbone, The
Charles Dickens.
Coach House. 1961. [1953]. Folklore and fairy tales.
A royal family falls on hard times, but the princess receives a magic fishbone from a fairy. Used just at the right time, the magic brings riches to the family.

Magic Fishbone, The.
11 min. Color. Animation. Produced by Kratky Films. 1982.
High-quality central-European animation helps make this a sensitive, audience-holding story about patience and judgment.
Audience: Ages 6-10
Distributor: Phoenix/BFA Films & Video
16mm film: $240 **Videocassette:** $140
Rental: $25

*****

"Magic Shop, The"
H. G. Wells.
Anthologized in *The Complete Short Stories of H. G. Wells.*
St. Martin's Press. 1987. Short stories—fantasy.
A boy leads his father into a genuine magic shop, where the shopkeeper performs fantastic tricks.

Magic Shop, The.
12 min. Color. Live action. Produced by Bert Van Bork with Clifton Fadiman. 1986.
The fine acting in this film contributes to the tension that climaxes when the young boy disappears. All ends happily ever after, as in the short story. Outside the performance of the tricks, the tale has little action.
Audience: Ages 10-Adult
Distributor: Britannica
16mm film: $420 **Videocassette:** $240
Rental: $21 Penn State University

Gift of the Magi, The and *The Magic Shop.*
28 min. Color. Live action. 1980.
A laser disc version of the same two titles distributed separately by Britannica (see above).
Distributor: Britannica
Laser disc: CAV format $129

*****

Make Way for Ducklings
Robert McCloskey (illus.).
Penguin USA. 1941. Realistic fiction.
A quietly entertaining story, *Make Way for Ducklings* follows the experiences of a duck family living in Boston. A policeman aids Mother Duck as she leads her brood through the traffic to a pond in the Public Garden.

Make Way for Ducklings.
11 min. Brown and White. Iconographic. Produced by Weston Woods. 1955.
Like the storybook, the film is both instructive and entertaining (Mom teaches her children how to survive when the ducks wander into traffic, for example). Fine narration and music strengthen the show, but it moves slowly and relies on brown-and-white drawings of limited interest to a present-day audience.
Audience: Ages 4-6
Distributor: Weston Woods
16mm film: $175 **Videocassette:** $60
Rental: $25 daily

Robert McCloskey Library, The.
58 min. Color. Iconographic and animated. Produced by Weston Woods. 1991.
Included in this tape anthology are adaptations of *Lentil*, *Make Way for Ducklings*, *Burt Dow: Deep-Water Man*, *Blueberries for Sal*, and *Time of Wonder.* See individual titles for full descriptions. An additional segment, *Getting to Know Robert McCloskey*, features the author commenting on his work.
Audience: Ages 4-8
Distributor: Children's Circle, Weston Woods
Videocassette: $19.95

No public performance rights

Smile for Auntie and Other Stories.
27 min. Color. Iconographic and animated. Produced by Weston Woods. 1985.
Included in this tape anthology are adaptations of *Smile for Auntie* (Diane Paterson), *Make Way for Ducklings* (Robert McCloskey), *The Snowy Day* (Ezra Jack Keats), and *Wynken, Blynken and Nod* (Eugene Field). See individual titles for full descriptions.
Audience: Ages 4-8
Distributor: Children's Circle, Weston Woods
Videocassette: $19.95
No public performance rights

★★★★★

Maltese Falcon, The
Dashiell Hammett.
Multiple editions. Mystery.
The search for an ornamental black bird encrusted with precious gems leads to multiple murders. A detective conspires with the criminals, becoming involved in the wrongdoing.

Maltese Falcon, The.
80 min. Black and white. Live action. Produced by Warner. 1931. Ricardo Cortez, Bebe Daniel, Dudley Digges.
This is a very good rendition of the novel, well paced and full of strong performances. Cortez plays the male lead as more of a lady charmer than Bogart does in the excellent 1941 remake, which surpassed this earlier version.
Reviews: *New York Times*, May 29, 1981, 26:5; *Variety*, June 2, 1931
Audience: Ages 14-Adult
Distributor: Videocassette not currently in distribution

Maltese Falcon, The.
101 min. Black and white. Live action. Produced by Warner/Henry Blanke. 1941. Humphrey Bogart, Mary Astor, Sidney Greenstreet.
An outstanding mystery and suspense film, this adaptation has retained its excellence over the years. Bogart's performance as the detective-hero is exceptional, and the movie is so well paced that it just glides along. John Huston served as both writer and director.
Reviews: *New York Times*, Oct. 4, 1941, 18:2; *Variety*, Oct. 1, 1941
Audience: Ages 14-Adult
Distributor: MGM/UA Home Video
Videocassette: $19.98
No public performance rights

Maltese Falcon, The.
101 min. Color. Live action. 1941. Humphrey Bogart, Mary Astor, Sidney Greenstreet.
A colorized version of the same title also distributed by MGM/UA Home Video (see above).
Distributor: MGM/UA Home Video
Videocassette: $19.98
No public performance rights

Maltese Falcon, The.
102 min. Black and white. Live action. 1941. Humphrey Bogart, Mary Astor, Sidney Greenstreet.
A laser disc version of the same title offered by MGM/UA Home Video (see above).
Distributor: Pioneer LDCA, Inc.
Laser disc: CLV format $34.98
No public performance rights

★★★★★

"Man and the Snake, The"
Ambrose Bierce.
Anthologized in *The Stories and Fables of Ambrose Bierce*. Stemmer House. 1977. Short stories—horror.
A snakekeeper who harbors the slithery creatures in his home has an overnight guest. Fed by an evening of stories on snakes, the visitor grows alarmed, with tragic results, at the sight of what seems to be a snake in his bedroom.

Man and the Snake, The.
26 min. Color. Live action. Produced by Elizabeth McKay/Sture Tydman. 1975.
The shots of the snakery, along with dialog about snakes escaping and charming humans, build a sense of foreboding in the film. Yet the production moves slowly. Suspense grows to a climax at the end, startling viewers who have not yet read the story with its surprise ending.
Reviews: *Booklist*, Feb. 1, 1976
Awards: Red Ribbon, American Film Festival; Chris Bronze Plaque, Columbus International Film Festival
Audience: Ages 14-Adult
Distributor: Pyramid Film & Video
16mm film: $525 **Videocassette:** $225
Rental: $75

★★★★★

Man Called Horse, A
Dorothy M. Johnson.
Ballantine. 1973. Historical fiction.
Set in the Dakota territory during the early 1800s, this details the adventure of an Englishman captured by Sioux Indians. He undergoes ritual torture to prove his mettle and is transformed into a great white chief.

Man Called Horse, A.
115 min. Color. Live action. Produced by Cinema Center/Sanford Howard. 1970. Richard Harris, Judith Anderson, Jean Gascon.
Based on an original story by Dorothy M. Johnson, the motion picture, in this case, preceded the book of the same name. Complete with graphic shots of blood and torture, the film details some of the tribal customs of the Dakota Sioux. Painful-to-watch rituals are somewhat balanced by the Englishman's survival and success in Indian society.
Reviews: *New York Times*, Apr. 30, 1970, 46:1; *Variety*, Apr. 29, 1970
Audience: Ages 16-Adult
Distributor: Fox Video
Videocassette: $59.98
No public performance rights

★★★★★

Man for All Seasons, A
Robert Bolt.
Random House. 1962. Drama.
Sir Thomas More, chancellor of England, will not approve King Henry VIII's divorce and then marriage to Anne Boleyn. Consequently, he is executed.

Man for All Seasons, A.
120 min. Color. Live action. Produced by Highland Films. 1966. Robert Shaw, Paul Scofield, Wendy Hiller.
Scripted by the playwright himself, the motion picture is an outstanding adaptation that captures the historical event with a flourish. The issue, for More, is the inescapable necessity of following his conscience.
Reviews: *New York Times*, Dec. 13, 1966, 60:1; *Variety*, Dec. 14, 1966
Awards: Academy Awards, Best Picture, Best Actor, Best Director, Best Screenplay, Best Cinematography, Best Costume Design; Golden Globe Awards, Best Dramatic Film, Best Actor
Audience: Ages 14-Adult
Distributor: Columbia TriStar Home Video
Videocassette: $19.95

No public performance rights

Man for All Seasons, A.
120 min. Color. Live action. 1966. Robert Shaw, Paul Scofield, Wendy Hiller.
A laser disc version of the same title offered by Columbia TriStar Home Video (see above).
Distributor: Pioneer LDCA, Inc.
Laser disc: CLV format $39.95
No public performance rights

★★★★★

"Man That Corrupted Hadlyburg, The"
Mark Twain.
Anthologized in *The American Short Story, Vol. 1*, edited by C. Skaggs. Dell. 1979. Short stories—realistic fiction.
A stranger, snubbed by the people of a supposedly pious town, returns after many years with a plan to avenge the earlier mistreatment.

Man That Corrupted Hadlyburg, The.
40 min. Color. Live action. Produced by Learning in Focus. 1980. Robert Preston, Fred Gwynne.
Stealing a page from *Our Town*, Robert Preston plays the role of the man seeking revenge for past ill-treatment. He also acts as narrator, interrupting the story periodically to explain what is happening. It is a technique that slows the pace too much for sustained audience interest.
Reviews: *Booklist*, Sept. 1, 1980
Audience: Ages 14-18
Distributor: Monterey Home Video
Videocassette: $24.95
No public performance rights

★★★★★

Man Who Loved Cat Dancing, The
Marilyn Dunham.
Harcourt Brace Jovanovich. 1972. Adventure.
After a disenchanted wife of the West leaves her husband, she is kidnapped by outlaws, one of whom she grows to love.

Man Who Loved Cat Dancing, The.
114 min. Color. Live action. Produced by MGM/Martin Poll, Eleanor Perry. 1973. Sarah Miles, Burt Reynolds, Lee J. Cobb.
At times the film lags, but the emotion between the wife and the captor she grows to love is convincing.
Reviews: *New York Times*, June 29, 1973, 17:1; *Variety*, June 27, 1973
Audience: Ages 14-Adult
Distributor: MGM/UA Home Video
Videocassette: $19.98
No public performance rights

★★★★★

Man Who Would Be King, The
Rudyard Kipling.
Multiple editions. Adventure.
Two adventurers, British soldiers in India during the 1880s, make their difficult way to a remote kingdom, where the inhabitants mistake one of them for the heir to Alexander the Great. He succumbs to his thirst for power.

Man Who Would Be King, The.
129 min. Color. Live action. Produced by John Foreman. 1975. Sean Connery, Michael Caine, Christopher Plummer.
The adventurers stumble upon unexpected wealth when the high priest decides one of them deserves Alexander the Great's treasure. Instead of taking to his heels with the riches, the taste of power keeps him rooted in the kingdom. Plummer portrays the writer, Kipling, who meets up with the adventurers. The

action involves some violence.

Reviews: *New York Times*, Dec. 18, 1975, 62:1; *Variety*, Dec. 10, 1975
Audience: Ages 10-Adult
Distributor: Fox Video
Videocassette: $19.98
No public performance rights

Man Who Would Be King, The.
129 min. Color. Live action. 1975. Sean Connery, Michael Caine, Christopher Plummer.
A laser disc version of the same title offered by Fox Video (see above).

Distributor: Image Entertainment
Laser disc: Widescreen CLV format $49.98
No public performance rights

★★★★★

Mandy's Grandmother
Liesel Moak Skorpen.

Dial Press. 1975. Realistic fiction.
Mandy has never seen her grandmother but has a mental picture of her from storybooks. When they meet, the grandmother is not at all like the storybooks. Mandy and her grandmother eventually bridge these differences.

Mandy's Grandmother.
30 min. Color. Live action. Produced by Andrew Sugarman. 1978. Maureen O'Sullivan, Kathryn Walker, Amy Levitan.
Though slightly slow-moving, this faithful-to-the-book version is a well-acted portrayal of a misunderstanding between generations and the beautiful resolution of that misunderstanding.

Audience: Ages 7-11
Distributor: Phoenix/BFA Films & Video
16mm film: $545 **Videocassette:** $310
Rental: $45

★★★★★

Mary Poppins
P. L. Travers.

Illustrated by Mary Shepard. Harcourt Brace Jovanovich. 1981. Fantasy.
Blowing in on an east wind, Mary Poppins—a nanny who's "practically perfect in every way"—arrives to tend the Banks children. She teaches them how to make even their chores fun, and Mr. Banks learns the value of spending time with his family.

Mary Poppins.
139 min. Color. Live action/Animation. Produced by Bill Walsh/Walt Disney. 1964. Julie Andrews, Dick Van Dyke, Ed Wynn.
This musical fantasy is a smooth and delightful blend of live action and animation, with an Academy Award-winning musical score by Richard and Robert Sherman. Set in London about 1910, *Mary Poppins* boasts two strong female characters: a very independent nanny, and the children's mother, who is active in the suffragette movement of the time. Special effects enhance an already beloved children's tale. With its fully developed parent-child plot, the film appeals to a wide audience. It is described in the *New York Times* as "a most wonderfully cheering movie...irresistible to kids and adults."

Reviews: *New York Times*, Sept. 25, 1964
Awards: Academy Awards, Best Actress, Best Music Score, Best Song, Best Visual Effects
Audience: Ages 3-Adult
Distributor: Buena Vista Home Video
Videocassette: $24.99
No public performance rights

Mary Poppins.
139 min. Color. Live action. Produced by Walt Disney. 1964. Julie Andrews, Dick Van Dyke.

A laser disc version of the same title offered by Buena Vista Home Video Home Video (see above).
Distributor: Image Entertainment
Laser disc: CLV format $44.99
No public performance rights

★★★★★

Marzipan Pig, The
Russell Hoban.
Illustrated by Quentin Blake. Farrar, Straus & Giroux. 1986. Fantasy.
A chain of events—beginning with a mouse eating a marzipan pig and also involving a clock, an owl, and a bee—brings out the interaction between living and nonliving things.

Marzipan Pig, The.
25 min. Color. Animation. Produced by Michael Sporn and Italtoons Corp. 1990.
Michael Sporn sticks closely to the tale as it unfolds in the book, producing a film animated in the sprightly style for which he is noted. He adds a nice dimension of humor to the antics of the owl in a production limited only by the episodic style of the original story.
Awards: Best Film of the Year, ASIFA Animation Festival; Silver Apple, National Education Film and Video Festival
Audience: Ages 5-10
Distributor: Lucerne Media
16mm film: $495 **Videocassette:** $295

Marzipan Pig, The.
25 min. Color. Animation. Produced by Michael Sporn and Italtoons. 1990.
A home video version of the same title distributed by Lucerne Media (see above).
Distributor: Family Home Entertainment
Videocassette: $14.95
No public performance rights

★★★★★

"Masque of the Red Death"
"Hop Frog"
Edgar Allan Poe.
Anthologized in *Tales of Terror.* Prentice Hall. 1985. Short stories—horror.
Evil Prince Prospero lives in luxury while plague attacks the surrounding countryside in the first tale. The second features a stunted dwarf who wreaks revenge on his tormentors.

Masque of the Red Death.
86 min. Color. Live action. Produced by George Willoughby/AIP. 1964. Jane Asher, Hazel Court, Nigel Green, Patrick Magee, Skip Martin, Vincent Price, David Weston.
The film adapts one Poe tale and works in another ("Hop Frog") beneath the main plot. A masterpiece of horror, the show stars Vincent Price as the devil-worshiping villain. Its footage was shot in beautiful surroundings in England.
Reviews: *New York Times*, Sept. 17, 1964, 52:6; *Variety*, June 24, 1964
Audience: Ages 15-18
Distributor: Vestron Video
Videocassette: $59.98
No public performance rights

Masque of the Red Death.
169 min. Color. Live action. 1964. Vincent Price.
A laser disc version of the same title offered by Vestron Video (see above). Also includes a second feature, *The Premature Burial*, adapted from another Poe tale.
Distributor: Image Entertainment
Laser disc: CLV format $49.95

No public performance rights

★★★★★

Master Thief
Jacob Grimm and Wilhelm K. Grimm.
Multiple editions. Folklore and fairy tales.
A master thief is challenged by his godfather, a count, to steal some "unobtainable" targets: the count's favorite horse from his stable, the count's bed sheet and his wife's wedding ring while they sleep, and officials from the church.

Jack and the Dentist's Daughter.
40 min. Color. Live action. Produced by Tom and Mimi Davenport. 1984.
Performed by a mostly black cast, in this version Jack accidentally falls in with a band of thieves and intentionally robs from them. His purpose in the film, not in the tale, is to prove himself worthy to his sweetheart's father by meeting his demands. The demands are almost exactly as in the original tale; probably the most difficult is stealing the father's sheets from his bed and a ring from his wife's hand in the thick of the night. Despite additions, such as the character of the sweetheart, the spirit of the original has been retained.
Audience: Ages 8-Adult
Distributor: Davenport Films
16mm film: $550 **Rental:** $55
Videocassette: $60 (with public performance rights)
Videocassette: $29.95 (no public performance rights)

★★★★★

Matter of Time, A
Roni Schotter.
Collins. 1979. Realistic fiction.
A sixteen-year-old girl's mother is dying of cancer; through the help of a social worker, the teenager copes with the problem of waiting for death.

Matter of Time, A.
30 min. Color. Live action. Produced by LCA. 1981.
This award-winning ABC After School Special is a very sensitive and well-acted story about dying.
Awards: Emmy Award, Outstanding Children's Entertainment Special; Outstanding Children's Program, National Council on Family Relations
Audience: Ages 14-18
Distributor: Coronet/MTI Film & Video
16mm film: $550 **Videocassette:** $250
Rental: $75

★★★★★

Maurice Sendak's Really Rosie
Maurice Sendak (illus.).
Harper & Row Junior Books. 1975. Drama, songs.
Published after the theatrical production, this book includes lyrics, text, and pictures. It stars Rosie, who makes a movie that includes her friends Alligator, Johnny, Pierre, and Chicken Soup, and the stories from their individual books.

Really Rosie.
25 min. Color. Animated. Produced by Sheldon Riss/Weston Woods. 1976.
Every inch the glamorous movie queen, self-confident Rosie "allows" her friends to perform in her production. The show therefore includes individual films/books described elsewhere in this volume (*Alligators All Around*, *One Was Johnny*, *Pierre*, and *Chicken Soup with Rice*), and set in the context of the larger story *Really Rosie*. For entertainment, only *Pierre* succeeds as well on its own as in this boisterous collected offering.

Reviews: *Booklist*, Mar. 1, 1977; *Horn Book*, June 1977; *Video Choice*, Oct. 1988
Awards: ALA Notable Film; Blue Ribbon, American Film Festival; CINE Golden Eagle
Audience: Ages 4-8
Distributor: Weston Woods
16mm film: $525 **Videocassette:** $60
Rental: $40 daily

Really Rosie.
27 min. Color. Animated. Produced by Weston Woods. 1985.
A home video version of *Really Rosie* distributed by Weston Woods (see above).
Distributor: Children's Circle, Weston Woods
Videocassette: $19.95
No public performance rights

★★★★★

Mayday! Mayday!
Hillary Milton.
F. Watts. 1979. Adventure.
Two boys survive an airplane crash and set out to get help for their injured parents.

Mayday! Mayday!.
50 min. Color. Live action. Produced by ABC Weekend Specials. 1983.
This is one of the finest and most exciting of the ABC Weekend Specials for young viewers. It is beautifully photographed in a wilderness setting, and the challenges to the two heroes are entirely believable.
Audience: Ages 8-11
Distributor: Coronet/MTI Film & Video
16mm film: $645 **Videocassette:** $250
Rental: $75

★★★★★

Midnight Ride of Paul Revere, The
Henry Wadsworth Longfellow.
Multiple editions. Poetry.
Paul Revere's famous ride to warn the American countryside of the coming of the British is recounted in verse.

Midnight Ride of Paul Revere, The (Second Edition).
10 min. Color. Animation. Produced by Sharon Hoogstraten. 1989.
This second edition of a Coronet release retains Longfellow's words and is more fully animated than the earlier version.
Audience: Ages 10-15
Distributor: Coronet/MTI Film & Video
16mm film: $290 **Videocassette:** $250
Rental: $75

★★★★★

Midsummer Night's Dream, A
William Shakespeare.
Multiple editions. Drama.
With the help of some magical juice, a fairy king adjusts the feelings of love among two couples. He also uses the potion on his fairy queen with comical results.

Midsummer Night's Dream, A.
133 min. Black and White. Produced by Warner/Max Reinhardt. 1935.
James Cagney, Dick Powell, Jean Muir, Ross Alexander, Olivia de Havilland, Mickey Rooney.
Cagney is quite effective as Bottom in a large-scale Hollywood remake of Max Reinhardt's Broadway production. The adaptation treats Shakespeare's text with great respect, but is somewhat melodramatic, a characteristic shared by other productions made in the days of the early sound film.

Awards: Academy Award, Best Cinematography
Reviews: *Variety*, Oct. 16, 1935
Audience: Ages 12—Adult
Distributor: Videocassette not currently in distribution

Midsummer Night's Dream, A.
111 min. Live action. Color. Produced by Rediffusion. 1964. Jill Bennett, Maureen Beck, John Fraser, Clifford Elikin, Benny Hill.
Shakespeare's verse is spoken in lively fashion in this delightful British remake. Playing Lysander, John Fraser employs gestures and expression to fine effect. The Pyramus and Thisbe play within the play is entertainingly performed. Only the detail of the actors' short hairstyles seems out of keeping with Shakespeare. Overall, the production is beautifully romantic; its music, composed by Felix Mendelssohn, is performed by the Philharmonic Orchestra.
Reviews: *Variety*, Feb. 10, 1965
Audience: Ages 12-Adult
Distributor: Video Yesteryear
Videocassette: $29.95

Midsummer Night's Dream, A (The Shakespeare Plays).
112 min. Color. Live action. Produced by BBC. 1982. Nigel Davenport, Geoffrey Lumsden, Helen Mirren, Cherith Mellor.
Produced in the tradition of the earlier Reinhardt film, this version is not quite as strong. The setting seems tightly confined, even within the open forest. Also, the Pyramus and Thisbe miniplay is not funny enough. Yet there are strong performances, too. Helen Mirren makes an enchanting Titania, and Cherith Mellor is a winning Helena. She appears, as noted in the *Shakespeare on Film Newsletter*, "tall, spindly, bespectacled, her hair awry, looking for all the world like a woman who has been jilted and who would expect a practical joke in poor taste at the hands of Lysander and Demetrius." This video edition is for institutional use only.
Reviews: *Times Literary Supplement*, Dec. 25, 1981; *Washington Post*, June 19, 1981; *Shakespeare on Film Newsletter*, Dec. 1983
Audience: Ages 12-Adult
Distributor: Ambrose Video
Videocassette: $249.95

Midsummer Night's Dream, A.
165 min. Color. Live action. Produced by Joseph Papp/ABC Video. 1982. Jeffrey DeMunn, Rich Leiberman, Christine Baranski, Deborah Rush.
This television version of a stage play is an uneven production. Among its drawbacks is an unappealing Puck, who shrieks lines and emits irksome giggles. Bottom's donkey head—ear muffs and a nose smudge—is decidedly unconvincing. On the other hand, Christine Baranski plays an aristocratic Helena with fine timing and keen, self-mocking humor. The enchanting setting includes birch trees, moss, and a bronze Cupid. The lighting seems better suited to stage, not adapted to the nearness of the television camera. However, it is used to fine purpose in at least one instance. Oberon is in the spotlight when he declares, "I am invisible." Poof! Suddenly the spotlight is switched off.
Audience: Ages 12-Adult
Distributor: Films for the Humanities & Sciences
Videocassette: $89.95

★★★★★

Mike Mulligan and His Steam Shovel
Virginia L. Burton (illus.).
Houghton Mifflin. 1939. Realistic fiction.
Mike Mulligan has not abandoned his steam shovel, despite the invention of new gas shovels. He attempts to prove

his steam shovel can dig a cellar for the Potterville town hall in one day.

Mike Mulligan and His Steam Shovel.
11 min. Color. Iconographic. Produced by Weston Woods. 1956.
The story entertains while it effectively deals with the concept of change. It ends happily as Mike meets his goal. Trapped in the cellar, the steam shovel becomes a furnace and Mike a janitor. Though faithful to the original, the film relies on the movement of only the camera and is slow paced.
Audience: Ages 4-8
Distributor: Weston Woods
16mm film: $175 **Videocassette:** $60
Rental: $25 daily

Mike Mulligan and His Steam Shovel and Other Stories.
33 min. Color. Iconographic and animated. Produced by Weston Woods. 1986.
Included in this tape anthology are adaptations of *Burt Dow: Deep-Water Man* (Robert McCloskey), *Moon Man*, and *Mike Mulligan and His Steam Shovel.* See individual titles for full descriptions.
Audience: Ages 4-8
Distributor: Children's Circle, Weston Woods
Videocassette: $19.95
No public performance rights

★★★★★

Miracle Worker
William Gibson.
Bantam. 1989. [1957]. Drama.
An account of Anne Sullivan's work with the blind and deaf child Helen Keller, this play follows the progress of teacher and student in the rebellious child's education.

Miracle Worker, The.
107 min. Black and white. Live action. Produced by United Artists/Playfilms/Fred Coe. 1962. Anne Bancroft, Patty Duke, Victor Jory, Andrew Prine.
Patty Duke plays Helen Keller and Anne Bancroft is Annie Sullivan in this best of the book's adaptations. Both stars won Oscars for their performances, which climax when Helen, forced to refill a water pitcher, finally makes the mental connection between a word and its concrete meaning.
Reviews: *New York Times*, May 24, 1962, 29:2; *Variety*, May 2, 1962
Awards: Academy Awards, Best Actress, Best Supporting Actress
Audience: Ages 10-Adult
Distributor: MGM/UA Home Video
Videocassette: $24.98
No public performance rights

Miracle Worker, The.
100 min. Color. Live action. Produced for television. 1979. Patty Duke Astin, Melissa Gilbert, Anne Seymour, Stanley Wells.
Patty Duke is Anne Sullivan in this version, which focuses on the early Sullivan-Keller encounters. The production is powerful, almost to the degree reached by the earlier version in which Patty Duke stars in the role of Helen Keller.
Audience: Ages 10-Adult
Distributor: Warner Home Video
Videocassette: $59.95
No public performance rights

★★★★★

Miss Nelson Is Missing
Harry Allard.
Houghton Mifflin. 1987. [1977]. Mystery.
Miss Nelson seems to have lost her unruly class's attention, so she disappears and is replaced by a mean substitute, Miss Swamp.

Miss Nelson Is Missing.
14 min. Color. Animated. Produced by LCA. 1979.

Young viewers are enchanted by this humorously portrayed story that is faithfully animated in the style of Henry Allard's book illustrations. As described in *Previews*, the film "retains the tongue-in-cheek humor of the book. The use of both adult and children's voices in the narration is especially effective. Children thoroughly enjoy this film."

Reviews: *Previews*, May 1980
Audience: Ages 5-11
Distributor: Coronet/MTI Film & Video
16mm film: $250 **Videocassette:** $250
Rental: $75

Fables of Harry Allard.
30 min. Color. Animation. 1979.
A home video version of two titles distributed separately by Coronet/MTI Film & Video: *Miss Nelson Is Missing* and *It's So Nice to Have a Wolf Around the House* (see above).

Distributor: New World Video
Videocassette: $14.95
No public performance rights

★★★★★

Mr. Little
Robert N. Peck.
Illustrated by Ben Stahl. Doubleday. 1979. Realistic fiction.
Unhappy with their new teacher, Drag and his friend play tricks on Mr. Little.

Joke's on Mr. Little, The.
24 min. Color. Live action. Produced by ABC Weekend Specials. 1982.
In this lively film, Drag and his friend play all the tricks on Mr. Little that students sometimes dream about but never dare to do. The show is great fun to watch; it provides an entertaining lesson in getting along with others.

Audience: Ages 8-11
Distributor: Coronet MTI
16mm film: $455 **Videocassette:** $250
Rental: $75

★★★★★

Mrs. Frisby and the Rats of NIMH
Robert C. O'Brien.
Illustrated by Zena Bernstein. Atheneum. 1971. Fantasy.
A cast of animal characters, including a crow and some super-intelligent rats, attempts to help Mrs. Frisby, a field mouse, move her home to safer ground. She, in turn, helps the rats.

Secret of NIMH, The.
84 min. Color. Animation. Produced by Don Bluth. 1982. Voices of John Carradine, Dom DeLuise, Hermione Baddeley, Derek Jacobi.
Don Bluth, a former Disney animator, produced this film as his first independent feature. The animation is exceptional, but the story drags in spots, becoming dark and somber. There is a fine musical score by Jerry Goldsmith, the crow is quite comical, and the character voices are enchanting, yet the film as a whole remains episodic and uninvolving.

Reviews: *New York Times*, July 30, 1982, C12:5; *Variety*, June 16, 1982
Audience: Ages 8-12
Distributor: MGM/UA Home Video
Videocassette: $19.98
No public performance rights

Secret of NIMH, The.
85 min. Color. Animation. 1982.
A laser disc version of the same title offered by MGM/UA Home Video (see above).

Distributor: Pioneer LDCA, Inc.
Laser disc: CLV format $24.98

No public performance rights

★★★★★

Moby Dick
Herman Melville.

Multiple editions. Adventure.

A whaleboat captain excites his crew into mounting a running battle with a great white whale. The captain seeks revenge on the whale, who previously cost him a leg.

Moby Dick.
116 min. Color. Live action. Produced by MGM/John Huston. 1956. Harry Andrews, Richard Basehart, Bernard Miles, Gregory Peck, Orson Welles.
John Huston and Ray Bradbury wrote a script that plays a bit unevenly in this adaptation of the classic book, which casts Gregory Peck as Captain Ahab. The result is a sporadically good production and a reasonably honest adaptation that is quite faithful to the details of whaling.
Reviews: *New York Times*, July 5, 1956, 18:1; *Variety*, June 27, 1956
Audience: Ages 14-Adult
Distributor: MGM/UA Home Video
Videocassette: $19.98
No public performance rights

★★★★★

"Molly Morgan"
John Steinbeck.

Anthologized in *The Portable Steinbeck*. Viking Penguin. 1971. Short stories—realistic fiction.

A pretty young school teacher takes a job in a central California town, winning over the townspeople with her diplomacy and intelligence. Haunted by the thought that a local drunk may be her shiftless but endearing father, she suddenly leaves.

Molly Morgan.
32 min. Color. Live action. Produced by Mac and Ava Motion Pictures. 1990.
Fine performances in this slice-of-life adaptation draw viewers into the story. The schoolteacher moves in with a warm family, whose characters contrast sharply with her own family, which we catch glimpses of in the production. Tasteful and well-acted, the film tells a personal story about inner conflict (between an imagined and a real father), at the same time capturing some California social history.
Audience: Ages 14-Adult
Distributor: Pyramid Film & Video
16mm film: $550 **Videocassette:** $395
Rental: $95

★★★★★

Molly's Pilgrim
Barbara Cohen.

Illustrated by Michael J. Deraney. Lothrop, Lee & Shepard. 1983. Realistic fiction.

A young Russian Jewish immigrant to the United States has difficulty adjusting to school life until she presents a report about the Pilgrims.

Molly's Pilgrim.
24 min. Color. Live action. Produced by Jeff Brown and Chris Pelzer. 1985.
This outstanding film has won awards for excellence both in film quality and as a children's story about the difficulties of accepting differences.
Reviews: *Booklist*, Feb. l, 1986; *Library Journal*, Oct. 15, 1986; *School Library Journal*, Mar. 1986
Awards: Blue Ribbon, American Film Festival; CINE Golden Eagle
Audience: Ages 6-12
Distributor: Phoenix/BFA Films & Video
16mm film: $535 **Videocassette:** $325
Rental: $50

★★★★★

Momataro, or Peach Boy

Multiple editions. Folklore and fairy tales.
An old woodcutter and his wife, who are childless, discover a boy inside of a giant peach. The boy grows quickly into a very strong young man and informs his parents that he must be off to fight the ogres that plague their land.

Peach Boy.
30 min. Color. Limited animation. Produced by Rabbit Ears. 1991. Narrated by Sigourney Weaver.
Soft watercolors fill the line drawings that illustrate this tale of the Japanese folk hero Momataro. A peasant woman doing laundry in a stream finds a huge peach that contains a boy. The boy grows into a young man, then sets out on a dangerous journey. Along the way he is joined by a pheasant, a dog, and an ape, who quarrel until their real enemies—the ogres—are encountered. Smith's watercolors brighten in tone when the clash between Momataro and the ogres begins.

Reviews: *Booklist*, June 15, 1991
Audience: Ages 4-10
Distributor: Uni Distribution Corp.
Videocassette: $9.95

★★★★★

"Monkey's Paw, The"
W. W. Jacobs.

Anthologized in *The Oxford Book of English Ghost Stories.* Oxford University Press. 1987. Short stories—horror.
A family who has lost a son is visited by an old shipmate who has a magical monkey's paw. The visit results in tragedy.

Monkey's Paw, The.
19 min. Color. Live action. Produced by Martha Moran. 1978.
Martha Moran has demonstrated top-quality sensitivity to the medium in this good production of the mystery-filled story.

Audience: Ages 14-17
Distributor: Phoenix/BFA Films & Video
16mm film: $425 **Videocassette:** $250
Rental: $60

Monkey's Paw, The.
27 min. Color. Live action. Produced by Stillife-Gryphon Films/LCA. 1983.
Augmented by trivial dialog, this is a slow telling of the frightening story. The acting appears less than perfect and scenes in which the magical monkey's paw are introduced inspire revulsion rather than awe.

Audience: Ages 14-17
Distributor: Coronet/MTI Film & Video
16mm film: $550 **Videocassette:** $250
Rental: $75

★★★★★

Moon Man
Tomi Ungerer (illus.).

Harper & Row Junior Books. 1967. Fantasy.
The moon wants to have fun, so it catches a shooting star and has some exciting experiences on Earth.

Moon Man.
8 min. Color. Animated. Produced by Weston Woods. 1981.
Against a background of jazz-style music, the film portrays the moon in motion: escaping from jail on earth, dancing, riding a rocket homeward. Animation enlivens the zesty tale. It is episodic, however, and somewhat slowly paced. As described in *Horn Book*, these features contribute to making the show "a mood piece that combines the liveliness

of Ungerer's drawings with imaginative filmmaking."

Reviews: *Horn Book*, Oct. 1981
Awards: Silver Award, Houston International Film Festival
Audience: Ages 4-8
Distributor: Weston Woods
16mm film: $195 **Videocassette:** $60
Rental: $20 daily

Mike Mulligan and His Steam Shovel and Other Stories.
33 min. Color. Iconographic and animated. Produced by Weston Woods. 1986.
Included in this tape anthology are adaptations of *Burt Dow: Deep-Water Man* (Robert McCloskey), *Moon Man*, and *Mike Mulligan and His Steam Shovel*. See individual titles for full descriptions.

Audience: Ages 4-12
Distributor: Children's Circle, Weston Woods
Videocassette: $19.95
No public performance rights

★★★★★

Morris Goes to School
Bernard Wiseman (illus.).
Harper & Row Junior Books. 1970. Humor.
In this comical tale, a moose named Morris experiences the thrills of learning the alphabet, counting, singing, spelling and so on. The idea of a moose going to school poses problems and opportunities that inspire laughter.

Morris Goes to School.
14.5 min. Color. Puppet animation. Produced by George McQuilkin. 1988.
This is joyous entertainment with an informational edge, a celebration of the rewards in learning. In vivid, three-dimensional animation, the motion picture remains true to the original storybook but adds elements—for example, a song about "feeding your brain" instead of watching television all day.

Reviews: *Booklist*, Apr. 1, 1989
Awards: CINE Golden Eagle Award
Audience: Ages 4-7
Distributor: Churchill Media
16mm film: $405 **Videocassette:** $305
Rental: $60

★★★★★

Morris's Disappearing Bag: A Christmas Story
Rosemary Wells (illus.).
Dial Press. 1975. Fantasy.
On Christmas Day, Morris the Rabbit is left out of the fun as his family trades toys until he makes use of the most interesting toy of all—a disappearing bag.

Morris's Disappearing Bag.
6 min. Color. Animated. Produced by Weston Woods. 1982.
This show has all the elements of appeal for the very young, from toys to feeling left out to a film finely paced for interest and understanding. As stated in *Horn Book*, "the spirit and the humor of the original come through."

Reviews: *Booklist*, Mar. 1, 1983; *Horn Book*, Apr. 1983; *School Library Journal*, May 1983
Awards: ALA Notable Film; Grand Prize, ASIFA Film Festival; First Prize, Birmingham International Film Festival; CINE Golden Eagle
Audience: Ages 4-6
Distributor: Weston Woods
16mm film: $195 **Videocassette:** $60
Rental: $20 daily

Christmas Stories.
30 min. Color. Iconographic and animated. Produced by Weston Woods. 1986.

Included in this tape anthology are adaptations of *Morris's Disappearing Bag* (Rosemary Wells), *The Clown of God* (Tomie de Paola), *The Little Drummer Boy* (Katherine Davis, Henry Onrati, and Harry Simeone), and *The Twelve Days of Christmas* (Robert Broomfield).

Audience: Ages 4-Adult
Distributor: Children's Circle, Weston Woods
Videocassette: $19.95
No public performance rights

★★★★★

Morte D'Arthur
Sir Thomas Malory.

Multiple editions. Adventure; romance.
Arthur becomes King of England, protects his realm with the help of the hundred knights of his round table and, at his death, orders that the sword symbolizing his power be thrown into the lake.

Knights of the Round Table.
115 min. Color. Live action. Produced by MGM/Pandro S. Berman. 1953. Robert Taylor, Ava Gardner, Mel Ferrer.
Lancelot, who was banished due to his love for the King's wife, Guinevere, returns to do battle in a version that frequently digresses from the progression of events in the novel.

Reviews: *New York Times*, Jan. 8, 1954, 17:2; *Variety*, Dec. 23, 1953
Audience: Ages 12-Adult
Distributor: MGM/UA Home Video
Videocassette: $19.98
No public performance rights

Knights of the Round Table.
116 min. Color. Live action. 1953. Robert Taylor, Ava Gardner, Mel Ferrer.
A laser disc version of the same title offered by MGM/UA Home Video (see above).

Distributor: Pioneer LDCA, Inc.
Laser disc: CLV format $34.98
No public performance rights

★★★★★

Most Wonderful Egg in the World, The
Helme Heine (illus.).

Atheneum. 1983. Fantasy.
Three hens quarrel about who is most beautiful, and a king settles the matter. Contending that what a hen can do is more important than how she looks, he devises a contest to see who can lay the most wonderful egg.

Most Wonderful Egg in the World, The.
6 min. Color. Animated. Produced by Weston Woods. 1986.
Entertaining and well-paced, this motion picture features appealing, watercolor style characters. The king promises to make a princess of whichever hen lays the most wonderful egg, but each lays a wonderful one in her own way. His majesty solves the problem this poses in a kingly fashion.

Reviews: *Booklist*, Apr. 15, 1987; *School Library Journal*, Sept. 1987
Awards: CINE Golden Eagle; Chris Statuette, Columbus International Film Festival
Audience: Ages 4-8
Distributor: Weston Woods
16mm film: $175 **Videocassette:** $60
Rental: $20 daily

Joey Runs Away and Other Stories.
24 min. Color. Iconographic and animated. Produced by Weston Woods. 1989.
Included in this tape anthology are adaptations of *Joey Runs Away* (Jack Kent), *The Most Wonderful Egg in the World* (Helme Heine), *The Cow Who Fell into the Canal* (Phyllis Krasilovsky), and *The Bear and the Fly* (Paula Winter). See individual titles for full descriptions.

Audience: Ages 4-8
Distributor: Children's Circle, Weston Woods
Videocassette: $19.95
No public performance rights

★★★★★

Mother Goose Nursery Rhymes.
Multiple editions. Folklore and fairy tales.
Mother Goose verses include Little Miss Muffet, Queen of Hearts, Humpty Dumpty, Old Mother Hubbard, and other lesser known stories in rhyme.

Mother Goose Stories.
11 min. Color. Animation. Produced by Ray Harryhausen. 1961.
Mother Goose comes alive from the storybook to magically conjure up a few of the traditional rhymes. Though not how the rhymes are introduced in print, the vehicle is an excellent way to tell stories like Little Miss Muffet, The Queen of Hearts, Humpty Dumpty, and Old Mother Hubbard on screen.
Audience: Ages 5-8
Distributor: Phoenix/BFA Films & Video
16mm film: $220 **Videocassette:** $125
Rental: $28

Songs from Mother Goose.
30 min. Color. Animated.
Mother Goose shows viewers her book and the characters come to life as the pages turn in this entertaining edition of Mother Goose stories. The tales are well—if not fully—animated.
Audience: Ages 4-6
Distributor: Golden Book Video
Videocassette: $9.95
No public performance rights

★★★★★

Mouse and the Motorcycle, The
Beverly Cleary.
Illustrated by Louis Darling. William Morrow and Co. 1965. Fantasy.
Learning to ride a boy's toy motorcycle, a mouse zips through the hotel in which he lives. The mouse comes to the boy's rescue in a time of need and is rewarded by the boy's letting him keep the toy motorcycle.

Mouse and the Motorcycle, The.
41 min. Color. Live action and puppet animation. Produced by Churchill Films. 1987. Ray Walston.
Combining live action with lifelike, three-dimensional animation, this is a humorously entertaining motion picture that faithfully portrays the book. The squeaky mouse voices are occasionally indistinct but overall the adaptation is superb.
Reviews: *Booklist*, Sept. 1, 1989; *Instructor*, Apr. 1988; *Video Librarian*, Aug. 1987
Awards: ALA Notable Children's Film; Chicago International Festival of Children's Films; CINE Golden Eagle; Silver Apple, National Educational Film and Video Festival; Ollie Award; Peabody Award
Audience: Ages 4-7
Distributor: Churchill Films
16mm film: $495 Video: $79 **Rental:** $75

Mouse and the Motorcycle, The.
41 min. Color. Animation. 1987. Ray Walston.
A home video version of the same title distributed by Churchill Media (see above).
Distributor: Strand VCI
Videocassette: $12.98
No public performance rights

Mouse and the Motorcycle, The (Special Edition).
90 min. Color. Animation. 1991. Ray Walston.
A home video version of two separate titles, *The Mouse and the Motorcycle* and *Runaway Ralph*, distributed by Churchill Media (see above).
Distributor: Strand VCI
Videocassette: $24.95
No public performance rights

★★★★★

Mufaro's Beautiful Daughters: An African Tale
John Steptoe (illus.).
Lothrop, Lee & Shepard. 1987. Folklore and fairy tales.
Set in Africa, this tale concerns a father whose daughters (one bad-tempered, the other good-natured) compete to become wife to a great king.

Mufaro's Beautiful Daughters.
14 min. Color. Iconographic. Produced by Weston Woods. 1989. Narrated by Terry Alexander.
Speaking clearly, the narrator adds an air of authenticity to the tale through his African accent. The kind daughter befriends a garden snake/hungry boy/old woman (the king in disguise). In the end, her haughty sister becomes her servant. The camera, not the characters, moves, yet the pictures, events, and pacing result in a lively production.
Audience: Ages 4-8
Distributor: Weston Woods
16mm film: $245 **Videocassette:** $120
Rental: $25 daily

★★★★★

"Murderer, The"
Ray Bradbury.
Anthologized in *The Stories of Ray Bradbury.* Knopf. 1980. Short stories—science fiction.
A young man, weary of electronic communication devices, decides to "murder" them by turning them off.

The Murderer.
28 min. Color. Live action. Produced by Andrew Silver. 1976.
Here is a nice workmanlike adaptation of one of Ray Bradbury's futuristic and, in this case, comic stories.
Audience: Ages 14-18
Distributor: Phoenix/BFA Films & Video
16mm film: $500 **Videocassette:** $300
Rental: $40

★★★★★

Mutiny on the Bounty
Charles Nordhoff and James N. Hall.
Little, Brown & Co. 1932. Historical fiction.
A crew of English sailors voyaging in the South Seas mutiny against a cruel captain, and the few who are loyal to him must share the fate of the mutineers.

Mutiny on the Bounty.
135 min. Black and white. Live action. Produced by MGM/Irving Thalberg, Albert Lewin. 1935. Clark Gable, Charles Laughton, Franchot Tone.
Laughton shines as the tyrant Captain Bligh, while Gable convincingly stages the mutiny in this adventure thriller of a novel based on actual fact. Though the mutineers cast off their captain in a tiny boat over three thousand miles from the nearest shore, he survives to wreak revenge.
Reviews: *New York Times,* Nov. 9, 1935, 19:2; *Variety,* Nov. 13, 1935
Awards: Academy Award, Best Picture
Audience: Ages 16-Adult
Distributor: MGM/UA Home Video

Videocassette: $19.98
No public performance rights

Mutiny on the Bounty.
185 min. Color. Live action. Produced by Arcola/Aaron Rosenberg. 1962. Trevor Howard, Marlon Brando, Richard Harris.
This pales next to the 1935 version, though the visual footage is highly pleasing. The film changes story details, portraying Christian as a dandy, not confining him to the ship when it lands in Tahiti but ordering him to go ashore, and having him die rather than keeping him alive after the mutineers settle on the island.
Reviews: *New York Times*, Nov. 9, 1962, 31:2; *Variety*, Nov. 14, 1962
Audience: Ages 16-Adult
Distributor: MGM/UA Home Video
Videocassette: $29.98
No public performance rights

Mutiny on the Bounty.
186 min. Color. Live action. 1962. Trevor Howard, Marlon Brando, Richard Harris.
A laser disc version of the 1962 remake of the same title offered by MGM/UA Home Video (see above).
Distributor: Pioneer LCDA, Inc.
Laser disc: CLV format $39.98, widescreen CLV format $39.98
No public performance rights

★★★★★

My Dancing White Horses
Alois Podharsky.
Translated from the German by Frances Hogarthe-Gaute.
Holt, Rinehart & Winston. 1955. Biography.
As World War II draws to an end, the owner of some famed Lipizzan stallions evacuates the horses to safety in Switzerland, along with a group of war refugees. Helped by several riding school students, they travel through difficult terrain, managing to evade capture.

Miracle of the White Stallions, The.
92 min. Color. Live action. Produced by Peter V. Harold/Walt Disney. 1963. Robert Taylor, Eddie Albert, James Franciscus.
This is a true story and the film has been faithfully adapted from the book. The book, however, is not a spellbinder and the film is relatively talky, slow-moving, and dull. Still, it has appeal for horse-lovers over age ten.
Reviews: *New York Times*, May 23, 1963
Audience: Ages 10-Adult
Distributor: Buena Vista Home Video (not currently in distribution)

★★★★★

"My Dear Uncle Sherlock"
Hugh Pentacost.
Anthologized in *Handle with Care*, edited by J. Kahn. Greenwillow. 1985. Short stories—mystery.
A boy, who shares with his uncle an interest in sleuthing, gets a chance to try detective work when a neighbor is robbed.

My Dear Uncle Sherlock.
24 min. Color. Live action. Produced by ABC Video. 1977. Robbie Rest, Royal Dare, John Carter, John Milford.
The special feelings of an uncle and nephew for each other bridge the generation gap and make this a warm and interesting detective story with a message: it pays to get involved with another's difficulties.
Audience: Ages 8-12
Distributor: Coronet/MTI Film & Video

16mm film: $455 **Videocassette:** $250
Rental: $75

★★★★★

My Friend Flicka
Mary O'Hara.
Harper & Row. 1973. [1941]. Realistic fiction.
A young boy chooses for his own a colt whose mother is a hard-to-handle mare. With work and determination, he trains the colt and it grows into an exceptional mare and friend.

My Friend Flicka.
89 min. Color. Live action. Produced by Ralph Dietrich/Twentieth Century Fox. 1943. Roddy McDowall, Preston Foster, Rita Johnson.
A fine adaptation that touches the heart, the film has held its impact over time. The boy's hard work with the colt pays off, imparting a lesson without being heavy handed. Meanwhile, the footage captures the splendor of the Rocky Mountains.
Reviews: *New York Times*, May 27, 1943, 21:4; *Variety*, Apr. 7, 1943
Audience: Ages 10-14
Distributor: Fox Video
Videocassette: $14.98
No public performance rights

★★★★★

My Grandson Lew
Charlotte Zolotow.
Illustrated by William Pène Du Bois. Harper & Row. 1974. Realistic fiction.
A boy with only distant memories talks with his mother about how he misses his grandfather's visits. Only then does he learn that his grandfather is dead.

My Grandson Lew.
13 min. Color. Live Action. Produced by Donald MacDonald. 1976.
An excellently performed adaptation of one of Charlotte Zolotow's best works, this film has earned two top awards for nontheatrical films. It is one of the finest films among those that deal with the difficult subject of death.
Awards: CINE Golden Eagle; Best of the Year, *Learning* Magazine
Audience: Ages 6-12
Distributor: Barr Films
16mm film: $270 **Videocassette:** $190
Rental: $50

★★★★★

My Mother Is the Most Beautiful Woman in the World
Becky Rehyer.
Illustrated by Ruth Gannett. Lothrop, Lee & Shephard. 1945. Folklore and fairy tales.
In the milling throng of wheat harvesters, a young girl loses her mother and cannot describe her except to say that she is the most beautiful woman of all. The Russian folktale climaxes when a particularly ugly woman claims the child, conveying the idea that beauty is in the eye of the beholder.

My Mother Is the Most Beautiful Woman in the World.
9 min. Color. Animation. Produced by Bosustow. 1968.
This is a sensitive rendering of a story about a girl who has lost her mother, and identifies her only as the most beautiful woman in the world. The limited animation is the only deterrent to an excellent film.
Audience: Ages 5-9
Distributor: Phoenix/BFA Films & Video
16mm film: $180 **Videocassette:** $110
Rental: $25

★★★★★

"My Old Man"
Ernest Hemingway.
Anthologized in *The Complete Short Stories of Ernest Hemingway*. Scribner. 1987. Short stories—realistic fiction.
A young boy recounts his days with his father, who rode horses as a jockey. In the process, he reveals the crooked nature of the horse races and his deep affection for his honorable father.

My Old Man.
27 min. Color. Live action. Produced by Larry Yust with Clifton Fadiman. 1969.
Like the story, this dramatization is told from the first-person viewpoint of the young boy. It presents exciting footage of horse races, life in Paris at sidewalk cafes, and the tender feeling between father and son, while raising the moral issue of fixed races. The film triumphs as a Hemingway adaptation.
Reviews: *Scholastic Teacher*, Nov. 2, 1970
Audience: Ages 12-Adult
Distributor: Britannica
16mm film: $680 **Videocassette:** $300
Rental: $18 Penn State University

My Old Man (and Discussion).
38 min. Color. Live action. 1969.
A laser disc version of the same title also distributed by Britannica (see above). Added to this version is the separate Britannica title *A Discussion of My Old Man.*
Distributor: Britannica
Laser disc: CAV format $129

★★★★★

My Side of the Mountain
Jean Craighead George (illus.).
Dutton. 1960. [1959]. Realistic fiction.
A thirteen-year-old boy runs away from home to explore the wilderness of the Canadian Rockies.

My Side of the Mountain.
100 min. Color. Live action. Produced by Paramount/Robert B. Radnitz. 1969. Theodore Bikel, Peggi Loder.
A fine film for young audiences, this production features a simple script and good performances by the central actors.
Reviews: *New York Times*, June 26, 1969, 44:2; *Variety*, Feb. 26, 1969
Audience: Ages 8-12
Distributor: Paramount Home Video
Videocassette available
No public performance rights

★★★★★

"Myra Meets His Family"
F. Scott Fitzgerald.
Anthologized in *The Price Was High: The Last Uncollected Stories of F. Scott Fitzgerald*, edited by Matthew J. Bruccoli. Harcourt Brace Jovanovich. 1979. Short stories—realistic fiction.
A young, money-hungry husband seeker finds herself an eligible victim. After learning of her reputation, he tricks her out of wanting to be his wife. She learns of his duplicity and cleverly turns the tables on him.

Under the Biltmore Clock.
70 min. Color. Live action. Rubicon Film Productions. 1984. Lenny Von Dohlen, Barnard Hughes, Sean Young.
The adaptation conveys events in the narrative without capturing the depth of Fitzgerald's writing.
Audience: Ages 14-Adult
Distributor: Coronet/MTI Film & Video

Videocassette: $125 **Rental:** $75

Under the Biltmore Clock.
70 min. Color. Live action. 1984. Lenny Von Dohlen, Barnard Hughes, Sean Young.
A home video version of the same title distributed by Coronet/MTI Film & Video (see above).
Distributor: New Line Home Video
Videocassette: $19.95
No public performance rights

Under the Biltmore Clock.
70 min. Color. Live action. 1984. Lenny Von Dohlen, Barnard Hughes, Sean Young.
A laser disc version of the same title offered by Coronet/MTI (see above).
Distributor: Pioneer LDCA, Inc.
Laser disc: CLV format $34.98
No public performance rights

★★★★★

Mysterious Island
Jules Verne.
Multiple editions. Science fiction.
Three Union soldiers and others escape the Civil War's siege of Richmond in a balloon and set down on an island in the South Seas. There they meet some unexpected creatures.

Mysterious Island.
101 min. Color. Live action. Produced by Ameran Films/Columbia. 1961. Joan Greenwood, Michael Craig, Herbert Lom, Michael Callan.
The adventure is lively enough, and the monsters have young audience appeal.
Reviews: *New York Times*, Dec. 21, 1961, 30:6: *Variety*, Dec. 13, 1961
Audience: Ages 12-Adult
Distributor: Columbia TriStar Home Video
Videocassette: $19.95
No public performance rights

★★★★★

Mysterious Tadpole, The
Steven Kellogg (illus.).
Dial. 1977. Fantasy.
Uncle McAllister sends Louis a mysterious gift from Loch Ness, Scotland. What is so mysterious about a tadpole? This one grows so enormous that Louis can't find a home for it until the day it retrieves a sunken treasure.

Mysterious Tadpole, The.
9 min. Color. Animated. Produced by Michael Sporn.
This well-paced animated version progresses from one humorous detail to the next. The tadpole/monster grows too big for the bathtub and moves to a local swimming pool. Finally, he "earns his own keep" by retrieving a treasure in the harbor.
Reviews: *Booklist*, Apr. 15, 1987; *School Library Journal*, June/July 1987
Awards: CINE Golden Eagle; Chris Plaque, Columbus International Film Festival
Audience: Ages 4-8
Distributor: Weston Woods
16mm film: $215 **Videocassette:** $110
Rental: $20 daily

Mysterious Tadpole and Other Stories, The.
34 min. Color. Animated and Iconographic. Produced by Weston Woods. 1989.
Included in this tape anthology are adaptations of *The Mysterious Tadpole* (Steven Kellogg), *The Five Chinese Brothers* (Claire Bishop), *Jonah and the Great Fish* (Warwick Hutton), and *The*

Wizard (Jack Kent). See individual titles for full descriptions.
Reviews: *Children's Video Report*, Feb./Mar. 1989
Audience: Ages 4-8
Distributor: Children's Circle, Weston Woods
Videocassette: $19.95
No public performance rights

N

adherence to book **film rating**

Nannabah's Friend
Mary Perinne.
Illustrated by Leonard Weisgard. Houghton Mifflin. 1989. [1970]. Realistic fiction.
Nannabah, a young Navajo shepherdess, recalls a time of loneliness, then chances upon another Navajo girl playing with miniature hogans for dolls. Created by Nannabah, the hogans are a link, and the two girls become friends.

Girl of the Navajos.
15 min. Color. Live action. Produced by Coronet. 1977.
The film, unlike the book, does not make clear the fact that Nannabah created the toys with which the other Navajo girl is playing. Still, this is a well-done motion picture that illustrates Navajo life for young viewers.
Audience: Ages 6-10
Distributor: Coronet/MTI Film & Video
Videocassette: $250 **Rental:** $75

★★★★★

Napping House, The
Audrey Wood.
Illustrated by Don Wood. Harcourt Brace Jovanovich. 1984. Humor.
This is a cumulative tale about a mound of sleepers—on top of granny is a child, then a dog, then a cat, then a mouse, then a troublemaking flea that disrupts them all.

Napping House, The.
5 min. Color. Iconographic. Produced by Weston Woods. 1985. Narrated by Melissa Leebaert.
In keeping with the storybook, the film is short and its brevity sustains the visual, iconographic technique in which only the camera moves. The narration is superb. Illustrations, adapted from the storybook, feature cool colors giving way to warm ones as the sleepers awaken.
Audience: Ages 4-6
Distributor: Weston Woods
16mm film: $115 **Videocassette:** $60
Rental: $15 daily

Happy Birthday Moon and Other Stories.
30 min. Color. Animated and iconographic. Produced by Weston Woods.
Included in this tape anthology are adaptations of *Happy Birthday, Moon* (Frank Asch), *Peter's Chair* (Ezra Jack Keats), *The Napping House* (Audrey Wood), *The Three Little Pigs* (Erik Blegvad), and *The Owl and the Pussy-Cat* (Edward Lear). See individual titles for full descriptions.
Reviews: *Children's Video Report,*

Feb./Mar. 1989
Audience: Ages 4-8
Distributor: Children's Circle, Weston Woods
Videocassette: $19.95
No public performance rights

★★★★★

Nate the Great and the Sticky Case
Marjorie Weinman Sharmat.
Illustrated by Marc Simont. Coward, McCann & Geoghegan. 1978. Mystery.
Nate, the great child detective, solves the case of his friend's missing dinosaur stamp.

Nate the Great and the Sticky Case.
19 min. Color. Live action. Produced by Paul Buchbinder. 1983.
After a brief, stilted start, this adaptation warms up into a mostly natural, endearing rendition that captures the mystery-solving character with a touch of humor that is well-suited to the books starring Nate the Great.
Audience: Ages 6-10
Distributor: Britannica
16mm film: $525 **Videocassette:** $300

★★★★★

Nate the Great Goes Undercover
Marjorie Weinman Sharmat.
Illustrated by Marc Simont. Putnam. 1974. Mystery.
In his first night case, Nate the Great tackles the mystery of the neighborhood garbage snatcher.

Nate the Great Goes Undercover.
10 min. Color. Animated. Produced by Nick Bosustow and Mitch Seltzer. 1978.
While the film is an accurate rendition of the garbage-can mystery, the humor and charm of the story seem better suited to the print medium.
Audience: Ages 5-10
Distributor: Churchill Media
16mm film: $240 **Rental:** $60

★★★★★

National Velvet
Eric Bagnold.
Multiple editions. Adventure.
An English girl wins a spirited horse in a lottery and decides to race it in the Grand National Steeplechase, a competition barred to female riders.

National Velvet.
125 min. Color. Live action. Produced by MGM. 1944. Mickey Rooney, Donald Crisp, Elizabeth Taylor, Anne Revere, Angela Lansbury.
Velvet Brown (Elizabeth Taylor) overcomes one obstacle after another, reaching her goal in fine style. The performances, along with an outstanding horse-racing sequence, contributed to the highly successful release of a film that has lost some of its impact over time.
Reviews: *New York Times*, Dec. 15, 1944, 25:2; *Variety*, Dec. 6, 1944
Awards: Academy Award, Best Supporting Actress
Audience: Ages 10-Adult
Distributor: MGM/UA Home Video
Videocassette: $19.98
No public performance rights

National Velvet.
124 min. Color. Live action. 1944. Elizabeth Taylor, Mickey Rooney.
A laser disc version of the same title offered by MGM/UA Home Video (see above).
Distributor: Pioneer LDCA, Inc.
Laser disc: CLV format $39.98
No public performance rights

★★★★★

Native Son
Richard Wright.
Harper & Row. 1940. Realistic fiction.
A poor, embittered twenty-year-old black man in Chicago during the 1930s accidentally suffocates his white employer's daughter. After a harrowing chase, he is caught and tried for the crime.

Native Son.
91 min. Black and white. Live action. Produced by James Prades and Michael Terr. 1950. Richard Wright, Jean Wallace, Gloria Madison, Nicholas Joy.
The low-budget adaptation offers an adequate dramatization of the plot. More natural than the later version, it still does not capture the depth of the novel. The production, which includes a narrator as well as actors, is not continually involving.
Audience: Ages 12-Adult
Distributor: International Film Forum
Videocassette: $39.95
No public performance rights

Native Son.
111 min. Color. Live action. Produced by Diana Silver Productions. 1986. Carroll Baker, Akosuwa Busia, Matt Dillon, Art Evans, Elizabeth McGovern, Geraldine Page.
The adaptation is too slow moving to be as powerful as the novel it portrays. Though the film tones down some aspects of the novel, it remains faithful to the basic story line.
Audience: Ages 12-Adult
Distributor: Vestron Video
Videocassette: $79.98
No public performance rights

★★★★★

Natural, The
Bernard Malamud.
Farrar, Straus & Giroux. 1961. [1952]. Realistic fiction.
A baseball player's career is stopped short by a bullet. Over a decade later he makes a comeback, despite his old injury, going on to win the World Series and his first love.

Natural, The.
137 min. Color. Live action. Produced by Tri-Star/Mark Johnson. 1984. Robert Redford, Robert Duvall, Glenn Close, Kim Basinger.
The production is uneven, but has appealing moments. It adapts selectively from Malamud's novel, achieving a more neatly packaged effect than the original, explaining matters the novel leaves open-ended.
Reviews: *New York Times*, May 11, 1984, C15:1
Audience: Ages 14-Adult
Distributor: Columbia TriStar Home Video
Videocassette: $19.95
No public performance rights

Natural, The.
134 min. Color. Live action. 1984. Robert Redford, Robert Duvall, Glenn Close, Kim Basinger.
A laser disc version of the same title offered by Columbia TriStar Home Video (see above).
Distributor: Pioneer LDCA, Inc.
Laser disc: CLV format $39.95
No public performance rights

★★★★★

Necessary Parties
Barbara Dana.

Harper & Row. 1986. Realistic fiction.
Teenager Chris decides to sue his parents after they announce their intentions to end their seventeen-year marriage.

Necessary Parties.
109 min. Color. Live action. Produced by Otto Salamon/WonderWorks. 1990. Alan Arkin, Barbara Dana, Julie Hagerty.
Author Barbara Dana also wrote the screenplay and acted with her husband Alan Arkin (who plays an eccentric, caring attorney) in this comically tender, superb drama that is true to the novel on which it is based.

Reviews: *Booklist*, Nov. 15, 1990; *Variety*, Nov. 23, 1988
Audience: Ages 11-Adult
Distributor: Public Media Video Video
Videocassette: $29.95

★★★★★

Never Cry Wolf
Farley Mowat.

Little Brown & Co. 1963. Nonfiction.
A man is left "alone" in the Arctic to study the behavior of wild wolves. He indeed finds himself alone, except for the company of native travelers.

Never Cry Wolf.
105 min. Color. Live action. 1983. Charles Martin Smith.
The production has some engrossing moments in the course of the scientist's relationship with the wolves. Comic touches occur during, for example, his eating mice to better understand the wolves. From the Arctic experience, which is based on an actual trip by the author Farley Mowat, the scientist comes to better understand himself.

Reviews: *Christian Century*, Feb. 29, 1984; *Commonweal*, Jan. 27, 1984
Audience: Ages 8-Adult
Distributor: Buena Vista Home Video (not currently in distribution)

Never Cry Wolf.
30 min. Color. Live action. Produced by Disney Educational Productions. 1984.
Feature films can often be shortened with little loss, or even some improvement, to the dramatization. This is one adaptation of a feature film based on a book that appears to have been improved in the cutting. The incident of the scientist's eating the mice is absent from this version.

Reviews: *Christian Century*, Feb. 29, 1984; *Commonweal*, Jan. 27, 1984
Audience: Ages 8-Adult
Distributor: Coronet/MTI Film & Video
16mm film: $630 **Videocassette:** $250
Rental: $75

★★★★★

Nicholas Nickleby
Charles Dickens.

Multiple editions. Realistic fiction.
Working at a cruelly run boarding school in Victorian England, Nicholas Nickleby loses his place when he intervenes on behalf of a student. Nicholas later becomes an actor, then a merchant, while struggling to save his family from an evil uncle.

Nicholas Nickleby.
106 min. Black and white. Live action. Produced by Ealing/John Groydon. 1947. Derek Bond, Cedric Hardwicke, Alfred Drayton, Sybil Thorndike.
The motion picture captures the spirit of the novel, though it does not adapt the work in its entirety. Some of the dramatic impact is lost in this translation to the screen.

Reviews: *New York Times*, Dec. 1, 1947, 27:2; *Variety*, Mar. 26, 1947

Audience: Ages 14-Adult
Distributor: Janus Films
Videocassette: $88

Nicholas Nickleby.
106 min. Black and white. Live action. Produced by Ealing/John Croydon. 1947. Derek Bond, Cedric Hardwicke, Alfred Drayton, Sybil Thorndike.
A home video version of the same title distributed by Janus Films (see above).
Distributor: HBO Video
Videocassette: $69.99
No public performance rights

★★★★★

Night Swimmers, The
Betsy Byars.
Illustrated by Troy Howell. Delacorte. 1980. Realistic fiction.
Pressed into housekeeping and brother tending when her mother dies, a teenage girl experiences frustration despite her attempts to follow her mother's management style.

Daddy, I'm Their Mama Now.
26 min. Color. Live action. A Disney Educational Production. 1984. Martin Tabor.
This is a well-done adaptation of the Betsy Byars book and a sensitive film about the relationships in a broken family.
Audience: Ages 12-Adult
Distributor: Coronet/MTI Film & Video
16mm film: $600 **Videocassette:** $450
Rental: $75

★★★★★

Night the Ghost Got In, The
James Thurber.
Creative Education. 1983. Short stories—humor.
A man taking a bath thinks he hears an unusual noise. His reaction sets off a series of hilarious events.

James Thurber's The Night the Ghost Got In.
16 min. Color. Live action. Produced by James Stitzel. 1976.
A little unevenly dramatized, this is still an audience-gripping film about an overactive imagination and its comical outcomes.
Audience: Ages 10-17
Distributor: Phoenix/BFA Films & Video
16mm film: $345 **Videocassette:** $200
Rental: $48

★★★★★

Night to Remember, A
Walter Lord.
Holt, Rinehart, and Winston. 1955. Nonfiction.
A passenger ship runs into an iceberg and begins to sink. The passengers and crew react to the sinking in highly individual ways.

Night to Remember, A.
123 min. Color. Live action. Produced by Rank. 1958. Kenneth More, Honor Blackman, Michael Goodliffe.
Produced in documentary style, this is a detailed account of the sinking of the Titanic. The disaster is told from the point of view of the second officer with sequences on various passengers.
Reviews: *Variety*, July 9, 1958
Audience: Ages 10-Adult
Distributor: Paramount Home Video
Videocassette available
No public performance rights

★★★★★

Nightingale, The
Hans Christian Andersen.

Multiple editions. Folklore and fairy tales.

A real nightingale amazes the emperor of China with its wondrous voice. When a jeweled, artificial songbird is favored at court, the real nightingale flies back to freedom. The artificial bird breaks down and the emperor, on his death bed, is revived by the return of the real nightingale.

Nightingale, The (Faerie Tale Theatre).
54 min. Color. Live action. Produced by Shelley Duvall. 1983. Mick Jagger, Bud Cort, Barbara Hershey.

Like most other Faerie Tale Theatre shows, this one opens with a preview of the other shows in the series. This is a thoroughly faithful adaptation of Andersen's tale, evoking through visuals, music, and convincing performances the mysterious atmosphere of an ancient Chinese kingdom. Death and the emperor's bad deeds are personified at the end with gruesome masks likely to frighten very young viewers. The theme of the real versus the artificial also appeals to an older audience. Other than the singing, there is little action, and the plot unfolds slowly.

Audience: Ages 8-Adult
Distributor: Fox Video
Videocassette: $14.98
No public performance rights

Nightingale, The.
54 min. Color. Live action. 1983. Mick Jagger.

A laser disc version of the same title offered by Fox Video (see above).

Distributor: Image Entertainment
Laser disc: CLV format $29.98
No public performance rights

Nightingale, The.
16 min. Color. Puppet animation. Produced by Coronet. 1984.

Puppet animation makes the characters seem heavy and cumbersome in this otherwise well-told story of the emperor and his feathered friend.

Audience: Ages 5-10
Distributor: Coronet/MTI Film & Video
16mm film: $385 **Videocassette:** $250
Rental: $75

Emperor and the Nightingale, The.
40 min. Color. Limited animation. Produced by Rabbit Ears. 1987. Narrated by Glenn Close.

An emperor, as imperious in the show as he is in the tale, insists on the capture of a real nightingale. When its plain appearance is compared to that of a jeweled artificial bird, discontent affects both bird and ruler. Glenn Close's narration conveys the heartache and clash of wills inherent in the tale, blending perfectly with Mark Isham's lilting music and Robert Van Nutt's oriental setting.

Reviews: *Booklist*, Feb. 1, 1988
Awards: Action for Children's Television Award
Audience: Ages 6-12
Distributor: SVS/Triumph
Videocassette: $14.95
No public performance rights

★★★★★

Noah's Ark
Peter Spier (illus.).

Doubleday. 1977. Bible stories.

Except for a poem at the beginning, this book is wordless. It shows in pictures Noah's family building the ark, then boarding it with the animals, and surviving the flood.

Noah's Ark.
27 min. Color. Animation. Produced by Joshua M. Greene. 1989. Narrated by James Earl Jones.
Produced in consultation with Peter Spier, this rendition is faithful both to his storybook art and the lyrical tone of the poem that begins it. The screenplay includes lines from the poem and adds narration not in the wordless book. True to the storybook art, fine animation is graced with all the thoughtful touches—two turtles, for example, are the last to board the ark. The show has awesome yet realistic majesty. Now booming, now gentle, the voices of James Earl Jones suits the story perfectly. Enhancing the animation and narration is a rich music score by Stewart Copeland.
Reviews: *Booklist*, Dec. 15, 1989; *Video Librarian*, Nov. 1989
Awards: Silver Apple, National Educational Film & Video Festival
Audience: Ages 4-10
Distributor: Lightyear Entertainment
Videocassette: $14.95
No public performance rights

★★★★★

Nobody's Family Is Going to Change
Louise Fitzhugh.
Putnam. 1975. [1974]. Realistic fiction.
A boy wants to be a tap dancer, and his older sister wants to be a lawyer. The sister pleads a case of children's rights.

Tap Dance Kid, The.
33 min. Color. Live action. NBC Special Treat/LCA. 1979.
Although the girl is almost too good in her legal argument to be believed, this is an excellent story about family members willing to talk to each other. It is a testimony to the respect to which children are entitled as individual people.
Awards: ALA Notable Film; Chris Plaque, Columbus International Film Festival; Emmy Award, Outstanding Children's Entertainment Special; NAACP "Image" Award
Audience: Ages 10-14
Distributor: Coronet/MTI Film & Video
16mm film: $500 **Videocassette:** $250
Rental: $75

Tap Dance Kid, The.
49 min. Color. Live action. 1979.
A full-length version of the same, abbreviated title also distributed by Coronet/MTI Film & Video (see above).
Distributor: Coronet/MTI Film & Video
16mm film: $750 **Videocassette:** $250
Rental: $75

★★★★★

"Noon Wine"
Katherine Anne Porter.
Anthologized in *The Collected Stories of Katherine Anne Porter.* Harcourt Brace Jovanovich. 1979. Short stories—realistic fiction.
An itinerant Swedish American hires on as a dairy hand and, though he is a good worker, brings disaster to his employer.

Noon Wine.
81 min. Color. Live action. Produced by Learning in Focus. 1985. Fred Ward, Lisa Hilbolt.
Excellent casting and a solid plot line make this one of the stronger short-story adaptations. Helton, the harmonica-playing Swedish worker, prompts good and then ill fortune, which ultimately results in a killing.
Audience: Ages 15-18
Distributor: Monterey Home Video
Videocassette: $24.95

No public performance rights

★★★★★

Norman the Doorman
Don Freeman (illus.).

Penguin USA. 1959. Fantasy.

Norman, a mouse-doorman in a museum of art, turns artist and enters his sculpture in a contest for humans.

Norman the Doorman.

15 min. Color. Iconographic. Produced by Weston Woods. 1971.

Lively narration enhances this imaginative tale. Using a mousetrap, Norman sculpts a mouse on a trapeze. His caption misspells the word *trapeze* (*trapeese*) but the sculpture itself wins the award. The film successfully conveys the clever fun of the storybook.

Reviews: *Booklist*, Sept. 15, 1973
Audience: Ages 4-6
Distributor: Weston Woods
16mm film: $195 **Videocassette:** $60
Rental: $25 daily

Norman the Doorman and Other Stories.

38 min. Color. Iconographic and animated. Produced by Weston Woods. 1989.

Included in this tape anthology are adaptations of *Norman the Doorman* (Don Freeman), *Brave Irene* (William Steig), and *Lentil* (Robert McCloskey). See individual titles for full descriptions.

Audience: Ages 4-8
Distributor: Children's Circle, Weston Woods
Videocassette: $19.95
No public performance rights

★★★★★

North Wind and the Sun
Jean de La Fontaine.

Illustrated by Brian Wildsmith. Oxford University Press. 1987. [1964]. Folklore and fairy tales.

To determine who is strongest, the North Wind and the Sun agree to a contest, which the Sun wins with gentleness and persistence.

North Wind and the Sun, The.

9 min. Color. Animation. Produced by Greatest Tales. 1977.

As with other Greatest Tales folklore adaptations, the film is strong in faithfulness to the original story but limited in animation.

Audience: Ages 6-10
Distributor: Phoenix/BFA Films & Video
16mm film: $230 **Videocassette:** $135
Rental: $30

North Wind and the Sun, The.

7 min. Color. Animation. 1962.

The old-world story is told with contemporary flair in this nicely paced production of the contest between the cold North Wind and the Sun.

Audience: Ages 5-8
Distributor: Coronet/MTI Film & Video
16mm film: $190 **Videocassette:** $125
Rental: $75

★★★★★

"Notes from a Lady at a Dinner Party"
Bernard Malamud.

Anthologized in *Rembrandt's Hat.* Farrar, Straus & Giroux. 1986. [1968]. Short stories—realistic fiction.

A beginning architect is invited to dinner at the home of his professor. At the party, he sits next to the professor's young wife, and an exchange of notes begins between them. The notes, and reactions of the professor to events at the dinner, reveal frustrations and hidden emotions among all three people.

Notes from a Lady at a Dinner Party.
25 min. Color. Live Action. Made-to-Order Productions. 1989.
The lighting is good and the staging is as described in the original, but the production drags. The actors play their roles in keeping with the short story. Except for some note-passing, not much happens in this version of a tale that brings out hidden feelings in the various relationships. The production seems to run twice as long as measured.
Audience: Ages 14-Adult
Distributor: Barr Films
Videocassette: $395 **Rental:** $50

★★★★★

Now One Foot, Now the Other
Tomie de Paola (illus.).
Putnam. 1981. Realistic fiction.
Bob has a special relationship with his grandfather, who helped him learn everything—including how to walk. When his grandfather has a stroke, Bob thinks it is time to reverse roles and help his grandfather learn to walk again.

Now One Foot, Now the Other.
24 min. Color. Live action. Produced by Donald MacDonald. 1986.
This is a touching film that crosses generations. The story of role reversals is well-told by a master filmmaker of the dramatic short.
Audience: Ages 8-15
Distributor: Filmfair Communications
16mm film: $470 **Videocassette:** $420
Rental: $50

★★★★★

Nutcracker, The
Multiple editions. Fantasy.
In this story within a story, Clara receives a nutcracker that she imagines is a prince cast under a spell. With the kiss of a maiden, the nutcracker resumes his princely shape just in time to battle the Mouse King and his army.

Nutcracker, The.
26 min. Color. Animation. Produced by Soyuzmult Film Studio. 1978. Narrated by Hans Conried.
Animated in a style of central Europe, with figures heavily drawn and not altogether graceful, this film has nevertheless won awards. Its strength lies in the simplicity with which the story is told, the graceful narration of Hans Conried, and the music of Tchaikovsky.
Awards: Golden Babe, Chicago Educational Film Festival
Audience: Ages 8-15
Distributor: Barr Films
16mm film: $550 **Videocassette:** $385
Rental: $50

O

adherence to book **film rating**

Occurrence at Owl Creek Bridge, An
Ambrose Bierce.
Creative Education. 1980. Short stories—historical fiction.
Bierce's story, set during the Civil War, focuses on one condemned man's thoughts as he stands on a bridge with a noose around his neck.

Occurrence at Owl Creek Bridge, An.
17 min. Black and white. Live action. Produced by Marcel Ichac, Paul de Roubaix. 1962.
Directed by Robert Enrico, this French film (the spare dialogue seems to be dubbed in English) closely follows the plot of Bierce's story, though it leaves more to conjecture. Only at the end of the drama is it revealed that the condemned man is just dreaming that he plunges into the water, escapes, and is reunited with his wife. With little dialogue, the film forces viewers to deduce the reason for the man's hanging and the identity of his loved one. Its black-and-white format is rather unspectacular.
Awards: Academy Award, Best Short Subject
Reviews: *Library Journal*, Jan. 15, 1971
Audience: Ages 14-Adult
Distributor: Films Inc.
16mm film: $445 **Videocassette:** $79

Occurrence at Owl Creek Bridge, An.
29 min. Black and white. Live action. 1962.
A full-length version of the same title distributed by Films Inc. (see above).
Awards: Academy Award, Best Live-Action Short Subject
Audience: Ages 14-Adult
Distributor: Video Yesteryear
Videocassette: $19.95

★★★★★

Of Human Bondage
Somerset Maugham.
Multiple editions. Realistic fiction.
Born with a club foot, Philip Carey grows up to study medicine. He becomes involved with an ungrateful woman, then settles down with someone he loves, for the first time undertaking what he wants to do instead of what he should do.

Of Human Bondage.
84 min. Black and white. Live action. Produced by RKO/Pandro S. Berman. 1934. Leslie Howard, Bette Davis, Frances Dee.

The production, Bette Davis's first vehicle to stardom, is still an emotionally rousing experience. Howard plays the lovestruck medical student with great sensitivity, and the performances of the supporting cast are quite strong.

Reviews: *New York Times*, June 29, 1934, 17:1; *Variety*, July 3, 1934
Audience: Ages 16-Adult
Distributor: KVC Entertainment
Videocassette: $19.95
Distributor: Video Yesteryear
Videocassette: $29.95
No public performance rights

Of Human Bondage.
99 min. Black and white. Live action. Produced by MGM/James Woolf. 1964. Laurence Harvey, Kim Novak, Nanette Newman.
The production is less than convincing. As in the novel, Philip is obsessed by his passion for an unscrupulous waitress.

Reviews: *New York Times*, Sept. 24, 1964, 46:2; *Variety*, July 1, 1964
Audience: Ages 16-Adult
Distributor: MGM/UA Home Video
Videocassette: $24.98
No public performance rights

★★★★★

Oh Boy! Babies!
Alison C. Herzig and Jane L. Mali.
Photos by Katrina Thomas. Little, Brown & Co. 1980. Nonfiction.
A group of sixth-grade boys takes an elective course in infant care with sometimes hilarious, sometimes tender results.

Oh, Boy! Babies!.
30 min. Color. Live action. Produced by Bruce and Carole Hart/NBC Special Treat. 1983.
A private school in New York is the setting for this film, whose many prizes attest to its excellence. The production is a smooth combination of entertainment and information.

Awards: Christopher Award, Columbus Film Festival; National Council of Christians and Jews Gold Mass Media Award
Audience: Ages 11-15
Distributor: Coronet/MTI Film & Video
16mm film: $500 **Videocassette:** $250
Rental: $75

★★★★★

Old Black Witch
Harry and Wende Devlin.
Illustrated by Harry Devlin. New York Parents Magazine Press. 1980. [1963]. Fantasy.
A family moves into an old home mysteriously sold to them for four hundred dollars, only to find that they must share it with a two-hundred-year-old witch.

Winter of the Witch.
25 min. Color. Live action. Produced by LCA and Parents Magazine Films. 1970. Burgess Meredith, Hermione Gingold.
Narrated by Burgess Meredith, the film features Hermione Gingold as the witch. This witch seems overbearing at first but goes on to become the endearing character everyone loves to watch. This is an exceptionally well-produced adaptation.

Reviews: *Booklist*, Sept. 15, 1973
Awards: CINE Golden Eagle
Audience: Ages 5-14
Distributor: Coronet/MTI Film & Video
16mm film: $425 **Videocassette:** $250
Rental: $75

★★★★★

Old Gringo, The
Carlos Fuentes.
Farrar, Straus & Giroux. 1985. Historical fiction.
A young spinster is courted by a general in the Mexican revolution of the early 1900s. An American writer, Ambrose Bierce, becomes a third major character on the scene.

Old Gringo.
119 min. Color. Live action. Produced by Columbia. 1989. Jane Fonda, Gregory Peck, Jimmy Smits.
Peck plays the aging journalist, Ambrose Bierce. The picture vividly recreates the setting and the exceptionally fine performances command attention, yet "something got lost in the translation from novel to screen." —*Variety*
Reviews: *Variety*, May 24, 1989
Audience: Ages 14-Adult
Distributor: Columbia TriStar Home Video
Videocassette: $19.95
No public performance rights

Old Gringo.
120 min. Color. Live action. 1989. Jane Fonda, Gregory Peck.
A laser disc version of the same title offered by Columbia TriStar Home Video (see above).
Distributor: Pioneer LDCA, Inc.
Laser disc: CLV format $39.95
No public performance rights

★★★★★

Old Yeller
Fred Gipson.
Illustrated by Carl Burger. Harper & Row. 1956. Historical fiction.
An adolescent farm boy of 1859 Texas becomes attached to a stray dog. They have adventures together but then the dog contracts rabies and has to be destroyed.

Old Yeller.
83 min. Color. Live action. Produced by Walt Disney. 1957. Dorothy McGuire, Fess Parker, Tommy Kirk.
This is one of the Disney studio's finest live-action films for young viewers, even though it was one of its first. The adaptation is straightforward with the addition of a fine sense of the outdoors. The audience joins in the boy's agony at making his most difficult decision.
Reviews: *New York Times*, Dec. 26, 1957, 23:4
Audience: Ages 8-12
Distributor: Buena Vista Home Video
Videocassette: $19.99
No public performance rights

Old Yeller.
83 min. Color. Live action. 1957. Dorothy McGuire, Fess Parker, Tommy Kirk.
A laser disc version of the same title originally offered by Buena Vista Home Video (see above).
Distributor: Image Entertainment
Laser disc: CLV format $34.99
No public performance rights

Old Yeller.
28 min. Color. Live action. Produced by Disney Educational Productions. 1980.
An abbreviated version of the same title originally offered by Buena Vista Home Video (see above). This version retains the basic plot but omits selected details.
Audience: Ages 8-12
Distributor: Coronet/MTI Film & Video

16mm film: $600 **Videocassette:** $250
Rental: $75

★★★★★

Oliver Twist
Charles Dickens.
Multiple editions. Realistic fiction.
A stray boy escapes from a poorhouse, falls into the clutches of a ruthless crook, then moves to a warm, upper middle class home. A half brother, who knows Oliver's heritage, tries to deprive the boy of his share of the family fortune.

Oliver Twist.
74 min. Black and white. Live action. 1933. Dickie Moore, Irving Pichel, Barbara Kent.
This is a low-budget film that looks the part. Featuring episodes that unfold sketchily and hurriedly, it is not one of the average or better adaptations of the Dickens classic.
Reviews: *New York Times*, Apr. 13, 1933, 15:3; *Variety*, Apr. 18, 1933
Audience: Ages 12-Adult
Distributor: KVC Entertainment
Videocassette: $19.95
Distributor: Video Yesteryear
Videocassette: $29.95

Oliver Twist.
116 min. Black and white. Live action. Produced by Cineguild/Ronald Neame. 1948. Alec Guinness, Robert Newton, Anthony Newley.
Capturing the spirit and events of Dickens' classic, this film, adapted by David Lean, condenses the story and eliminates some characters to good purpose. The adaptation is an outstanding feat of cinema, both visually memorable and expertly played. Later remade as a musical, this version is reputed as the finest of several Oliver films.
Reviews: *New York Times*, July 31, 1951, 17:2; *Variety*, June 30, 1948
Audience: Ages 12-Adult
Distributor: Janus Films
Videocassette: $88

Oliver Twist.
116 min. Black and white. Live action. 1948. Alec Guinness, Robert Newton, Anthony Newley.
A home video version of the same title distributed by Janus Films (see above).
Distributor: Paramount Home Video
Videocassette available
No public performance rights

Oliver Twist.
116 min. Black and white. Live action. 1948. Alec Guinness, Robert Newton, Anthony Newley.
A laser disc version of the same title offered by Janus Films (see above).
Distributor: Pioneer LDCA, Inc.
Laser disc: CLV format $34.95
No public performance rights

Oliver!.
146 min. Color. Live action. Produced by Columbia. 1968. Ron Moody, Oliver Reed, Mark Lester.
This is a musical motion picture in the grand old style, generally faithful to the novel. The 1948 adaptation is a closer match in overall mood and performances. There is discordance between the novel's serious themes, such as child labor abuse, and the energetic, spirited nature of this version. Yet high production values makes this a memorable film experience. Its technical aspects are first-rate.
Reviews: *New York Times*, Dec. 11, 1968, 57:1; *Variety*, Oct. 2, 1968

Awards: Academy Awards, Best Picture, Best Director, Best Art Direction—Set Decoration, Best Sound, Best Music Score, Best Choreography; Golden Globe Award, Best Musical Film
Audience: Ages 12-Adult
Distributor: Columbia TriStar Home Video
Videocassette: $19.95
No public performance rights

Oliver!.
146 min. Color. Live action. 1969. Ron Moody, Oliver Reed, Mark Lester.
A laser disc version of the same title offered by Columbia TriStar Home Video (see above).
Distributor: Pioneer LDCA, Inc.
Laser disc: CLV format $39.95
No public performance rights

Charles Dickens: Oliver Twist.
333 min. Color. Live action. Produced by Alexander Baron/BBC. 1985. Eric Porter, Frank Middlemass, Gareth Davies.
Beautifully staged with fine performances, this production is overlong for young audiences; some of the dialog is delivered with so authentic an English accent it may be lost on them. However, the show's faithfulness to the novel is unsurpassed. The remake includes characters (a friendly family, the Maylies) left out of previous versions and conveys the novel's grim contrast between the wealthy and impoverished. The author's hand in the production is unmistakably felt.
Audience: Ages 10-Adult
Distributor: Fox Video
Videocassette: $29.98

Once and Future King
Terence H. White.
Putnum. 1958. Folklore and fairy tales.
The novel profiles the rise and fall of King Arthur, who marries Guenevere and creates the Round Table to further his goal: the use of force in society not to seize power but to help the weak, rescue damsels in distress, and so forth.

Camelot.
181 min. Color. Live action. Produced by Jack L. Warner. 1967. Richard Harris, Vanessa Redgrave, David Hemmings.
Actually an adaptation of the Lerner and Lowe musical *Camelot*, which was based on White's novel, the film comes across as a sentimental romance without the feeling of magic merited by the original. The dash and daring of Lancelot give way in this adaptation to his mental anguish, as well as that of Arthur and Guenevere. Her dual devotion to Arthur and Lancelot is difficult to swallow. In the film Guenevere is sent to the stake for her offenses. In the novel her fate is milder; she takes the veil. Reviewers wrote disparagingly of the show's singing, though the music itself received high acclaim. The show has moments of fine acting. It was Jack L. Warner's last production for Warner Brothers.
Reviews: *New York Times,* Oct. 26, 1967, 54:1; *Variety*, Oct. 25, 1967
Awards: Academy Awards, Best Costume Design, Best Music Score, Best Art Direction/Set Decoration; Golden Globe Awards, Best Actor in a Musical, Best Original Song
Audience: Ages 14-Adult
Distributor: Warner Home Video
Videocassette: $29.98
No public performance rights

Camelot.
181 min. Color. Live action. 1967. Richard Harris, Vanessa Redgrave, David Hemmings.

A laser disc version of the same title offered by Warner Home Video (see above).
Distributor: Pioneer LDCA, Inc.
Laser disc: CLV format $29.98
No public performance rights

★★★★★

One Fish Two Fish Red Fish Blue Fish
Oh, the Thinks You Can Think!
The Foot Book
Dr. Seuss (illus.).
Beginner Books Random House. 1960. 1975. 1968. Concept books; humor. *One Fish Two Fish Red Fish Blue Fish* is a set of short stories about numbers, colors, and simple concepts, showing there are funny items everywhere. *Oh, the Thinks You Can Think!* is about how pleasurable it is to make up words and put them together with words that already exist. *The Foot Book* uses "silly feet" stories to teach concepts such as right and left, wet and dry, and slow and quick.

Dr. Seuss Beginner Book Video: One Fish Two Fish Red Fish Blue Fish; Oh, the Thinks You Can Think!; The Foot Book.
30 min. Color. Iconographic. Produced by Praxis Media and Random House Home Video. 1989.
This excellent film teaches concepts such as number, colors, and comparative adjectives, encouraging children to discover and even invent words on their own, and to imitate the narrator by repeating sounds they hear. The bright music and the jolly drawings add to the enjoyment of the basic lessons.
Reviews: *Children's Video Report*, Oct./Nov. 1989
Audience: Ages 4-8
Distributor: Random House Home Video
Videocassette: $9.95
No public performance rights

★★★★★

One Flew Over the Cuckoo's Nest
Ken Kesey.
Penguin USA. 1962. Realistic fiction.
A rabble-rouser transferred to a mental hospital incites patients against the iron hand of the head nurse.

One Flew Over the Cuckoo's Nest.
133 min. Color. Live action. Produced by Paul Zaentz, Michael Douglas. 1975. Jack Nicholson, Louise Fletcher.
The film is topnotch anti-establishment entertainment. Nicholson, as the rabble-rouser, is superb.
Reviews: *New York Times*, Dec. 21, 1975, II, 17:5; *Variety*, Nov. 19, 1975
Awards: Academy Awards, Best Picture, Best Actor, Best Actress, Best Director, Best Screenplay; Golden Globe Awards, Best Dramatic Film, Best Actor in a Drama, Best Actress in a Drama, Best Screenplay
Audience: Ages 15-Adult
Distributor: HBO Video
Videocassette: $29.98
No public performance rights

One Flew Over the Cuckoo's Nest.
133 min. Color. Live action. 1975. Jack Nicholson, Louise Fletcher.
A laser disc version of the same title offered by HBO Video (see above).
Distributor: Pioneer LDCA, Inc.
Laser disc: CLV format $39.95
No public performance rights

★★★★★

One Gallant Rush
Peter Buchard.
St. Martin's Press. 1965. Historical fiction. Commanded by a white officer, the first black regiment to be raised in the North during the Civil War storms a seemingly unassailable Southern fort. *Lay This Laurel* by Lincoln Kirsten and personal letters by Robert Gould Shaw were additional sources contributing to the production *Glory*.

Glory.
122 min. Color. Live action. Produced by Tri-Star Pictures/Freddie Fields. 1989. Matthew Broderick, Denzel Washington, Cary Elwes, Morgan Freeman.
This outstanding dramatization captures details and emotions of the 54th Regiment, the first official black fighting force of Massachusetts. The production achieves historic credibility with painful and spellbinding success. The setting, like the performances, smacks of authenticity. Rather than adapting a single book, the screenplay synthesizes several sources, including the white officer's letters. It achieves a vividly realistic flavor, climaxing with the one gallant rush described in that novel.
Reviews: *Variety*, Dec. 13, 1989
Awards: Academy Awards, Best Supporting Actor, Best Cinematography, Best Sound; Golden Globe Award, Best Supporting Actor
Audience: Ages 14-Adult
Distributor: Columbia TriStar Home Video
Videocassette: $19.95
No public performance rights

Glory.
122 min. Color. Live action. 1990. Matthew Broderick, Denzel Washington.
A laser disc version of the same title offered by Columbia TriStar Pictures Home Video (see above).
Distributor: Pioneer LDCA, Inc
Laser disc: Widescreen CLV format $39.95
No public performance rights

★★★★★

"One Thousand Dozen, The"
Jack London.
Anthologized in *Young Wolf: The Early Adventure Stories of Jack London* edited by Howard Latchman. Capra Press. 1984. Short stories—adventure.
David Rasmussen survives hardship after hardship to get his precious cargo of a thousand dozen eggs to Dawson, where the food shortage promises him a soaring profit.

One Thousand Dozen.
55 min. Color. Live action. Produced by William MacAdam/Norfolk. 1980. Narrated by Orson Welles. Neil Munro, Ray Whelan.
This is exceptional both for its historical content of the Yukon gold rush and for its literary impact as a captivating tale with a surprise ending. It runs through the gamut of emotions from hope to anger to exaltation to disappointment, while exposing the hardships of travel and existence in the Far North. Hands bleeding, determined David Rasmussen reaches his goal, arriving at Dawson with his precious cargo. But an ironic twist of fate robs him of ultimate success.
Audience: Ages 14-Adult
Distributor: Britannica
Videocassette: $99

★★★★★

One Was Johnny: A Counting Book
Maurice Sendak (illus.).
Harper & Row Junior Books. 1962. Concept books.

Centered around a boy named Johnny, this counting book introduces numbers by adding to the items in Johnny's room and then subtracting each item. In the end, all that is left is the one that was Johnny.

One Was Johnny.
3 min. Color. Animation. Produced by Sheldon Riss/Weston Woods. 1972. Directed by Maurice Sendak. Music by Carole King.
Lyrical and faithful to the book, this motion picture narrates the text in song. The pacing is rapid so that the show works best as an introduction to or review of numbers.
Audience: Ages 4-6
Distributor: Weston Woods
16mm film: $100 **Videocassette:** $60
Rental: $10 daily

Maurice Sendak Library.
35 min. Color. Animated. Produced by Weston Woods. 1989.
Included in this tape anthology are adaptations of *Alligators All Around, Pierre, One Was Johnny, Chicken Soup with Rice, In the Night Kitchen,* and *Where the Wild Things Are.* See individual titles for full descriptions. An additional segment, *Getting to Know Maurice Sendak,* features the author commenting on his work.
Reviews: *Children's Video Report,* Nov. 1, 1990
Audience: Ages 4-8
Distributor: Children's Circle, Weston Woods
Videocassette: $19.95
No public performance rights

★★★★★

"Open Window, The"
Saki.
Anthologized in *Great Ghost Stories,* edited by B. A. Schwartz. Messner. 1985. Short stories—horror.
Set in the country, where there is little to ruffle a man's nerves, this tale focuses on a fidgety gentleman in quest of relaxation. He finds instead a young girl who agitates him into imagining he spies two ghosts through an open window.

Open Window, The.
12 min. Color. Live action. Produced by Richard Patterson. 1972.
It is more obvious in the motion picture than in the story that the girl is fabricating the tragedy about the untimely death of two men. Nevertheless she is extremely convincing as she explains that the window is open in hopes that the two "dead" men will reappear any moment. The short story relies on words alone, but in the film, gestures, such as the restless hands of the man, heighten the aura of nervousness.
Awards: Jack London Award, National Educational Film and Video Festival
Audience: Ages 14-Adult
Distributor: Pyramid Film & Video
16mm film: $395 **Videocassette:** $195
Rental: $75

Open Window, The.
11 min. Color. Live action. 1972.
A home video version of the same title distributed by Pyramid Film & Video (see above). Also includes a 28-minute feature called *Child's Play,* another story by Saki.
Audience: Ages 14-Adult
Distributor: Monterey Home Video
Videocassette: $24.95
No public performance rights

★★★★★

Ordinary People
Judith Guest.
Viking Press. 1976. Realistic fiction.

An ordinary family begins to deteriorate when the oldest son drowns.

Ordinary People.
124 min. Color. Live action. Produced by Ronald L. Schwartz/Paramount/Wildwood. 1980. Donald Sutherland, Mary Tyler Moore, Judd Hirsch, Timothy Hutton.
Hutton plays the surviving younger brother who handles his fragile emotions with psychological help from Hirsch. Set in suburban Chicago, the film garnered a string of awards that attests to its excellence. Supporting actor Timothy Hutton, director Robert Redford, and screenwriter Alvin Sargent each won Oscars, Redford in his first major directing assignment. The outstanding adaptation also received an Oscar for Best Film of 1980.
Reviews: *New York Times*, Sept. 19, 1980, III, 6:5; *Variety*, Sept. 17, 1980
Awards: Academy Awards, Best Picture, Best Directing, Best Screenplay, Best Supporting Actor; Golden Globe Awards, Best Dramatic Film, Director, Best Actress, Best Supporting Actor
Audience: Ages 15-Adult
Distributor: Paramount Home Video
Videocassette available
No public performance rights

Ordinary People.
124 min. Color. Live action. 1980. Mary Tyler Moore, Donald Sutherland, Timothy Hutton.
A laser disc version of the same title offered by Paramount Home Video (see above).
Distributor: Pioneer LDCA, Inc.
Laser disc: CLV format $35.95
No public performance rights

★★★★★

Other Side of the Mountain, The
E. G. Valens.
Harper & Row. 1988. Biography.
Jill Kinmont, a world class skier, is paralyzed by an accident and must rebuild her life without the ability to move her body below the shoulders.

Other Side of the Mountain, The.
102 min. Color. Live action. Produced by Universal/Filmways/Larry Peerce. 1975. Marilyn Hassett, Beau Bridges, Belinda Montgomery.
This is a pleasant if almost too-even production of a heart-rending story, successful enough to inspire a sequel (*The Other Side of the Mountain, Part Two*, Universal 1977).
Reviews: *New York Times*, Nov. 15, 1975, 20:1; *Variety*, Mar. 19, 1975
Audience: Ages 12-Adult
Distributor: MCA/Universal Home Video
Videocassette available
No public performance rights

★★★★★

Otherwise Known as "Sheila the Great!"
Judy Blume.
Dell. 1986. [1972]. Realistic fiction.
Many new fears surface in a ten-year-old girl when she moves to a new home for the summer. Initially, she attempts to cover up her apprehension with bragging, but her new friends help her face reality and overcome her fears.

Otherwise Known as "Sheila the Great!"
24 min. Color. Live action. Produced by Calico Films. 1988.
Selected as an American Library Association notable film, this accurate and amusing adaptation was directed by the novelist's son. It is a gentle story of a ten-year-old girl's fears. Only an occasional flatness in the performance by the main character detracts from the production.

Reviews: *School Library Journal*, Apr. 1990; *Booklist*, Mar. 15, 1990
Awards: Crystal Apple, National Educational Film and Video Festival; ALA Notable Children's Film
Audience: Ages 6-12
Distributor: Barr Films
16mm film: $565 **Videocassette:** $395
Rental: $50

★★★★★

"Ounce of Cure, An"
Alice Munro.
Anthologized in *Dance of the Happy Shades and Other Stories.* McGraw-Hill. 1973. Short stories—realistic fiction.
In an engrossing short story, Elizabeth recalls her high school days and her impetuous actions following the inevitable breakup between herself and her first love.

Ounce of Cure, An.
26 min. Color. Live action. Produced by Janice Platt, Michael MacMillan, Seaton McLean. 1984.
Many original lines were added to this atmospherically filmed screenplay (set in the 1950s or 1960s; the era is not firmly established in the story). According to *Booklist*, "this adaptation imaginatively redirects the story's thrust from the babysitting fiasco to the turbulent emotions that motivated Elizabeth." It depicts Elizabeth drowning her sorrows in alcohol following the loss of her first boyfriend.
Reviews: *Booklist*, May 1, 1985
Awards: ALA Selected Films for Young Adults; Chris Bronze Plaque, Columbus International Film Festival
Audience: Ages 16-Adult
Distributor: Beacon Films Films
16mm film: $575 **Videocassette:** $149

Out of Africa
Isak Dinesen.
Modern Library. 1983. [1937]. Nonfiction.
In *Out of Africa*, Isak Dinesen (Karen Blixen) recounts the years 1914–1931 on her coffee plantation in Kenya. Other sources for the motion picture are Isak Dinesen's *Shadows on the Grass* and *Letters From Africa*, Judith Thurman's *Isak Dinesen*, and Errol Tzebinski's *Silence Will Speak* about Denys Finch Hatton and his relationship with Isak Dinesen.

Out of Africa.
150 min. Color. Live action. Produced by Sydney Pollack. 1985. Meryl Streep, Robert Redford, Klaus Maria Brandauer.
The motion picture is a richly romantic drama worth the watching for the magnifcent African setting alone. Beyond the breathtaking photography are a love story and glimpses of early twentieth-century native and immigrant ways. While the picture is long, it evokes a magical feel for the continent. The female lead, ignored by her husband, falls in love with a white hunter, Denys. Five sources have been skillfully synthesized into a unified whole to create a screenplay with characters whose complex natures are apparent on screen. Isak Dinesen comes across as a woman of keen intelligence and dogged determination. As described in the *New York Times*, the portrayal of her romance is less reflective of reality. "From Miss Dinesen's letters, one sometimes suspects that Denys was a creature of her own imagination, but that their 'affair' was no less real for being a passionate fantasy. The film can't agree to this—it is, after all, supposed to be a love story."
Reviews: *New York Times*, Dec. 18, 1985, C, 17:1; *Variety*, Dec. 11, 1985
Awards: Academy Awards, Best Picture, Best Director, Best Adapted Screenplay, Best Music Score, Best Cinematography; Golden Globe Award, Best Dramatic Film
Audience: Ages 14-Adult
Distributor: MCA Universal Home Video
Videocassette available
No public performance rights

★★★★★

Outsiders, The
S. E. Hinton.
Viking. 1967. Realistic fiction.
Poor boys in Tulsa, Oklahoma, known as "greasers," hide out when a rich society character is accidentally knifed to death.

Outsiders, The.
91 min. Color. Live action. Produced by Zoetrope/Warner. 1983. Ralph Macchio, Matt Dillon, Patrick Swayze.
The production, set in the 1960s, is a period piece that looks the part. Despite some fine performances and a screenplay that sticks closely to the novel, the film never quite realizes the full potential of its story. Still, the adaptation is above average.
Reviews: *New York Times*, Mar. 25, 1983, C 3:1; *Variety*, Mar. 23, 1983
Audience: Ages 15-Adult
Distributor: Warner Home Video
Videocassette: $19.98
No public performance rights

Outsiders, The.
91 min. Color. Live action. 1983. Ralph Macchio, Matt Dillon, Patrick Swayze.
A laser disc version of the same title offered by Warner Home Video (see above).
Distributor: Pioneer LDCA, Inc.
Laser disc: CLV format $29.98
No public performance rights

★★★★★

Owl and the Pussy-Cat, The
Edward Lear.
Multiple editions. Poetry.
In rhyming verse, an owl and a cat sail to a distant land to be married.

Owl and the Pussy-Cat, The.
3 min. Color. Iconographic. Produced by Weston Woods. 1971.
Adapted from the storybook version illustrated by Barbara Cooney, the film is a straight retelling set to music. There is a noticeable lack of motion in this adequate, rather uninvolving adaptation.
Audience: Ages 4-6
Distributor: Weston Woods
16mm film: $85 **Videocassette:** $45
Rental: $10 daily

Owl and the Pussycat, The.
7 min. Color. Animation. Produced by John Halas/BFA. 1981.
Stylized characters are cleverly animated in this recreation of the popular poem. Enhancing the animation is an engagingly lighthearted musical score.
Audience: Ages 7-10
Distributor: Phoenix/BFA Films & Video
16mm film: $170 **Videocassette:** $120
Rental: $17.50

Happy Birthday, Moon and Other Stories.
30 min. Color. Animated and iconographic. Produced by Weston Woods. 1989.
Included in this tape anthology are adaptations of *Happy Birthday, Moon* (Frank Asch), *Peter's Chair* (Ezra Jack Keats), *The Napping House* (Audrey Wood), *The Three Little Pigs* (Erik Blegvvad), and *The Owl and the Pussy-Cat* (Edward Lear). See individual titles for full descriptions.
Reviews: *Children's Video Report*, Feb./Mar. 1989
Audience: Ages 4-8
Distributor: Children's Circle, Weston Woods
Videocassette: $19.95
No public performance rights

Pig's Wedding and Other Stories, The.
39 min. Color. Iconographic and animated. Produced by Weston Woods. 1991.

Included in this tape anthology are adaptations of *The Pig's Wedding* (Helme Heine), *The Happy Owls* (Celestino Piatti), *The Selkie Girl* (Susan Cooper), *A Letter to Amy* (Ezra Jack Keats), and *The Owl and the Pussy-Cat* (Edward Lear). See individual titles for full descriptions.

Audience: Ages 4-8
Distributor: Children's Circle, Weston Woods
Videocassette: $19.95
No public performance rights

★★★★★

Owl Moon
Jane Yolen.
Illustrated by John Schoenherr. Putnam. 1987. Realistic fiction.
A girl and her father go *owling* together through the snow. In other words, they hoot to inspire a reply from a true owl.

Owl Moon.
8 min. Color. Iconographic. Produced by Weston Woods. 1990. Narrated by Jane Yolen.
This is a well-paced, peaceful film with text narrated by the author herself in the first person. Sound effects enhance the story's awed respect for nature. Viewers hear the hoots offered and answered as father and daughter are successful in their quiet quest to draw sound from an owl.
Audience: Ages 4-6
Distributor: Weston Woods
16mm film: $195 **Videocassette:** $100
Rental: $20 daily

Owl Moon and Other Stories.
35 min. Color. Iconographic and animated. Produced by Weston Woods. 1990.
Included in this tape anthology are adaptations of *Owl Moon* (Jane Yolen), *The Caterpillar and the Polliwog* (Jack Kent), *Hot Hippo* (Mwenye Hadithi), and *Time of Wonder* (Robert McCloskey). See individual titles for full descriptions.
Audience: Ages 4-8
Distributor: Children's Circle, Weston Woods
Videocassette: $19.95
No public performance rights

★★★★★

Ox-Bow Incident
Walter V. Clark.
Multiple editions. Realistic fiction.
A cowboy is unable to reason with a mob that unjustly lynches a farmer for a murder.

Ox-Bow Incident.
75 min. Black and white. Live action. Produced by Twentieth Century Fox/Lamar Trotti. 1943. Henry Fonda, Harry Morgan, Jane Darwell, Anthony Quinn.
While this piece of past realism is engrossing, it is at the same time difficult to watch because of the downbeat message it imparts about human behavior.
Reviews: *New York Times*, May 10, 1943, 15:2; *Variety*, May 12, 1943
Audience: Ages 12-16
Distributor: Fox Video
Videocassette: $19.98
No public performance rights

Ox-Bow Incident.
75 min. Black and white. Live action. 1943. Henry Fonda, Harry Morgan, Jane Darwell, Anthony Quinn.
A laser disc version of the same title offered by Fox Video (see above).
Distributor: Image Entertainment
Laser disc: CLV format $39.98
No public performance rights

P

adherence to book   film rating

"Painted Door, The"
Sinclair Ross.
Anthologized in *Great Canadian Short Stories: An Anthology* compiled by Alec Lucas. Dell. 1971. Short stories—realistic fiction.
In this story of love, betrayal, and trust, a handsome neighbor stays with Ann while her husband braves a treacherous blizzard to care for his elderly father.

Painted Door, The.
26 min. Color. Live action. Produced by Michael MacMillan, Janice Platt. 1984.
The wife seems more bitter, resentful, and unhappy with her marriage in the short story version of this taut dramatization, which uses flashbacks to embellish the original tale. Other than these minor changes, this acclaimed production identically follows the Sinclair Ross story.
Reviews: *Booklist*, Feb. 1, 1986
Awards: *Booklist* Editors' Choice; Chris Statuette, Columbus International Film Festival; Silver Plaque, Chicago International Film Festival
Audience: Ages 16-Adult
Distributor: Beacon Films
16mm film: $575 **Videocassette:** $149

★★★★★

Pandora's Box.
Multiple editions. Folklore and fairy tales.
This ancient Greek myth revolves around the beautiful Pandora, the first woman created, and sent with a wondrous golden box to Earth to plague men. Instructed by a man, Epimetheus, not to open the box, Pandora disobeys. She thereby unleashes the world's evils, which the box had contained along with one fine jewel known as hope.

Pandora's Box.
12 min. Color. Animation. Produced by Kevin Brown. 1978.
Pandora and Epimetheus are curiously represented as colored circles in animation that loosely follows the general storyline of the well-known Greek myth. In the classic myth, only hope remains in the box after all the world's troubles are unleashed. In the show, Pandora and Epimetheus cross a river to represent hopeful feelings. A jazzy musical score accents this modernistic adaptation, which stresses the concept that individuals must work to overcome their problems.
Audience: Ages 8-12
Distributor: Beacon Films
16mm film: $240 **Videocassette:** $149

★★★★★

Parent Trap, The
Eric Kastner.
Cape Publishing. 1937. Humor.
Susan and Sharon, twins who have never met, are sent to the same summer camp and become best friends. They pose as each other, exchanging places to become better acquainted with the parent they have never seen, then join forces to reconcile their parents. Ultimately the parents reunite, becoming, with the twins, a real family for the first time.

Parent Trap, The.
124 min. Color. Live action. Produced by George Golitzen/Walt Disney. 1961. Hayley Mills, Brian Keith, Maureen O'Hara.
This is a consistently good-natured and appealing film, an adaptation that keeps faith with the romantic premise love is forever. While its entertainment value is high, the show rests on a cheerful plot line that presents an optimistic view of divorce.
Reviews: *New York Times*, June 22, 1961
Audience: Ages 8-Adult
Distributor: Buena Vista Home Video
Videocassette: $19.99
No public performance rights

Parent Trap, The.
124 min. Color. Live action. 1961. Hayley Mills, Brian Keith, Maureen O'Hara.
A laser disc version of the same title originally offered by Buena Vista Home Video (see above).
Distributor: Image Entertainment
Laser disc: CLV format $39.99
No public performance rights

★★★★★

Passage to India, A
E. M. Forster.
Multiple editions. Historical fiction.
A young English woman touring India when it was under British rule in the 1920s accuses an Indian doctor of attempting to rape her during an outing to rural caves.

Passage to India, A.
163 min. Color. Live action. Produced by Columbia. 1984. Alec Guinness, Judy Davis, Victor Banerjee.
The movie is a careful and thoughtful adaptation of the original, rich in the atmosphere it evokes and in the human relations it profiles.
Reviews: *New York Times*, Dec. 14, 1984, C 10:1
Awards: Academy Awards, Best Supporting Actress, Best Music Score; Golden Globe Awards, Best English Language Foreign Film, Best Supporting Actress
Audience: Ages 14-Adult
Distributor: Columbia TriStar Home Video
Videocassette: $19.95
No public performance rights

Passage to India, A.
163 min. Color. Live action. 1984. Alec Guinness, Judy Davis, Victor Banerjee.
A laser disc version of the same title offered by Columbia TriStar Home Video (see above).
Distributor: Pioneer LDCA, Inc.
Laser disc: CLV format $44.95
No public performance rights

★★★★★

Patrick
Quentin Blake (illus.)
Jonathan Cape. 1968. Fantasy.
Vendors try unsuccessfully to sell Patrick their wares. Finally, he purchases a violin and plays music on it that envigorates everything and everyone he passes.

Patrick.
7 min. Color. Limited animation. Produced by Kratky Film/Weston Woods. 1973.
The film sustains interest through its bright colors, upbeat violin music, and the lively movements of a boy, a girl, a peasant couple in a cart, and others affected by the music. In this case, the limited animation works to advantage. Characters affected by the violin tune grow more animated as the picture progresses, in keeping with the spirited music.
Audience: Ages 4-8
Distributor: Weston Woods
16mm film: $175 **Videocassette:** $60
Rental: $20 daily

★★★★★

Paul Bunyan.
Multiple editions. Folklore and fairy tales.
Loggers popularized this tall tale, changing details along the way. In most versions, Paul Bunyan and Babe, his blue ox, felled forests, ate prodigious amounts of pancakes, and contributed to the forging of national and natural monuments such as the Grand Canyon.

Paul Bunyan and the Blue Ox.
6 min. Color. Puppet animation. Produced by Coronet. 1952.
The puppet animation works reasonably well in this earliest Coronet effort to retell the story of the mighty lumberjack.
Audience: Ages 4-8
Distributor: Coronet/MTI Film & Video
16mm film: $170 **Videocassette:** $125
Rental: $75

Paul Bunyan: Lumber Camp Tales.
11 min. Color. Animation. Produced by Coronet. 1962.
A good film for its time and the budgets of the period, this rendition is overshadowed by the later Disney version. Still, this version brings to life some lesser known Bunyan feats; for example, the lumberjack creates a giant flapjack griddle, forms a popcorn blizzard, and straightens the Big Onion River.
Audience: Ages 5-12
Distributor: Coronet/MTI Film & Video
16mm film: $270 **Videocassette:** $190
Rental: $75

Paul Bunyan.
17 min. Color. Animation. Produced by Disney. 1970.
Music and clever animation vividly recreate the stories of Paul and his ox Babe, who form the finest logging team in the West.
Audience: Ages 5-12
Distributor: Coronet/MTI Film & Video
16mm film: $455 **Videocassette:** $250
Rental: $75

Paul Bunyan.
11 min. Color. Animation. Produced by Lumin Films. 1970.
Trying to be all-inclusive of the Bunyan yarns, this film begins with Paul's fall from his parents' wagon, after which he is cared for by wolves. The limited animation detracts from the adaptation's overall impact.
Audience: Ages 7-12
Distributor: Phoenix/BFA Films & Video

16mm film: $265 **Videocassette:** $150
Rental: $35

Paul Bunyan.
30 min. Color. Limited animation. Produced by Rabbit Ears. 1990. Narrated by Jonathan Winters.
In a voice filled with genuine affection and a text packed with old-fashioned expressions, Winters narrates as if he were a long-time intimate of Paul Bunyan. The dissolves, pans, and zooms give the show's brightly colored illustrations a sense of whirlwind motion and an appropriate larger-than-life quality. The ending reflects today's environmental conscientiousness—the infamous logger turns tree-planter.
Reviews: *Booklist*, Oct. 1, 1990
Audience: Ages 4-10
Distributor: SVS/Triumph
Videocassette: $14.95
No public performance rights

★★★★★

"Paul's Case"
Willa Cather.
Anthologized in *The American Short Story, Vol. 2* edited by C. Skaggs. Dell. 1980. Short stories—realistic fiction.
A restless, beauty-loving young man steals money and has a fling in New York City, but must then face up to what he has done.

Paul's Case.
55 min. Color. Live action. Produced by Learning in Focus. 1980. Eric Roberts, Michael Higgins.
In a series hosted by Henry Fonda, this film depends heavily for most of the play on one character. Eric Roberts almost carries off this assignment.
Awards: Red Ribbon, American Film Festival
Audience: Ages 12-18
Distributor: Coronet/MTI Film & Video
16mm film: $815 **Videocassette:** $250
Rental: $75

Paul's Case.
52 min. Color. Live action. 1980. Eric Roberts, Michael Higgins.
A home video version of the same title distributed by Coronet/MTI Film & Video (see above).
Distributor: Monterey Home Video
Videocassette: $24.95
No public performance rights

★★★★★

Pecos Bill.
Multiple editions. Folklore and fairy tales.
The various versions of this tall tale feature a heroic lad who invents cow punching and cattle drives, uses a lariat made from a rattlesnake, and rides a wild mustang named Widowmaker. Taming the nastiest land and meanest cowpokes, he maintains a sunny disposition all the while.

Pecos Bill.
17 min. Color. Animation. A Disney Educational Production. 1986.
In peerless comic animation, Disney relates how Pecos Bill was nurtured and how he learned to outrun the antelope and ride a cyclone. The film also describes the folk hero's feats at both the Rio Grande and the Grand Canyon.
Audience: Ages 5-10
Distributor: Coronet/MTI Film & Video
16mm film: $330 **Videocassette:** $250
Rental: $75

Pecos Bill.
30 min. Color. Limited animation. Produced by Rabbit Ears. 1988. Narration by Robin Williams.
In this tall Texas tale, an abandoned infant who is raised by coyotes turns into the quintessential cowboy (Pecos Bill) after meeting up with one of his own kind, a cowboy who looks and sounds remarkably like John Wayne. Williams's voice twangs as he spouts Texan lingo and humorous asides. Using dissolve animation, the show features Pecos Bill creating the Grand Canyon, the Great Salt Lakes, and Death Valley. He meanwhile battles a tornado that he finally rides to heaven (in contrast to other versions, which have him ride it into the arms of his family or his intended, SlewFoot Sue).
Reviews: *Booklist*, Feb. 15, 1989 and Mar. 15, 1989; *School Library Journal*, Feb. 1989; *Video Librarian*, Sept. 1988
Awards: ALA Notable Film; Parents' Choice Award
Audience: Ages 4-10
Distributor: SVS/Triumph
Videocassette: $14.95
No public performance rights

Pecos Bill.
25 min. Color. Limited animation. 1988. Narrated by Robin Williams.
A laser disc version of the same title offered by SVS/Triumph (see above).
Distributor: Image Entertainment
Laser disc: CLV format $19.95
No public performance rights

★★★★★

Pegasus.
Multiple editions. Folklore and fairy tales.
Belleraphon, a young man, rides the winged horse Pegasus to slay a fire-breathing monster. The young man then takes a forbidden ride to Mount Olympus, home of the Greek gods.

Pegasus (Stories to Remember).
25 min. Color. Animation. Produced by Joshua M. Greene. 1990. Narrated by Mia Farrow.
Enraged at Belleraphon's audacity, Zeus has a gadfly sting the horse, which, as in the classic legend, throws his rider. This enchanting adaptation captures the magic of the original with a magnificent monster and an eventful story line to captivate viewers.
Reviews: *Booklist*, Dec. 15, 1990
Awards: Parents' Choice Award
Audience: Ages 6-14
Distributor: Lightyear Entertainment
Videocassette: $14.98
No public performance rights

★★★★★

Penrod
Booth Tarkington.
Illustrated by Gordon Grant. Grosset & Dunlap. 1970. [1914]. Realistic fiction.
Penrod Schofield, now twelve years old, no longer detests Marjorie Jones the way he did when younger. He joins a dance class to be near her and plans to take her to the Cotillion but is frustrated in his attempt.

Miss Rensdale Accepts.
17.5 min. Color. Live action. Produced by Sharon Johnston. 1989.
Despite exceedingly convincing performances, the show relies on content with which it may be difficult for today's young audiences to identify. The old-fashioned setting of a social dance class is the context for the refreshing discovery that in love there is sometimes justice after all.
Reviews: *Booklist*, June 1, 1990
Audience: Ages 8-12
Distributor: Filmfair Communications
16mm film: $425 **Videocassette:** $385
Rental: $45

★★★★★

Perseus and Medusa
C. J. Naden.
Illustrated by Ross M. Maden. Troll Associates. 1980. Folklore and fairy tales.
When Perseus sets out to kill the monster Medusa at the demand of King Polydectes, he finds help from the sympathetic god Hermes. Provided with a mirrorlike shield, a sword, and winged shoes, Perseus succeeds in his venture and uses the head of Medusa to rescue the maiden Andromeda.

Perseus.
20 min. Color. Animation. Produced by Brian Jackson. 1987.
Limited animation is skillfully used to recount the legendary feat involving the prince who sets out to kill Medusa.
Reviews: *Curriculum Products News Service*, Apr. 1988
Audience: Ages 8-14
Distributor: Barr Films
16mm film: $470 **Videocassette:** $330
Rental: $50

Clash of the Titans.
118 min. Color. Live action. Produced by MGM/Charles H. Schneer, Ray Harryhausen. 1981. Laurence Olivier, Harry Hamlin, Claire Bloom.
In this loose adaptation, Perseus overcomes obstacles to rescue the maiden Andromeda from kidnappers. Laurence Olivier plays Zeus; Claire Bloom is Hera. There are some captivating moments (with the flying horse Pegasus and the monster Medusa) but the whole seems overlong and episodic.
Audience: 6-12
Distributor: MGM/UA Home Video
Videocassette: $69.98
No public performance rights

Clash of the Titans.
118 min. Color. Live action. 1981. Laurence Olivier, Harry Hamlin, Claire Bloom.
A laser disc version of the same title offered by MGM/UA Home Video (see above).
Distributor: Pioneer LDCA, Inc.
Laser disc: CLV format $39.98
No public performance rights

★★★★★

Pet Show!
Ezra Jack Keats (illus.).
Macmillan. 1972. Realistic fiction.
Just as the neighborhood pet show is about to start, Archie's cat disappears. After winning the heart of an old lady, it reappears to also win a prize.

Pet Show.
13 min. Color. Live action. Produced by LCA. 1989.
This Ezra Jack Keats' story seems a weak base for a motion picture, as this live-action film ambles along to a not-too-dramatic conclusion.
Awards: CINE Golden Eagle
Audience: Ages 5-8
Distributor: Coronet/MTI Film & Video
16mm film: $380 **Videocassette:** $250
Rental: $75

★★★★★

Peter and the Wolf
Sergei Prokofiev.
Multiple editions. Folklore and fairy tales.
Designed to teach children the orchestra's instruments, this fairy tale concerns a boy who ignores his grandfather's warnings and tries to capture a wolf. The various characters are associated with instruments of the orchestra.

Peter and the Wolf.
14 min. Color. Animation. A Disney Educational Production. 1963.
An excellent musical score and the unbeatable Disney animation combine to make this adaptation a classic.

Audience: Ages 5-18
Distributor: Coronet/MTI Film & Video
16mm film: $380 **Videocassette:** $250
Rental: $75

★★★★★

Peter Pan
J. M. Barrie.
Multiple editions. Fantasy.
Peter Pan, a boy who flies, takes the Darling children—Wendy, John and Michael—to adventures in Never-Never Land with the fairy Tinker Bell and the evil pirate Captain Hook. Peter wants Wendy to fly away with him and be forever young, but she decides to return home and grow up.

Peter Pan.
76 min. Color. Animation. Produced by Walt Disney. 1953. Featuring the voices of Bobby Driscoll and Hans Conried.
J. M. Barrie's *Peter Pan*, the boy who won't grow up, comes to life in this beautifully animated film. The show includes mild violence in the menacing Captain Hook and a major discrepancy with the original. While the book ends darkly, with Wendy's growing up referred to as "the tragedy," the film lightens the ending by treating the children's experiences as a dream. As described in the *New York Times*, "The film does not hold to the spirit of the play. The whole adventure is treated as a dream and the crisis is dropped. Otherwise, a wholly amusing and engaging film."

Reviews: *New York Times*, Feb. 15, 1953
Audience: Ages 5-Adult
Distributor: Buena Vista Home Video (not currently in distribution)

Peter Pan.
76 min. Color. Animation. Produced by Walt Disney. 1953.
A laser disc version of the same title offered by Buena Vista Home Video Home Video (see above).

Distributor: Image Entertainment
Laser disc: CLV format $29.99, CAV format $39.99
No public performance rights

Peter Pan.
100 min. Color Live action. Produced by Richard Halliday. 1960. Mary Martin, Cyril Ritchard.
This classic picture captures on screen the Broadway stage production of *Peter Pan*. Perhaps the most memorable of several captivating songs from the production is "I Won't Grow Up." The picture as a whole won high acclaim when it was released. "In spirit, verve, performance and total execution, it was the best of the 'Pans.'" —*Variety*

Reviews: *Variety*, Dec. 14, 1960
Awards: Emmy Award, Best Actress in a Single Performance
Audience: Ages 5-Adult
Distributor: Image Entertainment
Laser disc: CLV format $29.95
No public performance rights

★★★★★

Peter's Chair
Ezra Jack Keats (illus.).
Harper & Row Junior Books. 1967. Realistic fiction.
Peter grows angry at his new sister Susie's inheriting his cradle, high chair, and so on. He decides to run away with

his dog Willie, then has a change of heart.

Peter's Chair.
6 min. Color. Iconographic. Produced by Weston Woods in consultation with Ezra Jack Keats. 1971.
The film, like the book, makes visible Peter's change of heart about his new sister. He confiscates a little chair she stands to inherit, then changes his mind and decides to paint it pink.
Audience: Ages 4-8
Distributor: Weston Woods
16mm film: $140 **Videocassette:** $60
Rental: $20 daily

Happy Birthday Moon and Other Stories.
30 min. Color. Animated and iconographic. Produced by Weston Woods. 1989.
Included in this tape anthology are adaptations of *Happy Birthday, Moon* (Frank Asch), *Peter's Chair* (Ezra Jack Keats), *The Napping House* (Audrey Wood), *The Three Little Pigs* (Erik Bledgvad), and *The Owl and the Pussy-Cat* (Edward Lear). See individual titles for full descriptions.
Reviews: *Children's Video Report*, Feb./Mar. 1989
Audience: Ages 4-8
Distributor: Children's Circle, Weston Woods
Videocassette: $19.95
No public performance rights

★★★★★

Petronella
Jay Williams.
Illustrated by Friso Henstra. Parents' Magazine Press. 1973. Folklore and fairy tales.
A dragon enchanter has imprisoned worthless Prince Frederick. To rescue Frederick, Princess Petronella performs three tasks demanded by the enchanter. She later captures and kisses the enchanter, whereupon he turns into a handsome prince.

Petronella.
13.25 min. Color. Puppet animation. Produced by Barbara Dourmashkin. 1978.
Puppets work well to tell this reversal of the old knight-in-shining-armor-who-rescues-the-fair-maiden story. This time the princess does the rescuing—-but with an unusual turn of events.
Awards: Chris Plaque, Columbus Film Festival
Audience: Ages 5-10
Distributor: Filmfair Communications
16mm film: $260 **Videocassette:** $89
Rental: $25

★★★★★

Petunia
Roger Duvoisin (illus.).
Knopf. 1962. [1950]. Humor.
Petunia the Goose grows conceited, thinking that just carrying a book makes her smart. Events prove otherwise.

Petunia.
10 min. Color. Animated. Produced by Weston Woods. 1971.
Lively and comical, this show "packs a wallop" in more than one way. Disaster strikes when "wise" Petunia the goose misinforms the barnyard animals that a box of firecrackers is a box of candy. Besides entertaining viewers, the film leads them and Petunia to attach value to reading—not just carrying—books. Sound effects enhance the amusing story.
Audience: Ages 4-8
Distributor: Weston Woods
16mm film: $235 **Videocassette:** $60
Rental: $20 daily

★★★★★

Phaeton
Adapted by Doris Gates.

Anthologized in *The Golden God: Apollo.* Illustrated by Constantinos CoConis. Viking 1973. Folklore and fairy tales.

Phaeton wants to drive the sun chariot across the sky, but when he proves unable to handle the horses, Zeus must destroy him in order to save the world.

Phaeton.

4.5 min. Color. Animation. Produced by Brian Jackson. 1987.

Phaeton is appropriately insistent about driving the sun chariot. He unfortunately persuades Zeus to grant his permission in this limited animation version of the age-old story.

Reviews: *Curriculum Products News Service*, Apr. 1988
Audience: Ages 8-12
Distributor: Barr Films
16mm film: $115 **Videocassette:** $80
Rental: $50

★★★★★

Phantom Tollbooth, The
Norman Juster.

Illustrated by Jules Feiffer. Random House. 1972. [1961]. Fantasy.

A bored young boy drives through a toy tollbooth and enters the fantastic Kingdom of Wisdom, which is enmeshed in a civil war between the City of Words and the City of Numbers.

Phantom Tollbooth, The.

90 min. Color. Live action and animation. Produced by MGM/Chuck Jones, Abe Levitow, Les Goldman. 1969. Butch Patrick as Milo.

The adaptation simplifies yet does justice to the novel. Beginning in live action, the production slips into animation once Milo passes through the tollbooth. The animation is quite fine, but the show has select appeal as the story appeals to a sophisticated audience. Visualized are characters such as Rhyme and Reason and the Demons of Ignorance. The film, like the book, demands continual concentration.

Reviews: *Variety*, Oct. 14, 1970
Audience: Ages 10-14
Distributor: MGM/UA Home Video
Videocassette: $12.95
No public performance rights

★★★★★

Philharmonic Gets Dressed, The
Karla Kushkin.

Illustrated by Marc Simont. Harper & Row. 1982. Realistic fiction.

A young visitor backstage is introduced to the orchestra members and their instruments.

Philharmonic Gets Dressed, The.

30 min. Color. Live action. Produced by Blue Penguin Productions. 1988.

This has a greatly enhanced story line that deviates from the book in order to establish a plot on which to hang the book's introduction to the instruments in a philharmonic orchestra.

As noted by *Booklist*, the film "will be especially enjoyed by music students."

Reviews: *Booklist*, Dec. 1, 1988
Audience: Ages 8-17
Distributor: Coronet/MTI Film & Video
16mm film: $595 **Videocassette:** $250
Rental: $75

★★★★★

Picture for Harold's Room, A
Crockett Johnson (illus.).
Harper & Row Junior Books. 1960. Fantasy.
Harold wants a picture for his wall, so he draws a house, town, the sea, high mountains he crosses over, and so on. He is stumped at the end about how to get home but comes up with a clever solution that highlights the difference between fantasy and reality.

Picture for Harold's Room, A.
6 min. Color. Animated. Produced by Weston Woods. 1971.
The few colors used in the film (purple and tan) highlight the power of Harold's crayon (and imagination). Since Harold journeys into his picture, the motion picture medium is ideal. The show's "...fine narration and a lovely string quartet provide gracefully textured accompaniment to the story of Harold's simply animated exploits." —*Booklist.*
Reviews: *Booklist*, May 1, 1972
Audience: Ages 4-8
Distributor: Weston Woods
16mm film: $175 **Videocassette:** $60
Rental: $20 daily

Amazing Bone and Other Stories, The.
33 min. Color. Iconographic and animated. Produced by Weston Woods. 1989.
Included in this tape anthology are adaptations of *The Amazing Bone* (William Steig), *John Brown, Rose, and the Midnight Cat* (Jenny Wagner), *A Picture for Harold's Room* (Crockett Johnson), and *The Trip* (Ezra Jack Keats). See individual titles for full descriptions.
Reviews: *Children's Video Report*, Apr./May 1989
Audience: Ages 4-12
Distributor: Children's Circle, Weston Woods
Videocassette: $19.95
No public performance rights

★★★★★

Picture of Dorian Gray, The
Oscar Wilde.
Multiple editions. Fantasy.
A young man embarks on a life of debauchery that registers, as the years pass, not on his physical self but on changes in a portrait that was made of him in his youth.

Picture of Dorian Gray, The.
110 min. Black and white. Live action. Produced by MGM/Pandro S. Berman. 1945. George Sanders, Hurd Hatfield, Donna Reed, Angela Lansbury.
As in the novel, Dorian Gray retains his youthful looks while the portrait of him ages. One day his conscience fills him with remorse because of the heartless person he has become and the portrait is restored to its original state while his physical self meets a more tragic end. An engrossing melodrama, this adaptation captures the spirit of the novel.
Reviews: *New York Times*, Mar. 2, 1945, 15:2; *Variety*, Mar. 7, 1945
Awards: Academy Award, Best Cinematography
Audience: Ages 16-Adult
Distributor: MGM/UA Home Video
Videocassette: $24.95
No public performance rights

Picture of Dorian Gray, The.
111 min. Black and white. Live action. 1945. George Sanders, Hurd Hatfield, Donna Reed, Angela Lansbury.
A laser disc version of the same title offered by MGM/UA Home Video (see above).
Distributor: Pioneer LDCA, Inc.
Laser disc: CLV format $34.98
No public performance rights

Dorian Gray.
92 min. Color. Live action. Produced by Harry Alan Towers. 1971. Helmut Berger, Richard Todd, Herbert Lom.
The production, which updates the story to late twentieth century, does not inspire any of the suspense and horror inherent in the tale. While a couple of the performances provide depth, the portrait, which is the key element in the story, appears rather lackluster.

Reviews: *New York Times*, Dec. 10, 1970, 58:4; *Variety*, Nov. 18, 1970
Audience: Ages 16-Adult
Distributor: Republic Pictures Home Video
Videocassette: $14.98
No public performance rights

★★★★★

Pied Piper of Hamelin, The
Robert Browning.
Multiple editions. Poetry.
Hired to rid Hamelin Town of an irksome horde of rats, the Pied Piper accomplishes his task. The townspeople then refuse to pay the piper, who punishes them by leading their children into a mountain from which they never return.

Pied Piper of Hamelin, The.
17 min. Color. Animation. Produced by Argo Sight and Sound. 1970. Narrated by Peter Ustinov.
Peter Ustinov reads the old story in rhyme as skillful animation reveals the tale of greed and honor.

Audience: Ages 8-12
Distributor: Phoenix/BFA Films & Video
16mm film: $340 **Videocassette:** $210
Rental: $49

Pied Piper of Hamelin, The.
11 min. Color. Limited animation. Produced by Coronet. 1980.
Adequately animated, this version of the old story is precisely true to the details in Browning's poetic tale.

Audience: Ages 7-12
Distributor: Coronet/MTI Film & Video
16mm film: $170 **Videocassette:** $130
Rental: $75

Pied Piper of Hamelin, The (Faerie Tale Theatre).
60 min. Color. Live action. Produced by Shelley Duvall. 1982. Eric Idle as the Pied Piper.
This is a tremendously lifelike rendition of the poem, complete with hordes of actual rats. While accurately relayed, it is set in a larger context. A boy visits the English countryside in 1840, and his guardian tells him the Browning tale. Adding to the realism, the townspeople converse during the delivery of the poem. Though some lines of verse are difficult for the very young to comprehend, the plot unfolds so vividly that the show appeals to a wide audience.

Audience: Ages 6-Adult
Distributor: Fox Video
Videocassette: $14.98
No public performance rights

The Pied Piper of Hamelin.
18 min. Color. Limited animation. A Pied Piper Production. 1983. Narrated by Orson Welles.
This is an accurate, artful rendition of the Robert Browning poem. Not immediately engaging, it warms up to a splendid and lyrical delivery of lines by Orson Welles. Visuals consist of brightly colored art in which movement is limited. Like the book, the film highlights the importance of keeping promises.

Reviews: *Horn Book*, Apr. 1984; *School Library Journal*, Apr. 1984
Awards: CINE Golden Eagle
Audience: Ages 8-14

Distributor: Churchill Media
16mm film: $315 **Videocassette:** $79
Rental: $60

Pied Piper, The.
8 min. Color. Animation. A Disney Educational Production. 1986.
In the original, the children of Hamelin are lured to a mysterious land; the Disney film names the place Garden of Happiness to soften the ending for sensitive young viewers.
Audience: Ages 4-8
Distributor: Coronet/MTI Film & Video
16mm film: $280 **Videocassette:** $195
Rental: $75

★★★★★

Pierre
Maurice Sendak (illus.).
Harper & Row Junior Books. 1962. Humor.
A delightfully funny tale about apathy, this book features Pierre, who just doesn't care about anything until a lion offers him a ride.

Pierre.
6 min. Color. Animated. Produced by Weston Woods. 1978. Directed by Maurice Sendak. Music by Carole King.
Set to music and sung by Carole King, the text accompanies adroitly animated art from the storybook. The singer's tone enhances the humor in the story, and creates a lilting rhythm of its own. The pace is lively, the lyrics are clearly understandable, and the show is delightfully amusing.
Audience: Ages 4-8
Distributor: Weston Woods
16mm film: $175 **Videocassette:** $60
Rental: $20 daily

Maurice Sendak Library.
35 min. Color. Animated. Produced by Weston Woods. 1989.
Included in this tape anthology are adaptations of *Alligators All Around*, *Pierre*, *One Was Johnny*, *Chicken Soup with Rice*, *In the Night Kitchen*, and *Where the Wild Things Are*. See individual titles for full descriptions. An additional segment, *Getting to Know Maurice Sendak*, features the author commenting on his work.
Reviews: *Children's Video Report*, Nov. 1, 1990
Audience: Ages 4-8
Distributor: Children's Circle, Weston Woods
Videocassette: $19.95
No public performance rights

★★★★★

"Pigeon Feathers"
John Updike.
Anthologized in *Pigeon Feathers and Other Stories*. Knopf. 1962. Short stories—realistic fiction.
A family moves to a farm, where the teenage boy, full of questions about life and death, finds peace in the quiet and beauty of the countryside.

Pigeon Feathers.
45 min. Color. Live action. Produced by Learning in Focus. 1987. Christopher Collet, Caroline McWilliams.
Though Caroline McWilliams is excellent, her performance cannot completely compensate for an uneventful script with its repeated voicing of questions about the meaning of life and afterlife.
Reviews: *New York Times*, Nov. 6, 1988; *Video Librarian*, Nov. 1988
Awards: CINE Golden Eagle
Audience: Ages 15-18
Distributor: Monterey Home Video
Videocassette: $24.95
No public performance rights

★★★★★

Pigs' Wedding, The
Helme Heine.
Macmillan. 1979. [1978]. Fantasy.
From far and wide, the pigs arrive to witness the marriage of Porker and Curly Tail. The couple clean their guests up and paint clothing on them, but nature leaves the pigs in a more familiar state at story's end.

Pigs' Wedding, The.
7 min. Color. Animated. Produced by Kratky Film, Prague/Weston Woods. 1990.
Full animation and a song during the wedding festivities complement the story. Nature intervenes on the day of the ceremony. It rains. Their "clothing" washed away, the pig guests frolic in the mud.
Audience: Ages 4-6
Distributor: Weston Woods
16mm film: $250 **Videocassette:** $125
Rental: $25 daily

Pigs' Wedding and Other Stories, The.
39 min. Color. Iconographic and animated. Produced by Weston Woods. 1991.
Included in this tape anthology are adaptations of *The Pigs' Wedding* (Helme Heine), *The Happy Owls* (Celestino Piatti), *The Selkie Girl* (Susan Cooper), *A Letter to Amy* (Ezra Jack Keats), and *The Owl and the Pussy-Cat* (Edward Lear). See individual titles for full descriptions.
Audience: Ages 4-8
Distributor: Children's Circle, Weston Woods
Videocassette: $19.95
No public performance rights

★★★★★

Pinballs, The
Betsy Byars.
Harper & Row. 1977. Realistic fiction.
Three young people are placed in the same foster home, where their differences finally give way to love and respect.

Pinballs, The.
31 min. Color. Live action. A Disney Educational Production. 1977. Kristy McNichol.
Kristy McNichol, as the most headstrong of the three protagonists who share the foster home, leads a fine cast. The story, in print and on film, exposes their difficult problems with a great deal of sensitivity.
Audience: Ages 8-14
Distributor: Coronet/MTI Film & Video
16mm film: $655 **Videocassette:** $495
Rental: $75

★★★★★

Pinocchio, the Tale of a Puppet
Carlo Collodi.
Multiple editions. Fantasy.
Old Geppetto carves a talking wooden puppet, Pinocchio, who, says the fairy, must prove himself to become a real boy. Untruthful, Pinocchio is punished for his lies with a longer and longer nose. A series of adventures lands the puppet inside a fish before he reforms and becomes a a real boy.

Pinocchio.
88 min. Color. Animation. Produced by Walt Disney. 1940. Featuring the voices of Dickie Jones and Evelyn Venable.
This captivating movie about the wooden puppet has dazzling animation and unforgettable characters. Because of some frightening scenes (the chase with the whale and Lampwick's transformation into a donkey), the Disney classic is unsuitable for very young audiences. Otherwise, the portrayal is topnotch entertainment.

Reviews: *New York Times*, Feb. 8, 1940
Awards: Academy Awards, Best Music Score, Best Song
Audience: Ages 8-Adult
Distributor: Buena Vista Home Video (not currently in distribution)

Pinocchio (Faerie Tale Theatre).
60 min. Color. Live action. Produced by Shelley Duvall. 1983. Pee Wee Herman, James Coburn, Carl Reiner, Lainie Kazan.
James Coburn makes a marvelous Geppetto and Laine Kazan is a convincing fairy in this amusing live-action adaptation. Though he seems more naive than mischievous, Pee Wee Herman is appropriately disobedient as Pinocchio. The wooden boy gets sidetracked by a gypsy who plans to change him into a donkey and by swindlers before being swallowed by a whale. Lending authenticity to the show, the characters and narrator speak English with an Italian accent. The setting, a small Italian town, is quite lifelike in this production; the fairy is a voluptuous-looking character.
Audience: Ages 6-10
Distributor: Fox Video
Videocassette: $14.98
No public performance rights

Pinocchio (Faerie Tale Theatre).
51 min. Color. Live action. 1983. Pee Wee Herman, James Coburn, Carl Reiner, Lainie Kazan.
A laser disc version of the same title offered by Fox Video (see above).
Distributor: Image Entertainment
Laser disc: CLV format $29.98
No public performance rights

*****

Pippi Longstocking
Astrid Lindgren.
Penguin USA. 1950. Humor.
Pippi, a nine-year-old Swedish girl, lives by herself with a horse and monkey. Defeating efforts by the police and others to reform her, Pippi tells fantastic tales and has a knack for involving herself in comic escapades. Sequels to this initial novel include *Pippi Goes on Board*, *Pippi in the South Seas*, and *Pippi on the Run*.

New Adventures of Pippi Longstocking, The.
100 min. Color. Live action. Produced by Columbia/Gary Mehlman, Walter Moshay. 1988. Tami Erin, Eileen Brennan, Dennis Dugan.
Altogether unconvincing, this motion picture is a slow-moving Americanized version that places Pippi in a small Florida community. She makes an enemy of an orphanage mistress due to her practical jokes, and the film spends considerable time on uninspired food fights. The character, not the plot, has been adapted from the literature, but instead of a fearless young girl, Pippi comes across as perennial troublemaker.
Reviews: *New York Times*, July 29, 1988, C11
Audience: Ages 8-12
Distributor: Columbia TriStar Home Video
Videocassette: $19.95
No public performance rights

New Adventures of Pippi Longstocking, The.
100 min. Color. Live action. 1988. Tami Erin, Eileen Brennan, Dennis Dugan.
A laser disc version of the same title offered by Columbia TriStar Home Video (see above).
Distributor: Pioneer LDCA, Inc.
Laser disc: CLV format $34.95
No public performance rights

★★★★★

Pit and the Pendulum, The
Edgar Allan Poe.

Multiple editions. Short stories—horror.
The horror story features a man who imagines himself to be his own father, a major torturer in the Spanish Inquisition.

Pit and the Pendulum, The.
80 min. Color. Live action. Produced by AIP/Roger Corman. 1961. Luana Anders, Anthony Carbone, John Kerr, Vincent Price, Barbara Steele.
The film skillfully builds the short story into a larger tale. Price is perfect as the demented hero and is supported by a good cast in this well-staged, but somewhat slow-moving adaptation.
Reviews: *New York Times*, Aug. 24, 1961, 25:3; *Variety*, Aug. 9, 1961
Audience: Ages 15-Adult
Distributor: Warner Home Video
Videocassette: $19.98

★★★★★

Planet of the Apes
Pierre Boulle.

NAL. 1968. [1963]. Science fiction.
Two astronauts unexpectedly land on a planet ruled by talking apes. The humans on this planet (Earth in the future) are silent and are kept in zoos or used as laboratory animals.

Planet of the Apes.
112 min. Color. Live action. Produced by Twentieth Century Fox/Mort Abrahams. 1968. Charlton Heston, Roddy McDowall, Kim Hunter.
Hailed as thought-provoking and entertaining, this adaptation is science fiction at its finest. Special effects enhance the delivery of the novel's tale. The picture won a special Oscar for its marvelous ape makeup.
Reviews: *New York Times*, Feb. 9, 1968, 55:2; *Variety*, Feb. 7, 1968
Awards: Academy Award, Best Makeup
Audience: Ages 12-Adult
Distributor: Fox Video
Videocassette: $19.98
No public performance rights

Planet of the Apes.
112 min. Color. Live action. 1968. Charlton Heston, Roddy McDowall, Kim Hunter.
A laser disc version of the same title offered by Fox Video (see above).
Distributor: Image Entertainment
Laser disc: Widescreen CLV format $59.98
No public performance rights

★★★★★

Pollyanna
Eleanor Porter.

Multiple editions. Realistic fiction.
Pollyanna brings joy to people in a small New England town in 1912. She transforms the town grump, reunites her aunt with an old love, and helps establish a new orphanage.

Pollyanna.
134 min. Color. Live action. Produced by George Golitzen/ Walt Disney. 1960. Hayley Mills, Jane Wyman, Karl Malden.
Climbing back into the house after sneaking to the town fair, Pollyanna falls and her legs are paralyzed. The cheery soul almost gives up on life, but the townfolk, touched by her love, rally her spirits as she leaves to have surgery. Though the picture seems overly long and serious, it features some outstanding performances.
Reviews: *New York Times*, May 20, 1960
Awards: Academy Award, Outstanding Juvenile Performance

Audience: Ages 5-Adult
Distributor: Buena Vista Home Video (not currently in distribution)

★★★★★

Ponies of Mykillengi
Lonzo Anderson.
Scribner. 1966. Adventure.
Children of Iceland ride their ponies into many adventures as they explore the varied landscape.

Ponies of Miklaengi.
25 min. Color. Live action. Produced by Daniel Smith/Gary Templeton. 1979.
Beautiful scenery of Iceland and bright young characters doing what children often want to do—riding ponies—make this an interesting film. Add an earthquake and the birth of a foal for an exciting tale that captures the wonder of nature: "The film succeeds as the book did in conveying the awesomeness of nature's miracles...." —*Horn Book*
Reviews: *Horn Book*, Feb. 1980
Audience: Ages 8-12
Distributor: Phoenix/BFA Films & Video
16mm film: $450 **Videocassette:** $260
Rental: $40

★★★★★

Portnoy's Complaint
Philip Roth.
Random House. 1969. Realistic fiction.
A Jewish boy in New Jersey falls victim to pent-up guilt associated with his ethnic heritage and his sexual longings.

Portnoy's Complaint.
101 min. Color. Live action. 1972. Richard Benjamin, Karen Black, Lee Grant.
Portnoy describes his sexual problems and family to his therapist. Though lines have been lifted directly from the novel, the spirit in this dull adaptation has been left behind. "Gone with the novel's...serious substructure, and with its exuberant, practically slapstick superstructure, is any real feeling of Alex's anguish." —*New York Times*
Reviews: *New York Times*, June 20, 1972, 35:1; *Variety*, June 21, 1972
Audience: Ages 15-18
Distributor: Warner Home Video
Videocassette: $64.99
No public performance rights

★★★★★

Pride and Prejudice
Jane Austen.
Multiple editions. Realistic fiction.
Mrs. Bennet, a nineteenth-century Englishwoman in an amiable family, plans to marry off her five daughters. One of them, spirited Elizabeth, resents the haughty airs of a Mr. Darcy, a man she ultimately agrees to marry.

Pride and Prejudice.
116 min. Black and white. Live action. Produced by MGM/Hunt Stromberg. 1940. Laurence Olivier, Greer Garson, Edmund Gwenn, Mary Boland, Melville Cooper, Edna May Oliver.
The cast, the set, and the screenplay join forces to make this an outstanding adaptation of the comedy-of-manners novel. Mr. Darcy's pride exudes a haughtiness that prejudices Elizabeth Bennet against him until the man reveals his true character.
Reviews: *New York Times*, Aug. 9, 1940, 19:1; *Variety*, July 10, 1940
Awards: Academy Award, Best Set Design
Audience: Ages 14-Adult
Distributor: MGM/UA Home Video
Videocassette: $19.98

No public performance rights

Pride and Prejudice.
226 min. Color. Live action. Produced by BBC. 1980. Elizabeth Garvie, David Rintoul.
The comic moments are more pronounced in this lengthy yet entertaining production than in the novel, and the females, even by their gestures, give the impression of being more opinionated.
Reviews: *London Sunday Times*, Jan. 27, 1980
Audience: Ages 14-Adult
Distributor: Fox Video
Videocassette: $29.98
No public performance rights

★★★★★

Prime of Miss Jean Brodie, The
Muriel Spark.
NAL. 1984. [1961]. Realistic fiction.
A teacher in an Edinburgh school influences her susceptible students in a detrimental fashion.

Prime of Miss Jean Brodie, The.
116 min. Color. Live action. Produced by Fox/Robert Fryer. 1969. Maggie Smith.
The novel loses impact in its translation to the screen. As in print, Miss Brodie so inspires her pupils that one scurries off to Spain to fight for France and dies. Miss Brodie is quite changeable and ultimately mentally unstable as their teacher. Maggie Smith commands attention and hearty applause for her superb performance in the role.
Reviews: *New York Times*, Mar. 3, 1969, 30:1
Awards: Golden Globe, Best Original Song
Audience: Ages 16-Adult
Distributor: Fox Video
Videocassette: $19.98
No public performance rights

★★★★★

Prince and the Pauper, The
Mark Twain.
Multiple editions. Adventure.
Look-alikes, one a street urchin and the other the Prince of Wales, exchange places. Confusion reigns when the king dies and the Prince must be crowned king.

Prince and the Pauper, The.
120 min. Black and white. Live action. Produced by Warner Brothers/Robert Lord. 1937. Errol Flynn, Claude Rains, Henry Stephenson, Barton MacLane, Billy Mauch, Bobby Mauch.
This is an action-packed tale befitting the swashbuckling image of Errol Flynn, backed by a well-suited musical score. Even in black and white, it provides fine entertainment for present-day audiences. The version adapts a book by Eric Portman and William Keighley based on the Mark Twain novel. Not in Twain's novel but in the picture is the idea that the Earl of Hartford knew of the boys' switch and tried to exploit it by assassinating the genuine prince. This minor change appears in a production that, as stated in the *New York Times*, is "an exciting make believe, gently humorous and melodramatically adventurous."
Reviews: *New York Times*, May 6, 1937, 23:1; *Variety*, May 12, 1937
Audience: Ages 10-Adult
Distributor: MGM/UA Home Video
Videocassette: $19.98
No public performance rights

Prince and the Pauper, The.
113 min. Color. Live action. Produced by International Film Production/Ilya and Alexander Salkind. 1978. Ernest Borgnine, Rex Harrison, Charlton Heston, Mark Lester, Oliver Reed, George C. Scott, Raquel Welch.
Plush sets, handsome costumes, and a star-studded cast do not raise this production, originally released as *Crossed Swords*, above average. Mark Lester is older than the parts warrant in his double roles of the young prince and the pauper.
Reviews: *New York Times*, Mar. 2, 1978, III 14:1; *Variety*, June 15, 1977
Audience: Ages 10-Adult
Distributor: Videocassette not currently in distribution

Prince and the Pauper, The.
24 min. Color. Animation. Produced by Walt Disney. 1990.
Mickey Mouse is both prince and pauper in this animated version of Mark Twain's story. Goofy comes to the aid of the prince when his father dies and leaves him the throne. Overall, the show is classic, slapstick-style entertainment. It has "stunning layouts," but "completely lost is the element of the prince learning what it's like to be a peasant or seeing the peasant adjust to the fruits and constraints of royalty." —*Variety*
Reviews: *Variety*, Nov. 14, 1990
Audience: Ages 6-10
Distributor: Buena Vista Home Video
Videocassette: $12.99
No public performance rights

★★★★★

Prince Caspian
The Voyage of the Dawn Treader
C. S. Lewis (illus.).
Macmillan. 1988 [1951]. 1988. [1952]. Fantasy.
In *Prince Caspian* the English children return to mythical Narnia to help restore it to the rule of the talking beasts. They join the Prince in the *Voyage of the Dawn Treader* to rescue some missing lords.

Prince Caspian and the Voyage of the Dawn Treader.
171 min. Color. Live action. Produced by BBC/Wonderworks/Paul Stone. 1989. Richard Dempsey, Susan Cook, Jonathan R. Scott, Sophie Wilcox, Jean Marc Perret, Samuel West.
Delightfully imaginative, this sequel to *The Lion, the Witch and the Wardrobe* captures the thrilling momentum of two enchanting plots. First young Prince Caspian champions the old Narnians in battle against the new. Next, two of the English children rejoin the Prince on a quest by sea to rescue seven lords. Their journey brings them into contact with slavers, a dragon, and the like.
Audience: Ages 8-12
Distributor: Public Media Video
Videocassette: $29.95
No public performance rights

★★★★★

Princess and the Pea, The
Hans Christian Andersen.
Multiple editions. Folklore and fairy tales.
A prince searches in vain for a true princess to marry. One day a storm drives to his castle a bedraggled maiden who claims to be a princess. The queen puts the maiden to the test, having her sleep on twenty mattresses and twenty eider-down beds that sit over a single pea. Unable to sleep due to the pea, the sensitive maiden proves her royalty.

Princess and the Pea, The (Faerie Tale Theatre).
60 min. Color. Live action. Produced by Shelley Duvall. 1983. Liza Minnelli, Tom Conti, Beatrice Straight.

True to the traditional tale, this delightfully comic version opens at the end with the pea on display in a museum. The rest of the production is a flashback that retains the classic story line but augments it with new characters. The prince has a fool companion, a somewhat silly king father, and an imperious queen mother. There is a wonderful warmhearted quality of friendship between the prince, the princess, and the fool. As the production progresses, other candidates for princess appear, but the prince's friendship with the storm-drenched maiden blossoms into love. She adds a dimension to the story, admonishing the prince for his superficial considerations in choosing a partner. Though it does not detract from the plot, the fool tries to warn the princess about the pea in this version. She cannot clearly hear his warning, though, and endures the sleepless night.

Audience: Ages 8-Adult
Distributor: Fox Video
Videocassette: $14.98
No public performance rights

Princess and the Pea, The (Faerie Tale Theatre).
50 min. Color. Live action. 1983. Liza Minnelli, Tom Conti, Beatrice Straight.
A laser disc version of the same title offered by Fox Video (see above).

Distributor: Image Entertainment
Laser disc: CLV format $29.98
No public performance rights

★★★★★

Princess Bride.
William Goldman.
Ballantine. 1987. [1974]. Adventure; humor.

Grandfather reads a bedtime story to a sick grandson. Set in a medieval land, the action-packed adventure involves a princess who consents to marry a prince upon discovering that her true love has been killed by pirates. When the princess is kidnapped, a mysterious stranger rescues her.

Princess Bride.
98 min. Color. Live action. Produced by Andrew Scheinmann, Rob Reiner. 1987. Cary Elwes, Mandy Patinkin, Chris Sarandon.
Adapted for the screen by the novelist himself, the production includes some exceptional scenes and characterizations. Comic bits interfere with the flow of the story on occasion, and a few of the lines are difficult to understand.

Audience: Ages 14-Adult
Distributor: New Line Home Video
Videocassette: $19.95
No public performance rights

Princess Bride.
98 min. Color. Live action. 1987. Cary Elwes, Mandy Patinkin, Chris Sarandon.
A laser disc version of the same title offered by Nelson Entertainment (see above).

Distributor: Criterion Collection
Laser disc: CLV format $34.98, Widescreen CLV format $39.95, Widescreen CAV format $79.95
No public performance rights

★★★★★

Prometheus and the Story of Fire
I. M. Richardson.
Illustrated by Robert Baxter. Troll. 1983. Folklore and fairy tales.

In this classic myth, Prometheus, sympathizing with winter-frozen humans, tricks the keeper of the gods' fire into giving him some; he then spreads fire throughout the world.

Prometheus.
18 min. Color. Animation. Produced by Brian Jackson Films. 1987.
Limited animation, skillfully applied, makes this an entertaining film about Prometheus's adventure with fire in defiance of the will of the gods.
Reviews: *Curriculum Products Review Service*, Apr. 1988
Audience: Ages 8-12
Distributor: Barr Films
16mm film: $425 **Videocassette:** $296
Rental: $50

★★★★★

Pudd'nhead Wilson
Mark Twain.
Multiple editions. Realistic fiction.
A mulatto slave woman exchanges her baby for one of her white master's.

Pudd'nhead Wilson.
87 min. Color. Live action. Produced by PBS. 1984. Ken Howard, Lise Hilboldt, Stephen Webber.
Filmed in West Virginia, this is an excellent adaptation of Twain's classic. The show was among the best received of the PBS American Playhouse offerings.
Audience: Ages 10-18
Distributor: MCA/Universal Home Video
Videocassette: $19.95
No public performance rights

★★★★★

Puss in Boots
Charles Perrault.
Multiple editions. Folklore and fairy tales.
A wily cat helps its master, a miller's son, gain wealth, land, and the hand of a beautiful princess by outsmarting an evil ogre.

Puss in Boots.
11 min. Color. Limited animation. Produced by Coronet. 1980.
Though the animation is limited, this film is full and faithful in plot development. Coronet has added a cat friend for the brilliant Puss in Boots.
Audience: Ages 5-10
Distributor: Coronet/MTI Film & Video
16mm film: $280 **Videocassette:** $195
Rental: $75

Puss in Boots (Faerie Tale Theatre).
60 min. Color. Live action. Produced by Shelley Duvall. 1984. Gregory Hines, Ben Vereen, Alfred Woodard.
Delightful acting by an all-black cast brings this classic to life. A dimension of humor is added as the miller's son alternates between exasperated anger at his cat and support of its plan to bring him riches. Performed by a human in costume, the cat proves itself crafty and loyal, as in the classic tale. New to the motion picture is the concept of a princess who is exceedingly poor due to the evil ogre. The dialog includes a few updated phrases—*he's a scream* and *are you out of your gourd*—that are entertaining but out of sync with the language used in traditional readings.
Audience: Ages 6-Adult
Distributor: Fox Video
Videocassette: $14.98
No public performance rights

Puss-in-Boots.
26 min. Color. Animation. Produced by Rankin-Bass. 1990.
This is another average television-style cartoon, which falls flat and seems weakly scripted.
Audience: Ages 4-8
Distributor: Lucerne Media
Videocassette: $195

★★★★★

Pygmalion
George Bernard Shaw.
Multiple editions. Drama.
A professor bets he can transform a Cockney flower girl into a lady of such pure speech that no one will detect her origins.

Pygmalion.
90 min. Black and white. Live action. Produced by Gabriel Pascal. 1938. Leslie Howard, Wendy Hiller, Wilfrid Lawson.
This is a joyous adaptation of the richly humorous play, exceptionally fine in its faithfulness to Shaw and in its cinematic strength. Howard is particularly marvelous as the professor.
Reviews: *New York Times*, Dec. 8, 1938, 34:2; *Variety*, Sept. 7, 1938
Awards: Academy Awards, Best Adaptation, Best Screenplay
Audience: Ages 14-Adult
Distributor: Janus Films
Videocassette: $88

Pygmalion.
90 min. Black and white. Live action. 1938. Leslie Howard, Wendy Hiller, Wilfrid Lawson.
A home video version of the same title offered by Janus Films (see above).
Distributor: New Line Home Video
Videocassette: $14.95
No public performance rights

Pygmalion.
96 min. Black and white. Live action. 1938. Leslie Howard, Wendy Hiller, Wilfrid Lawson.
A laser disc version of the same title offered by Janus Films (see above).
Distributor: Janus Films, Criterion Collection
Laser disc: CLV format $88 (with public performance rights)
Laser disc: CLV format $39.95 (no public performance rights)

My Fair Lady.
171 min. Color. Live action. Produced by Jack L. Warner. 1964. Rex Harrison, Audrey Hepburn, Stanley Holloway.
A film classic, this musical adaptation of Shaw's play won awards for excellence in several categories. Harrison makes a superb Professor Higgins, and the Lerner and Lowe songs ("The Rain in Spain," "Get Me to the Church on Time," "I Could Have Danced All Night") became classics in their own right.
Reviews: *New York Times*, Oct. 22, 1964, 41:1; *Variety*, Oct. 28, 1964
Awards: Academy Awards, Best Picture, Best Actor, Best Directing, Best Cinematography, Best Art Direction—Set Decoration, Best Sound, Best Music Score, Best Costumes; Golden Globe Awards, Best Musical, Best Actor in a Musical
Audience: Ages 12-Adult
Distributor: Fox Video
Videocassette: $29.98
No public performance rights

My Fair Lady.
170 min. Color. Live action. 1964. Rex Harrison, Audrey Hepburn, Stanley Holloway.

A laser disc version of the same title offered by Fox Video (see above).

Distributor: Image Entertainment
Laser disc: CLV format $44.98, Widescreen CLV format $69.98
No public performance rights

Q

adherence to book   film rating

Quarreling Book, The
Charlotte Zolotow.
Illustrated by Arnold Lobel. Harper & Row. 1963. Realistic fiction.
A story of the James family illustrates how one person's mood can start a chain reaction in feelings and behavior.

Quarreling Book, The.
16 min. Color. Live action. Produced by LCA. 1989.
A rather unexciting dramatization, this film follows the tribulations of a usually happy family turned to quarreling on a dismal day. The slow story is nevertheless faithful to the book.
Audience: Ages 4-8
Distributor: Coronet/MTI Film & Video
16mm film: $435 **Videocassette:** $250
Rental: $75

R

adherence to book   film rating

Ragtime
E. L. Doctorow.
Random House. 1975. Historical fiction.
The story is a patchwork saga of individuals living in pre-World War I America who are affected by current events. Included are interacting families and a black revolutionary.

Ragtime.
155 min. Color. Live action. Produced by Ragtime/Dino de Laurentiis. 1981. Mary Steenburgen, Howard E. Rollins, Jr., James Cagney, Elizabeth McGovern.
A fine cast carries this film beautifully, especially in the early part of the adaptation. Later, the focus is narrowed from the complex structure of the novel to the one strand in which the black character seeks justice.
Reviews: *New York Times*, Nov. 20, 1981, C, 10:5; *Variety*, Nov. 18, 1981
Audience: Ages 15-Adult
Distributor: Paramount Home Video
Videocassette available
No public performance rights

Ragtime.
156 min. Color. Live action. 1981. Mary Steenburgen, Howard E. Rollins, Jr., James Cagney, Elizabeth McGovern.
A laser disc version of the same title offered by Paramount Home Video (see above).
Distributor: Pioneer LDCA, Inc.
Laser disc: CLV format $39.95
No public performance rights

★★★★★

Raiders of the Lost Ark: The Storybook Based on the Movie
Les Martin and George Lucas.
Random House. 1981. Adventure.
An archaeologist and his girlfriend compete with the Nazis for possession of a biblical artifact.

Raiders of the Lost Ark.
115 min. Color. Live action. Produced by Lucasfilm/Frank Marshall. 1981. Harrison Ford, Karen Allen, Ronald Lacey.
The film is a stream of hair-raising adventures starring hero Indiana Jones (played by Ford). The frightening episodes may be a bit excessive, but the film is such a crowd pleaser that it was adapted into a storybook.
Reviews: *Variety*, June 10, 1981
Awards: Academy Awards, Best Art Direction—Set Decoration, Best Sound, Best Film Editing, Best Visual Effects
Audience: Ages 10-Adult

Distributor: Paramount Home Video
Videocassette available
No public performance rights

Raiders of the Lost Ark.
115 min. Color. Live action. 1981. Harrison Ford, Karen Allen, Ronald Lacey.
A laser disc version of the same title offered by Paramount Home Video (see above).
Distributor: Pioneer LDCA, Inc.
Laser disc: CLV format $29.95, CAV format $49.95
No public performance rights

★★★★★

Raisin in the Sun, A
Lorraine Hansberry.
Random House. 1969. [1961]. Drama.
A black family in a Chicago ghetto experiences conflict over how to spend a ten-thousand-dollar insurance payment.

Raisin in the Sun, A.
128 min. Black and white. Live action. Produced by Paman—Doris/David Susskind, Philip Rose. 1961. Sidney Poitier, Ruby Dee, Claudia McNeil.
The cast performs with outstanding sensitivity in a drama adapted for the screen by the original playwright.
Reviews: *New York Times*, Mar. 30, 1961, 24:1; *Variety*, Mar. 29, 1961
Audience: Ages 14-Adult
Distributor: Columbia TriStar Home Video
Videocassette: $14.95
No public performance rights

★★★★★

Ralph S. Mouse
Beverly Cleary.
Illustrated by Paul O. Zelinsky. William Morrow and Co. 1982. Fantasy.
Leaving the hotel that is home, a motorcycle-riding mouse named Ralph accompanies the boy Ryan to school. There Ralph becomes the subject of a classroom science experiment and a peacemaker between two hostile boys.

Ralph S. Mouse.
40 min. Color. Live action and dimensional animation. Produced by George McQuilken and John Clark Matthews. 1990. Karen Black, Ray Walston.
Like the book, the movie is delightfully entertaining and raises several issues that stimulate thoughts about friendship, school, and experimenting with animals. The music enriches a version that strays from the original only slightly, adding entertaining sequences that fit with the plot. The janitor, for example, becomes a "villain" out to catch the mouse-hero Ralph.
Reviews: *Booklist*, Mar. 15, 1991
Awards: Andrew Carnegie Award; ALSC Notable Film & Video; *Booklist* Best of the Best
Audience: Ages 4-12
Distributor: Churchill Media
16mm film: $495 **Videocassette:** $225
Rental: $60

Ralph S. Mouse.
40 min. Color. Live action and dimensional animation. 1990. Karen Black, Ray Walston.
A laser disc version of the same title also distributed by Churchill Media (see above).
Distributor: Churchill Media
Laser disc: CAV format $225

★★★★★

Ramona and Her Mother
Beverly Cleary.
Illustrated by Alan Tiegreen. William Morrow and Co. 1979. Realistic fiction.
At age seven, Ramona experiences jealousy, fear, and loneliness. She envies her older sister's closeness with their mother, fears that her parents will divorce, and handles her loneliness by preparing to run away. The sister also goes through a trying time with her hair.

Ramona: The Great Hair Argument.
27 min. Color. Live action. Produced by Atlantis Films, Lancit Media, and Revcom Television. 1988. Sarah Polley, Lori Chodos, Lynda Mason Green, Barry Flatman.
Ramona's older sister, Beezus, insists on getting her hair cut professionally and the result is disastrous. While the show generally corresponds to the incident in the book, it adds a sequence of imagination that features the fairy tale character Rapunzel. In the film, Aunt Bea and Mom remedy the hair disaster; in the book the disaster resolves itself.
Audience: Ages 6-11
Distributor: Churchill Media
16mm film: $435 **Videocassette:** $59
Rental: $60

Ramona: The Great Hair Argument.
27 min. Color. Live action. 1988. Sarah Polley, Lori Chodos, Lynda Mason Green, Barry Flatman.
A home video version of the same title distributed by Churchill Media (see above).
Audience: Ages 6-11
Distributor: Warner Home Video
Videocassette: $14.95
No public performance rights

Ramona: New Pajamas.
27 min. Color. Live action. Produced by Atlantis Films, Lancit Media, and Revcom Television. 1988. Sarah Polley, Lori Chodos, Lynda Mason Green, Barry Flatman.
In a show that closely matches action in *Ramona and Her Mother*, Ramona wears her new pajamas to school under her clothes. Later, feeling unappreciated, she decides to run away from home. Instead of protests, her mother helps Ramona pack and, in the process, tricks her into staying.
Audience: Ages 6-11
Distributor: Churchill Media
16mm film: $435 **Videocassette:** $59
Rental: $60

Ramona: New Pajamas.
27 min. Color. Live action. 1988. Sarah Polley, Lori Chodos, Lynda Mason Green, Barry Flatman.
A home video version of the same title distributed by Churchill Media (see above).
Distributor: Warner Home Video
Videocassette: $14.95
No public performance rights

Ramona: Ramona's Bad Day.
27 min. Color. Live action. Produced by Atlantis Films, Lancit Media, and Revcom Television. 1988. Sarah Polley, Lori Chodos, Lynda Mason Green, Barry Flatman.
From poor performance in school to her parents' fight at home, Ramona has one bad experience after another. Loosely based on action in *Ramona and Her Mother*, the show adds details such as Ramona's keeping a diary and her fantasy of what would happen to her if her parents divorced. It draws Uncle Hobart (from another book, *Ramona Forever*) into the action. The spirit of events and relationships are preserved despite these

changes.
Audience: Ages 6-11
Distributor: Churchill Media
16mm film: $435 **Videocassette:** $59
Rental: $60

Ramona: Ramona's Bad Day.
27 min. Color. Live action. 1988. Sarah Polley, Lori Chodos, Lynda Mason Green, Barry Flatman.
A home video version of the same title distributed by Churchill Media (see above).
Distributor: Warner Home Video
Videocassette: $14.95
No public performance rights

★★★★★

Ramona Forever

Beverly Cleary.
Illustrated by Alan Tiegreen. William Morrow and Co. 1984. Realistic fiction.
Now a third grader, Ramona experiences a new babysitting arrangement in which her sister Beezus is supervisor. She also meets her friend Howie's rich uncle, attends a wedding, loses a pet, and gains a baby sister.

Ramona: Goodbye Hello.
16.5 min. Color. Live action. Produced by Atlantis Films, Lancit Media, and Revcom Television. 1988. Sarah Polley, Lori Chodos, Lynda Mason Green, Barry Flatman.
Focusing on Ramona's relationship with her older sister Beezus, this show reveals both hostile and loving feelings. The girls overcome their bickering in the face of tragedy when their cat dies. Mostly in keeping with the original, the film changes some minor details—for example, the cat dies in the basement in the book, outdoors in the film.
Audience: Ages 6-11
Distributor: Churchill Media
16mm film: $435 **Videocassette:** $59
Rental: $60

Ramona: Goodbye Hello.
26.5 min. Color. Live action. 1988. Sarah Polley, Lori Chodos, Lynda Mason Green, Barry Flatman.
A home video version of the same title distributed by Churchill Media (see above).
Audience: Ages 6-11
Distributor: Warner Home Video
Videocassette: $14.95
No public performance rights

Ramona: The Perfect Day.
27 min. Color. Live action. Produced by Atlantis Films, Lancit Media, and Revcom Television. 1988. Sarah Polley, Lori Chodos, Lynda Mason Green, Barry Flatman.
Ramona's Aunt Bea marries Hobart, a man Ramona dislikes. Mostly in keeping with the character in *Romana Forever*, Hobart on screen differs in appearance. Instead of blond, curly hair, the movie's Hobart has dark, straight hair. Still, the film keeps to the general sequence of events and the spirit of the characters in the novel.
Reviews: *Booklist*, Feb. 15, 1989
Audience: Ages 6-11
Distributor: Churchill Media
16mm film: $435 **Videocassette:** $59
Rental: $60

Ramona: The Perfect Day.
27 min. Color. Live action. 1988. Sarah Polley, Lori Chodos, Lynda Mason Green, Barry Flatman.

A home video version of the same title distributed by Churchill Media (see above).
Distributor: Warner Home Video
Videocassette: $14.95
No public performance rights

Ramona: Siblingitis.
27 min. Color. Live action. Produced by Atlantis Films, Lancit Media, and Revcom Television. 1988. Sarah Polley, Lori Chodos, Lynda Mason Green, Barry Flatman.
The film centers on the approaching arrival of a third child in the Quimby family and Ramona's feelings concerning it. Some details stray from the original. The doctor who diagnoses Ramona's case of siblingitis is a woman on the screen, a man in *Ramona Forever*. Still, the general spirit and plot line of both the film and book versions match.
Reviews: *School Library Journal*, May 1989
Audience: Ages 6-11
Distributor: Churchill Media
16mm film: $435 **Videocassette:** $59
Rental: $60

Ramona: Siblingitis.
27 min. Color. Live action. 1988. Sarah Polley, Lori Chodos, Lynda Mason Green, Barry Flatman.
A home video version of the same title distributed by Churchill Media (see above).
Distributor: Warner Home Video
Videocassette: $14.95
No public performance rights

★★★★★

Ramona Quimby, Age Eight
Beverly Cleary.
Illustrated by Alan Tiegreen. William Morrow and Co. 1981. Realistic fiction.
Reaching the third grade, Ramona has an embarrassing experience in school. At home, she and her sister must prepare dinner as punishment for refusing to eat a meal their mother made. An irritable Sunday ends with a happy surprise.

Ramona: Mystery Meal.
27 min. Color. Live action. Produced by Atlantis Films, Lancit Media, and Revcom Television. 1988. Sarah Polley, Lori Chodos, Lynda Mason Green, Barry Flatman.
This is an entertaining show with a moral: appreciate what you have. Excerpting an incident from the book, it follows the Quimby girls as they prepare a mystery meal for their parents because they refused to eat the tongue served to them the previous night. The film follows closely the action in the book, adding a few details, such as Ramona's exotic imaginings at the mention of mystery meat for dinner.
Reviews: *Los Angeles Times*, Sept. 17, 1988
Audience: Ages 6-11
Distributor: Churchill Media
16mm film: $435 **Videocassette:** $59
Rental: $60

Ramona: Mystery Meal.
27 min. Color. Live action. 1988. Sarah Polley, Lori Chodos, Lynda Mason Green, Barry Flatman.
A home video version of the same title distributed by Churchill Media (see above).
Distributor: Warner Home Video
Videocassette: $14.95
No public performance rights

Ramona: The Patient.
27 min. Color. Live action. Produced by

Atlantis Films, Lancit Media, and Revcom Television. 1988. Sarah Polley, Lori Chodos, Lynda Mason Green, Barry Flatman.

When Ramona throws up in front of the whole class, her mother leaves work and brings her embarrassed daughter home. Ramona creates an oral book report at home, then forgets her embarrassment in the excitement of delivering it when she returns to school. There is an addition to the action drawn from *Ramona Quimby, Age Eight*; Aunt Bea drops in for a visit in the movie but not in the book. The spirit and plot lines of both versions are, however, closely matched.

Reviews: *School Library Journal*, May 1989

Audience: Ages 6-11

Distributor: Churchill Media

16mm film: $435 **Videocassette:** $59

Rental: $60

Ramona: The Patient.

27 min. Color. Live action. 1988. Sarah Polley, Lori Chodos, Lynda Mason Green, Barry Flatman.

A home video version of the same title distributed by Churchill Media (see above).

Distributor: Warner Home Video

Videocassette: $14.95

No public performance rights

Ramona: Rainy Sunday.

27 min. Color. Live action. 1988. Sarah Polley, Lori Chodos, Lynda Mason Green, Barry Flatman.

Moping at home on a rainy Sunday, Ramona is bored until her father takes the family out to dinner at the Whopperburger, where they meet a mysterious stranger. Taken mostly from *Ramona Quimby, Age eight*, the movie adds a sequence that is absent from the novel (Ramona's imagining herself outside playing in the rain). It also inserts an incident from another book (Ramona squeezing out a whole tube of toothpaste from *Ramona and Her Mother*). Yet the spirit and plot line are generally faithful to the original.

Reviews: *Booklist*, Feb. 15, 1989

Audience: Ages 6-11

Distributor: Churchill Media

16mm film: $435 **Videocassette:** $59

Rental: $60

Ramona: Rainy Sunday.

27 min. Color. Live action. 1988. Sarah Polley, Lori Chodos, Lynda Mason Green, Barry Flatman.

A home video version of the same title distributed by Churchill Media (see above).

Distributor: Warner Home Video

Videocassette: $14.95

No public performance rights

Ramona: Squeakerfoot.

27 min. Color. Live action. Produced by Atlantis Films, Lancit Media, and Revcom Television. 1988. Sarah Polley, Lori Chodos, Lynda Mason Green, Barry Flatman.

Among other incidents in the film, Ramona humiliates herself by cracking a supposedly hard-boiled egg on her face. The egg, it turns out, is raw. Using the visual medium to full advantage, the film adds a few details that are in keeping with, but not in, *Ramona Quimby, Age Eight*. Ramona, for example briefly imagines her head full of scrambled eggs.

Audience: Ages 6-11

Distributor: Churchill Media

16mm film: $435 **Videocassette:** $59

Rental: $60

Ramona: Squeakerfoot.
27 min. Color. Live action. 1988. Sarah Polley, Lori Chodos, Lynda Mason Green, Barry Flatman.
A home video version of same title distributed by Churchill Media (see above).

Distributor: Warner Home Video
Videocassette: $14.95
No public performance rights

★★★★★

"Ransom of Red Chief, The"
O. Henry.
Anthologized in *The Ransom of Red Chief and Other Stories.* Running Press. 1989. Short stories—adventure.
A boy kidnapped and held for ransom turns the tables on his three captors.

Ransom of Red Chief, The.
27 min. Color. Live action. 1978.
The impish kidnap victim in this adaptation of the O. Henry story will charm any viewer, and his antagonists will raise equal sympathy. This is a fine half-hour of entertainment, based on a strong screenplay with performers well-suited to their parts.

Awards: ALA Selected Film for Young Adults; CINE Golden Eagle; Chris Bronze Plaque, Columbus Film Festival
Audience: Ages 10-18
Distributor: Coronet/MTI Film & Video
16mm film: $500 **Videocassette:** $250
Rental: $75

★★★★★

"Rappaccini's Daughter"
Nathaniel Hawthorne.
Anthologized in *Twice Told Tales.* Multiple editions. Short stories—horror.
Dr. Rappaccini raises his daughter like a rare flower, sequestering her from the public and having her system absorb the poison of a plant. A scholar in a neighbor's rooming house falls in love with the daughter.

Rappaccini's Daughter.
57 min. Color. Live action. Produced by Perspective films/Robert Geller. 1980. Series host Henry Fonda.
Realistic in its Padua, Italy, setting, this adaptation evokes the chilling spirit of the original tale. The performances are quite believable; the ominous atmosphere surrounding the daughter is almost palpable.

Audience: Ages 15-18
Distributor: Monterey Home Video
Videocassette: $24.95
No public performance rights

★★★★★

Rapunzel
Jacob Grimm and Wilhelm K. Grimm.
Multiple editions. Folklore and fairy tales.
A witch catches a man stealing from her garden and demands he repay her with his daughter. Locked up in a tower, the daughter is nearly rescued by a prince, but the witch interferes. Finally, the prince and Rapunzel are united.

Rapunzel.
11 min. Color. Animation. Produced by Ray Harryhausen. 1955.
Animated in the fine style of Harryhausen, this film is a faithful interpretation of the Grimm story of a maiden harassed by a wicked witch.

Audience: Ages 6-10
Distributor: Phoenix/BFA Films & Video
16mm film: $225 **Videocassette:** $130
Rental: $29

Rapunzel, Rapunzel.
15 min. Color. Live action. Produced by Tom and Mimi Davenport. 1978.
For most of this production, a narrator explains events as the actors perform them. The technique is distancing, making this faithful dramatization rather uninvolving.
Audience: Ages 5-12
Distributor: Davenport Films
16mm film: $275 **Rental:** $30
Videocassette: $60 (with public performance rights)
Videocassette: $29.95 (no public performance rights)

Rapunzel.
10 min. Color. Animation. Produced by Somersaulter and Moats. 1981.
Film descriptions by the distributor say that symbols *coruscate* ("flash") along the picture borders as the story unfolds. The *coruscating* symbols distract and clutter the film. Inside the borders, however, a nice story is portrayed.
Reviews: *Booklist*, Apr. 15, 1981
Awards: CINE Golden Eagle; Chris Plaque, Columbus International Film Festival
Audience: Ages 4-8
Distributor: Coronet/MTI Film & Video
16mm film: $265 **Videocassette:** $170
Rental: $75

Rapunzel (Faerie Tale Theatre).
60 min. Color. Live action. Produced by Shelley Duvall. 1982. Jeff Bridges, Shelley Duvall, Gena Rowlands. Narrated by Roddy McDowall.
This adaptation is quite faithful to the original, with minor exceptions. The vegetable stolen in the tale is "rampion"; in the movie it is "radish." Added in the screen version is the explanation that the witch locks Rapunzel up because she believes "you can't trust men." In the movie, Rapunzel befriends a talking bird, who informs the witch about the secretive visits of the prince; in the tale Rapunzel herself divulges the truth. The motion picture concludes with the prince discovering not only Rapunzel in the wilderness but also twin children she has given birth to in the interim. Gena Rowlands is exceptionally convincing as the witch.
Reviews: *Variety*, Feb. 8, 1984
Audience: Ages 8-Adult
Distributor: Fox Video
Videocassette: $14.98
No public performance rights

Rapunzel (Faerie Tale Theatre).
51 min. Color. Live action. 1983. Jeff Bridges, Shelley Duvall, Gena Rowlands. Narrated by Roddy McDowall.
A laser disc version of the same title offered by Fox Video (see above).
Distributor: Image Entertainment
Laser disc: CLV format $29.98
No public performance rights

Rapunzel (Timeless Tales).
30 min. Color. Animation. Produced by Hanna-Barbera and Hallmark Cards. 1990. Hosted by Olivia Newton-John.
The live-action scene that starts the show seems a bit contrived, but the animated adaptation of the fairy tale is charming. It changes some details. Punished by the villain, the prince, instead of becoming blind, is changed into a dove, and he finds Rapunzel in the woods rather than the desert.
Audience: Ages 4-8
Distributor: Hanna-Barbera Home Video
Videocassette: $14.95
No public performance rights

★★★★★

Rascal
Sterling North.
Illustrated by John Schoenherr. Dutton. 1963. Nonfiction.
Set in Wisconsin in 1918, this volume deals with a baby raccoon named Rascal and his relationship with a lonely boy.

Rascal.
15 min. Color. Live action. A Disney Educational Production. 1981.
Not the best of the Disney films, this adaptation of the nonfiction book is reasonably entertaining. The film was initiated as a made-for-education production.
Audience: Ages 10-14
Distributor: Coronet/MTI Film & Video
16mm film: $390 **Videocassette:** $250
Rental: $75

*****

Rebecca
Daphne Du Maurier.
Doubleday. 1948. [1938]. Mystery.
An aristocratic landowner marries a shy woman who is haunted by thoughts of her predecessor, the landowner's first wife.

Rebecca.
132 min. Black and white. Live action. Produced by David O. Selznick. 1940. Laurence Olivier, Joan Fontaine, George Sanders, Judith Anderson.
Performed to the hilt, this best-selling novel adapted to film is masterfully suspenseful. Alfred Hitchcock directed the production. Along with gripping tension, it has moments of romance, humor, and drama. Particularly exceptional is the performance of the housekeeper by Judith Anderson.
Reviews: *New York Times*, Mar. 29, 1940, 25:2; *Variety*, Mar. 27, 1940
Awards: Academy Awards, Best Picture, Best Cinematography
Audience: Ages 16-Adult
Distributor: Fox Video
Videocassette: $19.98
No public performance rights

Rebecca.
132 min. Black and white. Live action. 1940. Laurence Olivier, Joan Fontaine, George Sanders, Judith Anderson.
A laser disc version of the same title offered by Fox Video (see above).
Distributor: Criterion Collection
Laser disc: CAV format $124.95, CLV format $69.95
No public performance rights

*****

Rebecca of Sunnybrook Farm
Kate Douglas Wiggin.
Multiple editions. Realistic fiction.
With her sunny personality, Rebecca Randall wins over the neighborhood when she moves to her aunt's farm. She continues to live there after her aunt dies.

Rebecca of Sunnybrook Farm.
80 min. Black and white. Live action. Produced by Twentieth Century Fox/Darryl F. Zanuck. 1938. Shirley Temple, Randolph Scott.
The story has been vastly transformed. In this musical version, a child star is a victim of an attempt to capitalize on her talents over the radio.
Audience: Ages 8-12
Distributor: Fox Video
Videocassette: $19.98
No public performance rights

Rebecca of Sunnybrook Farm.
161 min. Black and white. Live action. 1938. Shirley Temple, Randolph Scott.

A laser disc version of the same title offered by Fox Video (see above). Also includes a second feature, *The Little Colonel*.

Distributor: Image Entertainment
Laser disc: CLV format $49.98
No public performance rights

★★★★★

Red Badge of Courage, The
Stephen Crane.

Multiple editions. Historical fiction.
A young man caught up in the Civil War runs away from battle when he sees his friends dying around him, then returns to become a fine Union soldier.

Red Badge of Courage, The.
69 min. Black and white. Live action. Produced by MGM/Gottfried Reinhardt. 1951. Audie Murphy, Bill Mauldin, Douglas Dick, Royal Dano.
Not overplayed, this film is a realistic portrayal of people caught in the horrors of war. The natural performances suit the story superbly. "Gottfried Reinhardt's production backs the psychological intent of the story with realistic physical support." —*Variety*

Reviews: *New York Times*, Oct. 19, 1951, 22:2; *Variety*, Aug. 15, 1951
Audience: Ages 12-Adult
Distributor: MGM/UA Home Video
Videocassette: $24.98
No public performance rights

★★★★★

Red Carpet, The
Rex Parkin (illus.).

Macmillan. 1988. [1948]. Humor.
A story in rhyme, this tale follows the path of a nonstop red carpet rolled out by a hotel doorman. It finally comes to rest at the ferry, where it serves a surprisingly useful purpose.

Red Carpet, The.
9 min. Color. Iconographic. Produced by Weston Woods. 1955.
The great fun in this story lies in the novelty of the nonstop carpet and in the element of surprise at the end. (The carpet comes to rest at the feet of a visiting dignitary who debarks from the ferry.) Though only the camera moves, energetic narration and the rapid tempo of the music help simulate motion.

Audience: Ages 4-8
Distributor: Weston Woods
16mm film: $175 **Videocassette:** $60
Rental: $20 daily

★★★★★

Red Pony, The
John Steinbeck.

Penguin. 1959. [1945]. Realistic fiction.
A boy grows fond of a pony and spends a great deal of time with it to avoid his unhappy family. When the pony dies, the boy suspects a ranch hand has played a role in the death.

Red Pony, The.
89 min. Color. Live action. Produced by Republic/Lewis Milestone. 1949. Robert Mitchum, Peter Miles, Myrna Loy, Louis Calhern.
Peter Miles is excellent as the boy in this production, which is accompanied by an Aaron Copeland score. Steinbeck's novel is actually a compilation of four tales: *The Gift*; *The Great Mountains*; *The Promise*; and *The Leader of the People*. The film carefully adapts all of the first story and parts of the last two, picturing the red pony's death "with fidelity to the stabbing shock of Mr. Steinbeck's tale."—*New York Times*

Reviews: *New York Times*, Mar. 9, 1949, 33:2; *Variety*, Feb. 9, 1949

Audience: Ages 12-Adult
Distributor: Republic Pictures Home Video
Videocassette: $19.98
No public performance rights

Red Pony, The.
100 min. Color. Live action. Produced by Frederick Brogger. 1973. Jack Elam, Henry Fonda, Clint Howard, Ben Johnson, Maureen O'Hara.
In this version, the role of Billy Buck, which dominated the earlier film, is abandoned and emphasis falls on the father, who is so hardened that he has difficulty expressing his love for his son. Henry Fonda commands attention for his sensitive portrayal of the father. Included in the production is some harsh violence.
Reviews: *Variety*, Mar. 21, 1973
Awards: Peabody Award, Outstanding Drama Special
Audience: Ages 12-Adult
Distributor: Phoenix/BFA Films & Video
16mm film: $1,350 **Videocassette:** $585
Rental: $100

★★★★★

Red Room Riddle, The
Scott Corbett.
Illustrated by Geff Gerlach. Little, Brown & Co. 1975. Mystery.
Two boys enter an old abandoned mansion and find themselves in the company of a ghost and a bulldog. Led by the ghost, the boys make their way to a mysterious, glowing red room.

Red Room Riddle, The.
24 min. Color. Live action. Produced by ABC Weekend Specials. 1983. Christopher Hall, Billy Jacoby.
After a not-too-exciting opening, the fine cast turns this film experience into a spine-tingling, imagination-stirring pleasure. "This smoothly produced drama will send chills up the spines of young mystery fans." —*Booklist*
Reviews: *Booklist*, Aug. 1984
Audience: Ages 8-11
Distributor: Coronet/MTI Film & Video
16mm film: $455 **Videocassette:** $250
Rental: $75

★★★★★

Red Shoes, The
Hans Christian Andersen.
Multiple editions. Folklore and fairy tales.
A vain little girl wears inappropriate red shoes to church, and thinks only of them during the service. She later wears them to a ball instead of tending her sick old guardian. The shoes begin dancing of their own accord, not stopping until the girl's feet are cut off, and she repents of her vanity.

Red Shoes, The.
25 min. Color. Animation. Produced by Michael Sporn and Italtoons Corp. 1990. Narrated by Ossie Davis.
Hans Christian Andersen's religious fairy tale is transformed in time and place to present-day New York. Two black girls are best friends. Lisa, one of the girls, and her family win the lottery. Afterwards, Lisa becomes spoiled and arrogant until she puts on a pair of red shoes that bring her back to her senses and back to her best friend. Watercolor style animation, and upbeat, rhythmic music heightens the impact of this splendidly adapted values tale.
Awards: Gold Electra, Birmingham Film Festival; Special Award for Animation, Chicago International Film Festival; CINE Golden Eagle; Silver Medal, Parents' Choice Award
Audience: Ages 8-12
Distributor: Lucerne Media

16mm film: $495 **Videocassette:** $295

Red Shoes, The.
25 min. Color. Animation. Produced by Michael Sporn and Italtoons. 1990.
A home video version of the same title distributed by Lucerne Media (see above).
Audience: Ages 8-12
Distributor: Family Home Entertainment
Videocassette: $14.95
No public performance rights

★★★★★

Reluctant Dragon, The
Kenneth Grahme.
Multiple editions. Fantasy.
A dragon-wise young boy "arranges" a fight between a dragon and a knight to please the townspeople. In truth, the dragon is a poetry-loving beast that has absolutely no interest in fighting.

Reluctant Dragon, The.
28 min. Color. Animation. Produced by Walt Disney. 1941.
The delightful yet simple animation and characterization remain true to the storybook. This is a literary rather than a quarrelsome dragon that spouts poems for the dragon-wise little boy who befriends him. The boy helps the dragon prepare for a bout with the knight, Sir Giles, as in the book. Instead of the dragon's being slightly wounded, the show has the combatants simulate a wound to trick the crowd. The spirit in the print and video versions is identical.
Audience: Ages 4-8
Distributor: Buena Vista Home Video
Videocassette: $12.99
No public performance rights

Reluctant Dragon, The.
19 min. Color. Animation. A Disney Educational Production. 1980.
Young viewers will long remember the poem-loving, flower-smelling dragon, the bungling but lovable Sir Giles, and the sensible young boy in this ageless adaptation of the tale. The animation is full and brightly colored, with a charming simplicity well-suited to the tale.
Audience: Ages 4-8
Distributor: Coronet/MTI Film & Video
16mm film: $480 **Videocassette:** $250
Rental: $75

Reluctant Dragon, The.
12 min. Color. Animation. Produced by Bosustow Entertainment. 1981.
This straightforward adaptation opens with the boy shepherd, moves on to his encounter with the obstinately nonviolent dragon, and culminates with the mock fight between dragon and knight in which the dragon is speared. Faithful to the storybook, the film is imaginative and entertaining. It is a gentle discussion-prompter to the subject of fighting.
Awards: CINE Golden Eagle
Audience: Ages 4-8
Distributor: Churchill Media
16mm film: $260 **Videocassette:** $59
Rental: $50

★★★★★

Remarkable Riderless Runaway Tricycle, The
Bruce McMillan (illus.).
Apple Island Books. 1985. [1978]. Fantasy.
A discarded tricycle escapes from a trash heap to lead a chase through the town.

Remarkable Riderless Runaway Tricycle, The.

11 min. Color. Live action. Produced by John Sturner/Gary Templeton. 1982.
There is a great and adventurous chase in this non-narrated film of a tricycle that seems to have a mind of its own. "A meticulously created film that ranks among the best ever produced for children."—*Horn Book*

Reviews: *Booklist*, Aug. 1982; *Horn Book*, Oct. 1982
Audience: Ages 4-8
Distributor: Phoenix/BFA Films & Video
16mm film: $275 **Videocassette:** $175
Rental: $23

★★★★★

"Renegade, The"
Shirley Jackson.
Anthologized in *Hunting Women* edited by A. Ryan. Avon Books. 1988. Short stories—realistic fiction.
A family that has recently moved to the country discovers its dog likes to raid the neighbor's chicken coop.

Renegade, The.
19 min. Color. Live action. Produced by Rex Victor Goff. 1984.
A bit cluttered, the film is still a good adaptation of a story about a series of neighborhood incidents. There is so much action that some viewers may find it hard to follow.

Audience: Ages 14-16
Distributor: Phoenix/BFA Films & Video
16mm film: $450 **Videocassette:** $250
Rental: $40

★★★★★

"Rescue Party"
Arthur C. Clarke.
Anthologized in *The Arbor House Treasury of Modern Science Fiction* by R. S. Silverberg and M. H. Greenberg. Arbor House. 1980. Short stories—science fiction.
Space ship commander Alveron travels to rescue residents of a small planet about to be destroyed when its sun explodes. The planet's residents, however, are not what the travelers had expected.

Rescue Party.
21 min. Color. Live action. Produced by Bernard Wilets. 1978.
Accompanying notes from the distributor suggest that viewers will be compelled to think about the fate of their own planet as they watch this strange story of a small planet about to be destroyed by its exploding sun. However, the short story and its film version never quite generate the excitement and involvement needed to make this giant extrapolation.

Audience: Ages 12-18
Distributor: Britannica
Videocassette: $260

★★★★★

"Retrieved Reformation, A"
O. Henry.
Anthologized in *The Black Cabinet*, edited by Peter Lovesey. Carroll & Graf. 1989. Short stories—realistic fiction.
A safecracker is released from prison, falls in love, then faces a dilemma. Should he expose his past and use his criminal skills to rescue a child trapped in a safe?

O. Henry's "Jimmy Valentine."
30 min. Color. Live action. Produced by LCA. 1985. Victor Ertmanis, Mark Strong.
This film begins with an introduction of O. Henry as a prison inmate who uses his time to write stories; one of them is about a safecracker. The production proceeds with a moderately entertaining adaptation that remains true to the short story, including its surprise ending.

Awards: ALA Selected Film for Young Adults

Audience: Ages 12-Adult
Distributor: Coronet/MTI Film & Video
16mm film: $550 **Videocassette:** $250
Rental: $75

O. Henry's "Jimmy Valentine."
55 min. Color. Live action. 1985. Victor Ertmanis, Mark Strong.
A full-length version of the same, abbreviated title also distributed by Coronet/MTI Film & Video (see above).

Audience: Ages 12-Adult
Distributor: Coronet/MTI Film & Video
16mm film: $750 **Videocassette:** $250
Rental: $75

★★★★★

Return from Witch Mountain
Alexander Key.
Archway Paperbacks. 1984. [1978]. Science fiction.
Two young aliens with special powers have traveled to earth's Witch Mountain to seek their origins. As they return, one is kidnapped by two villains intent on using the powers.

Return from Witch Mountain.
95 min. Color. Live action. Produced by Walt Disney. 1978. Bette Davis, Christopher Lee, Kim Richards.
Bette Davis is at her most villainous as she kidnaps one of the young people endowed with special powers in this sequel to *Escape to Witch Mountain.* The picture is just plain fun.

Reviews: *New York Times*, July 14, 1978, III 14:5
Audience: Ages 8-15
Distributor: Buena Vista Home Video (not currently in distribution)

★★★★★

Revenge of the Nerd
John McNamara.
Dell. 1985. [1984]. Humor.
A computer wiz who is considered a nerd by his peers turns his genius to revenge.

Revenge of the Nerd.
31 min. Color. Live action. Produced by LCA and Robert Keeshan Associates. 1983. Manny Jacobs, Chris Barnes.
As in the original the "nerd" aims to take revenge on the boys who ridicule him and to impress a girl. He manages only to distance her from him. This short version has been effectively cut from a full-length film. The result is a slightly faster pace and greater adherence to the story.

Reviews: *Booklist*, Apr. 1, 1984; *School Library Journal*, May, 1984
Awards: ALA Selected Film for Young Adults; First Place, National Educational Film and Video Festival
Audience: Ages 10-15
Distributor: Coronet/MTI Film & Video
16mm film: $550 **Videocassette:** $250
Rental: $75

Revenge of the Nerd.
45 min. Color. Live action. 1983. Manny Jacobs, Chris Barnes.
A full-length version of the same, abbreviated title also distributed by Coronet/MTI Film & Video (see above).

Audience: Ages 10-15
Distributor: Coronet/MTI Film & Video
16mm film: $750 **Videocassette:** $250
Rental: $75

★★★★★

"Revolt of Mother, The"
Mary E. Wilkins Freeman.
Anthologized in *Selected Stories of Mary E. Wilkins Freeman.* Norton. 1983. Short stories—realistic fiction.
A man developing a New England farm continues to add to the farm building despite having promised his wife a new house. When she rebels in an unusual way, their love for each other is tested and revealed.

Revolt of Mother, The.
46 min. Color. Live action. Produced by Learning in Focus. 1988.
Slightly slow-moving but nevertheless charming, this story tells of a rebellious wife in the late nineteenth century. Her daughter and son learn from both her revolt and her subsequent behavior.
Audience: Ages 16-Adult
Distributor: Coronet/MTI Film & Video
16mm film: $750 **Videocassette:** $250
Rental: $75

Revolt of Mother, The.
46 min. Color. Live action. Produced by Learning in Focus. 1989.
A home video version of the same title distributed by Coronet/MTI Film & Video (see above).
Distributor: Monterey Home Video
Videocassette: $24.95
No public performance rights

★★★★★

Right Stuff, The
Tom Wolfe.
Bantam. 1984. [1979]. Nonfiction.
The novel concerns the birth of America's space program, woven around the activities of test pilot Chuck Yeager.

Right Stuff, The.
193 min. Color. Live action. Produced by Warner/Ladd. 1983. Sam Shepard, Scott Glenn, Ed Harris, Dennis Quaid.
Characteristic roles and real-life scenes of space flights and test flying combine with exaggerations on screen to make this a not-too-serious testimonial to frontier flights. The show deals mainly with the training and exploitation of astronauts, delving beneath the astronaut-hero surface with the help of some fine acting. "There's not a weak performance in the entire film."—*New York Times*
Reviews: *New York Times*, Oct. 21, 1983, C5:1
Awards: Academy Awards, Best Film Editing, Best Music Score, Best Sound
Audience: Ages 10-18
Distributor: Warner Home Video
Videocassette: $29.98
No public performance rights

Right Stuff, The.
193 min. Color. Live action. 1983. Sam Shepard, Dennis Quaid.
A laser disc version of the same title offered by Warner Home Video (see above).
Distributor: Pioneer LDCA, Inc.
Laser disc: CLV format $39.98
No public performance rights

★★★★★

Rip Van Winkle
Washington Irving.
Multiple editions. Short stories—fantasy.
Shiftless but loveable, Rip Van Winkle takes a rest in the Catskill Mountains, where he discovers Commander Henry Hudson drinking ale and playing ninepins. Twenty years later Rip wakes up to an independent America.

Rip Van Winkle.
19 min. Color. Animation. Produced by Bernard Wilets. 1970.
Beautifully drawn cells, animated mostly in iconographic style, tell this classic story very well. The production remains highly faithful to the original writing.
Awards: CINE Golden Eagle
Audience: Ages 8-16
Distributor: Britannica
Videocassette: $250

Rip Van Winkle (Faerie Tale Theatre).
60 min. Color. Live action. Produced by Shelley Duvall. 1985. Harry Dean Stanton, Talia Shire.
Directed by Francis Ford Coppola, this is a vivid dramatization that captures quite exactly Rip's shiftless but good-natured personality. There is an appropriately dreamlike quality to his comraderie in the mountains with Henry Hudson. Not present in Irving's tale but added to this adaptation is a conservation message: Hudson charges Rip with the responsibility of seeing that the people respect the land. Otherwise, the show matches closely the story line and characterization of the original.
Audience: Ages 12-Adult
Distributor: Fox Video
Videocassette: $14.98
No public performance rights

★★★★★

Robin Hood.
Multiple editions. Folklore and fairy tales.
Among various editions, *The Merry Adventures of Robin Hood* by Howard Pyle (Scribner's 1946) is often hailed as the classic. Its twenty-two stories recount the adventures in Sherwood Forest. Robin Hood, a Saxon rebel, takes to the forest and with a band of outlaws matches wits and brawn against traitorous Norman nobles, robbing the rich to help the poor and preserving the kingship for the absent King Richard.

Adventures of Robin Hood, The.
102 min. Color. Live action. Produced by Hal B. Wallis/Warner. 1938. Errol Flynn, Olivia de Havilland, Claude Rains, Basil Rathbone.
Errol Flynn has been described as the definitive Robin Hood, and this production does absolute justice to the action-packed literary classic. The Austrians are holding King Richard captive, and Robin Hood plans to raise the ransom by stealing from the rich. The film captures the personalities of legendary characters such as Little John, Friar Tuck, and Maid Marion, while Flynn enhances the Robin Hood role with a hearty dash of eye-sparkling humor and admirable athletics.
Reviews: *New York Times*, May 13, 1938, 17:2; *Variety*, Apr. 27, 1938
Awards: Academy Awards, Best Set Design, Best Music Score
Audience: Ages 9-Adult
Distributor: MGM/UA Home Video
Videocassette: $19.98
No public performance rights

Adventures of Robin Hood, The.
102 min. Color. Live action. 1938. Errol Flynn, Olivia de Havilland.
A laser disc version of the same title offered by MGM/UA Home Video (see above).
Distributor: The Voyager Company
Laser disc: CAV format $99.95, CLV format $49.95
No public performance rights

Story of Robin Hood and His Merry Men, The.
83 min. Color. Live action. Produced by Perce Pearce/Walt Disney. 1952. Richard Todd, Joan Rice, Peter Finch.

The adaptation is a faithful portrayal of Robin Hood and his Merry Men, who rob the rich to aid the poor. Though older than other versions, this is both straightforward and action-packed, with Robin Hood craftily emptying the treacherous Prince John's coffers to ransom King Richard and Maid Marion.

Reviews: *New York Times*, Jan. 27, 1952
Audience: Ages 7-Adult
Distributor: Buena Vista Home Video
Videocassette: $19.99
No public performance rights

Story of Robin Hood and His Merry Men, The.
83 min. Color. Live action. 1952. Richard Todd, Joan Rice, Peter Finch.
A laser disc version of the same title offered by Buena Vista Home Video (see above).

Distributor: Image Entertainment
Laser disc: CLV format $34.99
No public performance rights

Robin Hood.
26 min. Color. Animation. Produced by Rankin-Bass. 1972. This is an average animated production, limited to the very young in its cartoon-style appeal.

Audience: Ages 6-12
Distributor: Lucerne Media
Videocassette: $195

Robin Hood.
83 min. Color. Animation. Produced by Wolfgang Reitherman/Walt Disney. 1973. Featuring the voices of Brian Bedford, Phil Harris, Peter Ustinov, Andy Devine.
This well-animated feature has animals filling the roles. Prince John is a lion, Robin Hood is a fox, Little John is a bear, and so on. The changes reduce the romantic classic to episodic cartoon-style escapades. The idea of robbing the rich to give to the poor is retained (and the morality of this is discussed), along with the archery contest in Nottingham. New episodes, characters, expressions (for example, "we're busting out of here") are added. Though the original has broad appeal, this rendition speaks only to very young audiences. Others find the show flat and uninvolving.

Audience: Ages 4-8
Distributor: Buena Vista Home Video
Videocassette: $24.99
No public performance rights

Robin Hood.
104 min. Color. Live action. Produced by John Irvin Film/Working Title Production/Sarah Radclyffe. 1991. Patrick Bergin, Uma Thurman, Jurgen Prochnow.
This is a reasonably faithful adaptation, geared toward older audiences. Some updated language is used, and there is a brief love scene with bare flesh. At one point, Maid Marion disguises herself as a boy, but in the main, the production keeps to the incidents of the original with fine performances and splendidly realistic scenery.

Audience: Ages 16-Adult
Distributor: Fox Video
Videocassette available
No public performance rights

Robin Hood, Prince of Thieves.
120 min. Color. Live action. Produced by John Watson, Pen Densham, and Richard B. Lewis. 1991. Kevin Costner, Morgan Freeman, Christian Slater.
Diverting from the original, this version adds as a main character a Moor named Azeem. The audience first meets him

with Robin Hood in the dungeons of the Middle East, where the hero had gone to fight the Crusades. Robin helps Azeem escape, so the Moor, determined to repay the debt, journeys to England with Robin. From then on, the legend resumes its classic tack with some exceptions. The Sheriff of Nottingham has a witch-adviser who inspires him to hire Celts to fight in Sherwood Forest. They stage an onslaught, complete with burning arrows, and general havoc ensues. There are pluses to this remake. The contrast between the Moor and white society is marvelous, the Moor time and again demonstrating his clever thinking. There is, however, a more distant relationship between Robin and his Merry Men than in the original, with Robin acknowledging his social superiority to the other outlaws. At the same time, this Prince of Thieves seems to have less fun than the Robin Hood in literature. The production, as noted in the *New York Times*, includes "partial nudity." It also features some lusty jokes. The combination makes it most appropriate for older audiences.

Reviews: *New York Times*, June 14, 1991, C1; *Variety*, June 12, 1991
Audience: 14-Adult
Distributor: Warner Home Video
Videocassette: $24.98
No public performance rights

★★★★★

Robinson Crusoe
Daniel Defoe.

Multiple editions. Adventure.
Robinson Crusoe experiences a shipwreck and solitary survival on an island for thirty-five years. Without human contact for a quarter century, Crusoe finally meets a native named Friday.

Robinson Crusoe.
34 min. Black and white. Live action. Produced by W. A. Wetherell. 1936. Narrated by Don Carney.
An announcer narrates the old silent footage in this abridged adaptation of the book. The silent original was produced in Great Britain in 1927, then updated a generation later with music, sound effects, and narration by radio personality Don Carney.

Audience: Ages 15-Adult
Distributor: Video Yesteryear
Videocassette: $24.95
No public performance rights

Robinson Crusoe.
26 min. Color. Animation. Produced by Rankin-Bass. 1990.
The dialogue in this adaptation, which includes a talking parrot, is frivolous at best.

Audience: Ages 10-15
Distributor: Lucerne Media
Videocassette: $195

★★★★★

Rocking-Horse Winner, The
D. H. Lawrence.

Creative Education. 1982. Short stories—realistic fiction.
A boy predicts racetrack winners while riding a rocking horse. Ultimately he rides himself into a feverish frenzy with dire consequences.

Rocking-Horse Winner, The.
91 min. Black and white. Live action. Produced by Rank/Two Cities. 1949. John Mills, Valerie Hobson, John Howard Davies.
This is a strong but lengthy production of the short story.

Reviews: *New York Times,* June 9, 1950, 29:2; Variety, Dec. 21, 1949
Audience: Ages 15-Adult
Distributor: Janus Films

Videocassette: $88

Rocking-Horse Winner, The.
30 min. Color. Live action. Produced by LCA. 1977.
If viewers can endure the first few seconds of screeching parents with British accents, they will find a touching story nicely told in this adaptation of D. H. Lawrence's tale.
Awards: ALA Selected Films for Young Adults
Audience: Ages 15-Adult
Distributor: Coronet/MTI Film & Video
16mm film: $475 **Videocassette:** $250
Rental: $75

★★★★★

Roll of Thunder, Hear My Cry
Mildred D. Taylor.
Dial. 1976. Historical fiction.
The struggles of a Southern black family, the Logans, during the Depression unfold as seen through the eyes of eleven-year-old daughter Cassie.

Roll of Thunder, Hear My Cry.
135 min. Color. Live action. 1978. John Cullum, Morgan Freeman, Janet MacLachlan, Claudia NcNeil, Roy Poole, Lark Ruffin, Larry Scott, Rockne Tarkington.
The Mildred Taylor story is so powerful that it draws in the audience even in this mediocre production. As in the novel, events transpire from the viewpoint of young Cassie, the daughter. Some strong performances contribute to the realism of the production. As described in *Variety*, "the travails of a closely knit black family...were effectively presented despite slow pacing and a rather soft conclusion in dramatic terms."
Reviews: *Variety*, June 7, 1978
Audience: Ages 12-Adult
Distributor: International Video Entertainment
Videocassette: $14.95
No public performance rights

★★★★★

Romeo and Juliet
William Shakespeare.
Multiple editions. Drama.
Two innocent lovers of Verona, Italy, become deadly victims of a feud between their respective families.

Romeo and Juliet.
138 min. Color. Live action. Produced by Rank/Verona. 1954. Laurence Harvey, Susan Shentall, Flora Robson.
The production makes the idea of the dastardly feud between two proud famliies the primary focus. Even Shakespeare's language takes a backseat. As a couple in love, Romeo and Juliet seem stiff rather than passionate. The most effective feature of the production is the dramatic realism it creates. Its photography is outstanding. Costumes and furnishings are copied from paintings of the Renaissance; fashion leaps forward a century from the time of the play for the sake of more showy styles. There are also added scenes, such as the marriage between Romeo and Juliet in a medieval cloister.
Reviews: *New York Times*, Dec. 22, 1954: 28
Audience: Ages 14-Adult
Distributor: Films for the Humanities & Sciences
Videocassette: $89.95

West Side Story.
155 min. Color. Live action. Produced by Mirisch/Seven Arts. 1961. Natalie Wood, Richard Beymer, Russ Tamblyn, Rita Moreno.

The setting has been updated and moved to New York but the story line of star-crossed lovers divided by family feuding is the same. The lovers are Puerto Rican and white, while the "families" involved are their respective gangs. Memorable musical numbers ("Maria," "Tonight," "America") grace the captivatingly energetic production. Shakespeare used music as a vehicle in his works; one suspects the bard would have approved.

Reviews: *New York Times*, Oct. 19, 1961, 39:3; *Variety*, Sept. 27, 1961
Awards: Academy Awards, Best Picture, Best Supporting Actor, Best Supporting Actress, Best Director, Best Cinematography, Best Art Direction—Set Decoration, Best Sound, Best Music Score, Best Costumes; Golden Globe Awards, Best Musical, Best Supporting Actor, Best Supporting Actress
Audience: Ages 12-Adult
Distributor: MGM/UA Home Video
Videocassette: $19.98
No public performance rights

West Side Story.
150 min. Color. Live action. 1961. Natalie Wood, Richard Beymer, Russ Tamblyn, Rita Moreno.
A laser disc version of the same title offered by MGM/UA Home Video (see above).

Distributor: Criterion Collection
Laser disc: Widescreen CLV format $69.95, widescreen CAV format $124.95
No public performance rights

Romeo and Juliet.
152 min. Color. Live action. Produced by Dino de Laurentiis. 1968. Olivia Hussey, Leonard Whiting, Michael York. Featuring Laurence Olivier as the prologue speaker.

Perhaps the best of several adaptations of the tragic play, this production is still less than gripping. The version is notable for the youthfulness of the lead actors. It also won Oscars for its superb photography and costuming. In deference to modern filmmaking, the motion picture clads Juliet skimpily on her wedding night; Romeo is clothesless.

Reviews: *New York Times*, Oct. 9, 1968, 41:1; *Variety*, Mar. 13, 1968
Awards: Academy Award, Best Cinematography and Costume Design; Golden Globe, Best Foreign Film
Audience: Ages 15-Adult
Distributor: Paramount Home Video
Videocassette available
No public performance rights

Romeo and Juliet.
138 min. Color. Live action. 1968. Olivia Hussey, Leonard Whiting, Michael York.
A laser disc version of the same title offered by Paramount Home Video (see above).

Distributor: Pioneer LDCA, Inc.
Laser disc: CLV format $35.95
No public performance rights

Romeo and Juliet.
167 min. Color. Live action. Produced by BBC. 1978. John Gielgud, Rebecca Saire, Patrick Ryecart.
For the first time in the motion picture medium, fourteen-year-old Juliet is played by a fourteen-year-old actress, Rebecca Saire. Neither she nor Romeo inspire great sympathy separately, but together they are reasonably convincing. This is a mostly conventional adaptation, with some exceptional performances by the more minor characters: Celia Johnson makes a splendid nurse; Michael Hordern, a humorously fussy Capulet; and John Gielgud, a dignified Chorus. In contrast to the 1968 remake, which centers on the tragic love affair, the

present version focuses more on the play's subplots. This video edition is for institutional use only.

Reviews: *Los Angeles Times*, Mar. 14, 1979; *Variety*, Dec. 13, 1978
Audience: Ages 14-Adult
Distributor: Ambrose Video
Videocassette: $249.95

★★★★★

Roots
Alex Haley.
Dell. 1980. [1976]. Biography.
A young man is followed from his home village in Africa to America, where he experiences slavery and a stream of related events in his family life.

Roots (6 volumes).
540 min. Color. Live action. Produced by Warner. 1977. LeVar Burton, John Amos, Ben Vereen, Edward Asner.
The superb serial held audiences spellbound when released on television. It is a superior production that plays up the historical context and boasts strong performances by notable actors. Like the novel, the show details American social history through the experiences of its black main characters.

Reviews: *Variety*, Jan. 26, 1977
Awards: Emmy Award, Outstanding Limited Series; Gold Award, Houston International Film Festival
Audience: Ages 10-18
Distributor: Warner Home Video
Videocassette: $64.99 per volume
No public performance rights

★★★★★

"Rose for Emily, A"
William Faulkner.
Anthologized in *Dark Descent*, edited by David Hartwell. St. Martin's Press. 1987. Short stories—mystery.
A member of an upper-class Southern family, Miss Emily meets a Yankee who charms and "conquers" her. Though she plans a wedding, he presumably leaves her. She then buys arsenic, but its spine-tingling use is not revealed until after her death.

Rose for Emily, A.
30 min. Color. Live action. Produced by Lyndon Chubbuck/H. Kaye Dyal. 1983. Angelica Huston, John Carradine. Narrated by John Houseman.
The film, a flashback, begins with characters measuring a casket for Miss Emily. Suspense builds as the production unfolds. Like the short story, the film foreshadows the chilling conclusion during which relatives discover a skeleton and other tell-tale items in a locked bedroom. Riveting performances and expert narration heighten the tension until the film reaches its surprise ending.

Reviews: *English Journal*, Feb. 1984; *Library Journal*, Apr. 1, 1984; *School Library Journal*, Mar. 1984
Awards: CINE Golden Eagle; Honorable Mention, Columbus International Film Festival
Audience: Ages 16-Adult
Distributor: Pyramid Film & Video
16mm film: $525 **Videocassette:** $395
Rental: $95

★★★★★

Rosie's Walk
Pat Hutchins (illus.).
Macmillan. 1968. Humor.
Out for a leisurely walk, Rosie the Hen is oblivious to a hungry fox who is continually frustrated in his efforts to grab hold of her.

Rosie's Walk.
5 min. Color. Animated. Produced by Weston Woods. 1970.
The humor of the tale shines through this well-animated and narrated production. Viewers are in on the joke but not Rosie the Hen as the fox meets obstacle after obstacle (from a water drenching to an unexpected wagon ride) in his attempt to snare her. As described in *Booklist*, the show is "...wonderful visual slapstick."
Reviews: *Booklist*, June 15, 1971
Awards: Blue Ribbon, American Film Festival; CINE Golden Eagle
Audience: Ages 4-6
Distributor: Weston Woods
16mm film: $160 **Videocassette:** $60
Rental: $15 daily

Rosie's Walk and Other Stories.
32 min. Color. Iconographic and animated. Produced by Weston Woods. 1985.
Included in this tape anthology are adaptations of *Rosie's Walk* (Pat Hutchins), "*Charlie Needs a Cloak*," (Tomie de Paola), *The Story about Ping* (Marjorie Flack), and *The Beast of Monsieur Racine*. See individual titles for full descriptions.
Audience: Ages 4-8
Distributor: Children's Circle, Weston Woods
Videocassette: $19.95
No public performance rights

★★★★★

Rufus M.
Eleanor Estes.
Illustrated by Louis Slobodkin. Harcourt Brace Jovanovich. 1943. Realistic fiction.
Rufus Moffatt is a five-year-old with a very persistent and explorative personality, which gets him into many adventures.

Rufus M., Try Again.
13 min. Color. Live action. Produced by Martha Moran. 1977.
Taken from only one chapter of the book, the story focuses on a boy who really wants a library card and finally gets one. This excellent dramatization of the chapter draws the viewer into the spirit of the whole book about Rufus.
Awards: Chris Bronze Plaque, Columbus International Film Festival
Audience: Ages 6-10
Distributor: Phoenix/BFA Films & Video
16mm film: $300 **Videocassette:** $180
Rental: $42

★★★★★

Rumpelstiltskin
Jacob Grimm and Wilhelm K. Grimm.
Multiple editions. Folklore and fairy tales.
At the peril of death, a miller's daughter must prove to the king that she can spin gold from straw as her father claims. A magical little man spins the gold for her, demanding she repay him with her child unless she can guess his name.

Rumpelstiltskin.
7.5 min. Color. Limited animation. Produced by Halas and Batchelor. 1969.
Bright animation, spirited narration, and a brisk pace make this an adequate adaptation, but it is one with little character depth.
Audience: Ages 4-8
Distributor: Britannica
16mm film: $210 **Videocassette:** $210

Rumpelstiltskin.
12 min. Color. Animation. Produced by Perspective Films. 1981.
Smoothly animated from carefully drawn cells by Somersaulter and Moats, this is an involving adaptation of the old tale.
Reviews: *School Library Journal*, Nov. 1982

Audience: Ages 5-10
Distributor: Coronet/MTI Film & Video
16mm film: $295 **Videocassette:** $210
Rental: $75

Rumpelstiltskin (Faerie Tale Theatre).
60 min. Color. Live action. Produced by Shelley Duvall. 1982. Shelley Duvall, Herve Villachaize, Ned Beatty.
This dramatization follows the Grimm storyline, adding personality traits to the characters. The king appears to be a somewhat foolish and materialistic monarch who refuses to marry anyone without money. In the Grimm version, a messenger discovers and relays Rumpelstiltskin's name to the miller's daughter. In this screen version, the miller's daughter herself takes to the wood, where in the thick of night she discovers Rumpelstiltskin's name.
Audience: Ages 6-Adult
Distributor: Fox Video
Videocassette: $14.98
No public performance rights

Rumpelstiltskin (Faerie Tale Theatre).
40 min. Color. Live action. 1982. Shelley Duvall, Herve Villachaize, Ned Beatty.
A laser disc version of the same title offered by Fox Video (see above).
Distributor: Image Entertainment
Laser disc: CLV format $29.99
No public performance rights

Rumpelstiltskin.
30 min. Color. Animation. Produced by Hugh Campbell. 1985. Narrated by Christopher Plummer.
Christopher Plummer narrates this interesting animated version of the story. The illustrations will hold the attention of young viewers who are accustomed to less able animation in some television cartoons.
Audience: Ages 4-8
Distributor: Family Home Entertainment
Videocassette: $9.95
No public performance rights

Rumpelstiltskin.
84 min. Color. Live action. Produced by Golan Globus. 1987. Billy Barty, Amy Irving, John Moulder-Brown.
This is a poor attempt to turn the well-known fairy tale into a musical. Some of the actors appear inappropriate for their roles.
Audience: Ages 6-Adult
Distributor: Cannon Video
Videocassette available
No public performance rights

Rumpelstiltskin (Timeless Tales).
30 min. Color. Animation. Produced by Hanna-Barbera and Hallmark Cards. 1990. Hosted by Olivia Newton-John.
Instead of losing her life in this softened adaptation, the miller's daughter would be banished if she failed to spin straw into gold. Bright animation vividly brings the tale to life. Rumpelstiltskin seems less gruff than in the original, and the prince who marries the miller's daughter resents her common origins. She guesses Rumpelstiltskin's name not in dialogue but in song, a pleasant touch.
Audience: Ages 4-8
Distributor: Hanna-Barbera Home Video
Videocassette: $14.95
No public performance rights

Rumpelstiltskin.
12 min. Color. Animated. Produced by David Alexovich. 1990.

While this adaptation changes a few of the fairy tale's details, it features exceptionally fine animation and dialog. The king threatens not to have the miller's daughter put to death but to throw the miller into prison if his daughter fails to spin the straw into gold. Later the king threatens to lock her up forever. Outside such minor changes the screen version remains true to the tale and adds depth. It is an energetic production, with captivating characterization and artwork.

Audience: Ages 4-8
Distributor: Britannica
Videocassette: $79

★★★★★

Runaway Ralph
Beverly Cleary.
Illustrated by Louis Darling. William Morrow and Co. 1970. Fantasy.
Ralph, the mouse with the motorcycle, rides away from his hotel home to Happy Acres summer camp. There he is caught and caged until he rescues an outcast boy camper by proving him innocent of a crime.

Runaway Ralph.
40 min. Color. Live action and puppet animation. Produced by John Matthews/Churchill Media. 1988. Ray Walston.
Quite faithful to the original, this is a wonderfully realistic combination of live action and dimensional (puppet) animation. The voices of mice are occasionally hard to distinguish but in the main "this is a stellar sequel to Churchill's mouse and the motorcycle."—*Booklist*

Reviews: *Booklist*, Jan. 15, 1989; May 1988; *School Library Journal*, Sept. 1988
Awards: *Booklist* Editors' Choice
Audience: Ages 5-9
Distributor: Churchill Media
16mm film: $495 **Videocassette:** $79
Rental: $75

Runaway Ralph.
40 min. Color. Animation. 1988. Ray Walston.
A home video version of the same title distributed by Churchill Media (see above).

Distributor: Strand VCI
Videocassette: $12.98
No public performance rights

Mouse and the Motorcycle, The (Special Edition).
90 min. Color. Animation. 1991. Ray Walston.
A home video version of two separate titles, *The Mouse and the Motorcycle* and *Runaway Ralph*, distributed by Churchill Media (see above).

Distributor: Strand VCI
Videocassette: $24.95
No public performance rights

S

adherence to book   film rating

Sam and His Cart
Arthur Honeyman.
Illustrated by Michael De Waide. Wheel Press. 1977. Realistic fiction.
Sam, a boy with cerebral palsy, goes door to door in his cart, peddling lightbulbs. He is befriended by some, harshly treated by others. Relying on his own courage and his father's support, Sam survives the difficult days. He eventually becomes a successful author.

Sam.
25 min. Color. Live action. Produced by Daniel Hoffman. 1981.
A difficult subject is sensitively approached in this film about a boy with cerebral palsy, his relations with neighbors—both harsh and kind—and his special relationship with his father. It is a well-told, beautifully acted story of courage. While not the complete book (this account does not cover the boy's adult accomplishments), the film excellently presents the tone and intent of the author.
Awards: Red Ribbon, American Film Festival
Audience: Ages 8-15
Distributor: Barr Films
16mm film: $560 **Videocassette:** $350
Rental: $50

★★★★★

Sam, Bangs and Moonshine
Evaline Ness (illus.).
Holt, Rinehart & Winston. 1966. Realistic fiction.
A girl with a tendency to stretch the truth gets her friend and her cat in trouble.

Sam, Bangs and Moonshine.
15 min. Color. Live action. Produced by Robert Johnson. 1976.
Acting that is sometimes stiff is easily compensated for by the great settings and charm of the boy in trouble in this live-action adaptation of the award-winning book.
Reviews: *Booklist*, May 15, 1979
Audience: Ages 6-10
Distributor: Phoenix/BFA Films & Video
16mm film: $340 **Videocassette:** $215
Rental: $47

Sarah, Plain and Tall
Patricia MacLachlan.
Harper & Row. 1985. Realistic fiction.
Father, a widower, places an advertisement for a bride and mother for his two children. Sarah responds, coming to the farm from Maine for a month's trial at filling the position.

Sarah, Plain and Tall.
97 min. Color. Live action. Produced by William Self/Glenn Close/Hallmark Hall of Fame. 1991. Glenn Close, Christopher Walken, Lexi Randall.
The plot of the slight novel is retained and some emotional conflicts have been added. In the novel, young Anna eagerly welcomes her new "mother," but Anna is reluctant to accept Sarah in this screen version. Also the novel does not dwell on the father's feelings, hinting only at his initial shyness with Sarah, but the movie shows the father struggling with feelings of guilt, as if he were betraying his first wife. Otherwise, the production shows careful regard for incidents and character traits in the novel: Sarah's love for the sea, her strong-mindedness, and her experiences with a haystack and in a storm. The sense of social history in both versions builds this simple story into a fine piece of Americana.
Reviews: *Variety*, Feb. 3, 1991; *Washington Times*, Feb. 1, 1991
Awards: Emmy Award, Outstanding Editing for Miniseries or Special
Audience: Ages 8-Adult
Distributor: Republic Pictures Home Video
Videocassette: $89.98
No public performance rights

★★★★★

Scarlet Letter, The
Nathaniel Hawthorne.
Multiple editions. Historical fiction.
In Puritan times, Hester Prynne is convicted of adultery and must wear a scarlet *A* across her chest. The novel details the effect of her deed on four people: her lover (Reverend Arthur Dimsdale), her child, her husband, and herself.

Scarlet Letter, The.
70 min. Black and white. Live action. Produced by Darmour for Majestic. 1934. Colleen Moore, Hardie Albright, Henry B. Walthall.
The film concentrates on the community's reaction to the outcast rather than the relationship between man and woman. Walthall recreates his good performance as Roger Prynne (from an unavailable 1926 silent version), but it is surrounded by weaker performances from other actors. Colleen Moore seems especially out of place as Hester. A replay of the same basic script, this is not as fine as the 1926 silent version.
Reviews: *Variety*, Sept. 25, 1934
Audience: Ages 15-18
Distributor: KVC Entertainment
Videocassette: $19.95
Distributor: Video Yesteryear
Videocassette: $29.95
No public performance rights

Scarlet Letter, The.
240 min. Color. Live action. Produced by WGBH for The WGBH Collection/Rick Hauser, Herbert Hirschman. 1979. Kevin Conway, Meg Foster, John Heard.
This vividly realistic dramatization, a four-part program, boasts fine performances and close adherence to the novel. Actually, it has been faulted for sticking so closely to the novel and not adjusting the material more to the film medium. Voice-over narration uses Hawthorne's prose quite faithfully, acting as a bridge to the action. The authentic look and verbage, as described in *Variety*, result in "a respectable and literal but far from compelling, four-hour adaptation."
Reviews: *Variety*, Apr. 11, 1979
Audience: Ages 12-Adult
Distributor: Films for the Humanities & Sciences
Videocassette: $249
No public performance rights

Scarlet Letter, The.
90 min. Color. Live action. 1988.
Produced in Germany, this is a carefully detailed version whose appeal is limited

to young audiences that favor foreign films. The actors speak in German with English subtitles.

Audience: Ages 14-Adult
Distributor: Pacific Arts Video
Videocassette: $59.95
No public performance rights

★★★★★

Scarlet Pimpernel, The
Baroness Orczy.
Multiple editions. Historical fiction.
A dapper Englishman becomes Pimpernel, leader of a gang that rescues French aristocrats from the guillotine in 1792.

Scarlet Pimpernel, The.
98 min. Black and white. Live action. Produced by London Films. 1934. Leslie Howard, Merle Oberon, Raymond Massey.
Evoking the period of the French Revolution, this strong production captures the spirit of adventure with gusto and humor.

Audience: Ages 14-Adult
Distributor: KVC Entertainment
Videocassette: $19.95
No public performance rights

Scarlet Pimpernel, The.
97 min. Black and white. Live action. 1935. Leslie Howard, Merle Oberon, Raymond Massey.
A laser disc version of the same title offered by KVC Entertainment (see above).

Distributor: Image Entertainment
Laser disc: CLV format $39.95
No public performance rights

Elusive Pimpernel, The.
109 min. Color. Live action. Produced by British Lion Films/London Films. 1950. David Niven, Margaret Leighton, Cyril Cusack.
Less convincing than the 1934 adaptation, this production also lacks its excitement. The picture was originally filmed as a musical but the songs were ultimately cut. The character of the Pimpernel has a falseness of a different nature than in the original.

Reviews: *Variety*, Nov. 15, 1950
Audience: Ages 14-Adult
Distributor: Janus Films
Videocassette: $88

Scarlet Pimpernel, The.
150 min. Color. Live action. Produced by London Films. 1982. Anthony Andrews, Jane Seymour, Ian McKellen.
Location, performances, and costuming combine to make this an enchanting adaptation.

Reviews: *Variety*, Nov. 17, 1982
Audience: Ages 14-Adult
Distributor: Vestron Video
Videocassette: $69.98
No public performance rights

★★★★★

"Scorn of Women, The"
Jack London.
Anthologized in *The Unabridged Jack London*, edited by Lawrence Teacher and Richard E. Nicholls. Running Press. 1981. Short stories—realistic fiction.
A gold digger who struck it rich is waiting for his sweetheart to arrive. Meanwhile, a foreigner sets her sights on him but her plans are thwarted by a society lady and a local dance girl.

Scorn of Women, The.
52 min. Color. Live action. Produced by William MacAdam/Norfolk. 1980. Narrated by Orson Welles. Eva Gabor, Tom Butler, Kerrie Keane, Sarah Torgov.
This funny adaptation captures the spirit of the story, enhancing it with sharp character development. While all the roles are exceptionally well performed, the dance girl in particular is convincing in her earnest desire for Floyd (who mistakenly assumes he suddenly has three women chasing after him) to behave properly. Viewers gain a perspective on the role of women during the Klondike gold rush from a screen version that is both entertaining and informative.
Audience: Ages 14-Adult
Distributor: Britannica
Videocassette: $99

★★★★★

"Screaming Woman, The"
Ray Bradbury.
Anthologized in *The Stories of Ray Bradbury.* Alfred A. Knopf. 1980. Short stories—horror.
A young girl with an overactive imagination thinks that she hears a buried woman screaming from the grave.

Screaming Woman, The.
26 min. Color. Live action. Produced by Seaton McLean for Atlantis Films. 1986. Drew Barrymore, Alan Scarfe.
Author Ray Bradbury wrote the screenplay for this generally faithful adaptation of his short story. Slight variations include a name change for the young female character and a spine-tingling conclusion that eerily depicts a barely alive woman being rescued from the grave—a scene original to the video version.
Reviews: *Booklist*, Aug. 1990
Awards: Blue Ribbon, American Film & Video Festival
Audience: Ages 12-Adult
Distributor: Beacon Films
Videocassette: $149 **Rental:** $50

★★★★★

Secret Garden, The
Frances Hodgson Burnett.
Multiple editions. Realistic fiction.
An orphaned girl leaves India for England, where she moves in with her Uncle and helps restore her invalid cousin and her deceased aunt's garden to health.

Secret Garden, The.
92 min. Black and white with color sequence. Live action. Produced by MGM/Clarence Brown. 1949. Margaret O'Brien, Herbert Marshall, Dean Stockwell, Brian Roper.
This generally faithful adaptation is shot mostly in black and white with the scenes in the reborn garden slipping into color. The film focuses more on the realistic than magical element in the novel. A few details have changed. A raven, not a robin, leads Mary at first to the garden, and the role of Dickon's mother (a servant) is minimized. The garden itself seems more like a refuge than the magical place it is in the novel.
Reviews: *Variety*, Apr. 27, 1949
Audience: Ages 8-12
Distributor: MGM/UA Home Video
Videocassette: $19.98
No public performance rights

Secret Garden, The.
106 min. Color. Live action. Produced by BBC Video. 1975. Sarah Hollis Andrews, David Patterson, John Woodnutt.
This adaptation has a fine air of authenticity and is splendidly performed by all concerned. The scenery of the Yorkshire moors is enchanting. Servants speak with the appropriate accent, as does Dickon, the poor nature-loving lad who befriends Mary. As in the novel, the garden is a tonic that transforms the disagreeable

Mary, her sickly cousin Colin, and his spiritless father.

Audience: Ages 8-12
Distributor: Fox Video
Videocassette: $14.98
No public performance rights

★★★★★

"Secret Sharer, The"
Joseph Conrad.

Anthologized in *Short Stories of the Sea*, edited by G. C. Solley and E. Steinbaugh. Naval Institute Press. 1984. Short stories—adventure.
Shortly after a captain assumes command of a ship, he secretly helps a fugitive sailor escape from confinement for a crime.

Secret Sharer, The.
30 min. Color. Live action. Produced by Larry Yust with Clifton Fadiman. 1973.
The tension mounts as this well-acted, faithful adaptation progresses. Viewers gain a realistic look at life on board ship, while rooting for the captain and his stowaway to triumph in the end, which they do. As described in *Scholastic Teacher*, "The characterizations are strong, the setting appears authentic, and the cinematography is excellent."
Reviews: *Scholastic Teacher*, Oct. 1973
Audience: Ages 10-Adult
Distributor: Britannica
16mm film: $720 **Videocassette:** $300

★★★★★

Selfish Giant, The
Oscar Wilde.

Multiple editions. Fantasy.
A selfish giant experiences only winter in his garden until he shares it with neighborhood children.

Selfish Giant, The.
14 min. Black and white. Animated. Produced by Reiner Film/Weston Woods. 1971.
The film visualizes selfishness in a way young viewers can understand when the giant refuses, then allows, the children to play in his garden. However, it is difficult for young audiences to identify with the old giant himself. The film, like the book, succeeds for them on a surface level. Attached to the giant's death scene, though, is a deeper symbolism that reaches above the level of many viewers.
Audience: Ages 6-10
Distributor: Weston Woods
16mm film: $195 **Videocassette:** $60
Rental: $20 daily

Selfish Giant, The.
27 min. Color. Animated. Produced by Reader's Digest with Potter Productions. 1972.
Somewhat slow-moving, the film includes fine animated images of the cold, which create the impression of winter. The giant is appropriately contrite in this religious fantasy. As in the original, spring dawns when he opens his garden to children. Years pass. It is the winter of the giant's death, when the image of Christ appears in a conspicuous tree of spring to lead the giant to the garden of paradise.
Reviews: *Booklist*, Jan. 1, 1973; *Instructor*, Feb. 1973; *Religion Teacher's Journal*, Oct. 1973
Audience: Ages 6-12
Distributor: Pyramid Film & Video
16mm film: $495 **Videocassette:** $95
Rental: $75

★★★★★

Selkie Girl, The
Susan Cooper.

Illustrated by Warwick Hutton. Macmillan. 1986. Folklore and fairy tales.

A lonely fisherman spots three girls enjoying a respite from their lives as selkies—gray seals. He falls in love with one of the girls and steals her sealskin so she cannot return to the sea. They marry and have children before the selkie girl discovers where the fisherman has hidden her sealskin.

Selkie Girl, The.
14 min. Color. Iconographic. Produced by Weston Woods. 1991. Narrated by Jenny Agutter.
This is a winning rendition of the British legend, complete with a narrator whose authentic accent helps evoke a magical atmosphere. The fine pacing, clear, lively retelling, and maneuvers of the camera over descriptive illustrations make this a delightful adaptation of a tale with an edge of sadness. Content with her family on land, the selkie girl finally returns to the sea in a surprise ending that reveals she has another five children there.
Audience: Ages 4-10
Distributor: Weston Woods
16mm film: $245 **Videocassette:** $120
Rental: $25 daily

Pigs' Wedding and Other Stories, The.
39 min. Color. Iconographic and animated. Produced by Weston Woods.
Included in this tape anthology are adaptations of *The Pigs' Wedding* (Helme Heine), *The Happy Owls* (Celestino Piatti), *The Selkie Girl* (Susan Cooper), *A Letter to Amy* (Ezra Jack Keats), and *The Owl and the Pussy-Cat* (Edward Lear). See individual titles for full descriptions.
Audience: Ages 4-8
Distributor: Children's Circle, Weston Woods
Videocassette: $19.95
No public performance rights

★★★★★

Sense and Sensibility
Jane Austen.
Multiple editions. Realistic fiction.
Two sisters in eighteenth-century England fall in love, one with a disreputable gentleman and the other with a gentleman who does not have the "sense" to return her affection until a less worthy mate deceives him.

Sense and Sensibility.
174 min. Color. Live action. Produced by BBC. 1985. Irene Richard, Tracy Childs, Diana Fairfax.
The rich setting recreates eighteenth-century England vividly, and the acting quite splendidly captures the spirit and letter of the novel. Diana Fairfax is particularly exceptional.
Audience: Ages 16-Adult
Distributor: Fox Video
Videocassette: $29.98
No public performance rights

★★★★★

Sentinel, The
Arthur C. Clarke.
Illustrated by Lebeus Woods. Berkeley Publishing Group. 1986. [1967]. Science fiction.
In the year 2001, astronauts voyage to Jupiter. When the computer that operates their spaceship malfunctions, they attempt to shut it down.

2001: A Space Odyssey.
139 min. Color. Live action. Produced by MGM/Stanley Kubrick. 1968. Keir Dullea, Gary Lockwood, William Sylvester.
This landmark film considers space travel in the context of human history. The author himself helped adapt his tale to the screen. In its day, the production captivated audiences with sensational visuals. Some of the impact is lost, however, in the translation from a large to a small screen.

Reviews: *New York Times*, Apr. 4, 1968, 58:1; *Variety*, Apr. 3, 1968
Awards: Academy Award, Best Visual Effects
Audience: Ages 10-Adult
Distributor: MGM/UA Home Video
Videocassette: $19.98
No public performance rights

2001: A Space Odyssey.
139 min. Color. Live action. 1968. Keir Dullea, Gary Lockwood, William Sylvester.
A laser disc version of the same title offered by MGM/UA Home Video (see above).
Distributor: Criterion Collection
Laser disc: Widescreen CAV format $124.95, widescreen CLV format $59.95
No public performance rights

★★★★★

Separate Peace, A
John Knowles.
Macmillan. 1962. [1959]. Realistic fiction.
Two boys are thrown together as roommates in a prep school and must learn to be sensitive to each other's needs. Jealous of his roommate's popularity, one betrays a trust and causes a crippling accident.

Separate Peace, A.
140 min. Color. Live action. Produced by Paramount. 1972. Parker Stevenson, Scott Bradbury.
Set in the World War II era, the motion picture does not convincingly evoke the period. The roommates, moreover, share a complex relationship, not easily adapted to the screen.
Reviews: *New York Times*, Sept. 28, 1972, 55:1; *Variety*, Sept. 13, 1972
Audience: Ages 15-Adult
Distributor: Paramount Home Video
Videocassette available
No public performance rights

★★★★★

Seven Ravens, The
Jacob Grimm and Wilhelm K. Grimm.
Multiple editions. Folklore and fairy tales.
A seven-year-old girl sets out to rescue her seven brothers, who have been turned into ravens by a vengeful witch.

Seven Ravens, The.
21 min. Color. Animated. Produced by DEFA Studio. 1971.
Very full illustrations compensate in part for very limited animation in this version of the classic German fairy tale. "Created by European animators and accompanied by dramatic music, this is a beautiful version of the Grimm fairy tale." —*Booklist*
Reviews: *Booklist*, Sept. 15, 1973
Audience: Ages 5-11
Distributor: Coronet/MTI Film & Video
16mm film: $315 **Videocassette:** $250
Rental: $75

★★★★★

Seven Wishes of Joanna Peabody, The
Genevieve Gray.
Illustrated by Elton Clay Fax. Lothrop, Lee & Shepard. 1972. Fantasy.
A girl living in a tenement is granted seven wishes by an "Aunt Thelma," who lives in the television set. The girl's best wishes turn out to be ones that help others.

Seven Wishes of Joanna Peabody, The.
27 min. Color. Live action. Produced by ABC Children's Special. 1978. Butterfly McQueen.

"Aunt Thelma" overplays her role, and tenement life seems to be a bit overdramatized in this contemporary, Cinderella-type story of a girl who tries to make the most of her seven wishes.

Audience: Ages 8-14
Distributor: Coronet/MTI Film & Video
16mm film: $500 **Videocassette:** $250
Rental: $75

★★★★★

"Shadow, The"
Hans Christian Andersen.

Anthologized in *Hans Christian Andersen: The Complete Fairy Tales and Stories.* Doubleday. 1974. Short stories—fantasy.
A scholar loses his shadow, which encounters a woman called Poetry and grows into a man. In later years, the shadow visits the scholar, now a philosopher reduced by misfortune to a shadow of his former self. The two change places, the philosopher becoming a shadow who is ultimately killed.

Shadow, The.
25.5 min. Color. Live action. Produced by Leonard S. Berman. 1990.
Like the short story, this film is a haunting tale full of symbolism. The Shadow appears to be a fatter and more hostile character in the motion picture than in the short story. There is also a more ominous tone to the film, though the plot matches.

Audience: Ages 15-Adult
Distributor: Churchill Media
16mm film: $460 **Videocassette:** $250
Rental: $60

★★★★★

Shelter from the Wind
Marion Dane Bauer.

Houghton Mifflin. 1979. [1976]. Realistic fiction.
A girl runs away from home and finds a friend in an elderly neighbor, who has a horse that is gentle enough to train.

Rodeo Red and the Runaway.
33 min. Color. Live action. Produced by LCA. 1979. Geraldine Fitzgerald.
This shortened version of a longer film moves at a better pace and holds the audience well. Even so, some parts are a bit sluggish.

Audience: Ages 8-14
Distributor: Coronet/MTI Film & Video
16mm film: $500 **Videocassette:** $250
Rental: $75

Rodeo Red and the Runaway.
49 min. Color. Live action. Produced by LCA. 1979. Geraldine Fitzgerald.
A full-length version of the same, abbreviated title distributed by Coronet/MTI (see above).

Audience: Ages 8-14
Distributor: Coronet/MTI Film & Video
16mm film: $750 **Videocassette:** $250
Rental: $75

★★★★★

Shoeless Joe
W. P. Kinsella.

Ballantine. 1987. [1982]. Fantasy.
An Iowa farmer is inspired to build a baseball diamond on his land in hopes of resurrecting baseball star Shoeless Joe Jackson.

Field of Dreams.
106 min. Color. Live action. A Gordon Company Production. 1989. Kevin Costner, Amy Madigan, Gaby Hoffman.
An absolutely convincing adaptation, artfully handled, this live-action dramatization is a moving tribute to both baseball and dreams.

Audience: Ages 14-Adult
Distributor: MCA/Universal Home Video
Videocassette available
No public performance rights

Field of Dreams.
106 min. Color. Live action. 1989. Kevin Costner, Amy Madigan, Gaby Hoffman.
A laser disc version of the same title offered by MCA/Universal Home Video (see above).
Distributor: Pioneer LDCA, Inc.
Laser disc: CLV format $34.98
No public performance rights

★★★★★

Shoeshine Girl
Clyde Robert Bulla.
Illustrated by Alice Leigh Grant. Harper & Row Junior Books. 1975. Realistic fiction.
A girl sent to her aunt's house for a summer to correct her misbehavior finds a job in a shoeshine stand and matures when the owner of the stand is hurt in an accident.

Shoeshine Girl.
25 min. Color. Live action. Produced by LCA. 1980.
The script for this adaptation of Bulla's excellent story is the basis for a fine film. The casting and subsequent acting have rendered it into a tender story of a girl who grows through misfortune.
Reviews: *Instructor*, Dec. 1980
Awards: ALA Notable Children's Film; CINE Golden Eagle
Audience: Ages 9-12
Distributor: Coronet/MTI Film & Video
16mm film: $450 **Videocassette:** $250
Rental: $75

★★★★★

"Sight, The"
Brian Moore.
Anthologized in *Black Water*, edited by Alberto Manguel.
Crown. 1984. Short stories—realistic fiction.
New York City attorney Benedict Chipman's Irish housekeeper has a clairvoyant dream that leads her to believe death is imminent.

Sight, The.
26 min. Color. Animation. Produced by Janice Platt and William Weintraub. 1985. Cedric Smith, Frances Hyland.
A few unnecessary scenes from Brian Moore's short story are missing in this eerie drama, which contains haunting background music, inspired acting, and the short story's open ending.
Reviews: *Booklist*, Nov. 15, 1986
Audience: Ages 16-Adult
Distributor: Beacon Films
16mm film: $575 **Videocassette:** $149

★★★★★

Silas Marner
George Eliot.
Multiple editions. Realistic fiction.
A weaver retreats from the world when he is unjustly accused of robbery. He hoards his earnings, which are one day stolen, but acquires greater wealth by giving refuge to a homeless child.

Silas Marner.
91 min. Color. Live action. Produced by BBC. 1985. Ben Kingsley, Giles Foster, Jenny Agutter.
While the drama adheres to the surface details of the literary work, it changes the main character's mood. The novel profiles his absorption in the present and dismissal of the past but the film shows him pursuing activity with a vengeance that suggests an acid memory of the past. The show nevertheless succeeds as a splendidly detailed adaptation.

Reviews: *Times Literary Supplement*, Jan. 3, 1986; *Variety*, Mar. 25, 1987
Audience: Ages 14-Adult
Distributor: Fox Video
Videocassette: $29.98
No public performance rights

★★★★★

"Silver Blaze"
Sir Arthur Conan Doyle.
Anthologized in *The Memoirs of Sherlock Holmes*. Reader's Digest. 1987. Short stories—mystery.
A horse is stolen and its trainer killed, leaving just enough clues for Sherlock Holmes.

Silver Blaze.
31 min. Color. Live action. Produced by LCA. 1977. Christopher Plummer, Thorley Walters.
Christopher Plummer is at his best as Sherlock Holmes takes on the chore of finding a murderer and recovering a stolen horse. This is a fine version of an Arthur Conan Doyle mystery.
Audience: Ages 12-17
Distributor: Coronet/MTI Film & Video
16mm film: $475 **Videocassette:** $250
Rental: $75

★★★★★

Silver Chair, The
C. S. Lewis.
Illustrated by Pauline Diana Baynes Macmillan. 1988. [1953]. Fantasy.
In this third installment of The Chronicles of Narnia (*The Lion, The Witch, and the Wardrobe*; *Prince Caspian and the Voyage of the Dawn Treader*; *The Silver Chair*), an English boy and girl enter Narnia to find King Caspian's lost son.

Silver Chair, The.
169 min. Color. Live action. Produced by Paul Stone/BBC/WonderWorks. 1990.
This is a captivating flight into fancy with a touch of humor mixed in with the adventure and a healthy dose of realism in the bickering between the boy and the girl. As in the other Chronicles of Narnia installments, animation is tastefully combined with live action. The costumes are splendid and the performances convincing. Aslan, the Lion force of good, gives the children four tasks/signs to fulfill on their mission, involving flying creatures, giants, and so forth.
Audience: Ages 8-12
Distributor: Public Media Video
Videocassette: $29.95
No public performance rights

★★★★★

Silver Cow, The: A Welsh Tale
Susan Cooper.
Illustrated by Warwick Hutton. Atheneum. 1983. Folklore and fairy tales.
A Welsh farmer with a mean heart has his son watching cows instead of attending school. A magic silver cow emerges from a lake and brings the farmer good fortune until he decides to butcher the cow, who magically disappears, then reappears as a water lily.

Silver Cow, The.
13 min. Color. Iconographic. Produced by Weston Woods. 1986.
A narrator with a Welsh-sounding accent, strong character voices, and a fine plot complement the watercolor style pictures adapted from the storybook. The camera interacts with them to simulate motion in an engrossing production. At the end, the son escapes his ornery father and leaves home.
Awards: CINE Golden Eagle
Audience: Ages 6-10
Distributor: Weston Woods

16mm film: $235 **Videocassette:** $60
Rental: $25 daily

★★★★★

The Silver Pony
Lynd Ward (illus.).
Houghton Mifflin. 1973. Fantasy.
This wordless story with black-and-white pictures follows a boy's ride on a flying horse to faraway lands. He rescues a flood victim and an endangered lamb, then crashes to earth, where reality greets him with a pleasant surprise.

The Silver Pony.
7 min. Animated. Produced by Bosustow Entertainment. 1981.
A wordless film, this show effectively portrays the original.
Audience: Ages 4-8
Distributor: Churchill Media
16mm film: $160 **Videocassette:** $59
Rental: $50

★★★★★

"Silver Whistle, The"
Jay Williams.
Anthologized in *The Practical Princess and Other Liberating Fairy Tales*. Illustrated by Rick Schreiter. Parents Magazine Press. 1978. Folklore and fairy tales.
Prudence sets out into the world with her silver whistle, which proves to be of great assistance as she encounters a magic mirror, a curse, and a prince.

Silver Whistle, The.
16 min. Color. Puppet animation. Produced by Barbara Dumashkin. 1981.
The puppet animation in this film, though not up to the level of popular television puppetry, adequately portrays the story of a girl who sets out into the world taking only a silver whistle.
Audience: Ages 5-10
Distributor: Filmfair Communications
16mm film: $325 **Videocassette:** $89
Rental: $30

★★★★★

Sinbad the Sailor.
Multiple editions. Folklore and fairy tales.
Sinbad, a hero from the 1,001 tales in *Arabian Nights Entertainments*, embarks on seven fantastic voyages. His seventh and final voyage pits him face to face with angry elephants.

Sinbad the Sailor.
117 min. Color. Live action. Produced by RKO/Stephen Ames. 1947. Douglas Fairbanks, Jr., Walter Slezak, Maureen O'Hara.
The adventure is described as Sinbad's eighth voyage, but in *Arabian Nights Entertainments* the hero takes only seven voyages. This new adventure has Sinbad competing with evil characters to find the hidden treasure of Alexander the Great. En route, he falls in love with a rich and lovely adventuress who returns his affection. In a framing story, Sinbad relates his fantastic adventure to gullible friends. This production is fun, though its plot is rather loose. The set designs and Arabian fashions are quite elaborate.
Reviews: *New York Times*, Jan. 23, 1947, 31:2
Audience: Ages 9-Adult
Distributor: RKO/Turner Home Entertainment
Videocassette: $19.98
No public performance rights

Sinbad the Sailor.
117 min. Color. Live action. 1947. Douglas Fairbanks, Jr., Walter Slezak, Maureen O'Hara.

A laser disc version of the same title offered by RKO/Turner Home Entertainment (see above).

Distributor: Image Entertainment
Laser disc: CLV format $39.95
No public performance rights

Seventh Voyage of Sinbad.
89 min. Color. Live action. Produced by Columbia/Morningside. 1958. Kerwin Mathews, Kathryn Grant, Richard Eyer.
The show is lively, the effects (by Ray Harryhausen) are superb, and the narrative has magical charm. Strictly speaking, Sinbad was sold into slavery on his seventh voyage and assigned to collect elephant ivory. In this version Sinbad searches for the huge egg of a fantastic Arabian bird, the roc, to remedy his fiancée's problem: an evil magician has reduced her to a midget.

Reviews: *Variety*, Nov. 26, 1958
Audience: Ages 10-16
Distributor: Columbia TriStar Home Video
Videocassette: $14.95
No public performance rights

Seventh Voyage of Sinbad.
Color. Live action. 1958. Kerwin Mathews, Kathryn Grant.
A laser disc version of the same title offered by Columbia TriStar Home Video (see above).

Distributor: Pioneer LDCA, Inc.
Laser disc: CLV format $34.95
No public performance rights

★★★★★

Single Light, A
Maia Wojciechowska.
Harper & Row. 1968. Realistic fiction.
A girl who is deaf and mute discovers a priceless statue of the Christ child in a Spanish village church. Habitually ignored or mistreated, the girl becomes the center of attention when she takes the precious statue into the woods.

Single Light, A.
30 min. Color. Live action. Produced by LCA. 1984. William Atherton.
The characters are more deeply developed in the uncut 55-minute version, but little is lost in this shortened version, which sparkles with fine acting and an intensely dramatic plot. In particular, the longer version spends more time delving into the character of the deaf-mute star, but both versions are highly effective.

Awards: CINE Golden Eagle
Audience: Ages 12-Adult
Distributor: Coronet/MTI Film & Video
16mm film: $550 **Videocassette:** $250
Rental: $75

Single Light, A.
55 min. Color. Live action. 1984. William Atherton.
A full-length version of the same, abbreviated title also distributed by Coronet/MTI Film & Video (see above).

Distributor: Coronet/MTI Film & Video
16mm film: $750 **Videocassette:** $250
Rental: $75

★★★★★

Sister Carrie
Theodore Dreiser.
Multiple editions. Realistic fiction.
A Chicago restaurant manager of the early 1900s is reduced to poverty because of his love for a country girl.

Carrie.
118 min. Black and white. Live action. Produced by Paramount/William Wyler. 1952.
As in the novel, Carrie takes to the stage after losing her innocence in the city. The production proceeds to play up the drama rather than following the sociological emphasis given to the story by its original author.
Reviews: *New York Times*, July 17, 1952, 20:2; *Variety*, June 11, 1952
Audience: Ages 16-Adult
Distributor: Paramount Home Video
Videocassette available
No public performance rights

★★★★★

Skateboard Scramble
Barbara Douglass.
Illustrated by Alex Stein. Westminster Press. 1979. Realistic fiction.
Pushed by her father to win a skateboard contest, a girl chooses instead to lose to another girl whose handicapped brother would enjoy the trophy.

Different Kind of Winning, A.
27 min. Color. Live action. Produced by LCA. 1980.
While this dramatization remains true to the written version, its production qualities rank just above average. The show is a discussion starter for the topics of being a sports person, relating to parents, and initiating friendships.
Audience: Ages 10-15
Distributor: Coronet/MTI Film & Video
16mm film: $450 **Videocassette:** $250
Rental: $75

★★★★★

Skating Rink, The
Mildred Lee.
Houghton Mifflin. 1979. [1969]. Realistic fiction.
A teenager, Tuck Faraday, suffers from lack of confidence and a serious stutter. In the skating rink, he excels and finds an identity.

Skating Rink, The.
27 min. Color. Live action. Produced by LCA. 1975.
A shy teenage boy gains confidence after learning to skate. Fine acting and a realistic ending make this an exceptional production.
Reviews: *Variety*, Feb. 12, 1975
Awards: ALA Notable Film
Audience: Ages 12-Adult
Distributor: Coronet/MTI Film & Video
16mm film: $550 **Videocassette:** $250
Rental: $75

★★★★★

"Sky Is Gray, The"
Ernest Gaines.
Anthologized in *The American Short Story, Vol. 2,* edited by C. Skaggs. Dell. 1980. Short stories—realistic fiction.
James is a black boy with a toothache that takes him on an adventure into town, where he discovers the complexity of life.

Sky Is Gray, The.
46 min. Color. Live action. Produced by Learning in Focus. 1980. Olivia Cole, James Bond III.
This film has won many accolades for its portrayal of the life of a black boy in 1940s Louisiana. Olivia Cole is excellent and James Bond performs well, despite a touch of overacting.
Reviews: *Booklist*, Oct. 1, 1980
Awards: Blue Ribbon, American Film Festival
Audience: Ages 10-Adult

Distributor: Coronet/MTI Film & Video
16mm film: $835 **Videocassette:** $250
Rental: $75

Sky Is Gray, The.
46 min. Color. Live action. Produced by Learning in Focus. 1980. Olivia Cole, James Bond III.
A home video version of the same title distributed by Coronet/MTI Film & Video (see above).

Distributor: Monterey Home Video
Videocassette: $24.95
No public performance rights

★★★★★

Slake's Limbo
Felice Holman.
Scribner. 1974. Realistic fiction.
Desperate, thirteen-year-old Slake seeks refuge in New York City's grimy, dangerous subway tunnels until he is finally rescued from a near fatal accident.

Runaway.
58 min. Color. Live action. Produced by Peggy Zapple/WonderWorks. 1989.
A loose adaptation of Felice Holman's ALA Notable Book, *Slake's Limbo*, this entertaining video contains numerous changes. Joseph, a minor character in the book, is prominently featured in the plot of the video version, which also omits a climactic concluding episode in which Slake nearly loses his life.

Reviews: *Booklist*, June 1, 1991
Audience: Ages 9-14
Distributor: Public Media Video Video
Videocassette: $29.95

★★★★★

Slaughterhouse Five
Kurt Vonnegut, Jr.
Barron. 1985. [1969]. Science fiction.
In this anti-war story, a practicing optometrist jumps backward and forward in time fantasies that are interspersed with jumps in space.

Slaughterhouse Five.
104 min. Color. Live action. Produced by Universal. 1972. Michael Sacks, Valerie Perrine, Ron Liebman, Sharon Gans, Eugene Roche.
The motion picture is a time- and space-travel fantasy that alternates between Nazi prison camp, middle-class family life, and captivity by alien beings. Along the way, there are scenes with bare bodies and violence. It is a difficult-to-follow story, not made clearer in this film adaptation. "The problem with the film, as it was with the novel, is that it's really not outraged or outrageous enough." —*New York Times*

Reviews: *New York Times*, Mar. 23, 1972, 51:1; *Variety*, Mar. 22, 1972
Audience: Ages 14-Adult
Distributor: MCA/Universal Home Video
Videocassette: $19.95
No public performance rights

★★★★★

Sleeping Beauty, The (Briar Rose).
Multiple editions. Folklore and fairy tales.
Taking revenge for not being invited to the new princess's christening, an evil fairy sentences the princess to death in her teenage years by pricking her finger on a spinning wheel. Another fairy softens the sentence to a hundred-year sleep. Awakened by a prince, the princess lives happily ever after in the Grimm version of this tale. The version by Charles Perrault has the evil fairy return to plague the princess's happiness.

Sleeping Beauty.
75 min. Color. Animation. Produced by Walt Disney. 1959.
This classic film version is a cinematic feat of elaborate animation set to music from the Tchaikovsky ballet. Despite its technical excellence and accuracy, the production is lacking in strong emotional impact.
Audience: Ages 4-8
Distributor: Buena Vista Home Video (not currently in distribution)

Sleeping Beauty.
7 min. Color. Limited animation. Produced by Halas and Batchelor. 1969.
The production, which lacks both dialogue and characterization, is somewhat distancing. In this version, three kind faeries take the princess away from the castle and raise her in the forest to avert the evil prophecy, but to no avail. A highlight of the film is a convincingly frightening fight with a dragon. Overall, the colorful limited animation and brisk narration make this an adequate adaptation.
Audience: Ages 4-8
Distributor: Britannica
16mm film: $190 **Videocassette:** $190

Sleeping Beauty and Briar Rose, The.
15 min. Color. Puppet animation. Produced by Omega. 1970.
Puppets may not be the best medium for a film adaptation of the timeless story of good and evil. These particular puppets seem stilted and less animated than is necessary for a really fine film.
Audience: Ages 6-10
Distributor: Phoenix/BFA Films & Video
16mm film: $325 **Videocassette:** $195
Rental: $46

Sleeping Beauty (Faerie Tale Theatre).
60 min. Color. Live action. Produced by Shelley Duvall. 1983. Bernadette Peters, Beverly D'Angelo, Christopher Reeve, Carole Kane, Sally Kellerman.
A fairly faithful "Sleeping Beauty" lays within a larger tale in this dramatization. Part of the larger story is a prince's search for a suitable mate. This prince and his lackey stumble upon a woodsman, who briefs them on the plight of the famous Sleeping Beauty. During his conversation, the film switches into an enactment of the fairy tale up to her falling asleep and then back again to the forest where the woodsman tells the story. The prince too has a story to tell, about his vain search for a mate. Once, it took him to the land of a scheming princess who made indecent advances, suggesting the prince rip the pearls off her dress in a scene that seems too suggestive for young audiences. Sleeping Beauty also averts a mismatch in this version when her parents try to marry her off to get her out of the kingdom before the curse takes effect. In the Grimm tale, they only banish spinning wheels from the kingdom. The prince, intent on awakening Sleeping Beauty, finally leaves the woodsman and braves the castle walls to find his perfect princess.
Reviews: *Variety*, Feb. 8, 1984
Audience: Ages 12-Adult
Distributor: Fox Video
Videocassette: $14.98
No pubic performance rights

Sleeping Beauty (Faerie Tale Theatre).
60 min. Color. Live action. Produced by Shelley Duvall. 1983. Bernadette Peters, Beverly D'Angelo, Christopher Reeve, Carole Kane, Sally Kellerman.
A laser disc version of the same title offered by Fox Video (see above).
Distributor: Image Entertainment
Laser disc: CLV format $29.98
No public performance rights

Briar Rose: The Sleeping Beauty.
12 min. Color. Limited animation. Produced by Perspective Films. 1986.
Animation that is limited to one movement at a time and a weak narrator are the only flaws in this beautifully drawn story about the revenge of the snubbed witch.
Awards: First Prize, Chicago International Festival of Children's Films
Audience: Ages 6-10
Distributor: Coronet/MTI Film & Video
16mm film: $350 **Videocassette:** $250
Rental: $75

Sleeping Beauty.
90 min. Color. Live action. Produced by Golan Globus Production. 1989. Morgan Fairchild, Tahnee Welch.
A comical dwarf promises to help the queen, who pines for a child. He spends an overlong period concocting a charm and she bears the child, from which point the classic story line proceeds with an interlude of some acrobatic dancing.
Audience: Ages 6-Adult
Distributor: Cannon Video
Videocassette available
No public performance rights

Sleeping Beauty.
12 min. Color. Animated. Produced by David Alexovich. 1990.
As in the Perrault version, this film shows the evil fairy reappearing to destroy Sleeping Beauty's happiness after she is married and has two children named Dawn and Day. A fearful villain, the evil fairy turns herself into the prince's mother and other characters into bugs before she falls victim to her own wicked potion.
Audience: Ages 4-8
Distributor: Britannica
Videocassette: $79

Sleeping Beauty.
26 min. Color. Animation. Produced by Rankin-Bass.
This adaptation appears too long for such a limited production. The animation and voice tracks are erratic.
Audience: Ages 4-8
Distributor: Lucerne Media
Videocassette: $195

★★★★★

Smile for Auntie
Diane Paterson (illus.).
Dial Press. 1976. Humor.
Auntie sings, dances, and carries on to make her nephew smile. Ultimately, he smiles only when she stalks off in frustration threatening never to return.

Smile for Auntie.
5 min. Color. Animated. Produced by Weston Woods. 1979.
The narrator relates the tale as written, her voice relaying Auntie's words. Though the visuals are animated, characters' lips do not move. The little boy's smile at the end conveys a feeling of malice that is missing from the book.
Audience: Ages 4-8
Distributor: Weston Woods
16mm film: $160 **Videocassette:** $80
Rental: $15 daily

Smile for Auntie and Other Stories.
27 min. Color. Iconographic and animated. Produced by Weston Woods. 1985.
Included in this tape anthology are adaptations of *Smile for Auntie* (Diane Paterson), *Make Way for Ducklings* (Robert McCloskey), *The Snowy Day* (Ezra Jack Keats), and *Wynken, Blynken and Nod* (Eugene Field). See individual titles for full descriptions.

Audience: Ages 4-8
Distributor: Children's Circle, Weston Woods
Videocassette: $19.95
No public performance rights

★★★★★

Snow Queen, The
Hans Christian Andersen.
Multiple editions. Folklore and fairy tales.
A boy and girl romp through summer and winter together until a sliver of mirror pierces the boy's eyes and heart. Turning curt and mean, he is whisked away by the snow queen to her ice palace. His heart grows icy, but his young friend rushes to the rescue and finally melts his coldness with her tears.

Snow Queen, The.
21 min. Color. Animation. Produced by Greatest Tales. 1981.
Cut from Japanese film footage, this show offers only adequate animation and communication of the message that human feelings well-directed can overcome great obstacles.
Audience: Ages 6-12
Distributor: Phoenix/BFA Films & Video
16mm film: $445 **Videocassette:** $275
Rental: $65

Snow Queen, The (Faerie Tale Theatre).
60 min. Color. Live action. Produced by Shelley Duvall. 1984. Lance Kerwin, Melissa Gilbert, Lee Remick.
While this adaptation telescopes the girl Gerta's adventures in her pursuit of the boy Kay, it retains the basic plot. This screen version, like the story, has a talking reindeer transport Gerta to the ice palace, but the film is more explicit about Gerta's saving Kay from a life without love. On the other hand, Andersen's tale has the children chant a religious verse: "Where roses deck the flowery vale/There, Infant Jesus, thee we hail!" The screen version substitutes nonreligious words: "Cold be hot and friends be kind/When love unites the heart and mind." It captures beautifully the story line and secular themes in the Andersen original.
Audience: Ages 6-Adult
Distributor: Fox Video
Videocassette: $14.98
No public performance rights

★★★★★

Snow Bound
Harry Mazer.
Delacorte Press. 1973. Adventure.
A very self-confident boy offers a less confident girl a ride. When they are snowbound and the boy gets injured, it is the girl's strength that saves them.

Snow Bound.
32 min. Color. Live action. Produced by LCA (An NBC Special Treat). 1978.
This is an abridged version edited to accommodate classroom time. While it retains the basic plot and has lost none of the tension created by the original, some of the action has been noticeably cut.
Reviews: *Booklist*, Sept. 15, 1978
Awards: ALA Selected Film for Young Adults; Chris Bronze Plaque, Columbus Film Festival
Audience: Ages 12-Adult
Distributor: Coronet/MTI Film & Video
16mm film: $500 **Videocassette:** $250
Rental: $75

Snow Bound.
50 min. Color. Live action. Produced by LCA (An NBC Special Treat). 1978.
A full-length version of the same, abbreviated title also distributed by Coronet/MTI Film & Video (see above).
Audience: Ages 12-Adult

Distributor: Coronet/MTI Film & Video
16mm film: $750 **Videocassette:** $250
Rental: $75

★★★★★

Snow White and the Seven Dwarfs
Jacob Grimm and Wilhelm K. Grimm.
Multiple editions. Folklore and fairy tales. Jealous of her lovely stepdaughter, Snow White, a queen sends the child out to be killed by a huntsman. He spares her and she takes refuge in the home of seven dwarfs, only to face more attempts on her life by the wicked queen.

Snow White and the Seven Dwarfs (Faerie Tale Theatre).
53 min. Color. Live action. Produced by Shelley Duvall. 1983. Elizabeth McGovern, Vincent Price, Vanessa Redgrave.
This adaptation changes a few details but retains both the spirit and plot development of the Grimm tale. Adding depth to the classic, it creates memorable characters. This is a racially integrated set of dwarfs, who are friendly, grumpy, argumentative, and protective of Snow White. She is the picture of innocence, completely believable as someone with too trusting a nature. Instead of three attempts on her life, her stepmother makes two attempts before Snow White bites the poisoned apple. Also, the prince appears earlier in this version. Yet these changes make little difference in a production that richly relays the gist of the original. The queen is too frightening for preschool audiences.
Reviews: *Variety*, Oct. 10, 1984
Audience: Ages 6-Adult
Distributor: Fox Video
Videocassette: $14.98
No public performance rights

Snow White and the Seven Dwarfs.
53 min. Color. Live action. 1983. Elizabeth McGovern, Vincent Price, Vanessa Redgrave.
A laser disc version of the same title offered by Fox Video (see above).
Distributor: Image Entertainment
Laser disc: CLV format $29.98
No public performance rights

Snow White.
26 min. Color. Animation. Produced by Rankin-Bass. 1989.
The low-budget cartoon is no match for Disney-style animation. In this version, Snow White flees to the woods after the queen orders that the child be put to death.
Audience: Ages 6-10
Distributor: Lucerne Media
Videocassette: $195

Snow White.
85 min. Color. Live action. Produced by Golan Globus Productions. 1989. Diana Rigg, Billy Barty.
This is a vivid musical production of the fairy tale, with fine performances that sustain interest. The dwarfs are comical and the stepmother is so very wicked that preschool viewers may find her too frightening. The whole captures the magic of the original.
Audience: Ages 6-Adult
Distributor: Cannon Video
Videocassette available
No public performance rights

★★★★★

Snowman, The
Raymond Briggs (illus.).
Random House. 1978. Fantasy.
This wordless story features a boy and a snowman who comes alive, enters the boy's house, and flies through the sky with him to visit Santa and his reindeer.

Snowman, The.
26 min. Color. Animated. Produced by John Coates/Weston Woods. 1983.
Lively animation and music combine with the imaginative story line to make this fine entertainment, even though there is no narration. The feisty snowman puts on clothes, glasses, and dentures in the boy's house. Later, he rides a motorcycle and dances. While the production is full of action, very young viewers may find it somewhat long for a wordless film.
Reviews: *Booklist*, Jan. 15, 1984; *Horn Book*, Feb. 1984; *School Library Journal*, May 1984
Awards: ALA Notable Film; British Academy Award
Audience: Ages 4-6
Distributor: Weston Woods
16mm film: $525 **Videocassette:** $60
Rental: $40 daily

Snowman, The.
30 min. Color. Animated. Produced by John Coates/Weston Woods. 1989.
A home video version of the same title distributed by Weston Woods (see above).
Audience: Ages 4-8
Distributor: Children's Circle, Weston Woods
Videocassette: $14.95
No public performance rights

★★★★★

Snowy Day, The
Ezra Jack Keats (illus.).
Penguin USA. 1962. Realistic fiction.
One winter morning, Peter wakes up to a snowy day and enjoys the nature of it, making footprints in white powder and so on. Much to his dismay, he feels for a snowball that he earlier pocketed and learns that the cold white substance passes.

Snowy Day, The.
6 min. Color. Animated. Produced by Mal Wittman/Weston Woods. 1964.
The film, like the storybook, quietly celebrates snow through the eyes of a young black boy. Deftly animated visuals capture the wonder, joy, and sadness of the boy in relation to the snow.
Reviews: *Booklist*, May 1, 1972
Audience: Ages 4-8
Distributor: Weston Woods
16mm film: $175 **Videocassette:** $60
Rental: $20 daily

Smile for Auntie and Other Stories.
27 min. Color. Iconographic and animated. Produced by Weston Woods. 1985.
Included in this tape anthology are adaptations of *Smile for Auntie* (Diane Paterson), *Make Way for Ducklings* (Robert McCloskey), *The Snowy Day* (Ezra Jack Keats), and *Wynken, Blynken and Nod* (Eugene Field). See individual titles for full descriptions.
Audience: Ages 4-8
Distributor: Children's Circle, Weston Woods
Videocassette: $19.95
No public performance rights

★★★★★

Soldier Jack.
Anthologized in *Jack Tales*, edited by Richard Chase. Illustrated by Berkeley Williams, Jr. Houghton Mifflin. 1943. Folklore and fairy tales.

Released from the army, Soldier Jack has but two loaves of bread and these he gives to needy strangers. One stranger returns the favor with a magic bag that will capture whatever Jack desires and a glass that helps him know if a person will die. They are the keys to his future fortune.

Soldier Jack: An American Folktale.
40 min. Color. Live action. Produced by Tom and Mimi Davenport. 1988.
The film portrays Jack as a warm, friendly soldier. He uses his magic bag to rid a haunted house of three evil devils, characters who are convincing yet not too fearsome. Afterwards, Jack goes on to lead a contented life in the house, later using his magic glass and bag to capture Death, which threatens to seize the President's daughter. There is a nice edge of humor to this version, which strays slightly from the original by Jack's proceeding to marry the President's daughter.
Awards: CINE Golden Eagle; American Library Association Notable Film; Blue Ribbon, American Film Festival; Silver Apple, National Educational Film and Video Festival
Audience: Ages 8-Adult
Distributor: Davenport Films
16mm film: $550 **Rental:** $55
Videocassette: $60 (with public performance rights)
Videocassette: $29.95 (no public performance rights)

★★★★★

"Soldier's Home"
Ernest Hemingway.
Anthologized in *The Complete Short Stories of Ernest Hemingway.* Scribner. 1987. Short stories—realistic fiction.
A soldier in World War I returns home and finds it difficult to establish himself in his old community.

Soldier's Home.
42 min. Color. Live action. Produced by Learning in Focus. 1986. Richard Backus, Nancy Marchand.
An introduction by Henry Fonda is immediately followed by a voice-over narration repeating essentially the same message. This unfortunate beginning slows audience involvement, an effect from which the film never fully recovers.
Audience: Ages 15-Adult
Distributor: Coronet/MTI Film & Video
16mm film: $740 **Videocassette:** $250
Rental: $75

Soldier's Home.
41 min. Color. Live action. 1986. Richard Backus, Nancy Marchand.
A home video version of the same title distributed by Coronet/MTI Film & Video (see above).
Distributor: Monterey Home Video
Videocassette: $24.95
No public performance rights

★★★★★

Someone New
Charlotte Zolotow.
Illustrated by Erik Blegvad. Harper & Row Junior Books. 1978. Realistic fiction.
Told in the first person, this tale features a narrator who proclaims someone is gone, proceeds to pack up his old toys, and makes a self-discovery. He is someone new.

Someone New.
4 min. Color. Limited animation. Produced by Nick Bosustow. 1983.
While this animated version is admirably faithful to the storybook, its message seems better suited to the print medium.
Audience: Ages 6-9

Distributor: Churchill Media
16mm film: $125 **Videocassette:** $59
Rental: $50

★★★★★

Something Wicked This Way Comes
Ray Bradbury.
Simon and Schuster. 1962. Horror.
Mr. Dark arrives in town with a traveling carnival, to the excitement of two thirteen-year-olds, Will and Jim. The townsfolk, having their fantasies granted, begin to disappear. Through love, the boys, and subsequently the enslaved townspeople, are saved from evil.

Something Wicked This Way Comes.
94 min. Color. Live action. Produced by Peter Vincent Douglas/Walt Disney. 1983. Jason Robards, Jonathan Pryce, Diane Ladd. Narrated by Arthur Hill.
The show begins with a narrator introducing the story in Bradbury's own words, then becomes a good production of a slow-moving story. The dark fantasy is told from the point of view of thirteen-year-old Will, whose father (played by Jason Robards) saves him from evil. Adapted from an intricately woven book, the film is sometimes hard to follow. Scenes, such as one of a man physically dissolving, may inspire fright, as described by the *New York Times*: "A film best suited to children, though it may scare them at times."
Reviews: *New York Times*, Apr. 19, 1980
Audience: Ages 10-Adult
Distributor: Buena Vista Home Video
Videocassette: $19.99
No public performance rights

Something Wicked This Way Comes.
31 min. Color. Live action. 1984. Jason Robards, Jonathan Pryce, Diane Ladd. Narrated by Arthur Hill.
An abbreviated version of the same title distributed by Buena Vista Home Video (see above). This version retains the basic plot but omits selected details.
Audience: Ages 10-Adult
Distributor: Coronet/MTI Film & Video
16mm film: $655 **Videocassette:** $250
Rental: $75

★★★★★

Sound of Sunshine, Sound of Rain
Florence Parry Heide.
Illustrated by Kenneth Longtemps. Parents' Magazine Press. 1970. Realistic fiction.
The difference between a friend's perception and the real world of parks, grocery stores, and hazards confuses a blind boy.

Sound of Sunshine, Sound of Rain.
14.5 min. Color. Animation. Produced by Edna Godel Hallinan. 1984.
A story of a blind seven-year-old black boy, this film has won several awards for excellence. Its animation is based on the book's illustrations by Kenneth Longtemps.
Reviews: *Booklist*, May 15, 1984
Awards: Red Ribbon, American Film Festival; Notable Film, American Library Association; Ruby Slipper, International Children's Film Festival; First Place, Family Life Award, National Council on Family Relations
Audience: Ages 6-10
Distributor: Filmfair Communications
16mm film: $300 **Videocassette:** $270
Rental: $30

★★★★★

Sounder
William H. Armstrong.
Illustrated by James Barkley. Harper & Row. 1969. Historical fiction.

A well-meaning father of a black family in 1930s Louisiana steals bread for his hungry brood. Caught, he serves six years of hard labor, during which his son comes of age.

Sounder.
105 min. Color. Live action. Produced by Radnitz-Mattel/Robert B. Radnitz. 1972. Cicely Tyson, Paul Winfield, Kevin Hooks.
The film triumphs as a portrayal of black family loyalty, though it changes a few details of the novel. The family has one less child on screen, and the father's six-year absence is reduced to one year. Also the film ends hopefully with the family intact; both the father and the dog (Sounder) die at the close of the novel. Still, the basic story has been faithfully adapted. In one heart-rending scene, Kevin, the boy, makes a painstaking journey to visit his father, only to find he has been transferred to another labor camp. On the way, Kevin makes contact with a black school that gives him some cultural insight. He returns home and farms until his father reappears and the boy makes a weighty decision.
Reviews: *New York Times*, Sept. 25, 1972; *Variety*, Aug. 16, 1972
Audience: Ages 10-Adult
Distributor: Paramount Home Video
Videocassette available
No public performance rights

Sounder.
105 min. Color. Live action. 1972. Cicely Tyson, Paul Winfield.
A laser disc version of the same title offered by Paramount Home Video (see above).
Distributor: Pioneer LDCA, Inc.
Laser disc: CLV format $29.95
No public performance rights

★★★★★

Soup and Me
Robert Newton Peck.
Illustrated by Charles Lilly. Knopf. 1978. [1975]. Realistic fiction.
Rob and Soup find what is surely the largest pumpkin, but Janice, the class bully, threatens their chance at winning the Halloween contest.

Soup and Me.
24 min. Color. Live action. Produced by ABC Weekend Specials. 1977. Frank Cady, Shane Sinuto.
Pure fun to watch, the film adapts a storybook based on the author's experiences with his best friend, Soup, during their boyhood in rural Vermont. Soup's friend Rob, in keeping with reality, tells the story of their escapades as they try for the largest pumpkin and best costume at the Halloween party.
As predicted in *Booklist*, "Viewers will relish the ingenuity and careless ease with which Rob and Soup find trouble."
Reviews: *Booklist*, Oct. 15, 1978
Awards: Chris Bronze Plaque, Columbus International Film Festival
Audience: Ages 8-11
Distributor: Coronet/MTI Film & Video
16mm film: $455 **Videocassette:** $250
Rental: $75

★★★★★

Soup for President
Robert Newton Peck.
Illustrated by Ted Lewin. Knopf. 1978. Realistic fiction.
In a small Vermont town, Soup runs for class president and Rob manages his campaign.

Soup for President.
24 min. Color. Live action. Produced by ABC Weekend Specials. 1978. Shane Sinuto, Frank Cady.
The very well-chosen cast makes this film a delight. Rob's dilemma when he must choose between his best friend and his

dream girl is a plight to interest middle graders.

Audience: Ages 10-14
Distributor: Coronet/MTI Film & Video
16mm film: $455 **Videocassette:** $250
Rental: $75

★★★★★

Special Trade, A
Sally Wittman.
Illustrated by Karen Gundersheimer. Harper & Row Junior Books. 1985. Realistic fiction.
Bartholomew takes little Nellie for a daily stroll around the neighborhood. When Bartholomew and Nellie grow older, the aged man injures himself in a fall. Unable to take Nellie for their walks, Bartholomew is cheered when Nellie decides it is time to reverse their roles.

A Special Trade.
17 min. Color. Live action. Produced by Ron Underwood. 1979.
As a testimony to its production quality and tender story line, this film has won many awards for excellence. The two central characters—an old man and a girl (who ages several years in the film)—are excellent in this adaptation of the fine book.

Awards: Red Ribbon, American Film and Video Festival; Best of Festival, Canadian Children's Film Festival; *Instructor* Magazine Top Twenty; *Learning* Magazine Best of the Year; First Place, National Mental Health Association
Audience: Ages 6-12
Distributor: Barr Films
16mm film: $385 **Videocassette:** $270
Rental: $50

★★★★★

Spoon River Anthology
Edgar Lee Masters.
Macmillan. 1987. [1915]. Poetry.
History and ecology are brought together in the story of the lives of people settling along "Spoon River" in rural America.

Spoon River Anthology.
21 min. Color. Live action. Produced by Thomas G. Smith. 1976.
With beautiful scenery, old photos, and selected words from the book, producer Thomas G. Smith captures both the mood and the central message of the author.

Reviews: *Booklist*, Nov. 15, 1976
Awards: Chris Bronze Plaque, Columbus International Film Festival; CINE Golden Eagle
Audience: Ages 12-18
Distributor: Phoenix/BFA Films & Video
16mm film: $435 **Videocassette:** $250
Rental: $62

★★★★★

Stanley
Syd Hoff (illus.).
Harper & Row Junior Books. 1962. Fantasy.
Different from all the other cavemen, Stanley says "please" and "thank you" and treats the animals kindly. The others throw him out of their cave, whereupon Stanley builds himself a novel type of shelter—a house. His kindness to dinosaurs ultimately serves him (and the other cavemen) in good stead.

Stanley and the Dinosaurs.
15.5 min. Color. Dimensional animation. Produced by John Matthews. 1989.
The plot is the same in both versions but the show adds updated dialog, songs, and a few characters (the cave people's children). In the film version, the dinosaurs form a melodic quartet, producing music that helps carry the story forward. The lyrics stick to the storybook's

theme that there is value in being different; a few lines may be difficult for younger audiences to understand.

Reviews: *Booklist*, Feb. 15, 1990
Audience: Ages 4-8
Distributor: Churchill Media
16mm film: $435 **Videocassette:** $325
Rental: $60

★★★★★

Star Wars
Larry Weinberg and George Lucas.
Random House. 1985. [1978]. Science fiction.
Setting the scene for the battle between forces of good and evil in a far-off galaxy, this story introduces the characters Luke Skywalker, Han Solo, Princess Leia, Darth Vader, and the Forces. Also published by Random House (and adapted) are the sequels, *Empire Strikes Back* and *Return of the Jedi*. In *Empire Strikes Back*, the forces of good take refuge on an ice planet. Meanwhile, the evil Darth Vader tries again to take control of the universe. The final installment in the Star Wars trilogy pits Darth Vader against the hero Luke Skywalker in a climactic battle.

Star Wars.
121 min. Color. Live action. Produced by Lucasfilm/Gary Kurtz. 1977. Mark Hamill, Harrison Ford, Carrie Fisher.
Pivotal in film history for its stupendous special effects, the picture includes a thunderous battle involving fighting lasers and explosive planets. The adventurous saga begins with the faraway galaxy being ruled by an evil villain and is succeeded—but not outdone by—two sequels (see *The Empire Strikes Back* and *Return of the Jedi*).

Reviews: *New York Times*, May 26, 1977 III, 18:1; *Variety*, May 25, 1977
Awards: Academy Awards, Best Costumes, Best Film Editing, Best Music Score, Best Sound, Best Visual Effects
Audience: Ages 8-Adult
Distributor: Fox Video
Videocassette: $19.98
No public performance rights

Star Wars.
120 min. Color. Live action. 1977. Mark Hamill, Harrison Ford, Carrie Fisher.
A laser disc version of the same title offered by Fox Video (see above).

Distributor: Image Entertainment
Laser disc: CLV format $34.98, CAV format $64.98, Widescreen CLV format $69.98
No public performance rights

Empire Strikes Back, The.
124 min. Color. Live action. Produced by Lucas film/Gary Kurtz. 1980. Mark Hamill, Harrison Ford, Carrie Fisher, Billy Dee Williams.
Celebrated for phenomenal special effects and Oscar-winning sound, this Star Wars episode shows evil gaining ground in the battle against good. Yoda, a little creature, advises Luke Skywalker about the Force before Luke confronts Darth Vader. The conflict is resolved in *Return of the Jedi*.

Awards: Academy Awards, Best Sound, Best Visual Effects
Audience: Ages 8-12
Distributor: Fox Video
Videocassette: $19.98
No public performance rights

Empire Strikes Back, The.
124 min. Color. Live action. 1980. Harrison Ford, Mark Hamill.
A laser disc version of the same title offered by Fox Video (see above).

Distributor: Image Entertainment
Laser disc: CLV format $34.98, CAV format $64.98, Widescreen CLV format $69.98

No public performance rights

Return of the Jedi.
132 min. Color. Live action. Produced by Lucasfilm/Howard Kazanjian. 1983. Mark Hamill, Harrison Ford, Carrie Fisher, Billy Dee Williams.
Celebrated for its special effects, the movie features death-ray contraptions, cycles that fly, and so on. There is little in the way of character depth in the fight between good and evil, but the film introduces some fantastic new characters. It is more episodic than previous installments and difficult to understand without having seen them. The book, in this case, was adapted from the film.
Reviews: *New York Times*, May 25, 1983, C, 24:1
Awards: Academy Award, Best Visual Effects
Audience: Ages 8-12
Distributor: Fox Video
Videocassette: $19.98
No public performance rights

Return of the Jedi.
132 min. Color. Live action. 1983. Harrison Ford, Mark Hamill.
A laser disc version of the same title offered by Fox Video (see above).
Distributor: Image Entertainment
Laser disc: CLV format $44.98, widescreen CLV format $69.98
No public performance rights

★★★★★

Starstruck
Marisa Gioffre.
Scholastic. 1985. Realistic fiction.
A girl is torn between her ambition to be a performer and her mother's insistence that she prepare for an accounting career.

Starstruck.
31 min. Color. Live action. Produced by ABC After School Specials/LCA. 1981.
An all-too-real story of youthful ambition and parental hopes is told in a style that will hold the interest of most audiences who appreciate good acting and a well-designed story line. This is also available in a longer version that allows for fuller character development.
Reviews: *Variety*, Oct. 21, 1981
Awards: ALA Selected Film for Young Adults; Emmy Award, Outstanding Children's Special
Audience: Ages 14-18
Distributor: Coronet/MTI Film & Video
16mm film: $500 **Videocassette:** $250
Rental: $75

Starstruck.
46 min. Color. Live action. 1981.
A full-length version of the abbreviated title also distributed by Coronet/MTI Film & Video (see above).
Distributor: Coronet/MTI Film & Video
16mm film: $750 **Videocassette:** $250
Rental: $75

★★★★★

Steadfast Tin Soldier, The
Hans Christian Andersen.
Multiple editions. Folklore and fairy tales.
A one-legged tin soldier survives a perilous journey in the outside world only to be thrown into the fire along with the paper dancer who won his heart.

Staunch Tin Soldier, The.
27 min. Color. Live action and puppet animation. Produced by Ake Soderquist. 1967.

Set in Holland in 1830, this live-action version begins at a boy's birthday party. Hans Christian Andersen, who attends the party, takes out a box of tin soldiers and tells the story as visual representations of the castle, paper dancer, and other elements appear on screen. Puppet animation portrays the movement of the toys.

Audience: Ages 4-8
Distributor: Britannica
16mm film: $590 **Videocassette:** $300

Steadfast Tin Soldier, The.
30 min. Color. Iconographic. Produced by Rabbit Ears Productions and Random House Home Video. 1986. Narrated by Jeremy Irons.
David Jorgensen's beautiful illustrations and Mark Isham's heroic musical score (using trumpet, drum, celeste, calliope, and a variety of other instruments) enhance this simple story of a one-legged tin soldier who retains a brave and generous heart despite the troubles that he encounters. Jeremy Irons's narration conveys the theme: Be loving, loyal, and of strong heart, and don't let circumstances rule you.

Audience: Ages 6-12
Distributor: Random House Home Video
Videocassette: $14.95
No public performance rights

★★★★★

Stone Soup
Marcia Brown (illus.).
Scribner. 1982. [1947]. Folklore and fairy tales.
Three French soldiers cleverly trick a whole village into serving them a feast.

Stone Soup.
11 min. Color. Iconographic. Produced by Weston Woods. 1955.
The picture starts slowly, but interest builds as it progresses. Curious about the soldiers' plan to make stone soup, the villagers contribute ingredients until the dish becomes a splendid potpourri.

Awards: Award of Merit, Columbus Film Festival
Audience: Ages 6-10
Distributor: Weston Woods
16mm film: $175 **Videocassette:** $60
Rental: $25 daily

★★★★★

Stonecutter, The: A Japanese Folk Tale
Gerald McDermott (illus.).
Penguin USA. 1975. Folklore and fairy tales.
A stonecutter wishes he were as powerful as others. His wish is granted, and he is transformed first into a prince, then the sun, and finally a mountain, which proves less powerful than imagined as its foundation gives way to the chisel of another stonecutter.

Stonecutter, The.
6 min. Color. Animated. Produced by Gerald McDermott/Weston Woods. 1975. Narrated and directed by Gerald McDermott.
This fast-paced production features an abstract style of art that appeals especially to the imaginative viewer. Instead of the film spelling out the moral, viewers are left to conclude it as the end shows the stonecutter chipping away at the mountain. The film, in this case, preceded the book.

Audience: Ages 4-10
Distributor: Weston Woods
16mm film: $195 **Videocassette:** $60
Rental: $20 daily

Folktale from Two Lands.
16.5 min. Color. Very limited animation. Produced by Pieter Van Deusen. 1988. Narrated by Walker Edmiston.
Included in this short film anthology are two stories that deal with personal greed, "The Fisherman and His Wife" and "The Stonecutter." The fisherman's wife is more sympathetic here then in other versions. Absent from the show is the element of a storm rising as the wife grows greedier. Like the fisherman's wife, the stonecutter wishes to be more and more powerful until he becames a mountain. The mountain ironically falls victim to the chisel of a lowly stonecutter. Both films feature limited animation and story lines that are generally faithful to the originals.
Audience: Ages 5-9
Distributor: Churchill Media
16mm film: $415 **Videocassette:** $310
Rental: $60

★★★★★

Story—A Story, A
Gail E. Haley (illus.).
Atheneum. 1970. Folklore and fairy tales.
A weak old spider man cleverly accomplishes three seemingly impossible tasks. In return the African sky god awards him the golden box of stories, which he shares with the world.

Story—A Story, A.
10 min. Color. Limited animation. Produced by Weston Woods. 1973. Narrated by Dr. John Akar.
This engrossing film follows the spider man from one challenging task to the next as he captures a leopard, a hornet, and a fairy whom others never see. Set to African music and narrated with an African accent, this animated version enhances the printed retelling.
Audience: Ages 4-8
Distributor: Weston Woods
16mm film: $235 **Videocassette:** $60
Rental: $20 per day

Strega Nonna and Other Stories.
35 min. Color. Iconographic and animated. Produced by Weston Woods. 1985.
Included in this tape anthology are adaptations of *Strega Nonna* (Tomie de Paola), *Tikki Tikki Tembo* (Arlene Mosel), *The Foolish Frog* (Pete and Charles Seeger) and *A Story—A Story* (Gail E. Haley). See individual titles for full descriptions.
Audience: Ages 4-8
Distributor: Children's Circle, Weston Woods
Videocassette: $19.95
No public performance rights

★★★★★

Story about Ping, The
Marjorie Flack.
Illustrated by Kurt Wiese. Penguin USA. 1933. Adventure.
Escaping a spanking, a tardy duck named Ping gets separated from his family on the Yangste River in China.

Story about Ping, The.
10 min. Color. Iconographic. Produced by Weston Woods. 1955.
Though only the camera moves, the illustrations convey a realistic impression of life on the Yangste River. The plot is full of action as the lost duck narrowly escapes from a family bent on eating him.
Audience: Ages 4-6
Distributor: Weston Woods
16mm film: $175 **Videocassette:** $60
Rental: $20 daily

★★★★★

Story of Babar, The
Jean De Brunhoff (illus.).
Random House. 1937. Fantasy.
In this first tale about the elephant Babar, his mother is shot by a hunter and Babar flees to the city. There he meets the kind Old Lady, then returns to the forest to become king of the elephants. Sequels are *The Travels of Babar* in which Babar outsmarts the Retaxes, rhinoceroses that have declared war on the elephants. In *Babar the King*, the monarch builds a city for the elephants, and the Old Lady is bitten by a snake. *Babar and Father Christmas* follows Babar to the home of Father Christmas. In *Babar Comes to America* by Laurent De Brunhoff, Babar journeys from New York to Disneyland.

Babar and Father Christmas.
30 min. Color. Animation. Produced by Hi Tops Video/Alison Clayton. 1986. Narrated by Laurent De Brunhoff.
This is a brightly animated but slow-moving adaptation. It remains faithful to the original but changes a few details. In the adaptation, but not in the original, a rhinoceros competes with Babar to reach Father Christmas first. The movie has Babar reach his destination alone; a little dog accompanies him in the original. Lastly, the production adds a song at the conclusion. Missing is the spirit of adventure in the storybook during Babar's pursuit of Father Christmas.
Reviews: *Children's Video Report*, Dec. 1986
Audience: Ages 4-8
Distributor: Videocassette not currently in distribution

Babar Comes to America.
25 min. Color. Animation. Produced by Lee Mendelson and Bill Melendez. 1986. Narrated by Peter Ustinov.
This version adds to the plot in a storybook that is like a travelogue of Babar's journey. Unlike the book, the movie opens before Babar leaves for America. It draws from another book (*The Travels of Babar*), having the king and his queen start the journey in a hot air balloon. In America, they visit major cities, an auto factory, a drugstore, and so forth. Babar travels alone in the original, but with elephant companions in the adaptation. Little Arthur gets separated from the others, who search high and low for him. They are reunited in Hollywood, where they all land parts in a movie.
Reviews: *Booklist*, May 1, 1987
Audience: Ages 4-8
Distributor: Vestron Video
Videocassette: $14.98
No public performance rights

Babar the Movie.
79 min. Color. Animation. A Nelvana Production with The Clifford Ross Company. 1988.
The movie is a flashback in which King Babar recounts a past experience in a story he tells his children. Dramatized on screen and drawn largely from *Travels with Baber*, the story concerns the war between the rhinoceroses and the elephants. Not intended as a strict adaptation, the show changes details. It portrays a physical battle; the rhinoceroses torch a city and take captives. In the book, the enemies take off peacefully once Babar outsmarts them. He outsmarts them in the screen version too, but with a different tactic than in the original. Some catchy songs are built into the action. One spirited tune, about the politics of running a kingdom, has lyrics that speak to an older audience than the book. The production, though violent, is full of action, brightly colored animation, and charming character voices.
Reviews: *Children's Video Report*, Feb./Mar. 1990; *Variety*, July 26, 1989
Awards: Gold Award, Houston World Film and Video Festival
Audience: Ages 4-8
Distributor: Family Home Entertainment
Videocassette: $24.95

No public performance rights

Babar's First Step.
49 min. Color. Animation. A Nelvana Production with The Clifford Ross Company. 1989.
Now living in the palace as a king, Babar recounts his origins to his children in a tale drawn from the book *The Story of Babar*. The adaptation follows the elephant's adventures from his birth to the hunter's shooting his mother. The plot diverges from the storybook at this point. On screen, Babar then fights the hunter so the other elephants can escape; he is separated from them as a result.
Audience: Ages 4-8
Distributor: Family Home Entertainment
Videocassette: $14.95
No public performance rights

Babar Returns.
49 min. Color. Animation. A Nelvana Production with The Clifford Ross Company. 1989.
Drawn from *The Story of Babar*, this installment features the elephant living in the city with the kind Old Lady. Two old friends bring him home to the forest, where a hunter still threatens the elephants. In the storybook, Babar returns not because of a hunter but because he longs for his old companions, who then make him king. The movie has him defeat the hunter with a clever trick before they make him king. This leads to some cartoon-style antics; the hunter uses his gun to deflate Babar's car tire, gets drenched and so forth. There is a second video story, "The City of Elephants," drawn from *Babar the King*. Babar sets out to build an elephant city, the Old Lady gets bitten by a snake, and Babar dreams of winged elephants chasing misfortune away as in the book. Both video stories are set in the context of Babar recalling times past as he and a family member enjoy a nighttime snack.
Audience: Ages 4-8
Distributor: Family Home Entertainment
Videocassette: $14.95
No public performance rights

★★★★★

Story of Doctor Dolittle, The
The Voyages of Doctor Dolittle
Hugh Lofting.
Multiple editions. Fantasy.
A nineteenth-century English doctor is an eccentric veterinarian who talks to his animals. His saga begins in *The Story of Dr. Dolittle* and continues in *The Voyages of Doctor Dolittle*, which includes his journey to the South Seas in pursuit of the Great Pink Sea Snail.

Doctor Dolittle.
145 min. Color. Produced by Arthur P. Jacobs. 1967. Rex Harrison, Anthony Newley, Samantha Eggar.
The production is a musical that progresses slowly. Yet children take delight in the real animals that parade across the screen, including a trained chimp that answers the doctor's front door. The song "Talk to the Animals" won an Oscar.
Reviews: *New York Times*, Dec. 20, 1957, 55:1; *Variety*, Dec. 20, 1967
Awards: Academy Awards, Best Song, Best Visual Effects; Golden Globe Award, Best Supporting Actor
Audience: Ages 8-12
Distributor: Fox Video
Videocassette: $19.98
No public performance rights

★★★★★

Story of Ferdinand, The
Munro Leaf.
Illustrated by Robert Lawson. Penguin USA. 1936. Humor.

Though its owners had hoped it would do battle in the ring, a peace-loving bull prefers smelling flowers to fighting.

Ferdinand the Bull.
8 min. Color. Animation. A Disney Educational Production. 1960.
Straying from its more usual style, Disney this time produced a straight adaptation of the book. The brightness of Disney animation shines through, as reflected by the Oscar awarded to this production in 1938, when it was initially released.
Awards: Academy Award, Best Cartoon
Audience: Ages 5-10
Distributor: Coronet/MTI Film & Video
16mm film: $225 **Videocassette:** $170
Rental: $75

★★★★★

Story of the Dancing Frog, The
Quentin Blake (illus.).
Knopf. 1985. [1984]. Fantasy.
George the Frog and his once lonely owner, Aunt Gertrude, dance their way around the world.

Story of the Dancing Frog, The.
25 min. Color. Animation. Produced by Michael Sporn and Italtoons Corp. 1990.
Award-winning animation results in appealingly lively visuals as George the Frog dances on tour through Spain, Russia, and elsewhere...even after Aunt Gertrude receives a marriage proposal. The imaginative concept is amusingly executed.
Awards: Ace Award; Gold Medal, Parents' Choice Award
Audience: Ages 5-8
Distributor: Lucerne Media
16mm film: $495 **Videocassette:** $295

Story of the Dancing Frog, The.
25 min. Color. Animation. Produced by Michael Sporn and Italtoons Corp. 1990.
A home video version of the same title distributed by Lucerne Media (see above).
Distributor: Family Home Entertainment
Videocassette: $14.95
No public performance rights

★★★★★

Story of the Trapp Family Singers, The
Maria Augusta Trapp.
Larlin. 1978. [1949]. Biography.
A young governess tutors an Austrian widower's children, bringing them joy and falling in love with their father. The family of singers escapes the Nazis during a music festival.

Sound of Music, The.
173 min. Color. Live action. Produced by Twentieth Century Fox/Robert Wise. 1965. Julie Andrews, Christopher Plummer, Peggy Wood.
Wildly popular, this musical retains the story line of the print version but extends it with memorable songs ("My Favorite Things," "Climb Every Mountain," "Do Re Mi"). The film has been faulted for its obviousness but applauded for its strong appeal and a captivating performance by Julie Andrews. This motion picture is based on the Rodgers and Hammerstein play, which, in turn, is adapted from the biography.
Reviews: *New York Times*, Mar. 3, 1965, 34:1; *Variety*, Mar. 3, 1965
Awards: Academy Awards, Best Picture, Best Directing, Best Sound, Best Music Score; Golden Globe, Best Musical, Best Actress in a Musical
Audience: Ages 8-Adult
Distributor: Fox Video
Videocassette: $29.98

No public performance rights

Sound of Music, The.
173 min. Color. Live action. 1965. Julie Andrews, Christopher Plummer, Peggy Wood.
A laser disc version of the same title offered by Fox Video (see above).
Distributor: Image Entertainment
Laser disc: CLV format $54.98, widescreen CLV format $69.98
No public performance rights

★★★★★

Strange Case of Dr. Jekyll and Mr. Hyde, The

Robert Louis Stevenson.
Multiple editions. Horror.
Assuming two identities, a doctor concocts a drug that transforms his body into the physical symbol of his evil self.

Dr. Jekyll and Mr. Hyde.
63 min. Black and white. Live action. Produced by Paramount Artcraft. 1920. John Barrymore, Nita Naldi, Martha Mansfield.
This is a silent version of the classic. Barrymore, who uses facial contortion to achieve changes in character, is excellent in the starring role.
Reviews: *New York Times*, Mar. 19, 1920, 18:1; *Variety*, Apr. 2, 1920
Audience: Ages 14-Adult
Distributor: Republic Pictures Home Video
Videocassette: $19.98
No public performance rights

Dr. Jekyll and Mr. Hyde.
63 min. Black and white. Live action. 1920. John Barrymore, Nita Naldi, Martha Mansfield.
A laser disc version of the same title offered by Republic Pictures Home Video (see above).
Distributor: Pioneer LDCA, Inc.
Laser disc: CLV format $29.98
No public performance rights

Dr. Jekyll and Mr. Hyde.
98 min. Black and white. Live action. Produced by Paramount/Rouben Mamoulian. 1932. Frederic March, Miriam Hopkins, Rose Hobart.
Probably the most thrilling rendition of the classic horror story, this adaptation excels in pacing, performances, settings, and special effects.
Reviews: *New York Times*, Jan. 2, 1932, 14:2
Awards: Academy Award, Best Actor
Audience: Ages 14-Adult
Distributor: MGM/UA Home Video
Videocassette: $19.98
No public performance rights

Dr. Jekyll and Mr. Hyde.
98 min. Black and white. Live action. 1932. Frederic March, Miriam Hopkins, Rose Hobart.
A laser disc version of the same title offered by MGM/UA Home Video (see above).
Distributor: Pioneer LDCA, Inc.
Videocassette: Widescreen CLV format $34.98
No public performance rights

Dr. Jekyll and Mr. Hyde.
122 min. Black and white. Produced by MGM. 1941. Spencer Tracy, Ingrid Bergman, Lana Turner.

Concentrating more on the emotional and psychological dimensions than the 1932 version, this one includes dream sequences that do little to clarify the action. The screenplay is nevertheless well performed.

Reviews: *New York Times*, Aug. 13, 1941, 13:2; *Variety*, July 23, 1941
Audience: Ages 14-Adult
Distributor: MGM/UA Home Video
Videocassette: $24.98

★★★★★

Strega Nonna
Tomie de Paola (illus.).
Prentice Hall. 1975. Folklore and fairy tales.
Strega Nonna, a wise woman of Italy, hires Big Anthony to help with the chores, cautioning him never to touch her pasta pot. When he does, the pot overflows with nonstop pasta until Strega Nonna reappears and Anthony receives his "just desserts."

Strega Nonna.
12 min. Color. Animated. Produced by Weston Woods. 1978.
This lively motion picture conveys the imaginative humor of the book. Along with background music and character voices, the storyteller narrates in English with an Italian accent, which adds atmosphere to the tasty tale. *Booklist* describes the film as "a new masterpiece for viewers of all ages."

Reviews: *Booklist*, Sept. 15, 1978
Awards: Blue Ribbon, American Film Festival; CINE Golden Eagle; The *Learning* AV Award
Audience: Ages 4-Adult
Distributor: Weston Woods
16mm film: $215 **Videocassette:** $60
Rental: $20 daily

Strega Nonna and Other Stories.
35 min. Color. Iconographic and animated. Produced by Weston Woods. 1985.
Included in this tape anthology are adaptations of *Strega Nonna* (Tomie de Paola), *Tikki Tikki Tembo* (Arlene Mosel), *The Foolish Frog* (Pete and Charles Seeger) and *A Story—A Story* (Gail E. Haley). See individual titles for full descriptions.

Audience: Ages 4-8
Distributor: Children's Circle, Weston Woods
Videocassette: $19.95
No public performance rights

★★★★★

Suho and the White Horse
Yuzo Otsuka.
Translated by Yasuko Hirawa; illustrated by Suekichi Akaba. Viking Penguin. 1981. [1969]. Folklore and fairy tales.
Set in Mongolia, this legend attributes the origin of the horsehead fiddle to injustice suffered by a shepherd.

Suho and the White Horse.
10 min. Color. Iconographic. Produced by Weston Woods. 1982.
A governor renegs on his promise to give his daughter's hand in marriage to the winner of a horse race when that winner turns out to be a common shepherd. With only the camera moving, the film follows the shepherd's horse as it escapes to a musical fate.

Reviews: *Booklist*, Dec. 1, 1982
Awards: Ruby Slipper Award, International Children's Film Festival
Audience: Ages 6-10
Distributor: Weston Woods
16mm film: $175 **Videocassette:** $60
Rental: $20 daily

★★★★★

Summer of '42
Herman Raucher.
Putnam. 1971. Realistic fiction.
A middle-aged man nostalgically recalls his romance at age fifteen with a young war bride in 1942 New England.

Summer of '42.
103 min. Color. Live action. Produced by Warner Bros. /Richard Alan Roth. 1971. Jennifer O'Neill, Gary Grimes.
Not particularly profound, the show is fun to watch and particularly pleasing to hear, with its Oscar-winning score. Another highlight is its realistic view of male adolescence. The novel, in this case, was adapted from the screenplay. Its story is slim, a middle-aged man's memory of his first lustful experience, a mood piece rather than a densely plotted tale. It is dramatized tenderly and humorously; a seventeen-minute wordless sequence appears at the end. The motion picture was applauded for its direct treatment of the romanticism, achieved with the help of the objective camera. This matter-of-fact tone changes in the novel, where words replace camera shots; in the novel, for example, "sand dunes are described as 'sulking in the grass.'" —*New York Times*
Reviews: *New York Times*, Apr. 19, 1971, 51:1; *Variety*, Apr. 21, 1971
Awards: Academy Award, Best Music Score
Audience: Ages 16-Adult
Distributor: Warner Home Video
Videocassette: $19.98
No public performance rights

★★★★★

Summer Switch
Mary Rodgers.
Harper & Row Junior Books. 1982. Fantasy.
A boy about to attend summer camp and his father about to meet his boss wish they could trade places; their wish comes true.

Summer Switch.
31 min. Color. Live action. Produced by LCA/Highgate/ABC After School Specials. 1984. Robert Klein.
The role reversal ploy, this time between father and son, has been dramatized before, but few such movies are as fun to watch. The abridged version is good but not nearly as rich as the longer version also distributed by Coronet/MTI Film & Video (see below).
Reviews: *Booklist*, July 1985; *School Library Journal*, Aug. 1985
Audience: Ages 8-12
Distributor: Coronet/MTI Film & Video
16mm film: $550 **Videocassette:** $250
Rental: $75

Summer Switch.
46 min. Color. Live action. 1984. Robert Klein.
A full-length version of the same, abbreviated title also distributed by Coronet/MTI Film & Video (see above).
Distributor: Coronet/MTI Film & Video
16mm film: $750 **Videocassette:** $250
Rental: $75

★★★★★

Superlative Horse, The
Jean Merrill.
Illustrated by Ronni Solbert. W. R. Scott. 1961. Historical fiction.
Duke Mu, ruler of ancient China, loves horses and needs a chief groom for the royal stables. Han Kan wants the job but must first demonstrate his knowledge by choosing a superlative horse.

Superlative Horse, The.
36 min. Color. Produced by Urs Furrer. 1975.
Yanna Brandt directed a lovely and tender story of a young horse lover in ancient China. Han Kan's surprising

choice, which proves to be correct, indicates that one should not judge by outward appearances but by inner qualities.
Audience: Ages 8-14
Distributor: Phoenix/BFA Films & Video
16mm film: $550 **Videocassette:** $320
Rental: $45

★★★★★

Swimmy
Leo Lionni (illus.).
Pantheon. 1973. [1963]. Adventure.
Swimmy, a tiny fish, escapes being swallowed by a larger fish. He flees through the colorful, underwater world, and then, with another school of fish, outsmarts a hungry tuna.

Swimmy.
6 min. Color. Animation. Produced by Italtoons. 1987.
Faithful to the original art and story line, this adaptation enhances the original with movement and winning music. Swimmy's adventure occurs in the midst of a "group tour" of the colorful undersea world. In the process of outsmarting the tuna, Swimmy discovers the power of working as a team.
Awards: Gold Medal, Atlanta Film Festival
Audience: Ages 4-10
Distributor: Lucerne Media
16mm film: $300 **Videocassette:** $225

Five Lionni Classics—The Animal Fables of Leo Lionni.
30 min. Color. Animation by Giulio Gianini. Produced by Italtoons Corp./Random House Home Video. 1987.
Included in this tape anthology are adaptations of *Frederick*, *Cornelius*, *It's Mine*, *Fish Is Fish*, and *Swimmy*. See individual titles for plot summaries. Simple yet profound, these animal fables illustrate the power of imagination, the joy of discovery, and the importance of living together in harmony. The film versions remain true to the original art and manuscripts. Winning animation, along with equally winning music by Egisto Macchi, enhances the charm of the characters and the appeal of the storybooks.
Reviews: *Children's Video Report*, Feb. 1987
Audience: Ages 4-8
Distributor: Random House Home Video
Videocassette: $14.95
No public performance rights

Five Lionni Classics.
30 min. Color. Animation. Produced by Italtoons. 1987.
A public performance package of five separate Lionni titles for libraries, including *Frederick, Swimmy, Cornelius, Fish Is Fish*, and *It's Mine*. Each of these titles is also distributed individually by Lucerne Media (see above).
Audience: Ages 3-10
Distributor: Lucerne Media
Videocassette: $325

★★★★★

Swineherd, The
Hans Christian Andersen.
Multiple editions. Folklore and fairy tales.
A prince disguises himself as a swineherd and pursues a princess, whose character disappoints him.

Swineherd, The.
13 min. Color. Animated. Produced by Weston Woods. 1975.
Both funny and sad, this film captures the power in Andersen's tale as the swineherd grows to despise a princess who would kiss him to gain a musical toy. Character voices heighten the drama.

Awards: ALA Notable Film; Gold Plaque, Chicago Film Festival
Audience: Ages 4-8
Distributor: Weston Woods
16mm film: $295 **Videocassette:** $60
Rental: $25 daily

★★★★★

Swiss Family Robinson
Johann David Wyss.
Multiple editions. Adventure.
A Swiss family—parents and three sons—are on their way to New Guinea when a violent storm shipwrecks them onto a desert island. They live there for ten years before any contact with the outside world occurs.

Swiss Family Robinson.
126 min. Color. Live action. Produced by Bill Anderson, Basil Keys/Walt Disney. 1960. John Mills, Dorothy McGuire, James MacArthur.
The adaptation is hard to believe at times (the family builds a house complete with windows and conveniences), yet it captures the spirit of the novel and is highly entertaining. "It's hard to imagine how the picture could be better as a rousing, humorous and gentle-hearted tale of family love amid primitive isolation and dangers." —*New York Times*
Reviews: *New York Times*, Dec. 24, 1960
Audience: Ages 10-Adult
Distributor: Buena Vista Home Video (not currently in distribution)
No public performance rights

Swiss Family Robinson.
27 min. Color. Live action. A Disney Educational Production. 1979.
An abridged version of the same title offered by Buena Vista Home Video (see above). Complete with giant turtle for the young ones to play with as they come ashore, this slightly modernized adaptation is an exceptionally fine production.
Audience: Ages 10-Adult
Distributor: Coronet/MTI Film & Video
16mm film: $600 **Videocassette:** $250
Rental: $75

Swiss Family Robinson.
26 min. Color. Animation. Produced by Rankin-Bass. 1990.
Another low-cost, limited-animation effort, this production appeals mainly to very young, non-discriminatory audiences.
Audience: Ages 8-12
Distributor: Lucerne Media
Videocassette: $195

★★★★★

Sword in the Stone, The
Terence H. White.
Putnam. 1939. Folklore and fairy tales.
Twelve-year-old Wart, a servant boy, happens upon a sword that is embedded in a stone in medieval England. He quite easily pulls it out, becoming the legendary King Arthur.

Sword in the Stone, The.
79 min. Color. Animation. Produced by Ken Peterson/Walt Disney. 1963. Featuring the voices of Sebastian Cabot, Karl Swenson, Ricky Sorenson.
This animated film follows the young orphan from his tutelage by Merlin the Wizard (portrayed as somewhat of a buffoon) to his becoming the mythical King Arthur. The action is faithful to events of the novel, but characters lack depth and the magical feel of the original is largely missing. Set in the Dark Ages, the film adds modern references—mentioning helicopters, London Time, electricity—not in the book.
Reviews: *New York Times*, Dec. 26, 1963

Audience: Ages 4-10
Distributor: Buena Vista Home Video
Videocassette: $24.99
No public performance rights

Sword in the Stone, The.
79 min. Color. Animation. Produced by Walt Disney. 1963.
A laser disc version of the same title offered by Buena Vista Home Video Home Video (see above).
Distributor: Image Entertainment
Laser disc: CLV format $36.99
No public performance rights

T

adherence to book   film rating

Tailor of Gloucester, The
Beatrix Potter (illus.).
Multiple editions. Fantasy.
When a kind tailor grows ill, his work is completed by industrious little mice.

Tailor of Gloucester, The.
30 min. Color. Limited animation. Produced by Rabbit Ears. 1988. Narrated by Meryl Streep.
All the charm of Potter's own creations comes through in David Jorgenson's pastel-gray sketches, which feature the good-hearted tailor, his mice-seeking cat, and the busy mice who complete a waistcoat and make the tailor's fortune. Accompanying Meryl Streep's rich narration, there is a well-orchestrated musical arrangement including pipes and flutes.
Audience: Ages 4-8
Distributor: SVS/Triumph
Videocassette: $14.95
No public performance rights

★★★★★

Tale of Peter Rabbit and Other Stories, The
Beatrix Potter.
Multiple editions. Fantasy.
The tales involve childlike animals such as Peter Rabbit, who disobediently scampers into Mr. McGregor's garden, where he is trapped for a spell. Two mice are caught robbing a doll's house to furnish their own. When the frog Mr. Jeremy Fisher goes fishing, he is almost eaten himself.

Tales of Beatrix Potter, The.
91 min. Color. Live action. Produced by EMI/Richard Goodwin. 1971.
Beautifully performed by the Royal Ballet in animal masks, the adaptation appeals to a select audience. The version demands close attention and interpretation since the entire production (five episodes) is wordless. Among the characters portrayed are Peter Rabbit, the two bad mice, Jemima Puddle-Duck, Jeremy Fisher, and Mrs. Tiggy-Winkle.
Reviews: *New York Times*, July 1, 1971, 61:1; *Variety*, Apr. 14, 1971
Audience: Ages 6-10
Distributor: Janus Films
Videocassette: $88

Tale of Mr. Jeremy Fisher, The and *The Tale of Peter Rabbit.*
30 min. Color. Limited animation. Produced by Rabbit Ears. 1987. Narrated by Meryl Streep.

Two of Beatrix Potter's classics come to life in David Jorgenson's softly colored drawings. Accompanied by lyrical tunes, Streep serenely recounts the hazards faced by the main characters: a fisher frog wearing a macintosh and a garden-marauding rabbit dressed in a blue jacket with brass buttons.

Reviews: *Booklist*, Feb. 1, 1988
Awards: Red Ribbon, American Film & Video Festival
Audience: Ages 4-8
Distributor: SVS/Triumph
Videocassette: $14.95
No public performance rights

Tale of Mr. Jeremy Fisher, The and *The Tale of Peter Rabbit.*
23 min. Color. Limited animation. 1988.
A laser disc version of the same title offered by SVS/Triumph (see above).
Distributor: Image Entertainment
Laser disc: CLV format $19.98
No public performance rights

★★★★★

Tale of Two Cities, A
Charles Dickens.

Multiple editions. Historical fiction.
During the French Revolution, a man is sent to the guillotine because of the sins of his ancestors. Another man, his look alike, trades places with him for the sake of his wife.

Tale of Two Cities, A and *In the Switch Tower.*
70 min. Black and white. Live action. 1911 and 1915.
This is an abridged version of the first silent effort to portray Dickens's classic on film. As a companion piece, its producers added a melodrama about an ambitious railroad man, whose alcoholic father attempts to thwart a train wreck.
Audience: Ages 14-Adult
Distributor: Video Yesteryear
Videocassette: $29.95
No public performance rights

Tale of Two Cities, A.
121 min. Black and white. Live action. Produced by MGM/David O. Selznick. 1935. Ronald Coleman, Elizabeth Allen, Basil Rathbone, Edna May Oliver.
An outstanding cast makes this production the standard against which the several other adaptations of the Dickens novel are measured. Ronald Coleman is peerless as Sydney Carton. As in the novel, Lucie Manette's husband is sentenced to death. His look alike is a lawyer who loves her and so takes the prisoner's place.
Reviews: *New York Times*, Dec. 26, 1935, 21:2; *Variety*, June 1, 1936
Audience: Ages 14-Adult
Distributor: MGM/UA Home Video
Videocassette: $19.98
No public performance rights

Dickens: A Tale of Two Cities.
117 min. Black and white. Live action. Produced by Rank. 1958. Ian Bannen, Dirk Bogarde, Dorothy Tutin, Cecil Parker.
A reasonably faithful adaptation of the complex Dickens story, this lacks the vitality of the 1935 version.
Reviews: *New York Times*, Aug. 5, 1958, 23:1; *Variety*, Feb. 12, 1958.
Audience: Ages 14-Adult
Distributor: Films for the Humanities & Sciences
Videocassette: $89.95

Tale of Two Cities, A.
70 min. Color. Animation. 1984.
Reduced from the original story for children, this animated version will hold the younger audience but does not well serve the classic, which is geared to an older group.

Audience: Ages 8-14
Distributor: Vestron Video
Videocassette: $19.98
No public performance rights

★★★★★

Taming of the Shrew, The
William Shakespeare.
Multiple editions. Drama.
A younger sister cannot marry until her older, shrewish sister finds a mate. Petruchio takes on the challenge and tames the older sister.

Taming of the Shrew.
68 min. Black and white. Produced by United Artists. 1929. Mary Pickford, Douglas Fairbanks, Edwin Maxwell.
This is an abridged version of Shakespeare's play with additional dialogue written by and credited to Sam Taylor. Its pacing and performances are weaker than in subsequent remakes. Kate seems more angry than Shakespeare intended. She shatters windows and is plopped into slimy mud on her wedding night in a show that seems devoted to winning laughs. Also on this laser disc is the documentary "The Birth of a Legend."

Reviews: *New York Times*, Nov. 30, 1929, 23:1; *Variety*, Dec. 4, 1929
Audience: Ages 16-Adult
Distributor: Image Entertainment
Laser disc: CLV format $39.95
No public performance rights

Kiss Me Kate.
111 min. Color. Live action. Produced by MGM/Jack Cummings. 1953. Kathryn Grayson, Howard Keel, Ann Miller.
A step removed from the original, this motion picture is actually an adaptation of Cole Porter's Broadway musical based on the Shakespeare play. The show keeps to the original story line, adding memorable songs ("Too Darn Hot").

Reviews: *New York Times*, Nov. 6, 1953, 23:2; *Variety*, Oct. 18, 1953
Audience: Ages 14-Adult
Distributor: MGM/UA Home Video
Videocassette: $19.98
No public performance rights

Kiss Me Kate.
110 min. Color. Live action. 1953. Kathryn Grayson, Howard Keel, Ann Miller.
A laser disc version of the same title offered by MGM/UA Home Video (see above).

Distributor: Pioneer LDCA, Inc.
Laser disc: CLV format $39.98
No public performance rights

Taming of the Shrew, The.
126 min. Color. Live action. Produced by Columbia/Richard McWhorter. 1967. Elizabeth Taylor, Richard Burton, Michael York.
Elizabeth Taylor and Richard Burton make the perfect pair in this version of the Shakespeare play. The text and characters are somewhat off balance in the movie, which stresses the humor more pronouncedly than the play, but the show nevertheless succeeds as lighthearted entertainment.

Reviews: *New York Times*, Mar. 9, 1967, 43:1; *Variety*, Mar. 1, 1967
Audience: Ages 14-Adult
Distributor: Columbia TriStar Home Video

Videocassette: $19.95
No public performance rights

Taming of the Shrew, The.
122 min. Color. Live action. 1967. Elizabeth Taylor, Richard Burton, Michael York.
A laser disc version of the same title offered by Columbia TriStar Home Video (see above).
Distributor: Pioneer LDCA, Inc.
Laser disc: CLV format $34.95
No public performance rights

Taming of the Shrew, The.
127 min. Color. Live action. Produced by BBC. 1981. John Cleese, Simon Chandler.
In this version, Petruchio opts for verbal attacks rather than physical ones like starving or slapping. Performances are strong, making it seem less a conflict between gentleman and shrew and more a man-woman controversy. As stated in the *Seattle Times*, the production is "wonderfully hilarious." Its settings are simple yet atmospheric. This video edition is for institutional use only.
Reviews: *Seattle Times*, Jan. 25, 1981
Distributor: Ambrose Video
Videocassette: $249.95

★★★★★

Tarzan of the Apes
Edgar Rice Burroughs.
Multiple editions. Adventure.
Lord Greystoke, an infant, is shipwrecked on an island. Apes raise the boy, who eventually encounters white hunters and must decide whether to join civilization.

Tarzan, the Ape Man.
99 min. Black and white. Live action. Produced by MGM/Irving Thalberg. 1932. Johnny Weissmuller, Neil Hamilton, Maureen O'Sullivan.
In search of ivory, a hunting party including Jane (Maureen O'Sullivan) meets Tarzan. He kidnaps her, and she grows fond of him. Their joy is marred when some pygmies lower them into a pit, but elephants come thundering to the rescue.
Reviews: *New York Times*, Mar. 28, 1932, 11:2; *Variety*, Mar. 29, 1932
Audience: Ages 14-Adult
Distributor: MGM/UA Home Video
Videocassette: $19.98
No public performance rights

Tarzan, the Ape Man.
104 min. Black and white. Live action. 1932. Johnny Weissmuller, Neil Hamilton, Maureen O'Sullivan.
A laser disc version of the same title offered by MGM/UA Home Video (see above).
Distributor: Pioneer LDCA, Inc.
Laser disc: CLV format $34.95
No public performance rights

Tarzan, the Ape Man.
112 min. Color. Live action. Produced by MGM. 1981. Bo Derek, Richard Harris, Miles O'Keefe.
Including strictly adult situations (Bo Derek appears costumeless), this version departs from the intent and the letter of the original literary work. An explorer, his daughter, and a photographer meet Tarzan in Africa. Tarzan rescues her from disaster, and she "loses" her clothes.
Reviews: *New York Times*, Aug. 7, 1981, C 10:3; *Variety*, July 29, 1981
Audience: Ages 18-Adult
Distributor: MGM/UA Home Video
Videocassette: $79.98

No public performance rights

Tarzan, the Ape Man.
112 min. Color. Live action. 1981. Bo Derek, Richard Harris, Miles O'Keefe.
A laser disc version of the 1981 remake of the same title offered by MGM/UA Home Video (see above).
Distributor: Pioneer LDCA, Inc.
Laser disc: CLV format $34.95
No public performance rights

Greystoke: The Legend of Tarzan, Lord of the Apes.
130 min. Color. Live action. Produced by Warner/WEA Records. 1984. Christopher Lambert, Andie MacDowell, Ralph Richardson.
A man raised by apes rejoins society and his loving grandfather in this remake, which at times moves too slowly. Sticking more closely to the novel than other remakes, this one shows Greystoke's experiences with the apes, a Belgian explorer, and British society. It waxes strongest in the jungle; the ape makeup is especially splendid. Its spirit flags when the action moves to England; the second half of the production is so anti-upper class that interest dwindles. There are obvious cuts from what was a lengthy original, as well as some brief moments of bare bodies and violence. Glenn Close dubbed the voice of female lead Andie MacDowell.
Reviews: *New York Times*, Mar. 30, 1984, C, 5:1; *Variety*, Mar. 21, 1984
Audience: Ages 14-Adult
Distributor: Warner Home Video
Videocassette: $19.98
No public performance rights

Greystoke: The Legend of Tarzan, Lord of the Apes.
130 min. Color. Live action. 1984. Christopher Lambert, Andie MacDowell, Ralph Richardson.
A laser disc version of the same title offered by Warner Home Video (see above).
Distributor: Pioneer LDCA, Inc.
Videocassette: $39.98
No public performance rights

★★★★★

Teeny-Tiny and the Witch-Woman
Barbara Walker.
Illustrated by Michael Foreman. Pantheon. 1975. Folklore and fairy tales.
Three brothers ignore their mother's warning not to go into the forest where a witch woman lives.

Teeny-Tiny and the Witch-Woman.
14 min. Color. Animated. Produced by Weston Woods. 1980.
Beginning with brief live action of an old woman's gnarled hands, the animated thriller is so well adapted that very young audiences may find it too frightening.
Awards: CINE Golden Eagle; Gold Award, 23rd International Film & TV Festival of New York
Audience: Ages 6-10
Distributor: Weston Woods
16mm film: $295 **Videocassette:** $60
Rental: $25 daily

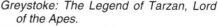

What's Under My Bed? and Other Creepy Stories.
35 min. Color. Iconographic and animated. Produced by Weston Woods. 1990.
Included in this tape anthology are adaptations of *What's Under My Bed* (James Stevenson), *Georgie* (Robert Bright), *Teeny-Tiny and the Witch-Woman* (Barbara Walker), and *The Three Rob-*

bers (Tomi Ungerer). See individual titles for full descriptions.

Audience: Ages 4-10
Distributor: Children's Circle, Weston Woods
Videocassette: $19.95
No public performance rights

★★★★★

"Tell-Tale Heart, The"
Edgar Allan Poe.
Multiple editions. Short stories—horror.
A murderer with a vivid imagination hears a sound that leads to his own undoing as the beat of the victim's heart grows louder and louder in his mind.

Tell-Tale Heart, The.
26 min. Black and white. Live action. Produced by Steve Carver/An AFI Film. 1973. Sam Jaffe and Alex Cord.
Like the short story, the film has the narrator tell this gruesome tale in the first person. The tempo increases as the climax approaches. Parts of the black-and-white footage seem overexposed, though the absence of color suits the starkness of the short story. The action echoes events in the story, but little happens, further reducing the appeal.

Audience: Ages 12-Adult
Distributor: Churchill Media
16mm film: $450 **Videocassette:** $89
Rental: $60

Tell-Tale Heart, The.
26 min. Black and white. Live action. 1973. Sam Jaffe and Alex Cord.
A home video version of the same title offered by Churchill Media (see above)

Distributor: Monterey Home Video
Videocassette: $24.95

★★★★★

Tenth Good Thing About Barney, The
Judith Viorst.
Illustrated by Erik Blegvad. Atheneum. 1977. [1971]. Realistic fiction.
A little boy mourns the death of his cat, buries it with his family and neighbor, and recounts nine good things about the pet. His mother urges him to think of ten good things, which the boy does.

Tenth Good Thing About Barney, The.
13 min. Color. Live action. Produced by Bernard Wilets. 1986.
There is a nice mix of action and conversation, voice-over, and dialog in this story about the death of a pet. After learning from his father that the pet, now buried, is helping grow flowers in the garden, the boy adds the tenth good thing about Barney. He learns, with his parents' help, that it's okay to feel sad and consoles himself with the thought that helping flowers grow is a pretty nice job for a cat.

Audience: Ages 6-Adult
Distributor: Aims Media
16mm film: $295 **Videocassette:** $260
Rental: $50

Tenth Good Thing About Barney, The.
13 min. Color. Live action. 1986.
A laser disc version of the same title also offered by Aims Media (see above).

Distributor: Aims Media
Laser disc: CAV format $240

★★★★★

Tess of the d'Ubervilles
Thomas Hardy.
Multiple editions. Realistic fiction.
A poor English farm girl of the late 1800s, Tess is seduced by a supposed relative. Another man falls in love with and marries her, then spurns her when he discovers her earlier misfortune.

Tess.
180 min. Color. Live action. Produced by Renn-Burrill. 1980. Nastassja Kinski, Peter Firth, Leigh Dawson.
Directed by Roman Polanski, the adaptation is lengthy yet involving. It falls short, though, of evoking the emotional impact achieved by the book.

Reviews: *New York Times*, Dec. 12, 1980, III 8:5; *Variety*, Nov. 7, 1979
Awards: Academy Awards, Best Art Direction, Best Cinematography, Best Costumes
Audience: Ages 16-Adult
Distributor: Columbia TriStar Home Video
Videocassette: $29.95
No public performance rights

Tess.
170 min. Color. Live action. 1979. Nastassja Kinski, Peter Firth, Leigh Dawson.
A laser disc version of the same title offered by Columbia TriStar Home Video (see above).

Distributor: Pioneer LDCA, Inc.
Laser disc: CLV format $39.95
No public performance rights

★★★★★

Tex
S. E. Hinton.
Delacorte. 1979. Realistic fiction.
A young man whose father is seldom home has an older brother who attempts to raise him in the face of societal prejudices and temptations such as drugs.

Tex.
103 min. Color. Live action. Produced by Walt Disney. 1982. Matt Dillon, Jim Metzler, Meg Tilly, Ben Johnson, Emilio Estevez.
The author herself makes a brief appearance as a teacher in this straightforward adaptation of her best-selling young adult novel. The well-done dramatization, directed by Tim Hunter, features two brothers who struggle to survive in a very broken home. As observed in the *New York Times*, "Mr. Hunter has followed Miss Hinton's book just about exactly." The result is a convincing movie that maintains a relaxed, humorous tone yet deals with issues such as drugs, alcohol, crime, and social differences. Both young men show an indomitable spirit that should inspire teenage viewers.

Reviews: *Christian Century*, Dec. 1, 1982; *New Yorker*, Oct. 4, 1982; *New York Times*, Sept. 28, 1982; C 17:3, *Newsweek*, Aug. 2, 1982
Audience: Ages 12-18
Distributor: Buena Vista Home Video (not currently in distribution)

Tex.
26 min. Color. Live action. A Disney Educational Production. 1982. Matt Dillon.
An abridged version of the same title originally offered by Buena Vista Home Video (see above). This is a fine trimming of the Disney feature.

Distributor: Coronet/MTI Film & Video
16mm film: $600 **Videocassette:** $250
Rental: $75

★★★★★

"Thank You, M'am"
Langston Hughes.
Anthologized in *Sudden Fiction: American Short-Short Stories*, edited by R. Shapard and J. Thomas. Gibbs M. Smith, Inc. 1986. Short stories—realistic fiction.
A boy tries to snatch an old woman's purse but ends up finding a good friend.

Thank You, M'am.
12 min. Color. Live action. Produced by Andrew Sugarman. 1976.
A strong story line and excellent acting by the crotchety old lady who takes a wayward boy under her wing make this a fine film.

Awards: ALA Notable Children's Film; Special Commendation, *Media & Methods* Magazine
Audience: Ages 8-14
Distributor: Phoenix/BFA Films & Video
16mm film: $260 **Videocassette:** $160
Rental: $25

★★★★★

There's a Nightmare in My Closet
Mercer Mayer (illus.).
Dial Press. 1976. [1968]. Fantasy.
Five-year-old Christopher decides to take matters into his own hands when no one will believe there's a nightmare in his closet.

There's a Nightmare in My Closet.
14 min. Color. Live action. Produced by Evergreen. 1987.
There's a real live but not-too-scary "nightmare" in this very nicely produced film about self-reliance. The monster grows more frightened than the well-armed (with toy gun and football helmet) little boy who bravely confronts the beast.

Reviews: *Booklist*, Mar. 1, 1988; *School Library Journal*, Apr. 1988
Audience: Ages 4-8
Distributor: Phoenix/BFA Films & Video
16mm film: $365 **Videocassette:** $265
Rental: $55

★★★★★

Theseus and the Minotaur.
Multiple editions. Folklore and fairy tales.
Theseus sets out to kill the terrible Minotaur, which has been demanding human sacrifices for years. The Minotaur lives in a labyrinth from which no human but Theseus escapes.

Theseus and the Labyrinth.
20 min. Color. Animation. Produced by Brian Jackson. 1987.
The narrative asks viewers to assume a great deal that is not supported by the visual presentation in this version of the old myth. They are told no one ever escapes the labyrinth, but the picture suggests little that is formidable. As a whole, the film does not create much emotional response.

Reviews: *Curriculum Products Review Service*, Apr. 1988
Audience: Ages 8-12
Distributor: Barr Films
16mm film: $470 **Videocassette:** $330
Rental: $50

★★★★★

Three Billy Goats Gruff, The
The Three Little Pigs
Multiple editions. Folklore and fairy tales.
In "The Three Billy Goats Gruff," two smaller goats fool a troll guarding a bridge while encouraging him to confront the largest goat, who promptly butts him into the stream. In "The Three Little Pigs," a wolf defeats and eats two little pigs that live in a straw house and a brick house. It is defeated by the sturdy brick shelter of the third little pig.

Three Billy Goats Gruff, The and *The Three Little Pigs.*
30 min. Color. Limited animation. Produced by Rabbit Ears. 1989. Narrated by Holly Hunter.

Holly Hunter masterfully voices the concerns of the smaller goats and weaker pigs as well as the cunning of the victorious creatures who successively foil a troll and a wolf. In their visual artistry, the two stories share similar color tones—a blending of yellow, greys, and blues.

Audience: Ages 4-8
Distributor: SVS/Triumph
Videocassette: $14.95
No public performance rights

Three Billy Goats Gruff, The and *The Three Little Pigs.*
23 min. Color. Limited animation. 1988.
A laser disc version of the same title offered by SVS/Triumph (see above).

Distributor: Image Entertainment
Laser disc: CLV format $19.95
No public performance rights

Three Little Pigs, The.
9 min. Color. Animation. A Disney Educational Production. 1956.
Full animation in the familiar Disney style won high acclaim for this delightful version of the old fairy tale.

Awards: Academy Award, Best Cartoon
Audience: Ages 4-10
Distributor: Coronet/MTI Film & Video
16mm film: $260 **Videocassette:** $195
Rental: $75

Three Little Pigs, The (Faerie Tale Theatre).
60 min. Color. Live action. Produced by Shelley Duvall. 1985. Billy Crystal, Jeff Goldblum, Valerie Perrine.
There are some nice features to this production, such as the comic personality of the wolf and the special effects when the first two pigs' houses come tumbling down. The classic tale is short, though, and this adaptation generously augments it with new details and characters. The first pig is concerned with riches, the second is a lover boy, and the third is a reader and an artist. New to the film is a fourth, voluptuous-looking female pig, who flirts even with the fox. Less violent than the classic, this adaptation has the first two pigs take refuge in the third pig's brick home. Some joke lines (calling the female pig "bacon bits") are lost on very young audiences. The wolf in this version is a hen-pecked husband whose wife drives him to hunt the pigs.

Audience: Ages 8-Adult
Distributor: Fox Video
Videocassette: $14.98
No public performance rights

Three Little Pigs, The.
9 min. Color. Iconographic. Produced by Weston Woods. 1988.
The adaptation is so well paced it lends an impression of movement to the visuals. Emphasis in this version, as in the original, is on the cleverness of the third little pig, who outwits and ultimately eats the wolf. Adapted from *The Three Little Pigs* as retold by Erik Blegvad (Atheneum 1980), the film shows how the third pig begins outsmarting the wolf with a brick house and continues his clever thinking thereafter.

Audience: Ages 4-8
Distributor: Weston Woods
16mm film: $140 **Videocassette:** $70
Rental: $20 daily

★★★★★

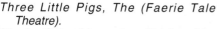

"Three Miraculous Soldiers"
Stephen Crane.

Anthologized in *Tales of War.* The Works of Stephen Crane, edited by Fredson Bowers, vol. 6. University Press of Virginia. 1970. Short stories—historical fiction.

Trapped between Confederate and Union soldiers, a girl takes a close-up look at the atrocities of the Civil War.

Stephen Crane's Three Miraculous Soldiers.
18 min. Color. Live action. Produced by Bernard Selling. 1976.
This is a good, low-budget film about the horrors of war as viewed by a young girl caught between opposing forces.
Audience: Ages 14-Adult
Distributor: Phoenix/BFA Films & Video
16mm film: $385 **Videocassette:** $225
Rental: $35

★★★★★

Three Musketeers, The
Alexandre Dumas.
Multiple editions. Historical fiction.
France's queen has given her diamond brooch to an English duke as a symbol of her affection. Unless D'Artagnan and the Musketeers retrieve it for her to wear on a certain occasion, the cardinal, enemy to the throne, will create political havoc.

Three Musketeers, The.
90 min. Black and white. Live action. Produced by Cliff Reid/RKO. 1935. Walter Abel, Paul Lukas, Ian Keith, Onslow Stevens, Ralph Forbes, Margot Grahame, Heather Angel.
Walter Abel is not a lively D'Artagnan in this overlong version of the Dumas story. "There is a deliberate, theatrical air about the business that limits the excitement." —*New York Times*
Reviews: *New York Times*, Nov. 1, 1935, 25:1; *Variety*, Nov. 6, 1935
Audience: Ages 10-Adult
Distributor: RKO/Turner Home Entertainment
Videocassette: $19.98
No public performance rights

Three Muskateers, The.
125 min. Color. Live action. Produced by MGM/Pandro S. Berman. 1948. Lana Turner, Gene Kelly, June Allyson, Van Heflin, Angela Lansbury, Vincent Price, Keenan Wynn, Gig Young.
This grandiose Hollywood studio production tells the Dumas story very well despite one or two shaky performances. Kelly, as D'Artagnan, performs so adroitly and acrobatically that he adds his own dimension of fun to the classic.
Reviews: *New York Times*, Oct. 21, 1948, 33:2; *Variety*, Oct. 20, 1948
Audience: Ages 10-Adult
Distributor: MGM/UA Home Video
Videocassette: $24.98
No public performance rights

Three Musketeers, The.
126 min. Color. Live action. 1948. Lana Turner, Gene Kelly, June Allyson, Van Heflin, Angela Lansbury, Vincent Price, Keenan Wynn, Gig Young.
A laser disc version of the same title offered by MGM/UA Home Video (see above).
Distributor: Pioneer LDCA, Inc.
Laser disc: CLV format $39.95
No public performance rights

Three Musketeers, The.
105 min. Color. Live action. Produced by Alexander Salkind. 1973. Michael York, Oliver Reed, Raquel Welch, Richard Chamberlain, Frank Finlay, Geraldine Chaplin, Faye Dunaway, Charlton Heston.
Although not a precise adaptation of the book, this is an admirable mixture of adventure, romance, and comedy. It is probably the most entertaining of the several versions on videocassette. There is less stress on characters than on events in this adaptation, and "the adventures are less swashbuckle than slapstick." —*New York Times*

Reviews: *New York Times*, Apr. 4, 1974, 52:1
Audience: Ages 10-Adult
Distributor: Videocassette not currently in distribution

★★★★★

Three Robbers, The
Tomi Ungerer (illus.).
Atheneum. 1971. [1962]. Fantasy.
Three robbers spend their stolen treasure on all the lost and abandoned children they can find.

Three Robbers, The.
6 min. Color. Animated. Produced by Weston Woods. 1972.
The narrator's dramatic reading heightens the tension in the story, making the three robbers out to be fearsome villains indeed. Animation effectively portrays the growth of the castle built by the robbers for the children. Instead of music, a type of rhythmic humming contributes to the energetic mood of the piece.
Audience: Ages 4-8
Distributor: Weston Woods
16mm film: $175 **Videocassette:** $60
Rental: $20 daily

★★★★★

Through Grandpa's Eyes
Patricia MacLachlan.
Illustrated by Deborah Ray. Harper & Row Junior Books. 1983. [1980]. Realistic fiction.
A boy visiting his blind grandfather finds that there are many other senses for "viewing" the world.

Through Grandpa's Eyes.
20 min. Color. Live action. Produced by Grey Havens Films. 1980.
This is a close following of a good book, resulting in a touching film about a blind man and his grandson. The actors cast in the two lead roles complement each other very well. Only a few scenes seem to stretch believability a bit.
Awards: Los Angeles County Commendation
Audience: Ages 8-15
Distributor: Barr Films
16mm film: $470 **Videocassette:** $330
Rental: $50

★★★★★

Thumbelina
Hans Christian Andersen.
Multiple editions. Folklore and fairy tales.
A childless woman is blessed with a miniature little girl only to have her stolen away by a toad. After the girl escapes, she is rescued by a mouse and readied for a wedding to a mole. Her final escape leads her to a flower prince.

Thumbelina.
9 min. Color. Limited animation. Produced by Greatest Tales. 1977.
This is one in a series of folklore films produced in Asia and adapted by Greatest Tales for English-speaking audiences. Though the animation is limited, it flows nicely for the duration of the film.
Audience: Ages 4-8
Distributor: Phoenix/BFA Films & Video
16mm film: $235 **Videocassette:** $145
Rental: $30

Thumbelina.
16 min. Color. Puppet animation. Produced by Coronet. 1981.
The puppet animation suits this story beautifully. Young viewers are not likely to forget Thumbelina's encounter with the big, ugly toad or her eventual happiness with the flower prince.

Audience: Ages 4-8
Distributor: Coronet/MTI film & Video
16mm film: $385 **Videocassette:** $250
Rental: $75

Thumbelina (Faerie Tale Theatre).
60 min. Color. Live action. Produced by Shelley Duvall. 1983. Carrie Fisher, William Katt, Burgess Meredith.
This is a lovely, live-action rendition of the traditional tale with impressive costuming and technical effects. Included in the show is a touch of singing, using lyrics that are in keeping with the basic story line. Though the show starts slowly, it builds into a warmly told tale with plenty of action and a fine finish.
Audience: Ages 4-Adult
Distributor: Fox Video
Videocassette: $14.98
No public performance rights

Thumbelina (Faerie Tale Theatre).
50 min. Color. Live action. 1983. Carrie Fisher, William Katt, Burgess Meredith.
A laser disc version of the same title offered by Fox Video (see above).
Distributor: Image Entertainment
Laser disc: CLV format $29.98
No public performance rights

Thumbelina.
30 min. Color. Limited animation. Produced by Rabbit Ears. 1989. Narrated by Kelly McGillis.
David Johnson's pastoral backdrops in misty shades of yellow, blue, and green lend a mystical quality to this classic tale of a tiny girl who is kidnapped by a fearsome toad, then befriended by other creatures. McGillis handles well the challenge of croaking like a toad and the conversations between mole, mouse, and Thumbelina.
Reviews: *Booklist*, Feb. 15, 1990
Audience: Ages 4-10
Distributor: SVS/Triumph
Videocassette: $14.95
No public performance rights

Thumbelina.
30 min. Color. Limited animation. 1989. Narrated by Kelly McGillis.
A laser disc version of the same title offered by SVS/Triumph (see above).
Distributor: Image Entertainment
Laser price: CLV format $19.95
No public performance rights

Thumbelina (Timeless Tales).
30 min. Color. Animated. Produced by Hanna-Barbera and Hallmark Cards. 1990. Hosted by Olivia Newton-John.
The production, nicely animated, includes some singing and raises the value question of the conflict that sometimes arises when pleasing everyone else means displeasing yourself.
Audience: Ages 4-8
Distributor: Hanna-Barbera Home Video
Videocassette: $14.95
No public performance rights

★★★★★

Tikki Tikki Tembo
Arlene Mosel.
Illustrated by Blair Lent. Holt, Rinehart & Winston. 1968. Folklore and fairy tales.
When a boy with a long name falls into a well, it takes so much time to alert others that from then on Chinese children are given short names.

Tikki Tikki Tembo.
9 min. Color. Iconographic. Produced by Weston Woods. 1974.

Though only the camera moves, pacing, narration, and dialog create a lively adaptation of the storybook.

Audience: Ages 4-8
Distributor: Weston Woods
16mm film: $175 **Videocassette:** $60
Rental: $20 daily

Strega Nonna and Other Stories.
35 min. Color. Iconographic and animated. Produced by Weston Woods. 1985.
Included in this tape anthology are adaptations of *Strega Nonna* (Tomie de Paola), *Tikki Tikki Tembo* (Arlene Mosel), *The Foolish Frog* (Pete and Charles Seeger), and *A Story—A Story* (Gail E. Haley). See individual titles for full descriptions.

Audience: Ages 4-8
Distributor: Children's Circle, Weston Woods
Videocassette: $19.95
No public performance rights

★★★★★

Time Machine, The
H. G. Wells.

Multiple editions. Science fiction.
Time Traveler journeys from the Victorian era far into the future (year 802,701), encountering short vegetarian creatures (Ebi) on land and apelike subterranean creatures (Morlocks) who confiscate the time machine.

Time Machine, The.
103 min. Color. Live action. Produced by MGM/George Pal. 1960. Rod Taylor, Yvette Mimieux, Alan Young, Sebastian Cabot.
The Victorian setting has been carefully recreated, but the action that occurs in the future is unconvincing. The main character, George, travels through time, not space, so that all his adventures occur in the same area of England. Before plummeting himself into the year 802,701, the film has George briefly step into the periods of the two World Wars and the year 1966. The view of the future is more optimistic than in the novel, and the movie in general seems somewhat dated.

Reviews: *New York Times*, Aug. 18, 1960,19:1; *Variety*, July 20, 1960
Awards: Academy Award, Best Special Effects
Audience: Ages 10-Adult
Distributor: MGM/UA Home Video
Videocassette: $19.98
No public performance rights

Time Machine, The.
103 min. Color. Live action. 1960. Rod Taylor, Yvette Mimieux, Alan Young, Sebastian Cabot.
A laser disc version of the same title offered by MGM/UA Home Video (see above).

Distributor: Pioneer LDCA, Inc.
Laser disc: CLV format $34.98
No public performance rights

★★★★★

Time of Wonder
Robert McCloskey (illus.).

Penguin USA. 1957. Realistic fiction.
Life on an island in summertime includes an array of experiences, which range from spotting ghostlike trees to preparing for a hurricane.

Time of Wonder.
13 min. Color. Iconographic. Produced by Weston Woods. 1961.
Like the book, the film captures the awe inspired by the island in summer but is more a static series of moods and impressions than a story.

Audience: Ages 4-8
Distributor: Weston Woods
16mm film: $195 **Videocassette:** $60
Rental: $25 daily

Owl Moon and Other Stories.
35 min. Color. Iconographic and animated. Produced by Weston Woods. 1990.
Included in this tape anthology are adaptations of *Owl Moon* (Jane Yolen), *The Caterpillar and the Polliwog* (Jack Kent), *Hot Hippo* (Mwenye Hadithi), and *Time of Wonder* (Robert McCloskey). See individual titles for full descriptions.
Audience: Ages 4-8
Distributor: Children's Circle, Weston Woods
Videocassette: $19.95
No public performance rights

Robert McCloskey Library, The.
58 min. Color. Iconographic and animated. Produced by Weston Woods. 1991.
Included in this tape anthology are adaptations of *Lentil*, *Make Way for Ducklings*, *Burt Dow: Deep-Water Man*, *Blueberries for Sal*, and *Time of Wonder*. See individual titles for full descriptions. An additional segment, *Getting to Know Robert McCloskey*, features the author commenting on his work.
Audience: Ages 4-8
Distributor: Children's Circle, Weston Woods
Videocassette: $19.95
No public performance rights

★★★★★

Tinder Box, The
Hans Christian Andersen.

Multiple editions. Folklore and fairy tales.
A soldier happens upon a witch who leads him to a tinder box. With the box, he can beckon three dogs that satisfy wishes. The witch and others come to a violent end in this tale, which concludes happily ever after for the soldier.

Tinder Box, The.
25 min. Color. Live action. Produced by Swedish Broadcasting Corp. 1967.
Introducing the tale is a gentleman narrator, who portrays Hans Christian Andersen. The narrator slips nicely into character voices at times. However the production places his retelling over live-action footage, a technique that results in a slow-moving film likely to lose audience interest. The violence is tastefully portrayed; viewers glimpse only a mock severed witch's head on the screen.
Audience: Ages 4-8
Distributor: Britannica
16mm film: $565 **Videocassette:** $300

★★★★★

"To Build a Fire"
Jack London.

Anthologized in *The Norton Book of American Short Stories*, edited by Peter S. Prescott. Norton. 1988. Short stories—realistic fiction.
A man who sets out on a journey across snow-covered wild lands is caught in a blizzard.

Jack London's To Build a Fire.
14 min. Color. Live action. Produced by Robert Stitzel. 1975.
This is an amazingly faithful and well-produced adaptation of the London story, filmed in spectacular wilderness.
Audience: Ages 12-Adult
Distributor: Phoenix/BFA Films & Video
16mm film: $300 **Videocassette:** $190
Rental: $44

★★★★★

To Have and Have Not
Ernest Hemingway.

Multiple editions. Historical fiction.
Operating off the coast of Florida, Harry Morgan uses his fishing launch to smuggle contraband so that he can support his family during the Depression.

To Have and Have Not.
100 min. Black and white. Live action. Produced by Warner/Howard Hawks. 1945. Humphrey Bogart, Lauren Bacall, Walter Brennan.
The movie changes elements of the novel, making Harry Morgan a charter boat captain who carries guns for the French and helps a singer escape the Nazis. Included in the engrossing film are a couple of songs and some outstanding dialog. William Faulkner and Jules Furthman wrote the screenplay. Whereas Hemingway sets the novel in Cuba and the Florida Keys in the 1930s, the film story occurs in France and Martinique during World War II. Morgan is a married man with children in the novel. On screen, he is single, and his romance with Bacall overpowers the other elements of the story. Both versions impart the theme that people need other people.
Reviews: *New York Times*, Oct. 12, 1944, 24:1; *Variety*, Oct. 11, 1944
Audience: Ages 16-Adult
Distributor: MGM/UA Home Video
Videocassette: $24.98
No public performance rights

To Have and Have Not.
101 min. Black and white. Live action. 1945. Humphrey Bogart, Lauren Bacall, Walter Brennan.
A laser disc version of the same title offered by MGM/UA Home Video (see above).
Distributor: Pioneer LDCA, Inc.
Laser disc: CLV format $34.98
No public performance rights

★★★★★

To Kill a Mockingbird
Harper Lee.
Harper & Row. 1961. [1960]. Realistic fiction.
A black man in the South is accused of raping a white woman and is defended by a capable white attorney, who must then explain his actions to family and friends.

To Kill a Mockingbird.
131 min. Black and white. Live action. Produced by Universal/Alan Pakula. 1962. Gregory Peck, Mary Badham, Robert Duvall.
This is an exceptionally powerful film in the 1960s tone of racial mistreatment and misunderstanding.
Reviews: *New York Times*, Feb. 15, 1963, 10:2; *Variety*, Dec. 12, 196
Awards: Academy Awards, Best Actor, Best Screenplay, Best Art Direction—Set Decoration; Golden Globe Awards, Best Actor, Best Music Score
Audience: Ages 12-Adult
Distributor: MCA/Universal Home Video
Videocassette available
No public performance rights

To Kill a Mockingbird.
132 min. Black and white. Live action. 1962. Gregory Peck, Mary Badham, Robert Duvall.
A laser disc version of the same title offered by MCA/Universal (see above).
Distributor: Pioneer LDCA, Inc.
Laser disc: CLV format $39.98
No public performance rights

★★★★★

Toby Tyler
James Otis.
Multiple editions. Adventure.
A young man runs away from home and spends ten unhappy weeks traveling with a circus. He learns the best place is home, despite chores and other unappealing duties.

Toby Tyler (Or Ten Weeks with a Circus).
96 min. Color. Live action. Produced by Walt Disney. 1960. Kevin Corcoran, Henry Calvin, Gene Sheldon.
This is an average Disney film from a thinly plotted book about a boy and a circus. While the novel brings out the grim aspects of nineteenth-century circus life, the film paints a cheery picture of the pleasures of such a life.
Reviews: *New York Times*, Apr. 20, 1960, 45:2; *Variety*, Dec. 22, 1965
Audience: Ages 8-15
Distributor: Buena Vista Home Video (not currently in distribution)

★★★★★

Tom Thumb

Multiple editions. Folklore and fairy tales.
A woodcutter and his wife have a son no larger than a person's thumb. To bring in money for the family, Tom embarks on a series of adventures that take him inside a cow's stomach, then inside a wolf's, and thanks to Tom's clever thinking, back home to his family again.

Tom Thumb.
98 min. Color. Live action and puppet animation. Produced by Galaxy/MGM/George Pal. 1958. Russ Tamblyn, Alan Young, Terry-Thomas, Peter Sellers.
Russ Tamblyn is an excellent Tiny Tom and Terry-Thomas is just the right master of villainy to delight young viewers. The story holds to the action of the original but is played with humor in this adaptation. *Variety* describes it as "a comic fairy tale with music that stacks up alongside some of the Disney classics."
Reviews: *New York Times*, Dec. 24, 1958; *Variety*, Dec. 3, 1958
Awards: Academy Award, Best Special Effects
Audience: Ages 4-10
Distributor: MGM/UA Home Video
Videocassette: $39.98
No public performance rights

Little Tom Thumb.
8 min. Color. Animation. Produced by Halas and Batchelor. 1969.
Not the traditional version of the tale, this film plot seems to combine in the story of "Tom Thumb" elements of "Hansel and Gretel" and "Jack and the Beanstalk." Tom has six brothers and his parents leave them all in the forest because there is too little food to eat. An ogre captures the children but Tom outwits him.
Audience: Ages 4-8
Distributor: Britannica
16mm film: $210 **Videocassette:** $210

Tom Thumb.
9.5 min. Color. Produced by A Bosustow Production. 1978.
This delightfully colorful version of the classic tale is adapted from *Eric Carle's Storybook: Seven Tales by the Brothers Grimm* (Franklin Watts 1976). The show mirrors the plot line and illustrations in the book.
Audience: Ages 5-10
Distributor: Churchill Media
16mm film: $215 **Videocassette:** $59
Rental: $50

★★★★★

Treasure Island

Robert Louis Stevenson.
Multiple editions. Adventure.
After receiving a treasure map, young Jim Hawkins embarks on a voyage in search of lost treasure. His ship is taken over by bloodthirsty pirates led by peg-legged Long John Silver.

Treasure Island.
105 min. Black and white. Live action. Produced by MGM/Hugh Stromberg. 1934. Lionel Barrymore, Wallace Beery, Nigel Bruce, Jackie Cooper.
Wallace Beery is a great Long John Silver in this action-packed motion picture. The acting and production are generally excellent, making this an absorbing adaptation, despite its being filmed before color dominated the industry.
Reviews: *New York Times*, Aug. 18, 1934, 5:5; *Variety*, Aug. 21, 1934
Audience: Ages 10-15
Distributor: MGM/UA Home Video
Videocassette: $19.98
No public performance rights

Treasure Island.
105 min. Color. Live action. Produced by MGM/Hugh Strombert. 1934.
A colorized version of the same title also distributed by MGM/UA (see above).
Audience: Ages 10-15
Distributor: MGM/UA Home Video
Videocassette: $19.98
No public performance rights

Treasure Island.
96 min. Color. Live action. Produced by Perce Pearce/Walt Disney. 1950. Bobby Driscoll, Robert Newton.
The production truly captures the spirit of the book, showing how the craving for adventure causes children—and adults—to wander into harm's way. Shot in England, the film is a coming-of-age tale in which young Jim Hawkins faces up to danger in a courageous moment.
Reviews: *New York Times*, Aug. 16, 1950
Audience: Ages 6-Adult
Distributor: Buena Vista Home Video
Videocassette: $19.99
No public performance rights

Treasure Island.
96 min. Color. Live action. 1950. Bobby Driscoll, Robert Newton.
A laser disc version of the same title originally offered by Buena Vista Home Video (see above).
Distributor: Image Entertainment
Laser disc: CLV format $34.99
No public performance rights

Treasure Island.
30 min. Color. Live action. A Disney Educational Production. 1979.
This excellent production tells the story of Jim Hawkins's adventures but does not carry each incident to as full a level of suspense or action as the available feature-length films.
Audience: Ages 8-15
Distributor: Coronet/MTI Film & Video
16mm film: $630 **Videocassette:** $250
Rental: $75

Treasure Island.
50 min. Color. Animation. Produced by Children's Video of America. 1988.
Animation of the quality of Saturday morning cartoons does not quite sustain this nearly hour-long story of Jim Hawkins and his search for treasure. The production is directed at a younger audience than the novel.
Audience: Ages 7-10
Distributor: Horizon Entertainment Group
Videocassette: $9.98

Treasure Island.
132 min. Color. Live action. 1990. Charlton Heston, Christian Bale, Oliver Reed.
This made-for-television movie captures the spirit of the classic. Thrilling and realistic, it is also beautifully filmed in Cornwall and Jamaica. Heston plays a convincing Long John Silver.

Audience: Ages 10-15
Distributor: Turner Home Entertainment
Videocassette: $79.98
No public performance rights

★★★★★

Treasure of Alpheus Winterborn, The

John Bellairs.
Bantam. 1985. [1978]. Mystery.
Anthony Monday begins at the library to follow clues left by treasure-hider Alpheus Winterborn. Before discovering the treasure, Anthony finds that others are following his detective movements.

Treasure of Alpheus Winterborn, The.
35 min. Color. Live action. Produced by Diane Asselin. 1990.
This is an exceptionally well-done, lightly suspenseful story of a boy who sets out to remedy his family's financial difficulties with the help of a friendly librarian. A not-quite-believable portrayal of the town banker who turns out to be a wimpish villain is the one flaw in the production.

Awards: Bronze Apple Award, National Educational Film and Video Festival
Audience: Ages 5-12
Distributor: Barr Films
16mm film: $595 **Videocassette:** $395
Rental: $50

★★★★★

Treasure Trap, The

Virginia Masterman-Smith.
Illustrated by Roseanne Litzinger. Four Winds Press. 1979. Mystery.
A new neighbor persuades Billy Beak to search the mansion of a long lost millionaire for treasure.

Haunted Mansion Mystery.
50 min. Color. Live action. Produced by ABC Weekend Specials. 1983.
This exciting adventure contains fully as much detail of a book as can be expected in a motion picture adaptation. Excellent pacing keeps the audience riveted to the screen, as predicted in *Booklist*: "An adaptation that will spellbind young viewers."

Reviews: *Booklist*, May 1, 1984
Audience: Ages 8-13
Distributor: Coronet/MTI Film & Video
16mm film: $645 **Videocassette:** $250
Rental: $75

★★★★★

Tree Grows in Brooklyn, A

Betty Smith.
Harper & Row. 1968. [1943]. Historical fiction.
A struggling family living in Brooklyn in the early 1900s includes ambitious Francie, her brother, her hardworking mother, and her loveable father, a singing waiter who drinks. Francie adores her father but is at odds with her mother.

Tree Grows in Brooklyn, A.
128 min. Black and white. Live action. Produced by Fox/Louis D. Lighton. 1945. James Dunn, Dorothy McQuire, Joan Blondell.
This period piece is precious just for the early twentieth century tenement life it recreates. Beyond this slice of realism is a heart-rending story, brought adroitly to the screen, of a family struggling to make it in America by the sweat of their brow. Francie romanticizes her father but there

is justification for her view. As in the novel, he dies and she comes of age with insight into the complexity of life and her mother. The tone is ultimately upbeat—hope survives.

Reviews: *New York Times*, Mar. 1, 1945, 25:5; *Variety*, Jan. 24, 1945
Awards: Academy Award, Best Supporting Actor
Audience: Ages 12-Adult
Distributor: Fox Video
Videocassette: $14.98
No public performance rights

Tree Grows in Brooklyn, A.
133 min. Black and white. Live action. 1945. James Dunn, Dorothy McQuire, Joan Blondell.
A laser disc version of the same title offered by Fox Video (see above).

Distributor: Image Entertainment
Laser disc: CLV format $49.98
No public performance rights

★★★★★

"Trifles"
Susan Glaspell.

Anthologized in *Plays*, edited by C. W. Bigsby. Cambridge University Press. 1987. Drama.
After a crime has been committed, two female neighbors review people and events to find the perpetrator. A farmer's wife has been jailed for her husband's murder; the two women envision her life and discover a motive for the crime.

Trifles.
21 min. Color. Live action. Produced by Martha Moran. 1979.
The action in the production revolves around two women who mostly sit at a kitchen table and talk. As they verbally solve the crime, the motion picture reenacts their thoughts. The plot corresponds to the play *Trifles* and the short story, "A Jury of Her Peers," on which the play was based.

Reviews: *Booklist*, Mar. 15, 1980
Audience: Ages 14-Adult
Distributor: Phoenix/BFA Films & Video
16mm film: $440 **Videocassette:** $275
Rental: $64

Trifles.
22 min. Black and white. Live action. Produced by Sandra Nervig/Centre Productions. 1983.
The production couples black-and-white visuals with sparse dialog that is sometimes overpowered by the sound effects. While it captures the spirit of the play, young adults may need a second viewing to understand the course of events.

Reviews: *School Library Journal*, Nov. 1984
Awards: Honorable Mention, Columbus International Film Festival; Gold Award, Houston International Film Festival
Audience: 16-Adult
Distributor: Barr Films
16mm film: $390 **Videocassette:** $240
Rental: $50

★★★★★

Trip, The
Ezra Jack Keats (illus.).

Greenwillow. 1978. Realistic fiction.
Louis imagines traveling to his old neighborhood and seeing witches who are really his friends in Halloween disguise.

Trip, The.
6 min. Color. Iconographic. Produced by Weston Woods in consultation with Ezra Jack Keats. 1980.
Only the camera moves as this film faithfully portrays the picture story of Louis's imaginings.

Audience: Ages 4-8
Distributor: Weston Woods
16mm film: $125 **Videocassette:** $60
Rental: $15 daily

Amazing Bone and Other Stories, The.
33 min. Color. Iconographic and animated. Produced by Weston Woods. 1989.
Included in this tape anthology are adaptations of *The Amazing Bone* (William Steig), *John Brown, Rose, and the Midnight Cat* (Jenny Wagner), *A Picture for Harold's Room* (Crockett Johnson), and *The Trip* (Ezra Jack Keats). See individual titles for full descriptions.
Reviews: *Children's Video Report*, Apr./May 1989
Audience: Ages 4-12
Distributor: Children's Circle, Weston Woods
Videocassette: $19.95
No public performance rights

★★★★★

Trouble with Miss Switch, The
Barbara Brooks Wallace.
Archway. 1981. [1971]. Fantasy.
An adventure to Witch Mountain by broomstick leads to an appearance before the witches council.

Trouble with Miss Switch, The.
48 min. Color. Animation. Produced by ABC Weekend Specials. 1980.
This adventure film in a fanciful setting was a network attempt at a long animation feature. Within the limits of budget for animation, it holds the audience quite well.
Audience: Ages 8-12
Distributor: Coronet/MTI Film & Video
16mm film: $455 **Videocassette:** $250
Rental: $75

★★★★★

Truck Song
Diane Siebert.
Illustrated by Byron Barton. Crowell. 1984. Realistic fiction.
In pictures accompanied by rhyming text, this book describes the journey of a transcontinental truck.

Truck Song.
17 min. Color. Live action. Produced by Bernard Wilets. 1988.
With splendid real-life visuals, this journey of a cross-country truck introduces a trucker's life to young viewers. The narration is clear and pleasantly slow paced. Rhythmic music has been added to the film with spirited lyrics, which are difficult to comprehend in a few spots. For truck lovers, the film is a live-action delight that shows the vehicle winding down canyons, stopped for fuel, crossing desert, and resting alongside other trucks.
Reviews: *Booklist*, Mar. 1, 1989; *Parents' Choice Magazine,* Sept. 1990
Audience: Ages 4-8
Distributor: Aims Media
16mm film: $295 **Videocassette:** $260
Rental: $50

Truck Song.
13 min. Color. Live action. Produced by Bernard Wilets. 1988.
An abbreviated version of the same title also distributed by Aims Media (see above). This version retains the basic plot but omits selected details.
Audience: Ages 4-6
Distributor: Aims Media
16mm film: $295 **Videocassette:** $260
Rental: $50

★★★★★

Twelve Angry Men: A Screen Adaptation

Reginald Rose .

Irvington. 1989. [1954]. Drama.

About to convict an eighteen-year-old of murder, a jury is persuaded to render another verdict by one dissenting member. The eighteen-year-old is a hard-nosed boy from the slums, charged with stabbing his father, a former convict.

Twelve Angry Men.

95 min. Black and white. Live action. Produced by Henry Fonda/Reginald Rose. 1957. Henry Fonda, Lee J. Cobb, E. G. Marshall, Ed Begley, Jack Klugman.

Reginald Rose, the playwright, elaborated on his own 1954 television play, developing it into this motion picture. It is a riveting melodrama that succeeds on multiple levels. The actors perform superbly and are cleverly photographed in ways that help build momentum. "Above all, they have made full use of the trenchant words and ideas of the author to plumb the characters of their principals." *—New York Times*

Reviews: *New York Times*, Apr. 15, 1957, 24:1; *Variety*, Feb. 27, 1957

Audience: Ages 16-Adult

Distributor: MGM/UA Home Video

Videocassette: $29.98

No public performance rights

Twelve Angry Men.

92 min. Black and white. Live action. 1956. Henry Fonda, Lee J. Cobb, E. G. Marshall, Ed Begley, Jack Klugman.

A laser disc version of the same title offered by MGM/UA Home Video (see above).

Distributor: Criterion Collection

Laser disc: CLV format $39.95

No public performance rights

★★★★★

Twelve Dancing Princesses, The

Jacob Grimm and Wilhelm K. Grimm.

Multiple editions. Folklore and fairy tales.

A father promises one daughter in marriage and his kingdom to the gentleman who discovers how his dozen daughters wear out their shoes each night. A soldier acquires a cloak that renders him invisible and solves the mystery.

Dancing Princesses, The (Faerie Tale Theatre).

60 min. Color. Live action. Produced by Shelley Duvall. 1984. Lesley Ann Warren, Peter Weller, Roy Dotrice.

Narrated by Roy Dotrice, the king, this captivating dramatization expands on the original. The mystery of how the princesses wear out their slippers is retained, but edges of comedy and drama are added. The king is beside himself, spending 5,400 francs on new shoes for his six (not twelve) daughters each day. The soldier solves the mystery, and chooses as his wife the eldest daughter, whose character is developed in depth, as cleverest of the lot. True to the original, the plot is further extended as the king plays an overprotective father whose daughters engage in their nightly frolic with good cause. The mood remains mostly light, and the father-daughters relationship is loving throughout. A few updated witticisms ("If I were you, I'd keep this [magic] cloak under wraps") build on the inherent humor.

Audience: Ages 6-Adult

Distributor: Fox Video

Videocassette: $14.95

No public performance rights

★★★★★

Twelve Days of Christmas, The.
Multiple editions. Songs.
This traditional carol recounts an increasing number of gifts received by a young woman during the Christmas season.

Twelve Days of Christmas, The.
6 min. Color. Iconographic. Produced by Q3 Limited London. 1972.
Lyrically and clearly sung, this adaptation relies on camera movements to simulate motion. The technique works so well that the film is nevertheless quite effective.
Audience: Ages 4-8
Distributor: Weston Woods
16mm film: $140 **Videocassette:** $70
Rental: $20 daily

Christmas Stories.
30 min. Color. Iconographic and animated. Produced by Weston Woods. 1986.
Included in this tape anthology are adaptations of *Morris's Disappearing Bag* (Rosemary Wells), *The Clown of God* (Tomie de Paola), *The Little Drummer Boy* (Katherine Davis, Henry Onrati, and Harry Simeone), and *The Twelve Days of Christmas* (Robert Broomfield).
Audience: Ages 4-Adult
Distributor: Children's Circle, Weston Woods
Videocassette: $19.95
No public performance rights

★★★★★

Twenty and Ten
Claire Huchet Bishop.
Illustrated by William Pène DuBois. Penguin. 1978. [1952]. Historical fiction.
In 1944 in German-occupied France, twenty young boarding school students outfox the Nazis by successfully hiding ten young Jewish children in a nearby cave.

Miracle at Moreaux.
55 min. Color. Live action. Produced by Janice Platt/WonderWorks. 1985, 1990. Loretta Swift.
This adeptly acted, beautifully filmed drama changes selected events from Claire Bishop's *Twenty and Ten.* In the book the convent's nun is arrested and ten Jewish children are hidden in a nearby cave; the film features only three Jewish children who live in the convent school with Sister Gabrielle and the students who help the runaways escape to freedom. None of the changes affect the impact of this emotionally involving production.
Reviews: *Booklist*, Nov. 15, 1990
Awards: President's Chris Award, Columbus International Film Festival; Best Drama Television Award, Samuel G. Engel International Festival; Gold Award, Houston International Film Festival; Grand Award, International Film & Television Festival of New York
Audience: Ages 10-14
Distributor: Public Media Video
Videocassette: $29.95

★★★★★

Twenty Thousand Leagues Under the Sea
Jules Verne.
Multiple editions. Adventure.
Three men are trapped on a submarine that travels the world. The ship is run by a Captain Nemo, who hates society but uses his fortune from sunken treasures to benefit those in need.

Twenty Thousand Leagues Under the Sea.
127 min. Color. Live action. Produced by Walt Disney. 1954. Kirk Douglas, James Mason, Paul Lukas, Peter Lorre.

This best of Disney films, with an all-star cast performing flawlessly and with spectacular effects for its day, is a must see. It pares the story down to basics, keeping the pace moving. The result is a full-length feature as thrilling and suspenseful as the novel.

Reviews: *New York Times*, Dec. 24, 1954, 7:2; *Variety*, Dec. 15, 1954
Awards: Academy Awards, Best Art Direction–Set Decoration, Best Special Effects
Audience: Ages 8-Adult
Distributor: Buena Vista Home Video
Videocassette: $19.99
No public performance rights

Twenty Thousand Leagues Under the Sea.
50 min. Color. Animation. Produced by William Hanna/Joseph Barbera. 1973.
Very young viewers will enjoy the sea monster scene and the villainous Captain Nemo in this Saturday-morning cartoon-style version of the famous Jules Verne story. The adaptation addresses a younger audience than the novel.

Audience: Ages 7-12
Distributor: Hanna-Barbera Home Video
Videocassette: $19.95
No public performance rights

Twenty Thousand Leagues Under the Sea.
52 min. Color. Animation. Produced by Rankin-Bass. 1990.
This is a mediocre animation effort, with a format that is less sophisticated than contemporary adolescent audiences.

Audience: Ages 10-15
Distributor: Lucerne
Videocassette: $195

★★★★★

Twice Told Tales
Nathaniel Hawthorne.
Multiple editions. Short stories—horror.
In "Rappaccini's Daughter," a doctor isolates his daughter by feeding her poison. In "Dr. Heidegger's Experiment," a doctor interferes with aging. The third tale, *The House of the Seven Gables*, is about the decay of an old Salem family.

Twice-Told Tales.
119 min. Color. Live action. Produced by Admiral Pictures. 1963. Vincent Price, Sebastian Cabot, Mari Blanchard.
Sebastian Cabot performs sympathetically and convincingly as Dr. Heidegger in an adaptation that includes a fine touch of humor. Vincent Price stars in an abbreviated *House of the Seven Gables* and also as Dr. Rappaccini in the most blood-curdling and least modified of the three tales. As stated in *Variety*, "the yarn least molested emerges most genuinely shuddery."

Reviews: *Variety*, Sept. 25, 1963
Audience: Ages 14-Adult
Distributor: MGM/UA Home Video
Videocassette: $19.98
No public performance rights

★★★★★

Two Loves for Jenny
Sandy Miller.
New American Library. 1982. Realistic fiction.
Two high school violin players aspire to mastery in musical performance. Ironically, the one who does not aim for a career in music wins the prize of a scholarship. The story focuses on their friendship.

Between Two Loves.
27 min. Color. Live action. A Disney Educational Production. 1984.

A story of two teenagers with high goals and also a deep interest in each other, this film is a gentle exploration of a teenage dilemma. The plot is a little slow to unfold.

Audience: Ages 12-16
Distributor: Coronet/MTI Film & Video
16mm film: $600 **Videocassette:** $500
Rental: $75

★★★★★

"Two Soldiers"
William Faulkner.

Anthologized in *Thirty Stories to Remember*. Doubleday. 1962. Short stories—historical fiction.

An eight-year-old boy in Tennessee rebels when his older brother enlists to fight in World War II. Intent on going to war also, the younger boy makes his way to Memphis, finds his soldier brother, and learns a lesson or two about life.

Two Soldiers.
30 min. Color. Live action. Produced by Jacob Bertucci. 1985.

A wonderful slice of life, the story and film concern love and responsibility in World War II America. The footage is realistic and the drama intense with an edge of amusement in the young boy's determination and success despite the troublesome adults that try stopping him. Intent on reaching his goal, he at one point brandishes a knife at others, then is sharply rebuked for his misconduct by the brother he so adores. The adaptation changes the story's point of view from first person (the young boy) to third person, yet it retains the spirit and content of the original.

Reviews: *Booklist*, Oct. 1, 1986; *English Journal*, Oct. 1986; *School Library Journal*, Nov. 1986
Awards: CINE Golden Eagle; Chris Plaque, Columbus International Film Festival
Audience: Ages 10-Adult
Distributor: Pyramid Film & Video
16mm film: $550 **Videocassette:** $395
Rental: $75

★★★★★

Ty's One-Man Band
Mildred Pitts Walter.

Illustrated by Margot Ladd Tomes. Four Winds. 1987. [1980]. Realistic fiction.

A boy meets an accomplished guitarist and decides to create his own band.

Ty's Homemade Band.
20 min. Color. Live action. Produced by Gary Templeton. 1983.

This is an adequate production of a story about a boy who decides to create his own band. Ty's choice of homemade instruments is interesting.

Reviews: *Booklist*, Sept. 1, 1984; *Horn Book*, June 1984
Audience: Ages 6-10
Distributor: Phoenix/BFA Films & Video
16mm film: $400 **Videocassette:** $250
Rental: $40

U

adherence to book   film rating

Ugly Duckling, The
Hans Christian Andersen.
Multiple editions. Folklore and fairy tales. An ugly "duckling" spends an unhappy year ostracized by others before it grows into a beautiful swan.

Ugly Duckling, The.
11 min. Color. Live action. 1953.
The reliance on real animals makes this unique among adaptations of the tale. Beginning with a 1950s family, the production appears dated. The children in the family listen to their mother narrate the story in their living room. During her discourse, the camera moves to the live animals and at intervals returns to the family setting.
Audience: Ages 4-8
Distributor: Britannica
Videocassette: $99

Ugly Duckling, The.
11 min. Color. Live action. Produced by Coronet. 1953.
Beautiful scenery adds interest to this live-action version of the story, which was produced in Europe.
Audience: Ages 4-8
Distributor: Coronet/MTI Film & Video
16mm film: $280 **Videocassette:** $195
Rental: $75

Ugly Duckling, The.
8 min. Color. Animation. A Disney Educational Production. 1955.
Great fun to watch, this is the finest of three versions of this story available from the same distributor.
Awards: Academy Award, Best Cartoon Short Subject
Audience: Ages 4-8
Distributor: Coronet/MTI Film & Video
16mm film: $225 **Videocassette:** $170
Rental: $75

Tale of the Ugly Duckling.
8 min. Color. Limited animation. Produced by Halas and Batchelor. 1969.
Bright animation and spirited narration combine with some amusing sequences (an elderly, short-sighted woman takes in the duckling for a time) to make this an entertaining adaptation despite the limited animation.
Audience: Ages 4-8
Distributor: Britannica
16mm film: $210 **Videocassette:** $210

Ugly Duckling, The.
17 min. Color. Puppet animation. Produced by Coronet. 1982.
All the characters appear as puppets in this slightly overlong adaptation of the classic tale.
Awards: CINE Golden Eagle
Audience: Ages 4-8
Distributor: Coronet/MTI Film & Video
16mm film: $405 **Videocassette:** $250
Rental: $75

Ugly Duckling, The.
30 min. Color. Iconographic. Produced by Rabbit Ears Productions. 1986. Narrated by Cher.
True-to-the-original story, this allegory follows a "duckling" in search of his right place in the world. Cher's straightforward narration, in which she speaks all the parts, Patrick Ball's subdued music and Robert Van Nutt's beautiful watercolors all support the simple but profound messages, concluding that a good heart is never too proud.
Audience: Ages 4-8
Distributor: Random House Home Video
Videocassette: $14.95

Ugly Duckling, The.
15 min. Color. Limited animation. Produced by Weston Woods. 1976.
Fine character voices and narration join captivating visuals in this story about the values of inner self and appearances.
Audience: Ages 4-8
Distributor: Weston Woods
16mm film: $275 **Videocassette:** $60
Rental: $20 daily

Ugly Duckling, The.
11 min. Color. Animation. Produced by Greatest Tales. 1980.
This is part of a series of folklore adaptations produced by Greatest Tales. The art in all the films seems stylized with a slightly oriental flavor, and the animation is a bit stiff. Yet the adaptations stick closely to the originals. In this particular version, some minor additions that update the tale include a hen who keeps calling the ugly duckling a "turkey."
Audience: Ages 4-8
Distributor: Phoenix/BFA Films & Video
16mm film: $260 **Videocassette:** $140
Rental: $34

Ugly Duckling and Other Classic Fairytales, The.
35 min. Color. Animated. Produced by Weston Woods. 1986.
Included in this tape anthology are adaptations of "The Ugly Duckling" (Hans Christian Andersen), "The Stonecutter" (Gerald McDermott), and "The Swineherd" (Hans Christian Andersen). See individual titles for full descriptions.
Audience: Ages 4-8
Distributor: Children's Circle, Weston Woods
Videocassette: $19.95
No public performance rights

Ugly Duckling, The (Timeless Tales).
30 min. Color. Animation. Produced by Hanna-Barbera and Hallmark Cards. 1990. Hosted by Olivia Newton-John.
In a short, live-action scene, two children, Kevin and Emily, introduce this entertaining adaptation. Its highlights include fine animation, a sense of family life among the ducks, songs that reinforce the plot, and a kind rabbit that takes in the ugly duckling and later rescues it from crocodiles. Generally, the story line keeps to the original.
Audience: Ages 4-8
Distributor: Hanna-Barbera Home Video
Videocassette: $14.95
No public performance rights

★★★★★

"Ugly Little Boy, The"
Isaac Asimov.

Anthologized in *The Complete Stories*. Vol. 1. Doubleday. 1990. Short stories—science fiction.

A group of scientists uses time warp to bring a Neanderthal boy to the present world. A kind nurse helps the boy adjust to the new life.

Ugly Little Boy, The.

26 min. Color. Live action. Produced by LCA. 1977. Kate Reid.

Media and Methods equates the development of a moving relationship in this film to that of Anne Sullivan and Helen Keller in the *The Miracle Worker*. Viewers, however, may be disturbed by the casting of a midget in the role of the little boy.

Reviews: *Media and Methods*, Dec. 1977; *Religion Teacher's Journal*, Mar. 1978

Awards: ALA-Notable Children's Film; ALA-Selected Film for Young Adults; Chris Bronze Plaque, Columbus International Film Festival

Audience: Ages 10-Adult

Distributor: Coronet/MTI Film & Video

16mm film: $475 **Videocassette:** $250

Rental: $75

★★★★★

Uncle Elephant
Arnold Lobel (illus.).

Harper & Row. 1981. Adventure.

An elephant's parents are lost at sea, so the boy elephant lives with his uncle. A loving bond develops between the uncle and his nephew before the parents are rescued and the family is reunited once again.

Uncle Elephant.

26 min. Color. Puppet animation. Produced by John Matthews. 1991.

Delightful, bright three-dimensional puppet animation brings this elephant family to life. Character traits have been added. In the film, the boy elephant is not only a lost soul but also a comedian who is upset because he can't seem to make people laugh. Sharing this and other feelings with his uncle, they grow closer so that the additions remain in keeping with the story. The boy and uncle put their feelings into songs that slow the action but fit in smoothly. Sad because his parents are lost, the boy elephant is cheered by his uncle's entertaining antics. There are wonderfully lifelike touches from human-style clothing to the young elephant rolling his eyes at a joke he doesn't find funny. He feels sad, excited, afraid, and happy, experiencing emotions that occur abruptly at times. Still, the production adds a dimension to the original story by dwelling on the feelings of the young elephant and his newfound friendship.

Reviews: *Booklist*, Jan. 1, 1992

Awards: *Booklist* Editors' Choice

Audience: Ages 4-8

Distributor: Churchill Media

16mm film: $535 **Videocassette:** $365

Rental: $60

★★★★★

"Unexpected, The"
Jack London.

Anthologized in *The Unabridged Jack London*, edited by Lawrence Teacher & Richard E. Nicholls. Running Press. 1981. Short stories—realistic fiction.

An Englishwoman living in the Yukon witnesses an unexpected crime, the killing of two of her companions. She insists on holding a trial for the murderer, who in the end, is hanged.

Unexpected, The.

53 min. Color. Live action. Produced by William MacAdam/Norfolk. 1980. Narrated by Orson Welles. John Candy, Cherie Lunghi, Patrick Bryner.

This is an apt but slow-moving dramatization of the dark tale. Despite the plodding pace, there is an edge of suspense to the production. The acting is quite fine and tension mounts at the end, but the middle seems overlong in its focus on Edith's preoccupation with the lawful course of action.

Audience: Ages 14-Adult
Distributor: Britannica
Videocassette: $99

V

adherence to book   film rating

Velveteen Rabbit
Margery Williams.
Multiple editions. Fantasy.
This is the story of the friendship of a boy and his toy rabbit, who discovers what it takes to become "real."

Velveteen Rabbit.
30 min. Color. Iconographic. Produced by Rabbit Ears Productions. 1985. Narrated by Meryl Streep.
This film, with soft drawings in pastels, narrated by Meryl Streep and scored with piano music by George Winston beautifully recreates the book. At the heart of the story is the special relationship that children develop with their toys. The tale shows viewers this relationship from the point of view of the toy—the Velveteen Rabbit—and also reveals what the power of their love can do.
Reviews: *Children's Video Report*, Apr. 1986
Audience: Ages 4-8
Distributor: Random House Home Video
Videocassette: $14.95
No public performance rights

★★★★★

Very Touchy Subject, A
Todd Strasser.
Delacorte. 1985. Realistic fiction.
Seventeen-year-old Scott struggles with adolescent urges in a summer that ends with his rescuing an attractively tempting neighbor from her unhappy household.

Can a Guy Say No?.
45 min. Color. Live action. 1988. Beau Bridges.
Slow moving and full of cliches, this film is not likely to change anyone's mind about sexual practices. The audience is likely to gain more from reading the book.
Audience: Ages 15-17
Distributor: Coronet/MTI Film & Video
16mm film: $750 **Videocassette:** $250
Rental: $75

Can a Guy Say No?.
32 min. Color. Live action. 1988. Beau Bridges.
An abbreviated version of the same, full-length title also distributed by Coronet/MTI Film & Video (see above).
Awards: Chris Statuette, Columbus International Film Festival; Bronze Award, National Educational Film and Video Festival

Distributor: Coronet/MTI Film & Video
16mm film: $595 **Videocassette:** $250
Rental: $75

★★★★★

Victor
Clare Galbraith.

Illustrated by William Commerford. Little, Brown & Co. 1971. Realistic fiction.
A ten-year-old boy moves from Mexico to the United States and finds many things different in his new country. Having difficulty adjusting to a new school and language, the boy wins the hearts of his classmates through a class project.

Victor.
26.5 min. Color. Live action. Produced by Dianne Haak Edson. 1989.
Very sensitively produced with excellent acting, this is a tender story of a boy and his family as they struggle with new customs and a new language.
Reviews: *Booklist*, Jan. 1, 1990
Awards: Golden Andy Award, Guidance Association; Silver Apple, National Educational Film and Video Festival
Audience: Ages 8-14
Distributor: Barr Films
16mm film: $595 **Videocassette:** $420
Rental: $50

★★★★★

Village of Round and Square Houses, The
Ann Grifalconi (illus.).

Little, Brown & Co. 1986. Folklore and fairy tales.
Grandmother explains why the men and women in a Cameroon village of Africa live in separate round and square houses.

Village of Round and Square Houses, The.
12 min. Color. Iconographic. Produced by Weston Woods. 1990. Narrated by Cheryl Lynn Bruce. Adapted by Ann Grifalconi and David R. Paight.
Lifelike sound effects and a narrator with an African accent help evoke the atmosphere of this village in which men and women have places to be apart and a time to be together.
Audience: Ages 6-10
Distributor: Weston Woods
16mm film: $235 **Videocassette:** $120
Rental: $25 daily

W

adherence to book film rating

Walt Disney's Dumbo
Adapted by Annie North Bedford and Dick Kelsey.
Illustrated by Walt Disney Studio. Western Publishing. 1988. [1946]. Fantasy.
This is the story of Dumbo, a baby circus elephant born with huge ears that make him the object of ridicule. Turning his "handicap" into an asset, Dumbo uses his ears to fly and rises to such stardom that he and his mother get their own circus train car.

Dumbo.
64 min. Color. Animation. Produced by Walt Disney. 1941. Featuring the voices of Ed Brophy, Sterling Holloway, Verna Felton.
This is an inspiring movie tale about mother love, how to turn a handicap into an asset, and most of all the message that it is okay to be different. In an incident at the beginning that some viewers may find objectionable, Dumbo mistakenly drinks some alcohol. Appealing songs grace the show's soundtrack. The production, as described in *Variety*, presents "a pleasant little story, plenty of pathos mixed with large doses of humor and lots of good music."
Reviews: *Variety*, Oct. 24, 1941
Awards: Academy Award, Best Music Score
Audience: Ages 4-8
Distributor: Buena Vista Home Video
Videocassette: $24.99
No public performance rights

★★★★★

War and Peace
Leo Tolstoy.
Multiple editions. Realistic fiction.
The intricate plot follows the lives and loves of Russians caught up in their country's war with Napoleon.

War and Peace.
208 min. Color. Live action. Produced by Carlo Ponti/Dino de Laurentiis. 1956. Audrey Hepburn, Henry Fonda, Mel Ferrer.
The cast of stars was treated, it seems, to a so-so script, which makes this version play even longer than it is. Spectacular battle scenes are saving bits and may be the reason for the film's Golden Globe Award. As an adaptation, the show is far simpler than the plot of the novel.
Reviews: *New York Times*, Aug. 22, 1956, 26:2; *Variety*, Aug. 22, 1956
Awards: Golden Globe Award, Best Foreign Language Film
Audience: Ages 16-Adult
Distributor: Paramount Home Video
Videocassette available

No public performance rights

War and Peace.
208 min. Color. Live action. 1956. Audrey Hepburn, Henry Fonda, Mel Ferrer.
A laser disc version of the same title offered by Paramount Home Video (see above).
Distributor: Pioneer LDCA, Inc.
Laser disc: CLV format $39.95
No public performance rights

War and Peace.
373 min. Color. Live action. 1967.
Produced in Russia, this very long but spectacular film has been dubbed in English for American audiences. It is so well done that it seems shorter then its Paramount competitor.
Reviews: *New York Times*, Apr. 19, 1968, 50:5; *Variety*, May 1, 1968
Awards: Academy Award, Best Foreign Film
Audience: Ages 16-Adult
Distributor: Kultur Video
Videocassette: $99.95
No public performance rights

★★★★★

War of the Worlds
H. G. Wells.
Multiple editions. Science fiction.
Panic is the keynote as England is invaded by Martians; their superior weapons allow the Martians to dominate the humans.

War of the Worlds.
85 min. Color. Live action. Produced by George Pal/Paramount. 1953. Gene Barry, Ann Robinson.
For 1953, and still today, the special effects in this film about a Martian invasion are spectacular. Fine pacing builds excitement in this science fiction thriller. Generally faithful to the original, it moves the invasion of Earth from London to a small southern California town. The film focuses on the violent, frightening events in the original.
Reviews: *New York Times*, Aug. 14, 1953, 10:2; *Variety*, Mar. 4, 1953
Awards: Academy Award, Best Special Effects
Audience: Ages 10-Adult
Distributor: Paramount Home Video
Videocassette available
No public performance rights

War of the Worlds, The.
85 min. Color. Live action. 1953. Gene Barry, Ann Robinson.
A laser disc version of the same title offered by Paramount Home Video (see above).
Distributor: Pioneer LDCA, Inc.
Laser disc: CLV format $29.95
No public performance rights

★★★★★

Watcher in the Woods
Florence Engle Randall.
Atheneum. 1976. Mystery.
A girl and her family move into an English mansion but have immediate feelings of uneasiness. The girl sets out to solve the mystery.

Watcher in the Woods.
83 min. Color. Live action. Produced by Walt Disney. 1981.

In a style that would make Sherlock Holmes proud, teenaged Jan pieces together the parts of a mystery of a girl who disappeared long ago from the old home that Jan and her parents now inhabit. This is a mystery yarn to hold an audience.

Audience: Ages 8-Adult
Distributor: Buena Vista Home Video
Videocassette: $19.99
No public performance rights

Watcher in the Woods.
25 min. Color. Live action. A Disney Educational Production. 1984.
An abbreviated version of the same, full-length title offered by Buena Vista Home Video (see above). This version retains the basic plot but omits selected details.

Audience: Ages 8-Adult
Distributor: Coronet/MTI Film & Video
16mm film: $600 **Videocassette:** $250
Rental: $75

★★★★★

Watership Down
Richard Adams.
Macmillan. 1972. Fantasy.
An anthropomorphic family of rabbits encounters endless difficulties as they try to establish a safe home, where they can live in peace.

Watership Down.
92 min. Color. Animation. Produced by Martin Rosen. 1978. Voices of John Hurt, Richard Briers, Ralph Richardson, Zero Mostel.
The stylized animation is perfect for this parable about a family of rabbits seeking a safe place to live. Zero Mostel adds a touch of humor in his performance of a captivating character voice for the sea gull.

Reviews: *New York Times*, Nov. 3, 1978; *Variety*, Oct. 18, 1978
Audience: Ages 10-18
Distributor: Warner Home Video
Videocassette: $19.98
No public performance rights

★★★★★

Wee Gillis
Munroe Leaf.
Illustrated by Robert Lawson. Viking Penguin. 1985. [1938]. Realistic fiction.
Wee Gillis has a choice to make. Should he care for cows in the Scottish Lowlands, or hunt stags with the Highlanders? Trying both, he builds skills that equip him for yet a third occupation—blowing bagpipes.

Wee Gillis.
19 min. Color. Live action. Produced by George McQuilkin and Pieter Van Deusen. 1984. Narrated by Roddy MacDonald.
This film enhances the original with breathtaking live-action scenes in Scotland. The scenes with real animals are particularly appealing. A storyteller narrates in English with a Scottish accent that adds to the authentic flavor. Despite these attractions, as noted in *School Library Journal*, "elementary children will find the pace a bit slow."

Reviews: *School Library Journal*, Nov. 1985
Audience: Ages 7-12
Distributor: Churchill Media
16mm film: $395 **Videocassette:** $290
Rental: $60

★★★★★

Wee Willie Winkie
Rudyard Kipling.
Penguin. 1988. [1900]. Short stories—adventure.

A mischievous six-year-old son of a colonel is the darling of the regiment. When he sees a soldier's sweetheart wander into enemy territory, he rushes to the rescue.

Wee Willie Winkie.
100 min. Black and white. Live action. Produced by Gene Markey. 1937. Shirley Temple, Victor McLaglen, C. Aubrey Smith.
Shirley Temple and Victory McLaglen complement each other excellently in this version of a Kipling story written for an adult audience. Addressing a younger audience, the film enhances Shirley Temple's Wee Willie Winkie role to feature her talents. The movie is loosely based on the original, in which the main character is a boy rather than a little girl. The colonel, Wee Willie Winkie's father in the story, is the tyke's grandfather in the movie. On screen, Wee Willie Winkie plays peacemaker between enemy troops; in the story the enemy simply retreats. As noted in the *New York Times*, some of the changes reduce the plot's credibility: "Mr. Kipling, by jingo, never would have dreamed of sending a kilted lassie against his precious Fuzzy-wuzzies...."
Reviews: *New York Times*, July 24, 1937, 12:1; *Variety*, June 30, 1937
Audience: Ages 6-Adult
Distributor: Fox Video
Videocassette: $19.98
No public performance rights

★★★★★

Welcome Home, Jellybean!
Marlene Fanta Shyer.
Scholastic. 1980. [1978]. Realistic fiction.
A mother whose mentally handicapped daughter has been institutionalized decides it is better to have her at home.

Welcome Home, Jellybean!.
30 min. Color. Live action. Produced by MTI. 1986. Dana Hill.
As a realistic look at the difficulty of a handicapped person living at home with a caring but pressured family, this is an excellent production.
Reviews: *Booklist*, Mar. 15, 1987; *School Library Journal*, Mar. 1987; *Science Books & Films*, Jan./Feb. 1987
Awards: ALA Selected Film for Young Adults
Audience: Ages 12-Adult
Distributor: Coronet/MTI Film & Video
16mm film: $500 **Videocassette:** $250
Rental: $75

What Mary Jo Shared
Janice May Udry.
Illustrated by Eleanor Mill. Albert Whitman & Co. 1966. Realistic fiction.
Mary Jo, a young black girl, must find something unusual to share in school. After much searching, she decides the perfect person to share would be her father, who is a doctor.

What Mary Jo Shared.
13 min. Color. Live action. Produced by Bernard Wilets. 1981.
This story of a girl who has trouble fulfilling an assignment is well photographed and sensitively produced. The strengh of Mary Jo's family is quite evident in the film. Like the book, the production builds to an unusual solution of the girl's problem that makes the story interesting to any student who experiences sharing time in class.
Audience: Ages 4-8
Distributor: Phoenix/BFA Films & Video
16mm film: $290 **Videocassette:** $175
Rental: $40

★★★★★

What Mary Jo Wanted
Janice May Udry.

Illustrated by Eleanor Mill. Albert Whitman & Co. 1968. Realistic fiction.

Mary Jo wants a puppy so badly that she even writes poems about one. When her parents agree to let her have one, the puppy disturbs the entire family at night until Mary Jo finds a happy solution for everyone.

What Mary Jo Wanted.

14.5 min. Color. Live action. Produced by Bernard Wilets. 1984.

Mary Jo's desire for a puppy leads to family warmth and imaginative solutions in this award-winning adaptation by a producer who is known for keeping as closely as possible to the original storybook. Even a somewhat weak performance by the girl does not deter from the gentleness of this film.

Reviews: *Booklist*, Sept. 15, 1983; *Early Childhood*, Feb. 1983; *Young Viewers*, Sept. 1986
Awards: CINE Golden Eagle; Learning Magazine-AV awards
Audience: Ages 4-10
Distributor: Barr Films
16mm film: $330 **Videocassette:** $230
Rental: $50

★★★★★

What's Under My Bed?
James Stevenson (illus.).

Greenwillow. 1983. Realistic fiction.

An endearing grandfather tricks his grandchildren into reducing their own fears at night, as they furnish logical explanations for all the old childhood fears that he recalls.

What's Under My Bed?.

8 min. Color. Animated. Produced by Weston Woods. 1990.

As delightful as the book, the film captures both the humor and lesson about groundless fears of the night. Both mediums feature a grandfather who, instead of preaching, leads the children into recognizing their own folly.

Audience: Ages 4-8
Distributor: Weston Woods
16mm film: $215 **Videocassette:** $110
Rental: $25 daily

What's Under My Bed? and Other Creepy Stories.

35 min. Color. Iconographic and animated. Produced by Weston Woods. 1990.

Included in this tape anthology are adaptations of *What's Under My Bed?* (James Stevenson), *Georgie* (Robert Bright), *Teeny Tiny and the Witch Woman* (Barbara Walker), and *The Three Robbers* (Tomi Ungerer). See individual titles for full descriptions.

Audience: Ages Ages 4-10
Distributor: Children's Circle, Weston Woods
Videocassette: $19.95
No public performance rights

★★★★★

When the Wind Stops
Charlotte Zolotow.

Illustrated by Howard Knotts. Harper & Row. 1987. [1962]. Realistic fiction.

A boy asks question after question: Where does the wind go when it stops? Where does the mountain go after the top? What happens to a train when it goes in the tunnel? His mother's answers show that nothing ends; there are only beginnings.

When the Wind Stops.

11 min. Color. Live action. Produced by Diane Haak and Bernard Wilets. 1986.

Wondrous photography communicates the awe inspired by the natural world and continuous cycle of life. The end of autumn is when winter begins, and so forth. Overall, this is a mood piece with plenty of dialogue but a minimum of action.

Reviews: *Booklist*, Apr. 1, 1987
Audience: Ages 4-8
Distributor: Aims Media
16mm film: $265 **Videocassette:** $195
Rental: $50

★★★★★

When We First Met
Norma Fox Mazer.
Scholastic. 1984. [1982]. Realistic fiction.
The son of a woman who killed a girl in an auto accident meets and falls in love with the sister of the dead girl.

When We First Met.
33 min. Color. Live action. Produced by LCA. 1984.
A few teenagers might identify with the problems of the protagonists in this soap opera-like story. The chief assets of the motion picture are the two charming and vibrant teenage characters.

Awards: Chris Statuette, Columbus International Film Festival
Audience: Ages 14-Adult
Distributor: Coronet/MTI Film & Video
16mm film: $550 **Videocassette:** $250
Rental: $75

When We First Met.
54 min. Color. Live action. Produced by LCA. 1984.
A full-length version of the same, abbreviated title also distributed by Coronet/MTI Film & Video (see above).

Distributor: Coronet/MTI Film & Video
16mm film: $750 **Videocassette:** $250
Rental: $75

★★★★★

Where the Wild Things Are
Maurice Sendak (illus.).
Harper & Row Junior Books. 1988. [1963]. Fantasy.
Sent to his room without dinner, young Max follows his imagination to a wonderful, scary place inhabited by huge wild creatures, who crown Max king of their domain.

Where the Wild Things Are.
40 min. Color. Live action. Produced by BBC Television. 1985. Karen Beardsley, Mary King.
An opera version of the popular Sendak story features a female singing Max's part. This may be off-putting to young viewers who will expect a male in the part of naughty Max. However, the monster characters, with their large heads and other features, are especially captivating. Maurice Sendak created the set designs and libretti, which remain faithful to the plot. Younger children may not be enthralled with the piercing effect of the music.

Reviews: *New York Times*, Mar. 29, 1987
Audience: Ages 6-Adult
Distributor: Films Inc.
Videocassette: $39.95

Where the Wild Things Are.
8 min. Color. Animated. Produced by Weston Woods in consultation with Maurice Sendak. 1988.
While the film starts slowly, it builds to a fine finish, with realistic sound effects accompanying the wonderfully imaginative visuals.

Awards: CINE Golden Eagle
Audience: Ages 4-8
Distributor: Weston Woods
16mm film: $195 **Videocassette:** $60
Rental: $20 daily

Maurice Sendak Library.
35 min. Color. Animated. Produced by Weston Woods. 1989.
Included in this tape anthology are adaptations of *Alligators All Around*, *Pierre*, *One Was Johnny*, *Chicken Soup with Rice*, *In the Night Kitchen*, and *Where the Wild Things Are*. See individual titles for full descriptions. An additional segment, *Getting to Know Maurice Sendak*, features the author commenting on his work.
Reviews: *Children's Video Report*, Nov. 1, 1990
Audience: Ages 4-8
Distributor: Children's Circle, Weston Woods
Videocassette: $19.95
No public performance rights

★★★★★

Whistle for Willie
Ezra Jack Keats.
Penguin USA. 1964. Realistic fiction.
Willie, a young black boy, goes about his life trying to whistle until he succeeds.

Whistle for Willie.
6 min. Color. Limited animation. Produced by Weston Woods. 1965.
This faithful adaptation combines animation with an iconographic-style visualization of the author's art. The sound effects of Peters attempting to whistle heighten the impact of his delightful story about achievement and the pride it inspires in him.
Audience: Ages 4-8
Distributor: Weston Woods
16mm film: $175 **Videocassette:** $60
Rental: $20 daily

Five Stories for the Very Young.
30 min. Color. Iconographic and animated. Produced by Weston Woods. 1986.
Included in this tape anthology are adaptations of *Changes, Changes* (Pat Hutchins), *Harold's Fairy Tale* (Crockett Johnson), *Whistle for Willie* (Ezra Jack Keats), *Drummer Hoff* (Barbara and Ed Emberly), and *Caps for Sale* (Esphyr Slobodkina). See individual titles for full descriptions.
Audience: Ages 4-6
Distributor: Children's Circle, Weston Woods
Videocassette: $19.95
No public performance rights

★★★★★

White Heron, A
Sarah Orne Jewett.
Creative Education. 1983. [1886]. Realistic fiction.
Sylvy admires a young hunter but is also concerned for the wildlife he hunts. When she is the first to sight a heron, her loyalties are torn but she decides not to disclose the heron's resting place.

White Heron, The.
26 min. Color. Live action. Produced by Jane Morrison. 1978.
Booklist calls this a "superb adaptation." A beautifully acted dramatization with a lovely setting in the wild, it is also a fine film about divided loyalties.
Reviews: *Booklist*, Apr. 5, 1979
Awards: Chris Plaque, Columbus International Film Festival
Audience: Ages 12-18
Distributor: Coronet/MIT Film & Video
16mm film: $500 **Videocassette:** $250
Rental: $75

★★★★★

Who Am I This Time? For Romeos and Juliets
Kurt Vonnegut, Jr.
Redpath Press. 1987. Realistic fiction.
A young actor is completely caught up in the roles he plays but becomes a recluse as soon as the play ends. A new leading actress courts the recluse in a charming and unusual way.

Who Am I This Time?.
56 min. Color. Live action. Produced by Rubicon Film Productions. 1987.
The almost hour-long show seems to fly by in this beautifully acted and directed adaptation of the Vonnegut story. It is a terrifically paced and emotionally moving film.
Audience: Ages 12-Adult
Distributor: Coronet/MTI Film & Video
Videocassette: $125 **Rental:** $75

★★★★★

Who Wants to Be a Hero?
Robert E. Rubinstein.
Putnam. 1985. [1979]. Realistic fiction.
A high school athlete encounters a mugging and rescues the victim. As the only witness, he struggles with the fear for his own safety before deciding to testify in court.

Who Wants to Be a Hero?
28 min. Color. Live action. Produced by Lyons Films. 1981.
There is plenty of action right from the start in this story of a good deed that ends in a moral dilemma. The acting is not quite believable. Still, this is a consciousness-raising production, as described in *School Library Journal*: "A timely, realistic film about the problems faced by those who agree to be witnesses in criminal trials."
Reviews: *School Library Journal*, Nov. 1982
Awards: ALA Selected Film for Young Adults
Audience: Ages 12-Adult
Distributor: Coronet/MTI Film & Video
16mm film: $500 **Videocassette:** $250
Rental: $75

★★★★★

Why Mosquitoes Buzz in People's Ears: A West African Tale
Retold by Verna Aardema.
Illustrated by Leo and Diane Dillon. Dial Books for Young Readers. 1975. Folklore and fairy tales.
A mosquito teases an iguana, starting a chain of events that ends in Mother Owl refusing to wake the sun and make it rise. After the true culprit, the mosquito, is discovered, it whines in the animals' ears to see if they are still angry.

Why Mosquitoes Buzz in People's Ears.
10 min. Color. Limited animation. Produced by Weston Woods. 1984.
Full of colorful, jungle animals, this film faithfully animates the chain of events that results in a terrible accident: a monkey swings frantically through the trees and breaks a branch that kills a baby owl, so Mother Owl won't hoot for the sun to rise. King Lion traces the events back to the mosquito, and it proceeds to buzz in people's ears.
Reviews: *Booklist*, Oct. 15, 1984; *School Library Journal*, Nov. 1984
Awards: CINE Golden Eagle; Chris Plaque, Columbus International Film Festival
Audience: Ages 4-8
Distributor: Weston Woods
16mm film: $235 **Videocassette:** $60
Rental: $20 daily

Emperor's New Clothes, The and Other Folktales.
30 min. Color. Iconographic and animated. Produced by Weston Woods. 1991.

Included in this tape anthology are adaptations of *The Emperor's New Clothes* (Hans Christian Andersen), *Why Mosquitoes Buzz in People's Ears* (Verna Aardema), and *Suho and the White Horse* (Yuzo Otsuka). See individual titles for full descriptions.

Audience: Ages 4-10
Distributor: Children's Circle, Weston Woods
Videocassette: $19.95
No public performance rights

★★★★★

Wild Swans, The
Hans Christian Andersen.
Multiple editions. Folklore and fairy tales.
A girl sets out to rescue her brothers, eleven princes who have been turned into wild swans by a sorcerer.

Wild Swans, The.
9 min. Color. Animation. Produced by Greatest Tales. 1976.
The animation is limited and somewhat stylized, but the production keeps closely to the original story line. As in other Greatest Tales films, the visuals were created in Asia.
Audience: Ages 6-10
Distributor: Phoenix/BFA
16mm film: $220 **Videocassette:** $130
Rental: $29

Wild Swans, The.
11 min. Color. Limited animation. Produced by Coronet. 1980.
Though the movement is limited, this nicely animated adaptation is faithful to the classic fairy tale about a princess who courageously saves her eleven brothers.
Reviews: *Instructor*, Nov./Dec. 1981
Audience: Ages 4-8
Distributor: Coronet/MTI Film & Video
16mm film: $280 **Videocassette:** $195
Rental: $75

★★★★★

Wilder Summer, The
Stephen Krensky.
Atheneum. 1983. Realistic fiction.
A wild but nice bunch of campers enjoys a summer of amusing activities and pranks.

Wilder Summer, The.
32 min. Color. Live action. Produced by LCA. 1984.
This is a fun-filled story of camp experience that will make viewers think about what might have happened to them or possibly provide some ideas for the next camp experience. The most rowdy incidents have been cut to produce this short version, which, at thirty-two minutes, is long enough.
Audience: Ages 10-14
Distributor: Coronet/MTI Film & Video
16mm film: $550 **Videocassette:** $250
Rental: $75

Wilder Summer, The.
54 min. Color. Live action. Produced by LCA. 1984.
A full-length version of the same, abbreviated title also distributed by Coronet/MTI Film & Video (see above).
Audience: Ages 10-14
Distributor: Coronet/MTI Film & Video
16mm film: $750 **Videocassette:** $250
Rental: $75

★★★★★

William's Doll
Charlotte Zolotow.
Illustrated by William Pène Dubois. Harper & Row. 1985. [1972]. Realistic fiction.
William is an object of scorn because he wants a doll; his understanding grandmother purchases the doll so that William can pretend he is a father.

William's Doll.
18 min. Color. Live action. Produced by Roberto Chiesa. 1981.
This adapts a Charlotte Zolotow story, written in soft, gentle tones that may be too peaceful for the movie medium. The film is a well-done, accurate portrayal of the book but lacks the spark needed to grip an audience.
Reviews: *Horn Book*, Apr. 1982; *School Library Journal*, Nov. 1982
Audience: Ages 4-8
Distributor: Phoenix/BFA
16mm film: $400 **Videocassette:** $225
Rental: $35

★★★★★

Wind in the Willows
Kenneth Grahame.
Multiple editions. Fantasy.
Focusing on Rat's liking for boats, Toad's attraction to motorcars and so forth, the novel describes the pleasures and antics of animal neighbors.

Adventures of J. Thaddeus Toad.
25 min. Color. Animation. A Disney Educational Production. 1981.
Disney adds fun and fantasy to this already-charming classic. Focusing on one of its characters, the show features a toad who drives his neighbors to distraction.
Audience: Ages 5-12
Distributor: Coronet/MTI Film & Video
16mm film: $600 **Videocassette:** $250
Rental: $75

Wind in the Willows.
34 min. Color. Animation. Produced by Walt Disney. 1949. Narrated by Basil Rathbone.
The four animal friends—Toad, Mole, Rat, and Mr. Badger—live along a river in the English countryside. They are delightfully animated characters, imbued with equal amounts of animal and human qualities. Returning from town, where he went to buy a motorcar, Toad discovers that a band of weasels and a gang of ferrets have seized Toad Hall. He and his three animal friends fight to regain Toad Hall, then have a victory banquet. The novel follows Toad through a harrowing string of adventures before the showdown at Toad Hall instead of the movie's simple trip to town to purchase a motorcar, but the change suits the limited time span, and the action is in keeping with Toad's character.
Audience: Ages 4-10
Distributor: Buena Vista Home Video
Videocassette: $12.99
No public performance rights

★★★★★

Wind Rose
Crescent Dragonwagon.
Illustrated by Ronald Himler. Harper & Row. 1976. Nonfiction.
A book about having a child, the informational text is built around the idea that childbearing should grow out of love.

Wind Rose.
21 min. Color. Live action. Produced by Don MacDonald. 1983.
This is a nicely done, rather whimsical film about what happens when a woman is having a baby.

Reviews: *Family Review*, Oct. 1984; *Horn Book*, June 1984; *School Library Journal*, Nov. 1984
Audience: Ages 10-14
Distributor: Phoenix/BFA Film & Video
16mm film: $450 **Videocassette:** $275
Rental: $68

★★★★★

Winnie-the-Pooh
The House at Pooh Corner
A. A. Milne.
Illustrated by Ernest H. Shepard. Dutton. 1988 [1926]. 1988. [1928]. Humor.
The boy Christopher Robin plays imaginary games with his toys as if they were real. Among them is Winnie the Pooh, a loveable bear who has comical adventures with other animals. In the sequel *The House at Pooh Corner*, Pooh Bear and Piglet build a house for their donkey friend Eeyore, the character Tigger is introduced, and the animals have new adventures.

Winnie the Pooh and the Honey Tree.
25 min. Color. Animation. Produced by Walt Disney. 1966. Narrated by Sebastian Cabot. Featuring the voice of Sterling Holloway.
The show adapts the chapter "In Which We Are Introduced to Winnie the Pooh" from the novel *Winnie-the-Pooh*. Pooh visits the Hundred-Acre Wood, where he climbs to the top of the honey tree to satisfy his sweet tooth. His friends, Christopher Robin, Rabbit, Gopher, and Owl, rescue him from a swarm of bees and pull him from a rabbit-hole in which he gets stuck. As in other Pooh films, the animation literally jumps from pages of the book. Cuddly Pooh and his honey tree dilemma appeals to younger audiences, while Christopher Robin's wisdom holds the attention of older children.
Audience: Ages 4-10
Distributor: Buena Vista Home Video
Videocassette: $12.99
No public performance rights

Winnie the Pooh and the Blustery Day.
24 min. Color. Animation. Produced by Walt Disney. 1968. Narrated by Sebastian Cabot. Featuring the voice of Sterling Holloway.
Adapted from the chapter "In Which Tigger Comes to the Forest and Has Breakfast" in *The House at Pooh Corner*, this film features a blustery "Windsday" in the Hundred-Acre Wood. Pooh Bear meets Tigger, is driven out of his house by a flood, rescues Piglet from a waterfall, and takes him home to live in Christopher Robin's bedroom. Viewers are overwhelmed by the horrible flood and delighted by the animals' heroics. The entertaining show also provides a lesson in friendship.
Awards: Academy Award, Best Cartoon
Audience: Ages 4-10
Distributor: Buena Vista Home Video
Videocassette: $12.99
No public performance rights

Winnie the Pooh and Tigger Too.
25 min. Color. Animation. Produced by Walt Disney. 1974. Narrated by Sebastian Cabot. Featuring the voice of Sterling Holloway.
The film adapts the chapter "In Which Tigger Is Unbounced" from *The House at Pooh Corner*. Tigger's bouncing, trouncing, and flouncing is driving all the other animals mad. Rabbit prescribes a cure that ends in disaster, leading everyone to conclude that Tigger's bounciness isn't so bad after all. In the course of the show, the energetic character sings "The most wonderful thing about Tiggers is I'm the only one." His uniqueness is the issue. Straight from the pages of the book comes a lesson about accepting friends for what they are.
Audience: 4-10

Distributor: Buena Vista Home Video
Videocassette: $12.99
No public performance rights

Winnie the Pooh and the Blustery Day.
25 min. Color. Animation. 1982.
A public performance version of the same title offered by Buena Vista Home Video (see above).
Distributor: Coronet/MTI Film & Video
16mm film: $600 **Videocassette:** $250
Rental: $75

Winnie the Pooh and the Honey Tree.
26 min. Color. Animation. A Disney Educational Production. 1982.
A public performance version of the same title offered by Buena Vista Home Video (see above).
Distributor: Coronet/MTI Film & Video
16mm film: $600 **Videocassette:** $250
Rental: $75

Winnie the Pooh and Tigger Too.
26 min. Color. Animation. 1982.
A public performance version of the same title offered by Buena Vista Home Video (see above).
Distributor: Coronet/MTI Film & Video
16mm film:: $600 **Videocassette:** $250
Rental: $75

Winnie the Pooh and a Day for Eeyore.
25 min. Color. Animation. Produced by Walt Disney. 1983. Featuring the voices of Paul Winchell and Dick Billingsly.
The adaptation is based on the *Winnie-the-Pooh* chapter "In Which Eeyore Has a Birthday and Gets Two Presents." It features doleful Eeyore, a very glum donkey who realizes everyone in the Hundred-Acre Wood has forgotten his birthday. But the animal inhabitants save the day for Eeyore with a chocolate cake, an exploding balloon, and a game of Pooh Sticks, prompting the bear to say, "Eeyore is okay. I guess we're all okay." This is animated storytelling at its best.
Audience: Ages 4-10
Distributor: Buena Vista Home Video
Videocassette: $12.99
No public performance rights

Winnie the Pooh and a Day for Eeyore.
16 min. Color. Animation. A Disney Educational Production. 1984.
A public performance version of the same title offered by Buena Vista Home Video (see above).
Awards: CINE Golden Eagle
Distributor: Coronet/MTI Film & Video
16mm film: $600 **Videocassette:** $250
Rental: $75

★★★★★

Witch Who Was Afraid of Witches, The

Alice Low.
Illustrated by Karen Gundersheimer. Pantheon. 1978. Fantasy.
Wendy, the youngest and weakest of the witches, learns that she can become someone on her own.

Witch Who Was Afraid of Witches, The.
12 min. Color. Animated. Produced by LCA. 1979.

Simple drawings and limited animation along with a narrator whose voice grates like a witch's detract a little from the charming story of the youngest and weakest witch. Yet, as noted in *EFLA Sightlines*, "...this film...does carry the subtle message that even the reticent child can eventually overcome fear, given the right support and encouragement."

Reviews: *EFLA Sightlines*, Fall 1980
Audience: Ages 8-11
Distributor: Coronet/MTI Film & Video
16mm film: $250 **Videocassette:** $230
Rental: $75

Witches, The
Roald Dahl.
Illustrated by Quentin Blake. Farrar, Straus & Giroux. 1983. Fantasy.
Turned into a mouse by a grand old witch, a boy defeats her plan to turn every other child in England into a mouse. The boy-mouse succeeds with the help of his wise grandmother.

Witches, The.
95 min. Color. Live action. Produced by Jim Henson Productions. 1989. Angelica Huston, Mai Zettering, Jasen Fisher.
The lively fantasy is marvelously dramatized in this convincing production. It echoes the action in the novel with a few exceptions. In the movie, before the boy changes into a mouse, he saves a baby in peril due to the lead witch. His grandmother is more anxious and reticent to expose her grandson-mouse to danger. Finally, a benevolent witch (not in the novel) changes the mouse back into a boy at the end. In the book, the main character remains a mouse. This change softens the frightening dimension of the story, brought out earlier by the grosteque appearance of the witches.

Reviews: *Variety*, Mar. 21, 1989
Audience: Ages 8-12
Distributor: Warner Home Video
Videocassette: $92.99
No public performance rights

★★★★★

Wizard of Oz, The
L. Frank Baum.
Multiple editions. Fantasy.
A tornado catapults fourteen-year-old Dorothy to a strange land, where she finds friends and learns she can only return home with help from the Wizard of Oz. He first has her obtain a broomstick kept by the Wicked Witch of the West.

Wizard of Oz, The.
93 min. Black and white. Live action. Produced by Larry Semon. 1925. Dorothy Dwan, Oliver Hardy.
Oliver Hardy of Laurel and Hardy fame plays the tin man in this silent version (with a musical score) of the Baum story. It has some unique characters: villains named Prime Minister Kruel, Ambassador Wikked, and Lady Vishuss, and a hero named Prince Kynd. For the production capabilities of 1925, this was a fine film, but it appeals mostly to film buffs today.

Reviews: *New York Times*, Apr. 14, 1925, 26:1; *Variety*, Apr. 22, 1925
Audience: Ages 8-15
Distributor: Video Yesteryear
Videocassette: $24.95
No public performance rights

Wizard of Oz, The.
102 min. Color, black and white. Live action. Produced by Mervyn LeRoy/MGM. 1939. Judy Garland, Frank Morgan, Margaret Hamilton.

This classic remains a lasting delight, complete with special effects such as monkeys that fly and apple trees with arms that throw fruit. All Dorothy wants is to return home to Kansas. Her companions—a scarecrow in quest of a brain, a tin man who desires a heart, and a lion in search of courage—come to captivating life in the show. Margaret Hamilton, the Wicked Witch, may frighten the very young or impressionable. As Dorothy, Judy Garland is equally convincing. Oscar winners are the musical score and the song "Over the Rainbow" in a production that entertains audiences today just as enchantingly as when it was first released.

Reviews: *New York Times*, Aug. 18, 1939, 16:2; *Variety*, Aug. 16, 1939
Awards: Academy Awards, Best Music Score, Best Song
Audience: Ages 6-Adult
Distributor: MGM/UA Home Video
Videocassette available
No public performance rights

Wizard of Oz, The.
102 min. Color, black and white. Live action. 1939. Judy Garland, Frank Morgan, Margaret Hamilton.
A laser disc version of the same title offered by MGM/UA (see above). Also includes a second audio track with commentary and outtakes.

Distributor: Criterion Collection
Laser disc: CAV format $99.95
No public performance rights

Wizard of Oz, The: 50th Anniversary Edition.
119 min. Color, black and white. Live action. 1939. Judy Garland, Frank Morgan, Margaret Hamilton.
A laser disc version of the same title offered by MGM/UA Home Video (see above). This edition includes the original theatrical trailer.

Distributor: Pioneer LDCA, Inc.
Laser disc: CLV format $29.98
No public performance rights

Wiz, The.
133 min. Color. Live action. Produced by Motown. 1978. Diana Ross, Michael Jackson, Lena Horne.
Taken from a Broadway show, this is a musical version of *The Wizard of Oz*. The all-black, very talented cast tells the story interestingly, but the musical is less effective an adaptation than the 1939 version. In this version, Dorothy, played by Diana Ross, is a twenty-four-year-old ghetto-dweller.

Reviews: *New York Times*, Oct. 26, 1978, 1:1; *Variety*, Oct. 4, 1978
Audience: Ages 10-15
Distributor: MCA/Universal Home Video
Videocassette available
No public performance rights

Wizard of Oz, The.
79 min. Color. Animation. Produced by Paramount. 1982. Voices of Lorne Greene and Aileen Quinn.
Entertainingly drawn and animated and with solid voice tracks provided by veteran actors Greene and Quinn, this version is still no match for the classic that stars Judy Garland.

Audience: Ages 5-10
Distributor: Paramount Home Video
Videocassette available
No public performance rights

Wizard of Oz, The.
79 min. Color. Animation. 1982. Voices of Lorne Greene and Aileen Quinn.
A laser disc version of the same title offered by Paramount Home Video (see above).

Distributor: Pioneer LDCA, Inc.
Laser disc: CLV format $29.95
No public performance rights

★★★★★

Wizard of Wallaby Wallow, The
Jack Kent (illus.).
Parents' Magazine Press. 1971. Fantasy.
A comical wizard prescribes a bottled spell to a mouse who wants to be something else; the mouse comes to the happy conclusion that the wisest course is to remain himself.

Wizard, The.
8 min. Color. Animated. Produced by The Wizard Production Partnership/Weston Woods. 1985.
Delightfully humorous, the film portrays the likable wizard with animated, "cheerily drawn illustration and with a marvelous narrator creating both primly dry wit and effective characterizations...." —*Booklist*
Reviews: *Booklist*, Oct. 15, 1985; *School Library Journal*, Sept. 1985
Awards: Chris Bronze Award, Columbus Film Festival
Audience: Ages 4-10
Distributor: Weston Woods
16mm film: $195 **Videocassette:** $60
Rental: $20 daily

Mysterious Tadpole and Other Stories, The.
34 min. Color. Animated and Iconographic. Produced by Weston Woods. 1989.
Included in this tape anthology are adaptations of *The Mysterious Tadpole* (Steven Kellogg), *The Five Chinese Brothers* (Claire Bishop), *Jonah and the Great Fish* (Warwick Hutton), and *The Wizard* (Jack Kent). See individual titles for full descriptions.
Reviews: *Children's Video Report*, Feb./Mar. 1989
Audience: Ages 4-8
Distributor: Children's Circle, Weston Woods
Videocassette: $19.95
No public performance rights

★★★★★

Words By Heart
Ouida Sebestyen.
Little, Brown, & Co. 1979. Historical fiction.
A black family leaves the South in 1910 to settle in rural Bethel Springs, where, as the only black family in the region, they encounter racism and prejudice from their neighbors.

Words By Heart.
110 min. Color. Live action. Produced by Martin Tanse. 1991. Robert Hooks, Charlotte Rae, Alfre Woodard.
Using much of the same dialogue from Sebestyen's highly regarded junior novel, this well-acted, poignant drama faithfully recreates the evocative story of a proud rural black family who must encounter tragedy before triumphing over racist attitudes and behavior.
Reviews: *Booklist*, Oct. 15, 1991
Audience: Ages 10-14
Distributor: Public Media Video
Videocassette: $29.95

★★★★★

Wuthering Heights
Emily Brontë.
Multiple editions. Realistic fiction.
Catherine Linton, daughter in a middle class nineteenth century English family, falls deeply in love with Heathcliff, a waif who has been raised by her family.

Wuthering Heights.
103 min. Black and white. Live action. Produced by Samuel Goldwyn. 1939. Merle Oberon, Laurence Olivier, David Niven.
Although not the complete story written by Emily Brontë, this version won an Oscar for cinematography and could well have won one for the excellent acting. Celebrated in the *New York Times*, the film was described as "Goldwyn at his best, and better still Emily Brontë at hers...goes straight to the heart of the book." Images of the lovers' ghosts going off together were added to soften the tragic ending, and the setting was changed from the Regency to the Georgian era. Otherwise the film keeps faith with the novel.

Reviews: *New York Times*, Apr. 14, 1939, 28:2; *Variety*, Mar. 29, 1939
Awards: Academy Award, Best Cinematography
Audience: Ages 14-Adult
Distributor: HBO Video
Videocassette: $19.98
No public performance rights

Wuthering Heights.
90 min. Black and white. Live action. 1954.
Produced in Mexico, this is a so-so adaptation of the novel. The production focuses on the servant grown rich, who returns to disrupt the life of a former love.

Audience: Ages 14-Adult
Distributor: Videocassette not currently in distribution

Wuthering Heights.
105 min. Color. Live action. Produced by Samuel Z. Arkoff. 1970. Anna Calder-Marshall, Timothy Dalton, Harry Andrews.
A perhaps too-fast paced film, this is a good adaptation of the book, with very believable performances by the two principal actors. Like the 1939 version, this one focuses only on the first half of the novel. It fails to inspire feelings of sadness or feverish romantic love, though the footage is beautifully photographed. This version makes obvious relationships that the novel leaves vague, declaring outright that Heathcliff is Cathy's half-brother.

Reviews: *New York Times*, Feb. 19, 1971, 23:1; *Variety*, Dec. 16, 1970
Audience: Ages 14-Adult
Distributor: HBO Video
Videocassette: $19.99
No public performance rights

★★★★★

Wynken, Blynken, and Nod
Eugene Field.
Illustrated by Barbara Cooney. Dutton. 1982. [1964]. Poetry.
Told in rhyme, this is the story of Wynken, Blynken, and Nod, who go sailing through the sky in a wooden shoe. Their true identity is revealed at the end; the three characters are really the two eyes and head of an infant in his cradle.

Wynken, Blynken, and Nod.
4 min. Blue and white. Iconographic. Produced by Weston Woods. 1971.
Though true to the storybook, the limited color and the symbolism that concludes this tale make it moderately appealing to very young audiences. Only the camera moves, although the story line in which the characters sail through the sky lends itself to fuller motion.

Audience: Ages 4-6
Distributor: Weston Woods
16mm film: $115 **Videocassette:** $60
Rental: $15 daily

Smile for Auntie and Other Stories.
27 min. Color. Iconographic and animated. Produced by Weston Woods. 1985.
Included in this tape anthology are adaptations of *Smile for Auntie* (Diane Paterson), *Make Way for Ducklings* (Robert McCloskey), *The Snowy Day* (Ezra Jack Keats), and *Wynken, Blynken and Nod* (Eugene Field). See individual titles for full descriptions.
Audience: Ages 4-8
Distributor: Children's Circle, Weston Woods
Videocassette: $19.95
No public performance rights

Y

adherence to book film rating

Yearling, The
Marjorie Kinnan Rawlings.
Illustrated by N. C. Wyeth. Macmillan. 1985. [1938]. Historical fiction.
A post-Civil War farm family in rural Florida includes a lonely boy who raises a pet fawn. When the much-loved animal destroys crops, the boy must kill it.

Yearling, The.
134 min. Color. Live action. Produced by MGM/Sidney Franklin. 1946. Gregory Peck, Jane Wyman, Claude Jarman, Jr.
This fine adaptation is as dramatically wrenching today as when it was initially released. The story reaches far beyond the level of a boy and his pet to the pain involved in growing up. The mother's reluctance to let herself love her only remaining son plays nicely into the boy's experience of love for his pet and is expertly conveyed. An additional bonus is an honest look at the hardships of frontier life.
Reviews: *New York Times*, Jan. 24, 1947, 18:2; *Variety*, Nov. 27, 1946
Awards: Academy Awards, Best Cinematography, Best Set Design, Special Oscar for Outstanding Child Actor to Claude Jarmen, Jr.; Golden Globe Award, Best Actor
Audience: Ages 10-Adult
Distributor: MGM/UA Home Video
Videocassette: $19.98
No public performance rights

Yearling, The.
129 min. Color. Live action. 1946. Gregory Peck, Jane Wyman.
A laser disc version of the same title offered by MGM/UA Home Video (see above).
Distributor: Pioneer LDCA, Inc.
Laser disc: CLV format $39.98
No public performance rights

★★★★★

Yentl, the Yeshiva Boy
Isaac Bashevis Singer.
Farrar, Straus & Giroux. 1983. [1962]. Historical fiction.
At the turn of the twentieth century, a Polish girl disguises herself as a boy so that she can acquire an education.

Yentl.
133 min. Color. Live action. Produced by Barbara Streisand, Rusty Lemorande. 1983. Barbara Streisand, Mandy Patinkin, Amy Irving.

This adaptation shows tender respect for the original short story but has been lengthened considerably by a series of award-winning songs. The film appeals mostly, as do Singer's stories, to Jewish audiences. It also attracts Streisand fans. Others may consider it overlong.

Reviews: *New York Times*, Nov. 18, 1983, C10:1; *Variety*, Nov. 2, 1983
Awards: Academy Award, Best Music Score; Golden Globe Award, Best Musical
Audience: Ages 14-Adult
Distributor: MGM/UA Home Video
Videocassette: $19.98
No public performance rights

Yentl.
134 min. Color. Live action. 1983. Barbara Streisand, Mandy Patinkin, Amy Irving.
A laser disc version of the same title offered by MGM/UA Home Video (see above).
Distributor: Pioneer LDCA, Inc.
Laser disc: CLV format $39.98
No public performance rights

★★★★★

"Young Goodman Brown"
Nathaniel Hawthorne.
Anthologized in *Young Goodman Brown and Other Tales,* edited by Brian Harding. Oxford University Press. 1988. Short stories—historical fiction.
A young man in Puritan New England embarks on a journey through the forest, during which he is joined by the Devil. His destination is a meeting of "witches," who are in fact his self-righteous but not-so-venerable neighbors.

Young Goodman Brown.
30 min. Color. Live action. Produced by Donald Fox. 1972.
Otherwise faithful to the short story, the film opens on some townspeople preparing to burn a "witch" at the stake. The production is as symbolic as the story and adds ominous special effects—for example, clouds churning in the sky overhead at the meeting of sinners who plan to induct young Goodman Brown. The effects and lighting help establish a dreamlike atmosphere, but the adaptation is unconvincing. It is distant from the audience and, at times, slow moving.
Awards: CINE Golden Eagle
Audience: Ages 14-Adult
Distributor: Pyramid Film & Video
16mm film: $550 **Videocassette:** $225
Rental: $95

★★★★★

Youth Who Could Not Shiver and Shake, The
Jacob Grimm and Wilhelm K. Grimm.
Multiple editions. Folklore and fairy tales.
A father sends his fearless and "stupid" son out to make his own way in the world. The boy sets out determined to learn how to shiver, shake, and feel fear. His search carries him to a haunted castle, where he spends three eventful nights.

Youth Who Wanted to Shiver, The.
8.5 min. Color. Animated. Produced by Nick Bosustow and C.B. Wismar. 1978.
Based on the retelling in *Eric Carle's Storybook: Seven Tales by the Brothers Grimm* (Franklin Watts 1976), the show features brightly colored animation, vivacious narration, and dialog voices. As in the Grimm version, the princess finally makes the youth shiver and shake with the help of some water and fish at the end of the tale.
Audience: Ages 4-8
Distributor: Churchill Media
16mm film: $190 **Videocassette:** $59
Rental: $50

Boy Who Left Home to Find Out About the Shivers, The (Faerie Tale Theatre).
60 min. Color. Live action. Produced by Shelley Duvall. 1985. Peter Mac Nicol, Christopher Lee, Dana Hill.
This delightful "horror" film seems more humorous than frightening and may in fact help allay a young viewer's fears about monsters of the night. The hero laughs at the very clever special effects that make the evil spirits visible. Close to the Grimm version, the show differs in its ending. The tale has the boy shiver and shake when the princess covers him with watery fish; the adaptation has him shiver and shake at the thought of falling in love. It then moves into a concept new to the story—getting the blues. Overall, this is a highly entertaining exploration of feelings through a reasonably faithful retelling of the classic tale.

Audience: Ages 4-Adult
Distributor: Fox Video
Videocassette: $14.98
No public performance rights

Boy Who Left Home to Find Out About the Shivers, The.
52 min. Color. Live action. 1983. Peter Mac Nicol, Christopher Lee, Dana Hill.
A laser disc version of the same title offered by Fox Video (see above).

Distributor: Image Entertainment
Laser disc: CLV format $29.98
No public performance rights

Z

adherence to book   film rating

Zack and the Magic Factory
Elaine Schulte.
T. Nelson. 1976. Adventure.
Zack, a young boy on his own, goes to live with his relative who owns a magic factory. He gets tangled up with thieves in pursuit of his relative's latest invention.

Zack and the Magic Factory.
50 min. Color. Live action. Produced by ABC Weekend Specials. 1983.
This is the first forty-five minutes of a two-part film, complete with blackouts for commercials. It offers more than anyone needs to see of Daisy Dabble and her Magic Factory—a factory more dabble than magic—in that she dips into this and that escapade without carrying much to a conclusion.
Audience: Ages 8-11
Distributor: Coronet/MTI Film & Video
16mm film: $645 **Videocassette:** $250
Rental: $75

★★★★★

"Zero Hour"
Ray Bradbury.
Anthologized in *Science Fiction*, edited by Sylvia Z. Brodkin and Elizabeth J. Pearson. Lothrop, Lee and Shepard. 1975. Short stories—science fiction.
A seven-year-old girl is playing a new and captivating game. Her mother notices that the girl's vocabulary is changing but doesn't understand the implications until the "zero hour."

Zero Hour.
21 min. Color. Live action. Produced by Bernard Wilets. 1978.
The well-constructed but less-than-exciting story falls short of the emotion that the title might lead viewers to expect.
Audience: Ages 12-Adult
Distributor: Britannica
Videocassette: $260

★★★★★

Zlateh the Goat
Isaac Bashevis Singer.
Anthologized in *Zlateh the Goat and Other Stories.* Translated by Elizabeth Shub; illustrated by Maurice Sendak.
Harper & Row Junior Books. 1966. Short stories—realistic fiction.
A boy sadly takes the family goat to town so he can sell it at Chanukah time. Caught in a winter storm, the goat and boy save each other when they take refuge in a brush shelter.

Zlateh the Goat.
20 min. Color. Live action. Produced by Weston Woods. 1973.
Though the motion picture is remarkably realistic, the show has long silences and is slow moving for today's audiences.

Awards: Gold Medal, Atlanta Film Festival; Silver Award, International Film & TV Festival of New York; Silver Plaque, Chicago Film Festival
Audience: Ages 8-12
Distributor: Weston Woods
16mm film: $375 **Videocassette:** $60
Rental: $25 daily

★★★★★

"Zoo"
Edward D. Hoch.
Anthologized in *Young Extraterrestrials*, edited by Isaac Asimov, Martin H. Greenberg, and Charles G. Waugh.
Harper & Row. 1984. Short stories—science fiction.
A Chicago family visits an interplanetary zoo where they are as much looked at as they are lookers.

Zoo.
10.5 min. Color. Live action. Produced by Advanced American Communications. 1990.
The limited animation and vividly colored characters work very well to tell a fanciful story of human and extraterrestrial interaction. However, viewers may grow weary of the long wait to get into the "zoo."

Audience: Ages 11-Adult
Distributor: Coronet/MTI Film & Video
Videocassette: $250 **Rental:** $75

★★★★★

Zorba the Greek
Nikos Kazantzakis.
Simon and Schuster. 1971. [1953]. Realistic fiction.
A friendly Greek peasant helps an Englishman relax, although their experience with two women is, in the end, unhappy.

Zorba the Greek.
142 min. Black and white. Live action. Produced by Fox/Rockley Cacoyannis. 1964. Anthony Quinn, Alan Bates, Lila Kedrova.
The most outstanding element of the dramatization is its depth of character. This, on its own, makes the production emotionally rousing. The old woman, played by Lila Kedrova, is splendidly realized. Anthony Quinn's Zorba is described in the *New York Times*: Though the story gives him no major conflict to overcome, "so large and fantastic is the character that he all but overwhelms the total scene..."

Reviews: *New York Times*, Dec. 18, 1964, 25:1; *Variety*, Dec. 16, 1964
Awards: Academy Award, Best Supporting Actress, Best Cinematography, Best Art Direction
Audience: Ages 16-Adult
Distributor: Fox Video
Videocassette: $24.98
No public performance rights

Appendix A:

Films for the Hearing Impaired

Abel's Island (home video version)
Adventures of Sherlock Holmes, The (1939)
Adventures of Tom Sawyer, The (1938)
Alexander and the Terrible, Horrible, No Good, Very Bad Day
Alice in Wonderland (1957)
All Summer in a Day
All Creatures Great and Small
Animal Farm (1955) (home video version)
Anne of Avonlea (home video version)
Anne of Green Gables (1985) (home video version)
Annie and the Old One
Around the World in Eighty Days
Astronomers, The
Back to the Future
Beauty and the Beast (Faerie Tale Theatre) (1983)
Bedknobs and Broomsticks
Ben and Me (home video version)
Black Stallion, The
Black Stallion Returns, The
Bollo Caper, The (public performance version)
Boy, A Dog, and a Frog, A
"Boys and Girls"
Boy Who Left Home to Find Out About the Shivers
Brian's Song
Brighton Beach Memoirs
Brothers Grimm Fairy Tales, The (Little Red Riding Hood; The Seven Ravens)
Caine Mutiny, The
Call of the Wild (1989)
Canterville Ghost, The (1944)
Cat in the Hat, The
Chaparral Prince, The
Children of a Lesser God
Cinderella (1964)
Cinderella (1984)
Civil War, The
Clan of the Cave Bear, The
Cop and the Anthem, The
Dancing Princesses, The
Different Kind of Winning, A
Dr. Seuss: Lorax, The
Dr. Seuss: On the Loose
Dr. Seuss Beginner Book Video: Cat in the Hat Comes Back; Fox in Socks; There's a Wocket in My Pocket!
Dr. Seuss Beginner Book Video: Dr. Seuss's ABC; I Can Read With My Eyes Shut!; Mr. Brown Can Moo! Can You?
Dr. Seuss Beginner Book Video: Hop on Pop; Marvin K. Mooney Will You Please Go Now!; Oh Say Can You Say?
Dr. Seuss Beginner Book Video: One Fish Two Fish Red Fish Blue Fish; Oh, the Thinks You Can Think!; The Foot Book
Drums Along the Mohawk
Dumbo (home video version)
Electric Grandmother, The
Electric Grandmother, The (home video version)
Elephant Who Couldn't Forget, The
Elephant's Child
Elves and the Shoemaker, The (Timeless Tales)
Emperor's New Clothes, The (Faerie Tale Theatre) (1984)

Emperor's New Clothes (Timeless Tales)
Empire Strikes Back, The
Escape to Witch Mountain
Fables of Harry Allard (Miss Nelson Is Missing; It's So Nice To Have a Wolf Around the House)
Fall of the House of Usher, The
Field of Dreams
Five Lionni Classics–The Animal Fables of Leo Lionni
Follow My Leader (public performance version)
Freaky Friday
Free to Be You & Me
Frog and Toad Are Friends
Frog and Toad Together
Gift of Love, The
Gift of the Magi
Glory
Gold Bug
Gold Bug, The (home video version)
Goldilocks and the Three Bears (1983)
Gone with the Wind
Goodbye, Mr. Chips
Grapes of Wrath, The
Grasshopper and the Ants
Great Escape, The
Greystoke: The Legend of Tarzan, Lord of the Apes
Gulliver in Lilliput
Hansel and Gretel (1955)
Hansel & Gretel (Faerie Tale Theatre) 1982)
Hansel and Gretel (1985) (17 min.)
Heart is a Lonely Hunter, The
Heidi (1937)
Heidi (1979)
Hero Ain't Nothin' But a Sandwich, A
Hound of the Baskervilles, The (1939)
How the Whale Got His Throat
How to Be a Perfect Person in Just Three Days
Hunchback of Notre Dame, The
Ira Sleeps Over
Ivanhoe
Jack-a-Boy
Jack and the Beanstalk (1977)
Jack and the Beanstalk (Faerie Tale Theatre) (1982)
Jack London's To Build a Fire
Journey to the Center of the Earth
Julius Caesar (1953)
Jungle Book (1967)
Kidnapped (1959)
King Kong
King Kong-Color Enhanced
Lassie Come Home
Legend of Sleeping Hollow (1990)
Little Big Man
Little Engine That Could, The
Little Lord Fauntleroy
Little Match Girl (1978)
Little Match Girl (1990) (home video version)
Little Princess, The
Little Women (1949)
Luck of Roaring Camp, The
Lyle, Lyle Crocodile (public performance version)
Madeline: the Musical
Magic Shop, The
Magic Well
Maltese Falcon, The
Man Called Horse, A
Man Who Would Be King, The
Mandy's Grandmother
Mary Poppins
Marzipan Pig (home video version)
Molly's Pilgrim
Monkey's Paw, The (1978)
Mother Goose Stories
Mouse and the Motorcycle, The (public performance version)
My Old Man
Native Son (1986)
Natural, The
Necklace, The (1979)
Never Cry Wolf
Now One Foot, Now the Other
Oh Boy! Babies
Old Gringo
Old Yeller
Oliver!
Open Window, The (public performance version)
Open Window, The (home video version)
Out of Africa
Ox-Bow Incident, The
Parent Trap
Passage to India, A
Pied Piper of Hamelin, The (1982)
Pinocchio (1983)
Planet of the Apes
Pride and Prejudice (1980)
Prime of Miss Jean Brody, The

Prince and the Pauper, The (1937)
Prince and the Pauper, The (Disney) (1990)
Princess and the Pea, The (Faerie Tale Theatre) (1983)
Princess Who Never Laughed, The
Puss in Boots (1984) (Faerie Tale Theatre)
Raiders of the Lost Ark
Ramona Series (home video version)
Goodbye Hello
The Great Hair Argument
Mystery Meal
New Pajamas
The Patient
The Perfect Day
Rainy Sunday
Ramona's Bad Day
Siblingitis
Squeakerfoot
Mystery Meal and Rainy Sunday
Squeakerfoot and Goodbye, Hello
Ransom of Red Chief, The
Rapunzel (1955)
Rapunzel (Faerie Tale Theatre) (1982)
Rapunzel (Timeless Tales)
Rascal
Rebecca
Rebecca of Sunnybrook Farm
Red Room Riddle
Red Shoes (1990) (home video version)
Return of the Jedi
Right Stuff, The
Rikki Tikki Tavi (home video version)
Rip Van Winkle (1985)
Robin Hood (1973)
Rocking-Horse Winner
Roll of Thunder, Hear My Cry
Rudyard Kipling's Classic Stories (How the Elephant Got His Trunk; How the First Letter Was Written; How the Whale Got His Throat)
Rufus M., Try Again
Rumpelstiltskin (Faerie Tale Theatre) (1982)
Rumpelstiltskin (Timeless Tales)
Rumpelstiltskin (1985) (home video version)
Sam
Scrooge (Fox) (1970)
Secret of NIMH, The
Secret Sharer, The
Selfish Giant, The (1972)
Sense & Sensibility
Shoemaker and the Elves (1962)
Single Light, A
Sleeping Beauty (Faerie Tale Theatre) (1983)
Snow Queen (Faerie Tale Theatre)
Snow White & the Seven Dwarfs (Faerie Tale Theatre) (1983)
Something Wicked This Way Comes
Sounder
Star Wars
Steadfast Tin Soldier (1986) (home video version)
Story of the Dancing Frog (home video version)
Sword in the Stone
Tale of the Frog Prince (Faerie Tale Theatre) (1982)
Tap Dance Kid, The
Tell-Tale Heart, The (home video version)
Tenth Good Thing About Barney, The
Three Little Pigs, The (Faerie Tale Theatre) (1984)
Thumbelina (Faerie Tale Theatre) (1983)
Thumbelina (1981) (16 min.)
Thumbelina (Timeless Tales)
Tom Sawyer (1973)
Tortoise and the Hare, The
Treasure Island (1950)
Treasure Island (1990)
Tree Grows in Brooklyn, A
Twelve Angry Men
Ugly Duckling, The (Timeless Tales)
Ugly Duckling (1986) (home video version)
Velveteen Rabbit (1985) (home video version)
Voyage to the Bottom of the Sea
Watcher in the Woods
Wee Willie Winkie
When the Wind Stops
When We First Met
Who Wants to Be a Hero?
Winnie the Pooh and a Day for Eeyore
Winnie the Pooh and the Blustery Day
Winnie the Pooh and the Honey Tree
Winnie the Pooh and Tigger Too
Witch Who Was Afraid of Witches, The
Witches, The
Wizard of Oz, The
Yentl

Silent Films

Angus Lost
Crack in the Pavement, A
Dr. Jekyll and Mr. Hyde
Hunchback of Notre Dame, The
Remarkable, Riderless Runaway Tricycle, The
Tale of Two Cities, A & In the Switch Tower
Wizard of Oz, The (1925)

Appendix B: Film and Video Distributors

Listings include the source distributor for those home video products that are sold by a hierarchy of distributors.

Aims Media
9710 De Soto Ave.
Chattsworth, CA 91311
(800) 367-2467

Ambrose Video
1290 Avenue of the Americas
Suite 2245
New York, NY 10104
(800) 526-4663

Barr Films
12801 Schabarum Ave.
Irwindale, CA 91706
(800) 234-7878

Beacon Films
Altschul Group
930 Pitner Ave.
Evanston, IL 60202
(800) 323-5448

Britannica Films
310 So. Michigan Ave.
Chicago, IL 60605
(800) 554-9862

Buena Vista Home Video
500 So. Buena Vista St.
Burbank, CA 91521
(818) 562-3560

Cannon Video
c/o Warner Home Video
4000 Warner Blvd.
Burbank, CA 91522
(818) 954-6000

Children's Circle
c/o Weston Woods
Weston, CT 06883-9989
(800) 543-7843

Churchill Films
12210 Nebraska Ave.
Los Angeles, CA 90025
(800) 334-7830

Columbia TriStar Home Video
Customer Service Department
3400 No. Riverside Dr.
Suite 1100
Burbank, CA 91505
(818) 972-8686

Coronet Films
108 Wilmont Rd.
Deerfield, IL 60015
(800) 621-2131

Criterion Collection
c/o The Voyager Company
1351 Pacific Coast Hwy.
Santa Monica, CA 90401
(800) 446-2001

Davenport Films
RR1
P.O. Box 527
Delaplane, VA 22025
(703) 592-3701

Direct Cinema
P.O. Box 10003
Santa Monica, CA 90410
(800) 525-0000

Family Home Entertainment
c/o LIVE Home Video
15400 Sherman Way
Suite 500
P.O. Box 10124
Van Nuys, CA 91410-0124
(800) 288-5483

Filmfair Communications
10621 Magnolia Blvd.
North Hollywood,CA 91601
(818) 985-0244

Films Inc.
5547 No. Ravenswood Ave.
Chicago, IL 60640
(800) 323-4222

Films for the Humanities & Sciences
P.O. Box 2053
Princeton, NJ 08543-2053
(800) 257-5126

Fox Video
P.O. Box 900
Los Angeles, CA 90213
(800) 800-2369

Golden Book Video
c/o Western Publishing
1220 Mound Ave.
Racine, WI 53404
(800) 558-9427

Hanna-Barbera Home Video
c/o Turner Home Entertainment
1 CNN Center
Atlanta GA 30348-5366
(404) 827-3936; (404) 827-4936

HBO Video
Warner Home Video
4000 Warner Blvd.
Burbank, CA 91522
(818) 954-6000

Image Entertainment
9333 Oso Ave.
Chatsworth, CA 91311-6089
(800) 473-3475

International Film Forum
1000 E. William St.
Carson City, NV 89701
(702) 887-1122

International Video Entertainment
c/o LIVE Home Video
15400 Sherman Way
Suite 500
P.O. Box 10124
Van Nuys, CA 91410-0124
(800) 288-5483

Janus Films
c/o The Voyager Company
1351 Pacific Coast Hwy.
Santa Monica, CA 90401
(800) 446-2001

KVC Entertainment
c/o Barr Films
12801 Schabarum Ave.
Irwindale, CA 91706
(800) 331-1387

Kultur Video
121 Highway 36
West Long Branch, NJ 07764
(800) 458-5887

Lightyear Entertainment
350 Fifth Ave.
Suite 5101
New York, NY 10118
(800) 229-7867

LIVE Home Video
15400 Sherman Way
Suite 500
P.O. Box 10124
Van Nuys, CA 91410-0124
(800) 288-5483

Lucerne Media
37 Ground Pine Rd.
Morris Plains, NJ 07950
(800) 341-2293

MCA/Universal Home Video
70 Universal City Plaza
Universal City, CA 91608
(818) 777-4000

MGM/UA Home Video
1000 W. Washington Blvd.

Culver City, CA 90232
(310) 280-6000

Monterey Home Video
5142 Clareton St.
Suite 270
Agoura Hills, CA 91301
(800) 424-2593

New Line Video
c/o Columbia TriStar Home Video
Customer Service Department
3400 No. Riverside Dr.
Suite 1100
Burbank, CA 91505
(818) 972-8686

New World Video
1440 So. Sepulveda Blvd.
Los Angeles, CA 90025
(310) 444-8100

Pacific Arts Video
11858 La Grange Ave.
Los Angeles, CA
(800) 538-5856

Paramount Home Video
5555 Melrose Ave.
Hollywood, CA 90038-3197
(213) 956-5000

PBS Video
1320 Braddock Place
Alexandria, VA 22314-1698
(800) 424-7963

Pennsylvania State University
Special Services Building
University Park, PA 16802
(800) 826-0132

Phoenix/BFA Film & Video
468 Park Avenue So.
New York, N.Y. 10016
(800) 684-5910

Pioneer LDCA, Inc.
2265 East 220th St.
Long Beach, CA 90810
(800) 526-0363

Public Media Video
5547 No. Ravenswood Ave.
Chicago, IL 60640
(800) 323-4222

Pyramid Film & Video
P.O. Box 1048
Santa Monica, CA 90406
(800) 421-2304

Random House Home Video
225 Park Ave. So.
New York, NY 10003
(800) 733-3000

Republic Pictures Home Video
12636 Beatrice St.
Box 66930
Los Angeles, CA 90066-0930
(310) 306-4040

RKO/Turner Home Entertainment
1 CNN Center
Atlanta GA 30348-5366
(404) 827-3936; (404) 827-4936

Strand VCI
3350 Ocean Park Blvd.
Santa Monica, CA 90405
(800) 922-3827

SVS/Triumph
c/o Columbia TriStar Home Video
Customer Service Department
3400 No. Riverside Dr., Suite 1100
Burbank, CA 91505
(818) 972-8686

Uni Distribution Corp.
80 Universal City Plaza
Universal City, CA 91608
(818) 777-4000

Vestron Video
c/o LIVE Home Video
15400 Sherman Way
Suite 500
P.O. Box 10124
Van Nuys, CA 91410-0124
(800) 288-5483

Video Communications, Inc.
6535 E. Skelly Drive
Tulsa, OK 74145
(918) 622-6460

Video Treasures
(800) 786-8777

Video Yesteryear
P.O. Box C
Sandy Hook, CT 06482
(800) 243-0987

The Voyager Company
1351 Pacific Coast Hwy.
Santa Monica, CA 90401
(800) 446-2001

Warner Home Video
4000 Warner Blvd.
Burbank, CA 91522
(818) 954-6000

Weston Woods
Weston, CT 06883-9989
(800) 243-5020

Age-Level Index

Young people understand visual messages and spoken words at an earlier age than they do written words, and older audiences appreciate a simple story well told. The result is that viewers of a wide age range can be entertained by a given motion picture. The task of identifying the most favorable audience for a film is further complicated by the power of the medium; young viewers are attracted by the motion and action, even if the story is not fully understood. This index attempts to identify the youngest age range at which a given motion picture is most likely to be understood.

Preschool and Kindergarten Films (Ages 4-5)

Primary Films (Ages 6–8)

Intermediate Films (Ages 9–11)

Middle School Films (Ages 12–14)

High School Films (Ages 15–18)

Awards Index

Academy Awards

Adventures of Robin Hood (1938) [Best Set Design, Best Music Score] 280
All Quiet on the Western Front [Best Picture, Best Directing] 9
Around the World in Eighty Days [Best Picture, Best Screenplay, Best Cinematography, Best Music Score] 20
Back to the Future [Best Sound Effects Editing] 23
Bambi [Best Song] 23
Becket [Best Screenplay] 34
Bedknobs and Broomsticks [Best Visual Effects] 35
Born Free [Best Song, Best Music Score] 41
Bound for Glory [Best Cinematography, Best Music Score] 41
Boys and Girls [Best Short Film] 43
Bridge on the River Kwai, The [Best Picture, Best Actor, Best Directing, Best Screenplay, Best Cinematography, Best Music Score] 45
Camelot [Best Art Direction-Set Decoration, Best Music Score, Best Costumes] 233
Captains Courageous [Best Actor] 53
Children of a Lesser God [Best Actress] 60
Country Cousin, The [Best Cartoon] 71
Cyrano de Bergerac [Best Actor] 74
Devil and Daniel Webster, The [Best Music Score] 70
Diary of Anne Frank, The [Best Supporting Actress, Best Cinematography, Best Art Direction-Set Decoration] 15
Doctor Dolittle [Best Song, Best Visual Effects] 317
Dr. Jekyll and Mr. Hyde [Best Actor, 324
Dumbo [Best Music Score] 355
Elmer Gantry [Best Actor, Best Supporting Actress, Best Screenplay] 85
Empire Strikes Back, The [Best Sound, Best Visual Effects] 312
Fantastic Voyage [Best Art Direction-Set Decoration, Best Visual Effects] 90
Glory [Best Actor] 235
Gone With the Wind [Best Picture, Best Actress, Best Supporting Actress, Best Directing, Best Screenplay, Best Cinematography, Best Set Design] 112
Good Earth [Best Actress, Best Cinematography] 112
Goodbye, Mr. Chips [Best Actor] 113
Grapes of Wrath, The [Best Directing, Best Supporting Actress] 114
Great Expectations [Best Cinematography, Best Art Direction] 115
Great Gatsby, The [Best Costumes, Best Song Score] 116
Hamlet (1948) [Best Picture, Best Actor, Best Art Direction-Set Decoration, Best Costumes] 121
Human Comedy, The [Best Original Story] 137
In the Region of Ice [Best Short Film] 145
Kon-Tiki [Best Documentary] 169
Lilies of the Field [Best Actor] 177
Little Mermaid, The (1989) [Best Music

American Film and Video Festival Awards

American Library Association Awards

ASIFA Animation Festival Awards
(for best contributions to international understanding)

Athens Film Festival Award

Atlanta Film Festival Award

Birmingham Film Festival Awards
(for films and videotapes that are both educational and entertaining)

Booklist Magazine Editors' Choice Award

British Emmy Awards

British Film Festival Awards

Canadian Children's Film Festival

Chicago Educational Film Festival

Chicago International Festival of Children's Films

Chicago International Film Festival Awards

CINE Golden Eagle Awards

(for quality and suitability of nontheatrical short subjects for entry in international film festivals)

Columbus Film Festival Awards

Emmy Awards

Golden Globe Awards

Grammy Awards

Guidance Association Awards

Houston World Film and Video Festival Awards

Instructor Magazine Awards

International Animation Film Festival Awards

International Children's Film Festival Awards

International Film and TV Festival of New York Awards

International Short and Documentary Film Festival Awards

Learning Magazine Awards

Media and Methods Magazine Awards

NAACP Awards

National Council of Christians and Jews Awards

National Council on Family Relations Awards

National Educational Film and Video Festival (National Educational Film Festival) Awards

Jack of Hearts [Honorable Mention] 152
Little Match Girl, The (1990) [Silver Apple] 181
Mouse and the Motorcycle, The [Silver Apple] 211, 288
Open Window, The [Jack London Award] 236
Otherwise Known as Sheila the Great [Crystal Apple] 237
Revenge of the Nerd [First Place] 278
Soldier Jack: An American Folktale [Silver Apple] 308
Treasure of Alpheus Winterborn, The [Silver Apple] 342

National Mental Health Association Awards

(for films in the field of mental health)

Special Trade, A [First Place] 311

Netherlands Fishkon Film Festival Awards

Boy, a Dog, and a Frog, A [Best Short Feature] 42

Ollie Award

(for achievements in television programming for children)

Mouse and the Motorcycle, The, 212

Parents' Choice Award

Caddie Woodlawn, 49
Dr. Seuss Beginner Books Video: The Cat In the Hat Comes Back, Fox In Sox, There's a Wocket In My Pocket!, 55
Story of the Dancing Frog, The, 318

Peabody Award

(for achievement and meritorious public service by electronically delivered programs)

Mouse and the Motorcycle, The, 212
Red Pony, The, 275

Samuel A. Engel International Film Festival Award

Miracle at Moreaux [Gold Award] 346

Teheran International Film Festival Award

Drummer Hoff [Golden Plaque] 82

Virgin Island International Film Festival Award

Apt. 3 [Gold Venus Medallion] 18

Subject Index

African Americans

Aging and the aged

Allegories

Alphabet

Ambition—see Personal traits–ambition

Animals

Animals—bears

Animals—birds

Animals—bison

Animals—bulls

Animals—camels

Animals—caterpillars

Animals—cats

Animals—chickens

Animals—crocodiles

Animals—deer

Animals—dinosaurs

Animals—dogs

Animals—ducks

Animals—elephants

Animals—fish

Animals—frogs and toads

Animals—geese

Animals—hippopotamuses

Animals—horses

Animals—kangaroos

Cave dwellers

Cerebral palsy—
see Physical disability—cerebral palsy

Chickens—see Animals—chickens

Child abuse

Childbirth

China

Christmas

Circus

Cities and towns

Civil War—see War—Civil War, United States

Clairvoyance

Clothing and dress

Concept books—colors

Concept books—counting

Concept books—direction

Concept books—months

Concept books—opposites

Concept books—shapes

Concept books—sounds

Conservation—see Ecology

Family life—brothers and sisters

Family life—divorce

Family life—fathers

Family life—grandparents

Family life—mothers

Family life—single parents

Family life—stepparents

Fantasy

Farm life

Fathers—see Family life—fathers

Fear—see Emotions—fear

Fire engines

Fish—see Animals—fish

Folk songs

Folklore—Africa

Folklore—Arabia

Folklore—China

Folklore—Denmark

Folklore—France

Folklore—Germany

Folklore—Great Britain

Folklore—Greece

Folklore—India

Folklore—Italy

Folklore—Japan

Folklore—Mongolia

Folklore—Norway

Folklore—Russia

Folklore—United States

Food

France

Friendship

Frogs—see Animals—frogs and toads

Frontier and pioneer life

Geese—see Animals—geese

Geology

Ghost stories

Gorilla—see Animals-monkeys and apes

Grandparents—see Family life—grandparents

Great Britain

Greece

Halloween—see also Ghost stories; Witches

Hatred—see Emotions—hatred

Health

Hippopotamuses—see Animals—hippopotamuses

Historical fiction

Holidays—see Christmas; Halloween

Horror stories

Horse racing

Horses—see Animals—horses

Humorous stories

Hunting

Imagination

Immigrants

India (British)

Indians of North America—see Native Americans

Moon

Moose—see Animals—moose

Mothers—see Family life—mothers

Mountaineering

Museums

Music and musicians

Mystery

Native Americans

Nature

Nonfiction

Nonsense verse

Poetry

Puritans

Reading

Religion

Revenge

Romantic fiction

Runaways

Russia

School stories

Science fiction

Sea stories

Self-awareness—see Personal traits—self awareness

Self-esteem—see Emotions—self esteem

Sex roles

Short stories

Tanzania

Teeth

Tibet

Towns—see Cities and towns

Toys

Travel—see also Sea stories

Trucks

Tugboats

War—Civil War, United States

War—French and Indian War, United States

War—Revolution, France

War—Revolution, United States

War—World War I

War—World War II

Witches

Word games

Work

Author/Film Title Index

C

D

E

F

G

N

O

P

Q

R

S

T

U

V

W

Y

Z